Energy and Security

Energy and Security

Strategies for a World in Transition

Second Edition

Edited by

Jan H. Kalicki and David L. Goldwyn

Woodrow Wilson Center Press
Washington, D.C.

Johns Hopkins University Press
Baltimore

EDITORIAL OFFICES

Woodrow Wilson Center Press
Woodrow Wilson International Center for Scholars
One Woodrow Wilson Plaza
1300 Pennsylvania Avenue NW
Washington, D.C. 20004-3027
www.wilsoncenter.org

ORDER FROM

Johns Hopkins University Press
2715 North Charles Street
Baltimore, Maryland 21218-4363
Telephone 1-800-537-5487
www.press.jhu.edu/books/

2 4 6 8 9 7 5 3

Library of Congress Cataloging-in-Publication Data

Energy and security : strategies for a world in transition / edited by Jan H. Kalicki and David L.
   Goldwyn.—Second edition.
      pages cm
   Revised edition of Energy and security : toward a new foreign policy strategy, published in
   2005.
   ISBN 978-1-4214-1186-6—ISBN 978-1-4214-1169-9
   1. Energy policy—United States. 2. National security—United States. 3. United States—
Foreign relations—2001– I. Kalicki, Jan H. II. Goldwyn, David L., 1959–
HD9502.U52E4543 2013
333.790973—dc23

                                                                                        2013019966

Woodrow Wilson International Center for Scholars

The Wilson Center, chartered by Congress as the official memorial to President Woodrow Wilson, is the nation's key nonpartisan policy forum for tackling global issues through independent research and open dialogue to inform actionable ideas for Congress, the Administration, and the broader policy community.

Conclusions or opinions expressed in Center publications and programs are those of the authors and speakers and do not necessarily reflect the views of the Center staff, fellows, trustees, advisory groups, or any individuals or organizations that provide financial support to the Center.

The Center is the home of *dialogue* television and radio, *The WQ* digital magazine, and Woodrow Wilson Center Press. Please visit us on the Web at www.wilsoncenter .org.

Jane Harman, Director, President, and CEO

For Jeannie and the Brothers Three,
whose love and support made this possible,
And for Jan, Van, Cy, and Howard, visionaries all, in memory

For Peter and Ted, for their guidance, wisdom, and example;
For my band of brothers, for always being there;
And for Cathy and Benjamin, my renewable sources
of energy, love, and joy

And what is a man without energy? Nothing, nothing at all.
—*Mark Twain, 1860*

Come senators, congressmen

Please heed the call

Don't stand in the doorway

Don't block the hall

For he that gets hurt

Will be he who has stalled

There's a battle outside

And it is ragin'.

It'll soon shake your windows

And rattle your walls

For the times they are a-changin'.
—*Bob Dylan, 1963*

Contents

Foreword

James R. Schlesinger

Ever since the industrial revolution, energy and the need to secure its supply have been fundamental to any position of power in the world. Yet as the global energy landscape continues to change, a series of underlying structural shifts in supply, demand, and trade are altering national and regional economics, energy and national security considerations, and geopolitics.

Over the next several decades, most projected increases in global energy consumption will come from nonmembers of the Organization for Economic Cooperation and Development (OECD), or "emerging" economies, led by China and India. With few exceptions, most notably in North America, these emerging economies (especially in the Asia-Pacific region and the Middle East) are also likely to dominate energy production growth. As a consequence, global trade patterns for energy are forecast to undergo dramatic shifts as well, which will encourage the forging of new international alliances and further complicate America's diplomatic efforts.

Yet against this backdrop, there is also good news. The United States is experiencing a substantial upsurge in domestic oil and gas production, reversing decades of production decline and increased reliance on imports. And as the editors and authors of this book make clear, the strategic implications of this emerging new American energy reality are nothing less than revolutionary.

Five years ago, US oil imports accounted for almost 60 percent of domestic demand, and forecasts indicated an increasing need for imports of liquefied natural gas. Today, net oil import dependence is less than 43 percent and is declining, and the United States is projected to be a net exporter of natural gas within the decade. The great majority of US oil and gas imports now come from this hemisphere, primarily from Canada, a friendly and highly stable neighbor.

Of course, Organization of the Petroleum Exporting Countries (OPEC) nations continue to play a critical role in supplying the global oil market, including America, Japan, and other key American allies in Europe and elsewhere, but here too the landscape is shifting. Forty years ago, the Arab Oil Embargo brought home America's (and the industrial world's) vulnerability to disruption of that supply. And while the embargo provided Middle Eastern producers with a formidable (albeit short-lived) political and economic weapon, the event also served as the impetus for a decades-long pursuit of improved efficiency, alternative transportation fuels, domestic production incentives, and research and deployment of renewable energy. It also spurred the establishment of the Strategic Petroleum Reserve and the formation of the International Energy Agency.

Ironically—and the editors emphasize this point—the resurgence of US production and the development of alternative fuels technologies actually present an opportunity for renewed engagement with OPEC producers—but on different terms—even though the increased US output means reduced reliance on exporter nations. Saudi Arabia's recent commitment to improved efficiency and reliance on solar energy and natural gas (in no small part to preserve more valuable oil resources for export) is just one example of (a) how oil producers with growing populations at home are increasingly adopting consumer perspectives while still maintaining their exporter postures and (b) how US technology and assistance are furthering that objective. Similarly, the transfer of shale gas technology to China can help accelerate the development of indigenous gas resources—further relieving pressure on global gas supplies and concurrently improving the environment to the extent that increased gas production reduces the use of coal.

In this, the second edition of their *Energy and Security* work, editors Jan Kalicki and David Goldwyn point to the urgent need—and the opportunity—to make energy a pillar of our national policy and institutions. As they correctly point out, this effort will require presidential leadership, with new initiatives and processes led by a focused White House staff, unless once again we wish these issues to be submerged by an alphabet soup of government agencies and congressional committees.

As the editors and authors point out, the economic, environmental, foreign policy, and national security opportunities of this new energy position are increasingly clear. Of course, there will be tradeoffs and choices to be made. As a sector, energy has been responsible for both significant investment and a large portion of US and OECD job growth—from suppliers to refineries, petrochemicals, and other manufacturing spinoffs. Coupled with slower economic growth and efficiency improvements, the growing use of cheap natural gas—which is displacing much higher carbon coal in our power plants—is largely responsible for the fact that US emissions of greenhouse gases (GHGs) are back to 1994 levels. Energy security remains a crucial dimension of US foreign policy, and reduced reliance on sources of foreign oil, including the Middle East, will allow our security policy to focus on emerging 21st-century threats, from terrorism to proliferation to cyber, although strategic and regional stability in the Middle East will still remain a high priority.

In the broadest terms, then, the relative power position of the West could be enhanced substantially, not only in energy but also in economic and security dimensions. To achieve this goal will require not only technology, however, but also strategy and political will. The world will watch closely and draw its conclusions as (or if) our government promotes energy development with the lease of more federal lands; supports increased energy links with our neighbors, including notably the long-planned Keystone XL pipeline from Canada to the US Gulf states; and permits increased exports of American natural gas.

The breadth and implications of these changing conditions persuaded the editors of *Energy and Security* not only to update, but also to substantially revise their book in its second edition. All leaders in their fields, some of the authors and topics are the same as in the first edition in 2005; others have newly joined to form an impressive team of writers. In this promising environment, the editors and authors explore how foreign policy can best advance US energy interests and how energy can be used to further broader US foreign policy interests. They do so by focusing on the main regions of energy development and supply and then by constructing an energy security strategy that takes into account the role of strategic reserves, technology, the environment, and sustainable development.

In part I of the book, for example, Dan Yergin analyzes the effects of supply diversification, by type as well as by provenance, on energy security, and Amy Jaffe and Ed Morse delineate the path forward for reducing reliance on OPEC. David Victor addresses the promise of natural gas. Bill Reilly focuses on the critical issue of safety, and Bill Ramsay addresses the challenge of global energy governance.

Subsequent parts of the book hone in on energy and security issues in key regions of the world, including the Arctic frontier, where Charles Emmerson offers a probing analysis of the confluence of energy prospects and environmental challenges. The regional discussion is equally rich elsewhere, from Pierre Noël's analysis of the new European energy landscape, to Robin West and Raad Alkadiri's assessment of the oil potential and challenges of Iraq, to a thorough analysis of Asia-Pacific issues— from Australian production to Chinese consumption—by Amy Jaffe, Ken Medlock, and Mike Herberg.

Part VI offers thoughtful and often cutting-edge conclusions and prescriptions for a new US energy security strategy. Melanie Kenderdine and Ernie Moniz offer an outstanding review of technology and energy; Charles Ebinger and John Banks examine critical issues of electricity access; Charles McPherson considers the challenges of governance, transparency, and development; and Michelle Patron and David Goldwyn propose improved ways of managing strategic reserves in the new energy environment. It is also a pleasure to see two thoughtful companion pieces on energy, environment, climate change, and national security, the first a policy framework and analysis of tradeoffs by Mike Levi, and the second a call for a new paradigm and strategy by Leon Fuerth. Then, critically, Frank Verrastro and Kevin Book address the challenge of politics, which if not resolved would make a coherent, forward-looking energy policy impossible.

This book also benefits from point–counterpoint between producing and consuming perspectives—as borne out by commentaries from Chakib Khelil of Algeria and Abdullah bin Hamad Al-Attiyah of Qatar, both former OPEC leaders, and Alexander Gorban from the Russian Foreign Ministry, as well as probing critiques from Bennett Johnston, a former Senate energy and natural resources committee chairman, and from my old colleague John Deutch.

Jan Kalicki, David Goldwyn, and their outstanding group of contributors draw on extensive experience with energy issues in both government and the private sector. In my view, this book could not be timelier or more important at this moment of opportunity for a new energy security strategy for the United States. It enables readers from government, industry, and academic institutions to analyze the most important global and regional issues from an integrated energy and foreign policy standpoint—and to develop powerful new approaches to the growing range of policy problems with an energy dimension.

We are truly in an age of transformation, but one that will evolve over decades. Just as we substituted coal for oil in utility boilers, we are now displacing coal with natural gas in power generation and oil with gas (in limited circumstances) in transportation. Renewables and nuclear power, as cleaner, nonfossil fuels, should still be part of the energy mix going forward, but as a nation we would be well advised to avail ourselves of the benefits of our enormous natural resource wealth in oil and natural gas and to ensure that its development is done prudently, in a manner consistent with the nation's economic, security, and environmental goals.

Foreword

Richard G. Lugar

Energy security affects every aspect of life in the United States, from the cars we drive and the price we pay at the gas pump to our vulnerability to terrorism and our relationships with other countries. In the extreme, our nation's vulnerability to global oil volatility and supply constraints can lead to conflict, whereas each day our national security and humanitarian objectives are challenged by energy-driven political, economic, and environmental concerns.

For decades, few leaders seemed to believe that meaningfully changing America's energy fortunes could be accomplished. Yet today's outlook is bright. From alternative fuels such as ethanol to innovation for efficiency gains, technological advances have brought economic and security gains in reducing oil dependence. Now, breakthroughs in horizontal drilling and hydraulic fracturing have enabled the economical extraction of shale gas and tight oil in the United States, bringing about a revolution in domestic production. The International Energy Agency (IEA) now projects that the United States will become the largest global oil producer in the mid-2020s and will become a net oil exporter by around 2030. The IEA also projects that the United States will surpass Russia as the world's largest natural gas producer, with production growing from 650 billion cubic meters (bcm) in 2011 to 850 bcm in 2035. These developments were unthinkable just a few years ago.

America's energy landscape has altered dramatically. History teaches the lesson that energy security will be found in diversity of supply and usage, and overreliance on any single source is a mistake. America's new domestic energy portfolio offers diverse sources of secure domestic supply that will benefit both our economy at home and our security objectives abroad.

Even as domestic oil production ramps up, oil will remain a globally traded commodity, and the supply and demand decisions of diverse international players will still affect the price Americans pay at the pump. The ability of oil markets to meet growing global demand will still depend largely on countries with promising resource endowments yet highly volatile political climates. Meanwhile, changes in the longstanding production and consumption patterns of regional natural gas markets could render significant geopolitical effects regardless of future US export policy. For example, in Eastern Europe, states are trying to alleviate their dependence on Russian natural gas by building liquefied natural gas (LNG) import facilities and engaging in domestic shale gas exploration. If successful, these efforts could ultimately alter centuries-old dynamics of Russian–Eastern European relations. Russia has reacted by seeking to reinforce its energy and economic ties with post-Soviet states and to expand its natural gas exports to key Asian countries, including China and longstanding US allies Japan and South Korea.

These are just some of the global trends clearly indicating that the continued energy security of the United States and its allies will remain a critical facet of broader American national security interests. I have long believed that the United States should align its diplomatic priorities to meet energy security challenges. I have encouraged the North Atlantic Treaty Organization (NATO) to give closer consideration to energy security for several years and am pleased that Lithuania opened a NATO-accredited center of excellence in 2012 to strengthen allied interoperability on energy security matters. I pushed Congress to authorize the creation of the position of special envoy and coordinator for international energy affairs within the Office of the Secretary of State, which has precipitated realignment of diplomatic resources into the new Energy Resources Bureau. Since the

establishment of these positions in December 2007, successive coordina-
tors have worked to better integrate energy within the US foreign policy
agenda. Another important initiative has been the promotion of good governance in the extractive industries, including a law I wrote with Senator
Ben Cardin. Transparency contributes to multiple economic and national
security goals, including promotion of a better investment climate for US
businesses and improved reliability of commodity supplies.

The chapters of *Energy and Security: Strategies for a World in Transition* demonstrate a comprehensive understanding of the myths and realities
surrounding the massive development of American unconventional oil and
gas reserves. David Victor explains security, geopolitical, and environmental effects that may occur should other countries seek to emulate the shale
gas revolution in the United States. I took particular interest in his view that
shale gas may help mitigate the "resource curse" that plagues many gas-
exporting countries. The mismanagement of energy resources has long per-
petuated fraud, wasteful spending, corruption, military adventurism, and
instability. In some cases, these developments have had a direct impact on
American national security and humanitarian interests. This is yet another
area where there is clear evidence of the need to further incorporate energy
issues into our national security priorities.

Julia Nanay and Jan Kalicki also provide insight on the international
implications of increased American oil and natural gas production. They
note that this increased production has eliminated Russian plans for LNG
sales to the United States, contributed to lower spot gas prices in Europe,
and raised the prospect that Russia will face American and Australian competition as it seeks to gain a larger market share in Asia. The authors also
make the important point that continued Russian resource development is
essential to keeping global markets well supplied and is thus firmly within
American interests. Indeed, Russia's need for foreign investor assistance
in developing its unconventional oil and gas, which is likely essential for
maintaining Russian production levels, may prove to be an area in which
Russia's interests converge with those of the United States. It could even
provide a new medium for cooperation in Russian–American energy relations, which have often been contentious in recent decades.

Robin West and Raad Alkadiri's chapter on Iraq, Iran, and the Gulf region reflects the reality that oil and gas development at home will not insulate the United States from resource disruptions abroad. This point is
one that is especially important to communicate to the public as the effects
of increased American oil production are considered. The authors explain

why the United States will continue to seek to protect the free flow of oil from the Middle East, while also discussing the interrelated sources of continued instability in that critical region. Their lucid analysis of the possible effects of Syrian instability on Middle Eastern oil and gas production despite Syria's own very modest reserves is especially worthwhile. American policy-makers should keep these energy-related potential outcomes in mind as the conflict there unfolds.

For the United States to maximize the benefits of its newly profitable oil and gas reserves, continued efforts will be needed to ensure that these resources are developed in a safe and environmentally appropriate manner. William K. Reilly's examination of the consequences of the 2010 Macondo blowout illustrates that one catastrophe can have industrywide damaging impacts and can lead to severe erosion of public confidence in the industry. Reilly's recommendation that those engaged in shale gas and tight oil development work together to minimize the risk of a large accident by defining and implementing best practices deserves serious consideration. If carried out, it could improve public perceptions of shale gas and tight oil development and promote robust environmental stewardship.

Jan Kalicki and David Goldwyn have assembled an all-star cast of contributors, who have drawn on their extensive government and private sector experience to provide an exceptional survey of the most important energy and national security issues facing the United States today. The way that these matters are ultimately addressed will have significant repercussions both at home and abroad. This volume offers valuable guidance to American policy-makers as they continue to position the United States to bolster its energy security and protect its national security interests in what is still a very new and somewhat unknown environment. This book should be required reading for policy-makers, industry leaders, academics, students, and members of the general public who wish to better grasp the interrelated energy and national security issues that will, in my view, profoundly influence US prosperity at home and national security interests abroad in the coming years and decades.

Foreword

Jane Harman

Energy security has eluded generations of Americans, even as every president since Richard Nixon has warned of the dangers of dependency on foreign oil. But the discovery of energy resources in North America is a game changer. Today, the United States is on the verge of vaulting from being a net *importer* to being a net *exporter* of oil and natural gas by 2030—or even earlier.

This *quest*—to borrow Daniel Yergin's term—for an energy solution will have enormous economic, environmental, and geopolitical implications for the United States and the world. More than 100 years ago, when he was the president of Princeton, Woodrow Wilson said, "We live in an age disturbed, confused, bewildered, afraid of its own forces, in search not merely of its road but even of its direction." In 2013, our nation is at a similar crossroads—and the new energy landscape positions America to lead.

Energy is absolutely critical to all aspects of our daily lives—from food; to clothing; to the cars, trains, and airplanes that take us from point A to point B; to houses and buildings; to the lighting, cooling, and heating that many take for granted; to the omnipotent information technology infrastructure that increasingly runs our lives. Energy security is national security.

When the Wilson Center and Johns Hopkins University Press published the first edition of this book in 2005, experts were convinced that the United States would continue to depend on oil and gas imports for over half of our energy needs. How wrong they were! The editors of this volume describe the new energy reality, which stems mainly from three sources: commercial development of huge amounts of "unconventional" shale oil and natural gas in the United States; deepwater and ultradeepwater development of more "conventional" oil and gas from western Australia to the Gulf of Mexico; and growing amounts of Canadian oil and gas, both onshore and offshore.

At home, building our capacity to produce shale oil and natural gas will create jobs and foster economic growth. At the same time, we need to find responsible ways to extract those resources without endangering our environment, particularly our water supply. Already, the use of shale natural gas in energy supplies generates around half the amount of carbon dioxide as the use of coal, thus having less of an impact on the rise of global warming.

The editors of *Energy and Security: Strategies for a World in Transition* believe that the most serious mistake would be to misuse this new era of energy self-sufficiency to proclaim energy "independence"—the unfortunate slogan of too many Americans on both sides of the aisle. For one thing, such a course flies in the face of the reality of a global oil market and a globalizing natural gas market. For another, such an isolationist move would unravel our political–economic alliances and undermine world trade and growth, on which our own growth and security depend.

To explore this and the other tough policy issues that stem from new energy innovations, this edition brings together a stellar group of scholars and practitioners in the worlds of energy, security, and foreign policy. Prominent energy and foreign policy experts in their own right, Jan Kalicki has been senior scholar with the Wilson Center and Kennan Institute since 2001 and David Goldwyn served as the first special energy envoy and coordinator for Hillary Rodham Clinton, the former secretary of state. Both are thoughtful energy advisers who have played leading roles on energy, trade, and investment issues in the joint commissions cochaired by Vice President Al Gore in the Clinton administration.

Like the Wilson Center, this book bridges the worlds of scholarship and policy and offers actionable ideas for key decision-makers. Its editors are part of a new, pragmatic policy generation that seeks to tear down outdated ideological divides and bureaucratic and political stovepipes. As a former nine-term member of Congress who served on the House Energy and Commerce, Armed Services, Intelligence, and Homeland Security Committees, I know that political rhetoric inside the Beltway can become heated and destructive. How shortsighted! America leads if we take off our ideological blinkers, understand the new energy landscape, and make the most of its opportunities.

Acknowledgments

At a weak moment, we agreed with our wonderful editor, Joseph Brinley, to update the first, 2005 edition of this book, titled *Energy and Security: Toward a New Foreign Policy Strategy*.

The product is this second edition, with a new subtitle: *Strategies for a World in Transition*. As the subtitle suggests, much has changed—and much is changing—in energy and security. We discovered quickly that we could not just do an update; we had to make major revisions to reflect nothing less than a revolution in the world of energy:

- The fulcrum of energy demand is moving from West to East.
- The foundation of energy supply is expanding from East to West.
- Markets are even more crucial as states weather recession and dysfunction.
- The United States is now a resource-secure, rather than a resource-constrained, nation, endowing us with new and powerful tools to enhance our national, economic, and climate security.

These and other fundamental changes certainly create challenges, but they also create opportunities for energy producers and consumers, who are more and more the same. Since 2005, there has been increased understanding of the deep connections of energy with the economy and politics, national and global security, the climate, and the environment.

Even if hardly sufficient, there has been some progress in organizing our government to manage this interconnected network that will determine the quality of life of future generations.

The good news was that many of the authors in the first edition were ready to embark with us on this second, overhauled edition. We are joined by additional contributors, as we all recognized the wider and more global breadth of our subject. We are fortunate that top-tier authorities are again on the roster for this second edition—including the first and the current US secretaries of energy (writing in his prior academic capacity); former heads of the Environmental Protection Agency and the Central Intelligence Agency; a former secretary and deputy secretary of defense; a former White House chief of staff; two former Senate committee chairs (of both parties); several former heads of the Organization of the Petroleum Exporting Countries, the International Energy Agency, and the US Energy Information Administration; and a number of leading scholars and industry executives. European, American, Russian, Middle Eastern, and African writers all make this one of the most international sets of energy experts gathered in one volume.

In addition to Joe Brinley, we are grateful for the enthusiastic support of Jane Harman, Mike Van Dusen, and Blair Ruble at the Woodrow Wilson Center; for the editorial assistance of Cory Gill and Leigh Hendrix; and for our manuscript and copyeditors, led by Linda Stringer, vice president and senior editor at Publications Professionals LLC. We deeply appreciate the continuing advice and counsel of our good friend Daniel Yergin. And we were encouraged every step of the way by our wives, Jean and Cathy, and by Jan, Sasha, Peter, and Benjamin—the older of whom remembered the long hours required for the first edition but thought, mistakenly, that the hours would be shorter in a second round. Once again we knew we were excited by this project, but once again their enthusiasm made it a joy.

We extend our appreciation to all and, of course, especially to the contributors to this book. For any errors of omission or commission, we cheerfully accept responsibility.

JHK and DLG
Washington, DC, and Harwich Port, MA
June 2013

Abbreviations

ACER	Agency for the Cooperation of Energy Regulators
ADB	Asian Development Bank
AIOC	Azerbaijan International Operating Company
ANP	Agência Nacional do Petróleo, Gás Natural e Biocombustíveis, or National Agency of Petroleum, Natural Gas, and Biofuels (Brazil)
APEC	Asia-Pacific Economic Cooperation
API	American Petroleum Institute
ARPA-E	Advanced Research Projects Agency–Energy
ASEAN	Association of Southeast Asian Nations
bcf	billion cubic feet
bcfpd	billion cubic feet per day
bcm	billion cubic meters
bpd	barrels per day
BRICs	Brazil, Russia, India, and China
BTC	Baku–Tbilisi–Ceyhan (pipeline)

BTE   Baku–Tbilisi–Erzurum (pipeline)
Btu   British thermal units
CAFE   corporate average fuel economy (standards)
CCS   carbon capture and sequestration
CEER   Council of European Energy Regulators
CEO   chief executive officer
CFE   Comisión Federal de Electricidad, or Federal Electricity
           Commission (Mexico)
CNG   compressed natural gas
CNOOC   China National Offshore Oil Corporation
CNPC   China National Petroleum Corporation
CO_2 carbon dioxide
COS   Center for Offshore Safety
CPC   Caspian Pipeline Consortium
CSSD   Center for Sustainable Shale Development
DOE   US Department of Energy
DOI   US Department of the Interior
DRC   Democratic Republic of the Congo
ECE   energy critical elements
EIA   US Energy Information Administration
EITI   Extractive Industries Transparency Initiative
EOP   Executive Office of the President (United States)
EOR   enhanced oil recovery
EPA   US Environmental Protection Agency
EPCA   Energy Policy and Conservation Act (United States)
ESPO   East Siberia–Pacific Ocean (pipeline)
EU   European Union
FCPA   US Foreign Corrupt Practices Act
FERC   Federal Energy Regulatory Commission
G-8   Group of Eight
G-20   Group of 20
GASP   Group against Smog and Pollution
GDP   gross domestic product
GESS   global energy security system
GHG   greenhouse gas
GiZ   Deutsche Gesellschaft für Internationale Zusammenarbeit, or
           German Society for International Cooperation
GW   gigawatts
HEU   highly enriched uranium

ICE	Intercontinental Exchange
IEA	International Energy Agency
IEF	International Energy Forum
IFI	international financial institution
ILDC	Israel Land Development Company
IMF	International Monetary Fund
INPO	Institute of Nuclear Power Operations
IOC	international oil company
IPCC	Intergovernmental Panel on Climate Change
IPEEC	International Partnership for Energy Efficiency Cooperation
IRENA	International Renewable Energy Agency
JNOC	Japan National Oil Company
JOGMEC	Japan Oil, Gas, and Metals National Corporation
KA-CARE	King Abdullah City for Atomic and Renewable Energy
KDP	Kurdistan Democratic Party
KMG	KazMunaiGaz (national oil company of Kazakhstan)
KNOC	Korea National Oil Corporation
KOGAS	Korea Gas Corporation
KRG	Kurdistan Regional Government
LED	light-emitting diode
LNG	liquefied natural gas
LWR	light-water reactor
Mcf	thousand cubic feet
MDGs	Millennium Development Goals
MEDEA	Measurements of Earth Data for Environmental Analysis
MIST	Mexico, Indonesia, South Korea, and Turkey
MIT	Massachusetts Institute of Technology
mmbpd	million barrels per day
mmt	million metric tons
MPZ	main pay zone
MTBE	methyl tertiary butyl ether
MW	megawatts
NATO	North Atlantic Treaty Organization
NBP	national balancing point
NCOC	North Caspian Operating Company
NEB	National Energy Board (Canada)
NEPAD	New Partnership for Africa's Development
NGL	natural gas liquid
NGO	nongovernmental organization

NiMH	nickel metal hydride
NOC	national oil company
NPC	National Petroleum Council
NPT	Treaty on the Nonproliferation of Nuclear Weapons, or Nonproliferation Treaty
NRC	Nuclear Regulatory Commission
NYMEX	New York Mercantile Exchange
OECD	Organization for Economic Cooperation and Development
OFID	OPEC Fund for International Development
ONGC	Oil and Natural Gas Corporation (India)
OPEC	Organization of the Petroleum Exporting Countries
PAN	Partido Acción Nacional, or National Action Party (Mexico)
PCAST	President's Council of Advisors on Science and Technology
PdVSA	Petróleos de Venezuela (state energy company of Venezuela)
PEMEX	Petróleos Mexicanos (state petroleum company of Mexico)
PennFuture	Citizens for Pennsylvania's Future
PER	Public Expenditure Review
ppm	parts per million
PPP	purchasing power parity
PRD	Partido de la Revolución Democrática, or Party of the Democratic Revolution (Mexico)
PRI	Partido Revolucionario Institucional, or Institutional Revolutionary Party (Mexico)
PRS	Poverty Reduction Strategy
PWYP	Publish What You Pay
QER	quadrennial energy review
QP	Qatar Petroleum
R&D	research and development
RD&D	research, development, and demonstration
REE	rare earth element
RFS	Renewable Fuel Standard (United States)
ROZ	residual oil zone
SEC	US Securities and Exchange Commission
SEFA	Sustainable Energy for All
SMR	small modular reactor
SO_2	sulfur dioxide
SOCAR	State Oil Company of Azerbaijan Republic
SPR	US Strategic Petroleum Reserve
TANAP	Trans Anatolian Pipeline

TAP	Trans Adriatic Pipeline
TAPI	Turkmenistan–Afghanistan–Pakistan–India (pipeline)
tcf	trillion cubic feet
TCGP	Trans-Caspian Gas Pipeline
TCO	TengizChevroil
TPAO	Turkish Petroleum Corporation
TZ	transition zone
UAE	United Arab Emirates
UN	United Nations
UNDP	United Nations Development Program
UNFCCC	United Nations Framework Convention on Climate Change
USGS	US Geological Survey
WHO	World Health Organization
WTI	West Texas Intermediate
YPF	Yacimientos Petrolíferos Fiscales (state energy company of Argentina)

Energy and Security

Introduction

Jan H. Kalicki and David L. Goldwyn

The American energy landscape has changed radically since 2005, but public perceptions have not caught up. Almost as laggard is the understanding of America's renewed energy endowment and its global implications on the part of many political leaders and decision-makers. In the United States, the structure of federal policy-making undermines the government's ability to understand market shifts and formulate and deploy energy policy to serve US interests. Our fractious politics make long-term planning daunting. In this book, we seek to help citizens, analysts, and policy-makers understand the dynamics shaping this new energy landscape, the challenges and opportunities it presents, and the range of available policy options. If we can identify and pursue the necessary policies, our renewed energy endowment will help strengthen our partnerships, foster growth, and reduce greenhouse gas (GHG) emissions at scale.

A Renewed US Energy Endowment

Thanks to technological advances in energy production and consumption, increased private investment, and some wise government policies, American oil and gas production has revived.[1] Energy efficiency in vehicles, buildings, and appliances has advanced; solar and wind energy are growing rapidly (albeit from a small base); imports of crude oil and natural gas are declining; and the historically nearly equal correlation between economic growth and energy consumption has been broken.[2] The United States is more self-sufficient in energy than at any time since the 1960s and is growing more so every year. Although the United States has long obtained at least half of its total oil consumption from domestic sources, projections show that only 36 percent will come from abroad by 2035.[3]

These technological advances have profound implications for the US economy. In 2012, reduced imports will have improved the US balance of trade by about $471 billion (in 2005 dollars).[4] Oil and gas production and the construction of infrastructure to carry that supply to market have been the third-largest source of employment growth since 2000.[5] An October 2012 analysis indicates that unconventional oil and gas drilling will have led to the creation of 1.7 million US jobs in 2012 and predicts that this number could increase to 3 million by 2020.[6] It also finds that growing unconventional exploration and production will have added $62 billion to federal and state revenues in 2012.

The technology boom has also had positive effects on climate security. US natural gas is cost competitive with coal and has half its carbon intensity. The US Energy Information Administration (EIA) forecasts that natural gas will constitute a growing share of the US energy mix while the share of coal will decline.[7] Over five years from 2012, approximately 27 gigawatts (GW), or roughly 8.5 percent, of coal capacity are expected to phase out.[8] EIA also predicts that the substitution of natural gas for coal will play an important part in causing US energy-related emissions to decline by 1 percent annually until 2035, and it now appears entirely possible that the Obama administration could meet its target of a 17 percent reduction of 2005 carbon dioxide (CO_2) levels by 2020, even without legislative action.[9] The changing US energy demand structure—after years of research, development, and policy encouragement—is another key factor contributing to projected declines in annual emissions.

Domestic Policy Challenges Ahead

In addition to the shifts discussed, the United States has also become a net exporter of petroleum products and, if policy permits, may become a net exporter of natural gas and a limited exporter of crude oil. Dramatic increases in US natural gas production, thanks to shale and tight gas, can convert the United States from a gas importer to a gas exporter by 2020.[10] Natural gas production drove average US natural gas prices from a high of $8 per thousand cubic feet (Mcf) in 2008 to less than $3 per Mcf in 2012 — thus creating lucrative export opportunities to higher-priced foreign markets.

However, Americans still perceive the United States as resource constrained. Legislators express concern that US exports of petroleum products will leave us short of supply or that liquefied natural gas (LNG) exports will increase domestic prices. Little empirical evidence suggests that either worry is well founded.[11]

Others are ready to declare US energy independence, including a potential end of the US need to project military power in the Middle East and to maintain commitments to the stability of major energy producers.[12] Yet as long as oil remains a globally priced strategic commodity, the United States and global economies will be subject to disruption, economic harm, and therefore the threat of oil as a political weapon. Even if we imported no oil, the strategic nature of the commodity would require the United States to remain deeply concerned about global supply and freedom of navigation.

The recent, yet rapid, impact of combining the old technologies of horizontal drilling and hydraulic fracturing accounts for some of the public skepticism. Many find it hard to believe that this new resource endowment is real or sustainable. Some resistance is born of fear.[13] The world has witnessed several major human and environmental disasters since 2007, each born of negligent energy operations and inadequate regulatory supervision and controls. The Macondo oil spill of 2010, the Fukushima nuclear meltdown of 2011, and reports of water contamination and methane emissions coinciding with shale gas development in Pennsylvania have made many wary of the new energy boom.

A third area of public concern stems from a misinformed fear that climate security will be compromised by the emergence of new natural gas resources. In the United States and Europe, there are concerns that widespread, low-cost availability of natural gas will delay the development of large-scale renewable energy,[14] rather than limit and reduce GHGs by creating a scalable substitution for coal-based power generation. Renewable alternatives are growing in market share and may prove more scalable over the longer term, but concerns over natural gas that are based more on fear than on fact should not prevent major carbon, economic, and energy security improvements over the coming two to three decades.

Energy and the Shifting Geopolitical Landscape …

The focal point of global energy demand has shifted to the East. For decades, major energy suppliers focused on the United States and Europe. Energy demand is now most intense in China, South Korea, India, and the Arabian Gulf. These new economic links are strengthening ties between Middle Eastern, African, and Latin American producers and East and South Asian consumers, thereby creating new arenas for international competition. The energy shift to the East may reduce Western influence with producing nations. The United States and its allies will thus be required to reengage Asian partners with shared strategic interests to maintain old alignments.

However, technological advances and increased North American production should provide the United States and its allies with distinct advantages. To ensure the adequacy and diversity of supply to meet growing demand, the United States and its partners in the Organization for Economic Cooperation and Development (OECD) historically encouraged countries with significant reserves of oil and gas to open their markets to foreign investment and encouraged countries that restricted access to national oil companies to invest to meet global demand. This strategy gave added power to countries such as Saudi Arabia and Russia and obliged the West to cultivate good relations with autocratic regimes in Iraq, Libya, and Venezuela.

This landscape has changed substantially. The United States, Canada, and Australia are now popular places for investors looking to produce energy, while more traditional producers, such as Russia, require Western technology and know-how for deepwater, tight oil and gas,[15] and enhanced oil recovery development. If they wish to remain leaders in energy production, these traditional producers may also need Western capital and project management.

This shift has powerful implications for energy and foreign policy. Democratic, stable governments that are not members of the Organization of the Petroleum Exporting Countries (OPEC), such as the United States, Canada, and Brazil, are now empowered to play leading roles in helping the world meet growing oil demand. Similarly, the United States, Australia, and potentially Canada can help meet global demand for natural gas beyond the lead suppliers of the 1990s and 2000s, including Russia and Qatar.

... But Not the End of History

Although these changes are dramatic and in many ways positive, they are likely to have limited effect on the US economy's vulnerability to oil supply disruptions. Oil prices are formed by global supply and demand and by expectations of future supply availability. A disruption in global supply from local disturbances, such as the Libyan revolution of 2011 or Iran's recurrent threats to block the Strait of Hormuz, can send global prices skyward and inflict pain on the US and global economies. Rapid increases in oil demand, such as the Chinese-led global demand increases of 2003 and 2004, can also result in rapid price escalation. Supply and demand balances can also be disrupted by government policies, such as OPEC's decisions to cut back supplies to elevate declining prices in 1986 and 1998, or by leaps in technology, such as potential breakthroughs in batteries or second-generation biofuels.

Recent political developments clearly demonstrate these realities. The onset of the Arab Upheaval in 2011 coincided with a major global recession and high oil prices. In particular, civil war in Libya disrupted 1.4 million barrels per day (mmbpd) in oil supply and sent Brent oil prices from $103 per barrel of oil in January to $123 per barrel in April 2011. It also indicated continuing need for national governments to help limit oil market volatility. Saudi Arabia boosted oil production to lessen the economic pain from rising global oil prices, and the United States and the International Energy Agency (IEA) collaborated to activate the coordinated emergency response mechanism to free new oil supply to make up for lost Libyan supply.

Mounting US, European Union (EU), and other sanctions on Iran further demonstrate that the geography of oil consumption is immaterial when we face a significant disruption in global oil supply. US and EU sanctions caused Iranian exports to decrease by nearly 400,000 barrels per day (bpd) by mid-2012. US law requires the government to penalize any nation that imports or transports Iranian oil,[16] unless the president determines that the market is not adequately supplied or unless he provides waivers for countries that have substantially reduced their oil imports from Iran. This waiver authority recognizes that neither the US nor the global economy could tolerate a major self-imposed decrease in access to oil supply in a tight market, especially given the eurozone crisis and tentative economic growth in the United States and elsewhere.

Given these concerns, maintaining a diplomatic coalition to pressure Iran clearly requires management of oil price volatility. In June 2012, the Group of 20 (G-20) issued its first-ever statement on the oil market, announcing that nations stand ready to use strategic reserves if needed.[17] The revival of Iraqi oil production, a return of previously disrupted Libyan supply, Saudi Arabia's successful efforts to increase production to record levels of 10.3 mmbpd in June,[18] and supply increases from US tight oil and Canadian oil sands have mitigated the price impacts of coordinated actions to curtail Iranian exports. Although US imports of crude oil stayed at historic lows of 41 percent in 2012—only 8 mmbpd in June[19]—the importance of securing supply for others has rarely been higher.

Opportunities for Global Energy Policy

Although increased domestic oil and gas production cannot protect the United States from oil price shocks, it will still provide significant foreign policy benefits. Increased oil production places downward pressure on prices worldwide. It enhances our ability to work with the IEA and suppliers with spare capacity, including Saudi Arabia, to lessen the risk of oil supply disruptions and, if necessary, manage them. Similarly, our domestic natural gas boom has already lowered global LNG prices by eliminating the need for US LNG imports. US exports based on Henry Hub prices[20] to other markets would give rise to competitive pressures for gas and price relief to countries that pay oil-linked prices of $12 to $18 per million British thermal units for gas while the United States pays $2.75. Furthermore, US oil and LNG exports to countries such as India, China, and Japan could provide the impetus needed for those countries to finally renounce Iranian exports in the face of Iran's growing nuclear weapons capability.

The United States also stands to gain from helping others to access the technology to develop their own sources of tight oil or gas. Doing so would expand global energy supply and reduce other countries' vulnerability to coercion or monopoly pricing from single or limited suppliers. For example, assisting Eastern European countries in developing the regulatory frameworks to attract investment and require safe practices in shale gas development may help to break up Gazprom's longstanding monopoly in those countries. For China, India, and other nations that have depended on coal for power generation, natural gas is becoming an affordable, scalable alternative, with major potential global environmental benefits.[21] Efforts by the United States and its allies to finance the conversion of electric power from coal to natural gas in these countries through international financial institutions such as the World Bank would go far to limit global warming.

The Challenges Ahead

In addition to the opportunities listed previously, the United States will face many future challenges. First, energy poverty is a growing concern. Although the IEA estimated that 1.3 billion people lacked access to energy services in 2002, it anticipates only a slight reduction by 2030.[22] This situation is more than a humanitarian matter. The stability of governments often depends on their ability to deliver electricity. Many of the countries most severely affected by energy poverty are those where stability is necessary for US and global security interests. India and Pakistan both experience recurring summer blackouts, and power supplies remain precarious in Afghanistan, Iraq, Nigeria, and Yemen.

Second, safety concerns remain across the energy complex, from oil spill response in deep and Arctic waters, to nuclear safety after Fukushima, to the need for best practices in air and water protection from development of oil and gas from tight formations, and finally to the need for coal mine safety.[23] Cyber threats and cyber security represent major challenges for energy and other critical infrastructure.[24]

Third, multiple forums[25] have been launched to address climate change, but none yet has the agility and capacity to negotiate meaningful and timely reductions in GHG emissions to avert a 2-degree increase in global temperatures by 2050.

Fourth, the ability of energy-producing governments to manage the business and revenues from production transparently and for the good of their people remains a chronic issue. Recently, there has been some significant progress. Thirty-six countries, including the United States, are members of the Extractive Industries Transparency Initiative (EITI), which offers voluntary standards for disclosure of extractive industry revenues by countries and companies.[26] The Dodd–Frank legislation[27] contains a provision requiring the disclosure of payments made to governments by all companies listed in US stock exchanges. Adoption of open auction systems has grown, including the use of blind auctions by Libya, Iraq, and Algeria. Yet the quality of governance has yet to improve substantially, with greater transparency or with the development of civil society organizations.[28]

America's enhanced energy position also creates a wide range of global and regional opportunities and challenges. We have the resources to deploy energy as a vehicle of our foreign policy. However, optimal outcomes are often hindered because the United States lacks an adequate policy structure for integrating its energy and foreign policy interests. Similar problems frustrate progress at the international level.

Foreign Policy Opportunities and Challenges

Although many US agencies have cooperative relationships with foreign counterparts, the separation of national security and domestic policy-making makes it highly challenging to muster these programs to advance our interests. Some steps have been taken since 2009 to try to address these structural weaknesses. President Barack Obama launched the White House Office of Energy and Climate Change Policy to integrate energy and environmental issues. However, this office lasted only two years and primarily addressed climate and domestic energy policies. Issues that arose later in the Obama administration, such as the safety of shale gas development, the need to replace lost Libyan supply, and the use of the Strategic Petroleum Reserve, were taken up in an ad hoc fashion by a small but able group of officials drawn from the National Economic Council, the Council on Environmental Quality, and the Domestic Policy Council. Other issues, such as permitting the Keystone XL pipeline, did not receive comprehensive interagency review. For still other issues, such as assessing whether the nation's pipeline and transport infrastructure is adequate to move newfound supplies of oil from the US Midwest to refineries in the East, West, or Gulf Coast, there is no forum for review and assessment.

Despite these issues, a quick tour of federal agencies also illustrates the potential for creative policy-making. The US Department of Energy has cooperative programs with China on electric vehicles and energy efficiency, and the Department of the Interior has international training programs for geological characterization and resource assessment as well as offshore licensing. The Treasury Department's Office of Technical Assistance helps educate central banks and finance ministries on how better to manage resource revenues. The State Department's Global Shale Gas Initiative introduces countries to the methods of safely and efficiently developing unconventional gas, and its Energy Governance and Capacity Initiative helps potential oil and gas suppliers develop their resources in a competitive, transparent, and safe manner.

The State Department is taking tangible steps to integrate energy and foreign policy. The Global Shale Gas and Energy Governance and Capacity Initiatives use "all of government" approaches to muster multiple agencies behind coordinated programs. Additionally, in November 2011, the department launched the new Bureau of Energy Resources. This bureau will focus on existing energy supply relationships, on the promotion of energy governance, on the deployment of new energy technologies, and on the energy transformation of developing nations.[29]

Policy coordination is also limited at the international level. For many US partners, such as Saudi Arabia, China, India, Nigeria, and Brazil, energy policy is led at the chief-of-state or head-of-government level, bolstered by an energy minister. In the United States, multiple ministers address policy fragments. The secretary of the treasury leads on coordinating the use of strategic oil reserves because of the macroeconomic impact of oil prices. The State Department and White House episodically engage suppliers such as Saudi Arabia. President Obama's first secretary of energy focused heavily on domestic energy technology and famously said, "I don't do OPEC,"[30] subsequently leaving international coordination to a capable deputy. Although policy on shale gas and domestic production was led by a senior member of the Domestic Policy Council, a senior member of the National Economic Council coordinated policies on emergency response, and duties were divided on LNG exports. The Executive Office of the President has numerous finance experts and a macroeconomist, but only one serious energy economist was employed in the president's first term.

The international architecture for energy policy is similarly fragmented. The IEA remains the world's premier institution for assessing global energy trends and is a superb forum for addressing issues of energy-consuming nations. But it is handicapped by the absence of China and India as members, nations that constituted 31 percent of global energy consumption in 2012. Both countries are wary of joining a group in which voting is heavily weighted toward the United States and European countries. Other institutions exist as potential forums for coordination on energy issues, but they too are not without flaws.[31] The G-20 has a robust collection of producers and consumers. There is also precedent within the G-20 for addressing international energy markets. Its 2009 communiqué called for an end to inefficient energy subsidies, and its 2012 communiqué produced a first statement on the oil market itself. But the G-20 is a meeting, not an institution. It provides useful head-of-government contact but is informal, largely virtual, and not always transparent. OPEC and other forums, such as the Saudi-hosted International Energy Forum (IEF), lean more toward producer interests, although the IEF is bringing producers and consumers together on such important matters as energy data transparency.

Regional Opportunities

The United States must address these structural barriers to an effective international energy policy as well as to an effective foreign policy, while showing leadership to find a way to better coordinate international stewardship of global energy markets. The United States will remain an indispensable global power and will have intertwined energy and foreign policy concerns in nearly every world region.

Western Hemisphere

In our own hemisphere, the key issue will be the extent of our commitment to maximizing our enormous resource potential.[32] In the United States, there is huge tight oil potential in the Bakken and Midwest region; oil and liquids potential in Texas, Oklahoma, and Arkansas; and tight gas potential in the Marcellus and Utica shale formations. Arctic Alaska and Canada have great oil potential, as does remaining off-limits acreage in the eastern Gulf of Mexico and the mid-Atlantic. Canada has the ability to produce up to 5 mmbpd from oil sands in Alberta and Saskatchewan by 2020, and British Columbia holds 388 trillion cubic feet in gas and liquids.[33] Under new PRI (Partido Revolucionario Institucional, or Institutional Revolutionary Party) leadership, Mexico is seriously considering importing foreign expertise and capital into its oil sector to develop its underexplored deepwater side of the Gulf of Mexico, as well as its own shale gas formations, which appear to be a mirror image of the prolific Eagle Ford shale.

These developments pose serious policy issues. For the United States, the public's water and air safety will require improved standards and practices. In Canada, uncertainty over siting the Keystone XL pipeline has threatened to cap Canada's traditional market for oil, with major potential impacts on the Canadian economy. That risk has led Canadians to accelerate moves to welcome foreign investment in upstream assets and to approve pipelines running to their West Coast, looking to Asian markets rather than south to the United States. And in Mexico, declining oil production threatens its economic stability at a time when a US recession has hurt its export potential and trafficking of guns and narcotics has scared off investment in the industrial north. The potential opening of Mexico's hydrocarbon sector could require revising a major tenet of the Mexican Revolution—the ban on foreign ownership of natural resources.

In Latin America, the pendulum is moving away from free and open energy markets to increased state interference. This trend is evident in Argentina, where the government has moved effectively to expropriate Spanish energy assets; in Brazil, with its nationalist backlash clothed in a regulatory and safety agenda; in Ecuador, which flouts its bilateral investment treaty commitments; and in Venezuela, which some foreign companies have left because of changing business conditions and investment risks. All those who tout a North American energy renaissance hope for a revived Mexican hydrocarbon sector. But will a United States that no longer needs Venezuela's heavy oil or that exports LNG to South America be committed to playing a significant role in the post–Hugo Chávez era—and, if so, will it do so for broader political concerns, rather than for energy or economic reasons?

Europe and Eurasia

European autonomy, especially the autonomy of nations wholly dependent on Russia for gas, will depend on the ability to diversify supply.[34] Europe's climate change goals will require affordable supplies of gas to substitute for coal and to offset the currently high cost of renewable energy. Eurasian states need alternative export routes to support their freedom of action. Such alternatives will reduce the ability of Russia to use its transportation infrastructure to extract monopoly prices for transshipment and at times for political leverage. To these ends, the United States has supported alternative pipelines and LNG supplies and increased partnership ties in Europe. In the future, we can help accelerate deployment of shale and energy-efficiency technologies, which are sustainable contributions to energy security and economic growth.

In Eurasia, Kazakhstan is expanding production significantly, both in existing fields such as Tengiz and in prospective fields such as Kashagan, much of which will be carried by the CPC (Caspian Pipeline Consortium) pipeline, with expanded volumes over 1.4 mmbpd across Russia to the Black Sea. Azerbaijan is entering a new phase of oil and gas development that can help supply Europe with a southern corridor and real gas-on-gas price competition. Turkmenistan also holds enormous gas potential, but its president has yet to allow significant foreign investment beyond China in its major onshore fields.

Russia's energy path remains challenging. Russia has launched new openings with foreign companies for oil development in the Barents and Kara Seas, unconventional energy in Siberia, and offshore gas in the Far North. Yet the fiscal terms for those developments are uncertain, and a history of changing terms for foreign partners gives pause. As Western markets pose growing challenges, Russia is shifting east, increasing gas development and exports from Sakhalin and potentially other fields in the future, and completing its East Siberia to Pacific Ocean pipeline, which will carry up to 1 mmbpd to Asia by 2015. Despite years of negotiation, it has not yet reached agreement with China on pricing for gas, a situation that is further complicated by Beijing's 30 billion—and prospectively 60 billion—cubic meters of annual imports from Turkmenistan.[35]

The Middle East and North Africa

The Arab Upheaval is ongoing. The new regional emphasis on internal development will raise both domestic demand for energy and the threshold price at which oil- and gas-producing nations can fund national budgets. Although significant unrest has not reached substantial energy exporters such as Saudi Arabia or the United Arab Emirates, the potential for disruption remains high.

The region's role in global oil and gas supply is also shifting. Egypt may become a net gas importer rather than an exporter, while Israel may realize self-sufficiency in natural gas and even export natural gas or electric power.

Libya's leadership, laws, and investment framework are in flux. Iraq has made strides in recovering its prewar levels of oil production and is producing enough natural gas and power to revive economic activity within its borders. However, concerns regarding security, infrastructure, and continued disputes over control of Kurdish oil and gas exports make its full potential uncertain.[36]

Sub-Saharan Africa

With the exception of Nigeria and, to a lesser extent, South Africa and Angola, US engagement in Sub-Saharan Africa has been episodic and limited to counterterrorism, antipiracy, and humanitarian issues. Yet emerging African energy producers will face great challenges in managing the business and the revenues from oil production and in averting the resource curse issues that have plagued their neighbors.

It is an open question whether the United States will remain engaged on these issues. On the one hand, terrorist and Islamic extremist threats of the kind spreading from Algeria to Mali compel Western as well as African Union attention. On the other hand, Western failure to aid these nations adequately in channeling more resources into electricity and other development will likely lead them to seek assistance from other countries, such as those in East and South Asia. These countries may, in turn, realize increased diplomatic, economic, and energy leverage in Africa at Western expense.[37]

Asia and the Pacific

The energy paths of China, India, and other non-OECD countries will dominate their diplomatic relations with producing nations, their own security perceptions, the intensity of conflict over disputed maritime borders (and resources), and—to no small extent—the fate of the global climate. The region will account for at least half the total increase in total energy demand by 2035.[38] Each country depends heavily on coal for power generation yet has nascent potential to develop natural gas resources. Increasing demand for oil and petroleum products can either push these nations into a rerun of US energy history—with close ties to the Middle East and autocratic African regimes to secure ample supplies—or a more efficient and self-sufficient path.

This region also has new major energy producers. Australia is slated to become the world's largest LNG exporter by 2020. Smaller countries also have the potential to punch above their weight in energy supplies and politics: Papua New Guinea and Timor-Leste have large new LNG projects under way. Myanmar is now rejoining the family of nations and has vast resources that could help develop that country if used wisely.

These developments will raise challenging policy questions for the United States. For example, will we actively support natural gas development in these countries as a scalable alternative to coal? Will we export LNG to other Asian economies, beyond Japan, South Korea, and Taiwan? Will we interpose ourselves as facilitators or take a greater role in disputes between China and its neighbors in the South and East China Seas?[39]

The Domestic Dimension

The structural difficulties of thoroughly integrating energy issues into US foreign policy and showing energy leadership have been regrettably augmented by increased political polarization over the past five years.[40] In the 2008 US presidential election campaign, there seemed to be consensus that the threat of human-made emissions to the global climate was real, that domestic and multilateral actions were necessary, and that a market-based solution involving the world's major emitters was required.

However, our polity seems to have regressed since then to renewed doubts about global warming—despite all evidence to the contrary—as well as reflexive opposition to measures to reduce emissions of chemicals and toxins. Infrastructure has also proved divisive. In 2009, the Obama administration permitted the Alberta Clipper, a cross-border 400,000 bpd oil pipeline from Canada to Wisconsin, without much national debate. However, the similar Keystone XL pipeline, which was to bring 515,000 bpd of Canadian oil to the US Gulf Coast, encountered a major opposition campaign by environmental groups. Other initiatives, including plans for LNG export terminals in the East, Gulf, and West Coasts and even a proposed doubling of Alberta Clipper volumes without the need for an additional line, have also encountered opposition.

Certainly, legitimate issues are at play in these controversies, yet the all-or-nothing approach of core constituencies in both major US political parties, plus the inability of political leaders from both parties to negotiate solutions, has left US energy policy in disarray. President Obama signaled a renewed commitment to combat climate change in his 2013 inaugural address. Given congressional opposition, that commitment may well take the form of regulating emissions from power plants and other stationary sources, which would be a significant step.

In addition, US leaders can look abroad to discern alternative paths forward. The United Kingdom and Norway have adopted policies that foster energy production and targets to put their economies on a path to reduced emissions and improved industrial competitiveness. Even Saudi Arabia is embarking on a major energy-efficiency, solar energy, and nuclear energy plan to help end the use of oil for power generation for both fiscal and climate reasons. We believe a more balanced, science-based set of energy and environmental solutions is possible and could garner public support with strong political leadership. The foreign policy and national security benefits of a well-calibrated policy make this approach imperative.[41]

The Scope of This Volume

The first edition of this book, published in 2005, focused on the need for the United States to lead on energy reform at home so that it could lead abroad. The core challenges, at a time of rising import dependence and rising emissions, were to implement demand-side measures at home, to invest in technology, to collaborate with others on collective energy security, to diversify sources abroad, to address the consequences of the resource curse for important producers, to foster international coalitions to improve stability (especially by engaging China and India), and to recognize that energy and security are linked so that policy-makers would integrate those policies to make them more effective.

This new edition recognizes significant progress so far on this agenda and the work that remains, which is made both easier and more challenging by the new energy landscape. In many ways, the United States has led at home. Our reduced energy dependence is a result of reduced demand, which is reinforced by government policies, and increased supply. The United States has also advanced an international agenda that promotes energy development and transparency abroad, including the safe and efficient use of tight oil and gas technology.

In this new edition, we sustain our focus on energy security, regional politics, and the building blocks of a new energy economy, while emphasizing a radically new energy landscape and its wider implications. The new issues we address are (a) the effects of the gas revolution from shale to LNG, (b) the new energy frontiers from tight oil to the Arctic, (c) the rising agenda of safety concerns across the energy complex, (d) the problem of energy poverty, (e) the infrastructure needed to modernize our power grids, (f) a pathway to climate security in the current political and economic environment, and (g) the challenges and opportunities of these changes for our national security and regional politics around the globe.

Developments on these matters will follow multiple routes, but they will all culminate, in the aggregate, in either more or less energy security: the affordable, reliable access to the resources a nation needs to sustain national power. Success requires US leadership that recognizes and seizes these opportunities and musters the will to rally both public and private sectors behind advancing this goal. If we can achieve a coherent approach at home, we can wield our resources and our technology abroad to advance a safer, healthier, freer, and more prosperous planet.

Notes

1. See Richard G. Newell and Stuart Iler, "The Global Energy Outlook," chapter 1 of this volume, and Melanie A. Kenderdine and Ernest J. Moniz, "Technology Development and Energy Security," chapter 17 of this volume.

2. US Energy Information Administration (EIA), "EIA's AEO2012 Includes Analysis of Breakthroughs in Vehicle Battery Technology," *Today in Energy* (blog), July 2, 2012, http://205.254.135.7/todayinenergy/detail.cfm?id=6930.

3. EIA, *Annual Energy Outlook 2012 with Projections to 2035* (Washington, DC: Energy Information Administration, 2012).

4. Edward L. Morse, Eric G. Lee, Daniel P. Ahn, Aakash Doshi, Seth M. Klein, and Anthony Yuen, "Energy 2020: North America, the New Middle East?" *Citi GPS: Global Perspectives and Solutions*, March 20, 2012.

5. Richard Henderson, "Employment Outlook 2010–2020: Industry Employment and Output Projections to 2020," *Monthly Labor Review*, January 2012, http://www.bls .gov/opub/mlr/2012/01/art4full.pdf.

6. Daniel Yergin, "The Real Stimulus: Low-Cost Natural Gas," *Wall Street Journal*, October 22, 2012, http://online.wsj.com/article/SB10000872396390444734804578062331199029850.html.

7. EIA, *Annual Energy Outlook 2012*.

8. EIA, "27 Gigawatts of Coal-Fired Capacity to Retire over Next Five Years," *Today in Energy* (blog), July 27, 2012, http://www.eia.gov/todayinenergy/detail .cfm?id=7290#.

9. EIA, *Annual Energy Outlook 2012*. See also David Hone, "Can the United States Meet Its Energy Emissions Target?," *The Great Energy Challenge* (blog), September 9, 2011, http://www.greatenergychallengeblog.com/2011/09/09.

10. See David G. Victor, "The Gas Promise," chapter 3 of this volume.

11. Charles K. Ebinger, Kevin Massy, and Govinda Avasarala, "Liquid Markets: Assessing the Case for US Exports of Liquefied Natural Gas," Policy Brief 12-01, Brookings Energy Security Initiative, Washington, DC, 2012. See also Michael Levi,

"A Strategy for US Natural Gas Exports," Policy Brief 2012-04, Hamilton Project, Brookings Institution, Washington, DC, 2012.

12. Mark Mills, "US Can Become an Energy Export Nation," *Politico*, July 25, 2012, http://www.politico.com/news/stories/0712/78978.html.

13. Michael T. Klare, "The New 'Golden Age of Oil' That Wasn't," *European Energy Review*, October 8, 2012, http://www.europeanenergyreview.eu/site/pagina.php?id =3891.

14. Fiona Harvey, "'Golden Age of Gas' Threatens Renewable Energy, IEA Warns," *Guardian*, May 29, 2012, http://www.guardian.co.uk/environment/2012/may/ 29/gas-boom-renewables-agency-warns.

15. *Tight oil* consists of light crude oil contained in low-permeability formations, often shale or tight sandstone, whose production requires the same hydraulic fracturing and often the horizontal well technology used in the production of shale gas. It is different from *shale oil*, which is manufactured from oil shale by heating kerogen-rich rock. *Tight gas* is natural gas produced from low-permeability reservoir rocks, whose production also requires hydraulic fracturing and often horizontal drilling to produce the well at economic rates.

16. Office of Foreign Assets Control, Department of the Treasury, "Iranian Financial Sanctions Regulations," *Federal Register* 77, no. 38 (May 23, 2011): 11724–35, http://www.treasury.gov/resource-center/sanctions/Programs/Documents/fr77_11724 .pdf.

17. "G20 Summit Communiqué: Full Text," *Telegraph* (London), June 20, 2012, http://www.telegraph.co.uk/finance/g20-summit/9343250/G20-Summit-communique -full-text.html.

18. "Interview with Ali Al-Naimi," *Gulf Oil Review* 1, no.1 (London: Petroleum Policy Intelligence, June 2012).

19. EIA, "US Crude Oil and Liquid Fuels Supply, Consumption, and Inventories," *Short Term Energy Outlook* (blog), July 10, 2012, http://www.eia.gov/forecasts/steo/ tables/?tableNumber=9#endcode=201312&periodtype=m&startcode=201201.

20. A key natural gas distribution hub in Louisiana, Henry Hub lends its name to the pricing point for natural gas futures contracts traded on the NYMEX (New York Mercantile Exchange) and over-the-counter swaps traded on the ICE (Intercontinental Exchange).

21. According to the IEA's "Golden Age of Gas" scenario, by 2035 the world will have seen a reduction in CO_2 emissions by 740 metric tons because of the global transition from coal to gas.

22. IEA, *World Energy Outlook 2012* (Paris: Organization for Economic Cooperation and Development/IEA, 2012), 529.

23. See William K. Reilly, "Valuing Safety Even When the Market Doesn't Notice," chapter 4 of this volume.

24. See Daniel Yergin, "Energy Security and Markets," chapter 2 of this volume, and Leon Fuerth, "National Security, Energy, Climate Change: New Paradigm, New Strategy, New Governance," chapter 22 of this volume.

25. Examples include the United Nations climate negotiations, Clean Energy Ministerial and Major Economies Forum. William Ramsay suggests that "minilateralist" alternatives may be more productive. See William C. Ramsay, "Energy Sector Governance in the 21st Century," chapter 6 of this volume, and Michael Levi, "Energy, Environment, and Climate: Framework and Tradeoffs," chapter 21 of this volume.

26. The US EITI stakeholder group launched in February 2013, completing US candidacy.

27. The full text of the Dodd–Frank Wall Street Reform and Consumer Protection Act is available at http://www.sec.gov/about/laws/wallstreetreform-cpa.pdf.

28. See Charles McPherson, "Governance, Transparency, and Sustainable Development," chapter 19 of this volume.

29. Hillary Rodham Clinton, "Energy Diplomacy in the 21st Century," address to Georgetown University, Washington, DC, October 18, 2012.

30. Samuel R. Avro, "Energy Secretary Admits to Naiveté over OPEC Remarks," *Consumer Energy Report*, February 19, 2009, http://www.energytrendsinsider.com/2009/02/19/energy-secretary-admits-naivete-over-opec-remarks/.

31. See William C. Ramsay, "Energy Sector Governance in the 21st Century," chapter 6 of this volume.

32. See Shirley Neff and Angelina LaRose, "North America," chapter 15 of this volume, and Thomas F. "Mack" McLarty, "Latin America," chapter 16 of this volume.

33. Morse et al., "Energy 2020."

34. See Pierre Noël, "Europe's Gas Supply Security: Unfinished Business," chapter 7 of this volume.

35. See Julia Nanay and Jan H. Kalicki, "Russia and Eurasia," chapter 8 of this volume.

36. See J. Robinson West and Raad Alkadiri, "Iraq, Iran, and the Gulf Region," chapter 10 of this volume, and Fareed Mohamedi, "North Africa and the Mediterranean," chapter 11 of this volume.

37. See Phillip van Niekerk and Aaron Sayne, "Sub-Saharan Africa," chapter 12 of this volume.

38. This projection is according to the International Energy Agency's New Policies scenario, as described in IEA, *World Energy Outlook 2012*.

39. See Amy Myers Jaffe and Kenneth B Medlock III, "China, India, and Asian Energy," chapter 13 of this volume, and Mikkal Herberg, "Japan, Southeast Asia, and Australia," chapter 14 of this volume.

40. See Frank Verrastro and Kevin Book, "The Challenge of Politics," chapter 23 of this volume.

41. See Leon Fuerth, "National Security, Energy, Climate Change: New Paradigm; New Strategy; New Governance," chapter 22 of this volume.

Part I

The Global Framework

Part I of this volume sets forth a framework for understanding the political economy of energy and the ways that actions of nations and organizations affect both energy security and foreign policy. The key elements are (a) the outlook for supply and demand, (b) the role of markets and the evolving national requirements for energy security, (c) the role of the Organization of the Petroleum Exporting Countries (OPEC) in influencing oil prices, (d) the growing abundance and accessibility of natural gas as fuel for power and transport, (e) the need for new standards in the safe production of oil and gas, and (f) the need to update the international organizations that consuming states created in 1974 and to increase the global space to engage new consumers and new challenges.

In the first edition of this book, published in 2005, we identified the driving forces of the world of energy as supply and demand, technological change, OPEC's ability to limit supply, and the power of consuming nations to undertake policies to shape their own destiny. The consuming nations were largely resource constrained; they faced declining reserves

19

and demand in excess of supply and were focused on measures to constrain demand for reasons of economic and national security.

Three of these key drivers are still salient: supply and demand, technological change, and the policy choices of consuming countries, particularly as they consider energy security, fuel diversity, and climate change as policy goals. But technology is shifting the balance of power in energy. The huge jump in production of unconventional oil and gas in the United States over the past five years has changed expectations about the availability of fossil fuels and has reversed the reserve and production profiles of countries that had been in decline. North American self-sufficiency in liquids is now a realistic prospect: the United States and Canada both enjoy tight oil and shale gas booms, and Mexico appears poised to adjust policies that have left it rich in reserves but declining in production.

The role of OPEC, however, may change significantly over the coming decades, affecting its ability to influence the market, its cohesion, and its ability to achieve its goal of managing oil flows to maximize the revenues of its members. OPEC is still projected to maintain a significant share of total world production. Saudi Arabia will likely remain the largest oil exporter and continues to hold the largest spare capacity in the world, although it faces increasing questions about that role going forward. The leading gas exporters will include non-OPEC suppliers such as the United States, Australia, and soon East Africa. These shifts portend changes in foreign relations and perceptions of energy security around the world.

The authors in part I agree in numerous areas on the likely patterns of supply and demand over the next 25 years and the challenges to be faced. Although the share of total global energy production that comes from fossil fuels will fall, their share will still remain the largest by far. Energy demand will increase, with the largest growth coming from the developing world, particularly China and India. Oil will remain the primary transportation fuel, and inroads made by alternative fuels such as natural gas, biofuels, and electricity will be relatively small. Changes in the electricity fuel mix could be significant, particularly if the shale gas revolution can take hold outside of the United States. US shale gas success has already significantly offset US coal demand. Among the questions that part I seeks to address are the following:

- What shifts in the global fuel mix and energy demand are likely to be seen over the next two decades?

- What impact will changing production patterns, in part caused by booms in unconventional fuel production, have on energy security and geopolitics?
- What impact will low-probability, high-impact accidents such as the Macondo oil spill and Fukushima nuclear incident have on the industry's operating culture and on global energy trends?
- Will institutions such as the International Energy Agency (IEA) and OPEC continue to play the same role in energy governance?

Richard Newell and Stuart Iler assess global energy forecasts in chapter 1. In chapter 2, Daniel Yergin looks at changing definitions of energy security and possible ways to improve global energy security through technology, robust markets, and supportive policy. David Victor expounds on the promise of the global natural gas boom in chapter 3. William Reilly demonstrates, in chapter 4, the vital nature of safety as a tenet of industry culture in the wake of accidents such as Macondo and Fukushima. In chapter 5, Edward Morse and Amy Myers Jaffe look critically at the role that OPEC may play over the coming decades. And in chapter 6, William Ramsay explores a number of institutions aimed at ensuring good governance in the energy sector and the failure of multilateral organizations and treaty processes to address global climate change before suggesting an alternative path rooted in bilateral and "minilateral" diplomacy.

In chapter 1, Richard Newell and Stuart Iler analyze the assumptions behind a spectrum of different energy projections—those prepared by companies, governments, and other organizations—to provide a comprehensive, nuanced view of what the global energy sector (supply, demand, trade, efficiency, fuel mix, and so forth) could look like over the next 20 or more years. The authors suggest that though fossil fuels will continue to dominate the fuel mix, their overall share will continue to fall, and that coal and oil have either already reached or will soon reach their peak consumption in the Western Hemisphere. At the same time, they note that overall energy consumption in the Eastern Hemisphere will increase substantially, with particular growth in the demand for oil, natural gas, and electricity. On a global scale, renewables will be the fastest-growing fuel source by percentage, but according to most projections, they will represent only 7 to 18 percent of primary energy consumption in 2035, given their relatively small starting base. Newell and Iler also find that in some long-term forecasts, global emissions of carbon dioxide (CO_2) are expected to flatten out between 2030 and 2040 and that the adoption of additional policies aimed at limiting climate change would bring those emissions down further. To facilitate a better-informed discussion, Newell and Iler consider the policy, technology, and other assumptions that make up these different energy projections, helping to explain why forecasts of the same time period can often present widely varying results.

In chapter 2, Daniel Yergin argues that "the major risk to supplies over the next decade or two is not geology but geopolitics," such as the Arab Uprising, potential disputes over energy chokepoints such as the Strait of Hormuz, and tensions that may arise in times of limited energy supply. Yergin explains that energy security, previously thought of simply as an oil supply question, should be considered as a multidimensional concern. He also demonstrates how what he calls an "integrated oil shock" can paralyze an entire region. Among the principles of energy security Yergin identifies are spare capacity and strategic reserves; the need for robust dialogue and cooperation between producers and consumers; the importance of a technology-driven industry; and the ability of large, flexible, and well-functioning markets to self-modulate in times of fluctuation. He points to a major new risk to energy security—the cyber vulnerability of the energy system. Yergin concludes that by planning for disruptions—whether supply based, physical, cyber, or financial—countries can limit the impacts and be more prepared.

In chapter 3, David Victor, who describes (half tongue in cheek) the natural gas industry as "manic-depressive" and "prone to wild swings in mood," states that while the US shale gas revolution has swung energy analysts toward euphoria, plenty could still go wrong in a nascent industry. The discovery of shale gas, coupled with the ability to produce it relatively inexpensively, has created a huge boon to the domestic industry and has led to environmental benefits as a result of offsetting coal demand, but it is not yet known whether the revolution can be repeated abroad. He suggests that the best role for the United States in spreading shale gas development is to focus on helping countries to develop strong regulatory frameworks, on ensuring that the US industry sets a good example in terms of responsible development, and on allowing foreign investment to promote the spread of technology while letting the market develop at a natural pace.

In chapter 4, William Reilly pans the idea that catastrophic events are often—or ever—the result of unpredictable and unpreventable coincidences. Reilly provides considerable evidence that even low-probability, high-impact events can be mitigated through the development of a culture of safety and through serious examination of all incidents, no matter how small, for indicators of a pattern or potential for a larger disaster. He argues that in addition to industry executives and regulators, analysts and investors should play a role in placing a premium on safety and responsible operations. Reilly concludes that high-risk industries should learn from the lessons of Macondo and Fukushima and that industry leaders have strong incentive to pull up the bottom performers in their sectors to prevent catastrophes that would damage the entire sector.

In chapter 5, Amy Jaffe and Ed Morse note OPEC's remarkable and even enigmatic durability in sustaining a coalition of state-controlled economic management in a world of liberalized economies. Although OPEC's monarchies and other regimes look stable in the short term, Jaffe and Morse find it inevitable that demographic pressures and domestic constituencies will challenge the ability of OPEC governments to support coalition decisions. Moreover, the authors note that OPEC may have sown the seeds of its own destruction. By holding back investment in production and allowing prices to rise dramatically, OPEC spurred massive consumer investment in efficiency measures and alternative fuels. Rising prices also drove the technological development that has now shifted the balance of energy power back to the Western Hemisphere, with the massive tight oil boom in the United States, the investment in unconventional oil in Canada, and the ultradeepwater investment in the Gulf of Mexico and offshore Brazil. While acknowledging OPEC's remarkable durability, Jaffe and Morse warn that the organization's future will depend on how OPEC manages rising demand in its population, the integration of Iraq, and the loss of market share it may face as the Western Hemisphere becomes a potential export competitor.

In chapter 6, William Ramsay examines existing energy institutions, such as OPEC, the IEA, and the International Energy Forum (IEF), in an effort to determine whether those institutions are able to address vital challenges such as dealing with climate change, reducing energy poverty, and promoting energy sustainability. Ramsay finds that energy diplomacy today has not yet evolved enough to be effective; instead it has become unwieldy and inadequate. OPEC is oriented largely toward supply management. The IEA is frequently hindered by limitations of membership and ability to interact with nonmembers on policy issues. The IEF at present is aimed primarily at promoting data transparency in the energy sector. Ramsay concludes that multilateralism, in broad terms, is not the answer to many modern challenges and that countries should attempt bilateral or "minilateral" diplomacy to bring together parties with shared interests and common incentives so that they can address vital problems and find solutions.

In his commentary on part I, Chakib Khelil is sanguine concerning both OPEC's future and continued US engagement in the Middle East. Khelil notes that Newell and Iler forecast that OPEC will still be the largest contributor to global oil supply in 2035, with OPEC nations still holding 80 percent of global oil reserves. The challenge with Newell and Iler's forecast—and others—is that they have vastly different outcomes for the call on OPEC, thereby making security of demand uncertain and complicating the investment that Jaffe and Morse call for in their chapter. Noting that the organization's success is helping to balance the market during both Gulf Wars and the Libyan and other crises, Khelil finds OPEC necessary and effective, and he predicts that the changes in governance that Jaffe and Morse forecast will strengthen OPEC rather than weaken it. Citing Dan Yergin's views on interdependence, Bill Ramsay's recognition of OPEC and IEA cooperation, Victor's anticipation of a more global gas market, and US strategic interests in the Middle East, Khelil expects that the United States will remain committed to its strategic partners and to defense of the increasingly busy Strait of Hormuz in 2035 and beyond.

Chapter 1

The Global Energy Outlook

Richard G. Newell and Stuart Iler

Introduction

In this chapter, we explore the principal trends that are shaping the future energy landscape. We take a long-term view, on the timescale of a generation, by looking 25 years into the past, taking stock of the current situation, and projecting 25 years into the future. We view these trends at a global scale, as well as assess the key regional dynamics that are substantially altering the energy scene. The shift from West to East in the locus of energy growth and the turnaround of North American gas and oil production are the most pronounced of these currents.

We thank Paul Appleby (BP), Linda Doman (US Energy Information Administration), Matthew Frank (International Energy Agency), and Todd Onderdonk (ExxonMobil) for their assistance, including reviewing and verifying figures for their respective organizations. We also thank Robert Schwiers (Chevron) for helpful comments.

25

We place significant strategic value on the projection of alternative future energy scenarios for the purpose of informing business investment, domestic public policy, foreign policy, international trade, and other decisions. Some trends may appear neutral but require reaction in response to changing conditions. Other developments present opportunities that can be seized on. Still others may look distinctly negative, requiring risk mitigation or prodding us like the Chinese philosopher Lao Tzu that "if you do not change direction, you may end up where you are heading." In many or even most cases, whether particular trends look positive or negative will depend on one's point of view. Given that the bounds of uncertainty may be large, projections 25 years into the future must be done with humility, and there is considerable value in exploring multiple scenarios.

Major Shifts in the Energy Landscape

Several aspects of the energy landscape have changed significantly since the last edition of this book in 2005. Expected growth in global energy consumption has come down, and regional growth expectations have shifted more strongly eastward. At the same time, unconventional oil and especially natural gas are poised to play a more significant role in fulfilling the world's energy needs, while lingering uncertainty remains regarding the place of nuclear power in the energy mix. Nonhydro renewables are now making measurable inroads into the electricity mix, as are biofuels as a component of liquid transport fuels. On both fronts, the ability of existing energy infrastructure to accommodate renewables is being tested, requiring new approaches and additional investment.

In the previous edition, Adam Sieminski anticipated that world energy consumption would increase about 50 percent from 2010 levels by 2030, reaching almost 340 million barrels per day (mmbpd) of oil equivalent, not including nonmarketed biomass.[1] Current expectations are now generally lower, with comparable estimates in the range of 300 to 330 mmbpd of oil equivalent in 2035, five years later (see table 1.1, on page 31 of this chapter). Projections of future oil consumption follow a similar pattern. In the last edition, estimated oil demand grew to 124 mmbpd by 2030, whereas the highest current projections are in the range of 110 mmbpd for 2035 (table 1.5, later in this chapter). These lower projections of both overall energy consumption and oil demand reflect a number of developments, including the lasting impact of the global economic downturn, higher energy prices, and improved energy efficiency because of policy interventions.

Past and current fuel share projections show both similarities and differences. The expected share of petroleum 20 to 25 years hence has decreased significantly from 38 percent to around 30 percent (excluding nonmarketed biomass). At the same time, although the overall share of fossil fuels appears likely to remain above 75 percent and possibly closer to 80 percent, this estimate is significantly lower than the almost 90 percent share estimated for 2030 in the last edition of this volume.

New technologies such as horizontal drilling and hydraulic fracturing have made previously untapped reserves of oil and natural gas profitable and are beginning to shift regional supply dynamics. The abundance and location of these unconventional sources, coupled with patterns of demand, have the potential to significantly change the energy trade balance in certain parts of the world (figure 1.2, later in this chapter). Shale gas, in particular, has radically altered the outlook for North American natural gas production, shifting the United States from a position of increasing liquefied natural gas (LNG) importation to one in which it is preparing to export natural gas. This shift is, in turn, having ripple effects on spot market prices for natural gas, the global LNG market, and international price structures for natural gas contracts.

Oil sands and now tight oil are having a similar effect on the North American liquids front, although at this time the magnitude of impact is less pronounced than for unconventional gas. Still—when coupled with increased fuel economy, dampened liquids demand, and increased biofuels and natural gas liquids production—this increase in petroleum production has placed North America on a path to net self-sufficiency in liquids over roughly the next 20 to 25 years.

How the incident at the Fukushima nuclear reactor in Japan will affect the future of nuclear energy is still unclear. Some countries have announced plans to reevaluate, reduce, or completely dismantle their nuclear programs, though the form and timing of implementation are still in flux. General issues surrounding nuclear energy have changed little since the last edition: economically it remains a relatively expensive electricity source, and concerns about safety, waste disposal, and nuclear material proliferation have not subsided, particularly in light of the Fukushima incident. However, fast-growing Asian economies such as China and India, as well as some Middle Eastern countries, are looking for large-scale nonfossil sources of power and so have turned to nuclear energy as a part of their electricity mix. Whether the presence of nuclear power in the energy supply mix increases substantially may be driven largely by the extent of efforts to mitigate carbon emissions and the effects of climate change; if such efforts are significant, nuclear power may be much more economically competitive.

Types of Energy Scenarios

Energy outlooks—in the form of detailed quantitative projections of energy consumption, supply, technologies, prices, and other variables— are one way to explore future energy trends; the impacts of energy use; and the implications of current, expected, and potential policies. Some organizations, including the US Energy Information Administration (EIA) and the International Energy Agency (IEA), provide multiple scenarios within each of their energy outlooks. One benefit of this approach is a better understanding of how critical assumptions affect the results from these organizations' respective energy models. Some other organizations, such as ExxonMobil and BP, do not publish multiple scenarios (though they may internally perform sensitivity analysis), and as such their projections are presented as a single benchmark or "best guess" scenario. In all cases, some of the key factors that differentiate models and scenarios are assumptions regarding economic and population growth, policies, energy prices, and expected technological innovation and deployment.

   Energy scenarios can be grouped into roughly three types: (a) reference case or current policy scenarios, (b) best guess or expected value scenarios, and (c) alternative policy and technology scenarios. Reference case and current policy scenarios assume that existing market and technology trends—and particularly current policy—will continue into the future. Examples include the EIA's Reference Case scenario and the IEA's Current Policies scenario. These types of scenarios provide a very useful baseline against which the effect of new policy proposals and significant technology or market changes can be measured, and they avoid judgments about policy proposals that have not yet been put into law. By construction, however, these scenarios capture only the current state of policy—which can be very important to the energy system—and we know from experience that policy usually does, in fact, change rather than remain stagnant.

Technological change can also be discontinuous or abrupt at times, rather than incremental along a continuous path. Alternative policy and technology scenarios are therefore an important complement to business-as-usual projections.

One alternative approach is to consider a scenario of what one might reasonably expect will occur with future policy developments—that is, a best guess of those policies most likely to be adopted given recent policy trends. This second group of energy scenarios, which could be labeled as *expected* or *new policy* scenarios, include projections made by private companies such as ExxonMobil and BP, as well as the IEA's New Policies scenario. For example, despite current political uncertainty, ExxonMobil's *Outlook for Energy* expects policies in member countries of the Organization for Economic Cooperation and Development (OECD), China, and many other non-OECD countries to place a cost on carbon dioxide (CO_2) emissions of $80, $30, and $20 per ton by 2040, respectively.

The third group is a much wider range of alternative policy and technology scenarios, which take this type of exploration one step further—envisioning a future where political action and technological capabilities go beyond current trends, plans, and proposals. The IEA's 450 scenario is a useful example, where assumptions are based on the steps necessary to limit greenhouse gas (GHG) concentrations in the atmosphere to 450 parts per million (ppm) of CO_2 equivalent. This scenario includes more vigorous climate-related policy action than is assumed in the New Policies scenario or other major energy outlooks, translating into significant GHG reductions over the projection period and significant energy system changes for all of the world's major economies.[2] In addition to the Reference Case, the EIA produces a range of alternative scenarios, considering significant variations in economic growth, oil prices, and implementation of US policy proposals.[3]

World Primary Energy Consumption

Global primary energy consumption[4] is on a path to grow in the range of 30 to 35 percent over the next generation, reaching about 700 quadrillion British thermal units (quads) or 340 mmbpd of oil equivalent by 2035, including all energy sources (figure 1.1 and table 1.1).[5] Scenarios assuming the continuance of current policies tend to show significantly higher

Figure 1.1. World Primary Energy Consumption Trends

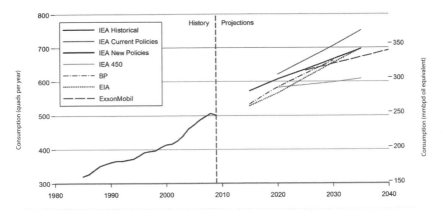

Sources: BP, *BP Energy Outlook 2030* (London: BP, 2012); ExxonMobil, *2012: The Outlook for Energy: A View to 2040* (Irving, TX: ExxonMobil, 2012); IEA, *World Energy Outlook 2011* (Paris: OECD/IEA, 2011); IEA, *World Energy Statistics and Balances*, 2011 ed. (Paris: OECD/IEA, 2011), doi:10.1787/enestats-data-en; EIA, *International Energy Outlook 2011* (Washington, DC: EIA, 2011).

Note: For clarity, the left vertical axis begins at 300 quads rather than at zero. BP and EIA projections do not include traditional, nonmarketed biomass energy consumption.

consumption growth (about 10 percent higher in absolute terms), illustrating the influence of policy on moderating the overall growth of energy consumption. In contrast, scenarios assuming very substantial reductions in CO_2 emissions, along the lines of the IEA's 450 scenario, could limit energy consumption growth to half that amount (about 16 percent) if pursued.

Historically, this rate of growth is much slower in percentage terms than the rate of growth in both of the two previous 25-year periods, from 1960 to 1985 (107 percent growth) and from 1985 to 2010 (67 percent growth). In absolute terms, however, a roughly 80 mmbpd of oil equivalent increase from 2010 to 2035 is only about 20 percent lower than the just over 100 mmbpd of oil equivalent increase from 1985 to 2010—a period of rapid global growth—and is essentially equal to the 80 mmbpd of oil equivalent increase experienced from 1960 to 1985. All in all, although the energy consumption growth rate is clearly slowing, the absolute magnitude of additional supply that will be required to meet increased energy needs over

Table 1.1. World Primary Energy Consumption

Years and Scenarios	Total Primary Energy Consumption		
	Quads	Oil Equivalent (mmbpd)	Total Growth over Prior 25 Years (%)
1960[a]	151	74	n.a.
1985[b]	313	153	107
2010 (including all biomass)[c]	524	257	67
2035			
IEA Current Policies[d]	752	368	44
IEA New Policies[d]	697	341	33
ExxonMobil[e]	676	331	29
IEA 450[d]	609	298	16
2010 (only marketed biomass)[c]	479	235	n.a.
2030 BP[f]	663	325	38[f]
2035 EIA[g]	698	342	46

Sources: As noted.

Note: n.a. = not applicable. The conversion rate is 1 quad per 0.49 mmbpd of oil equivalent. Fuel-specific energy consumption figures from each source were converted to primary energy in quads using a consistent set of rules to ensure comparability across sources; details are available from authors on request.

a. Arnulf Grubler, "Energy Transitions," in *Encyclopedia of Earth*, ed. Cutler J. Cleveland (Washington, DC: Environmental Information Coalition, National Council for Science and the Environment, 2008).

b. IEA, *World Energy Statistics and Balances*, 2011 ed. (Paris: OECD/IEA, 2011), doi:10.1787/enestats-data-en.

c. Two sets of consumption numbers are given for 2010, the first from IEA (*Key World Energy Statistics 2012* [Paris: OECD/IEA, 2012]) and the second from BP (*Statistical Review of World Energy June 2012* [London: BP, 2012]). The first includes all biomass energy consumption, both marketed and nonmarketed; the second includes only marketed biomass.

d. IEA, *World Energy Outlook 2011* (Paris: OECD/IEA, 2011).

e. ExxonMobil, *2012: The Outlook for Energy: A View to 2040* (Irving, TX: ExxonMobil, 2012).

f. *BP Energy Outlook 2030* (London: BP, 2012). The value for BP is for 2030 rather than 2035, and the total growth is over 20 years.

g. EIA, *International Energy Outlook 2011* (Washington, DC: EIA, 2011).

the next 25 years is roughly similar to what has been required over the past two generations. Nonetheless, this increment is on top of an already sizable consumption base.

Factors Driving Regional Energy Consumption

Energy consumption can be decomposed into three factors: population, gross domestic product (GDP) per capita, and the energy intensity of economic activity (i.e., energy per unit of GDP). This approach can be expanded to include carbon emissions, with the addition of a factor for the carbon intensity of energy.[6] Given this relationship, the growth of energy consumption (or carbon emissions) is directly related to the growth of these constituent factors. This simple relationship is useful for quickly grasping the underlying factors driving energy consumption as well as understanding what may be required to moderate the growth of energy consumption or emissions.

Policy-makers, of course, tend to promote the growth of per capita income, a key driver of energy consumption growth. And although population is a fundamental determinant of economic activity and energy needs, population dynamics are driven by forces largely outside the domain of energy markets and policies. Policy-makers, the energy industry, and other stakeholders therefore tend to focus on reducing the last two of these factors—energy intensity and the emissions intensity of energy—to achieve economic, environmental, and energy security objectives.

Current Regional Differences

Regionally, North America and Europe–Eurasia have significantly higher levels of both income and energy use per person than the rest of the world, with income per capita at almost 2 to 4 times the levels of Central and South America and the Middle East, and 4 to 12 times the levels of Asia and Africa (table 1.2). Energy use follows suit, with North America and Europe–Eurasia consuming energy at two to nine times the per capita level of other regions, excluding the Middle East. Because of its energy-intensive industrial base and degree of energy price subsidization, the Middle East consumes an unusually high amount of energy given its stage of overall

Table 1.2. Current Regional Distribution of Key Energy Drivers, 2009

Key Energy Drivers	World	North America	South and Central America	Europe–Eurasia	Africa	Middle East	Asia
Population[a] (millions)	6,765 (100%)	470 (7%)	451 (7%)	892 (13%)	1,009 (15%)	195 (3%)	3,749 (55%)
GDP[a] (trillion 2010 dollars PPP)	71 (100%)	17 (24%)	4 (6%)	20 (28%)	3 (4%)	2 (3%)	24 (34%)
Primary energy consumption[a,b] (quads)	500 (100%)	109 (22%)	22 (4%)	117 (23%)	27 (5%)	25 (5%)	186 (37%)
CO_2 emissions[a,b] (billion metric tons)	28.8 (100%)	6.2 (21%)	1.0 (3%)	6.3 (22%)	0.9 (3%)	1.5 (5%)	12.0 (42%)
GDP/population[c] ($1,000/person)	10	37	10	22	3	12	6
Energy consumption/GDP[c] (1,000 Btu/dollar)	7	6	5	6	9	10	8
Energy consumption/population[c] (million Btu/person)	74	231	50	131	27	128	50
CO_2 emissions/energy consumption[c] (million metric tons/quad)	58	57	44	54	34	60	65

Source: IEA, *World Energy Outlook 2011* (Paris: OECD/IEA, 2011).

Note: Btu = British thermal units; PPP = purchasing power parity.

a. Regional shares of the world total are shown in parentheses.

b. The sum of regions is less than the world total because only the latter includes oil transport bunkers.

c. The ratios in the bottom four rows are calculated from the values in the first four rows.

economic development. Asia contains over half of the world's population and, although it is still largely developing, accounts for more than a third of global GDP, primary energy consumption, and carbon emissions.

Regional Population Growth

A range of scenarios indicates that the growth in these factors over the next 25 years will be very different across regions. Most projections focus on a moderate population growth scenario in which global population reaches about 8.6 billion by 2035, or 26 percent higher than 2009 levels. Europe–Eurasia will have the slowest growth, roughly flat at perhaps 2 to 4 percent total growth, whereas population growth in Africa will likely be over 50 percent and potentially as high as 70 percent, or 720 million additional people. Similarly, projections for the Middle East show population growth of about 50 percent over the next generation. The Americas and Asia are on a population growth path of perhaps 20 to 25 percent, roughly in the middle of the two other regional extremes.[7] However, Asia is starting from a much higher population base, adding a projected 725 million people (similar to Africa), compared with an additional 200 million people in the Americas over the next 25 years. In absolute terms, about 45 percent of global population growth looks likely to occur in the East (Asia and the Middle East), with another 40 percent of the growth occurring in Africa. At the same time, significant uncertainty exists around these moderate population growth figures, and current United Nations population projections for 2035 range from 8.0 billion to 9.2 billion—that is, plus or minus 7 percent—compared with the 8.6 billion medium variant.[8]

Regional GDP Growth

A different set of regional patterns emerges when considering GDP. The major outlooks assume roughly 2.5-fold growth in global GDP from 2010 to 2035, when measured in terms of purchasing power parity (PPP), or closer to a doubling of GDP when measured using market exchange rates.[9] Across the different outlooks, regional GDP growth projections over this 25-year period (in PPP terms) are in the range of 70 to 80 percent for Europe–Eurasia, 85 to 95 percent for North America, 150 to 175 percent for the Middle East and Africa, and 230 to 250 percent for Asia.[10] Somewhat greater divergence exists in views about Central and South American GDP growth (about 130 percent for the IEA and ExxonMobil outlooks compared with 170 percent for that of the EIA).

In absolute terms, more than 60 percent of global income growth appears likely to occur in the East (Asia and the Middle East), about 30 percent in North America and in Europe–Eurasia, and the remainder in Central and South America and in Africa. Uncertainty surrounding the continuance of rapid growth in emerging economies, especially in Asia, could therefore have significant consequences for global energy demand moving forward, as it did over the past decade.

Regional Energy Consumption Growth

Over the next 25 years, Asia and the Middle East will experience close to half the world's population growth and over 60 percent of its income growth, forming a potent combination that implies about 70 percent of global energy consumption growth will occur in the East. All developing regions of the world—Asia, the Middle East, Africa, and South and Central America—will likely see energy consumption growth in excess of 40 percent, and some regions may see growth of 60 to 70 percent or more over the 2010 to 2035 period.

Despite the consistency of population and economic growth projections across the major energy outlooks—as well as the relative regional shares in energy consumption growth—considerable variation occurs in the resulting levels of energy demand. In some cases, this difference is due to assumptions that current policies remain unchanged—leading to higher consumption growth across the board (as in the EIA Reference Case and the IEA Current Policies scenarios)—or to assumptions of very stringent climate policy and much lower demand growth (as in the IEA 450 scenario). Carbon emissions tend to follow energy consumption estimates closely, with the amount depending on assumptions about climate policy.

However, even among central cases such as the IEA New Policies scenario and the ExxonMobil outlook, some considerable differences exist in energy consumption growth. Generally speaking, ExxonMobil projects significantly lower energy demand growth, both globally and for most major regions.[11] ExxonMobil's outlook, for example, has essentially zero net energy consumption growth in North America and Europe–Eurasia through

2035, and 29 percent growth globally—compared with 33 percent global growth in the IEA New Policies scenario.

Energy Efficiency and Energy Intensity

Two main subcomponents tend to determine the energy intensity of the economy: the energy efficiency of the capital stock (such as vehicles and equipment) and the overall structure of the economy (such as the relative shares of the manufacturing and service sectors). As such, reductions in energy intensity can occur both through improvements in energy efficiency and through a shift toward services as a larger share of economic activity (although at a global level such shifts are offset if manufacturing simply moves from one location to another).

Trends in the industrial[12] share of GDP are useful indicators of energy intensity differences among countries and where they are headed. For example, 34 percent of US GDP was associated with industry in 1980 but had declined to 20 percent by 2010. In contrast, the industrial shares of the economies of China and India have remained relatively steady. China's industrial share barely changed from 48 percent in 1980 to 47 percent in 2010, and India's share increased moderately from 24 percent to 27 percent during that period.[13]

Economic projections highlight how countries' economic structures are likely to evolve over the next few decades. For instance, macroeconomic forecasts have the industrial share of US shipments (by value) remaining roughly steady between 2010 and 2035, decreasing only slightly from approximately 22 percent to 21 percent over that period.[14] In contrast, recent World Bank estimates have the industrial share of GDP for China dropping to about 35 percent by 2030, compared with 47 percent in 2010.[15]

Without improvements in energy efficiency and energy intensity, energy consumption would grow by more than 120 percent globally in the Exxon-Mobil outlook, for instance, rather than by 30 percent. Even more striking are such differences for the OECD and non-OECD countries when considered separately: energy demand is nearly flat in the OECD countries when expected efficiency and intensity improvements are included, compared with 90 percent growth without these gains. In the non-OECD countries, projections show 60 percent compared with more than 250 percent growth with and without such developments, respectively.[16]

Potential Future Regional Differences

Regional differences in growth rates will significantly affect the potential future distribution of key energy drivers in 2035; here we use the IEA New Policies scenario as a central example (table 1.3). Although North America and Europe–Eurasia are on track to maintain the highest levels of GDP and energy consumption per capita, the Middle East, Asia, and South and Central America should experience significant increases by that time. This is not necessarily the case for Africa, which in most outlooks is assumed to experience population increases that consume the majority of gains in income growth or alleviation of energy poverty. The energy intensity of GDP decreases for all regions and for the world as a whole, indicating continued uptake of energy-efficient technologies and a relatively higher share of services than of manufacturing in economic growth. Finally, all regions show a decline in the carbon intensity of energy, reflecting the spread of renewables, the use of nuclear power, and the potential use of other technologies such as carbon capture and storage (with the last playing a greater role in scenarios with substantial CO_2 reductions).

Implications for Regional Trade

These shifting regional patterns of demand, coupled with changing sources of supply, have the potential to alter energy trade balances around the world (figure 1.2). One striking trend is the reduction of the energy trade imbalance in North America, with the Americas overall looking increasingly self-sufficient in energy. Over the next few decades, North America is likely to close this gap through the combination of two trends: modest consumption growth at the same time as a continued turnaround in supply, owing in large part to unconventional sources of oil and natural gas in Canada and the United States. In contrast, most other regions of the world become either greater importers or exporters, following historical trends. Net importers are Europe, China, India, and the rest of the Asia-Pacific region, while the former Soviet Union, the Middle East, Africa, and South and Central America continue to export increasing quantities of fossil fuels (the majority of which is oil, with growing levels of natural gas). The need for increased imports of all types is most acute for China, India, and other Asian countries,

Table 1.3. Potential Future Regional Distribution of Key Energy Drivers, 2035

Key Energy Drivers	World	North America	South and Central America	Europe–Eurasia	Africa	Middle East	Asia
Population[a] (millions)	8,556 (100%)	571 (7%)	558 (7%)	930 (11%)	1,730 (20%)	293 (3%)	4,474 (52%)
GDP[a] (trillion 2010 dollars PPP)	176 (100%)	32 (18%)	10 (6%)	36 (20%)	7 (4%)	7 (4%)	84 (48%)
Primary energy consumption[a,b] (quads)	697 (100%)	118 (17%)	34 (5%)	136 (19%)	37 (5%)	42 (6%)	310 (45%)
CO_2 emissions[a,b] (billion metric tons)	36.4 (100%)	5.7 (16%)	1.3 (4%)	6.2 (17%)	1.2 (3%)	2.3 (6%)	18.3 (50%)
GDP/population[c] ($1,000/person)	21	57	18	39	4	23	19
Energy consumption/GDP[c] (1,000 Btu/dollar)	4	4	3	4	5	6	4
Energy consumption/population[c] (million Btu/person)	81	207	61	146	21	144	69
CO_2 emissions/energy consumption[c] (million metric tons/quad)	52	48	38	46	31	55	59

Source: New Policies scenario, in IEA, *World Energy Outlook 2011* (Paris: OECD/IEA, 2011).

Note: Btu = British thermal units; PPP = purchasing power parity.

a. Regional shares of the world total are shown in parentheses.

b. The sum of regions is less than the world total because only the latter includes oil transport bunkers.

c. The ratios in the bottom four rows are calculated from the values in the first four rows.

Figure 1.2. Shifting Energy Trade Balances: 1990, 2010, and 2030

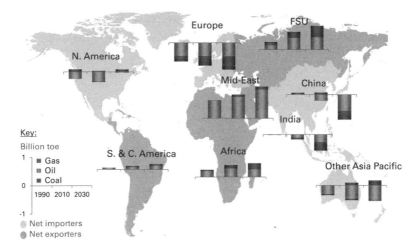

Source: Used with permission from BP, *BP Energy Outlook 2030* (London: BP, 2012).

Note: FSU = Former Soviet Union; toe = metric tons oil equivalent.

although European natural gas import needs will also continue to climb, especially with the desire to reduce CO_2 emissions and concerns about nuclear power.

The Global Energy Mix

We turn now from overall energy consumption trends to the specific fuels and technologies that supply those energy needs. The energy mix has important implications for the economic, environmental, and security performance of the global energy system. The mix changes slowly, but it does change. A key focus is often the share of energy supply from fossil fuels—coal, oil, and natural gas—relative to other energy sources, such as nuclear power, renewable electricity sources, and biofuels (table 1.4). The fossil fuel share provides a high-level indication of the diversity of the energy system, its dependence on (eventually) exhaustible resources, and its environmental impact. It also signals, of course, the continued overall importance of fossil fuels to the global energy system.

Table 1.4. Fuel Shares of Global Primary Energy

Years and Scenarios	Fuel Shares of Primary Energy (%)					
	Coal	Oil	Natural Gas	Total Fossil	Nuclear	Renewables
1960[a]	37	28	11	76	0	24
1985[b]	25	39	19	82	5	13
2010 (including all biomass)[c]	26	33	22	82	5	13
2035:						
IEA Current Policies[d]	29	28	24	81	6	14
IEA New Policies[d,e]	23	28	24	76	7	18
IEA 450[d,e]	15	26	22	63	11	26
ExxonMobil[f]	20	32	26	79	7	14
2010 (only marketed biomass)[c]	29	36	25	90	6	4
2030 BP[g,h]	29	28	28	84	7	9[h]
2035 EIA[h,i]	30	31	25	86	7	7[h]

Sources: As noted.

Note: Oil includes crude and natural gas liquids but not biofuels (which are included in Renewables). The Total Fossil column is the sum of Coal, Oil, and Natural Gas.

a. Arnulf Grubler, "Energy Transitions," in *Encyclopedia of Earth*, ed. Cutler J. Cleveland (Washington, DC: Environmental Information Coalition, National Council for Science and the Environment, 2008).

b. IEA, *World Energy Statistics and Balances*, 2011 ed. (Paris: OECD/IEA, 2011), doi:10.1787/enestats-data-en.

c. Two sets of fuel shares are given for 2010. The first, from IEA (*Key World Energy Statistics 2012* [Paris: OECD/IEA, 2012]), includes all biomass energy consumption, both marketed and nonmarketed; the second, from BP (*Statistical Review of World Energy June 2012* [London: BP, 2012]), includes only marketed biomass.

d. IEA, *World Energy Outlook 2011* (Paris: OECD/IEA, 2011).

e. Carbon capture and storage plays a minor role in the New Policies scenario and is an important abatement option in the 450 scenario. In both cases, its effect is greater near the end of the projection period.

f. ExxonMobil, *2012: The Outlook for Energy: A View to 2040* (Irving, TX: ExxonMobil, 2012).

g. BP, *BP Energy Outlook 2030* (London: BP, 2012). The values for BP are for 2030 rather than 2035.

h. EIA and BP renewable shares do not include traditional, nonmarketed biomass energy consumption.

i. EIA, *International Energy Outlook 2011* (Washington, DC: EIA, 2012).

The fossil fuel share of global primary energy actually increased from 76 percent to 82 percent during the period from 1960 to 1985 as the world industrialized, whereas traditional biomass-based renewables remained roughly constant in absolute terms and fell as a share. In the subsequent 25 years from 1985 to 2010, the global fossil share remained constant at 82 percent. Note that projections from the EIA and BP show much higher fossil shares because they do not include nonmarketed biomass in renewables.

The future share of fossil fuels looks almost certain to decline, with the magnitude of that decline depending on the stringency of actions to address climate change. In scenarios assuming climate policy actions along current trends—such as the IEA New Policies scenario and ExxonMobil outlook—the fossil share decreases to 76 to 79 percent by 2035. In the IEA 450 scenario, the fossil share falls to 63 percent, which—although a very substantial reduction—signals that even under stringent climate policy scenarios, fossil fuels are likely to remain a majority share of global energy for at least the next few decades. Despite this focus on fuel *shares*, it is also important to keep in mind that—with the exception of ExxonMobil's outlook for coal and the IEA 450 scenario for coal and oil—all of the major projections show *absolute increases* in the consumption of every fuel, regardless of shifting shares.

Fuel Shares

We turn now to a look at specific fuels.

Oil

Although oil consumption rose much more than any other fuel from 1960 to 1985—from 28 percent to 39 percent of global energy—its share had declined to 34 percent by 2010. The downward trend in oil's share is set to continue to about 30 percent by 2035, plus or minus 2 percent. As discussed in greater detail later in the chapter, fuel shares of aggregate consumption tend to mask the dependence of certain end-use sectors on particular fuels. Transport stands out (by far) as the least diverse sector in these terms, with more than 95 percent of world transport energy needs being met by oil and other liquids.[17]

Coal

Despite the maturity of coal as an energy source, its history over the past 25 years is one of resurgence compared with the period from 1960 to 1985, a time when natural gas and especially oil expanded rapidly. Although coal's share in primary energy consumption is now lower than its 37 percent share 50 years ago, coal actually grew more than any other fuel source from 1985 to 2010, stabilizing at about 26 percent by the end of that period. Because of coal's emissions of CO_2 and other pollutants, the future of coal—more than any other fuel—will depend on actions taken to mitigate climate change and local air pollution. As a result, projections have the coal share falling to 20 to 23 percent under recent policy trends, or as low as 15 percent if actions such as those in the IEA's 450 scenario are undertaken.

Natural Gas

The share of natural gas rose from 11 percent in 1960 to 19 percent in 1985 and had doubled to 22 percent by 2010; its annual consumption increased almost twofold from 1985 to 2010. Across all major projections, both the share and absolute amount of natural gas in primary energy consumption remain steady or increase between now and 2035, particularly in the ExxonMobil outlook, where the natural gas share rises to 26 percent.

Renewables

Renewables include a variety of electricity sources—hydroelectric, biomass, wind, geothermal, and solar—as well as biofuels and traditional nonmarketed biomass and waste fuels. The measured renewable share depends heavily on whether traditional nonmarketed biomass and waste fuels are included (as in IEA and ExxonMobil figures) or whether only marketed renewables are included (as in EIA and BP figures). Including nonmarketed biomass (which is a significant source at 9 percent of global energy), renewables currently meet about 13 percent of global energy consumption needs, with 4 percent coming from marketed renewables. Renewables are the fastest-growing energy source in percentage terms, and projections suggest that the total renewables share will reach 14 to 18 percent by 2035 or up to 26 percent in scenarios with dramatic CO_2 reductions. The share of marketed renewables could double over this 25-year period.

Nuclear

The emergence of nuclear power has been a significant development over the past half-century. Its share of primary energy consumption rose from zero in 1960 to 5 percent of global energy by 2010 and in most projections will rise to around 6 or 7 percent by 2035. In scenarios with very substantial CO_2 reductions (for example, the IEA's 450 scenario), nuclear power becomes a more competitive source of low-carbon power, resulting in a nuclear share of up to 11 percent—double the current share.

End-Use Sector Fuel Shares and Diversity

Fuel shares as a fraction of aggregate consumption do not highlight differences among end-use sectors—transport, industry, and residential and commercial buildings—in their dependence on particular fuels or in their fuel diversity and ability to substitute among alternative options. Given that supply diversity is an important component of energy security, understanding these connections helps identify areas of risk and vulnerability.

For instance, although the world's transportation system is fueled almost entirely by liquids (95 percent), the industrial sector obtains approximately 29 percent, 23 percent, and 26 percent of its delivered energy directly from oil, natural gas, and coal, respectively—and another 15 percent from electricity, which is itself diversely fueled.[18] Residential and commercial buildings also rely on a diversity of fuel sources, including 18 percent, 36 percent, and 7 percent of their delivered energy directly from oil, natural gas, and coal, respectively, and 38 percent from electricity.[19] The most significant global shift projected for these sectoral energy shares is for residential and commercial buildings, which are becoming more reliant on electricity (50 percent share in 2035) rather than directly consuming natural gas, oil, and coal.[20] Although the oil share of transport fuel consumption is very likely to decline, it will continue to serve the vast majority of transport needs for the foreseeable future, even in scenarios assuming significant policy change and innovation. For example, the oil share of transport energy consumption falls to 88 percent in the IEA's

New Policies scenario, whereas it falls to 76 percent in the 450 scenario; in other words, although biofuels, electricity, and natural gas make greater inroads into transport, oil maintains its dominance.

Carbon Dioxide Emissions

Future emissions of CO_2 from fossil energy combustion follow directly from overall trends in energy consumption, coupled with forecasts of the carbon intensity of the energy mix. As discussed previously, both of these key trends vary widely across future energy projections, principally as a function of differing assumptions about the path of future energy and environmental policy. The resulting range of energy-related carbon emissions trajectories is large, corresponding to the three types of scenarios introduced earlier: (a) at the high end, scenarios that hold current policies constant (EIA Reference Case and IEA Current Policies); (b) in the middle, scenarios that assume the addition of new policies along recent policy trends (ExxonMobil outlook and IEA New Policies); and (c) the IEA's 450 scenario at the low end (figure 1.3). For moderate projections along recent policy trends, global CO_2 emissions increase by about 16 percent from 31 billion metric tons annually in 2010 to 36 billion metric tons in 2035. In contrast, with unchanged current policies, CO_2 emissions could rise 40 percent to 43 billion metric tons. With actions targeting a 450 ppm concentration, emissions would need to fall 30 percent from 2010 levels to less than 22 billion metric tons by 2035.

Distinguishing among regions (tables 1.2 and 1.3), moderate policy scenarios tend to yield flat or declining emissions in North America and Europe–Eurasia moving forward, but they allow for moderate emissions growth in other regions before leveling off. The IEA New Policies scenario, for example, has OECD CO_2 emissions declining about 10 percent from 2010 levels by 2035, whereas non-OECD emissions increase by about 50 percent. In contrast, in the IEA 450 scenario, OECD emissions must decline 50 percent and non-OECD emissions 10 percent from 2010 levels, together achieving a 30 percent reduction in total global emissions.

To understand how these different energy projections relate to climate impacts, one finds it informative to draw from the Intergovernmental Panel on Climate Change (IPCC), which has produced a set of emissions scenarios and likely associated temperature changes (figure 1.4). These scenarios make clear that to map energy and emissions to climate impacts, one must

Figure 1.3. Diverging Policy Assumptions and World Energy–Related CO_2 Emissions

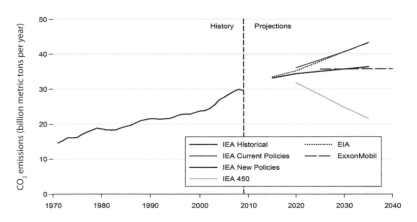

Sources: ExxonMobil, *2012: The Outlook for Energy: A View to 2040* (Irving, TX: ExxonMobil, 2012); IEA, *World Energy Outlook 2011* (Paris: OECD/IEA, 2011); IEA, *World Energy Statistics and Balances*, 2011 edition (Paris: OECD/IEA, 2011), doi:10.1787/enestats-data-en; EIA, *International Energy Outlook 2011* (Washington, DC: EIA).

Note: Historical data from IEA use the reference approach to estimating emissions.

Figure 1.4. IPCC Emissions Scenarios and Associated Temperature Increases

a. World CO_2 emissions

b. Equilibrium global average temperature increases above preindustrial levels

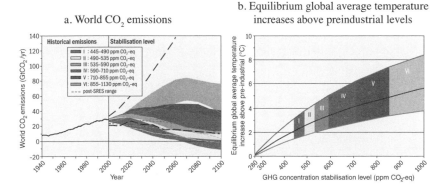

Source: IPCC, *Climate Change 2007: Synthesis Report—Contribution of Working Groups I, II, and III to the Fourth Assessment Report of the Intergovernmental Panel on Climate Change* (Geneva: IPCC, 2007).

Note: SRES = Special Report on Emissions Scenarios. Panel b shows IPCC's best estimate and "likely" range of temperature impacts.

look well beyond the next 25 years, because the long-term stock of GHGs is what really matters.

Nonetheless, moderate policy scenarios that have emissions peaking globally within the next 25 years (e.g., the ExxonMobil outlook)—assuming that emissions decline gradually thereafter—correspond roughly to IPCC emission scenario group III and an atmospheric CO_2 concentration of 550 to 600 ppm of CO_2 equivalent. The IPCC's best estimate of the associated global mean temperature increase is about 3.0 to 3.5°C (5.5 to 6.5°F), with a likely range of 2.0 to 5.0°C (3.5 to 9.0°F). For the IEA 450 scenario to actually achieve 450 ppm (and a 2.0°C expected temperature target), post-2035 emissions would need to fall faster than shown in the most stringent emission scenario in figure 1.4. However, if new policies do not further restrain CO_2 emissions from business-as-usual trends, CO_2 concentrations will tend toward 700 ppm of CO_2 equivalent or greater.

The Role of Electricity

Electricity represents close to 40 percent of worldwide primary energy consumption, a role that will be increasing going forward. In terms of end-use energy consumption, electricity is growing much faster than direct use of fuels. Given the importance of electricity to the energy system, it is important to consider (a) what the current roles of different fuels and technologies for electricity generation are and (b) how the fuel mix may change in the future. In 2010, the global electricity generation mix was 41 percent coal, 22 percent natural gas, 16 percent hydro, 13 percent nuclear, 5 percent oil, and 4 percent other renewables, including wind, geothermal, solar, and biomass or waste.[21]

As with overall energy consumption, electricity generation has risen substantially over time, and such increases will continue (figure 1.5). In addition to population and income growth, how much electricity consumption grows will depend in part on the extent to which future policies (a) encourage energy conservation through efficiency programs and (b) reduce carbon emissions through pricing or other means. As shown in figure 1.5, global electricity generation is on a path to grow about 80 percent by 2035, plus or minus approximately 10 percent depending on future policy developments.[22] Over the longer term, widespread electrification of the transportation sector has the potential to dramatically affect the consumption of electricity, the fuels and technologies for generating electricity, and the use of oil for trans-

Figure 1.5. Growth of Electricity, with Generation Sources, Depending on Fuel Prices, Environmental Policy, and Technology Innovation

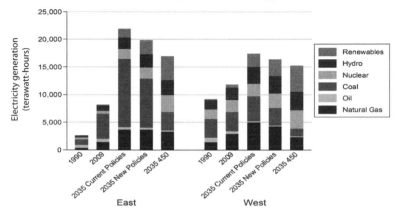

Source: IEA, *World Energy Outlook 2011* (Paris: OECD/IEA, 2011).

Note: East comprises Asia and the Middle East; West is the rest of the world.

port. Research indicates, however, that the vast majority of such changes—if they unfold—will likely occur after our 25-year time horizon.[23]

The trend of increasing electricity demand holds for both the East (Asia and the Middle East) and the West (the rest of the world), though in 2009 the East was just approaching the electricity generation levels that the West had reached in 1990. In the future, growth of electricity consumption will be much faster in the East than in the West, with the East growing 2.4-fold while the West grows about 40 percent by 2035. The East will likely surpass the West in terms of absolute electricity generation by the 2020 to 2025 period.

Another divergence between the East and the West is the anticipated amount of coal use for electricity generation. Although coal consumption is likely to be roughly flat or declining in the West, it could increase dramatically in the East unless policies inhibit its expansion. In both major regions, generation from hydro, other renewables, and nuclear power is set to rise, especially if ambitious climate policies unfold. Use of natural gas for electric power generation is likely to continue to increase in every region because of that fuel's low air emissions compared to coal, attractive construction cost profile, and (particularly recently) reasonable fuel prices. Only under substantial carbon reduction scenarios (e.g., the IEA's 450 scenario) would natural gas power in the West decline, although it increases in the East under all three of the IEA's scenarios. Finally, the role for oil in electricity generation is set to diminish regardless of the region or scenario. In the subsections that follow, we further consider coal, nuclear, and renewable electricity briefly—all energy sources used largely or exclusively for the production of electricity.

Coal

We find it striking that total coal consumption grew by about the same amount (roughly 50 quads) in the first decade of the 21st century as it did over the last four decades of the 20th century (i.e., 1960–2000) (figure 1.6). In fact, coal grew more than any other energy source and constituted almost half the total growth in global energy use from 2000 to 2010, with the major part of this growth being for the power sector in emerging economies. The global coal share of electricity generation stood at 41 percent in 2010, almost twice the size of the next largest fuel for electricity, natural gas.[24] We do not expect, however, this dramatic upward trend to continue. Even scenarios assuming no new policies that would inhibit coal—and therefore representing the highest projected coal consumption—have coal growth rates that are significantly lower than that seen during 2000 to 2010.

Under current trends, coal consumption will likely continue to grow but then level off within the next couple of decades. How much global coal consumption grows; exactly when it levels off; and whether, when, and how fast it starts to decline will depend heavily on ongoing developments in environmental policy (both conventional pollution and CO_2) and the availability of substitute electricity sources at reasonable cost. With a moderate to stringent cost applied to carbon emissions, coal consumption would decline substantially, as illustrated by the ExxonMobil and IEA 450 scenarios (where, for example, coal declines by one-third from 2010 levels).

Renewables

Renewable electricity sources—such as hydro, wind, biomass,[25] geothermal, and solar—have the advantage of negligible air emissions and fuel

Figure 1.6. World Coal Consumption, 1960–2040

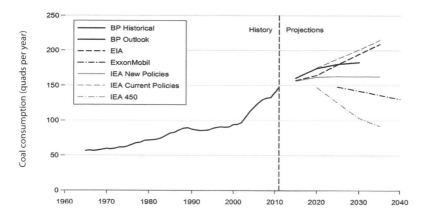

Sources: BP, *BP Energy Outlook 2030* (London: BP, 2012); BP, *Statistical Review of World Energy June 2012* (London: BP, 2012); ExxonMobil, *2012: The Outlook for Energy: A View to 2040* (Irving, TX: ExxonMobil, 2012); IEA, *World Energy Outlook 2011* (Paris: OECD/IEA, 2011); EIA, *International Energy Outlook 2011* (Washington, DC: EIA, 2011).

operating costs and have been the fastest-growing part of the energy mix in percentage terms, albeit from a relatively small base. Because of their higher capital costs, however, renewable sources remain relatively expensive on average compared to fossil fuel alternatives. In 2010, renewables constituted about 20 percent of global electricity generation, the vast majority of which (16 percent) was hydro, and the remainder other renewables (2.0 percent wind, 1.4 percent biomass, 0.3 percent geothermal, and 0.3 percent solar). Renewable sources are favored to the extent that clean energy, diversification, and climate change mitigation are a priority. As an illustration, the share of renewable electricity generation by 2035 in the IEA's Current Policies, New Policies, and 450 scenarios grows to 23 percent, 30 percent, and 46 percent, respectively.

Although all major analyses see the share of renewables in the energy mix growing, policies to promote the use of renewables for electricity generation—particularly in the form of subsidies—have been a critical factor in driving renewables growth given their cost relative to fossil fuels. For example, in the IEA's New Policies scenario, cumulative subsidies for renewables total almost $5 trillion between 2011 and 2035, with nearly

$250 billion in 2035 alone.[26] Government fiscal constraints in the wake of the Great Recession could pose a mounting challenge to renewables subsidies, potentially leading to alternative support mechanisms, including mandates, carbon pricing, or both. Continued cost reductions and mechanisms to address intermittency through energy storage, demand-side management, market structures, and smarter transmission networks are also crucial to continued growth in renewables.

Nuclear Electricity

The nuclear share of electricity generation stood at 13 percent in 2010,[27] and world nuclear capacity and generation are expected to increase significantly over the next several decades. In the IEA's New Policies scenario, nuclear power generation rises 70 percent, and nuclear capacity rises from 375 gigawatts (GW) in 2010 to more than 630 GW by 2035, and more so with more stringent CO_2 policies.[28] Similarly, ExxonMobil's outlook anticipates 80 percent growth in nuclear capacity by 2040, though as with other sources, this growth rate is lower than ExxonMobil's prior estimates because of effects of the Fukushima incident.[29] Following this trend, we see that although the IEA's *World Energy Outlook 2012* still includes substantial global growth in nuclear capacity, the total for 2035 is 50 GW (8 percent) lower in the 2012 edition than in the 2011 edition.[30]

These global trends can, however, overshadow differences among countries and regions. For example, between 2009 and 2035 in the IEA's New Policies scenario, more than 40 percent of global nuclear capacity growth takes place in China alone. This scenario projects substantial increases in other developing countries as well, such as two-thirds and 10-fold growth in Russia and India, respectively. In contrast, many of the capacity additions in the OECD are to replace retiring plants, leading to total OECD nuclear capacity growth of only 16 percent over this period.[31] In the 2012 IEA update, OECD nuclear capacity is basically level.[32]

As mentioned previously, the incident at the Fukushima Daiichi nuclear power station in Japan has had definite and potentially long-lasting effects on the role of nuclear electricity in the global energy mix. A number of countries are reviewing their nuclear programs, are reducing their capacity, or are completely phasing out the use of nuclear energy. In an effort to explore the ramifications of a world with lower nuclear supply, the IEA developed the Low Nuclear Case, which assumes the following: no new reactors in OECD countries, 50 percent lower capacity additions in non-OECD countries than under the New Policies scenario, and somewhat shorter average lifetimes for nuclear reactors.[33]

These modifications result in several notable outcomes. The first is that world nuclear capacity decreases by 15 percent over the projection period, rather than rising 60 percent. Instead, electricity demand is met by an additional 80 GW of coal-fired capacity, 122 GW of additional natural gas electricity generation, and 260 GW of additional renewables capacity.[34] Moreover, in a future with both stringent climate goals and restricted generation from nuclear sources, the required contribution from renewables, energy efficiency, and carbon capture and storage would be even more significantly increased.

The Role of Petroleum and Other Liquids

Petroleum and other liquids have been an essential source of energy for a variety of reasons, including their high energy density and transportability, and thus especially for transportation applications. In the future, demand for oil and other liquids is likely to continue to grow—albeit at a slower pace—and they will likely remain the world's largest energy source for at least the next couple of decades. With at least three-fourths of that growth occurring in emerging economies of the East, petroleum trade will shift eastward. At the same time, although the share of supply of the Organization of the Petroleum Exporting Countries (OPEC) will almost surely increase, the emergence of unconventional liquids (e.g., oil sands and biofuels) and tight oil is moderating that trend. Coupled with low demand growth, these supply dynamics are pushing North America, in particular, toward net balance in liquids supply and demand over the next 20 to 25 years.

Liquids Demand

Global consumption of petroleum and other liquids is on a path to grow to roughly 105 to 110 mmbpd by 2035, or 15–20 mmbpd higher than current levels of about 90 mmbpd. With the exception of the IEA's 450 scenario, all major projections show world oil consumption increasing over the next several decades by 20 percent or more compared with 2010 levels (table 1.5). In both absolute and percentage terms, however, the growth of oil

Table 1.5. Liquids Consumption

Years and Scenarios	World (mmbpd)		West (mmbpd)		East (mmbpd)	
	Amount Consumed	Total Growth over Prior 25 Years	Amount Consumed	Total Growth over Prior 25 Years	Amount Consumed	Total Growth over Prior 25 Years
1960[a]	22	n.a.	20	n.a.	2	n.a.
1985[b]	59	37 (171%)	46	26 (133%)	14	11 (501%)
2010[b]	87	28 (48%)	52	6 (14%)	35	22 (161%)
2035:						
EIA[c]	112	25 (28%)	60	8 (15%)	52	17 (48%)
IEA Current Policies[d]	111	23 (26%)	55	3 (5%)	56	20 (57%)
IEA New Policies[d]	104	16 (19%)	51	−1 (−1%)	52	17 (48%)
IEA 450[d]	86	−1 (−2%)	41	−11 (−21%)	45	10 (27%)
ExxonMobil[e]	110	22 (25%)	57	5 (9%)	52	17 (49%)
OPEC[f]	110	22 (25%)	55	3 (6%)	55	19 (57%)
2030 BP[g]	103	16 (18%)[g]	51	−1 (−1%)[g]	52	16 (45%)[g]

Sources: As noted.

Note: n.a. = not applicable. East comprises Asia and the Middle East, whereas West is the rest of the world. Biofuels are included in liquids, with projected biofuel consumption for 2035 varying by source: approximately 5 mmbpd for EIA; 3, 4, and 8 mmbpd for IEA's Current Policies, New Policies, and 450 scenarios, respectively; approximately 5 mmbpd for ExxonMobil; and 5 mmbpd for BP in 2030.

a. United Nations Statistical Office, World Energy Supplies, 1950–1974, Statistical Papers Series J, no. 19 (New York: Department of Economic and Social Affairs, Statistical Office, United Nations, 1976).

b. BP, Statistical Review of World Energy June 2012 (London: BP, 2012).

c. EIA, International Energy Outlook 2011 (Washington, DC: EIA, 2011).

d. IEA, World Energy Outlook 2011 (Paris: OECD/IEA, 2011). Regions are allocated proportional shares of world oil bunker consumption.

e. ExxonMobil, 2012: The Outlook for Energy: A View to 2040 (Irving, TX: ExxonMobil, 2012).

f. OPEC, World Oil Outlook 2011 (Vienna: OPEC, 2011).

g. EIA, Annual Energy Outlook 2012 with Projections to 2035 (Washington, DC: Energy Information Administration, 2012). The values for BP are for 2030 rather than 2035, and the total growth is over 20 years.

Figure 1.7. Eastward Shift of Liquids Consumption

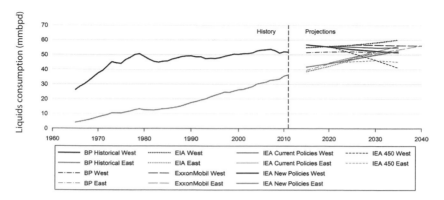

Sources: Data from BP, *BP Energy Outlook 2030* (London: BP, 2012); BP, *Statistical Review of World Energy June 2012* (London: BP, 2012); ExxonMobil, *2012: The Outlook for Energy: A View to 2040* (Irving, TX: ExxonMobil, 2012); IEA, *World Energy Outlook 2011* (Paris: OECD/IEA, 2011); EIA, *International Energy Outlook 2011* (Washington, DC: EIA, 2011).

consumption is slowing under these scenarios compared with the previous two generations.

The upward trend in world oil consumption also masks very different outlooks for the West and East (table 1.5 and figure 1.7). Although oil consumption in the West has been historically much higher than in the East, projections across a range of scenarios indicate that by 2030 to 2035 they will have equalized. Rising population and GDP per capita in the East are leading to greater consumption of all energy sources, including an approximately 50 percent increase in liquids consumption over the next 25 years. In contrast, the West appears close to reaching a plateau in oil demand—or *peak oil demand*—a threshold that OECD countries as a bloc probably passed in 2005. The flattening of oil consumption in advanced industrial countries is due to a combination of saturated demand for transportation services, government regulation of automotive fuel economy, and higher fuel prices. As a result, the vast majority of oil growth will be for transport in the emerging economies of the East, where vehicle ownership currently stands at about one-tenth or less the level in OECD countries.

Oil Resources and Liquids Supply

Worldwide recoverable oil resources[35] (both proved and unproved) currently stand at 5 trillion barrels or more, split roughly equally between
conventional sources and unconventional sources, the latter including
extra-heavy oil, tar sands (bitumen), and oil shale (kerogen).[36] When conventional and unconventional resources are considered together, North
America contains the most by far (more than 2 trillion barrels, including
bitumen and kerogen). With respect to conventional resources, the Middle
East ranks highest—with well over 1 trillion barrels of proved reserves or
other potentially recoverable conventional oil.

Worldwide proved oil reserves[37] tell a somewhat different story, however, and stand at about 1.5 trillion barrels, 73 percent of this amount
in OPEC countries, 52 percent in the Middle East, 14 percent in North
America, and less than 2 percent in the United States.[38] Concerns about the
physical availability of global oil resources are therefore largely misplaced.
Nonetheless, significant aboveground issues are associated with the location and governance of available conventional reserves, as well as technical, financial, environmental, and political challenges to the development
of much of the unconventional resource base.

Given the global distribution of oil reserves, most projections not surprisingly foresee an increasing production share for OPEC (tables 1.6 and
1.7). OPEC's share of supply stood at 40 percent in 2010 (the same as when
it was formed in 1960) but is likely to increase to 45 to 50 percent over
the next couple of decades.[39] The OPEC members of the Gulf Cooperation Council—Saudi Arabia, the United Arab Emirates, Kuwait, Qatar, and
Bahrain—account for about half of OPEC's production, represent a similar
share of its incremental production potential, and hold all available spare
crude oil production capacity. The strategic importance of these countries
is apparent.

A range of potential country-level sources can supply a global liquids
market of 100 mmbpd to as much as 115 mmbpd if demanded (table 1.7).
The IEA has a stagnant outlook for non-OPEC liquids supply, but most
other forecasts still see the potential for increased non-OPEC production.
The distribution of production between OPEC and non-OPEC countries,
and among countries within these blocs, will depend on market prices,
country-level energy and environmental policy and fiscal regimes, the
degree of political and military conflict, and as yet unknown technological innovations and resource discoveries. Saudi Arabia, Iraq, the United

Table 1.6. Global Liquids Production

Years and Scenarios	Liquids Production (mmbpd)			OPEC/Non-OPEC Shares (%)
	World	OPEC	Non-OPEC	
1960	22[a]	9[b]	13	40/60
1985[c]	59	16	43	28/72
2010[c]	87	35	52	40/60
2035:				
EIA[d]	112	47	65	42/58
IEA Current Policies[e]	111	57	54	51/49
IEA New Policies[e]	104	52	51	51/49
IEA 450[e]	86	41	45	48/52
OPEC[f]	110	49	61	45/55
2030 BP[g]	103	46	57	45/55

Sources: As noted.

a. United Nations Statistical Office, *World Energy Supplies, 1950–1974*, Statistical Papers Series J, no. 19 (New York: Department of Economic and Social Affairs, Statistical Office, United Nations, 1976).

b. OPEC, *OPEC: Annual Statistical Bulletin 2008* (Vienna: OPEC, 2008).

c. EIA, International Energy Statistics database, http://www.eia.gov/cfapps/ipdbproject/.

d. EIA, *International Energy Outlook 2011* (Washington, DC: EIA, 2011).

e. IEA, *World Energy Outlook 2011* (Paris: OECD/IEA, 2011).

f. OPEC, *World Oil Outlook 2011* (Vienna: OPEC, 2011).

g. BP, *BP Energy Outlook 2030* (London: BP, 2012). The values for BP are for 2030 rather than 2035.

States, Canada, Brazil, and Venezuela hold the greatest potential for incremental liquids production.

Most unconventional production will occur in non-OPEC countries, with major sources including Canada (oil sands) and the United States (biofuels and possibly coal-, gas-, and biomass-to-liquids), as well as China (biofuels, coal-to-liquids) and Brazil (biofuels) (table 1.7). The exception is Venezuelan extra-heavy oil, which has substantial production potential if the country can overcome significant financial, technical, and political hurdles to its development. Tight oil is also an increasingly important supply source in the United States. We consider North American oil production specifically in more detail in the next subsection.

Table 1.7. Country-Level Sources of Conventional and Unconventional Liquids Production

Country or Region	Liquids Production (mmbpd)		
	2010	2035	Change, 2010–35
United States	9.7 (0.9)	11–15 (2–3)	1–5 (1–2)
Canada	3.4 (1.5)	5–7 (3–5)	2–4 (2–4)
Mexico	3.0	1–2	–2—1
Total North America	16.1 (2.4)	17–24 (5–8)	1–8 (2–6)
Russia	10.1	10–14	0–4
China	4.3	4–6 (0–2)	0–2 (0–2)
Caspian area	2.9	4–5	1–2
Brazil	2.7 (0.5)	4–6 (1–2)	1–3 (0–1)
OECD Europe	4.6 (0.2)	3	–2—1
Other non-OPEC	11.1 (0.4)	10–12 (0–1)	–1–1
Total non-OPEC	**52 (3.5)**	**52–70 (6–13)**	**0–18 (2–9)**
Saudi Arabia	10.5	11–15	1–5
United Arab Emirates	2.8	2–3	0
Kuwait	2.5	3–4	0–2
Qatar	1.4	2–3	0–1
Total Gulf Cooperation Council (excluding Oman)	17.2	18–25	1–8
Iran	4.3	3–4	–1–0
Iraq	2.4	4–8	2–5
Total Middle East OPEC	23.9	25–37	2–13
Nigeria	2.5	2–5	0–2
Venezuela	2.4 (0.6)	3–6 (2–5)	0–3 (1–4)
Angola, Algeria, Libya, Ecuador	6.1	4–6	–2–0
Total OPEC	**35 (0.6)**	**40–52 (2–5)**	**5–17 (1–4)**
Total world	**87 (4.2)**	**100–115 (8–18)**	**13–23 (4–14)**

Sources: For 2010, EIA, International Energy Statistics database, http://www.eia.gov/cfapps /ipdbproject/. For 2035, author estimates of plausible country-level production that would support a 100 mmbpd to 115 mmbpd liquids market.

Note: Liquids include crude oil and condensates, natural gas plant liquids, unconventional liquids, other hydrocarbon refinery feedstocks, and refinery gains. Unconventional liquids include biofuels, oil sands, extra-heavy oil, and xTLs (coal-, gas-, and biomass-to-liquids). Shale oil/tight oil is included in total liquids but not unconventional. Unconventional portion of production is indicated in parentheses.

North American Oil Production

North America has the potential to significantly increase its oil production over the next several decades, particularly through use of its unconventional resources. A 2011 study by the National Petroleum Council (NPC)[40] on North American oil and gas resources provides a comprehensive distillation of recent developments.[41] The NPC's study concluded that the potential oil and natural gas supply in North America is larger than previously thought and, in the case of gas, much larger. Importantly, the study also found that realizing the benefits of these resources will depend on "safe, responsible, and environmentally acceptable production and delivery."[42]

The United States is the world's third-largest oil producer, following Saudi Arabia and Russia (table 1.7). Including Canada and Mexico—the sixth- and seventh-largest producers, respectively—North America produced almost 20 percent of global liquids in 2010. In the future, increased production in the United States and Canada should more than offset continued declines in Mexico, with total increases of as much as 50 percent on the high side over the next two to three decades. Coupled with a flattening of liquids consumption growth, these production increases are putting North America on a path toward net self-sufficiency in liquids by 2035. All the major energy outlooks reinforce this view.

The turnaround in US liquids production began in 2007 after a more than 30-year slide. US liquids production now stands at its highest level in 20 years. As a result, the United States, Saudi Arabia, and Russia are now roughly on par as the world's largest producers of liquids and appear likely to maintain similar production levels going forward. The largest US gains have come from onshore production in the lower 48 states and through the application of advanced techniques such as enhanced oil recovery and horizontal drilling or hydraulic fracturing technology transferred from the shale gas experience. Development of shale and other tight oil has expanded rapidly in formations such as the Bakken (North Dakota and Montana) and the Niobrara (Colorado and Wyoming), as well as the liquids-rich areas of shale gas plays, such as the Eagle Ford (Texas). The rapid learning and deployment of technologies for extracting shale gas have not been fully transferred to oil opportunities yet, so predicting how expansive these opportunities will be is difficult. On the high side, tight oil could contribute as much as 3 mmbpd to North American production by 2035.[43]

In addition to tight oil, natural gas liquids production has expanded, along with the substantial growth in dry gas production from shale gas, and could contribute as much as 3 mmbpd to US[44] and 4 mmbpd to North American liquids supply.[45] US biofuels have been another source of growth in liquids, driven by federal and state tax credits, the federal Renewable Fuel Standard program, and high oil prices. Already close to 1 mmbpd, production of ethanol and other biofuels could potentially double over the next generation, depending on the commercialization of advanced biofuel production techniques and the stability of the US federal Renewable Fuel Standard mandates.[46]

Potentially the largest growth in North American petroleum production over the next quarter-century could come from unconventional Canadian oil sands (i.e., bitumen). Production from Albertan oil sands stood at 1.6 mmbpd in 2011 and could more than triple to 5.0 mmbpd by 2035, including both surface mining and in situ production processes.[47] Whether oil sands production develops to this extent will depend on world oil prices (given its relatively high cost) and the degree to which local environmental impacts and concerns related to CO_2 emissions can or must be addressed. In any event, most major projections of future liquids supply assume that Canadian oil sands production will expand along this path.

The Role of Natural Gas

In terms of prospective production, consumption, and trade, no other major fuel source has seen as much change as natural gas since the 2005 edition of this volume. In fact, 2005 marked a turning point for US natural gas production because of the shale gas revolution, and the ripple effects of this transformation are still unfolding in North America and around the world. These effects include the impact of unconventional gas development on supply diversity, global LNG markets (and potential North American LNG exports), and long-term contracts—particularly their relationship to spot natural gas prices and the price of oil.

Along current policy, market, and technology trends, a substantial increase in world natural gas consumption (of at least 45 percent) is likely between 2010 and 2035 (table 1.8). Aside from scenarios with rapid CO_2 reductions (e.g., the IEA's 450 scenario), gas consumption in the West is set to grow 20 to 30 percent between 2010 and 2035, while corresponding total growth in the East is expected to be much higher, about 90 to 110 percent. Under more stringent CO_2 reduction efforts, natural gas consumption would grow much more slowly, but it would likely still grow—in contrast

Table 1.8. Natural Gas Consumption: Global History and Projections

Years and Scenarios	World (bcfpd)		West (bcfpd)		East (bcfpd)	
	Amount Consumed	Total Growth over Prior 25 Years	Amount Consumed	Total Growth over Prior 25 Years	Amount Consumed	Total Growth over Prior 25 Years
1960[a]	44	n.a.	43	n.a.	1	n.a.
1985[b]	159	116 (266%)	143	100 (233%)	17	16 (2,471%)
2010[c]	319	159 (100%)	226	83 (58%)	93	76 (460%)
2035:						
EIA[d]	462	144 (45%)	287	61 (27%)	175	82 (89%)
IEA Current Policies[e]	492	174 (54%)	297	71 (31%)	195	102 (111%)
IEA New Policies[e]	460	141 (44%)	274	48 (21%)	185	93 (100%)
IEA 450[e]	375	56 (18%)	211	−15 (−7%)	164	72 (77%)
ExxonMobil[f]	514	195 (61%)	305	79 (35%)	209	116 (126%)
2030 BP[g]	462	143 (45%)	269	43 (19%)	193	100 (108%)

Sources: As noted.

Note: bcfpd = billion cubic feet per day; n.a. = not applicable. East comprises Asia and the Middle East; West is the rest of the world.

a. United Nations Statistical Office, *World Energy Supplies, 1950–1974*, Statistical Papers Series J, no. 19 (New York: Department of Economic and Social Affairs, Statistical Office, United Nations, 1976).

b. BP, *Statistical Review of World Energy June 2012* (London: BP, 2012).

c. IEA, *Natural Gas Information 2012* (Paris: OECD/IEA, 2012).

d. EIA, *International Energy Outlook 2011* (Washington, DC: EIA, 2011).

e. IEA, *World Energy Outlook 2011* (Paris: OECD/IEA, 2011).

f. ExxonMobil (2012) figures include flaring, which would tend to elevate implied growth relative to the 2010 IEA figures, which do not include flaring. See Exxon-Mobil, *2012: The Outlook for Energy: A View to 2040* (Irving, TX: ExxonMobil, 2012).

g. BP, *BP Energy Outlook 2030* (London: BP, 2012). The values for BP are for 2030 rather than 2035, and the total growth is over 20 years.

to oil, which shows zero growth, and coal, which substantially declines in such projections (e.g., the IEA's 450 scenario).

Regional Gas Consumption

A number of factors will combine to produce significant changes in the international gas landscape over the next several decades. Although demand is likely to increase in all major regions, the supply sources for each region vary significantly. Figure 1.8 illustrates ExxonMobil's outlook of how regional natural gas consumption growth will be supplied over the 2010 to 2040 period. Other projections from the IEA and BP depict qualitatively similar dynamics, although quantitative comparisons are difficult given available data. Whereas the Middle East and Africa will be able to support the vast majority of their additional gas needs through local conventional production, Latin America and especially North America will turn increasingly to local unconventional sources of natural gas—in part to offset declining conventional supplies. In contrast, although the Asia-Pacific region is likely to turn to local unconventional sources as well, it will also need increments in LNG and pipeline imports of an even larger magnitude to meet its burgeoning demand growth. Significant uncertainty exists about whether Asian unconventional gas will grow to levels seen in North America. The composition of additional gas supply needs in Europe looks similar to that in Asia, albeit at a more modest scale. The increasing importance of unconventional gas and of LNG as a viable way to transport natural gas from producing to consuming regions stands out as a key element of this unfolding picture.

North American Unconventional Gas Development

The United States is now the world's largest producer of natural gas and, in combination with Canada, accounts for 25 percent of global production. The turnaround in US gas production is due to the application of horizontal drilling and hydraulic fracturing techniques to shale gas deposits. Shale gas development took on significant scale in the Barnett Shale formation (Texas) in the early 2000s and accelerated significantly around 2007. Shale gas drilling then expanded rapidly to the Fayetteville (Arkansas), Woodford (Oklahoma), Haynesville (Louisiana and Texas), and Marcellus (Pennsyl-

Figure 1.8. Changes in Gas Consumption and Supply Sources by Region and Type, 2010–40

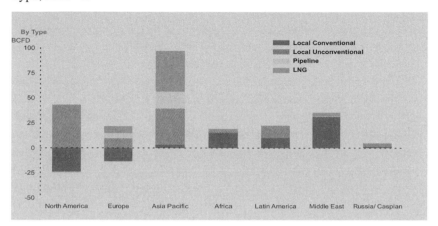

Source: Used with permission from ExxonMobil, *2012: The Outlook for Energy: A View to 2040* (Irving, TX: ExxonMobil).

vania and West Virginia) formations. As prices dropped in reaction to this dramatic supply shift, production began to focus more on the liquids-rich deposits of the Eagle Ford (Texas) and Bakken (North Dakota) formations, where output could be sold into liquids markets at price multiples several times higher than for dry gas.

As a result of these developments, US shale gas production increased 13-fold, from 2 billion cubic feet per day (bcfpd) in 2005 to 26 bcfpd by the middle of 2012, and now constitutes over 30 percent of US dry gas production. US natural gas proved reserves grew 50 percent from 2005 to 2010 and now stand at their highest levels ever.[48] Estimates of technically recoverable gas resources (proved and unproved) have, in turn, been updated and stand at about 2,203 trillion cubic feet[49]—a natural gas resource base that could support supply for five or more decades at current or even greatly expanded levels of use.[50] Canada and Mexico also have significant shale gas deposits, with the Bakken formation extending into Canada and continuing into the Colorado Group.

The greater availability of supply sources that are producible at competitive prices has led to a much more positive outlook for future US natural gas production, with current projections placing shale gas at about 50 per-

cent of US dry gas production by 2035.[51] Natural gas has also become the
favored fuel for new electric power capacity additions, as well as current
dispatch, because of current low prices and expectations of continued low
to moderate price levels for many years. Low conventional air pollutant
emissions and CO_2 emissions half the level of those from coal-based power
add to the appeal of natural gas relative to coal.

At the same time, the rapid expansion of shale gas production has
brought with it significant public concerns about its environmental impact
on water and air resources, particularly in regions without a recent significant oil and gas industry presence. Although these concerns have not
resulted in a significant slowdown in US shale gas production in major
producing regions, environmental rules have been strengthened in many
places, and some countries (such as France and Bulgaria) have banned
hydraulic fracturing altogether. Several reports, including some from the
Secretary of Energy Advisory Board, the IEA, and the NPC, have made
recommendations for continuously improving the environmental performance of shale gas extraction using hydraulic fracturing techniques and for
ensuring the public's confidence that it is safe.[52]

For example, the IEA put forward a set of "Golden Rules" in seven
high-level categories: (a) measure, disclose, and engage; (b) watch where
you drill; (c) isolate wells and prevent leaks; (d) treat water responsibly;
(e) eliminate venting, minimize flaring and other emissions; (f) be ready to
think big; and (g) ensure a consistently high level of environmental performance.[53] Although many companies already follow most of these recommendations, the IEA estimated that applying these rules across the board
could increase the overall financial cost of developing a typical shale gas
well by an estimated 7 percent.[54] Although not trivial, this cost is not a
substantial enough hurdle to significantly impede future shale gas development, were environmental compliance costs to rise in response to increased
regulation.

Unconventional Gas Implications for Exports and the International Gas Market

Another implication of the shale gas boom is that the United States has
moved from a position of declining production and increasing imports to
one in which developers are moving forward with plans to export LNG. In
fact, the same LNG import and regasification terminals that were reopened

or constructed in the mid- to late-2000s are now seeking to export LNG to take advantage of the substantial price differentials between US spot prices and delivered LNG prices abroad. Natural gas prices are more than twice as high in Europe and four times as high in Asia than those in the United States. Although considerable uncertainty still exists over the timing and magnitude of US exports—which hinge on both permit approvals and project financing—LNG exports from the lower 48 states could begin as soon as 2016, with the United States becoming a net natural gas exporter soon after 2020 if current trends persist.[55]

Domestic benefits of such exports include economic growth, job creation, and the supply stability that would come from an additional demand outlet for currently oversupplied US natural gas markets. Internationally, the availability of North American supply sources would also have a dampening effect on prices abroad and could further encourage the delinking of long-term natural gas contract prices that are directly tied to the price of oil. Increased US gas production has already redirected LNG shipments (originally meant to satisfy US demand) to the Atlantic and Pacific Basins, thereby loosening international LNG markets.

Shale gas deposits are also not limited to North America, and substantial resources are thought to exist in China, Argentina, Australia, Europe, and elsewhere.[56] Although commercial development of these resources is still at an early stage, it has the potential to significantly shake up international gas market dynamics and upset the previously growing influence of Russia and other large natural gas exporters on international gas markets. Russia, Iran, and Qatar alone collectively contain more than 50 percent of the world's proved gas reserves, and members of the Gas Exporting Countries Forum,[57] formed in 2001, together control close to 70 percent of proved gas reserves and over one-third of production.[58]

The main potential stumbling block to US export permit approvals is the possible impact of gas exports on domestic natural gas prices, which would be negligible for small export amounts but more sizable if the full amount of export capacity for which approval has been sought was actually built. As of late 2012, applications had been submitted for more than 20 bcfpd of natural gas export capacity, but only one project (Sabine Pass, for up to 2.2 bcfpd) had received the necessary approvals from both the US Department of Energy and the Federal Energy Regulatory Commission. Although 2.2 bcfpd is only 3 percent of current US natural gas consumption, 20 bcfpd equals a 30 percent share of the same. Any price increases associated with natural gas exports would, of course, be self-moderated by reduced demand for such exports on world markets, as well as encouragement of new supply sources in response to the higher prices.

Conclusion

Many aspects of the global energy outlook appear similar to those of the past, but significant movement is afoot. Although the energy system evolves slowly because of the very large and long-lasting installed capital base, it does change—and sometimes it changes faster than we expect. Although energy consumption continues to grow, it is growing at a slower rate as energy continues to decouple from economic growth because of structural transformation in the economy and technological improvements in energy efficiency. Fossil fuels will continue to dominate the energy mix, but their share is falling, and for the first time the absolute level of some fossil fuels looks ready to plateau and then potentially decline. Coal and oil are each already at or near their peak consumption in the West, and global coal consumption may level off and then decrease over the next two to three decades if policies unfold as expected.

Because of this changing outlook for energy consumption and the way it is fueled, major long-term energy projections are starting to foresee global CO_2 emissions flattening out by 2030 to 2040 if policy trends persist, rather than rising inexorably. These projections incorporate substantial improvements in energy efficiency, continued policy supports for renewable energy, sizable growth in nuclear power, and an explicit or implicit cost on CO_2 emissions rising to significant levels in both OECD and non-OECD countries. If climate change and other environmental risks are to be given more weight, even more will need to be done. In contrast, if these technology and policy changes do not unfold as expected, future energy consumption and emissions could be much higher.

The locus of demand growth has shifted strongly eastward and is pulling with it the attention of project investment, equipment sales, trading relationships, policy-makers, and geopolitical strategists. The capital equipment side of both energy production (e.g., electricity generation technology) and use (e.g., vehicle technology) has emerged as a strategic economic issue. Regarding global trade in fuels, although many regions look set to continue along historical trends—with the Middle East, Africa, and the former Soviet Union exporting increasing amounts to an increasingly import-dependent Europe and Asia—North America is undergoing a historic shift. The dramatic turnaround in oil and gas production coupled with moderate energy consumption growth has placed North America on a path to net balance in fuels over the next 20 to 25 years. The application of horizontal drilling and hydraulic fracturing technology to shale gas and oil plays is having a long-term effect on the US outlook that is still unfolding, while Canada's vast oil sands are both a tremendous resource and a formidable environmental challenge.

These North American developments will continue to have global effects and open up opportunities for market innovation and project development, while at the same time challenging existing relationships and structures. Although these North American energy dynamics will have clear benefits to the United States and Canada in terms of trade, economic development, and employment, they do not alone guarantee energy security. North America will continue to be deeply connected to the global oil market regardless of how much oil is produced locally and may become more connected to the global natural gas market. Those markets will continue to be subject both to the beneficial effects of diverse supply sources and trade and to the adverse influences of strategic actions by states and supply disruptions associated with political and military unrest.

From an environmental point of view, the rise of unconventional fuels brings with it both near-term opportunities and significant long-term challenges. Abundant, low-price natural gas can make more polluting, conventional, coal-based electric power easier to phase out—a trend that is now happening in some cases purely because of market forces. However, all types of energy production bring their own environmental impacts, and over the longer term, greater abundance of fossil fuels will increase the need either for ways to mitigate fossil emissions (such as carbon capture and storage) or for low-cost alternatives. Private and public innovative efforts will therefore continue to be essential. At the same time, the strong incentive to develop these ample unconventional resources raises an equally strong imperative to do so in a manner that continuously lowers the environmental footprint of their production and use.

In the context of this global energy outlook, energy security can be enhanced by the key market conditions of diverse, competitive energy trade; proper pricing of energy, including environmental impacts; and incentives for a robust energy distribution network. Reducing exposure to energy risks through energy efficiency, diversifying options through research and development of alternative fuels and technologies, and insuring against disruptions through wise use of strategic reserves and spare production capacity can also improve energy security. From the perspective of private planning and investment, the ongoing transformation of the energy system will open up new demand, supply, and arbitrage opportunities, as well as present substantial uncertainties in policy, technology, and market dynamics that will require robust investment and hedging approaches.

Notes

1. Adam E. Sieminski, "World Energy Futures," in *Energy and Security: Toward a New Foreign Policy Strategy*, ed. Jan H. Kalicki and David L. Goldwyn (Washington, DC, and Baltimore: Woodrow Wilson Center Press and Johns Hopkins University Press, 2005), 21–50. Note that these fuel share comparisons do not include traditional, nonmarketed biomass energy. This approach ensures an accurate comparison with the previous edition's figures, which also excluded nonmarketed biomass energy.

2. IEA, *World Energy Outlook 2011* (Paris: OECD/IEA, 2011).

3. Shell has taken a somewhat different approach to energy scenario develop ment, formulating more complex scenarios that differ across a number of societal, policy, economic, and technological dimensions. For example, in the Shell Scramble scenario, "policymakers pay little attention to more efficient energy use until supplies are tight. Likewise, greenhouse gas emissions are not seriously addressed until there are major climate shocks." See Shell, *Shell Energy Scenarios to 2050* (The Hague: Shell International, 2009), 4. See also Shell, *Signals and Signposts: Shell Energy Scenarios to 2050* (The Hague: Shell International, 2011). In a second Shell scenario, called Blueprints, "growing local actions begin to address the challenges of economic development, energy security and environmental pollution." See Shell, *Shell Energy Scenarios*, 4. Because the most recent Shell scenarios at the time of this writing were produced in 2008 and are published at a lesser level of detail, we do not include them in detail here with more recent projections dating from 2011.

4. *Primary energy consumption* refers to the direct use at the source, or supply to users without transformation, of crude energy (i.e., energy that has not been subjected to any conversion or transformation process).

5. The conversion rate is 1 quad per 0.49 mmbpd of oil equivalent.

6. The relationship between these factors and energy consumption (or carbon emissions) is sometimes referred to as the *Kaya Identity*. The equation for energy consumption can be written $E = E/GDP \times GDP/Pop \times Pop$. The extended equation for carbon emissions is $CO_2 = CO_2/E \times E/GDP \times GDP/Pop \times Pop$.

7. EIA, *International Energy Outlook 2011* (Washington, DC: EIA, 2011). See also IEA, *World Energy Outlook 2011*.

8. United Nations, *World Population Prospects: The 2010 Revision* (New York: United Nations), http://esa.un.org/unpd/wpp/.

9. This difference is largely due to substantially different measures of Asian GDP growth when measured in PPP (about 3.5-fold growth) compared to market exchange rates (about 1.7-fold growth). See EIA, *International Energy Outlook 2011*; IEA, *World Energy Outlook 2011*.

10. EIA, *International Energy Outlook 2011*; ExxonMobil, *2012: The Outlook for Energy: A View to 2040* (Irving, TX: ExxonMobil, 2012); IEA, *World Energy Outlook 2011*.

11. The exception is Africa, where ExxonMobil projects higher energy consumption growth than any of the other major outlooks.

12. According to the World Bank definition, *industry* "comprises value added in mining, manufacturing…, construction, electricity, water, and gas." See World Bank, "Industry, Value Added (% of GDP)," in the World Development Indicators database, http://data.worldbank.org/indicator/NV.IND.TOTL.ZS.

13. World Bank, "Industry, Value Added."

14. EIA, *Annual Energy Outlook 2012 with Projections to 2035* (Washington, DC: Energy Information Administration, 2012).

15. World Bank and the Development Research Center of the State Council, People's Republic of China, *China 2030: Building a Modern, Harmonious, and Creative High-Income Society* (Washington, DC: World Bank, 2013).

16. ExxonMobil, *2012: The Outlook for Energy*.

17. EIA, *International Energy Outlook 2011*.

18. EIA, *International Energy Outlook 2011*. Note that these shares do not include nonmarketed energy consumption.

19. EIA, *International Energy Outlook 2011*.

20. EIA, *International Energy Outlook 2011*.

21. IEA, *Key World Energy Statistics 2012* (Paris: OECD/IEA, 2012).

22. EIA, *International Energy Outlook 2011*; ExxonMobil, *2012: The Outlook for Energy;* IEA, *World Energy Outlook 2011*.

23. For example, the EIA includes a High Technology Battery case that explores the effects of battery technology breakthroughs and the use of electric vehicles. See EIA, *Annual Energy Outlook 2012*. In this scenario, significant improvements in technology help reduce vehicle battery costs for consumers, which in turn leads to greater sales of electric vehicles (24 percent of new light-duty vehicle sales in 2035 compared with 8 percent in the Reference Case). However, turnover of the entire light-duty vehicle fleet is slow, and although the resulting reduction in US liquids consumption in 2035 is measurable, it is modest at about 400,000 barrels per day.

24. IEA, *Key World Energy Statistics 2012*.

25. When biomass is combusted, it releases emissions, but CO_2 is also removed from the atmosphere during biomass growth. Ongoing research is investigating the full life-cycle emissions of biofuels and their potential effects on climate change. The typical accounting protocol used in projections is to assume biomass has net zero CO_2 emissions.

26. IEA, *World Energy Outlook 2011*.

27. IEA, *Key World Energy Statistics 2012*.

28. IEA, *World Energy Outlook 2011*; IEA, *Key World Energy Statistics 2012*.

29. ExxonMobil, *2012: The Outlook for Energy*.

30. IEA, *World Energy Outlook 2012* (Paris: OECD/IEA, 2012).

31. IEA, *World Energy Outlook 2011*.

32. IEA, *World Energy Outlook 2012*.

33. IEA, *World Energy Outlook 2011*.

34. IEA, *World Energy Outlook 2011*.

35. *Recoverable resources* include volumes that are judged likely to be ultimately producible, including proved reserves, future reserve growth, and as yet undiscovered resources.

36. ExxonMobil, *2012: The Outlook for Energy*; IEA, *World Energy Outlook 2011*.

37. *Proved oil reserves* are the subset of oil resources that have been demonstrated with reasonable certainty (often taken to be 90 percent) to be recoverable under existing economic and operating conditions.

38. EIA International Energy Statistics database, http://www.eia.gov/cfapps /ipdbproject.

39. For several reasons—most notably the energy crises of the 1970s, subsequent increases in non-OPEC production, and the resulting oil surplus of the 1980s—OPEC's share was much lower through the 1980s than it was either before or after that decade.

40. The National Petroleum Council is a federal advisory committee whose sole purpose is to advise, inform, and make recommendations on oil and natural gas at the request of the US secretary of energy.

41. NPC, *Prudent Development: Realizing the Potential of North America's Abundant Natural Gas and Oil Resources* (Washington, DC: NPC, 2011).

42. NPC, *Prudent Development*, 8.

43. NPC, *Prudent Development*.

44. EIA, *International Energy Outlook 2011*.

45. NPC, *Prudent Development*.

46. EIA, *Annual Energy Outlook 2012*.

47. National Energy Board, *Canada's Energy Future: Energy Supply and Demand Projections to 2035* (Ottawa: National Energy Board, 2011).

48. EIA, *US Crude Oil, Natural Gas, and Natural Gas Liquids Proved Reserves, 2010* (Washington, DC: EIA, 2012).

49. EIA, *Annual Energy Outlook 2012*.

50. NPC, *Prudent Development*.

51. EIA, *Annual Energy Outlook 2012*.

52. Secretary of Energy Advisory Board, *Shale Gas Production Subcommittee Second Ninety Day Report* (Washington, DC: US Department of Energy, 2011); IEA, *Golden Rules for a Golden Age of Gas: World Energy Outlook Special Report on Unconventional Gas* (Paris: OECD/IEA, 2012); NPC, *Prudent Development*.

53. IEA, *Golden Rules for a Golden Age of Gas*.

54. IEA, *Key World Energy Statistics 2012*.

55. EIA, *Annual Energy Outlook 2012*.

56. EIA, *World Shale Gas Resources: An Initial Assessment of 14 Regions outside the United States* (Washington, DC: EIA, 2011).

57. Forum member countries are Algeria, Bolivia, Egypt, Equatorial Guinea, Iran, Libya, Nigeria, Oman, Qatar, Russia, Trinidad and Tobago, and Venezuela.

58. EIA, International Energy Statistics database.

Chapter 2

Energy Security and Markets

Daniel Yergin

Energy security is squarely on the agenda again. Once more, the impact of energy on both foreign policy and the global economy is starkly clear. The dependence on energy systems and their growing complexity and reach underline the need to understand the risks and requirements of energy security in the 21st century. This chapter addresses two questions: What are the new dimensions of energy security? And what are the key principles for energy security?

Since the start of this century, a periodically narrowly balanced oil market and volatile prices—combined with geopolitical turmoil—have fueled concerns about energy security. The problem is not one of running out. Breakthroughs in production technology from what is called "unconventional" oil and gas—tight oil and shale gas in North America, Canadian oil sands, and "presalt" offshore resources—have allayed fears of shortage. To cite one critical indicator, US oil production rose 44 percent between 2008 and mid-2013.

The major risk to supplies over the next decade or two is not geology but geopolitics. Regional and social turmoil unsettles the Middle East. The "Arab Upheaval" that swept over North Africa and the Middle East, beginning in

2011, disrupted oil supplies, upended the strategic balance, and added a fear premium to the price of oil. Rising tensions over Iran's nuclear program have led to sanctions on Iranian oil exports. Iran responded with repeated threats to close the Strait of Hormuz, and anxiety has risen about the safety of oil and natural gas production and transport in the Arabian (Persian) Gulf.

Iraq could move toward the top of the list of the world's oil producers. But much uncertainty exists about its future political orientation, its relationship to Iran, the vulnerability of its production facilities to sabotage and violence, and even its durability as a unitary nation. Meanwhile, jihadism and global terrorism threaten the entire supply system.

The risks are hardly limited to the Middle East and North Africa. Over the past decade, political conflicts have disrupted significant amounts of oil supplies far afield from the Arabian Gulf—in Nigeria and Venezuela, both major producers. The large resource potential in the South China Sea, though still unproved, is raising concerns about the impact of geopolitical rivalry in those waters. Around the world, resource nationalism is resurging, which could restrain and distort the energy investment that is needed to be able to fuel global economic growth.

That energy security has come to loom so large results also from the new era in the global economy—the rapid economic growth in emerging market nations. This connection became clear around 2004 when the economic expansion of these countries—and particularly their need for oil and other commodities—reached world scale and went on to contribute significantly to what became the upward surge in oil prices.

Virtually all growth in oil demand in the decades ahead is expected to be in these emerging market nations. China and India, as well as Middle Eastern and other countries, will require substantial new energy supplies to support their rapid economic growth. That necessity creates a great challenge in terms of ensuring that such supplies will be developed in a timely way—and the great risk that, if not properly managed, commercial competition could turn into geopolitical rivalry. Adroit diplomacy will be needed on the part of both developed and developing nations, especially the United States and China. The pressing need for energy locates energy security firmly at the top of the agenda for these two nations.

Widening the Meaning of Energy Security

The very concept of *energy security* is taking on wider meaning. No longer does it mainly encompass just the flow of oil, as central as that is and as it has been for four decades. Natural gas was formerly a national or regional fuel. But the development of long-distance pipelines and the growth of liquefied natural gas have turned natural gas into much more of a global business.

The electric power blackouts that hit the northeast of the United States in 2003, and those that followed in Europe and Russia, demonstrated the vulnerability of complex transmission systems and generated great concern about the reliability of electricity supply. The danger was driven home in 2012, when a blackout in India cut off electricity to about 700 million people—almost one-tenth of the world's entire population.

Indeed, energy security now extends to the entire infrastructure of energy supply that supports both America's economy and the global economy—pipelines and tankers as well as refineries, storage facilities, generating facilities, transmission lines, and distribution systems. This vast network was not designed with disruption and terrorism in mind, but its operations now have to be managed with that continuing danger in view. The result is to create new and complex responsibilities for both industry and government, including communication and coordination between them. There is still much to be learned—and done—in this arena.

These dangers are embedded in something that the world had not seen, at least in modern times, until recent years: integrated energy shocks. This situation first became evident in 2005 when Hurricanes Katrina and Rita struck the Gulf of Mexico's energy complex. Everything seemed connected, and everything was down at the same time: oil and natural gas production and undersea pipelines in the gulf and—onshore—receiving terminals, refineries, natural gas–processing plants, long-distance pipelines, and electricity. The storms showed how fundamental was the electricity system on which everything else depended. The huge earthquake and tsunami that struck Japan in 2011, in addition to bringing death and destruction, also took down the region's power system, thereby immobilizing communication and transportation, disrupting the economy and global supply chains, and paralyzing efforts to respond to the tragedy. In 2012, the US mid-Atlantic—New York City, New Jersey, and Connecticut—experienced an integrated energy shock when Superstorm Sandy knocked out power and disrupted fuel supplies, paralyzing the region and causing great hardship. Lower Manhattan went dark, as did many other areas; hospitals were evacuated because of lack of power; fuel for emergency vehicles was perilously short; and first responders were lost in the "fog of war" owing to the blackout of information. In China, India, and other developing countries, chronic shortages of electric power continue to demonstrate the costs of unreliability.

Moreover, what could be a danger of enormous proportions looms in the years ahead: the Internet and reliance on complex information technology systems have created a whole new range of vulnerabilities for energy and electric power around the world. Electronic paths are now open for those who wish to disrupt those energy systems. Warning of cyber dangers in his 2013 State of the Union Address, President Barack Obama put, at the top of the list, the threat "to sabotage our power grid."[1]

Yet less visible and every bit as important as the risks is a compensating reality. New sources of oil and gas, technological advances for both energy production and consumption, and the lessons learned and the institutional development that has come with those lessons—these enable policy-makers and industry decision-makers to manage energy shocks and weather whatever storms may lie ahead. Relations between producing and consuming countries are generally based much more on interdependence and cooperation than in the past, although sharp rifts persist with some nations and new conflicts continue to appear. Still, these more cooperative relations provide a crucial foundation for handling and minimizing shocks.

For the longer term, a renewed commitment to new technologies and energy research and development holds promise of further diversification, although neither the timing nor the certainty is as sure as some may hope. At the very least, the realities—the huge scale of the energy supply system, the inevitable time lags, and the requirements for commercial proof—push off the major effect of renewables and new alternatives by one to two decades.

"Safety and Certainty in Oil"

In other words, energy security requires continuing commitment and attention—today and tomorrow. Of course, energy security is hardly a new concern. It has been a recurrent issue for more than a century, ever since oil became critical to transportation. It came clearly to the fore on the eve of World War I, when Winston Churchill, as First Lord of the Admiralty, converted the Royal Navy from coal to oil. As a result, the British fleet began to shift from Welsh coal as the source of its propulsion to Persian— Iranian—oil. In addressing the risks associated with this historic move, Churchill declared, "Safety and certainty in oil lie in variety and variety alone."[2] His words at the beginning of the 20th century are no less apt for the 21st century—for he was articulating the fundamental principle of energy security: diversification of supply. In recent years, the "unconventional revolution" in oil and natural gas has been making a new and unexpected contribution to diversification.

The Unconventional Oil and Gas Revolution

As late as 2008, when oil prices spiked to $147.27 per barrel, US oil and gas production were thought to be on a long-term decline, thereby making the United States more and more dependent on imported oil and eventually a major importer of natural gas as well. But the outlook has been transformed by what has become known as the revolution in unconventional oil and natural gas. It began with the yoking together of two technologies—hydraulic fracturing and horizontal drilling—to liberate natural gas trapped in dense shale rock.

The combination of hydraulic fracturing and horizontal drilling transformed the United States from a country that seemed destined to be short of gas into one endowed with abundant, relatively low-cost natural gas. Shale gas went from being a mere 2 percent of total gas production at the beginning of this century to almost 45 percent at this writing. Among other results, the United States overtook Russia as the world's largest natural gas producer.

Then oil explorers began applying these technologies to previously unproductive rocks. The result is the surge in what has become known as "tight oil." The increase in production is world class: in volumetric terms, between 2008 and the beginning of 2013, the increase is equivalent to the entire output of Nigeria and almost the total of Iran's exports before sanctions were applied in 2012.

Generally unanticipated were the economic effects of this revolution. The most immediate was in job creation—supporting more than 1.7 million jobs—because the development of shale gas and tight oil involves long supply chains, with substantial sums being spent across the United States. By 2020, the jobs supported could reach 3 million.[3]

This shift in production has given new life to the idea of energy independence. Richard Nixon proffered this idea during the 1973 oil crisis, despite the best efforts of his speechwriters, who thought the idea unrealistic. Every president since has held out the promise that the United States could return to self-sufficiency and thus, it was thought, become less vulnerable to Middle East turmoil and high prices. But as production went down and imports continued to rise, energy independence continued to seem unrealistic, a quixotic goal—until this revolution in unconventional oil and natural gas.[4]

Yet based on what is known today, the United States will continue to be an oil importer for a very long time. It will become not energy independent but rather energy *less* dependent. In that process, the country will become more integrated, in energy terms, with its largest trading partner, Canada.

This rebalancing of world oil and gas provides the United States with more resilience and with many economic benefits. But energy security, for all the reasons previously described, will continue to be a matter of overriding importance.

Further Dimensions of Energy Security

The standard definition of *energy security* is pretty straightforward: the availability of sufficient supplies at affordable prices. Yet thinking of it in several different dimensions is helpful. The first is *physical security*—protecting the assets, infrastructure, supply chains, and trade routes. In terms of trade routes, the Strait of Hormuz, through which oil passes out of the Arabian Gulf, is the best known of the chokepoints for world supplies.

However, pipelines and transmission lines around the world are also chokepoints. Security requires the provisioning for quick replacements and substitution, when need be. Such planning includes not only strategic petroleum reserves, but also, for instance, generators that can be quickly deployed when the power system is crippled by an integrated energy shock.

Second, access to energy is critical. *Access to energy* means the ability to develop and acquire energy supplies—physically, contractually, and commercially. Barriers and restrictions to energy trade not only impede energy flows in general but also make adjustments to disruptions more difficult.

Third, energy security is a system. That is, it involves national policies and international institutions that are designed to respond in a coordinated way to disruptions, dislocations, and emergencies as well as to help maintain the steady flow of supplies. It was for this reason, in the first place, that the International Energy Agency (IEA) was set up after the first oil crisis in 1973–74.

Finally, and crucially, energy security requires policies and a business climate that promote investments and development and innovation to ensure that adequate supplies and infrastructure will be available, in a timely way, in the future. Energy development can take a long time and thus requires a consistent flow of investment, as well as fiscal and regulatory regimes that allow those funds to flow. The same can be said of the long-term funding of research and development required for future innovation.

Oil-importing countries tend to think in terms of security of supply. Energy-exporting countries turn the question around. They talk of "security of demand" for their oil and gas exports, on which they depend to generate economic growth and a very large share of government revenues — and to maintain social stability.

The 10 Principles of Energy Security

As policy-makers approach energy security, experience suggests 10 key principles as follows.

Principle 1: The Importance of Diversification

First, Churchill's maxim of a century ago continues to hold true — diversification of supply is one of the main guarantors of security and, indeed, is the starting point for energy security. Widening the sources of supply lessens the impact of any particular disruption and provides opportunity for compensating supplies. This principle of diversification extends to energy transportation and infrastructure as well. And it also serves the interests of suppliers by creating a more stable market for their exports.

Principle 2: The Position of the United States in the Global Oil Market

Second, both policy-makers and the public need to recognize that there is only one oil market. The United States is part of a global oil market, an extraordinarily huge logistical system that moves about 90 million barrels of oil around the world every day. US security resides in the stability of this global market. Even with the turn toward increasing domestic production and decreasing imports, to consider being "independent" of the global market is not realistic.

Principle 3: The Need for a Security Margin

Third, energy security requires a *security margin*—that is, the availability
of extra supply that can replace supplies that have been disrupted. This
margin takes two forms. One is *spare capacity*—extra capacity above normal output levels that can be put into production quickly. A critical component of spare capacity is the 1.5 million to 2 million barrels per day
that Saudi Arabia explicitly maintains, at some cost, as policy. This unused
but available Saudi capacity was called into play in 1990 to replace the
shutdown of Iraqi and Kuwaiti oil fields and again when Iraq's output was
disrupted during and after the 2003 war. It was used in 2011 when Libyan
production was disrupted and in 2012 to compensate for the reduction in
Iranian exports resulting from sanctions.

At the same time, the emergency stocks, such as the US Strategic Petroleum Reserve (SPR), with 700 million barrels at this writing, and similar reserves in other industrial countries, are the frontline defense against
serious disruptions in supply. These stocks are held as part of the system
created for coordinated release and sharing under the auspices of the IEA.
The SPR and the strategic stocks of other countries constitute an insurance
policy against major disruptions and the resulting threat to gross domestic
product.

The SPR comes with a temptation to use it in market-management
schemes to deal with temporary price fluctuations. This temptation must be
resisted. If the SPR is used as a tool of price management, it will be deval-
ued as an instrument and lose its legitimacy. More important, its use as a
price management tool will discourage increases in production and investment and, at the same time, retard markets from adjusting to shifts in supply and demand. And there is an additional obvious risk: oil released from
the SPR may temporarily reduce prices, but what happens when, after the
release is completed, prices revert to higher levels? The government may
well find itself drawn into a much longer process of market management
than was anticipated, depleting the reserve in the meantime.[5]

Principle 4: The Role of Well-Functioning Energy Markets

Fourth is the role of markets themselves in dealing with disruptions. Large,
flexible, and well-functioning energy markets contribute to security by absorbing shocks and allowing supply and demand to respond more quickly

and with much greater ingenuity than is possible within a controlled system. Markets can often more efficiently and effectively—and far more quickly—resolve shortfalls and disruptions than more centralized direction.

The oil market today is far more flexible than it was in earlier decades, which is a big positive. Intervention and controls can be highly counterproductive, hindering the system from swiftly shifting supplies around to adjust to changes in the market or disruptions in supply. Resisting the temptation to micromanage markets in the face of political pressures is essential. It would be well to remember that the famous US gasoline lines that followed the 1973 and 1979 crises were largely the result of price controls and a cumbersome allocation system that prevented suppliers from moving gasoline from places where it was not needed to places where it was. The negative, unintended, and perverse effects of heavy-handed regulation were a main consequence of the controls of the 1970s.

This lesson, it seems, needs to be recalled whenever a disruption occurs. Charges of "gouging" are a staple of disruption, often accompanied by hearings, investigation, and litigation. But what may not be understood is that, by focusing on gouging rather than resupplying, authorities may be hindering recovery. The invocation of gouging and the threat of punishment act as a disincentive to people applying ingenuity to get supplies into the market as fast as possible. And it can lead to outcomes with a much higher economic and social cost: people sitting in a gasoline line for hours, growing angrier and angrier. Market participants should be concentrating on finding and moving supplies as quickly as possible; they should not be immobilized by the threat of investigation, litigation, penalties, and jail time.

Principle 5: The Importance of Building Relationships with Exporting Nations

Fifth, building cooperative relations, based on common interests, with nations that produce and export energy is critical. Since the 1980s, most oil-exporting nations—though not all—have come to recognize the mutuality of interest between themselves and the importing nations. While consumers need supplies at reasonable prices, producers need markets. Their national revenues depend on those markets. It is in the producers' interest to be seen as credible suppliers on whom buyers can count. Thus, most exporters are deeply interested in *security of demand*—stable commercial relations with their customers, whose purchases often provide a significant part of their national revenues. This mutual interdependence helps create the framework for a continuing dialogue and cooperation between producers and consumers.

Principle 6: The Need to Ensure Cooperative Relations among Importing Nations

Sixth, similar efforts need to go into maintaining an ongoing dialogue and cooperative energy relations among importing nations. This principle holds true whether they are the other industrial nations; the new "globalizers," such as China and India, whose demand for imported energy is increasing dramatically; or lower-income, developing nations. The IEA, whose members are countries belonging to the Organization for Economic Cooperation and Development, is a critical bulwark for these purposes. It promotes cooperation, helps coordinate energy policies, tests contingencies, develops common frameworks, and provides mechanisms for responding to energy emergencies. In the aftermath of the Gulf Crisis of 1990 to 1991, the IEA and the Organization of the Petroleum Exporting Countries, representing exporters, began a dialogue aimed at promoting a better understanding across a range of oil and natural gas topics. One result has been the creation of the International Energy Forum, whose members represent 90 percent of the world's production and consumption of oil and natural gas. The International Energy Forum is charged with creating greater transparency on energy production and demand, and on inventories, so that world markets can operate on the basis of better information.[6]

Principle 7: The Importance of High-Quality Information

Seventh, when markets become tight or disrupted—and inventories are drawn down and prices rise—the public's fear can, through panic buying, turn into self-fulfilling prophecies. Finger pointing, rancorous clamor, and search for conspiracies and manipulation—and the thundering charges of "gouging"—can take over and obscure the real issues and hinder the practical solutions. Whatever the politics, the results can be bad policy. Psychology can be calmed, anxieties and panic allayed with the flow of high-quality information to the public and by facilitating the exchange of information within the industry that makes possible more rapid adjustments to market disruptions.

That last point is an important issue in the United States. Repeatedly, the ability to respond effectively to crises has been hindered by the inability of companies to share market data and information because of antitrust laws. In due course, an antitrust waiver is issued, but the cost of "due course" can be very high—because valuable time is lost. It would make great sense to have an automatic antitrust waiver go into effect with the declaration of a disruption or crisis rather than have to relearn the issues and reinvent the wheel while lives hang in the balance and ambulances, police cars, and utility repair trucks stand immobilized because of lack of fuel.

Principle 8: The Importance of a Robust Domestic Industry

Eighth, a healthy, technologically driven, domestic energy industry is an important element of energy security. This means an oil and gas industry that can continue to explore and produce in the United States in an environmentally sound way but that is also efficient and operates under reasonable and predictable rules with timely decision-making by government regulators. The technological leadership of the US-based industry is also a source of strength. The power industry will require continuing innovation and diversification in the next wave of new generation capacity.

Principle 9: The Role of Research and Development

Ninth, a commitment to research and development and innovation across a broad spectrum is fundamental to energy security. In the long term, innovation is the engine both for achieving broadly based diversification and for establishing the basis for a transition to new energy systems later in this century. Much investment has already gone for this purpose. No one can be sure what the mix of energy sources will be two or three decades hence. How much of it will be similar to today, albeit more efficient, and how much of it will be going in new directions? How much market share will go to renewables and alternatives?[7] Certainly local and global environmental concerns will loom larger. Together with energy security and the reality of growing world demand, all these considerations make a compelling case for significant and consistent investment in energy research and development across a broad front. Here is where commitment by the federal government is crucial, working in cooperation with universities, research labs, and the private sector and in collaboration with other countries.

Principle 10: The Importance of Planning for Disruptions

One final principle remains. It is really a matter of mindset: to work on the assumption that disruptions of and threats to energy security will occur and to plan that they will occur. This assumption leads to operational results. One is to practice—to conduct drills as to how to respond. The second is to pre-position knowledge. Such pre-positioning means not only response plans, but also such basic things as who needs to talk to whom across public and private sectors. This preparation will help dissipate that aforementioned "fog of war," as a decision-maker described the situation during the 2012 Superstorm Sandy. In that crisis, confusion was generated and days were lost simply because of the lack of names and phone numbers of whom to call.

Energy: A "Hinge" of the World Economy

Since the rise of industrial society, the energy system has been a target in warfare. In World War II, both the Allies and the Axis powers tried to disrupt the other's petroleum supplies. Nazi U-boats came close to severing the flow of oil from the Western Hemisphere to Britain and the Allied forces in Europe. Later in the war, both the Nazi-controlled Romanian oil fields at Ploesti and Germany's synthetic fuel plants were main targets of Allied bombings. By the time the Germans developed the first jet fighter, they were so short of oil that they had to use oxen to pull the jet onto the runway, to conserve aviation fuel.[8]

However, in the aftermath of the oil embargo of 1973 and the Iranian Revolution of 1978–79, the principal focus of energy security became somewhat narrower. It centered on the reliability of the flow of oil, principally from the Middle East, and the response to and management of any disruptions. The terrorist attacks of September 11, 2001, widened the focus again, back to the whole system—that is, the security of the infrastructure, the entire supply chain that stretches around the world from production and gathering facilities to distribution to consumers.

Not only are terrorists seeking to wreak havoc and kill innocent people; they are also intent on waging economic warfare against the global economy. When Osama bin Laden threatened to attack the "hinges" of the American and world economy, he meant the critical infrastructure that runs the modern economy, such as transportation, communications, information technology, financial, health, food, and of course energy. For terrorists from the Middle East, for whom Saudi Arabia is centrally in their sights, the energy system looms as an all too obvious target for disrupting both the economy and society—and hitting, in the words of al Qaeda spokesmen, "the provision line and the feeding artery of the life of the crusader nation."[9] Ayman Al-Zawahiri, successor to bin Laden as leader of al Qaeda, declared that the mujahideen should "focus their attacks on the stolen oil of the Muslims" until an al Qaeda caliphate ruled the Arabian Peninsula.[10] The reality of this threat was made all too clear in 2013 when jihadists seized a large natural gas facility that operates a major Algerian gas field deep in the Sahara desert, killing a large number of workers, though failing in their main objective of blowing up the plant.

Tankers, which move well over half the world's oil, have already been singled out as targets. In addition to apprehensions about attacks on tankers on the high seas, particular concern exists about coordinated assaults that would scuttle ships and close down such critical shipping channels as the Strait of Hormuz and Bab el Mandeb, at the entrances respectively to the Arabian Gulf and the Red Sea. But a no less critical risk is the Strait of Malacca, between Malaysia and Indonesia, through which passes a quarter of world trade, including huge volumes of oil; the strait is already subject to attacks by pirates.[11]

In the aftermath of 9/11, much effort has gone into addressing the security of energy infrastructure within the United States. Ports, for instance, are much better protected than previously. Still, observers maintain that there is much more to do. Homeland security experts continue to warn that energy, along with other infrastructure, is poorly protected.

Providing such protection is not an easy job. The range is very wide—from pumping stations, gathering plants, and terminals, to tankers and pipelines, to refineries, power stations, and transmission lines, to distribution networks. Moreover, the scale in the United States is enormous: facilities to handle almost 14 million barrels per day of imports and exports, 4,000 offshore platforms, 144 refineries, 175,000 miles of oil pipelines, 5,800 operational power plants, 157,000 miles of high-voltage electricity transmission lines and millions of miles of distribution wires, 278,000 miles of natural gas transmission lines, more than 400 underground gas storage fields, and much more. In today's circumstances, some types of facilities, such as nuclear power plants, are much more secure than others.

Attacks could take the form of physical assaults on port facilities, refineries, petrochemical plants, compression stations, dams, transmission lines, and substations. These types of attacks are easier to visualize. No less dangerous, however, would be another form—coordinated cyber attacks and electromagnetic attacks that would seek to break into control systems and take over control or disrupt them. There is nothing fanciful about that possibility. Tens and tens of thousands of sites on the Internet are aimed at hackers. Some of them contain explicit instructions on how to launch an attack on energy and other infrastructure. Computers and notes recovered from al Qaeda operatives have included plans and diagrams for US energy facilities.[12]

"A Cyber Pearl Harbor"

In the past few years, cyber vulnerability has moved to the top of energy security concerns. And with good reason. Both government agencies and private companies are subject to an ever-growing number of cyber attacks and entry.

Already, by 2010, the US director of national intelligence identified cyber security as one of the top threats to the United States. "The information infrastructure," said the annual Threat Assessment, is "severely threatened." Even companies that are supposed to be among the most protected have become subject to successful attack. Increasing resources are going into efforts to protect against cyber threats, yet cyber security will continue to be a big challenge. As the director of national intelligence said in 2012, "We currently face cyber environments where emerging technologies are developed and implemented faster than governments can keep pace." He added that highly publicized attacks on well-known organizations "underscore the vulnerability of key sectors of the US and global economy."[13]

What the vulnerabilities of this new age might look like was made starkly clear at 11:08 a.m. on August 15, 2012, in Saudi Arabia. Employees of Saudi Aramco, the world's largest oil company, were at home preparing for a holiday. But at that moment, after a month of probes, a virus named Shamoon was launched into the company's computers. It wiped clean—burned—the hard drives of more than 30,000 computers. Everything was gone—e-mails, working files, documents, commercial data, addresses, and whatever else was stored in the hard drives—and presumably much of it was also pilfered by the attackers. It was all replaced with a single image—a burning US flag. Almost two weeks were needed to restore central computer services. By then a subsequent attack had been launched on Qatar's natural gas industry.

One Saudi described the assault as a "scorched earth" attack. As bad as it was, it could have been much worse. "The main target in this attack was to stop the flow of oil and gas to local and international markets," a Saudi Aramco official told the press. If the attack had succeeded to that degree, it would have disrupted production of more than 10 percent of total world oil, with potentially long-lasting impact on fields and equipment and panic and disruption in the global economy. "Thank God," the official added, "they were not able to achieve their goals."[14] Computers for production run on isolated systems, and, as Saudi oil minister Ali Al-Naimi explained, "There are protective devices which did not allow it."[15]

As to the perpetrators, the Saudis concluded that an "organized foreign group" was behind the attacks.[16] Although a group that called itself the Cutting Sword of Islam launched the attacks from four continents, only one country—Iran—was generally assumed to be behind the attackers.[17]

Two months after the attack, then–defense secretary Leon Panetta called it the alarm bell for what may be ahead. Describing the United States as being in a "pre-9/11 moment," he raised the level of threat to that of "a cyber Pearl Harbor" attack on critical infrastructure that, augmented by "physical attack," would "paralyze and shock the nation." His biggest worries included the vulnerability of "transportation systems, power systems, energy systems."[18] In 2013, Iranian cyber intrusions into the control mechanisms for various parts of the US energy infrastructure were reported.[19]

In terms of "critical infrastructures," the electric power system ranks among the most critical. The operations of everything else—from aviation and hospitals to the financial industry to government itself—depend on it. The paralysis from Hurricanes Katrina and Rita, and then Superstorm Sandy, give some indication of what a major cyber attack on the electric system would be like.

In the 1960s and 1970s, computers were deployed to manage the generation and distribution of electricity and to integrate the grid. In the years since, the system has become more sophisticated and integrated—and increasingly "smarter." All this makes the system more efficient. But it also makes the system more vulnerable.

The potential marauders cover a wide range—from hackers and disgruntled employees, to governments, to terrorists or anarchists or other nonstate actors seeking to wreak digital havoc. The point of entry could well be through the ubiquitous computer systems that monitor and control every kind of industrial process and that are now connected into large information networks.

In the face of risks for the electric grid and other critical infrastructure, nations are struggling to design policies and capabilities to repel the growing cyber threat. The US Department of Defense has created a Cyber Command. It is also developing a new doctrine in which a major attack on critical infrastructure, including energy, would constitute an act of war that would justify military retaliation. But these moves need to be matched by company efforts and bolstered with considerable investment and focus. A study by the US National Infrastructure Advisory Council concluded that "the public–private sector component of the infrastructure protection mission is not receiving the high priority that is commensurate with its vital importance" and that "the private sector generally does not receive the intelligence information it needs."[20]

Altogether, new security architectures have to be introduced into systems that were designed without such security in mind. And they need to be coordinated with other countries. After all, it takes only a fraction of a millisecond for an attack to hit a server from anywhere in the world.

Resilience

A new approach is emerging to deal with this wide range of threats to the energy sector (as to other critical infrastructures). It goes by the name of *resilience*. The intent is "to reduce the magnitude and/or duration of disruptive events."[21] For the electric power sector, it has four elements:

- *Robustness*: the ability to absorb shocks and keep operating
- *Resourcefulness:* the ability to skillfully manage a crisis as it unfolds
- *Rapid recovery:* the ability to get services back as quickly as possible
- *Adaptability:* the ability to incorporate lessons learned from past events to improve resilience[22]

The US—and global—energy system was not designed with these new kinds of threats in mind. A gap exists, as the Silent Vector research project identified, between the traditional safety costs that the private sector internalizes and preparation for "terrorist strikes" that are "intentional and focused, designed for maximum catastrophic impact."[23] Homeland security expert Stephen Flynn summarized the problem in simple terms: "Security is not free."[24] Building a higher degree of security into the energy infrastructure has a continuing cost, and one way or another that cost ultimately will need to be folded both into the cost of homeland security that the nation bears and into the price of energy in the marketplace. That is a requirement for the enhanced energy security that America requires in this new era.

Preparing for the Unexpected

This chapter quoted earlier one British prime minister, Winston Churchill, on energy security. It ends by quoting another. When Margaret Thatcher was interviewed for *The Commanding Heights: The Battle for the World Economy*, she remarked, "Remember Thatcher's Law." Asked what that law was, she replied, "The unexpected happens. You had better prepare for it."[25]

One must be very mindful of surprises, whether in the Middle East, or in places not being thought about in those terms today, or much closer to home. Thus, Thatcher's Law remains a very good guiding principle—indeed, an essential one—to keep in mind both now and in the future about the critical matter of energy security. That means not only expecting the unexpected but certainly also preparing for it.

Notes

1. Barack Obama, "Remarks by the President in the State of the Union Address," US Capitol, Washington, DC, February 12, 2013, http://www.whitehouse.gov /the-press-office/2013/02/12/remarks-president-state-union-address.

2. Winston Churchill, Parliamentary Debates, House of Commons, July 17, 1913, 1474–77. See also Daniel Yergin, *The Prize: The Epic Quest for Oil, Money, and Power* (New York: Free Press, 2008), 137–47.

3. IHS, *America's New Energy Future: The Unconventional Oil and Gas Revolution and the US Economy* (Englewood, CO: IHS, 2012); Daniel Yergin, *The Quest: Energy, Security, and the Remaking of the Modern World* (New York: Penguin, 2012), chapter 16 and 263–65.

4. Yergin, *The Quest*, 269–71.

5. See Michelle Patron and David L. Goldwyn, "Managing Strategic Reserves," chapter 20 of this volume, for another perspective.

6. Yergin, *The Quest*, 275–77. See also William Ramsay, "Energy Sector Governance in the 21st Century," chapter 6 of this volume, for an extensive analysis and assessment.

7. World Economic Forum and IHS Cambridge Energy Research Associates, *Energy Transitions: Past and Future* (Davos, Switzerland: World Economic Forum, 2013).

8. Yergin, *The Prize*, chapters 16–19.

9. Gal Luft, "A Crude Threat," *Baltimore Sun*, April 6, 2004, http://articles.baltimoresun.com/2004-04-06/news/0404060002_1_pipeline-attacks-iraq-sabotage.

10. Al Zawahiri made this comment in an interview with Al-Sahab TV on September 11, 2005. See Middle East Media Research Institute, "Newly Released Video of al-Qaeda's Deputy Leader Ayman Al-Zawahiri's Interview to Al-Sahab TV," Special Dispatch 1044, Middle East Media Research Institute, Washington, DC, http://www.memri.org/report/en/print1550.htm.

11. "Signs of Revived Qaeda Are Seen in Latest Strikes and New Tapes," *New York Times*, October 13, 2002; US Department of Homeland Security, *The National Strategy for the Physical Protection of Critical Infrastructure and Key Assets* (Washington, DC: Government Printing Office, 2003); Matthew Hunt, "Bleed to Bankruptcy: Economic Targeting Tactics in the Global Jihad," *Jane's Intelligence Review* 19, no. 1 (2007): 14–17; Donna J. Nincic, "The 'Radicalization' of Maritime Policy: Implications for Maritime Energy Security," *Journal of Energy Security*, December 14, 2010, http://www.ensec.org/index.php?option=com_content&view=article&id=269:the-radicalization-of-maritime-piracy-implications-for-maritime-energy-security&catid=112:energysecuritycontent&Itemid=367.

12. Thomas Hegghammer, *Jihad in Saudi Arabia: Violence and Pan-Islamism since 1979* (Cambridge, UK: Cambridge University Press, 2010), 215.

13. James R. Clapper, "Unclassified Statement for the Record on the Worldwide Threat Assessment of the US Intelligence Community for the Senate Select Committee on Intelligence," January 31, 2012, http://www.hsdl.org/?view&did=699575.

14. "Saudi Arabia Says Cyber Attack Aimed to Disrupt Oil, Gas Flow." *Reuters*, December 9, 2012, http://www.reuters.com/article/2012/12/09/saudi-attack-idUSL5E8N91UE20121209.

15. Camilla Hall and Javier Blas, "Aramco Cyber Attack Threatened Production," *Financial Times*, December 10, 2012, http://www.ft.com/cms/s/0/5f313ab6-42da-11e2-a4e4-00144feabdc0.html#axzz2RPdyGhEi.

16. Ahmad Abdullah, "Foreign Group behind Aramco Cyber Attacks, Reveals Inquiry," *Saudi Gazette*, December 10, 2012, http://www.saudigazette.com.sa/index.cfm?method=home.regcon&contentid=20121210145504.

17. Nicole Perlroth, "In Cyberattack on Saudi Firm, US Sees Iran Firing Back," *New York Times*, October 23, 2012, http://www.nytimes.com/2012/10/24/business/global/cyberattack-on-saudi-oil-firm-disquiets-us.html?pagewanted=all&_r=0.

18. Leon Panetta, "Remarks by Secretary Panetta on Cybersecurity to the Business Executives for National Security, New York City," October 11, 2012, US Department of Defense News Transcript, http://www.defense.gov/transcripts/transcript.aspx?transcriptid=5136. See also Mark Thompson, "Panetta Sounds Alarm on Cyber-War Threat," *Time*, October 12, 2012, http://nation.time.com/2012/10/12/panetta-sounds-alarm-on-cyber-war-threat/.

19. Siobhan Gorman and Danny Yadron, "Iran Hacks Energy Firms, US Says," *Wall Street Journal*, May 23, 2013, http://online.wsj.com/article/SB10001424127887323336104578501601108021968.html.

20. National Infrastructure Advisory Council, *Intelligence Information Sharing: Final Report and Recommendations* (Arlington, VA: National Infrastructure Advisory Council, US Department of Homeland Security, 2012), ES-2, ES-4. See also Center for Strategic and International Studies Commission on Cybersecurity for the 44th Presidency, US Department of Homeland Security, *Cybersecurity Two Years Later* (Washington, DC: Center for Strategic and International Studies, 2011); Charles Ebinger and Kevin Massy, "Software and Hard Targets: Enhancing Smart Grid Cyber Security in the Age of Information Warfare," Policy Brief 11-01, Brookings Energy Security Initiative, Washington, DC, 2011.

21. Alfred R. Berkeley III and Mike Wallace, *A Framework for Establishing Critical Infrastructure Resilience Goals: Final Report and Recommendations by the Council* (Arlington, VA: National Infrastructure Advisory Council, US Department of Homeland Security, 2010), 5.

22. Stephen E. Flynn, "Homeland Insecurity: Disaster and DHS," *American Interest* 4, no. 5 (2009): 19–26; Stephen E. Flynn, "Recalibrating Homeland Security," *Foreign Affairs* 90, no. 3 (2011): 130–40; Berkeley and Wallace, *A Framework for Establishing Critical Infrastructure Resilience Goals*, 5.

23. See the findings in Center for Strategic and International Studies, "Silent Vector: Issues of Concern and Policy Recommendations," Center for Strategic and International Studies, Washington, DC, September 2003, http://chnm.gmu.edu/cipdigitalarchive/files/125_CSISSilent-Vector-Brief0903.pdf.

24. Stephen E. Flynn, "The Neglected Home Front," *Foreign Affairs* 83, no. 5 (2004): 28.

25. Daniel Yergin and Joseph Stanislaw, *The Commanding Heights: The Battle for the World Economy* (New York: Touchstone, 2002), 105–6.

Chapter 3

The Gas Promise

David G. Victor

Natural gas is a manic-depressive industry that is prone to wild swings in mood. For decades, drillers had few incentives to hunt for gas. The industry was a niche backwater to the much more lucrative business of drilling for oil. Then, starting in the United States in the late 1980s, a host of regulatory and market reforms opened the market and created a vibrant and highly competitive industry that was flush with new supplies. A decade later, analysts swung back to depression as US supplies ran short and most experts envisioned a future heavily dependent on imports via liquefied natural gas (LNG) from overseas. The countries that expected to be the world's big gas suppliers—such as Russia, Algeria, and Qatar, with massive gas resources underground—even made the first moves to set up a cartel that might corner supplies and drive

Many thanks to Linda Wong for research assistance; to the Global Agenda Council on Energy Security for discussions; and to Jim Jensen, John Deutch, Jan Kalicki, and David Goldwyn for their comments.

up prices much as the Organization of the Petroleum Exporting Countries has tried to do in oil. Policy-makers braced for a nasty and brutish future because they assumed the country would depend on foreigners for natural gas just as it did for most of its oil.

For the past few years, the US natural gas industry has swung back to euphoria. A surge of new supplies, mainly from shale deposits unlocked through innovations in "fracking" and horizontal drilling, has created a revolution. At the turn of the millennium, just 1 percent of US gas came from shale; by 2011, that share had risen to 30 percent.[1] US gas prices, which averaged just over $9 per million British thermal units in 2008, plunged below $3. Low prices have been good for consumers, but they also drive the next mood swing within the industry. Investors who made big bets on LNG imports because they assumed that gas within North America would be scarce and expensive are now exploring the opposite business strategy: exporting American gas as LNG to the rest of the world.[2]

This chapter explores the origins and implications as innovations in shale gas, along with LNG, affect the rest of the world's gas industry. It looks at not just the effects on economies but also the effects on the environment and geopolitics. Throughout, I make one central argument. Analysts and industrialists alike are prone to focus on what is new in gas and manically extrapolate the latest trends into the future. The innovations in shale gas are real and profound. However, so far, the revolution is mainly an American affair that is still short lived. A lot could go wrong, especially as firms try to deploy shale gas technologies in the rest of the world. Thus, many of the plausible implications of this revolution for energy security and geo-politics—for example, new gas supplies could make Europe much less dependent on Russian gas exports and force Russia to reform its stodgy gas industry—are still not evident. However, the environmental benefits are already clear. Low gas prices in the United States, along with tighter regulation of coal, have allowed a massive shift toward gas in the US electric industry, leading to much lower US emissions of gases that cause global warming and possibly even greater reductions in the future. The potential economic effects of inexpensive gas are also clear. Within the United States, inexpensive shale gas is creating large numbers of jobs in gas production as well as in the industries that are intensive users of gas, leading industrialists in Japan, Europe, and other locales where gas is a lot more expensive to focus on how they, too, can enjoy the benefits of cheap gas.

I also argue that, on balance, the United States has a compelling interest in having this innovation spread quickly and globally. The country might benefit a bit if it kept cheap gas at home, but the global environmental and security benefits of a truly global gas revolution are much greater. A coherent US policy strategy must start with the realization that most of what will determine the fate of the gas revolution depends on national investment and drilling policies in dozens of other countries. US policy-makers could do a lot to impede the shale gas revolution, but they can do little to push it faster than it will spread on its own. Where the United States can perhaps have the greatest influence is in helping countries adopt the right regulations while, at the same time, opening the US market to foreigners, who will learn about shale-based technologies and spread those innovations into their home markets. The most difficult test for a gas-friendly policy strategy lies with China. The potential for China to clean the air by switching from coal to gas is huge, but Chinese investors face many political obstacles to participating in the North American gas market and learning, in practical terms, how to deploy shale and other unconventional gas technologies.

The Gas Industry in Historical Context

For most of its history, gas has been a poor stepchild in the oil industry. Found accidentally while the industry was drilling for oil, gas was a problem to be managed while hunting for the real liquid prize. Gas was a nuisance because it was flammable, often highly pressurized, and difficult to handle and transport. Until large networks of gas pipelines along with credible users of gas emerged, the easiest thing for drillers to do was to flare the gas. That practice is still widespread today. For example, in the Bakken area of western North Dakota, where drilling for shale oil is extensive, more than one-third of the gas produced alongside the oil is flared.[3] Although many programs exist to help governments cut flaring and venting, worldwide about 5 percent of annual global gas production is wasted this way.[4] On your next night flight over the Arabian (Persian) Gulf, an epicenter of flaring, look down and you will see the luminescent result.

Because building pipeline networks and lining up customers who will use gas is a risky affair, in most of the world large gas networks have arisen only through active intervention of government, including tight regulation, long-term contracts, and state ownership. State intervention reduced risk, but it made for a dull industry with few incentives to find new sources of supply or new customers. All that changed in the United States and a few other countries as market-oriented approaches to economic management rose in prominence starting in the 1970s. Along with other pivotal industries, such as airlines, trucking, and telecommunications, the United States deregulated its natural gas. Deregulation forced the dismantling of long-term contracts, separating the trading of gas from the more monopolistic business of actually operating pipelines, and it created markets where gas could be traded freely. In time, the price for gas was derived through gas-on-gas competition rather than through indexing to other fuels such as oil.

New markets, along with new technologies, helped inspire new uses for gas—especially in electricity. Cheap gas helped fuel a boom as electric utilities and speculators built many new gas-fired electric power plants. In the late 1990s, in fact, 84 percent of total new electric generation capacity built in the United States was designed to burn gas.[5] Competitive independent power producers loved natural gas because gas-fired electric plants were cheaper and easier to build than coal plants, thereby lowering the fixed capital needed to enter the industry. Low capital requirements and competitive gas markets meant that gas plants would be easy to switch on and off as needed to compete with other sources of electricity. These market-oriented trends also fueled the gas industry's manic tendencies. Rapid growth in gas-fired electric generators during the 1990s led analysts and investors to extrapolate a future in which US gas consumption would keep soaring. Huge demand for gas and the expectation that US domestic supplies would run short led inexorably to the conclusion that massive amounts of LNG would be needed to fill the gap. Indeed, the US gas market's high level of competition and the assumption that the United States was the market of last resort for LNG supplies led many LNG suppliers to evaluate all new projects on the basis of whether they could compete in America.

While these market-oriented reforms happened in the United States and a few other regions—notably in England and Wales—the shift to markets was slow or stillborn in the rest of the world. Most countries put state-owned enterprises in charge of gas and electricity, and the incumbents understandably did not want change. Even in continental Europe, where reformers passed strong laws requiring market competition, true progress toward competitive gas and electric markets has been slow. In fact, scholars who have studied and compared market liberalization around the world find that most gas and electric market reforms get stuck in a middle ground where governments pass laws requiring competition but do not dismantle the state enterprises and contracts that would allow for genuine competition except (if at all) around the margins.[6]

The failure of market reforms in most countries and the cost of moving gas long distances combine to explain why a global gas industry does not really exist. Rather, many hundreds of local markets are, at best, loosely coupled. Unlike oil, which is easy to move once on a ship, physical arbitrage of gas is a lot trickier. At distances of more than 1,000 or 2,000 miles, pipelines are not economical. Transport at greater distances requires LNG, which is an expensive proposition as well. The countries that historically have been the biggest buyers of LNG—Japan initially and now South Korea as well—have been willing to pay almost anything for gas because they have essentially no fossil fuels at home. For them, a global gas market exists in the sense that gas moves planetary-scale distances, such as from Doha to Tokyo, about 7,500 miles by ship. But the paramount desire for energy security and the need to avoid disrupting uncompetitive local monopolies have made Japanese buyers of LNG uninterested in truly competitive markets that might see their cargoes redirected to other countries. This situation also helps explain why gas prices in Japan are about five times those in the United States. Overall, in 2011, just 10 percent of global gas consumption moved as LNG.[7] The contrast with oil, which has been a global commodity for decades, is striking. Although the oil market suffers from some fragmentation because only a few refineries (mainly in the Arabian Gulf and Asia) are designed so that they can process any kind of crude, as a practical matter nearly every country's oil market pulses to the same global economic forces. That is not yet true for gas.[8]

Whether gas becomes a truly global commodity and the geopolitical effects of the global gas trade will depend centrally on the United States—the world's largest user of natural gas and the epicenter of most innovation in the industry. Moreover, although many factors will shape the US industry, two clusters of innovation will play central roles.

One, much in the news today, is new methods of production, such as fracking of shale combined with horizontal drilling. Although these technologies have entered the public mind only recently, the key innovations have, in fact, had a much longer gestation period. Starting in the mid-1970s, the US federal government partnered with the gas industry to conduct research and development; the key innovations emerged in the mid-1980s at Mitchell Energy, a Texas gas company that worked for another decade to perfect by the late 1990s an innovative drilling technique called *slick-water fracturing* that made fracking economical.[9] Almost another decade passed before other companies helped deploy the best combinations of technologies at the scale needed to have a substantial impact on US gas supply and prices. As late as 2007, most analysts expected that the United States would be short on home-produced gas and would need to import from Canada (by pipeline) and abroad (by LNG); by 2010, almost no analyst believed that vision because the effects of massive home-produced shale were apparent.

Although shale gas has proved to be the newest, most visible major source of gas, in reality gas has many diverse sources. Tapping some will require little or no innovation, such as the massive conventional gas resources in Russia, Iran, and Qatar, as well as big new finds in places such as Mozambique. Beyond shale, other unconventional sources of gas include coal-bed methane—a cutting-edge technology two decades ago that is now widely understood and still accounts for nearly one-tenth of US gas production.[10] China is making big bets on this gas source and is likely to scale it up before turning to shale. Massive new gas plays in the Arctic are now coming into focus. Today's story may be shale gas in America, but the next new thing in gas might well be geography or technology that is quite different in a few years time. Looking over the horizon, we could, in a decade or more, be focused on a cluster of innovations that make it economic to produce natural gas from methane hydrates, and even further into the future, we may see innovations in ultradeep natural gas. Indeed, quite a lot of evidence suggests the planet is geologically awash in methane.

The other, equally important cluster of innovations concerns transportation of gas. LNG is particularly important because it allows truly global interconnection of gas markets. The idea that gas could be compressed, cooled, and put on tankers for long-haul travel has been around for a long time. The first LNG cargo sailed in 1959 from the US Gulf Coast to Britain. Britain soon imported LNG from Algeria, the first commercial LNG train. The United States entered into the LNG business as an exporter from the Cook inlet (in rural coastal Alaska) to Japan—a project that shipped its first cargo in 1969. After the Arab Oil Embargo—when the cost of oil that powered much of Japan's electric grid soared—Tokyo poured money into LNG projects, gold plating them in exchange for a guaranteed supply. The Pacific Basin, huge in size and dominated by Japan, became the world's largest LNG trading zone. LNG was a boring, uncompetitive, costly industry dominated by Japanese buyers.

A project in Trinidad, conceived in the 1990s, helped eliminate gold plating by allowing flexibility in where the gas was sold: when prices were higher in Spain, the ships sailed there, but when prices were more dear in the large US market, the ships went to America.[11] The Atlantic Basin, because it was smaller and linked some competitive national gas markets (notably the United States), invited this form of destination flexibility, which is still slow to appear in Asia. As volumes of LNG grow from swing suppliers, such as Qatar, that sit between the Atlantic and Pacific Basins, gradually these basins are likely to yield a more global market, with global prices net the cost of the shipping. The Atlantic Basin is approaching that point; the Pacific is still far away.

Putting innovations in gas production together with innovations in LNG helps explain why today's gas revolution is so interesting. Big new supplies, such as from shale, could cut the cost of gas while diversifying the sources of supply. Even countries that do not have shale gas of their own (or do not create the regulatory environment that encourages shale supplies) will feel the effects of the shale revolution if LNG connects competitive gas markets globally.

Before we turn to the many consequences that could flow from this revolution, it is important to remember that these trends arise in an industry that is prone to wild swings in mood. A lot could unfold in ways that even the best analysts do not anticipate. A few years ago the best forecasting arm of the US government—the Energy Information Administration (EIA), whose forecasts are benchmarks for many energy contracts—took a careful look back over 16 years of forecasting and assessed its own performance. Although the EIA excelled in a few areas, one of its worst track records was in forecasting gas prices. As shown in figure 3.1, when gas prices were low, the EIA models assumed they would stay low and rise gradually with depletion. When they were high, the EIA assumed that prices would fall with time as new supplies and imports (notably through LNG) came online. As is typical with resource depletion models, the forecasts were driven mainly by real-world events rather than a deep capacity to predict the kinds of fundamental changes in markets that have come with shale gas.

The history of exuberance, despair, and error by the best forecasters is a warning that much can change in unpredictable ways.

Security, Geopolitical, and Ecological Consequences

Large transformations in energy are rare, and they usually unfold slowly. The shale revolution, by contrast, is moving with striking speed in the United States even as its fate globally remains quite uncertain.[12] Through diffusion of the technology or trade in gas via LNG, the effects of new shale supplies could be felt globally and quickly. In the future, the conse-

Figure 3.1. Annual Energy Outlook Natural Gas Wellhead Prices

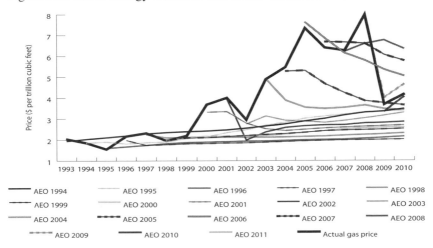

Source: EIA, *Annual Energy Outlook Retrospective Review: Evaluation of 2011 and Prior Reference Case Projections* (Washington, DC: EIA, 2012).

Note: AEO = Annual Energy Outlook. The actual price of gas is shown by a solid black line. Gray and patterned lines represent AEO projections.

quences could be many. I focus on three: energy security, geopolitics, and the environment.

Energy Security

Energy security is one of those terms that is particularly popular because it has no precise meaning. For me, it means reliable provision of energy services at manageable cost. Reliability allows investors and energy users to plan around their energy systems; manageable cost allows them to do more in life than buy energy. Almost any system can be made nearly perfectly reliable at nearly infinite cost—witness the elegant and reliable power supply on the international space station, for example—but manageable costs are much harder to combine with reliability. As a practical matter, energy security has two main flavors because, as economies mature, energy bifurcates into two main applications: transportation and electricity. Figure 3.2 shows this bifurcation for the US economy, but most modernizing economies follow similar patterns.

Figure 3.2. Primary Energy Consumption in the United States, 2010

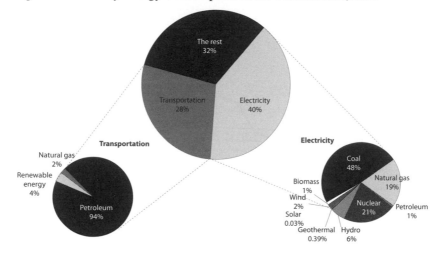

Source: EIA, *Annual Energy Review 2010* (Washington, DC: EIA, 2011).

In transportation, oil is king and so far has no serious rivals. In the United States, oil powers 94 percent of all transportation services. The balance comes mainly from a small role for biofuels blended with gasoline. Oil's dominance is hard to change because oil-based fuels are liquid at most temperatures and have a high energy density, which means that relatively little space and weight in cars, trucks, and airplanes are required to store fuel. Refilling a car at the local gasoline station takes just about three minutes and transfers energy at a rate of 6 megawatts per hour; by contrast, the best electric vehicle charging systems transfer at rates 100 times smaller. There is no shortage of innovative visions that could change that fact, involving, for example, much better battery-based electric storage and new charging systems.[13] So far, however, these visions are not practical realities.

The other flavor of energy security is electricity. Electricity is an energy carrier, not a fuel. In theory, other energy carriers, such as hydrogen, could work as well, but the hydrogen economy is more the work of dreamers than practical people. (Full disclosure: the first academic paper I ever wrote was about hydrogen-fueled aircraft. It was something fun to think and write about in graduate school but never amounted to anything practical.) Electricity is king because it is extremely flexible, mostly safe, pristine at the point of use, and relatively easy to make reliable.[14] Because most people live in cities, there is a special premium on energy carriers that can be wired directly to the final user while moving pollution and other externalities of power production far outside the urban area. In 1900, less than 2 percent of the world's primary energy was carried as electricity to its final users;[15] by 2010, that fraction had risen to more than 35 percent and is likely to keep going up.[16]

How could the gas revolution affect these two flavors of energy security? In transportation, gas has made few inroads. Some countries that are rich in gas and worried about dependence on imported oil give special incentives to switch vehicles to gas, but in practice that switching is rare except in fleet vehicles (e.g., taxis, buses, delivery trucks) that return to the same filling stations every night. As long as oil remains a tolerable rival, the coordination problems in switching infrastructures—in this case, from liquid fuel refilling stations to natural gas, along with switches in storage tanks and pipelines—are likely to outweigh the benefits for nearly all users.

Because infrastructure coordination is so difficult, I doubt much switching from oil to gas will occur unless the price differentials are massive. Already today in the United States, the price per unit of energy of oil-based fuels is more than seven times that of natural gas; before the surge in shale gas supplies around 2006, gas was only about half the price of oil.[17] (This severe decoupling of oil and gas prices is not yet evident in most of the rest of the world, where gas and oil prices are much more closely linked—often explicitly linked in contracts.) Despite the sevenfold price advantage for gas, little switching from oil to gas has taken place in the United States, except in some fleet vehicles. Programs to build infrastructure exist (e.g., a program for LNG along transcontinental highways, which is particularly promising for long-haul trucks that can easily store LNG and whose fuel bills are so huge that they have a strong incentive to make the move), but none is likely to make much of a dent in oil. Interesting visions (though far from realities) also see liquid fuels made from gas that can "drop" into the existing gasoline infrastructure; methanol is today's leading contender. When it comes to imagining ways to get off oil, technicians are bubbling with visions, but the realities are fewer.

That leaves energy security of the electric flavor, and here the gas revolution is likely to be much bigger news. The challenge for gas, however, is that it is just one of many rivals, and each fuel brings its own challenges for energy security. In 2012, India suffered two massive blackouts, which were linked in part to underinvestment in coal supply infrastructure and power plants. China, too, has suffered energy insecurities linked to coal when the network of mines, coal-transporting railroads, and power plants could not grow as quickly as demand for electric power. Boosting gas might help these countries create more reliable power supplies, but in practice they are finding that it is costly and difficult to build a gas supply infrastructure. Both countries are investing in gas, but both see energy security mainly coming from better coal supply systems and a bigger network of coal-fired generators. In part, electricity security comes from storing fuel, which is much costlier for gas than coal. A typical coal plant has a pile of coal worth 30 days sitting on hand, requiring little more than a plot of land and gravity to hold it in place. Most gas-fired electric plants have little storage and rely on real-time delivery of their fuel and contracts for storage. Other generators of electricity face even greater challenges with storage, such as wind (which does not always blow) and solar (which suffers at night or on cloudy days). Even at small market shares, these intermittent and highly variable renewable supplies have actually made some electric grids less secure.[18]

Cheap gas is already having a big impact on the shares for coal and gas in the US electric system. In 2010, coal accounted for nearly half of US electric supply (see figure 3.2). Over the next two years, that share dropped to one-third and is now at parity with gas. In my 20 years of studying energy systems, I have never seen such a huge shift in major fuels over such a short time.

So far, however, this dramatic shift to gas in the American electric grid has had little net effect on energy security. Cheap gas has kept retail electric prices today a bit lower than they would be otherwise, and dependence on gas will allow utilities to avoid costly upgrades for older coal-fired power plants to comply with tighter new environmental regulations. (Thanks partly to cheap gas, utilities will, in the coming decade, retire perhaps one-fifth of the coal fleet rather than upgrade those units.[19]) Most utilities, however, see growing dependence on gas as a threat to energy security because of the fuel's history of price volatility and the difficulty of creating stable long-term pricing for gas supplies. Gas that is cheap, even if just for some periods, can reduce diversity in power networks because it undercuts the financial viability not just of coal but also of new nuclear and renewable energy projects. Already these patterns are evident in parts of the US grid that have moved most extensively to gas, such as the Northeast, where gas for power plants competes with other uses, such as home heating, and the gas supply network cannot meet all needs during periods of maximum demand.

Geopolitics

The gas revolution could affect the political behavior of importers as well as exporters. If gas importers felt more secure, they might behave differently politically. Germany and France, for example, might be less beholden to Russia if they had more diverse and less costly gas supply options. So far, however, the revolutions rooted in shale gas supplies and LNG have not had much effect on energy imports anywhere in the world. In the United States, the shale revolution has mostly offset declines in domestic supplies—total US gas imports (most of which come by pipeline from Canada) have barely changed over the past decade. Of the countries that depend most on imported LNG for gas—Japan (which imported 92 percent of gas as LNG in 2010) and South Korea (which imported more than 98 percent of gas as LNG)—neither has much shale at home. Japan, with nearly all its nuclear reactors shut in the aftermath of Fukushima, has actually become more dependent on imported gas (and other fuels) in recent years.

In the future, a shale revolution, along with expanded supplies of LNG, could have the most immediate geopolitical effects in Western Europe. Today, about one-quarter of Europe's gas comes from Russia at prices indexed partly to oil, which makes European gas three or four times the cost of gas in the United States. This huge differential (which is reflected, as well, in electricity tariffs) has led energy-intensive European industries to lament their competitive disadvantage just as a host of gas-intensive industries, such as those producing ammonia, are investing in large expansions in the United States. With weak economies across the Organization for Economic Cooperation and Development (OECD), one of the few spots of bright news for economic growth comes in the form of low US gas prices. So far, the political implications of this growth are evident only within countries—with gas-intensive firms inside the major OECD countries pressuring their governments to keep cheap gas at home (in the United States) or to emulate American policies and cut local energy prices (in Europe and Japan).

Even small new shale supplies at home along with extra LNG that Americans do not need to import could help lower prices and force the whole European gas supply industry to become more competitive. So far, however, that possibility is imaginary. The shale revolution is starting to take off slowly in the United Kingdom. In France, environmental groups have created a ban on fracking before anyone has even learned much about the country's potential. New shale plays in Poland and Ukraine are just now beginning, with possibly large but still unknown potential for production. Overall, European shale gas resources appear to be much smaller than those already being developed in North America, but exploration in Europe remains at an early stage. One of the central lessons from the US shale revolution is that not only drilling technology but also a host of regulatory rules (e.g., requirements for well spacing) are needed, as well as market conditions (e.g., ownership of underground resources and access to pipelines) that still do not exist in most of Europe.

If the gas revolution washes into Europe, its gas producers—especially in Russia—will feel the biggest effects. Russia's prized position as supplier to Europe is based on a legacy of long-distance pipelines and the country's massive conventional gas resources. In turn, Russia has earned from $42 billion to $60 billion per year in the past six years from selling gas mainly to Europe. Lower prices could radically cut those revenues just as Russia faces much higher costs for new fields and pipelines. Producing and transporting gas from possible new Russian projects off Murmansk or on the Yamal Peninsula (both places with lots of gas underground but a sketchy investment climate aboveground) are barely economic today even with high gas prices. The shale revolution could seal that gas underground. Fewer exports and lower prices give less surplus cash for other things that the Russian state (which taxes gas exports and has a controlling interest in the gas pipeline monopolist Gazprom) might want to do. A Russia forced to live on a smaller state budget would probably be one that would encourage other kinds of economic activity, would seek trade with other countries, and would probably be less hostile to Western interests. Exactly that happened in the late 1990s, when low oil and gas prices forced fiscal probity on the Russian state: Russian foreign policy became less aggressive. Beyond Russia, lower export revenues will likely also cut into transit fees charged by Belarus and Ukraine—countries already under pressure as Russia and its customers build costly pipelines around these sometimes erratic transit points. In Asia, where Russia has bold plans to export gas and electricity, Russian suppliers face competition from LNG (e.g., from Australia) and China's own fledgling gas industry. Although the need to compete with cheap gas is terrible news for Russia, the exact effects on Russian politics and industrial policy are not easy to predict.

The demise of Gazprom as a monopoly—which is probably essential if Russia is to become more competitive as a gas supplier—has been forecast many times but has yet to happen. The Russian state might insulate itself from the loss of gas export revenues because it earns much more selling oil abroad than selling gas.

Elsewhere in the world, the shale gas and LNG revolutions could help lower surplus revenues and thus dampen the resource curse that has distorted the politics of other gas-exporting nations, such as Indonesia and Bolivia. It will also underscore a maxim that has long explained investment patterns in the gas industry (and to a lesser degree oil): what matters for gas production is not just resources underground but also the context aboveground, because that context determines whether firms will make the capital-intensive, long-lived investments typical of big gas export projects. That maxim explains why Trinidad is a powerhouse of LNG exports in the Atlantic Basin, but just 80 miles away, Venezuela sits on huge gas resources yet exports none. It also helps explain why firms operating in Qatar have aggressively tapped the world's largest gas field—the "north dome" in the middle of the Arabian Gulf—but on the Iranian side of that same field, there is almost no drilling. A more competitive global gas industry, linked with more cost-effective LNG and supplied with a more diverse array of shale-based producers, will make this maxim even more important. Huge amounts of gas will be left underground in parts of the world that are hostile to modern gas investment strategies aboveground.

Environment

In one area, the environment, the effects of the gas revolution are already tangible. Modern gas-fired electric power plants emit just two-fifths the carbon dioxide (CO_2) of coal-fired plants for the same amount of electricity output. The big shift to gas has thus caused a plunge in emissions of CO_2, the leading human cause of global warming. Figure 3.3 illustrates the importance of this shift in the United States, where annual US emissions of CO_2 are perhaps 400 million metric tons lower than they would be if coal still accounted for nearly half the US electric power sector. That is a huge number—about 8 percent of all US CO_2 emissions and about double the size of the European Union's progress in complying with the Kyoto Protocol.[20] This outcome could be ephemeral if gas prices rise. Indeed, at

Figure 3.3. CO_2 Emissions from US Energy Consumption, by Major Source

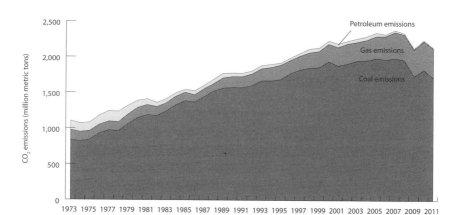

Source: EIA, *June 2012 Monthly Energy Review* (Washington, DC: EIA, 2012), table 12.1.

this writing (spring 2013), some US utilities are switching back to coal because the price of natural gas has risen, and around the world, costly gas has been a boon to coal-fired power generation. Today's American love affair with gas does not, of course, reflect a serious national global warming policy, and it will not deliver the 50 percent to 80 percent reduction in emissions most nations need to achieve to collectively stop global warming. But it is a big step in the right direction that also buys time for deeper cuts.

Shale gas is not automatically good news for the environment, however. Fracking has raised concerns about pollution of underground water supplies, triggering of small earthquakes, and even air pollution from all the trucks and drilling activities. Major concerns have arisen over the 1 million to 7 million gallons of water typically used to open a single well with fracking.[21] Some evidence indicates that gas fracking could lead to higher emissions of methane (the main component of natural gas but also a strong global warming gas), which could offset some of the global warming benefits from a dash to gas. A huge literature is amassing about how such challenges can be monitored and managed.[22] With best practices, the impacts on water and on leakage of methane will prove easy to manage.

Conclusions and Implications

As we look to the future, what can be done to accelerate the gas revolution and help it spread globally? That question is on many minds these days, especially in the United States, which has been at the center of the gas revolution and has a big stake in its success elsewhere in the world. New gas supplies and lower prices could help reduce world dependence on gas suppliers such as Russia. It could enrich US firms that have perfected the technology and also make it easier for countries around the world to cut emissions of warming gases—an outcome that would benefit the entire planet, including the United States, by lessening the rate of global warming.

Traditional foreign policy tools will not be very useful. What matters most for the spread of the gas production and transportation technologies will be the internal regulations that other countries adopt. At present, most of the world is not yet open for fracking. Some countries, such as France, have banned the practice. More common is the lack of regulatory and market frameworks that would encourage private firms (which are the experts in the technology) to take risks. For example, huge shale deposits in Argentina and Mexico are unlikely to be tapped much. Argentina recently nationalized the only competent gas company in the country and has a record of expropriating foreign investors. Mexico's constitution forbids private actors from most oil and gas drilling, and political gridlock has made this restriction impossible to change, although several recent Mexican administrations (including the current one) have sought greater political and economic space for foreign investment in tandem with Mexican partners. Across China and India—two coal-rich countries that could clear the air and cut warming emissions if they used more gas—a host of market barriers make shale and other promising gas sources hard to exploit.[23] The United States cannot change the fundamentally national prerogatives, but it can do three things to help tip the balance.

First, the United States must continue working to ensure that its industry—which is the model for a global shale gas revolution—offers a good example. That means, especially, monitoring and managing the environmental side effects of shale production so that the United States does not offer salient examples of what could go wrong with the technology.

Second, the United States should help where it can with direct technical assistance in the writing of regulations and other support for countries that seek it. (Such a program is already under way in the State Department.) I suspect, though, that most of the world's promising shale gas markets—

such as in China or Poland—are unlikely to need or want much foreign assistance.

Third, the United States should make sure that its own shale gas market is open to foreign investment so that foreigners can learn (and Americans can benefit from the influx of capital). The pivotal player is China, which today uses more coal than the rest of the world combined. Inexpensive, clean alternatives to conventional coal offer the best way for China to clear its air and lower its emissions. Foreign companies can play a role—and many are already in the early stages of shale gas exploration in China—but as a practical matter, nothing will happen at scale in China's energy system unless the country's state-owned national champions are centrally involved. Yet when those companies try to invest in North America, they find themselves entangled in security reviews—such as reviews by the Committee on Foreign Investments in the United States and similar reviews in Canada—that unwisely block the spread of this important technology. Wariness about theft of intellectual property and unfair contracting is understandable, but those legitimate worries have been an excuse to meddle in commercial transactions that, if allowed to proceed, would advantage the country over the long term.

The gas revolution is fundamentally the product of commercial incentives. So far, the stars are aligning in ways that could transform energy security, geopolitics, and the energy system's impact on the environment in ways that almost nobody predicted even five years ago. Government, especially in the United States, can help industry and other stakeholders focus on the long-term transformative potential for these technologies—especially as the shale revolution spreads worldwide.

Notes

1. IHS Global Insight, *The Economic and Employment Contributions of Shale Gas in the United States*, prepared for America's Natural Gas Alliance (Washington, DC: IHS Global Insight, 2011), http://www.ihs.com/images/Shale_Gas_Economic_Impact_mar2012.pdf.

2. W. David Montgomery, Robert Baron, Paul Bernstein, Sugandha D. Tuladhar, Shirley Xiong, and Mei Yuan, *Macroeconomic Impacts of LNG Exports from the United States* (Washington, DC: NERA Economic Consulting, 2012).

3. John Kemp, "Column: Bakken's Flaring Gas Is Only Part of the Story," *Inside US Oil*, July 30, 2012, https://customers.reuters.com/community/newsletters/oil_us/IOA_Jul_30_2012.pdf. See also Clifford Krauss, "In North Dakota, Flames of Wasted Natural Gas Light the Prairie," *New York Times*, September 26, 2011.

4. Michael F. Farina, *Flare Gas Reduction: Recent Global Trends and Policy Considerations* (Fairfield, CT: GE Energy, 2011).

5. US Energy Information Administration (EIA), "Most Electric Generating Capacity Additions in the Last Decade Were Natural Gas-Fired," *Today in Energy* (blog), July 5, 2011, http://www.eia.gov/todayinenergy/detail.cfm?id=2070.

6. My colleagues and I have studied this phenomenon in electric utilities, foreign investment in independent power producers, oil supply, gas, and now coal. Everywhere we look, the same patterns of partial reforms emerge. See David G. Victor and Thomas C. Heller, eds., *The Political Economy of Power Sector Reform: The Experiences of Five Major Developing Countries* (Cambridge, UK: Cambridge University Press, 2007); Erik J. Woodhouse, "The Obsolescing Bargain Redux? Foreign Investment in the Electric Power Sector in Developing Countries," *Journal of International Law and Politics* 38, no. 102 (2006): 121–246; David G. Victor, Amy M. Jaffe, and Mark H. Hayes, eds., *Natural Gas and Geopolitics: From 1970 to 2040* (Cambridge, UK: Cambridge University Press, 2006); David G. Victor, David R. Hults, and Mark C. Thurber, eds., *Oil and Governance: State-Owned Enterprises and the World Energy Supply* (Cambridge, UK: Cambridge University Press, 2012); David G. Victor and Richard K. Morse, "Living with Coal," *Boston Review*, September–October 2009.

7. Andrew Walker, "The Global LNG Market: A Look Back and a Look Forward," *LNG Industry*, Summer 2012.

8. For an overview of the industry and projections, in particular see MIT Energy Initiative, *The Future of Natural Gas: An Interdisciplinary MIT Study* (Cambridge, MA: Massachusetts Institute of Technology, 2011), http://mitei.mit.edu/publications/reports-studies/future-natural-gas.

9. Alex Trembath, Jesse Jenkins, Ted Nordhaus, and Michael Shellenberger, "Where the Shale Gas Revolution Came From: Government's Role in the Development of Hydraulic Fracturing in Shale," Breakthrough Institute Energy and Climate Program, Breakthrough Institute, Oakland, CA, 2012. See also Daniel Yergin, *The Quest: Energy, Security and the Remaking of the Modern World* (New York: Penguin, 2012).

10. EIA, *Annual Energy Outlook 2011 with Projections to 2035* (Washington, DC: EIA, 2011).

11. Rob Shepherd and James Ball, "Liquefied Natural Gas from Trinidad and Tobago: The Atlantic LNG Project," in *Natural Gas and Geopolitics: From 1970 to 2040*, ed. David G. Victor, Amy M. Jaffe, and Mark H. Hayes (New York: Cambridge University Press, 2007), 268–318.

12. John Deutch, "The Good News about Gas: The Natural Gas Revolution and Its Consequences," *Foreign Affairs* 90, no. 1 (2011): 82–93.

13. Steve Chu and Arun Majumdar, "Opportunities and Challenges for a Sustainable Energy Future," *Nature* 488, no. 7411 (2012): 294–303.

14. See Charles K. Ebinger and John P. Banks, "Electricity Access in Emerging Markets," chapter 18 in this volume.

15. Vaclav Smil, "Energy in the Twentieth Century: Resources, Conversions, Costs, Uses, and Consequences," *Annual Review of Energy and the Environment* 25 (2000): 21–51.

16. ExxonMobil, *2012: The Outlook for Energy: A View to 2040* (Irving, TX: ExxonMobil, 2012).

17. James Jensen, *Fostering LNG Trade: Developments in LNG Trade and Pricing* (Brussels: Energy Charter Secretariat, 2009).

18. See David Talbot, "The Great German Energy Experiment," *MIT Technology Review,* July–August 2012; Günther Keil, "Germany's Energy Supply Transformation Has Already Failed," Europäisches Institut für Klima und Energie, Berlin, December 2011. See also Warren Katzenstein, Emily Fertig, and Jay Apt, "The Variability of Interconnected Wind Plants," *Energy Policy* 38, no. 8 (2010): 4400–10.

19. Electric Power Research Institute, "PRISM 2.0: The Value of Innovation in Environmental Controls—Summary Report," Electric Power Research Institute, Palo Alto, CA, 2012.

20. For more on the real effect of Kyoto, see David G. Victor, *Global Warming Gridlock: Creating More Effective Strategies for Protecting the Planet* (Cambridge, UK: Cambridge University Press, 2011). For more detail on the impacts of gas on greenhouse gas emissions see National Petroleum Council (NPC), *Prudent Development: Realizing the Potential of North America's Abundant Natural Gas and Oil Resources* (Washington, DC: NPC, 2011), chapter 4.

21. See, for example, Jean-Philippe Nicot and Bridget R. Scanlon, "Water Use for Shale-Gas Production in Texas, U.S," *Environmental Science and Technology* 46, no. 6 (2012): 3580–86.

22. Secretary of Energy Advisory Board, *Shale Gas Production Subcommittee Second Ninety Day Report* (Washington, DC: US Department of Energy, 2011). See also, John Deutch, "The US Natural-Gas Boom Will Transform the World," *Wall Street Journal*, August 14, 2012, http://online.wsj.com/article/SB10001424052702303343404577514622469426012.html; Michael R. Bloomberg and George P. Mitchell, "Fracking Is Too Important to Foul Up," Washington Post, August 23, 2012, http://www.washingtonpost.com/opinions/fracking-is-too-important-to-foul-up/2012/08/23/d320e6ee-ea0e-11e1-a80b-9f898562d010_story.html.

23. Jane Nakano, David Pumphrey, Robert Price Jr., and Molly A. Walton, *Prospects for Shale Gas Development in Asia: Examining Potentials and Challenges in China and India* (Washington, DC: Center for Strategic and International Studies, 2012). China's own assessments of its energy future see a much larger role for gas and a larger role for low-emission technologies generally. See Han Wenke and Yang Yufeng, "China Energy Outlook: Executive Summary," Energy Research Institute, Beijing, 2012, http://www.eri.org.cn/uploadfile/Executive_Summary.pdf.

Chapter 4

Valuing Safety Even When the Market Doesn't Notice

William K. Reilly

A common feature in major industrial accidents is the occurrence of several incidents in the same timeframe, any one of which might not be sufficient to cause a catastrophe but taken together combine to doom a deep-sea oil rig, an ocean liner, or a refinery. Such was the case with BP's Macondo explosion and spill in April 2010: an ineffective cementing job; a misreading of pressure tests or, more precisely, a decision to trust one reassuring pressure test while discounting another troubling one; premature displacement of heavy muds with lighter seawater; failure to notice an indicator that gas was rising in the drill pipe; late activation of the blowout preventer; and finally a decision to allow high-pressure methane to release up through the rig rather than to divert it over the side, thereby exposing it to the source of ignition, which blew up the rig.[1]

After-action reviews frequently dwell on the improbability of a concatenation of misfeasance. Such reviews have a reassuring exculpatory subtext: the highly improbable event could never have been planned for or prevented; a series of somewhat familiar mistakes freakishly coincided.

The explanation of unimaginable coincidences, however, invariably falls to a detailed examination. How could a decision to invest so much confidence in a cement job have been made in a well that was known to pose significant pressure problems? How could the integrity of the cement formula not have been tested given the unusual well characteristics coupled with the operator's lack of confidence in the cementing contractor? And the questions continue, as gauges indicating trouble were misread, disregarded, or overlooked.

Major disasters have precursors. Transocean, the owner of the Deepwater Horizon drilling rig working the Macondo well for BP, had had an eerily similar accident a year before the Macondo event in the North Sea on a rig working for a different major oil and gas producer: a loss of well control and a high-pressure blowout of gases. The gases, fortunately, did not ignite. Although the event was carefully analyzed and critiqued by an insurance company, the knowledge from that examination did not receive widespread circulation. Similarly, the foundering of the *Costa Concordia* cruise ship in shallow waters off the Italian coast had its own precedent event. The same ship's hull was damaged when it hewed too close to the shore. BP, too, had a very public and tragic precedent—the disastrous explosion in its Texas City Refinery just five years before Macondo—and BP also experienced a serious spill from a ruptured pipeline in Alaska four years before. When many things go wrong and result in a disaster, a review of a company's history invariably reveals a troublesome pattern, a history of warning events from which its people did not learn.

Risky Industries, Exemplary Safety Records

Many risky industries operate with exemplary safety records. DuPont historically has led the chemical industry by all measures of worker safety and days lost to accidents. Oil giants Shell, Chevron, and ConocoPhillips have admirable track records, as does ExxonMobil in the aftermath of the 1989 *Exxon Valdez* disaster. BP, too, had an enviable record for having reduced slips and falls among its employees. In fact, BP executives were present on the Macondo rig the evening of the explosion to confer recognition for exemplary safety.

Ensuring Process Safety

The disjunction between standard metrics of workplace safety and process safety has been a theme of several reviews of the Macondo disaster. The frequency of inspections; the testing and monitoring of pumps, valves, pipe-line, and hose integrity; the replacement schedules for equipment subject to wear and tear; and simulated accident drills—these constitute some of the key measures of process safety. For failure to attend to these measures, a company-sponsored review of the Texas City Refinery explosion headed by former Secretary of State James A. Baker III as well as reviews by official bodies such as the presidentially appointed National Commission on the BP Deepwater Horizon Oil Spill and Offshore Drilling, cited BP.[2]

The responsibility for ensuring process safety lies primarily with the operating company's managers. Engineers are familiar with the requisite maintenance of complex engineering systems. They know and have experience with the machinery, equipment, fuels, and performance histories of the systems they oversee. But the engineers operate within a company culture, and a company's culture of safety is set and reinforced by its leadership and at every intervening level. Corporate culture can tolerate, or even promote, excessive cost cutting, which indeed characterized BP before the Texas City Refinery explosion and also the Alaskan pipeline spill.

BP's ranks of experienced professionals were seriously depleted when oil prices plunged in the 1990s, prompting the company to shed large numbers of senior operators. Buyouts created incentives for senior engineers and managers to retire early—not just at BP but at other oil companies too. Studies and formal reviews conducted of BP agree that a rigorous and pervasive cost-reduction policy operated without regard for the warnings of managers at the Texas City Refinery in the years preceding the fire, to note one prominent example. Numerous requests from refinery supervisors that more funds be allocated to maintenance and repair went unheeded by senior executives in London.

BP's failure to conduct frequent tests of the integrity of oil pipelines in Alaska was an issue of serious concern to the executives of other industry leaders who raised such issues with John Browne, BP's chief executive officer (CEO). The executives argued strongly for BP to increase funding for maintaining its transmission network. Accounts indicate that Browne rebuffed their entreaties. Soon thereafter, 3,000 barrels of oil flowed out of a ruptured BP pipeline.

The Need for Increased Scrutiny

It is not known how much, if any, special scrutiny BP's board devoted to the company's process safety after Texas City and the Alaskan pipeline spill. Process safety is not an area easily understood and overseen by lay-persons. Metrics shared within the oil industry, as with other companies in risky industries, regularly record slips and falls, and board committees keep a close watch on these familiar categories: lost workdays, total re-cordable injuries, and deaths of both employees and contractors.

Indicators of process safety receive far less if any regular examination by many boards. When the more familiar worker safety numbers are posi-tive, improving, or among the best in the industry, boards can be lulled into an unwarranted complacency. The record of BP's repeated experience of positive worker safety coupled with its dysfunctional process safety should prompt boards in other companies to demand that management compile practical, understandable, and meaningful measures of process safety. Senior engineers know how to do so. Several major oil companies have rigorous systems for inspecting processes and measuring their ef-fectiveness. But boards generally do not get educated in such systems or become familiar with what they mean. An important lesson from the Macondo disaster and the investigations and reports that followed it is that process safety deserves the greatest attention from senior executives and from the boards to whom they report.

During the past several years, a number of initiatives have been under-taken to design a systematic hierarchy of leading process safety indicators. In 2006, a guide published by the UK Health and Safety Executive set out a detailed methodology but warned that only a few key performance indicators could usefully serve for high-level review.[3] The US Chemical Safety and Hazard Investigation Board's 2007 final investigation report on the Texas City Refinery accident made a number of recommendations.[4] The Organization for Economic Cooperation and Development published guidance in 2008 regarding chemical accident prevention, preparedness, and response.[5] In 2010, the American Petroleum Institute (API) published a recommended four-tier approach aimed at downstream or refinery op-erations,[6] and the International Association of Oil and Gas Producers in 2011 followed with its own report directed at upstream or exploration and production operations.[7] Both the upstream and downstream reports used a four-tier approach in which tier 1 involved serious loss of primary contain-ment, tier 2 involved less serious loss of containment, tier 3 included near misses indicating challenges to safety systems, and tier 4 was associated with operating discipline and management system conditions. The col-lection and classification of information in these categories, supported by published examples, create a common system for comparing performance among companies and allow boards and senior management to exercise oversight.

Regulators also have an important role in demanding process safety performance, and they too appear to have ignored frequent warning signals from BP's experience. Despite BP's worrisome history beginning with the Texas City Refinery fire, together with the convincing critique of BP's neglect of process safety and its ruthlessly dominant cost-cutting culture, there is no evidence that regulators at the federal or state level exercised special scrutiny of the company. Detailed interviews with US Department of the Interior inspectors and their superiors conducted by the department and the US Coast Guard reveal no awareness of BP's culture nor any more concentrated attention to their performance beyond that directed at any other company.

These interviews also reveal a surprising "check-the-box" approach to inspections by government officials, who freely acknowledged ignorance of key tests for pressure and other routine well management operations. How could BP's challenged safety performance be so well known in the oil industry that other industry CEOs thought they must bring their concerns to Browne's attention yet it escaped notice by the regulators?

An overworked, underfinanced, and undertrained inspector force in the Gulf of Mexico, with each inspector accountable for oversight of 55 rigs, contributed to the lax culture on Macondo. British officials point to a pattern of oil industry executives lobbying for robust budgets for the British regulators because they recognize the industry's stake in rigorous enforcement of safety. The American oil industry might well learn from British experience and bring its influence to bear with Congress and the administration to address problems of underfinancing, undercompensating, or overworking inspectors and supervisory officials.

The Need for Scrutiny from Analysts and Investors

Beyond the industry and government, however, financial exposure created by risks run by companies and their management seems to be of little interest to the investor community. On the face of it, this situation defies belief. The Macondo disaster destroyed 50 percent of BP's market value. More than two years later, the company's share price continues to be depressed relative to the pre-Macondo value. How can it be that Wall Street disregards safety and fails to scrutinize safety performance and assess exposure to potentially value-destroying events? Yet CEOs in several industries that have suffered calamitous accidents report that they never are asked about safety in their quarterly calls with analysts. Cruise industry executives and chemical company CEOs say that although they sometimes attempt to initiate discussion of safety on these calls, analysts seem uninterested and do not follow up. And, reportedly, never do the analysts themselves raise the issue.[8] Corporate leaders who are accustomed to opening every internal company meeting with a safety briefing and who take pride in putting safety among the company's core values report that Wall Street appears uninterested. Indeed, Wall Street can punish a company that acts too prudently with respect to investing in risk control and reduction if such actions affect quarterly earnings and other short-term financial indicators. One executive of a cruise line who had included a helipad on a new ship found himself criticized for having allocated funds for emergency medical evacuations; the analyst noted that such events were infrequent, and cheaper means of evacuation were common on other ships.[9]

Nor do investors place a noticeable premium on the safety performance of a company. Explanations for this lack of interest point to a focus on the short-term horizon typical of analysts' interests and the statistical improbability of a major accident. Wall Street appears to see safety as the purview of managers and their regulators. Analysts may consider that they have no visibility or specialized understanding of safety indicators, although an intimate familiarity with an industry will lead to awareness of comparative best practices and of who has them and who does not.

Without investor interest and scrutiny, a company's exemplary safety record will have to be set by a company's CEO and reinforced by the company's culture, because the market will not reward it. And in the event of an accident experienced by a competitor, the stock price of all companies in the sector typically will fall. Such was true after the federal government shut down 31 exploratory wells in the deepwater Gulf of Mexico, including those operated by companies innocent of any implication in Macondo. And it also occurred when the *Costa Concordia* grounding resulted in canceled bookings on all cruise fleets.

Those experiences illustrate the extraneous risks run by a well-managed and safety-conscious entity from the errant behavior of a competitor that is inattentive to safe operations. Through no fault of its own and despite an exemplary safety regime, a company could well suffer from loss of consumer confidence in the entire industry, as occurred in the cruise industry after the *Costa Concordia* disaster, or from a government shutdown pending inspections, safety reviews, and permit revisions. Such was the experience of offshore oil drillers after Macondo.

Nuclear Accidents and Safeguards

Accidents in the nuclear industry have had even more draconian consequences for reactor operators located thousands of miles away. Consider Germany's decision to accelerate the phase-out of all of its reactors after the 2011 Fukushima nuclear disaster in Japan, disregarding German nuclear operators' unblemished safety record. After the 1979 Three Mile Island accident in Pennsylvania, when fears were raised of a catastrophic reactor meltdown and large-scale evacuations were contemplated, the US nuclear industry formed a self-auditing association known as the Institute of Nuclear Power Operations (INPO).[10] Staffed by experienced engineers from the nuclear navy, INPO regularly conducts exacting and detailed inspections of the 64 American nuclear power stations with their 104 reactors. These inspections include four-week preparatory and review sessions and two-week on-site visits to the stations. INPO is renowned for the rigor and ratcheting up of its evaluations, which focus on best practices. A score of 1 is hard won and highly valued. A score of 5, when communicated to the Nuclear Regulatory Commission (NRC), results in shutting down the reactor and has also led to the dismissal of top management. And as one nuclear utility CEO said to me, "A score of 1 this year, even if you maintain precisely similar performance, means that you will not receive a 1 next year because INPO raises the bar every year."[11] INPO does not lobby for the industry, nor does it advocate the nuclear cause in public relations as a trade association would. It does not publicize its scores, nor are the graded companies allowed to do so. Grades go only to the NRC, the insurer of the companies, and the companies themselves.

The industry created INPO because it understood after Three Mile Island that all nuclear operators were at risk from an accident at any one reactor. Self-interest created a culture of genuine no-nonsense self-policing. By all measures, it has worked.

The National Commission on the BP Deepwater Horizon Oil Spill and Offshore Drilling recommended that the oil industry learn from the nuclear industry and create an entity modeled on INPO.[12] As the offshore oil industry has moved from the relatively shallow coastal shelf into the ocean's deeper waters, the pressure, complexities, technological challenges, and

consequent risks have increased. Finding, accessing, and recovering oil under 5,000 feet of water and a further 13,000 feet of ocean floor is a modern
marvel—scarcely a generation old. The oil industry failed to adapt its risk
management to the transition, except in its creation of the drilling technology breakthrough.

The Need to Restore Public Confidence

Stunning though the technical mastery may be, the concomitant upgrading
of risk management for such precarious new explorations failed to keep
pace. As the former CEO of BP, Tony Hayward, said to the cochair of the
National Commission on the BP Deepwater Horizon Oil Spill and Offshore
Drilling shortly after the explosion, fire, and spill, "We have no adequate
subsea containment capability."[13] Resourceful experimentation and trial
and error by BP in close cooperation with the federal government resulted
in the creation of a capping stack that ultimately tamed the gushing well
and staunched the flow. The absence of subsea monitoring equipment and
the primitive calculation of the flow rate in the early weeks of the spill,
however, prolonged the period of heavy oil releases and sapped the confidence of the country in industry and government alike. A vocal minority of
observers questioned whether the risk of drilling in deep water was worth
the candle. The industry itself, not just BP, had to restore public confidence.

The new Center for Offshore Safety (COS) was the industry's response.
Modeled to some extent on INPO but also drawing from the International
Council of Chemical Associations' Responsible Care program and other
examples of self-regulation, COS is led by a highly respected former Shell
chief scientist, Charlie Williams. The center is budgeted and empowered
to conduct inspections and audits, to prescribe best practices, and to reassure the top performers in the industry that they will not be embarrassed
or compromised in the eyes of the regulators and the public by the mistakes of a few. COS has the apparent authority to do what the CEOs who
counseled Browne could not do—document his company's shortcomings
through audits and communicate more widely about his refusal to respond.
COS also has the charge of attending to the lessons of Macondo—instrumentation shortfalls, lack of response capability, and unrealistic worst-case
assumptions.

COS has begun with an inclusive membership of drilling contractors,
operators, science companies, and manufacturers that operate in deep wa-

ter. Every deepwater participant, if a member of the API, must join COS. Non-API members are welcome. The early focus is on safety performance indicators developed cooperatively with regulators from the US Department of the Interior and Coast Guard officials, who are routinely included at the table. A safety and environmental management system audit is required of members and offered to all. COS has identified improved and detailed planning and drills to prepare to manage losses of well control, and has identified increased availability of prebuilt, prestaged, and pretested equipment in the event of a spill.

In parallel with the creation of COS, major oil companies created the Marine Well Containment Corporation, with a focus on ensuring adequate and widely available access to the accoutrements of emergency response—capping stacks, booms, skimmers, and the like. In sum, the oil industry learned the key lessons of Macondo. Drilling in deep water is far more risky than on the coastal shelf and requires more rigorous and sophisticated care with respect to management, instrumentation, monitoring, and—in the event of a mishap—collaborative response. For in the most visible and risk-prone industries, where lives and public resources are most seriously exposed, everyone is in it together: everyone has a stake in avoiding an accident, and everyone must cooperate in preventing one.

Mutually Reinforcing Industry and Regulators

The core lesson of the BP Macondo disaster is that only industry at the top of its game, continuously improving in its practices and performance, coupled with a capable, well-resourced regulator, can reduce the inherent risks in a complex industrial undertaking. Furthermore, the incentives from investors, insurers, and other stakeholders in the financial sector need to become much more aligned to reward a culture of safety. Those are lessons we have learned the hard way, with the deaths of 11 men; the destruction of the rig; the despoliation of the Gulf of Mexico and many places along the coast; and the impacts on marine life, on the economies of the Gulf states, and on the residents of the region. The financial risks to a company that experiences a spill are greater now than before Macondo. The government of Brazil came down hard on Chevron after a spill in its waters. And the government of China was similarly aggressive in assessing penalties against ConocoPhillips for seepage in Bohai Bay. External costs to both companies exceeded $50,000 per barrel spilled, and those costs did not include employee and equipment downtime, cleanup costs, distraction of management, and injury to reputation. The US Clean Water Act fine for a spill after a finding even of gross negligence is $4,300 per barrel, a fraction of the assessments by Brazil and China.

Shale's Promise

The dramatic growth of the shale gas industry has some elements in common with the experience of deepwater drilling. Hydraulic fracturing, a technique dating to the 1940s, and the more recent technology of horizontal drilling have combined to access vast amounts of hydrocarbons previously considered unrecoverable, and they do so at a reasonable cost. The resulting finds of significant shale plays in several states are transforming the nation's energy economy and creating hundreds of thousands of jobs[14] along with a surge of growth in North Dakota, Texas, Ohio, Pennsylvania, and New York. Natural gas, tight oil, and liquids are flowing to the market in quantities that promise to reduce import demand and even add to exports. Natural gas available at low prices is allowing a displacement of coal from roughly half of US electricity generation down to one-third, while the contribution of gas has risen from roughly one-fifth to one-third of electricity generation.

Although the shale gas industry has much in common with conventional gas development, the sheer magnitude of the enterprise, like the movement of the offshore industry from shallow coastal waters to the deep ocean, poses significant new challenges. Some characteristics of shale development are similar to drilling for conventional oil or gas: design and execute a leak-proof casement and punch cleanly through an aquifer to reach deep veins of shale rock. But the volumes of water required and the generation and disposal of potentially contaminated wastes are posing new challenges to areas such as New York and Pennsylvania that are unaccustomed to managing the modern resurgent petroleum industry. Wastewater treatment plants are not typically designed to process shale gas residuals. And instances of sending wastes inappropriately to unprepared landfills have been reported.[15] There is also debate about just how much methane, a potent greenhouse gas, is released when shale gas is extracted and transported. Efforts are under way to determine the extent of methane leaks, with estimates running from less than 1 percent to as much as 4 percent. Capturing methane releases is urgently necessary to ensure the contribution of natural gas to carbon reductions and to comply with more rigorous regulation by the US Environmental Protection Agency. Given that any released gas has value, the industry's self-interest is doubly manifest. And finally, a gas boom, like any boom, means a surge of activity—population, housing pressures, development, water use, heavy truck traffic—introduced into previously sedate rural environments. The industrialization associated with the shale gas boom is probably the one unavoidable consequence of the development.

The Necessity of Industry Best Practices

In the controversies reported of wildcat drillers contaminating groundwater or discharging wastewater irresponsibly, industry leaders have offered a familiar defense: done responsibly by experienced companies, drill pipes are sealed from surrounding aquifers and wastewater is either reinjected into deep wells or treated and recycled. Yet once again, as with oil industry outliers, responsible operators are at risk of poor practice by less conscientious companies. The field calls at minimum for an industrywide standard of best practices. Techniques are available to ameliorate the undesirable by-products of much shale gas development. *Green completion*, whereby gas and liquid hydrocarbons are separated, with the hydrocarbons treated or sold rather than flared, is one such technique. Relying on deep saline aquifers for the water source in such techniques has proved effective in the Eagle Ford shale play in Texas.

Industry's preference has been to favor regulation by the states rather than the federal government, arguing that the highly diverse characteristics of geologies in the different shale reserves lend themselves better to localized, specialized oversight. And it is undeniable that issues of water use and allocation, housing needs, and traffic generation are typically addressed locally in the United States. Moreover, the issue of water use does not appear to rise to a level of national concern. According to a study by the Massachusetts Institute of Technology (MIT) Energy Initiative, in no state is the industry responsible for more than 1 percent of water consumption, and typically, the industry uses much less water.[16] Moreover, the MIT Energy Initiative found that for every 1 million British thermal units (Btu) produced by shale gas, about 1 gallon of water is required, which compares favorably for water intensity with other energy sources. Other studies consider that water demand for shale gas can range as high as 4 gallons per million Btu.

One downside to the abundance of shale gas and the resulting fall in the price of natural gas is the impact on renewable energy technologies. Though the costs of renewables are declining, they are not yet cost-effective for widespread deployment without subsidies or mandates. Intermittent sources such as wind and solar also continue to need the kind of baseload electricity generation that natural gas–fired plants provide. Thus, although gas is a necessary partner to intermittent renewables, any significant expansion of wind or solar power will encounter headwind as long as the price of natural gas remains low.

Shale gas development, like deepwater drilling, offers too many advantages for the nation to forgo its contribution. Development of shale gas offers a renewed competitiveness to industries such as chemicals and steel as they avail themselves of cheap feedstocks and gas-fired electricity. It offers greenhouse gas reduction as gas replaces coal and puts the nation on a course toward meeting US commitments on climate made in Copenhagen in 2009. And shale gas development creates an upsurge in new jobs and flourishing local economies. Nevertheless, the shoddy practices of some operators and the deviation from responsible practices by a few could damage the industry's reputation and impede public acceptance.

In 2013, a number of foundations, energy companies, academic centers, and environmental organizations joined forces to create the Center for Sustainable Shale Development (CSSD), based in Pittsburgh, Pennsylvania, to define best practices in the exploration and development of natural gas in the Marcellus shale area.[17] This independent center would define protocols and promote responsible methane controls and efficient water use. The CSSD appears to be modeled on COS, which was established by the petroleum industry in response to the Macondo BP oil spill and fire and pursuant to a recommendation of the National Commission on the BP Deepwater Horizon Oil Spill and Offshore Drilling. Companies would have a means of holding their peers to high standards of practice, thus ensuring that laggards do not discredit the industry. Both regulators and local officials considering drilling applications would thus be able to consult a company's adherence to CSSD policies when deciding whether to approve a permit application. This commitment to serious and specific self-regulation could go a long way toward reassuring the public regarding the safety of fracking.

Shale gas development is yet another instance of a resourceful industry using a new mix of technologies and having to confront and manage a new set of challenges. The situation calls once again for defining and initiating best practices in conjunction with regulators and exceeding expectations by doing more than the regulations require—the choice typical of the best performers. The new center offers promise that the industry recognizes this challenge.

Conclusion

Recent accidents have demonstrated the importance of a company culture that declares safety not just a priority but also a core value. The accidents make clear the importance of leadership to ensure that safety is not subordinated to cost controls. They demonstrate that slips and falls and lost workday numbers are not surrogates for process safety. Boards should require and review practical measures of process safety and performance, comparative indicators when available, and best practices in comparable companies, just as they routinely review workplace safety. Both regulators and investment analysts need a more intimate understanding of company cultures and safety performance. And in high-risk industries, companies have an incentive to create processes for identifying and ratcheting up the performance of their competitors when confronting behavior that risks a catastrophe likely to damage the entire sector. The oil industry's new COS has the promise to perform that function, although its presence within the industry's trade association and principal lobbyist, the API, is not optimal. A distinct physical presence in Houston, respected leadership, and stated commitments to independence all indicate sensitivity to the potential conflicts of interest in an enterprise that responds to a serious industrywide challenge. The oil industry can be said to "get it," though the lesson of Macondo was hard in the loss of 11 lives, in serious environmental damages, in the loss of livelihoods and jobs, and in capital destruction of calamitous proportions. Other industries would do well to learn from this experience.

Notes

1. National Commission on the BP Deepwater Horizon Oil Spill and Offshore Drilling, *Deep Water: The Gulf Oil Disaster and the Future of Offshore Drilling* (Washington, DC: National Commission on the BP Deepwater Horizon Oil Spill and Offshore Drilling, 2011), http://www.oilspillcommission.gov/final-report, especially chapters 4, 8, and 9.

2. James A. Baker III, Frank L. "Skip" Bowman, Glenn Erwin, Slade Gorton, Dennis Hendershot, Nancy Leveson, Sharon Priest, Isadore "Irv" Rosenthal, Paul V. Tebo,

Douglas A. Wegmann, and L. Duane Wilson, *The Report of the BP US Refineries Independent Safety Review Panel* (London: BP, 2007). See also National Commission on the BP Deepwater Horizon Oil Spill and Offshore Drilling, *Deep Water*.

3. UK Health and Safety Executive, *Developing Process Safety Indicators: A Step-by-Step Guide for Chemical and Major Hazard Industries* (London: Crown, 2006).

4. US Chemical Safety and Hazard Investigation Board, *Investigation Report: Refinery Explosion and Fire* (Washington, DC: US Chemical Safety and Hazard Investigation Board, 2007).

5. Organization for Economic Cooperation and Development (OECD), *Guidance on Developing Safety Performance Indicators Related to Chemical Accident Prevention, Preparedness, and Response for Public Authorities and Communities/Public* (Paris: OECD, 2008).

6. API, "Process Safety Performance Indicators for the Refining and Petrochemical Industries," ANSI/API Recommended Practice 754, API, Washington DC, 2010.

7. International Association of Oil and Gas Producers, "Process Safety: Recommended Practice on Key Performance Indicators," Report 456, International Association of Oil and Gas Producers, London, 2011.

8. Personal communication with multiple analysts and calls with five CEOs who do not wish to be identified.

9. Personal communication with a cruise industry executive.

10. INPO, "About Us," http://www.inpo.info/AboutUs.htm.

11. Anonymity required because of INPO practice.

12. National Commission on the BP Deepwater Horizon Oil Spill and Offshore Drilling, *Deep Water*.

13. *National Commission on the BP Deepwater Horizon Oil Spill and Offshore Drilling Hearing before the Committee on Energy and Natural Resources*, 112th Cong., US Senate, First Session, January 26, 2011.

14. See, for example, IHS Global Insight, *The Economic and Employment Contributions of Shale Gas in the United States*, prepared for America's Natural Gas Alliance (Washington, DC: IHS Global Insight, 2011), v, 1, 4, http://www.ihs.com/images/Shale_Gas_Economic_Impact_mar2012.pdf.

15. See, for example, "Our Look at Seeps, Leaks, and Spills," Marcellus-Shale.us, at http://www.marcellus-shale.us/seeps_leaks_spills.htm.

16. MIT Energy Initiative, *The Future of Natural Gas: An Interdisciplinary MIT Study* (Cambridge, MA: MIT, 2011), 43–44, http://mitei.mit.edu/publications/reports-studies/future-natural-gas.

17. CSSD strategic partners include Chevron, Citizens for Pennsylvania's Future (PennFuture), the Clean Air Task Force, CONSOL Energy, the Environmental Defense Fund, EQT Corporation, Group against Smog and Pollution (GASP), Heinz Endowments, the Pennsylvania Environmental Council, Royal Dutch Shell, and the William Penn Foundation. For more information, see http://sustainableshale.org.

Chapter 5

OPEC: Can the Cartel Survive
Another 50 Years?

Amy Myers Jaffe and Edward L. Morse

When the five founding members of the Organization of the Petroleum Exporting Countries (OPEC) met to create the organization in 1960, they could not in their wildest dreams contemplate that the oil producer group would come to be seen as the most successful commodity cartel in history. Indeed it is hard to understand today's petroleum world without taking into account OPEC's central position. The producer group played an instrumental role in reshaping the structure of the global oil industry in the 1960s and 1970s by changing the rules of the game and forcing the revamp of the governance of the sector. By nationalizing both the ownership of oil and gas reserves and the terms and conditions for future investment, OPEC's oil-exporting members became a shining symbol of geoeconomic power in a lopsided world of financial haves and have nots.

OPEC remains one of the most remarkable success stories and also one of the most extraordinary anomalies in the global economy. Its success for more than half a century defied a trend toward the Washington-led shift to market-based capitalism and globalization. In an era marked by market liberalization, the retreat of the state from intervention in the economy, and the spread of the political and economic values associated with competition, OPEC remains a noteworthy exception: a persistent, state-run anticompetitive force in the world marketplace.

OPEC's remarkable endurance at the center of the global petroleum market is both an economic puzzle and an intriguing subject, even an enigma of world politics. It is an economic puzzle because it is such a striking anachronism. For the past three-quarters of a century, governments have been retreating from playing more than a guiding role in their economies. They have relinquished the use of economic instruments both at home and at their borders, except in the most extreme of circumstances; they have fostered deregulation and liberalization of markets and have reaffirmed free-market principles even when in temporary retreat, such as during the aftermath of the economic recession of 2008; and they have promoted unfettered flows of capital, goods, services, and to a surprising extent even labor. The assumption has been that free flows foster greater efficiencies and higher growth, leaving citizens at home better off economically.

OPEC countries have resisted the increasingly open global environment for trade and investment. Instead, they have sought to defy market forces and control the price of oil through government interference and manipulation of markets through the artificial regulation of energy supply and investment. State-owned enterprises dominate most OPEC countries' oil and petrochemical sectors; quasi-authoritarian governments distribute investment capital, jobs, and public spending on a noncompetitive, selective basis that is usually determined by traditional patronage networks and informal relationships, particularly in the oil-rich Arabian Gulf region. A recent article in *Foreign Affairs* notes, "Arab states with oil reserves and revenues deployed this wealth to control the economy, building patronage networks, providing social services, and directing the development of dependent private sectors. Through these funds, Arab rulers connected the interests of important constituencies to their survival and placated the rest of their citizens with handouts in times of crisis."[1]

More than a half-century after Iran, Iraq, Kuwait, Saudi Arabia, and Venezuela met in Baghdad to lay out OPEC's blueprint, the political environment for OPEC is changing dramatically, opening the possibility that its members' societies will undergo the same kind of liberal transformations seen in other parts of the globe. This pressure on OPEC governments will represent a major challenge to the organization, one that may ultimately lead to the demise of its cohesiveness and effectiveness. In the short run, the ability of the Arab monarchs and Iranian mullahs to hold onto the reins of power seems stable. Limited reforms combined with repression and economic handouts have kept political opposition at bay. In the long run, however, as expectations of the population increasingly need to be met with broadly distributed benefits, the absolute power of OPEC heads of state will diminish—and with it, the ability of OPEC leaders to force unilateral decisions on their populations for the sake of a functioning cartel. The voices and interests of individual domestic constituencies will find their way into OPEC deliberations, complicating them and hindering the organization's ability to make the cohesive decisions needed to control global prices.

Democracy is struggling for a more solid footing in Kuwait and Iraq, and prospects for some change loom in almost every OPEC member state. With dramatic and domestically driven violence against status quo governments across the Arab and larger oil-producing world, an increasing restiveness by populations led to the Libyan revolution and the more widely and more popularly, if inaccurately, called movement, "Arab Spring." The roots of the Arab Spring can be found from the confluence of many factors, but the drop in per capita income that unfolded in the face of higher revenues along with high levels of unemployment in countries in the Middle East and North Africa have been major catalysts. Against this backdrop of possible internal political liberalization, OPEC will face a tough series of new challenges to its ability to buck the trend of globalization and free-market principles and sustain its anomalous, dominant price-setting role. In this chapter, we discuss the emerging factors that may push market forces to overwhelm OPEC's historical regulatory coalition and to bring to oil the same liberalization that has characterized trade in manufactured goods and services.

History of OPEC: Drivers of Policy

Before the formation of OPEC, an international oligopoly of multinational oil companies regulated the global supply of oil through a series of geographic market-sharing agreements. US regulators also played a role through the Railroad Commission of Texas, which rationed excess US oil supplies in an effort to even out a boom-and-bust cycle that tended to bring about deleterious rises and collapses in oil prices and created volatility in the reliability of supply.

The major companies controlled all aspects of the industry, including oil exploration and production, distribution, and processing. Access to oil was provided through concessionary agreements under which the companies paid host governments royalties on the basis of a somewhat arbitrarily set price for crude oil. It was against this context that five key oil-producing countries—Iran, Iraq, Kuwait, Saudi Arabia, and Venezuela—banded together in 1960 to try to counterbalance the market power of the international oil companies with an oligopoly of their own.[2] Thus, the essentially defensive nature of OPEC was apparent at the very origins of the organization, when the five founding members came together to stave off oil revenue reductions that the international majors were trying to impose on them to counter broader market trends.[3] These trends included a new Soviet strategy, in the context of the Cold War, to strike bilateral deals to sell cheap oil to Europe and a decision by the United States to impose mandatory quotas on oil imports in 1958 following voluntary import restraints. The quotas were designed to protect the maturing and costly production base in the United States against lower-cost oil from abroad, particularly from the founding members of OPEC. By 1960, US domestic prices rose to an average of $2.80 per barrel, while prevailing prices for internationally traded oil fell to $1.80.

OPEC's founders pushed two policy changes to secure their revenue objectives. First, they sought to put pressure on the companies operating in their territories to urge the US government, in turn, to reduce, if not eliminate, the quotas so as to gain revenue through volume. Second, the producers wanted to raise their revenues at the expense of the companies operating in their countries by gaining revenue sharing. Ultimately, the producers also hoped to raise prices.

By the late 1960s, certain OPEC countries, starting with Iran and Iraq (and later a new member, Libya), widened their ambitions to include the nationalization of oil fields in an effort to prevent international oil companies from underproducing local oil fields to squeeze economic concessions from the OPEC host governments. In June 1968, OPEC adopted a Declaratory Statement of Petroleum Policy, which proclaimed the "permanent and inalienable sovereignty" of the governments over their natural resources and called on OPEC members to acquire the greatest possible interest in existing oil concessions.

In 1967, King Faisal of Saudi Arabia introduced a new concept for oil producers to use their market power. Saudi Arabia threatened to wield an "oil weapon" in the form of a supply embargo against the United States and United Kingdom if they supported Israel in a war against fellow Arab states. But the embargo was less than effective as the United States orchestrated, by lifting rationing orders of the Railroad Commission of Texas, an increase in US oil production by 1 million barrels per day (mmbpd), thereby reducing the impact of Arab cutoffs to the United States and the United Kingdom.

By 1973, however, as rising demand eroded US surpluses, OPEC was able to launch an effective embargo coinciding with a new Arab–Israeli war, thereby putting OPEC on the geopolitical map in a manner that no other institution in the developing world had accomplished. Through the 1970s, OPEC upped its game, with many members nationalizing their oil concessions, leading to a massive deintegration of the international oil industry. The major international players, which had built and dominated the upstream or producing areas, were cut off from ownership of those resources, which devolved to national oil companies in the producer countries.

In subsequent years, OPEC refocused on its original revenue-protecting role, and after 1998, the organization was spectacularly successful at forging agreements to limit supplies to produce higher prices.[4] Previous concerns about the effect of rising oil prices on the global economy faded as OPEC's leaders were determined to avoid being seen as delivering benefits to Western consumers at the expense of their own citizens. OPEC governments henceforth favored the realization of greater short-term revenue, which could best be achieved not by bringing on line new production, but rather by curtailing output.[5]

Enjoying increased market power to push prices higher and thereby earn higher revenues, OPEC members have been careful not to overinvest in new productive capacity. OPEC's total sustainable production capacity did not rise between 1998 and 2005, despite a rising demand for OPEC crude supply. As shown in table 5.1, capacity gains made through added investments in Iran, Saudi Arabia, Kuwait, Algeria, Qatar, and Libya barely managed to offset losses in Iraq, Nigeria, Venezuela, and Indonesia.[6]

OPEC's price aggrandizement efforts were helped by additional constraints on investment in production and infrastructure over the 1990s and early 2000s in most OPEC countries because of tight state treasuries and rising social pressures as well as debilitating regional wars and economic sanctions. OPEC capacity growth failed to keep pace with rising demand from emerging markets led by the BRICs (Brazil, Russia, India, and China, but especially China) as demand rose to high levels and stressed supplies.[7]

Table 5.1. OPEC Production Capacity, 1998–2012, Selected Years

Member Country	Production Capacity (mmbpd)				
	1998	2001	2003	2005	2012
Saudi Arabia	9.80	9.90	10.15	10.30	11.80
Iran	3.70	3.80	3.80	4.00	3.50[a]
Iraq	2.80	3.05	2.20	1.80	3.30
Kuwait	2.40	2.40	2.50	2.60	3.10
UAE	2.40	2.45	2.50	2.40	2.90
Qatar	0.72	0.75	0.75	0.82	0.75
Venezuela	3.30	3.10	2.50	2.50	2.40
Nigeria	2.05	2.30	2.30	2.30	1.80
Libya	1.45	1.45	1.45	1.60	1.55
Algeria	0.88	0.88	1.15	1.35	1.20
Total	30.85	31.38	30.45	30.57	35.90
Call on OPEC	25.85	28.23	29.2	29.87	30.60
Spare capacity	5.00	3.15	1.25	0.70	5.30

Sources: Energy Intelligence Group and International Energy Agency.

a. Because of sanctions imposed in 2011, Iran was producing some 2 mmbpd in 2012, with 1.5 mmbpd of spare apacity.

The mismatch of OPEC's flagging investment and rising global demand reduced OPEC's spare production capacity sharply, making it easier to agree to restrain output. Nominal oil prices increased almost 15-fold from a low of about $10 per barrel in 1998 to a peak of close to $150 in the summer of 2008, as OPEC implemented one successful production-sharing agreement after another, thereby reaping a vast windfall that was helped by lost production capacity in Iraq, Nigeria, and Venezuela. The revenue consequences were astonishing. In 2000, OPEC members earned an estimated $251 billion from exports ($280 billion in constant 2005 dollars); by the end of the decade, collective revenues reached $771 billion in nominal dollars ($690 billion in constant 2005 dollars). By 2012, their collective revenues reached a record $1.05 trillion (nominal—$895 billion in real 2005 dollars).[8]

But from its very success, OPEC may have sown the seeds of its eventual demise. The organization faces a much rockier future than it has weathered in the past, with implications for potentially revolutionary change in the structure of the oil industry and global energy markets even as total earnings soar. The changes, brought about by the combination of sustained high oil prices and rapid social change across the Middle East, could have dramatic geopolitical consequences. Materially, long-term shifts may rekindle US geopolitical and economic power while leaving the Middle East economically and strategically adrift.

For every action, there is a reaction. Exceedingly high oil prices stimulated massive investment by private capital both in oil exploration outside of OPEC countries (particularly in unconventional resources in the industrial world) and in alternative sources of energy around the globe. The financial pressure of oil import bills on major economies has triggered consuming countries to reduce consumption, thereby targeting higher energy efficiency while taking a giant bite out of oil demand. In addition, the second and third decades of this century appear to be ushering in revolutionary changes in the uses of natural gas, which is becoming increasingly abundant in a variety of countries.

These uses include the conversion of natural gas into diesel and jet fuel as well as the direct use of natural gas, either as compressed natural gas or as liquefied natural gas, in the car and truck fleets. As a result, oil consumption should continue to fall in Organization for Economic Cooperation and Development (OECD) countries—notably in the United States—in the years ahead, potentially limiting OPEC's influence over the West and shifting any burden of OPEC's policies more squarely on emerging Asian countries such as China and India. At the same time, internal political conflicts inside most OPEC member countries could easily curb oil production growth, while fuel subsidies to OPEC's domestic consumers stimulate internal oil demand to new heights, potentially shrinking OPEC's share of exportable oil to levels that could greatly reduce its market power.

Looming Challenges for OPEC

How OPEC meets five major challenges will determine the future of the organization in the 21st century. The members of OPEC have been remarkably adaptable in the past in meeting challenges, both individually and collectively. It remains to be seen how the producer group will be able to steer an adaptive course in the years ahead.

Challenge 1: Rising Internal Demand and Falling Capacity

Rising internal demand and stagnant or even falling upstream capacity mean that OPEC's share of the export market is likely to decline over time, thereby limiting the cartel's market power. OPEC now has the fastest-growing rate of petroleum product consumption in the world, with resulting erosion of export capacity along with spare capacity. The situation is only worsening with new commitments to keep the peace at home. These commitments require not just higher spending but also higher subsidies. Oil product and electricity prices, in particular, are substantially below global market levels. OPEC consumption of refined products has been growing rapidly, from 5.4 mmbpd in 2002 to 8.26 mmbpd in 2011.[9] The increases are driven by economic expansion, high population growth, and extremely large subsidies to electricity and gasoline prices. Throughout the Gulf Cooperation Council, members such as Saudi Arabia and Kuwait struggle to meet rising electricity demand and have resorted to burning increasing amounts of fuel and crude oil for power generation despite negative environmental consequences and the loss of potential export revenues.

Fuel subsidies are crippling in high-population countries. They create a treadmill effect in which the subsidies serve as a budgetary drain for both the government and the national oil company, leaving reduced funds to reinvest in expanding oil production as internal oil demand grows. At the extreme, the combination of rising oil demand and flagging domestic production can lead to governance and economic crises.

In 2007, the *New York Times* quoted a report by CIBC World Markets that calculated that "soaring rates of consumption in Russia, in Mexico, and in member states of the Organization of the Petroleum Exporting Countries would reduce crude oil exports by as much as 2.5 million barrels a day by the end of the decade."[10] Other major OPEC countries such as Iran and Algeria face similar prospects and could become net oil importers, with dire economic consequences.[11]

The future of OPEC's share of tradable oil remains controversial. Conventional wisdom suggests that as global oil demand grows, OPEC will need to play a major role in satisfying demand growth, nearly all of which is expected to come from emerging market economies. Even as the International Energy Agency (IEA) notes in *World Energy Outlook 2012* that the resurgence of production in North America represents a "sea change" in the global outlook,[12] the IEA also thinks that after 2020 OPEC will have to increase its market share as global demand increases by some 7 mmbpd above the 2012 level.

But this conventional wisdom might well be wrong. OPEC's exportable surplus had a recent peak of 24.2 mmbpd in 2007, when the organization's market share was 60.1 percent. Exports were down almost 0.8 mmbpd in 2011, even as Saudi Arabia increased production by nearly 2 mmbpd to replace Libyan crude oil. If demand continues to grow at its recent rate, which saw total OPEC demand rising by 17 percent from 2007 through 2011, by 2015 OPEC demand will increase by 1.4 mmbpd to 9.6 mmbpd, and by 2020 demand will exceed 11.2 mmbpd, a total increase of 3 mmbpd from 2012 to the end of the decade.

This increase in demand will erode the exportable surplus of almost every OPEC country, the most glaring exception being Iraq. Meanwhile, if North America, Russia, Kazakhstan, and Brazil continue to grow at recent rates and if the United States and other OECD countries see a drop in their total petroleum product requirements, non-OPEC output would, as was the case in the 1980s, see a growing share of tradable oil. In that scenario, OPEC's market share would actually decline. OPEC countries would be in a bind in their ability to control prices, and increased domestic spending pressures would create a double bind: it would be difficult to reduce output and risk revenue, and a declining market share could actually cause the organization's pricing power to decline.

Challenge 2: Governance Issues

Governance issues will weigh increasingly on OPEC's members, and some will become more "democratic," thereby making it harder to forge agreements that require sacrificed revenue. In light of the Arab Spring, many oil-producing countries—not only those in OPEC—need to sustain social and economic expenditures at significantly higher levels. Budgetary (fiscal) break-even prices for oil are rising—in some cases, dramatically (see table 5.2). The fiscal challenges, whether in relatively impoverished Nigeria or in the wealthy Gulf Cooperation Council countries, raise the possibility that these countries may lose revenue, thereby making it difficult for them to publicly agree to curtail production as part of an OPEC production-sharing agreement. In addition, OPEC negotiations increasingly face the scrutiny of members of the public and their representatives (in parliaments and other governing bodies), thereby constraining the flexibility of

Table 5.2. Fiscal Break-Even Prices for Selected Oil Producers in the Middle East and North Africa

	Break-Even Price ($ per barrel)	
Country	2008	2012
Algeria	56	105
Bahrain	75	119
Iran	90	117
Iraq	111	112
Kuwait	33	44
Libya	47	117
Qatar	24	42
Saudi Arabia	49	71
United Arab Emirates	23	84

Source: Data from International Monetary Fund statistics.

heads of state and oil ministers to make large concessions during OPEC deliberations.

In some countries, greater democratic participation makes it difficult to spend money to increase production capacity. In other countries, particularly Iraq, democratic bodies might well insist on higher production even at the expense of OPEC obligations (see later discussion in this chapter).

Challenge 3: Iraq's Reintegration

Reintegrating Iraq could be tricky if global demand growth is not sufficiently strong. As a founding member of the group, Iraq is unlikely to want to break from the organization. Yet for more than half of the producer group's history, Iraqi production has been handicapped by three wars, a severe sanctions regime, and reconstruction. Iraq hit peak production just before the outbreak of the Iran–Iraq War in 1980, 20 years after OPEC was founded. As of 2012, Iraqi production was still below that level because of domestic and global impediments. Now that Iraq's political system has become more democratic, the sensibilities of average Iraqis have more bearing on OPEC deliberations about Iraq's resumption of a quota assignment. Many Iraqis resent that for more than half of OPEC's existence, other producers have increased market share while Iraq could not lift production. This resentment has led to a refusal to rejoin any quota system until Iraqi output tops 6 mmbpd, slightly more than double 2012's level. Depending on market conditions, this Iraqi position could turn out to be a serious challenge to OPEC unity and overall OPEC output controls.

The IEA's report on Iraq's oil potential paints an optimistic picture of Iraq's future production profile on the basis of a combination of fiscal requirements, huge potential, and increased security facilitating the country's ability to attract investment capital from abroad.[13] Although the road to enhanced production (like the path to greater stability) is mined with difficulties, the consequences for oil markets are enormous and need to be considered as well.

Challenge 4: Saudi Arabia's Changing Role

Unless it constrains oil demand much further, Saudi Arabia may no longer be able to maintain its enforcer role of threatening to flood oil markets to instill discipline within OPEC. Over the years, Saudi Arabia has taken on a special role of maintaining price discipline within OPEC by serving as the group's disciplinarian. By maintaining excess production capacity, the kingdom is a "swing producer" that can flood the market and drive down prices to punish producers who refuse to abide by OPEC agreements.[14] But by 2012, Saudi Arabia had less spare capacity immediately available (only about 1 mmbpd to 2 mmbpd) than in the past and has had to shift to areas that have more complex geology and that require greater technological intervention.[15]

Moreover, in light of new regional and internal challenges, Saudi Arabia faces competing priorities with higher spending requirements on social services and defense. The pressure for higher defense and social spending makes it harder for the government to justify a massive campaign to expand its oil sector. In sum, it will not be as easy for Saudi Arabia to mobilize a major price war as time goes on, thereby reducing its ability to police OPEC by threatening to drive prices lower to punish members who cheat on quotas. If market conditions deteriorate, it is unclear whether OPEC will be able to maintain cohesion minus the policing mechanism of Saudi spare capacity (figure 5.1).

Figure 5.1. Saudi "Overproduction" Could Overshoot to the Downside: Historical Case in 1997–99

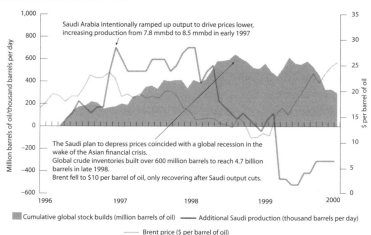

Sources: EIG and Citi Research.

Challenge 5: The Emergence of Unconventional Oil and Gas

Unconventional oil and gas are challenging OPEC's market dominance and dramatically changing OPEC's customers with geopolitical implications. Instead of being a major destination for OPEC surpluses, North America could become a potential export competitor. Emerging technological and market changes that accompanied the radical rise in prices after 2002 are rapidly becoming the defining feature of oil markets in the 21st century. High prices have made it economical to develop resources that had been known to exist but had previously been out of economic reach. Four new supply streams are emerging to challenge the dominance of the conventional crude oil under the control of OPEC's members:

- *Biofuels.* In 2013, biofuels constitute some 2 mmbpd, or 2.5 percent, of global oil.
- *Oil sands.* These deposits are a large part of OPEC member Venezuela's reserve base and a substantial part of the reserve base of non–OPEC member Canada, supplying some 3.7 mmbpd of oil liquids, or 4 percent of global oil.[16]

- *Deepwater deposits*. Located 2 to 5 kilometers under sea level and another 5 to 8 kilometers beneath the seabed, deepwater deposits have grown from virtually no production in 2000 to 5 mmbpd by the end of 2012, or 6 percent of global production.
- *Tight oil*. Production of tight oil exceeded 1.5 mmbpd by the end of 2012, or 1.6 percent of global production.

These four sources of supply, together with incremental output from Iraq, combine to provide a potential supply challenge to OPEC that is reminiscent of conditions from the mid-1980s through the 1990s, when incremental non-OPEC and OPEC production challenged OPEC's ability to balance the market. Whether OPEC again faces such a challenge depends in large part on the pace of global demand growth and especially on whether China maintains the rapid pace of demand growth of the first decade of this century.[17]

The main potential obstacles to the emergence of significant supply sources outside of OPEC are environmental risks and prevailing prices. With respect to the latter, there is little doubt that three unconventional sources of supply—deepwater resources, oil sands, and tight oil—require prices that are significantly higher than what prevailed before 2002. Deepwater resources require prices in 2010 dollars of $50 to $60 to sustain long-term exploitation. Oil sands developments in Canada have a wide range of minimum prices, but they are undoubtedly a bit higher than the range for deepwater resource development. And tight oil, also wide ranging in minimum price level to allow for commercial development, is somewhat higher than deepwater resources.

Hence, OPEC faces a dilemma. As long as fiscal break-even prices are high and rising to levels above $70 per barrel, OPEC production policies are likely to subsidize production in competitive non-OPEC oil. But it is the combination of external production from these unconventional sources and production from within—whether from Iraq or Venezuela or elsewhere—that is likely to challenge OPEC policy coherence.

The challenge from deepwater resources has been high, but it also stalled in the second decade of this century.[18] However, deepwater discoveries of oil and natural gas remain robust, and chances are that oil and gas discoveries in the Gulf of Mexico; in offshore West Africa and East Africa; in the Eastern Mediterranean; and in the deep waters around India, Australia, and China will yield huge development projects in the years ahead.

Oil sands in Canada look likely to continue to grow at a steady pace of some 0.2 mmbpd per year for at least a decade, if not two decades (figure

Figure 5.2. Canadian Oil Production through 2020

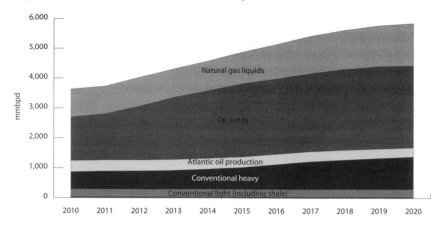

Source: Canadian Association of Petroleum Producers.

5.2). That means an increase of 2 mmbpd in this decade and another 2 mmbpd in the next decade. That slow but steady tortoise-like growth results in a formidable source of supply that not only can help furnish the US market but also—with outlets to the Pacific and Atlantic Basins opening in the future—can challenge OPEC's market share as well.

However, the shale and tight oil revolution, combined with the reduction in US petroleum product consumption, poses the greatest challenges to OPEC. These challenges are unfolding rapidly. In the brief five years after 2007, US net petroleum product imports fell by 4.5 mmbpd. Although 4.5 mmbpd is lower than the oil output of Russia, Saudi Arabia, the United States, or China, it is greater than the total oil production of any other country in the world. And it appears that this footprint will shrink even more rapidly in the next decade.[19]

The surge in US production is already knocking key OPEC exporters out of the US market, and the growth in both US and Canadian sour crude oil production could have a similarly limiting effect on exports to the United States from Venezuela and the Middle East. In the period between 2008 and 2012, light sweet crude exports to the United States and Canada fell from 2.6 mmbpd to about 1.0 mmbpd, reducing significantly the premiums commanded by West African and Mediterranean crude streams over Brent, a light sweet crude oil classification. The exports appear to be falling on an accelerating basis, and in a few years there could be no room for light sweet crude exports into North America, reducing further their value on international markets.

Sour crudes look likely to have an even greater fall in North America. Canadian crude oil exports to the United States will likely surge by 2015 with the development of new pipelines from Canada into the United States. This development is happening at a time when US production of sour crude in the Gulf of Mexico is resurging as the drilling moratorium in the Gulf of Mexico has ended and new production grows. The result will be increased challenges for OPEC crude oil exports into the US Gulf Coast, which has the highest concentration of refining upgrading capacity in the world.

Producers in Venezuela and the Middle East are thus likely to find it difficult to maintain their foothold in the United States. The problem is that there is no other concentration of refining upgrading capacity on a meaningful scale. Hence, they will have three choices: (a) maintaining their market share by pricing to meet competition from Canada, (b) discounting the price of their crude in other markets, and (c) shutting in production.

No matter how OPEC perceives the problem, the choices are not enviable and could lead to a period of disarray, much like that of the 1980s, when the producer group had less influence on market price trends. If OPEC's share of tradable oil falls to a very low level through a combination of rising competition from non-OPEC unconventional supplies and higher demands for OPEC oil for domestic use, its capability to function as a commodity cartel will be hampered.

Thus, what is unfolding in Iraq, potentially elsewhere in OPEC, and in North America is deeply challenging to the OPEC status quo—and particularly to the Saudi status quo.

OPEC's Future and US Policy Options

As OPEC crude gets pushed out of the US market, Asian buyers such as China and India are likely to become the countries that most depend on OPEC. At the same time, it is possible that US production increases, combined with falling demand, could leave the United States in a position to export surpluses to the global market. Those changes to the market dynamic have several geopolitical implications.

OPEC's ability to use oil sales as leverage to adversely influence the United States will be greatly reduced. Although the US and global economy will still be sensitive to oil price shocks, the United States as a large oil and gas producer and exporter will receive a compensating offset of higher energy sector revenues from any OPEC cutback. The United States will also be able to target its own exports to allied countries in Europe or to Japan, should those countries be threatened with a supply cutoff by OPEC. Instead of being able to target the United States and constrain its superpower prerogatives, OPEC's policy changes will have an impact that falls more squarely on Asia and particularly on China.

On the flip side, however, the United States will similarly lose its ability to threaten OPEC members with tight economic sanctions against oil sales, unless Asian buyers such as China, India, and Japan are willing to go along with US goals. The United States already came up against this problem in 2012 when it tried to tighten sanctions against Iran in an effort to influence Tehran's nuclear policies. But the US effort fell short in inducing China, Japan, India, and South Korea to make substantial reductions in purchases from Iran.

A more energy-sufficient United States will also be freer to engage in an international agenda of democracy promotion and human rights, which might weaken the relationship the United States has with authoritarian governments in major oil-producing states.

The longstanding US policy to promote diversification of oil and gas supplies around the world holds even more promise now. As investment in unconventional oil expands internationally, the monopoly power of OPEC is likely to wane considerably, possibly spelling the end of its anomalous rule that has kept free trade and open markets out of the oil business.

It has never been clear why the United States has not done more to eliminate the energy security and global economic risks posed by OPEC. But the United States now has the opportunity to recapture the status it had in the 1960s, when it was able to play a swing producer role to stabilize the oil market in the face of conflicts in the Middle East and other geopolitical events.

The challenges to OPEC are indeed formidable. But they looked equally formidable in the mid-1980s, when oversupply and falling demand led to declining prices, even as OPEC's second- and third-largest producers, Iran and Iraq, were at war with one another. Never count OPEC out, given its more than half-century of survival. But the obstacles to a rebirth of OPEC's power are large.

Notes

1. F. Gregory Gause III, "Why Middle East Studies Missed the Arab Spring," *Foreign Affairs* 90, no. 4 (2011): 81–90.

2. The founding of OPEC came in the aftermath of the 1956 Suez Crisis in which Egyptian leader Gamal Abdel Nasser had raised the specter of a successful populist campaign of anticolonialism, nationalizations, and Pan-Arabism and created an environment whereby oil-producing countries became dissatisfied with the status quo, which was permitting the world's largest private oil companies to control the absolute level and flow of money to their national treasuries. As described by the organization's secretariat, the 1960s were OPEC's formative years, during which the organization sought "to assert its Member Countries' legitimate rights in an international oil market dominated by the 'Seven Sisters' multinational companies." See OPEC, "Brief History," OPEC, Vienna, 2013, http://www.opec.org/opec_web/en/about_us/24.htm.

3. OPEC's original aim was to wrest higher fixed crude oil prices and royalty tax payments for host governments of oil producers from the international oil companies that owned and operated Middle East and South American oil fields under concessionary terms in the post–World War II period. As the 1960s progressed, the OPEC countries ultimately gained the upper hand in negotiations with the international oil companies and took control of their own national oil resources through massive nationalization of in-country oil field and infrastructure assets. OPEC's actions to "assert its member countries' legitimate rights" and to gain "a major say in the pricing of crude oil on world markets" made history in 1973, when the organization initiated its famous oil embargo that rocked the international community and quadrupled the price of oil. See OPEC, "Brief History." Although OPEC's membership originally included only 5 countries, today the membership has expanded to 12: Saudi Arabia, Venezuela, Kuwait, Iraq, Iran, the United Arab Emirates, Qatar, Libya, Nigeria, Algeria, Indonesia, and Angola.

4. Following an unexpected nosedive in oil prices to below $10 a barrel in 1998 in the aftermath of the Asian financial crisis of that same year, OPEC unity was galvanized. By 2000, as demand began to recover, OPEC set a more aggressive path to increase prices to within a range of $22 to $28 a barrel. OPEC's new stance reflected popular domestic sentiments in producer countries that governments were not doing enough to deliver economic benefits to a substantial portion of the population.

5. A rich literature exists on the subject of the tradeoffs between volume and price with respect to OPEC revenue. The most recent contributions to these debates are found in Dermot Gately's pieces in the *Energy Journal*. See Dermot Gately and Hillard G. Huntington, "The Asymmetric Effects of Changes in Price and Income on Energy and Oil Demand," *Energy Journal* 23, no. 1 (2002): 19–55; Dermot Gately, "How Plausible Is the Current Consensus Projection of Oil below $25 and Persian Gulf Oil Capacity and Output Doubling by 2020?," *Energy Journal* 22, no. 4 (2001): 1–28; Dermot Gately, "OPEC's Incentives for Faster Output Growth," *Energy Journal* 25, no. 2 (2004): 75–96.

6. Edward L. Morse and Amy Myers Jaffe, "OPEC in Confrontation with Globalization," in *Energy and Security: Toward a New Foreign Policy Strategy*, ed. Jan H. Kalicki and David L. Goldwyn (Washington, DC, and Baltimore: Woodrow Wilson Center Press and Johns Hopkins University Press, 2005), 65–95.

7. The four BRICs saw combined oil demand rise 55 percent to 18 mmbpd, and China alone saw demand rise by 94 percent. Demand growth in the Middle East showed

a parallel story, growing 54.4 percent over the decade to 7.89 mmbpd, with Kuwait and Saudi Arabia leading the growth path with more than 70 percent increases in both countries. See BP, *BP Statistical Review of World Energy 2012* (London: BP, 2012) for these and related data.

8. See Energy Information Administration (EIA), "OPEC Revenues Fact Sheet," EIA, Washington, DC, December 21, 2012, http://www.eia.gov/countries/regions-topics.cfm?fips=OPEC&trk=c.

9. See OPEC, *OPEC: Annual Statistical Bulletin 2006* (Vienna: OPEC, 2006); OPEC, *OPEC: Annual Statistical Bulletin 2012* (Vienna: OPEC, 2012).

10. Clifford Krauss, "Oil-Rich Nations Use More Energy, Cutting Exports," *New York Times*, December 9, 2007.

11. Already, former OPEC member Indonesia has flipped from being a net oil-exporting country to a net oil-importing country because of flagging oil production in aging oil fields combined with soaring demand driven by fuel subsidies. Those fuel subsidies, which by the late 1990s had reached almost one-quarter of the Indonesian government's entire federal budget, caused such massive economic dislocation for the Indonesian government that the longtime rule of President Suharto ended as a result.

12. See the executive summary of IEA, *World Energy Outlook 2012* (Paris: OECD/IEA, 2012) at http://www.iea.org/publications/freepublications/publication/English.pdf.

13. IEA, *Iraq Energy Outlook: World Energy Outlook Special Report* (Paris: OECD/IEA, 2012), http://www.worldenergyoutlook.org/media/weowebsite/2012/iraqenergyoutlook/fullreport.pdf. See also J. Robinson West and Raad Alkadiri, "Iraq, Iran, and the Gulf Region," chapter 10 of this volume, for further discussion of the challenges to Iraq's oil production.

14. For a discussion of the various examples of Saudi Arabia's fulfilling this responsibility, see Amy M. Jaffe and Ronald Soligo, "Market Structure in the New Gas Economy: Is Cartelization Possible?," in *Natural Gas and Geopolitics: From 1970 to 2040*, ed. David G. Victor, Amy M. Jaffe, and Mark H. Hayes (Cambridge, UK: Cambridge University Press, 2006), 439–64.

15. Saudi Arabia has spent $14 billion in the half-decade after 2005 trying to increase its capacity to produce oil from 10 mmbpd to 12.5 mmbpd. This increase has proved difficult, and Saudi Arabia, whose capacity at the end of 2012 was estimated at 11.5 mmbpd, was still working on the giant Manifa field to meet its 12.5 mmbpd immediate-term capacity target.

16. This level is expected to rise to 5.0 mmbpd of total liquids, or 5.5 percent of global supplies, which are expected to rise by 2020 to about 93 mmbpd.

17. Evidence is growing that just as China's gross domestic product growth is estimated to decelerate to below 6 percent per year by 2020, so too will its demand for oil decelerate, particularly as oil is displaced in many of its nontransportation roles. For a discussion of China's energy outlook, see Amy Myers Jaffe and Kenneth B Medlock III, "China, India, and Asian Energy," chapter 13 of this volume.

18. The challenge stalled in two critical areas: (a) in the United States, which had about 35 percent of deepwater production before the BP Macondo disaster of April 2010, when a moratorium was placed on production and when US output was about 1.75 mmbpd, and (b) in Brazil, where huge technological challenges; a government policy to favor the national oil company, Petrobras, and to force local content requirements on all development; and the unusual circumstances surrounding a near-miss accident

by Chevron in the deep offshore are combining to stymie efforts to reach 4 mmbpd by 2020.

19. For a full discussion of the US supply outlook, see Richard G. Newell and Stuart Iler, "The Global Energy Outlook," chapter 1 of this volume, and Shirley Neff and Angelina LaRose, "North America," chapter 15 of this volume.

Chapter 6

Energy Sector Governance
in the 21st Century

William C. Ramsay

Today's institutions of international governance in the energy sector are more a consequence of political events than of any systematic approach to build the infrastructure of an international dialogue to address common energy challenges. They reflect forces unleashed after the Second World War, when key colonial powers were too occupied with their own reconstruction—a situation that led in turn to a gradual erosion of their influence in former colonies and a growing awareness among newborn nations that they were not securing an adequate return on their natural resources.[1] This chapter examines the current array of institutions focused on energy; assesses their ability to address the urgent challenges of reaching energy sustainability, reducing energy poverty, and adapting energy systems to the consequences of climate change; and suggests a new path forward that is centered in bilateral diplomacy rather than in new organizations or treaties.

Three Core Institutions

Three organizations are central to institutional governance in the energy sector:

- The *Organization of the Petroleum Exporting Countries* (OPEC) grew out of this growing resource nationalism and the desire of producing countries to manage their own hydrocarbon patrimony. OPEC's political cohesion occurred only 13 years after its formation in 1960 on the occasion of the 1973 Yom Kippur War, when it confronted the West with a new political weapon: oil.[2]
- The *International Energy Agency* (IEA) was the defensive political reaction to the 1973 Arab Oil Embargo of the United States and the Netherlands. Its focus was consumer political solidarity and the immediate building of a defensive mechanism that would deny OPEC the use of oil as a political tool. In the ensuing years, OPEC and the IEA learned more about each other as institutions and through a proliferation of bilateral contacts.[3] Then 10 years of Iraqi adventurism convinced producers and consumers that they shared a strong collective interest in stable oil markets—even if stability was in the eye of the beholder. But emergency preparedness in oil today will need to evolve with global oil consumption patterns: as gas markets converge, greater coordination in gas market crises will be needed, and as grids stitch together across regions, greater effort will be needed to ensure the security of electricity supply. Multilateral efforts here will most likely be driven by market "train wrecks" forcing attention to these emerging needs.
- The *International Energy Forum* (IEF) had its beginnings in a long and relatively unproductive dialogue between oil producers and consumers that began in parallel with the creation of the IEA. Ultimately the dialogue led to the establishment of the IEF. The IEF now has a full-time secretariat in the Saudi Arabian capital, Riyadh, and is providing a positive place for oil producers and consumers to cooperate by airing issues that would have been impossible just a few years ago.

These three organizations—OPEC, the IEA, and the IEF—form the core of the international energy dialogue. Over the years, IEA has become much broader than oil and the IEF is seeking a place in gas, but OPEC remains firmly focused on oil and really considers gas as only a source of natural gas liquids.

Other Institutions

Other ad hoc institutions deal with specialized agendas, as described in the following summaries:

- *The Energy Charter.* Following the collapse of the Soviet Union, the Energy Charter Treaty laid down the legal framework for investments in the oil and gas sectors of the former Soviet Union.[4] But Russia's unwillingness to ratify the treaty has severely undercut its utility to investors.[5] Russians believe the European Union (EU) promotes discriminatory practices that negatively affect Russian commercial interests in Europe.
- *The United Nations Framework Convention on Climate Change and the Intergovernmental Panel on Climate Change.* The United Nations Framework Convention on Climate Change (UNFCCC) was created to address the abatement of all forms of greenhouse gas (GHG) contributing to global warming. It established a scientific panel under the Intergovernmental Panel on Climate Change (IPCC) to assess the science of climate change. Although suffering some political missteps, the IPCC has made compellingly clear that the world is on a collision course with irreversible consequences if it does not begin to rein in ever-increasing emissions of GHGs—particularly in the energy sector, where the burning of fossil fuels is by far the greatest source of carbon dioxide (CO_2) emissions.[6] Current emissions are taking the planet toward an average temperature change of 6°C by the end of the century—a cataclysmic scenario, but one we are nonetheless following.
- *Specialized agencies.* Narrow-focus organizations are too numerous to list here, but a few examples will make the point:
  - The *International Renewable Energy Agency* (IRENA) was established to advance deployment of nonpolluting renewable energy. IRENA got off to a rocky start, but under new management, it is establishing a positive role in promoting renewable energies to contribute to a more sustainable energy mix.[7]
  - The *International Partnership for Energy Efficiency Cooperation* (IPEEC) took life at the German-hosted Group of Eight (G-8) Summit at Heiligendamm. The IPEEC is now housed at the IEA, where it determines its own work plan and budget. It is currently chaired by India.[8]
  - *Regional energy organizations* include the Association of Southeast Asian Nations; the Latin American Energy Organization; the Shanghai Cooperation Organization, which includes Russia, China, and

several states in Central Asia; the Asia-Pacific Economic Cooperation, which includes the states of the Pacific Basin; the Observatoire Méditerranéen de l'Energie, which covers the littoral states of the Mediterranean; and the South African Development Community, which covers the countries of southern Africa and others. These organizations have various mandates and differing levels of competence.

These were the institutions of the past. But are they up to today's challenges?

The New Context of the 21st Century

Developments in global society and its economy are creating different conditions within which international organizations will have to function. In the past, just over a billion and a half of the world's population were overwhelming beneficiaries of the great majority of the world's abundance. Western Europe and the United States, along with elites in every country around the world, have happily shared among themselves the benefits of world productivity over the past two centuries—give or take a few decades. Those days are over.

Since 1988 in China and a bit later in India, hundreds of millions of people have been lifted from poverty—and large numbers now form a muscular middle class that wanders the world's tourist destinations as others have before. Earlier, the Asian Tigers (Hong Kong, Singapore, South Korea, and Taiwan) raised the standard of living of large portions of their large populations, and other emerging nations are gaining speed. These new voices will demand to be heard, and they are developing the economic and political clout to make it happen. Organizations that do not find a way to incorporate these new voices will be sidelined.

An unfortunate parallel development is that while the income gap between industrial and emerging nations is narrowing, all countries are suffering deepening internal chasms between their own rich and poor. The stresses from this inequality are visible around the world from anti–Wall Street demonstrations to the Arab Spring.

Three Unanswered Challenges

For the 21st century, three energy-related issues require much greater attention and much more concerted effort: energy sustainability, reduction of energy poverty, and, unfortunately now, adaptation of energy systems to the consequences of climate change. The institutions in place today were not designed to address these issues and cannot do so in their present form. Can they rise to these challenges? Or does the world need different institutions?

Energy Sustainability

Mitigating climate change requires reducing GHGs. Anxiety about the adequacy of the world's energy resources and our ability to mobilize them to meet our development needs was a 20th-century issue. Security of supply remains an issue, but means are available to deal with most threats. Increasing collaboration between the IEA and China, plus greater cooperation between producers and consumers, makes most oil market disruption scenarios relatively manageable—albeit with price consequences. At prevailing prices for hydrocarbons, massive new resources are becoming available. The concern now is far less the adequacy and security of the fossil fuel resources. The concern is knowing that we cannot afford to burn fossil fuels if we hope to inhabit the planet (unless we capture and store a large proportion of their CO_2 emissions).

Since the 2008 financial collapse, the world has moved GHG mitigation to a distant burner, putting economic recovery first. In the Organization for Economic Cooperation and Development (OECD), the high cost of stimulating renewables has come up against budget stringency and consumer rebellion. Feed-in tariffs and subsidies have been slashed. In emerging countries, promoting economic growth has quite understandably been a higher priority than addressing the threat of climate change, which has consequences that may emerge only later in the century. Renewing capital stock anywhere for greater energy efficiency requires a growth environment. Abundant gas is providing an appealing lower-carbon bridge in the power sector, reducing substantially the need for nuclear power and actually backing higher-carbon coal out of the power mix—in some markets. Perversely, cheaper gas in the United States means the United States burns less coal, thereby reducing world coal prices, making traded coal cheaper in Europe than oil-indexed gas, and resulting in greater coal consumption in Europe. Emissions around the world are increasing, and there is no international organization with a sufficiently strong mandate to do more than raise the alarm.

Reduction of Energy Poverty

Reducing energy poverty—that is, giving an increasing proportion of the world's population access to affordable, secure, and sustainable energy—is the second global challenge. An estimated 1.3 billion people have no electricity access now, and as the world's population grows, the percentage changes little. Around the world, collecting traditional biomass dominates the working days of large numbers of women, and the inefficient combustion of traditional biomass causes more premature deaths from respiratory-related diseases among women and children than from malaria.

The United Nations (UN) Millennium Development Goals do not have an energy-specific objective. Yet reaching the goals will require much more universal access to modern energy services. The real cost of fixing poverty is relatively small in the scheme of things, but emerging and developing countries require massive investment in their power sectors in the coming decades. Investors are not prepared to venture into these areas without policy reforms to raise energy and power prices closer to market parity. Official development assistance is minuscule compared to the investment requirements for power transmission and distribution. No institution has a strong enough mandate to address this challenge.

Adaptation of Energy Systems

Adaptation means responding to the implications of climate change for energy supply, energy transformation, or transportation infrastructure. Rising sea levels alone will present huge challenges because power plants around the world are at sea level for cooling purposes. Refineries dot our coastlines, as do strategic oil storage sites. Shipping infrastructure, gas liquefaction, and regasification facilities are at sea level. Extreme heat buckles rails, thereby impairing rail transport of fuels. It is not hard to conjure a long and worrying list of energy and energy infrastructure challenges that will result from our failure to prevent climate change.

Can Today's Institutions Meet These Challenges?

The question to be answered is whether the existing institutions can serve the needs of humanity in shaping a stable, sustainable energy future in the 21st century or whether we need something else. If the conclusion is that we need something else, what are the practical approaches that might permit defining and building those institutions? Can we reinforce existing organizations or expand their mandates? Can public policy-making do a better job of creating the conditions within which the world's economic operators will deploy their efforts to achieve our collective policy objectives?[9]

Traditional methods of dialogue need to evolve so that there are more opportunities for virtual debates, teleconferencing, and consensus building among core states. Energy diplomacy has become unwieldy and inefficient. Too much effort goes into the process, and not enough effort goes into concrete outcomes. Meanwhile, the world's most serious energy challenges go unanswered.

OPEC's only strategy over the years has been supply management. A highly skilled professional secretariat has developed over the years despite member interference in staffing and careful control over what OPEC is able to say as an institution. OPEC's ability to use its only policy tool has been hampered by each country's efforts to maximize its own revenues. OPEC members do not have a common view on how to maximize revenues because of differing resource bases, investment policies, and aspirations of their oil sectors.

OPEC does not play an organizational role in climate change talks, consistent with its members' vigilance in limiting the scope of OPEC Secretariat activities. OPEC's focus is oil. Consideration of gas intrudes to the extent that gas produces liquids. OPEC's ability to shape supply policy in unconventional oil is nearly zero: Venezuela's Orinoco Oil Belt is not subject to oil production quotas. OPEC's most recent member—Angola—has a growth agenda that is entirely at odds with the supply management goals of the organization. Iraq, recovering from 30 years of conflict, has OPEC quota-busting aspirations that are not negotiable inside OPEC. Just attaining OPEC's core supply policy will remain elusive when so many OPEC members are working at cross-purposes.

Recent high oil prices have led to greater spending by OPEC governments, which now find that meeting their national budgets drives production policies rather than considerations of resource depletion policy. Today, OPEC countries, which control 60 percent of the world's conventional oil reserves, contribute only 33 percent of world oil production. If OPEC remains focused on revenue requirements first and supply policy second, it is hard to see how this international organization will have the ability—even if it had the interest—to contribute to meeting the challenges of sustainability, energy poverty, or adaptation.[10]

OPEC members do have a mechanism for addressing energy poverty and development through the OPEC Fund for International Development (OFID). OFID had an assistance budget of nearly $760 million in 2011, largely in energy, agriculture, and transport projects in 60 countries around the world, with 52 of these countries in the poorest regions of Africa and Asia. OFID will continue to make a valued contribution to the development agenda, but it is not a policy body.

The IEA has evolved considerably over the years from its initial nearly unique focus on oil security. IEA work has dramatically expanded into every fuel and energy technology, climate change, and efficiency. Its initial focus on the short term now reaches to 2050. The previously hermetically sealed discussions among industrial countries now welcome and incorporate a broad diversity of nonmembers. The IEA sees itself as a policy formulation body and an energy policy adviser for any country seeking energy policy advice.

The IEA struggles with its limited membership and is in constant internal debate about whether its substantive energy policy mission can be achieved without a broader membership. Much time has been spent exploring different categories of associate membership or formal links with countries outside the OECD. The key candidates for closer relationships are China, India, and Russia.

The Chinese currently have no interest in formally joining an organization that requires collective decision-making in times of oil crisis. Yet the Chinese are deeply interested in the various policy options tried by the various IEA countries in search of workable solutions for themselves. They regularly send senior policy-makers to IEA conferences, workshops, and other meetings and appear to value the substantive dialogue. In addition, China has recognized the merit of collective responses to world oil market tensions. After years of close communication during oil market crises, China may already have made the policy decision to coordinate (voluntarily) in clearly crisis-driven strategic oil stock draw actions. Considerable benefit is already being derived from this substantive collaboration between the IEA and China, even if it has no more formality than a memorandum of understanding addressing cooperation.

Russia would be happy to join the IEA to enhance its international stature, but it is not of a mind to adhere to the principles that bind the agency. So far, its status as an OECD accession country has not led it to

apply for IEA membership. Perhaps World Trade Organization accession
will provide some indication of Russian intent. President Vladimir Putin
must know his old muscular formula of strengthening state control has
its own limits—if for no other reason than that he must soon address the
decline in Russia's expected revenue streams from both oil and gas. The
IEA will need to await a clearer definition of how Russia plans to manage this sector before committing a great deal of effort to higher-profile
collaboration.

India would not be able politically to join a "rich man's club" and is
in any case not ready to subscribe to the principles that bind the IEA.
India's bureaucrats are very well versed in the pros and cons of the most
up-to-date energy policies, but internal rigidities and bureaucratic complexity limit how effective collaboration can be. Nonetheless, the Indians
are enthusiastic interlocutors on energy policy, and any process that sus-
tains the substantive engagement of Indian policy-makers in the broader
international dialogue is sufficient for now. The IEA's memorandum of
understanding with India, anchored in the country's Ministry of Power,
has proved to be an efficient channel for substantive work to flow back
and forth.

Most important for the IEA is to engage these major players in its policy
discussions. An improvement in the energy-efficiency policies of any of
the big three would have significant global influence. An improved investment climate in any of the three would be of global benefit. Engaging any
of the three in a voluntary collective response to an oil crisis would have a
much more stabilizing effect on markets than the IEA acting alone.

Regarding climate change, the IEA has contributed substantial intellectual and policy input to the sustainability agenda. Agency statistics on
carbon emissions and renewables underpin the policy analysis. Ever since
the inception of climate change talks, the IEA has furnished energy sector
policy and data input to the work of the Climate Change (formerly Annex I) Expert Group. The IEA has a wealth of energy market analysis and
policy evaluation skills to offer to the sustainability agenda and does not
need a broader IEA membership to carry out that work.

On energy poverty, the IEA has made several significant contributions
to understanding the extent and origins of the world's energy poverty.
Through its annual publication *World Energy Outlook*, the agency has generated credible numbers defining the challenges of the world's energy poor.
It has tried to estimate the real cost of addressing much of the poverty
agenda. It has raised the profile of the corrosive effect of energy subsidies

on emerging economies. The IEA can continue to advance analysis and policy options for mitigating energy poverty, but it needs a clearer mandate to do so from its governing board. Even armed with such a mandate, the agency is not a development assistance body, nor does it have a development policy mandate. That work must be done elsewhere.

The International Energy Forum is still carving out its niche in promoting a better energy dialogue between producers and consumers of energy. In today's world, the duality of energy producers and consumers inherent in the IEF mandate is obsolete, reflecting earlier tensions between major exporters and major importers of crude oil. The IEF of today is trying to break away from that narrow definition, but its mandate is restrictive, its resource base is small, and its close oversight by members render it unlikely to venture far beyond oil and possibly gas. Unless the 40 or 50 countries involved in the IEF totally rewrite its mandate, the IEF is likely to remain limited to the niche functions of enhancing transparency in oil and gas markets and providing an unthreatening venue where energy ministers can meet.

What Next?

International organizations do not exist to relieve countries of their obligations to meet the challenges of the 21st century. International organizations can bring together experts and policy-makers, conduct independent research to define the challenges, and explore policy options for addressing those challenges. But they cannot do the work themselves, and few can do more than exert peer pressure.

Although many international organizations oversee binding commitments by their members, more often than not national priorities or circumstances will trump those commitments. Countries are very careful not to yield much sovereignty to international organizations, and sanctions for noncompliance are either weak or not applied. The only real sanction occurs when the peers in the organization believe deeply enough in the mandate of the organization to apply bilateral pressure to the offending state.[11]

Furthermore, just as international organizations cannot resolve these 21st-century challenges through their own actions, neither can governments by themselves. The role of international organizations is to establish the policy context, communicate it with clarity, and put in place the instructions so that economic operators will know how to react. They do so through clear policy articulation, regulatory procedures, rule writing, standards, and oversight. At the national level, there is the potential for sanctions with teeth as long as there is clarity in the terms of the understanding between the state and the economic players.

Inclusiveness or Impact?

International organizations can provide coherence in defining international policies and practices. But each country around the table is focused on its own competitiveness. Each is concerned about the success of its national champions. Each country wants to negotiate the best terms for its citizens. But if, at the end of the day, countries are not committed and willing to mobilize their economic operators to accomplish the agreed policy objectives, international organizations can do nothing.

Welcoming 210 countries to the UN General Assembly is very inclusive. The General Assembly gives everyone a voice, but how likely is it to reach any useful conclusions? After 24 years, nearly 100 countries at the UNFCCC are still stalemated. Twenty-seven countries in the EU can adopt bold policies, but those policies often get lost later in national implementation. Thirty countries at the IEA can generate punchy policy recommendations, but no one is obliged to follow them. Eight countries at the G-8 Summit can generate comprehensive communiqués, but the eight represent a small fraction of humanity. The G-8 offered second-class seats for the "plus" countries that it invited to the party, thereby creating a two-class system. What can 20 countries at the Group of 20 (G-20) do? We are now testing that.

The G-20's composition is much more representative: it includes the North and South; the East and West; and the developed, developing, and emerging. The majority of the world's population is represented. The G-20 is not far from George W. Bush's Major Economies Forum on Energy and Climate, which was designed to group the major CO_2 emitters (less Iran) around a table negotiating in *comité restraint*.[12] In the EU, a core of three or four countries formulates the major strategies to deal with the euro crisis. In the North Atlantic Treaty Organization, a few core countries set the agenda. In OPEC, it is the same. And in the UN, the Security Council has the final word, which is often "no" from one of the council's permanent five members if the issue is controversial.

For Hard Decisions, Whom to Invite?

A move is already being taken to identify a critical mass of countries specific to any given issue, find among this core group a plausible approach to the issues, and carry that strategy back to the broader population of countries. This approach is not democratic. Initially, many countries will be left out and will not like it. But without a core of deeply interested countries that operate on roughly the same wavelength, there is little likelihood of advancing the agenda. Moisés Naím, the former editor of *Foreign Policy*, has spoken of "minilateralism."[13] Many of our 21st-century agendas are too time sensitive for drawn-out, inconclusive debates.

Some issues cannot be resolved in UN-dimension groupings. Even smaller groups need some measure of cohesion or common purpose. In climate change, the biggest players are still at fundamental odds. Industrial countries need to start reducing their GHG emissions, and they want everyone else to do the same. But emerging and developing countries still need to increase emissions as they lift their populations out of poverty. The compromise can be found in equating reduction efforts from trends, not by demanding net reductions in emissions from 1990 levels. But politicians are not ready for this concept because they have spent the past 20 years arguing that everyone should commit to reduced emissions targets from 1990 levels, as agreed at Kyoto in 1997. That outcome is just one of the many flaws of the Kyoto Protocol.

What If Neither Mini nor Multi Works?

There are occasions when an issue is critical and we cannot find a top-down solution. And there are occasions when we collectively recognize that announcing ever more challenging targets is mere posturing. An alternative approach, which has been discussed and apparently dismissed, is the sectoral approach, or the bottom-up solution. All countries use modern technologies to make glass, aluminum, cement, steel, and other base commodities. Industrial standards can be set, and commitments to improve them can be negotiated. Appliance standards are converging worldwide because there is a world market to be won and everyone wants a share. Countries can take simple measures, such as reaching a global agreement on the wattage that powers standby functions in electronic gear. Narrow agreements can be reached in many places that, in the aggregate, have significant influence.

The UN Convention on the Law of the Sea was in negotiation for more than a decade and ultimately was not ratified by the United States. Yet cooperation in and under the seas has progressed relatively well where there is an immediate economic or security need (watch the South China Sea). If the world cannot set international commitments for an issue as urgent as climate change and if minilateralism founders on a fundamental disagreement, then we should continue the broad multilateral talks to meet the political agenda. But in addition, we should adopt a more aggressive strategy of identifying bottom-up solutions through collective ad hoc efforts. The longer we wait to address climate change, the more it will cost the world in cash and in hardship.

Adaptation

A wealth of research is going on in the multitude of adaptation challenges in a number of sectors. The challenges are being defined, and scenarios are emerging in water, agriculture, disease control, demographics, migration, and more. The UNFCCC provides for work on adaptations that are focused initially on the short term and on capacity building among the signatory countries. In a later phase, UNFCCC work will implement measures to respond to the consequences of climate change. But adaptation work in the UNFCCC does not have a strong political impetus behind it. Working groups plod on and papers circulate, but there is little action.[14]

In October 2009, US Presidential Executive Order 13514 created the US Interagency Climate Change Adaptation Task Force. The task force is composed of all the relevant departments of government at the federal level and has links to states and municipalities. It does not have a strong link with the rest of the world. The task force is building a database, defining and assessing the risks, exploring options, contracting public works, and trying to raise awareness. In one concrete example of civil works under way, Louisiana Highway 1 is being raised to the height of the 500-year storm. Adaptation will require input from all, including meteorologists, energy companies, and crisis management authorities, just to begin to identify the magnitude of the problem. Many, if not most, problems will be local, but the effort to find solutions would benefit from collective reflection. Throughout time, civilization's urban landscape has been built around water, but biblical allusions to lost civilizations suggest that humans did not find acceptable solutions the last time the water rose. In 2012, Hurricane

Sandy showed just how vulnerable our coastal installations are to rising water levels. One hopes that Sandy will serve as a wake-up call for anticipating abnormal weather events and that the hurricane may have washed some of the sand from under climate skeptics' feet.

Climate change and adaptation are topics that should be taken up in the G-20. As was the practice in the G-8 in the past, various aspects of the issue should be assigned to the relevant specialized international bodies. If no organization has the skill set required, the appropriate national authorities should be convened under the G-20 and chaired by a troika of past, present, and future chairs. We need to avoid the almost inevitable political impulse to seek a global convention or treaty on adaptation. Today, the increasing willingness to link extreme weather to incipient climate change would force politicians to seize on the negotiation of a convention or treaty as an expedient and low-cost way to meet the political need to "do something." Subjecting the adaptation agenda to negotiation would paralyze it.

Alleviation of Energy Poverty

The problem is not the lack of financial resources necessary to alleviate energy poverty. According to IEA calculations, the money spent subsidizing fossil fuel consumption around the world is a multiple of what is necessary to eliminate all but the worst poverty, and it would go some way toward addressing infrastructure needs.[15] Also, the vast sums of money earned on resource exploitation around the world would easily finance the necessary energy infrastructure if the export revenues did not disappear through corruption. The major impediment to broader access to modern energy in the majority of emerging and developing countries is not a lack of money. It is poor governance and the lack of a functioning market. No one wants to build a power plant where electricity is not paid for and where the state controls the fuels needed for power generation or their prices. All the official development assistance in the world and the collective efforts of every international organization can do little if improvements in energy sector governance do not come first.

Rather than exploring what kind of new international organization should deal with energy poverty, the world should focus on policy reforms and governance. The major emerging countries, such as India, China, South Africa, Indonesia, Brazil, and the former Soviet bloc countries (including Russia), all know full well what policies are needed to achieve greater sta-

bility in their markets—and they have sufficient financial muscle to resolve their own problems. The rest of the world should encourage them to
make these hard policy calls. How can we expose other smaller countries
to the range of policies that have worked elsewhere? A cultural change is
required. More emphasis should be put on understanding, writing, and implementing feasible policy reforms rather than writing grant applications.
Many of the policy changes will require higher prices for energy or lower
subsidies. Countries will need considerable encouragement to make these
changes, and our diplomacy to this end would be more effective if we dealt
with our own subsidy programs by way of example.

Existing international organizations should focus on implementing better policies in their member states and beyond and on empowering their
private sectors to get on with the work. People in the poorest of countries
know that they must pay for energy, and they will struggle to pay for better
energy because they know the consequences of not having it.

In a Nutshell

The world is not adequately addressing the challenges of the 21st century:
energy sustainability, climate change, energy poverty, and adaptation. Existing international energy and financial organizations cannot do enough—
but creating new ones is not the answer. The IEA is evolving in many of the
right directions and is expanding its substantive reach. It will find a useful
role. OPEC and the IEF serve different purposes and can contribute only
marginally, if at all, to the big four challenges.

Bilateral diplomacy will be at the origin of new directions in multilateralism. Just a few countries with a shared concern about a global or regional
challenge will seek a mechanism to adapt to the issue. Others will eventually be engaged. National self-interest will need to evolve beyond a narrow
focus on trade balances to embrace issues crucial to the common good of
the world. We are certainly not there yet, but the issues press.

New inclusive organizations, conventions, and treaties are not the answer. We should use the G-20 to assign narrow challenges to competent
bodies. We should use the UN to give everyone air time. But most important, we must get clear instructions to the economic operators and give
them the ability to operate by cleaning up governance everywhere. Guidance on appropriate policies can come from international organizations,
but instructions must come from the state.

Top-down international diplomacy is not working. Answers to climate change are already being found on the ground, and these answers should be nurtured to grow and converge with other solutions that come from the bottom up. A convergence of local solutions can be fostered by bringing together groups of national or industrial bodies responsible for a particular task. Tasks assigned by the G-20 or another body may serve to empower and to draw financing for grassroots efforts. We cannot allow the dogged pursuit of broad political consensus or the narrow pursuit of national interests to block real progress on these critical agendas.

Notes

1. See African Studies Center, "Resistance, Nationalism, and Independence," activity 4, module 7b, of the *Exploring Africa!* curriculum, Michigan State University, East Lansing, http://exploringafrica.matrix.msu.edu/students/curriculum/m7b/activity4.php.

2. For more information on the development of OPEC, see Amy Myers Jaffe and Edward L. Morse, "OPEC: Can the Cartel Survive Another 50 Years?," chapter 5 of this volume, and OPEC's website at http://www.opec.org.

3. Duco Hellma, Cees Wiebes, and Toby Witte, *The Netherlands and the Oil Crisis: Business as Usual* (Amsterdam: Amsterdam University Press, 2004).

4. To learn more about the Energy Charter, see http://www.encharter.org.

5. Sergei Kolchin, "Why Russia Refuses to Ratify the Energy Charter," RIA Novosti, April 4, 2006, http://en.rian.ru/analysis/20060407/45451331.html.

6. John T. Houghton, Yihui Ding, David J. Griggs, Maria Noguer, Paul J. van der Linden, Xiaosu Dai, Kathy Maskell, and Cathy A. Johnson, eds., *Climate Change 2001: The Scientific Basis—Contribution of Working Group 1 to the Third Assessment Report of the Intergovernmental Panel on Climate Change* (Cambridge, UK: Cambridge University Press, 2001), http://www.ipcc.ch/ipccreports/tar/wg1/.

7. For more information about IRENA, see http://www.irena.org.

8. For more information about IPEEC, see http://www.IPEEC.org.

9. Michael Levi, "Energy, Environment, and Climate," chapter 21 of this volume.

10. Edward L. Morse and Amy Myers Jaffe, "OPEC in Confrontation with Globalization," in *Energy and Security: Toward a New Foreign Policy Strategy*, ed. Jan H. Kalicki and David L. Goldwyn (Washington, DC, and Baltimore, MD: Woodrow Wilson Center Press and Johns Hopkins University Press, 2005), 65–95.

11. Xavier Philippe, "Sanctions for Violation of International Humanitarian Law," *International Review of the Red Cross* 90, no. 870 (2008): 359–70. See also W. Michael Reisman, "Sanctions and International Law," Faculty Scholarship Paper 3864, Yale Law School Legal Scholarship Repository, New Haven, CT, 2008, http://digitalcommons.law.yale.edu/fss_papers/3864/.

12. For a description of the forum, see http://www.majoreconomiesforum.org.

13. Moisés Naím, "Minilateralism: The Magic Number to Get Real International Action," *Foreign Policy* 173 (July–August 2009): 135–36, http://www.foreignpolicy.com/articles/2009/06/18/minilateralism?page=0,0.

14. Michael Levi, "Energy, Environment, and Climate," chapter 21 of this volume.

15. See the International Partnership for Energy Efficiency Cooperation website at http://www.IPEEC.org.

Commentary on Part I

Chakib Khelil

The six excellent chapters in part I, "The Global Framework," give me a welcome opportunity to share views on five important issues that will weigh increasingly on the energy world: the geopolitical and economic context, oil supply and demand, security of demand, implications for US policy, and the role of the Organization of the Petroleum Exporting Countries (OPEC) in oil market stability.

Geopolitical and Economic Context

Ever-changing geopolitics and global economics have always shaped the oil market's evolution and stability. Despite threats at times over the past 50 years from this phenomenon to OPEC's very existence, OPEC has been recognized as a big success story. It has been particularly successful in securing oil supplies to the world economy when most needed while consolidating its role as the unquestioned stabilizing force in the market. By

157

the same token, it has achieved its goal of "securing a steady income to the producing countries."[1] The past 15 years offer striking examples of the critical role that OPEC has played so successfully despite big upheavals in geopolitics and economics.

The Iraqi invasion of Kuwait in 1990 led instantly to a sharp cut in oil supply that prompted OPEC countries to use their large spare production capacities to make up for the lost output. Consequently, prices returned to their preinvasion levels.

The financial crisis that started in late 1997 in Asia led to a global economic downturn and weakened demand for oil the following year, sending prices down to near one digit. These events led OPEC to seek cooperation from large non-OPEC exporting countries such as Mexico, Norway, and Russia and then to adjust supply to balance the market and stabilize prices at a sustainable level.

The attack on the World Trade Center and the Pentagon on September 11, 2001, introduced the world to global instability, weakening the world economy and demand for oil late that year. OPEC sought assistance from non-OPEC countries and stabilized the oil market.

The attempted coup in Venezuela (2002), the crisis in Nigeria (2003), and the invasion of Iraq by coalition forces in the same period posed a serious challenge to the world economy as almost 4 million barrels per day (mmbpd) disappeared from the market. OPEC faced this major challenge by immediately increasing output to make up for the unavailable supply from those countries and to reestablish market stability.

In 2008, the financial crisis led to a brutal downturn in economic growth, oil demand, and oil prices by the end of that year. An ongoing debate still rages over whether the high oil price in early 2008, followed by its sharp free fall later that year, was controlled by speculative activity or by market fundamentals. But OPEC made a dramatic decision that December in Oran, Algeria, to balance the market and stabilize prices. This historic decision, and the others that preceded it, demonstrated the strength of OPEC when its members acted with unanimity and faithfully applied the organization's decisions.

Today, wars and high geopolitical tensions in the Middle East continue to pose a serious risk of disruption to oil production and export flow. In the recent past, exports were curtailed not only from OPEC member countries such as Iraq, Libya, and Iran but also from non-OPEC countries such as Yemen, Syria, and Sudan. In all of these cases, nobody denies that OPEC continued to meet these challenges by ensuring secure supplies to the world economy and stabilizing the market.

Major Shifts in Demand and Geopolitical Risks

Throughout the past perilous 15 years, China began its dramatic rise as an oil market powerhouse, thus becoming an inescapable part of the global price equation. Then the consolidation in the mid-2000s of China and emerging Asia as major oil importers, combined with a sudden upsurge in geopolitical uncertainties and risks in the Middle East region following the second allied war in Iraq, constituted a paradigm shift in market determinants.

In addition to oil supply, demand, and economic factors, operators started factoring in geopolitical uncertainties and the risks associated with them. Oil prices reached new highs, integrating exceptional price risk premiums for potential disruptions of oil production and trade flows.

High oil prices, in turn, benefited the development of unconventional resources of shale gas and then shale oil in the United States. This phenomenon meant that oil prices stabilized around a relatively high level that was required to reward big spending by companies developing shale oil reserves in the United States.

Supply and Demand

Most now believe that the world oil market and, for that matter, the future globalized gas market are operating against a background of ample resources of hydrocarbons.[2] But demand has shifted to the less energy-efficient emerging economies in the East from the more energy-efficient developed economies of the West, while the refining industry has become more globalized. Because OPEC controls some 80 percent of the world oil reserves, most market analysts expect it to play an important role in this new market environment by securing needed additional oil supplies, stabilizing the market, and safeguarding world economic growth.

The authors of part I agree that by 2035 fossil fuels will still constitute the dominant component (roughly 70 to 80 percent) of the global energy mix, and oil share will remain almost as significant as it is today. They also agree that additional oil demand will be led by the Asia-Pacific region, primarily by China and India. By end user, the transportation sector will continue to be the largest consumer of oil despite the potential competition from natural gas–derived fuels. An important consideration, however, is that oil consumption by the less energy-efficient emerging

countries would be less sensitive to economic downturns and consequently would be more stable and predictable than oil consumption by
developed economies.

Considering a range of different global energy projections, Richard
Newell and Stuart Iler anticipate that the world will need about 15 mmbpd
to 20 mmbpd of additional oil supplies by 2035. Their analysis reveals that
non-OPEC countries cannot meet this incremental demand and that OPEC
countries will probably have to provide about 10 mmbpd to 15 mmbpd to
close the gap.[3] These estimates do not raise objections because they reflect
the ranges of other organizations such as the International Energy Agency
(IEA) and OPEC. Within these prospects, OPEC member states Iraq and
Venezuela can be expected to play a key role to satisfy this additional demand by 2035, because both have huge conventional and unconventional
oil reserves that could be developed within a more stable and positive investment climate.

OPEC's Call for Security of Demand

OPEC's call for "security of demand" stems from its fears that long-term
investments for additional capacity may go unrewarded if future demand
remains tainted by uncertainties of unconventional oil supplies and prices.
The IEA found in its *World Energy Outlook 2012* that high oil prices would
favor a higher level of shale oil production in the United States, whereas
low oil prices would limit the contribution of shale oil to North American
self-sufficiency.[4] But each IEA scenario, if materialized, would mean a different call on new OPEC production capacity.

OPEC's projected world oil demand reference scenario is closer to other
global forecasts summarized by Newell and Iler, but three other scenarios
guide OPEC strategic thinking for the same period until 2035: the high
economic growth, low economic growth, and non-OPEC liquid supply
surge scenarios. What these three scenarios demonstrate, however, is their
lack of sustainability. The first scenario needs to be underpinned by unsus-
tainably high oil prices over the whole period, and the second and third
scenarios lead to a price collapse that discourages a supply surge from non-
OPEC sources.

But most of all, the three scenarios show that high uncertainty exists
about the call for OPEC oil, which should worry OPEC countries about
developing new reserves until the outlook for shale oil and oil sands output

becomes clearer. Until then, a period of instability and volatility is likely to prevail in the oil market.

Implications for US Policy

North America will be a net gas exporter by 2015 and could become a net oil exporter by 2035. I agree with Ed Morse and Amy Myers Jaffe that this major development will strengthen US geopolitical and economic power.[5] This new status will have important policy implications for the United States both domestically and globally. My particular view is that US policy will likely continue to maintain the strategic alliances forged with key member countries of OPEC.

Domestically, the greatest effect will be larger domestic and foreign investments in the US energy sector for development of new gas-based petrochemical ventures and power plants, thus fueling economic growth and job creation. As William Reilly also makes clear, expanded US and, indeed, global energy development depends increasingly on systemic safety improvements that are, in fact, in industry's own best interest.

Globally, lower oil and gas imports and future liquefied natural gas exports—the consequence of a far-reaching natural gas renaissance analyzed by David Victor[6]—will reshape global trade, reset gas sale purchase contracts, affect exporting- and importing-country economies in differing ways, and ultimately strengthen the US dollar.

But although the United States could further reduce its dependence on Middle East oil, it will not do so totally for a number of reasons:

- The United States has strategic alliances with several countries in the Middle East that it will likely maintain.
- Middle East oil remains a key strategic component of the global oil market in the longer term.
- Quantities of oil and liquefied natural gas crossing the Strait of Hormuz will increase in time, thus making this passage even more critical to the global oil and gas market than it is today.
- By continuing its presence in the Arabian Gulf, the United States will help oversee the flow to major consuming regions in Asia and Europe, including its closest allies.
- Despite future North American self-sufficiency, the United States and the global economy will still rely on the surplus production capacity

of the Middle East, particularly Saudi Arabia and potentially Iraq,[7] not only for emergencies as it did already several times before in world crises, but also for underpinning world economic growth and ensuring oil market and price stability. Unlike the case in the 1960s, it is improbable that the United States could play a future swing producer role to stabilize the oil market.

The Role of OPEC in Oil Market Stability

OPEC needs a clear view on a functioning oil market and outlook (which I call *visibility*), as well as stable and predictable prices, to secure additional supplies to the world economy and to ensure market stability. As William Ramsay points out, the ongoing dialogue among the IEA, OPEC, and the International Energy Forum on oil market data transparency is important to reach a broad, shared consensus view on demand, supply, and commercial inventories as well as on surplus production capacity needs for emergency situations.[8] More broadly, as Daniel Yergin points out, just as customers need reliability of supply, most exporters look for security of demand, and "this mutual interdependence helps create the framework for a continuing dialogue and cooperation between producers and consumers."[9]

On the one hand, stable markets and predictable prices facilitate timely decisions by OPEC countries on huge investments required to increase production capacities, secure supplies to the world economy, and balance the market for the future. On the other hand, OPEC countries continue to rely largely on oil revenues to finance their ambitious economic programs and social needs. These revenue needs have increased with population growth and the demand for better living standards. OPEC history shows that such revenue needs apply to all OPEC member countries irrespective of their political system in place. I also believe that with better governance in OPEC countries, the organization would be strengthened rather than weakened because the economies of member countries could become more diversified and oil revenues could be better shared and used for the benefit of their populations.

I agree with Newell and Iler that OPEC will play an even more important role than today in meeting world oil demand and will ensure market stability for the period ending in 2035. According to Newell and Iler, the OPEC share is likely to increase from 40 percent in 2010 to 45 to 50 percent by 2035. This increase would be valid were OPEC to develop a capacity of no more than about 45 mmbpd to 50 mmbpd by 2035 compared with 35 mmbpd today.[10]

To Sum Up

Throughout its 50-year history, OPEC has been highly successful in facing up to complex and risky geopolitical and economic challenges, in ensuring oil market and price stability, in guaranteeing security of supply to the world economy, and in preserving and consolidating the organization's interests. Oil prices reached new highs by the mid-2000s, integrating an exceptional risk premium that, in turn, facilitated the shale oil revolution in the United States. Although high oil prices are here to stay, most would expect that by 2035 OPEC's oil contribution will still make it the largest shareholder in global oil supply.

OPEC needs to have a better visibility on the call for its oil to justify huge investments in new production capacity while meeting the increasing revenue needs of its member countries' populations. Lacking better visibility, the market will likely enter a period of greater instability and volatility.

As a net gas exporter in the near future and potentially a net oil exporter by 2035, the United States will be strengthened geopolitically and economically but will likely preserve its strategic alliances with the main OPEC member countries, which are key components for well-functioning oil and gas markets and the world economy.

Notes

1. OPEC Statute, article 2, resolution II.6, approved by the Conference in January 1961, Caracas, http://www.opec.org/opec_web/static_files_project/media/downloads/publications/OS.pdf.
2. Richard G. Newell and Stuart Iler, "The Global Energy Outlook," chapter 1 of this volume. See also David G. Victor, "The Gas Promise," chapter 3 of this volume.
3. Richard G. Newell and Stuart Iler, "The Global Energy Outlook," chapter 1 of this volume.
4. IEA, *World Energy Outlook 2012* (Paris: OECD/IEA, 2012).
5. Edward L. Morse and Amy Myers Jaffe, "OPEC: Can the Cartel Survive Another 50 Years?," chapter 5 of this volume.
6. David G. Victor, "The Gas Promise," chapter 3 of this volume.
7. Daniel Yergin ("Energy Security and Markets," chapter 2 of this volume) points out correctly that Iraq must resolve political, legal, and infrastructure issues to be able

to tap commercially its large oil resource base. See also J. Robinson West and Raad Alkadiri, "Iraq, Iran, and the Gulf Region," chapter 10 of this volume.

8.   William C. Ramsay, "Energy Sector Governance in the 21st Century," chapter 6 of this volume.

9.   Daniel Yergin, "Energy Security and Markets," chapter 2 of this volume.

10.   Richard G. Newell and Stuart Iler, "The Global Energy Outlook," chapter 1 of this volume.

Part II

Europe, Eurasia, and the Arctic

After the global framework in part I, this and the following parts turn to a discussion of regional issues before the concluding part on a new energy security strategy. Part II discusses Europe and its search for gas supply security—from pipelines to liquefied natural gas (LNG) shipments to domestic natural gas from shale. Part II then turns to Russia and Eurasia. Russia has the world's largest gas reserves, and its oil exports now rival those of Saudi Arabia. Eurasia's oil reserves in the Caspian Sea region are equivalent to those of the North Sea, and the gas reserves rival those of Iran. Finally, part II examines the new frontier region of the Arctic and considers whether its abundant hydrocarbon resources can be developed safely without unacceptable risks to the environment.

In a turn of history's wheel, the West's former Soviet adversaries have become partners not only in discouraging proliferation and terrorism but also potentially in enhancing global energy security and reducing dependence on the Middle East. At the same time, new, unconventional tight oil and shale gas resources have the potential to create large domestic opportunities in the European and Eurasian region, much as they do in the United States and other parts of the world. The issues for US and Western policy are how best to reduce dependence on only a few energy suppliers and how to promote shared energy security through multiple sources— from unconventional fuels to multiple pipelines. Shared energy security is a particular challenge in Europe. As highlighted in chapter 7, western members of the European Union (EU) enjoy a greater diversity of supply than their eastern partners. Shale gas development in Central and Eastern Europe, including Ukraine, could significantly reduce EU dependence on Russian gas supplies—and could help alleviate this dilemma for the EU and its neighborhood.

These and related issues are addressed by Pierre Noël, who considers energy conflict, cooperation, and gas supply security in Europe; by Julia Nanay and Jan Kalicki, who analyze growth prospects for and challenges to developing and transporting Russian and Eurasian oil and gas; and by Charles Emmerson, who takes a necessarily longer view of Arctic resource development, environmental implications, and prospects for multilateral cooperation.

In chapter 7, Pierre Noël takes a close look at Europe's diversification of natural gas supplies, present and future. While recognizing the continued importance of piped gas supplies from Russia, Noël points to growing natural gas sources that will reduce Europe's energy dependence: piped gas supplies from the Caspian Sea and North Africa; LNG imports from Africa, the Middle East, and farther afield; and the promise of increased domestic natural gas production from shale deposits, particularly in Central and Eastern Europe. Whereas previously the eastern members of the EU, which depended almost entirely on Russian gas, felt the greater insecurity, they now have a greater prospect for shared security through multiple energy sources, domestic as well as foreign. That scenario, in turn, provides new energy and foreign policy opportunities, including the phase-out of long-term, oil-linked gas contracts with Gazprom and the development of a unified, transparent, and competitive gas market in the EU—and potentially beyond the EU to Ukraine and even Russia itself.

In chapter 8, Julia Nanay and Jan H. Kalicki argue that changing Western market realities—from lessened demand growth to increased diversity of domestic and foreign supplies—have "completely upended Russia's vision for the country's next generation of gas export projects," leading Russia to plan for increased oil and gas exports to the Asian markets. Completion of the Eastern Siberia–Pacific Ocean pipeline and Far Eastern LNG terminals will be only a prelude, however, to increased oil and gas competition with Australian, Southeast Asian, and Middle Eastern producers. In the absence of extensive investment, they see Russia as increasingly challenged to produce as much oil and gas as in the past, which in turn will require major reforms in its investment environment. Similarly, they assess growing oil and gas production in Azerbaijan and Central Asia, which is finding its way increasingly to European and Asian markets rather than primarily Russian markets. They argue that regional pipeline development should move from its zero-sum past to a positive-sum future, where pipelines from Russia and Eurasia can become mutually complementary and contribute, along with unconventional fuels and LNG, to a more stable and secure pan-European energy space.

In chapter 9, Charles Emmerson describes the somewhat ironic emergence of oil and gas resources in the Arctic as a consequence of greater access through a melting ice cap. The challenge is to develop these resources in a safe way for the environment and in a cooperative way for the member states of the Arctic Council—Canada, Denmark (through Greenland), Iceland, Finland, Norway, Russia, Sweden, and the United States. These states can band together to develop an environmentally friendly investment regime for this frontier region. Moreover, the changing energy market, the great expense, and the sheer technical complexity of Arctic projects could easily extend development timelines to mid-century and beyond.

In his commentary on part II, the director of the Russian Foreign Ministry's Department of Foreign Economic Cooperation, Alexander Gorban, has assumed the commentator's role taken by former energy minister and first deputy foreign minister Viktor Kalyuzhny in the first edition. Like Kalyuzhny, Gorban notes that energy security is just as important from Moscow's perspective as from that of Washington or Brussels and that Russian interests are determined by the country's dual role as a leading producer–exporter and a large consumer, which means the state must strike an optimum balance. In addition, he considers it axiomatic that the state must maintain control over the main oil and gas pipelines as "the only mechanism of effective state regulation available today," while believing that multiple pipelines should continue to develop throughout the region on "strictly commercial terms" without advancing political agendas. In the gas market, he notes that complementary, long-term supply–demand arrangements will promote global stability and security, but he also recognizes the need to balance such arrangements with those appropriate to future domestic shale gas development in Europe as well as potentially in Russia, China, and elsewhere. In both oil and gas, Russia is developing new production capacity in the Far North and the Far East, which will translate into new "energy export bridges" to Europe, Asia, and the Pacific, complementing those concluded earlier with the West.

Chapter 7

European Gas Supply Security: Unfinished Business

Pierre Noël

The European Gas Crisis, Four Years On

The security implications of Europe's natural gas supply situation have been a key theme of the international energy security discourse in the post–Cold War era. Dependence on Russian natural gas has been Europe's equivalent of US dependence on Middle Eastern oil: it has been the main point of intersection between energy realities and foreign policy challenges, the issue that has made energy an integral part of foreign and security policy thinking—what political scientists would call the *securitization* of energy.[1]

The concerns arose from a number of factors: rapid growth in Europe's natural gas consumption until 2005; even more rapid growth of imports as European production declined; Europe's reliance on a very small number of external suppliers; dominance of long-term, bilateral contracts between national, often government-backed gas utilities in Europe and government-controlled foreign suppliers; asymmetric dependence of Central and Eastern

European countries vis-à-vis Russia; and finally—and crucially—Russia's pushback under Vladimir Putin against the Euro–Atlantic realignment in the post-Soviet space (including key gas transit country Ukraine), Russia's effort to regain influence in Central and Eastern Europe, and Russia's apparent willingness to use energy exports as a tool to achieve those goals. The political situation in Ukraine—especially the high level of corruption in and around the gas industry and the very high level of market power Ukraine enjoyed as a transit services supplier—did not receive a lot of attention in Europe,[2] even though retrospectively those factors appear as a major source of gas supply insecurity.

The gas supply crisis of January 2009 was largely perceived as a validation of those concerns. Russian gas supplies to Europe were cut off for two full weeks as the failure of Kyiv and Moscow to agree on the renewal of their gas supply contract ended in the disruption of transit flows through Ukraine. The crisis launched a period during which energy—and especially gas—security became a central policy theme in Europe and a focus of nearly every EU rotating presidency.

In November 2008, two months before the crisis, I wrote that the fundamental problem Europe faces and must address is the absence of a pan-European competitive wholesale market for gas.[3] Over four years on, risks have gone down significantly with growing availability of liquefied natural gas (LNG) in Western Europe and the coming online of Nord Stream, bypassing the Ukrainian transit corridor. However, a smarter gas market concept for the European Union (EU), as well as national investments and market reforms by Central and Eastern European countries, remain critical to unifying Europe and addressing gas supply security for all Europeans.

Some Real Progress but Policies Remain Problematic

Dependence on Russian gas is not an issue for the EU *as a whole*. EU gas imports have actually diversified continuously and very significantly ever since the 1980s.[4] The real problem is that the EU has been split between its own East and West. A handful of Western European countries overwhelmingly dominated EU gas consumption and imports (including Russian gas) but also enjoyed a relatively high level of supply diversity. The so-called new member states, in contrast, were small gas markets that depended highly on Russia. In the context of President Putin's high-pressure foreign policy toward Europe, the bilateral relationships between Western European gas companies and Gazprom, which are supported by governments, were perceived in the new member states as crimes against European solidarity. The gas supply insecurity syndrome of Central and Eastern Europe was perceived as anti-Russian paranoia by economic elites and most political elites in Germany, Italy, and France.

The solution is (a) for Central and Eastern Europe to directly address their short-term gas supply security problem by increasing the resilience of their energy systems to gas supply disruptions through specific measures and (b) at the EU level for Brussels to concentrate fully on reviving its single gas market project. The emergence of an integrated, pan-European market would make Russian gas contestable in Central Europe, therefore limiting the security risks and political implications of gas import dependence.

The past four years saw two major positive developments. The first was the bypassing of Ukraine by the coming online of Nord Stream in 2011 (and South Stream likely by 2015). This event significantly reduces the risk of gas supply disruptions in the EU, because Ukraine is no longer able to use Europe as a hostage in its gas negotiations with Russia. The second development is the transformation of the Northwestern European gas market through the dynamics of commoditization, integration, and globalization.

The bypassing of Ukraine benefits the whole of Europe, even though Central Europe probably benefits disproportionately because, as the 2009 crisis showed, Central European countries are far more exposed than Western Europe to the risk of Ukrainian transit disruption. However, the process of commoditization and globalization of the gas market has largely escaped Central and Eastern Europe, where the contestability of Russian gas has progressed only marginally. Even the prospects for shale gas production now seem brighter in Northwestern Europe—particularly the United Kingdom—than in Central Europe, where exploration has proved disappointing and public opposition strong in some countries. Therefore, the split between East and West in terms of gas supply security might have widened since 2008. As far as Ukraine is concerned, Nord Stream has seriously weakened—and South Stream will sever—its de facto solidarity with the EU, to the benefit of European supply security but with serious geopolitical implications for the country.

It also appears that the few Central and Eastern European countries (such as Bulgaria and the Baltic states) that may have a serious short-term supply security issue—that is, a limited ability to meet final energy demand in case of Russian gas disruption—have not addressed the issue seriously or systematically. The European Commission, however, has used the crisis to revive a project to regulate the security of gas supply[5] that will not induce any national government to take gas supply security any more seriously than they already do.[6]

Consistent with my 2008 recommendation, the EU has indeed redoubled its policy efforts to build a single gas market. However, serious questions have arisen regarding the regulatory concepts and policy approach promoted by Brussels under its single gas market agenda. What emerges in Europe is a patchwork of tightly regulated, interconnected *national* gas systems governed by ever more detailed and complex rules that Brussels then wants to harmonize.[7] Under certain conditions—such as very large price zones, found in Northwestern Europe, most with direct access to the international LNG market—this system may mimic the short-term outcome of a genuine integrated market (i.e., price equalization), but it lacks the integrated market's main characteristics and sources of social benefits, especially decentralized investment in infrastructure development and the link between the short term and the long term provided by deep, liquid futures and financial derivatives markets.

The EU—and especially the European Commission—should be commended for the renewed emphasis on gas market integration since 2009. However, it is unclear if the market design that Europe has selected can deliver a pan-European gas market. Most member states in Central and Eastern Europe seem almost as cut off from Northwestern Europe at the turn of 2013 as they were four years before.[8]

Since the gas crisis, the European Commission has also wasted a lot of time, energy, and ultimately credibility in the pursuit of an external gas supply policy, essentially trying to solve a nonexistent problem (access to non-Russian gas) through a noncredible solution (a merchant pipeline through Europe and Turkey to Central Asia that will cost multibillion euros). The external energy policy agenda is even widening and the European Commission—here again supported by most EU member states in Central and Eastern Europe—has clearly signaled its ambition to scrutinize gas import contracts and ultimately get involved in their negotiation.[9]

The policy recommendations of November 2008 remain largely valid, even if international gas markets and the Gazprom-backed pipelines have actually reduced gas supply security risks in Europe.

Global LNG's Transformation of Western Europe

The economic organization of the gas industry in Western Europe has entered a period of rapid and profound change. In 2005, the industry looked fairly similar to what it had been 25 years earlier, but by 2015 it will look very different from what it was in 2005. The twin processes of commoditization (gas is increasingly traded on short-term markets as opposed to long-term contracts with an oil-indexed price) and globalization (the European gas system is increasingly integrated with the international LNG market) have important geopolitical implications because they change the nature of the relationship between Gazprom and its largest European clients.

Two developments have triggered the ongoing restructuring. First the spot price for gas—which in Northwestern Europe has converged with the British spot price, NBP (national balancing point)—has been durably below the oil-indexed price of traditional long-term import contracts (see figure 7.1). The reasons for that development include the economic downturn; the strong rise in oil prices; the rapid growth in global LNG exports, especially from the Middle East; and large new LNG import facilities coming online in the United Kingdom, France, the Netherlands, and Italy. The LNG import rate into Europe has grown more than 50 billion cubic meters (bcm) per year between 2008 and 2011 (see figure 7.2) or more than 10 percent of total EU consumption, in a context where demand declined by more than 10 percent and net imports were roughly flat. Second, spot-priced gas has been effectively available to large customers, traders, and brokers in Northwestern European markets. The reasons for that development are that national regulators have become more willing and able to enforce EU rules on pipeline access; the EU competition authorities have obtained from incumbent gas companies the release of entry capacity into their home markets; and merchant investments have increased interconnection capacity between the United Kingdom and the continent.

As a result of these developments, importers of oil-indexed gas started losing money and asked for contracts to be renegotiated in an effort either to move away (partly or fully) from oil indexation in favor of spot prices or to reduce (or abolish) the minimum volumes that importers have to pay for in a given year—or both.[10] The process of renegotiation was apparently quick with some exporters (especially Norway's Statoil) but long and painful with Gazprom, which defended the old model until all its major clients in Europe (and its historic strategic partners) had taken it to arbitration. Whether Gazprom would have lost in the courts is unclear, but any victory

Figure 7.1. British Spot Price, Oil-Indexed Price, and Average German
Import Price

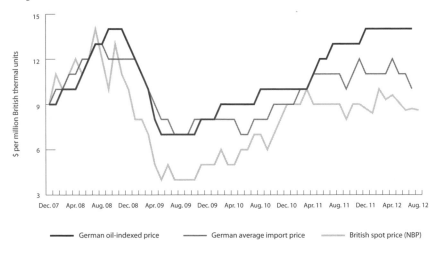

Sources: Data from Bloomberg and German Federal Ministry of Trade. Oil-indexed formula is
from Howard Rogers of the Oxford Institute for Energy Studies.

would have been a pyrrhic one: European utilities could always bankrupt
their money-losing gas businesses, which would be another way of terminating the import contracts.

The commoditization of gas is a self-reinforcing process. As more and
more gas is sold and bought on hubs, liquidity increases and prices become
more credible, thereby reducing the rationale for oil indexation and even
for long-term contracts. Therefore, the transition away from long-term oil-
indexed contracts is unlikely to be reversed, although important barriers to
the emergence of liquid and deep spot and forward markets in Northwestern Europe remain.[11]

Shale Gas in Western Europe: A Stillborn Revolution?

Interestingly, the globalization of Western European gas is raising new security concerns. In the United Kingdom, a rapid transition is under way
from self-sufficiency to large-scale imports; this change has made gas sup-

Figure 7.2. LNG Imports into Europe by Exporters and Importers, 1999–2011

a. Exporters

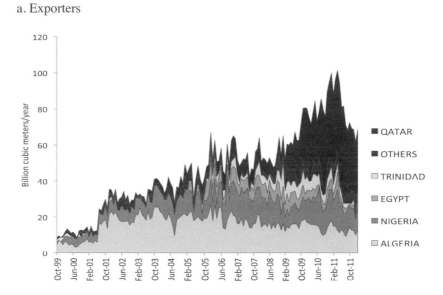

b. Importers

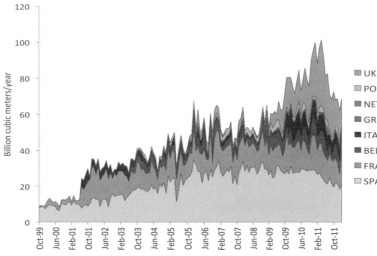

Sources: Data from Poten Partners Database and Bloomberg.

ply security one of the main issues in the energy policy discourse for nearly a decade. The market has delivered massive new import capacity, thanks to pipelines from both Norway and the continent and large LNG terminals, which ensure a diversified supply and access to the international market. Studies—including some commissioned by the government—have shown that the level of security of supply enjoyed by the British market remains very high despite the transition to imports.[12] UK politicians, however, are concerned about growing import dependence from a limited number of LNG suppliers (mostly in Africa or the Middle East) and their perception that the United Kingdom now requires a higher level of underground storage. Another concern is potential competition with East Asia for supply in a global market with intercontinental LNG arbitrage.

The winners in the UK gas security debate have been the shale gas explorers. Since Cuadrilla Resources made what it says is a major discovery in Lancashire in September 2011, the United Kingdom has been the most promising country in Europe for shale gas production. Exploration work was suspended after seismic activity induced by hydraulic fracturing was reported, but the government allowed companies to resume work in late 2012. The United Kingdom enjoys a relatively wide political consensus that, given the right regulatory framework and scrutiny, a new source of indigenous gas production is a good thing for the country. Britain may be the first place in Europe where shale gas is produced commercially. It is too early, however, to tell whether shale gas will have a discernible effect on UK gas supply; local opposition, which runs very high in prospective areas, could still derail it, just as local opposition is preventing serious exploitation of the country's onshore wind potential.

Elsewhere in Western Europe, the shale gas potential looks increasingly unlikely to materialize. A 2012 report by the International Energy Agency (IEA) summarizes the situation in France, where most of Western Europe's reserves are located but where hydraulic fracturing was banned by a law passed nearly unanimously in parliament with support from the Sarkozy government.[13] This bleak situation has gotten even bleaker since publication of the IEA report, as hopes of a reopening of the issue were dashed early in the Hollande presidency in an energy policy speech by President François Hollande,[14] and the definite character of the ban was confirmed in the first of his six-monthly press conferences.[15] Extraordinary political developments would now be necessary for shale gas production to take off in France.[16] Other geologically promising countries, such as Sweden or Germany, have various combinations of a very low level of political support for shale gas, a very high level of public opposition, and disappointing exploration results. A point often missed by commentators—and completely overlooked by the IEA report—is that it is very difficult to build a political case for shale gas in countries where natural gas consumption is rapidly declining and the security of the gas supply is not considered a pressing issue. In the short to medium term, gas faces a very difficult situation because it is displaced by subsidized renewables and cheap coal in electricity generation and by electricity and efficiency investment in industrial and residential heating. In the longer term, energy policies in Europe are focused on deep decarbonization of the power and heat sectors, creating a significant challenge for natural gas.

Fundamental Alteration of European Company Relations with Gazprom

The commoditization and globalization of the Western European gas market is generating a high degree of frustration with Gazprom and Russia. Gazprom has long been—and to some extent still is—in denial about the transformation of the Western European gas market.[17] Sergei Komlev, head of contracts and price formation at Gazprom Export, has been touring the European conference circuit for more than three years defending the business model that all his large clients were suing Gazprom to reform. The Russian leadership has interpreted the transition away from long-term oil-indexed contracts as an anti-Russian move engineered by the European institutions.

Indeed, the globalization and commoditization of Western European gas have quickly and profoundly altered the 40-year-old relationship between Western European gas companies and Gazprom. They will have important political implications as continental European gas-importing companies—a powerful pro-Russian lobby with their national governments[18]—can be expected to become more indifferent. Over time, politicians in key countries, such as Germany, France, and Italy, will realize that a "special relationship" with Moscow brings little supply security benefits. This realization, in turn, should go some distance in bridging the East–West gap regarding perceptions of Russia and foreign policy approaches toward Moscow. The restructuring of the Western European gas industry will illustrate the power of marketization in alleviating the foreign policy liabilities of energy import dependence. Russian gas will certainly remain quantitatively important—its market share could actually increase if Gazprom shifts from a price strategy to a quantity strategy—but because Russian gas is economically contestable, it will become more politically tenable.[19] The big prize for Europe is the commoditization of gas east of Germany, Switzerland, and Italy. Progress there has been limited, however.

Little Changing in the East

In their first *Market Monitoring Report*, the EU's new Agency for the Cooperation of Energy Regulators (ACER) and the Council of European Energy Regulators (CEER), after describing the positive evolutions in Western European gas markets, acknowledge that

> a vast area of the Eastern and South-Eastern EU has no gas hubs and, being mostly landlocked, no LNG. This lack of sufficient diversity in supplies, coupled with little connectivity between national markets (and insufficient backhaul flows from the West), makes this region particularly vulnerable to security of supply and market abuse dangers.[20]

The idea that because a place is far away from the coast it has no LNG and hence little supply diversity is a stark recognition by ACER and CEER that there is no "European" gas market.[21] There is very little trade between East and West despite most of Central Europe sitting alongside large pipeline systems carrying Russian gas westward. Before 2009, no one ever mentioned the possibility of such trade. During the gas crisis, however, the supposedly impossible happened: some gas came from west to east.[22] For most of the countries of Central and Eastern Europe, their isolation from Western Europe has no physical cause.[23] The "Berlin Wall of Gas," as I have called it, which is the root cause of Europe's gas security problem, is a policy and regulatory issue. The problem has to do with the organization of the gas transport industry under EU rules; the gas policies of some countries in Central Europe; and specific legal arrangements, to which Russia is a party, which govern some large transit pipelines.

   In terms of European gas transport regulation, what is needed is the ability to contract for and trade in point-to-point transport capacity on long-distance pipelines, irrespective of national borders.[24] This situation may sound trivial to gas experts from North America, but it is anathema to EU regulators, because it falls foul of the market design chosen by the European Commission in the early 2000s and codified by the 2009 Third Energy Package.

A related and necessary change is opening access to three key transit pipelines that could make Russian gas contestable deep into Central Europe: the Yamal–Europe pipeline across Poland, the pipeline across Romania and Bulgaria and into Greece and Turkey, and the Trans Austria Gas pipeline across Austria into Italy. The current legal arrangements governing these pipelines, which Gazprom has used for years to prevent backhaul transactions from West to East, essentially amount to preventing the resale of Russian gas by Western European importers to companies in Central Europe—a practice that the EU banned long ago. In 2011, Poland renegotiated, with the help of the European Commission, the intergovernmental agreement with Russia that governs the operation of the Yamal pipeline. Although views diverged as to what exactly had been achieved—with the European Commission claiming that under the new agreement backhaul transactions would be possible, while Polish officials were less sure—very little seems to have happened since that would suggest a serious restructuring.[25]

Finally, there is a need for deregulation of wholesale gas markets in Central European countries. In Poland and Romania—to take two of the largest gas markets in the region—the price of gas is maintained way below the import price through a weighted average of imports from Russia and gas produced locally, the latter being sold at prices close to its cost.[26] Such practices amount to subsidizing imports from Russia; they also destroy incentives to bring non-Russian gas in from Western Europe.

Since 2009, so much spot-priced gas has been looking for a way to reach consumers in Central and Eastern Europe—who are captives of oil-indexed gas—that any significant progress on the aforementioned issues would have transformed these markets and with them the European gas security landscape. The only market where spot-priced gas has indeed put serious pressure on oil-indexed contracts is the Czech Republic, which is directly connected to Germany, and to a lesser extent Austria and Slovakia, which are along the same pipeline system.

The paradox is that the EU and national governments have had big plans for gas market integration and security of supply in Central Europe. They have been discussing investments into various pipelines and LNG terminals that are supposed to give the region access to non-Russian gas—such as Nabucco or the Krk terminal in Croatia—or to increase interconnection between national markets. Some of these interconnectors have been

built—for example, between Hungary and Romania.[27] However, most
of these projects, starting with the flagship Nabucco pipeline, have been
shelved or abandoned because they were fundamentally not economical.
There are new ideas and projects (for the Baltic states, the Danube region,
the North–South Gas Corridor, etc.) but they all are more or less conceived
on the same flawed model of subsidizing infrastructure to complete the
internal market to ensure security of supply. In terms of completing the
market, very serious progress can be made, without building anything, by
reforming EU regulatory concepts and national gas policies, as we have
seen. In countries that are out of reach of a decently functioning European
gas market, such as the Baltic states, insuring against the risk of gas supply disruption can be done relatively cheaply without Brussels subsidizing
uneconomical pipelines.[28]

In the meantime, the limited progress in integrating Western and Eastern
Europe has political implications. First, it contributes to entrenching Central European governments' resistance to the EU climate change policy. Unless gas supply security improves, such countries will be highly reluctant to
let gas displace coal—and the larger economies of Central Europe, such as
Poland and the Czech Republic, are very coal intensive.[29] Beyond energy
policy, the persistence of gas supply insecurity could fuel resentment vis-
à-vis Brussels and Western European countries, thus playing into the hands
of nationalist and, in some countries, pro-Russian political forces.

Large-scale unconventional gas production in Central Europe would
make the European pipeline regulatory failure less critical. However, hopes
have been seriously dampened recently by disappointing exploration results, including those in Poland. In December 2012, ExxonMobil, a leading
foreign participant in the sector, decided to pull out and sold its exploration
licenses to a local company after concluding that the gas it found could
not be exploited economically.[30] In other countries, public opposition runs
high, and Bulgaria (like France) banned hydraulic fracturing. It is certainly
too early to write off unconventional gas as a significant source of supply in
Central and Eastern Europe, but this source is unlikely to make a difference
in the coming 10 to 15 years.

The Bypassing of Ukraine

The building by Gazprom and Western European energy companies of
large undersea pipeline systems that bypass the Ukrainian transit corridor

is one of the most consequential developments of this decade for European gas. The first line of Nord Stream, linking Russia to Germany under the Baltic Sea, was completed in June 2011. Once the second line is finished, the system will have an annual capacity of 55 bcm, nearly 15 percent of total European gas consumption and more than a third of Russian exports to Europe. A final investment decision was made on the building of South Stream under the Black Sea on November 14, 2012. Once finished, South Stream's capacity will be 63 bcm per year. Therefore, by 2015 or 2017, Gazprom and its partners will have created enough shipping capacity to bypass Ukraine entirely, assuming Russian exports to be around 150 bcm per year.[31]

The economics of the bypassing of Ukraine are complex, and its political implications are profound. Financial economist Chi Kong Chyong has shown that Nord Stream is a profitable investment under almost any scenario of European gas consumption.[32] The value of the pipeline system derives mostly from not paying the Ukrainian transit fee, which over three decades more than repays the capital cost. The economics of South Stream are more complex: it only becomes profitable if Ukraine is incapable of credible commitments on gas import prices and transit fees.[33] Gazprom has an incentive to prepare the groundwork for South Stream—which it has been doing for several years—in order to discipline Ukraine. However, if Ukraine becomes convinced that Gazprom will bypass it entirely at any cost, then its winning strategy is to violate its long-term commitments and try to maximize the rent from its transit monopoly before that rent disappears—thereby triggering the building of South Stream.[34] Again, this scenario fits very well with the sequence of events since the signing of the Ukraine–Russia agreements that put an end to the crisis of January 2009.

For Ukraine, the implications will be very serious. The value of its gas transit infrastructure will be brought to zero, depriving Naftogaz of billions of dollars in annual revenue. Ukraine is by far the largest of Gazprom's export markets that is entirely captive. Its transit monopoly acted as a check against Russia's market power. Ukraine now will have a choice between paying very high gas prices and experiencing creeping reintegration into Moscow's political orbit. Sustained high prices would reduce consumption, which will be painful, will be politically costly, and will create alternative supply options. The most promising are the development of its important conventional and unconventional gas potential, including shale gas; imports from Western Europe using existing (and increasingly under-

utilized) infrastructure;[35] and LNG imports on the Black Sea. All of these
options require serious institutional reforms of the energy industry—notably to allow meaningful, long-term involvement of foreign investors—that
have proved elusive for 20 years.[36]

The bypassing of Ukraine transfers rent from Kyiv to Moscow. It also
removes Ukraine's ability to take Europe hostage in its gas bargaining with
Moscow, a shared interest of the EU and Russia. However, Russia and the
EU may not have the same preferences regarding the political future of
Ukraine. In that respect, the bypassing pipelines will force Ukraine's ruling elite to reveal their true strategic preferences. If they are serious about
their Euro–Atlantic choice (or, more basically, their choice to be a viable,
sovereign, and democratic country), they will have to implement profound
and very difficult institutional and political reforms that would—among
many other benefits—allow Ukraine to move away from its perverse gas
relationship with Russia and become a modern energy economy. Europe
(and others) can help, and the structural weakening of Ukraine will make
real conditionality possible. Over the past decade the EU has been very na-
ive in its engagement of Ukraine, and Kyiv has been expert at making the
best of this naiveté.[37] This game is now over. Gazprom's bypassing project
is truly a game changer.

Summary and Conclusions

Since the European gas supply crisis of January 2009, the diversification of
gas supply in Western Europe has accelerated. Rapid and profound change
in the economic organization of the industry has followed, with short-term
markets playing a much bigger role. Russian gas is now contestable everywhere in Northwestern Europe, including northern Germany. Large importers of Russian gas have lost their captive customer base in their home
markets and therefore are loosening and marketizing their relationship with
Gazprom. Finally, the bypassing of Ukraine removes the single biggest risk
of gas supply disruption to EU countries.

Conversely, there has been little progress in integrating Western and
Eastern Europe by reforming the regulation and operation of the large
existing long-distance gas pipeline infrastructure. The model promoted
by Brussels for completing the internal market is the longest and most
complex route possible to a destination that could be approached, if not
reached, quickly through simpler alternative regulatory reforms. Simi-

larly, Brussels has failed to incentivize member states to invest in increasing the resilience of their energy systems to gas supply disruptions. The new regulation on gas supply security, despite its extreme complexity and apparent sophistication, will not be more effective than the directive it replaced. Improvements to EU gas supply security have been delivered mostly from the outside. If only they could be met by comparable progress from the inside, Europe's gas security problem could become history. We are not there yet.

Dependence on Russian gas remains an acute political problem in countries such as the Baltic states, where it is perceived as the last vestige of the preindependence era. However, economic calculations show that these countries could buy high levels of insurance against risks of supply disruption at a reasonable cost.[38] In Central Europe, governments should stop regulating wholesale gas markets and lobby Brussels to amend the Gas Target Model in a way that would allow point-to-point capacity trading on long-distance pipelines. Meanwhile, they should seriously assess their short-term resilience to gas supply disruptions and implement cost-effective measures to improve it.[39] In Ukraine, the country's ruling elite must decide whether they want to address their dependence on Russian gas through institutional and legal reform of the energy sector or through creeping, de facto reintegration into Moscow's political orbit. Being bypassed as a transit corridor, they can no longer address this issue by blackmailing Gazprom and taking Europe hostage.

That said, EU natural gas consumption peaked in 2005 and is now declining everywhere in Europe. In the residential sector, high gas prices and efficiency policies have triggered efficiency investment and fuel switching. Industrial demand is also switching to electricity or moving out of Europe altogether. Power generation should be a growth market for gas given Europe's climate change objectives and reliance on coal. However, the aggressive deployment of highly subsidized renewables (wind and solar), the fall in coal prices (in part because of the US shale gas revolution), and the collapse of the EU carbon price (compounded by renewable deployment) have made gas uneconomical as a fuel for power generation. In the large markets of Western Europe that account for the bulk of demand and imports, Russian exports have been severely hit by the combination of growing LNG availability, Norway's willingness to move to spot pricing, and declining consumption. For most of Europe, dependence on Russian gas is unlikely to be an important determinant of the continent's economic and security situation in the coming years.

Notes

1. Ole Wæver, "Securitization and Desecuritization," in *On Security*, ed. Ronnie D. Lipschutz (New York: Columbia University Press, 1995), 46–86.

2. For an exception, see Jonathan Stern, *The Future of Russian Gas and Gazprom* (Oxford, UK: Oxford University Press, 2005), 86–96.

3. Pierre Noël, "Beyond Dependence: How to Deal with Russian Gas," ECFR Policy Brief 9, European Council on Foreign Relations, London, 2008.

4. Russian gas represented 80 percent of imports in 1980 against 35 percent today. See Noël, "Beyond Dependence."

5. Regulation (EU) 994/2010 of October 20, 2010. The full text of the regulation is available at http://eur-lex.europa.eu/LexUriServ/LexUriServ.do?uri=OJ:L:2010:295: 0001:0022:EN:PDF.

6. For a detailed critique of the regulation, see Pierre Noël and Sachi Findlater, "On the Draft Regulation on Gas Supply Security," memo to the European Commission, Electronic Policy Research Group, University of Cambridge, Cambridge, UK, 2009. See also Pierre Noël, "Ensuring Success for the EU Regulation on Gas Supply Security," Occasional Paper, Electronic Policy Research Group, University of Cambridge, Cambridge, UK, 2010; Pierre Noël, "The EU Regulation on Gas Supply Security (994/2010): A Case Study in EU Energy Policy-Making," presented to the Electronic Policy Research Group–National Economic Research Associates Winter Seminar, University of Cambridge, Cambridge, UK, December 9, 2011.

7. Such harmonization, a task of immense complexity, is at the heart of implementing the so-called EU Third Liberalization Package.

8. European regulators themselves acknowledge this difficulty.

9. European Commission, "On Security of Energy Supply and International Cooperation: 'The EU Energy Policy—Engaging with Partners beyond Our Borders,'" COM(2011) 539 Final, Brussels, 2011.

10. Jonathan Stern and Howard Rogers, "The Transition to Hub-Based Gas Pricing in Continental Europe," Oxford Institute for Energy Studies, Oxford, UK, 2011.

11. These barriers include the continuing regulation of storage (which may actually come back to the United Kingdom instead of being abandoned in continental Europe); a lack of political understanding and support for gas market integration; a lack of trust between the British and continental governments (especially the French, German, and Belgian governments) on gas matters; and, finally, a flawed EU model for gas transport regulation and pricing (as I have already mentioned and will return to later).

12. See the excellent report by Pöyry Energy Consulting, *GB Gas Security of Supply and Options for Improvements: A Report to Department of Energy and Climate Change* (Oxford, UK: Pöyry Energy Consulting, 2010), https://www.gov.uk/government /uploads/system/uploads/attachment_data/file/47872/114-poyry-gb.pdf.

13. IEA, *Golden Rules for a Golden Age of Gas: World Energy Outlook Special Report on Unconventional Gas* (Paris, OECD/IEA, 2012), 122–30.

14. The speech, delivered on September 14, 2012, is available (in French) at http:// bit.ly/W8T1zq.

15. President Hollande held the press conference on November 13, 2012. The transcript of his remarks is available at http://bit.ly/VOfBgm.

16. The IEA report states, "In the Golden Age Case, we assumed a reversal of the ban on hydraulic fracturing. Shale gas production rises after 2020 to reach 8 bcm in

2035." Given the politics of shale gas in France, this scenario should be considered highly speculative. See IEA, *Golden Rules for a Golden Age of Gas*, 126.

17. In June 2010, Alexei Miller, the chairman of Gazprom's Management Committee, was still trying to convince audiences that LNG was no competitive threat to Gazprom. See Alexei Miller, "Natural Gas: Energy of the 21st Century," speech at the 13th Annual General Assembly of the European Business Congress, Cannes, France, June 10–11, 2010.

18. See Rawi Abdelal, "The Profits of Power: Commerce and Realpolitik in Eurasia," *Review of International Political Economy* (published online April 3, 2012): 1–36.

19. Pierre Noël, "A Market Between Us: Reducing the Political Cost of Europe's Dependence on Russian Gas," EPRG Working Paper 0916, Electricity Policy Research Group, University of Cambridge, Cambridge, UK, 2009.

20. ACER and CEER, *Annual Report on the Results of Monitoring the Internal Electricity and Natural Gas Markets in 2011* (Ljubljana and Brussels: ACER and CEER, 2012), 122.

21. Would the US Federal Energy Regulatory Commission write that San Francisco has no access to shale gas or that because Illinois is landlocked it lacks access to LNG?

22. Mostly this gas came from intracompany flows carried out by Gaz de France and E.ON to supply their affiliates in Central Europe.

23. The remote and tiny Baltic States are an exception. See Sachi Findlater and Pierre Noël, "Gas Supply Security in the Baltic States: A Qualitative Assessment," *International Journal of Energy Sector Management* 4, no. 2 (2010): 236–55.

24. See Paul Hunt, "Entry–Exit Transmission Pricing with Notional Hubs: Can It Deliver a Pan-European Wholesale Market in Gas?" Oxford Institute for Energy Studies, Oxford, UK, 2008. See also Graham Shuttleworth and Jeff Makholm, "Foundation for Regulating Pipelines," presented at the Florence School of Regulation Summer Course on Regulation of Energy Utilities, Florence Italy, 2011; David Newbery, "State of the Union: Achieving the Internal Market," presented at the European Energy Market Conference on State of the Union: Energy Policy, Florence Italy, May 10, 2012.

25. Recently, the competition authorities of the EU launched proceedings against Gazprom after raiding its offices in various countries of Central and Eastern Europe. Although little is known about the grievances, contractual practices amounting to resale restrictions (mimicking the defunct destination clauses) are probably part of what the European Commission is after.

26. Romania also bans the export of locally produced gas, a practice one finds hard to reconcile with the very basic principles of European economic law and the idea of a single market—but Brussels seems to tolerate it.

27. Market participants say that little trade is actually happening.

28. See Pierre Noël, Sachi Findlater, and Chi Kong Chyong, "The Cost of Improving Gas Supply Security in the Baltic States," EPRG Working Paper 1203, Electricity Policy Research Group, University of Cambridge, Cambridge, UK, 2012.

29. Both Poland and the Czech Republic have civilian nuclear programs, but those programs will not make a difference for at least a decade (maybe closer to two), if they ever do.

30. "Exxon Sells Shale Gas Licenses to Polish Refiner PKN," *Reuters*, December 7, 2012. Separately, in March 2012, a report by the Polish Geological Institute estimated the country's reserves to be a 10th of the number published in the widely quoted

study sponsored by the US Department of Energy's Energy Information Administration in April 2011. See IEA, *Golden Rules for a Golden Age of Gas*, 123–24. However, Chevron continues with exploration under a separate Polish license.

31. See Chi Kong Chyong, "Gazprom's Bypass Strategy and Russo–Ukrainian Gas Bargaining: South Stream Case Study," presentation at the Electricity Policy Research Group, University of Cambridge, Cambridge, UK, 2012, 5.

32. Chi Kong Chyong, Pierre Noël, and David M. Reiner, "The Economics of the Nord Stream Pipeline System," EPRG Working Paper 1026, Electricity Policy Research Group, University of Cambridge, Cambridge, UK, 2010.

33. Chyong, "Gazprom's Bypass Strategy."

34. Chyong, "Gazprom's Bypass Strategy."

35. In 2012, several transactions were realized. See "Ukraine Starts to Import Some Gas from Western Europe," *Reuters*, November 6, 2012.

36. Edward Chow and Jonathan Elkind, "Where East Meets West: European Gas and Ukrainian Reality," *Washington Quarterly* 32 (January 2009): 77–92.

37. See Marine Confavreux Zimmermann, "Securing Gas Transit? Co-operation between the European Commission and Ukraine" (MPhil diss., University of Cambridge, 2012).

38. Noël, Findlater, and Chyong, "Cost of Improving Gas Supply Security." The Baltic States could also move away from Russian gas altogether through a single buyer for LNG, but doing so would violate EU law. See Pierre Noël, "Singapore, Helsinki, or Brussels: Policy Approaches to Baltic Gas Security," presentation at the Electricity Policy Research Group–Center for Energy and Environmental Policy Research Annual Conference, Stockholm, July 12, 2012, http://bit.ly/13eZPBx.

39. We had tried to do this for Bulgaria. See Florent Silve and Pierre Noël, "Cost Curves for Gas Supply Security: The Case of Bulgaria," EPRG Working Paper 1031, Electricity Policy Research Group, University of Cambridge, Cambridge, UK, 2010.

Chapter 8

Russia and Eurasia

Julia Nanay and Jan H. Kalicki

A New Landscape

Russia and the countries of Eurasia have faced dramatically changing oil and gas market conditions since 2008, when the oil price spiked to $145 a barrel in July only to plunge to $39 a barrel the following February. The price has risen steadily since, and although the region's oil and gas export-reliant economies have breathed a collective sigh of relief, their dependence on high oil prices will create future vulnerabilities.

Many of these countries are on the verge of costly investments in new, complex oil and gas projects and export infrastructure, the payoffs from which may not be realized until a decade out, when the oil and gas price environment may be influenced by increased unconventional resource supplies in the United States and elsewhere. For Russia, this means expensive new investments in fields and infrastructure in East Siberia, the Yamal Peninsula, the Timan-Pechora Basin, and offshore. In Azerbaijan, new Caspian gas field investments and the construction of gas export pipelines to the West are underway. For Kazakhstan, the next phases of several giant projects—Kashagan, Tengiz, Karachaganak, the Caspian Pipeline Consortium (CPC) pipeline, and an intensive domestic gasification program—will require enormous capital commitments and continued effective risk management.

In Turkmenistan, the next phases of its giant onshore Galkynysh gas field are soon to be targeted for major outlays. Uzbekistan is looking for investors as it continues to struggle with meeting domestic energy demand while trying to free up more natural gas for export. And Ukraine, confronted with Russian gas pipeline bypasses that will increase its supply vulnerabilities, is finally opening its own resources to investors.

Greater energy self-sufficiency in the United States, lessened European gas demand, and rising Asian oil and gas demand will spur reassessments on project selection, timing, and investor roles. As long as oil prices remain at reasonably high levels, governments will feel that they can dictate the terms of engagement. Conversely, they cannot control the shifting market conditions that underpin investment decisions.

Radical Supply Shifts

Changed Western market realities, for example, have completely upended Russia's vision for the next generation of the country's gas export projects. Russia will now need to become a more significant supplier of liquefied natural gas (LNG) to Asia in addition to its traditional role of piping gas to Europe.

Gearing up for the highly competitive Asian gas trade will pose challenges, especially when significant growth in Russian LNG supplies may be a decade away and some projects will be based in harsh Arctic settings with high hurdle rates. In earlier LNG project planning stages, Gazprom was banking on sales to the United States, where it had built a staff and thought it understood the market. That was before 2010, when the United States and Russia began to rival each other as the world's largest gas producers. The shale gas revolution has transformed the United States from a gas buyer to a gas producer and global market influencer, tempering rising price expectations. Not only has this shift ended Russian LNG plans for the US market, but its effects are already reverberating in European markets as well.

Because the United States no longer needs to import LNG, US-bound supplies can now be sent to Europe and Asia. More LNG in Europe, in turn, has helped drive spot gas prices lower on the continent and caused Gazprom to reduce its prices in 2011 and 2012, thereby cutting into its margins, even as it embarks on numerous expensive upstream and infrastructure projects.[1] In addition, under the Third Energy Package, a legislative package for an internal gas and electricity market that has been adopted by the European Union (EU), competition rules call for equal access to EU markets (including by other Russian companies) at the same time as they require Gazprom to unbundle its pipeline assets from its gas supplies.

While Gazprom's European business will need to adapt to EU competition mandates, the United States, by 2017, will likely be exporting LNG, before Gazprom can count on exports from its Vladivostok LNG project to Asian customers. The US rise as a force in global gas markets already poses challenges for Russia, but these problems will be more acute if exports from the United States, together with giant projects in Australia and elsewhere, come to dominate Asian markets.

One likely scenario will be increased pressure on long-term natural gas contracts in the region. This will likely occur as increased LNG becomes available from Australia, Turkmenistan continues to increase its natural gas supplies to China and conceivably the Asian subcontinent, and Qatar possibly moves in the future to lift its moratorium on increased natural gas production and LNG exports. Given Gazprom's historic opposition to shorter-term or spot pricing for natural gas in Europe, it would be ironic if increased Russian LNG supplies undermined long-term contracts and accelerated natural gas price competition in Asia. This will likely be a longer-term process, however, because of the lead time required for Russian exports and Moscow's need to shore up Asian confidence in the reliability of its supply. Failure to agree on gas pricing with China, as well as Russian price and supply disputes with Belarus, Turkmenistan, and Ukraine, will affect Asian consumer perceptions of Russian supplies, requiring Russia to review not only its gas export strategy but also its chosen instruments—from companies to contracts—for carrying it out.

The US-driven changes in global gas markets are also affecting oil. By stepping up domestic production of shale oil, the previously high US dependence on imported crude, which reached 8.5 million barrels per day (mmbpd) in 2012,[2] will be markedly reduced. Interestingly, 18 percent of East Siberia–Pacific Ocean (ESPO) crude exports from the Far East port of Kozmino were shipped to the United States in 2012—placing it just behind Japan and China. This picture has changed radically as US imports diminish and Chinese imports will increase, in light of the June 21, 2013, agreements between Rosneft and CNPC, and after a planned pipeline spur expansion is completed from ESPO to the Chinese border.[3] Russia and, in particular, Kazakhstan and

Turkmenistan will seek increasingly to drive their oil and gas exports toward high-demand countries in Asia, such as China, India, Japan, and South Korea.

Russia has been more successful in diversifying toward Asian markets with oil than with gas. Operational in December 2012, the second phase of Russian state monopoly Transneft's ESPO oil pipeline has the capacity to transport 600,000 barrels per day (bpd) to Kozmino,[4] with about 420,000 bpd expected to be shipped in 2013, 480,000 to 500,000 bpd in 2014, and 600,000 bpd in 2015.[5] Since 2009, Russian state oil company Rosneft has been shipping 300,000 bpd through a pipeline spur to China under ESPO's first phase. With nearly 1 mmbpd of Russian export capacity for oil to move to the east, sizable oil flows will be directed away from Europe.

This trend toward increased Russian oil exports to Asia was reinforced during President Xi Jinping's March 2013 visit to Moscow, when Rosneft committed to nearly double its supplies to the China National Petroleum Corporation (CNPC) over 25 years and then secured a $2 billion long-term loan from the China Development Bank. The loan will help finance its recent purchase of TNK-BP, which in turn has made Rosneft the world's largest publicly traded oil company. However, Rosneft's increased supply to CNPC will require a second pipeline link, triggering a significant dispute with Transneft, which does not wish to divert resources from ESPO's terminus and demands that Rosneft cover the entire expense of additional pipeline transport to China, thus introducing new fissures in the state energy establishment. At the St. Petersburg Economic Forum on June 21, 2013, Rosneft and CNPC solidified their relationship when they signed an Intergovernmental Agreement that committed Rosneft to supply CNPC with an additional 365 million tons of oil over 25 years, equivalent to 14.6 million tons per year (280,000 bpd) in return for a sizeable prepayment.

In 2013 the largest purchaser of ESP crude exports was Japan, followed by China, South Korea, the Phillippines, Singapore, and (now in sixth place) the United States with just 6.1 percent.[6] If US imports continue to decline and, under the June 2013 CNPC–Rosneft agreement, Chinese imports continue to increase, this picture could shift radically. Instead of the United States as a preferred destination, the focus will be increasingly on high-demand countries in Asia, such as China, India, Japan, and South Korea. Not only Russia but also, to a degree, Kazakhstan will compete with Middle East exporters, including Iran, if and when it circumvents or emerges from sanctions.

For Eurasia, the export picture differs between the eastern and western Caspian countries. Since 2009, countries to the east have begun orienting greater volumes of their oil and gas to China, which has financed and built infrastructure to promote these flows. On the western side, namely Azerbaijan, the target markets for oil and gas are in the west, accessed largely through Georgia to Turkey and Europe.

Azerbaijan and its national oil and gas company SOCAR (State Oil Company of the Azerbaijan Republic) have relied on international oil companies (IOCs) to finance and build its infrastructure projects, whereas Kazakhstan has relied on IOCs working with its national oil company, KazMunaiGaz (KMG), and Russia's state pipeline company, Transneft, for its major oil exports through Russia and, more recently, on Chinese banks and state companies for networks to the east. Turkmenistan has relied increasingly on Chinese companies and banks, although it is now seeking to diversify its exports, such as to South Asia. In the future, Russian exporters will also be forced to compete with Turkmen supplies of up to 65 billion cubic meters (bcm) per year to China. Furthermore, Iran has participated in the financing and construction of a smaller second gas export pipeline from Turkmenistan that opened in 2010.

US companies so far have their major oil-producing and oil infrastructure investments in Kazakhstan. The TengizChevroil (TCO) joint venture was the region's first major contract.[7] Signed in 1993, it has become the country's flagship oil project, accounting for more than one-third of current national output. TCO has been coupled with the CPC export network to the Russian Black Sea port of Novorossiysk. CPC's planned doubling of capacity to more than 1.4 mmbpd by 2015 will create the region's largest oil export pipeline. US companies also participate in Kazakhstan's onshore Karachaganak gas and condensate field,[8] one of the biggest gas fields in Eurasia, and in the offshore Kashagan oil field,[9] the world's largest oil discovery since Alaska's Prudhoe Bay.

US Responses to the New Regional Landscape

The United States has tied its energy-related foreign policy in Russia and Eurasia largely to three factors, none of which involves direct dependence on imports from this region. First, Washington sees the states of Eurasia as critical geopolitically—adjoining not only Russia and China, but also the Middle East and Southwest Asia, whose independence from their larger and more powerful neighbors should be strongly supported. From Eurasia, pipelines can bring new supply sources to global markets. Also, until the North Atlantic Treaty Organization (NATO) military presence ends in Afghanistan, Eurasia remains an important military transshipment route to and from that conflict area. Second, Russia and other oil-producing countries of Eurasia, none of which are members of the Organization of the Petroleum Exporting Countries (OPEC), are important for the development and delivery of reliable oil and gas supplies to meet the needs of global markets at a reasonable cost. An added bonus is that a number of oil and gas projects are driven by US and EU companies. Third, US commercial interests in Azerbaijan, Kazakhstan, Russia, and Ukraine keep Washington engaged with possible future involvement of US energy companies in Turkmenistan and Uzbekistan.

The United States has made promoting energy supply diversification through new pipeline routes a key function of its involvement in Eurasia.[10] Hence, the United States supports EU efforts to create more transparent and interconnected gas markets across the continent and to bring gas from Azerbaijan and Turkmenistan to European consumers, bypassing Iran and Russia. Washington also wants to see a North–South energy and trade corridor—a new Silk Road—develop from Central Asia for gas and other supplies to Afghanistan, Pakistan, and India, thereby providing economic development opportunities and a measure of stability for these countries after 2014, when US forces are drawn down from Afghanistan. Turkey, a NATO ally, has been a key pipeline and policy partner in the southern Caspian for projects orienting toward the West, and it now plays a growing role vis-à-vis Iran and the wider Middle East, despite growing political unrest under the Erdogan government.

In the broader energy sphere, the United States recognizes Russia's and Eurasia's oil market stabilizing role. Overall oil production in Russia, Azerbaijan, Kazakhstan, and Turkmenistan reached an estimated 13 mmbpd in 2012, with the majority from Russia, which produced nearly 10.4 mmbpd (exceeding peak Soviet output) in 2012.[11] Russia's output rivals that of OPEC's Saudi Arabia, and together they have an undeniably critical role in keeping markets well supplied. In 2012, Russia, Azerbaijan, Kazakhstan, and Turkmenistan exported about 6.5 mmbpd of crude to world markets, although only a little more than 1 mmbpd was through non-Russian routes.[12] Oil export levels from Russia and the Caspian region approach those of Saudi Arabia, which sells just over 7 mmbpd abroad. Thus, these oil exports complement Saudi exports, and both are essential to the stability of global markets. If Kazakhstan's Kashagan oil field reaches its full potential, regional exports could increase markedly, exceeding volumes from Saudi Arabia, unless, of course, the Kingdom increases its own export capacity as it has considered doing in the past.

Perhaps the biggest US policy challenge in Eurasia will be to maintain the continued, longer-term commitment required by both energy and geopolitical realities. After combat forces withdraw from Afghanistan, as challenges increase in the Middle East and other regions, and as domestic budget pressures mount, there may well be less patience for high-level political and economic support. Yet its countries' contribution to global energy security and to continued balance among Russia, China, the Middle East, and Europe, as well as the region's limited capacity to withstand independently the pressures of their neighbors and a possibly increased Islamic extremist threat, call for continued US and Western engagement, not only in the public sphere but also in the private sphere.

Regional Responses to the New Realities

Azerbaijan and Kazakhstan, with the active involvement of IOCs, jointly produce about 2.5 mmbpd of crude. UK-led[13] and US-led consortia dominate oil production and oil export projects in these two countries. The region's second most important gas producer and exporter, after Russia, is Turkmenistan, and in future years, Azerbaijan will become an important gas producer and exporter as well.

Although the global market will continue to be strong for oil exports from all parts of the region, gas markets are not yet unified and will offer greater returns to the suppliers that make the first inroads and secure the first contracts. As David Victor shows in chapter 3 of this volume, Asian markets are a particularly good example of price differentials in long-term contracts, even if these differentials can be expected to erode over time. Thus, Russia, Kazakhstan, and Turkmenistan—as well as other leading gas suppliers such as Australia, Qatar, and potentially the United States—are greatly interested in which countries secure contracts in Asia currently that may tend to crowd out other suppliers later. Teaming up with foreign gas producers and marketers, BG, BP, Chevron, Eni, ExxonMobil, and Shell, for example, can substantially increase their global market prospects and will, in turn, have significant long-term bearing for Russian and Eurasian relations with the US and EU governments.

In the near term, with sufficient new investment, Russian companies will be able to sustain oil production by developing new fields in the Timan-Pechora Basin, East Siberia, and the Yamal Peninsula. In the longer term, however, Russia will need the technology, money, and management skills that only foreign investors can bring to develop onshore tight oil, shale oil and shale gas, and deposits located offshore.

Russia's continental shelf is the largest in the world: its combined territory—not counting the Arctic Lomonosov Ridge, which Russia claims—exceeds 2.4 million square miles, of which more than 1.5 million may yield oil and gas, with the majority of resources expected to be in the Kara and Barents Seas. Although the offshore area is likely to hold some oil, the larger part of reserves and production will likely be gas.[14] Arctic gas projects will be expensive, given the region's harsh drilling conditions and remote locations. In a world that may be increasingly awash in cheaper shale gas—alongside cheaper LNG developments in other less challenging regions—Arctic gas may have a hard time competing, whereas onshore tight and shale oil could also come to compete with Arctic oil.[15]

In April 2012, to encourage more rapid development of the Arctic with the help of foreign investors, the Russian government proposed a series of tax incentives that investors hope will be enacted in 2013, despite a history of fits and starts in the state tax regime. Production from new shelf developments will receive varying levels of beneficial treatment depending on location and development challenges linked to field depth, ice conditions, and required infrastructure.[16]

Despite pressures from nonstate companies, offshore licenses are still reserved for Russia's national oil companies, Rosneft and Gazprom. Unless and until this situation changes, foreign investors have to partner with these companies. In turn, Rosneft and Gazprom are increasingly rivals over new shelf licenses. With up to 20 percent of Russia's gas output by 2020, Rosneft also is already challenging Gazprom's export monopoly over gas.

Rosneft rapidly concluded three joint ventures for the offshore areas after the pending tax incentives were unveiled, the first two in April 2012 with ExxonMobil and Eni, and the third in May 2012 with Statoil. At first glance, all three arrangements benefit, at least initially, Rosneft, which receives 66.67 percent in each of the three joint ventures, seemingly free, with its costs carried by its partners in the offshore exploration phase. In contrast, Rosneft's partners will hope to recoup their share of benefits in the production phase and from other Russian fields. ExxonMobil (which expanded its Arctic acreage access in February 2013) will explore in the Kara, Chukchi, Laptev, and Black Seas; Statoil in the Barents and Okhotsk Seas; and Eni in the Barents and Black Seas. Rosneft will also join its IOC partners in projects outside Russia. In the case of ExxonMobil, they will work together in the United States and Canada. Eni will potentially work with Rosneft in North Africa and Europe, and Statoil will work with Rosneft in the Norwegian Barents Sea. Each foreign partner can bring advantages to Rosneft for its domestic technology, capital, and project management needs, as well as for its overseas ambitions.

For the foreign partners, Rosneft brings greater access to key onshore projects, most immediately in West Siberia's tight oil and heavy oil deposits and in southern Russia's oil shale, for which these companies expect to receive tax concessions. In signing these deals, Russia picked three partners that have the experience or access it seeks beyond offshore exploration expertise and technology. In the case of ExxonMobil, for example, which has increased its unconventional oil and gas development capacity since acquiring the US company XTO Energy in 2009, Russia wants technology for unconventional fossil fuels such as the huge Bazhenov formation in West Siberia, which may hold more tight oil than the giant US Bakken shale play in North Dakota. Tight oil development requires the same horizontal well and hydrofracturing methods that are used for shale gas, and the hardest to recover (including Bazhenov and Achimov) would qualify for zero mineral export tax for up to 15 years under government proposals before the Duma.[17]

Statoil is second in the European gas market after Gazprom, which wishes to cooperate with the Norwegian company because Europe is still key for Russian gas. Eni is partnering with Gazprom in the Blue Stream gas pipeline to Turkey and in building the South Stream gas pipeline to Southeastern and Central Europe and Italy. Rosneft is seeking to work with Eni in Algeria, which is Europe's third-largest gas supplier after Russia and Norway. All three foreign investors have enjoyed generally good relations with Russia over many years of mutual projects, and other investors are certainly possible for both offshore and onshore prospects, given the great frontier areas still to be developed.[18]

But perhaps Rosneft's most interesting breakthrough is its purchase of Russia's third-largest producer, the privately held joint venture TNK-BP. Announced in October 2012, the acquisition—completed in March 2013—has catapulted Rosneft to becoming the largest publicly listed oil and gas producer, with more than 4.5 mmbpd of oil equivalent, exceeding ExxonMobil's production. The deal is also expected to lead to a 19.75 percent BP stake in Rosneft, with two seats on its nine-member board.[19] BP will also work jointly with Rosneft in the Russian upstream. When fully implemented, the deal portends serious policy and commercial issues. In policy terms, the Russian state role will have greatly increased in oil, in the direction of the state's paramount position in gas, a political fault line between government reformers such as Deputy Prime Minister Arkady Dvorkovich and Kremlin statists such as Igor Sechin. Commercially, Rosneft's other partners will have to contend with

BP board influence and a possible risk of access to confidential bidding information. Its vice president for shelf projects is also a former ExxonMobil employee in Moscow.

Competition in Pipelines

Because Russia's gas future is still tied significantly to Europe, it will work hard to defend its predominant position in certain countries, which it could potentially ask BP, Eni, and Statoil to support. In the north, a third line of Nord Stream is to be commissioned, with talks about extending this line to the UK market, even though the first two lines are only half-full. In Southeastern, Eastern, and Central Europe and the Balkans, for example, Gazprom is the sole source of natural gas for some countries and vigorously lobbies against any alternative non-Russian pipelines that might carry gas into these captive markets. Still looking to start up its 63 bcm per year South Stream pipeline in 2016 in partnership with Eni, EDF, and Wintershall, Gazprom will work hard to head off competing supplies to core European markets.[20]

Underlying these pipeline plans is continued uncertainty about the sustainability of Russian gas production. Russian gas producers are expected to need $730 billion by 2035 to replace their current production of 655 bcm per year. In addition, a large share of Gazprom's 35 trillion cubic meters of reserves are in difficult to access areas. Nor are 25 trillion cubic meters in gas reserves forecast for East Siberia and the Far East yet confirmed.

An alternative gas pipeline is expected to be built from Azerbaijan, mainly from gas projects that are spearheaded by BP and Statoil.[21] Although Azerbaijan's gas will likely compete with Gazprom in Southeastern and Central Europe and the Balkans, Statoil wants to steer the majority of supplies from Turkey to Italy through its Trans Adriatic Pipeline (TAP) project.[22] Since BP has sealed an alliance with Rosneft, its approach to new gas pipelines into Europe may be influenced by its growing ties to Russia.

Over the coming years, a new gas pipeline, the Trans Anatolian Pipeline (TANAP) is envisaged for construction across Turkey. TANAP is planned to carry initially 6 bcm per year into western Turkey in 2018 and, from there, an additional 10 bcm per year into Europe by 2020. The gas will be sourced from the second phase of Azerbaijan's Shah Deniz field.[23] TANAP would be expandable to 31 bcm per year by 2026 and eventually 60 bcm per year. The extra capacity could some day accommodate additional future regional gas production. It would connect on the border between Turkey and Georgia to the expanded and upgraded (existing) Baku–Tbilisi–Erzurum (BTE) gas pipeline.[24] On Turkey's western side, TANAP will connect into a new pipeline network for Europe. The choice for the network to Europe was made in June 2013, with the Statoil-based TAP winning the competition.[25] The network of southern corridor piplines still needs to be constructed, and its future viability will depend on political stability in the countries it crosses.

An undersea Trans-Caspian Gas Pipeline (TCGP) that would connect Turkmenistan's gas resources to Western markets through Azerbaijan was initially promoted by the United States and the EU in the late 1990s. The failure to negotiate a deal with Saparmurat Niyazov, who was then president of Turkmenistan, put the effort on ice for a decade. After Nizayov's death, Turkmenistan discovered the giant onshore South Yolotan–Osman field. In 2011, this field was renamed the Galkynysh gas field (uniting the South Yolotan–Osman and Yashlar–Minara fields) and is now viewed as the world's second largest after the North Pars–South Pars offshore field straddling Iran and Qatar. The Galkynysh field holds as much as 26.2 trillion cubic meters of reserves, according to UK firm Gaffney, Cline & Associates.[26] The potential of growing output from the Turkmen onshore, due largely to Galkynysh, means that sufficient gas should be available to supply numerous pipelines, including a TCGP.

The United States and the EU would like their IOCs to obtain access to the giant Galkynysh field to bring it to both Western and South Asian markets, bypassing Iran and Russia. Ashgabat has focused on the proposed Turkmenistan–Afghanistan–Pakistan–India (TAPI) gas pipeline, which would diversify its supplies toward the southeast and avoid Russian opposition to gas heading west to Europe. In turn, Washington endorses TAPI as a way to support Afghanistan, to provide India and Pakistan with an alternative source of gas to Iran, and to help increase South Asian cooperation, all by using Turkmenistan as a supplier. In fact, all the potential participants support TAPI, but the obstacles remain huge, given the ongoing conflicts in Afghanistan and between India and Pakistan and given Turkmenistan's refusal thus far to support IOC development of the necessary upstream gas resources, despite advice from the Asian Development Bank (ADB) to the contrary. This position may be changing. Ashgabat is showing increased interest in diversifying its export routes and markets, as well as obtaining advanced, safe technology to manage high-sulfur gas reserves. While the ADB performs a financing study, the Turkmen government may well begin to comprehend the magnitude of effort and expense involved in building TAPI and securing both its route and its markets and may eventually accept a limited form of IOC engagement in Galkynysh as a surer way to achieve its goal.

Although the United States and the EU view the southern Caspian as a major source of new gas for exports, Gazprom, as discussed earlier, has pursued the South Stream gas pipeline as its own alternative to supply the EU with Russian gas, mirroring the planned gas export route from Azerbaijan through the new Southern Corridor pipeline.

The country that will feel the greatest negative fallout from South Stream is Ukraine. In 2011, about 70 percent, or just under 104 bcm, of Russian gas (of a total 150 bcm shipped to Europe) transited Ukraine to Europe. In 2012, the transit of Russian gas across Ukraine diminished by 19.1 percent from 2011, or by 19.9 bcm to 84.3 bcm per year.[27] This amount is about 60 percent of the 142 bcm capacity of Ukraine's export system to Europe.

Competitors of Ukraine include Russian gas exports across Belarus. In 2012, Gazprom shipped 44.3 bcm across Belarus, and this output is slated to rise to as much as 60 bcm per year now that Gazprom owns 100 percent of state company Beltransgaz.[28] Unpaid gas debts and future price discounts gave Gazprom the stick and carrot finally to take over Belarus's state gas company. The takeover was completed in December 2011.[29] Of comparable size to the future Belarus artery is the 55 bcm per year Nord Stream pipeline, which runs 1,220 kilometers (744 miles) under the Baltic Sea from Vyborg, Russia, on the Gulf of Finland to Greifswald, Germany. Coupled with South Stream, these three export routes will be able to fully substitute for Ukraine, thus ending Kyiv's leverage on Russian energy prices and supplies. In addition, Gazprom has announced plans to build two more Nord Stream pipelines with further capacity of 55 bcm per year, with a goal of targeting the UK market.

This pipeline competition will likely continue, but an even bigger uncertainty faces any new, expensive planned gas pipeline into Europe—whether it be South Stream, the Southern Corridor, or additional branches of Nord Stream. That possibility is, as previously noted, the potential development and supply of unconventional gas that can eventually be sourced from within Europe or from the United States as LNG exports.

Future Prospects for Ukraine and Central Asia

At this writing, Ukraine is in a phase of violent reaction against Russian pressures to join a newly formed Eurasian customs union instead of an association agreement with the EU. Against the historical backdrop of Russian-oriented regions in the East (as well as Crimea) and Europe-oriented regions in the West, public protests have increased against the outgoing Yanukovich government's pro-Russian tilt and pervasive corruption, with the pendulum swinging from Russia to the EU. The country's ultimate fate remains uncertain, although even a European-oriented government will need to maintain pragmatic relations with its huge northern neighbor.

Despite these uncertainties, one clear result is that Russia will seek to accelerate alternative, non-Ukrainian energy transit routes to the north and the south. At the same time, Ukraine will step up its efforts to become more energy self-sufficient. For that reason, Kyiv will do everything possible to welcome companies with money and technology to exploit Ukraine's vast holdings of shale gas, ranked among the biggest in Europe by the US Energy Information Administration. Just after Moscow announced its IOC partners for offshore projects with Rosneft, in May 2012 it was Kyiv's turn to pick partners for two shale gas prospects: Chevron for the Yuzivske field in western Ukraine, and Shell, which concluded a production-sharing agreement in January 2013 for eastern Ukraine's Oleske field.

Ukraine has been historically the largest post-Soviet market for Russian gas, but since 2010, it has been forced to pay higher prices than under earlier long-term agreements with Gazprom and it is seeking to dilute the Russian company's monopoly position with domestic supplies. State company Naftogaz Ukrainy has reduced its Russian purchases, plans to substitute more of its imports with domestic shale gas in the future, and will likely seek assistance in substituting overpriced and unreliable Russian supplies in response to Ukraine's new tilt to the West. Here, Azerbaijan could play a critical role with increased natural gas exports from its Shah Deniz field.

Russia can apply military and political pressure on Kyiv, up to increased autonomy and even secession by Crimea and Ukraine's pro-Russsian eastern provinces. Those draconian options aside, energy remains a point of pressure for Moscow, whose winter cutoffs of natural gas are vividly remembered not only in Ukraine but also in southeastern Europe. For example, Russia could conclude preferential economic and energy agreements with Crimea and the eastern provinces. Gazprom has also presented Naftogaz Ukrainy with a $7 billion bill for gas it did not purchase but was obliged to take under its 2009 "take or pay" contract. In response to the anti-Russian turn of events in Kyiv, Moscow has suspended its offer of reduced gas prices and a $15 billion credit. It is likely to push hard for repayment or energy asset takeovers, as in the case of Belarus, and Ukraine will need prompt countervailing assistance from the International Monetary Fund and the EU, US, Azerbaijan, and others.

While Ukraine tries to transition from its dependence on Russia and offers a somewhat improved environment for foreign investment, it is attracting IOCs not just to its onshore shale gas prospects but also to offshore areas in the Black Sea, which could represent attractive gas development opportunities to supply European markets. In August 2012, the Ukrainian government awarded an ExxonMobil-led consortium—which also included Shell, Romania's Petrom, and state exploration company Nadra Ukrayny—the Skifske deepwater natural gas field, one of the country's biggest offshore prospects.

Looking at the future of Eurasia, we may see a divided picture, with the eastern part increasingly oriented toward Asian markets and the western, toward Europe. Turkmenistan has committed growing volumes of gas to the Chinese market, with a third 25 bcm per year pipeline (Line C) being built from its border across Uzbekistan and Kazakhstan to China. The goal is eventually to export 65 bcm per year of Turkmen gas to China, up from about 21.5 bcm in 2012.

Kazakhstan is also building jointly with China a domestic gas network, the Beineu–Bozoi–Shymkent Gas Pipeline, from some of its western fields to its southern consuming regions.[30] The goal is eventually to tie this new pipeline from western Kazakhstan into the export pipeline from Turkmenistan, which crosses eastern Kazakhstan on its way to China. Kazakhstan is already connected with a 200,000 bpd oil pipeline that takes output from CNPC-partnered western and south-central Kazakh fields to refineries in China's Xinjiang Autonomous Region.[31] The Kazakhstan–China Oil Pipeline, which supplements the CPC pipeline, is planned to double in capacity to 400,000 bpd by 2015 and could be further expanded later. Together with the ESPO spur from Russia, it brings current pipeline access to the Chinese market from the Russia and Eurasia region to 500,000 bpd. For many Kazakh producers, the option to sell oil to China may eventually prove attractive, and growing volumes could flow east from projects that are not necessarily partnered with Chinese companies.

Conclusions

Many uncertainties face the oil and gas sectors of Russia and Eurasia over the next decade, and more surprises are likely in store. Five years ago, few would have predicted the global supply changes resulting from the revolution in North American production. Likewise, the outlook 10 years from now for shale gas development in China and its broader effect on Asian gas markets is hard to predict. Also hard to predict is the level of potential shale gas production in Europe and of US LNG exports, which may hit both European and Asian markets before 2020.

For both Russia and Kazakhstan, the question is whether they can maintain high oil production levels over the next decade and at what cost. With the Kazakhs seeking to use Kashagan to double current oil production of about 1.6 mmbpd, what if future phases of this massive project are delayed again because of high costs or other operational problems?

If Turkmenistan is to reach its potential as a major global gas producer and exporter, the government will need to make decisions about future development of its giant onshore Galkynysh field. In the future, bringing on new phases and maximizing returns will be difficult without involving the IOCs — particularly if Ashgabat wants actually to export to the southeast through the TAPI or to the west through the TCGP. Such financially and geopolitically challenging pipeline projects will require IOC involvement, but IOCs will develop pipelines only if they have a stake in the gas field that will feed those pipelines. In the meantime, Ashgabat has retained service companies to help develop Galkynysh in its initial phase.

US energy companies will continue to engage actively in Russia and Eurasia, given the extent of the region's resources and increased availability on competitive terms. More broadly, US and other Western companies bring the technology, know-how, and financial muscle needed to develop the next generation of projects. For host governments in Eurasia, particularly those in Azerbaijan and Kazakhstan, US backing is an important political statement for their leaders. Turkmenistan's proximity to Iran will make its relationships with the US government and US companies more sensitive. Significant political will is needed to resist this pressure as well as Russian pressure to avoid projects like the TCGP.

Although the US government is at present engaged, withdrawal of combat forces from Afghanistan, increased challenges in the Middle East, reorientation to Asia and the Pacific, and a more general retrenchment will create future challenges. Yet it is important to recognize Eurasia's influence on future US and global energy security, the need to maintain a stable balance among the neighboring powers, and the desirability of continued development of oil and gas resources in Russia and in the other countries of Eurasia.[32] Nor can this recognition be subcontracted to mid-government levels, however talented, when presidents and prime ministers press their national and company causes in this critical region.

In the energy sphere, deep engagement can bring long-term mutual benefits. For example, Chevron cooperates with its Kazakh and Russian partners in the CPC pipeline, which will deliver, when expanded, more than 1.4 mmbpd to global markets. In Russia, ExxonMobil is able to bring its unconventional resource expertise and technology to the Bazhenov and Achimov formations in West Siberia and its offshore capabilities to the Arctic. In Ukraine, Chevron and Shell are bringing their unconventional gas technology and expertise to the onshore, while ExxonMobil and Shell will tackle the deepwater offshore.

As the Russian and Eurasian energy landscape evolves, competitive pressures and often tensions between nationalization and privatization will continue, but new opportunities for cooperation will also arise. As IOCs and national oil companies develop joint stakes inside and outside the region, their roles and those of their governments will argue for increased cooperation. It is not impossible to foresee a new balance involving Russian, Eurasian, and US energy exports as each of these players becomes both a greater producer and a greater consumer, with increasing interest in the growth and stability of the global energy market.

The opportunity for plus–plus solutions and the need for agile and creative leadership are clear. One final uncertainty emerges: will enough oil and gas players rise to the occasion as a new generation of leaders comes to power?

Notes

1.   Gazprom had to downgrade its production forecasts for 2012 and 2013 to 500 billion cubic meters (bcm) per year, 13 bcm per year less than it produced in 2011. See Argus, "Gazprom Downgrades Output Forecast," *Argus FSU Energy*, November 22, 2012. But its 2012 production was less, reaching only 487 bcm. The downward pressure on Gazprom's output is linked to lower gas demand in Europe, where higher prices under long-term oil-indexed contracts have been eroding the Russian company's market share. Whereas Alexei Miller, the chief executive officer of Gazprom, had predicted that its market cap would rise above $1 trillion, in fact Gazprom's market cap dropped below $100 billion by 2013.

2.   US Energy Information Administration, "Total US Crude Oil Imports Continue to Decline in 2012 but Regional Differences Persist," *This Week in Petroleum* (blog), March 20, 2013, http://www.eia.gov/oog/info/twip/twiparch/2013/130320/twipprint .html. US crude oil imports were the lowest for any year since 1997. See also Richard G. Newell and Stuart Iler, "The Global Energy Outlook," chapter 1 of this volume.

3. This information is from a high-level source at Transneft, May 27, 2013.

4. Actual oil volumes through ESPO to Kozmino in 2013 are expected to reach 440,000 bpd. See Platts, "Russia to Export 440,000 b/d ESPO Crude in 2013," *Oilgram News*, November 22, 2012.

5. PFC Energy Russia and Caspian Service, "Russia: Who Will Fill the ESPO Pipeline?," March 11, 2013.

6. Platts. "Russian ESPO oil exports to grow this year," *Platts Oilgram*, January 23, 2014.

7. TCO ownership is as follows: Chevron (50 percent), ExxonMobil (25 percent), KMG (20 percent), and LUKoil (5 percent).

8. Under the Karachaganak Petroleum Operating production-sharing agreement, BG holds 29.25 percent, Eni holds 29.25 percent, Chevron holds 18.00 percent, LUKoil holds 13.50 percent, and KMG holds 10.00 percent.

9. Under the North Caspian Operating Company (NCOC) production-sharing agreement for Kashagan, Eni, ExxonMobil, KMG, Shell, and Total each hold 16.81 percent, plus ConocoPhillips holds 8.40 percent and Inpex holds 7.56 percent. ConocoPhillips is selling its stake, with India's Oil and Natural Gas Corporation (ONGC) announcing its intention to purchase, subject to government approvals and the exercise of preemption rights. Current foreign stakeholders have already declined preemption, but Chinese companies will also be bidders for the ConocoPhillips stake if KMG also decides not to preempt.

10. See Jan H. Kalicki, "Caspian Energy at the Crossroads," *Foreign Affairs* 80, no. 5 (2001): 120–34.

11. Argus, "Russian Crude Output Hits Record High," *Argus FSU Energy*, January 10, 2013.

12. Azerbaijan exported about 792,000 bpd in 2012, mostly through western-oriented routes, although a small amount was shipped through a pipeline to Russia. Kazakhstan exported more than 1.3 mmbpd in 2012, largely through the CPC pipeline. Additional volumes were shipped through the Atyrau–Samara pipeline, by tanker and rail exports to Georgia's Batumi port, and 213,000 bpd were shipped to China. Turkmenistan exported about 100,000 bpd, some through the Baku–Tbilisi–Ceyhan (BTC) pipeline. Russian oil exports to countries outside the former Soviet Union reached 4.23 mmbpd in 2012.

13. Shareholders in the Azerbaijan International Operating Company (AIOC) are BP, 35.78 percent; SOCAR, 11.65 percent; Chevron, 11.28 percent; Inpex, 10.96 percent; Statoil, 8.56 percent; ExxonMobil, 8.00 percent; Turkish Petroleum Corporation (TPAO), 6.75 percent; Itochu, 4.30 percent; and ONGC, 2.72 percent. In 2012, ONGC agreed to buy US company Hess's stake in the Azerbaijan International Operating Company and the BTC pipeline.

14. US Geological Survey, "Circum-Arctic Resource Appraisal: Estimates of Undiscovered Oil and Gas North of the Arctic Circle," USGS Fact Sheet 2008-3049, 2008, http://www.anwr.org/images/pdf/USGS_Oil_gas_Arctic_2008_estimate.pdf.

15. See Charles Emmerson, "The Arctic: Promise or Peril?," chapter 9 of this volume.

16. Most difficult and receiving the most tax incentives would be fields in the northern sections of the Kara and Okhotsk Seas and in the Bering and Laptev Seas. The next highest level of concessions would be for the Barents and Pechora Seas and the southern sections of the Kara and Okhotsk Seas. Lower benefits would accrue to fields in the Baltic

and deepwater Black Sea. Finally, the least concessions would be for fields in the Azov and Caspian Seas and the shallow waters of the Black Sea.

17. Argus, "Offshore Tax Breaks Delayed," *Argus FSU Energy*, November 15, 2012.

18. Despite accepting an offer it could not refuse to give Gazprom majority control of the giant Sakhalin II offshore gas field in 2006, Shell won an agreement with Gazprom in April 2013 for additional joint development of the Russian Arctic, as well as shale oil and gas exploration in Khanty-Mansiysk.

19. Rosneft paid BP $17.1 billion in cash and 12.84 percent of its treasury shares. BP then bought an additional 5.66 percent of Rosneft shares from the state holding company, Rosneftegaz for $4.8 billion, leaving the UK company with $12.3 billion in cash and a total stake of 19.75 percent.

20. South Stream partners are Gazprom (50 percent), Eni (20 percent), EDF (15 percent), and Wintershall (15 percent).

21. BP is the operator of Azerbaijan's offshore Shah Deniz gas field, the likely operator of an expected project to develop the offshore Azeri–Chirag–Gunashli fields' deep gas layers, and the operator of the offshore Shafag and Asiman fields, which are likely to hold gas.

22. TAP partners are Norway's Statoil (42.5 percent), Switzerland's Axpo (42.5 percent), and Germany's E.ON (15.0 percent).

23. Shah Deniz partners are BP, the operator (25.5 percent); Statoil (25.5 percent); SOCAR (10 percent); Iran's Naftiran Intertrade Company (10 percent), Total (10 percent), LUKoil (10 percent), and TPAO (9 percent).

24. BTE partners include all the members of the Shah Deniz gas and condensate field except Iran's Naftiran Intertrade Company. TANAP's partnership structure may change, but its initial makeup is SOCAR (51 percent), Turkey's BOTAŞ (5 percent), TPAO (15 percent), BP (12 percent), Statoil (12 percent), and Total (5 percent).

25. The alternative to TAP that was not chosen is Nabucco West, the shareholders of which were Austria's OMV (33.34 percent), with Romania's Transgaz, Bulgarian Energy Holding, Turkey's BOTAŞ, and Hungary's FGSZ splitting the remainder. By April 2013, FGSZ had lowered its share to 13.1 percent. OMV, which also in April acquired Germany's RWE 16.67 percent stake, sold 9 percent of this holding to GDF Suez in May.

26. Argus, "South Yolotan Reborn," *Argus FSU Energy*, November 25, 2011.

27. Interfax, "Tariff for Gas Transit via Ukraine in 2013 to Be Some $3.10 per 1,000 cu per 100 km, Says Offering Memo," Interfax News Wire, February 11, 2013, http://www.interfax.co.uk/ukraine-news/tariff-for-gas-transit-via-ukraine-in-2013-to -be-some-3-10-per-1000-cu-per-100-km-says-offering-memo/.

28. Interfax, "Gas Transit through Belarus 44.3 bcm in 2012," Interfax News Wire, February 8, 2013, http://www.interfax.co.uk/russia-energy-news/gas-transit-through -belarus-44-3-bcm-in-2012/.

29. This information is from a PFC Energy Russia and Caspian Service memo of December 12, 2011, titled "Belarus: Gazprom Takeover Brings Benefits."

30. The Beineu–Bozoi–Shykment Gas Pipeline is a joint venture between KMG (50 percent) and CNPC (50 percent).

31. The Kazakhstan–China Oil Pipeline is a joint venture between KMG (50 percent) and CNPC (50 percent).

32. The Russian Federation–Kazakhstan–Belarus Customs Union is to become part of a new Eurasian Union in which pipeline and other transport infrastructure is planned to be merged.

Chapter 9

The Arctic: Promise or Peril?

Charles Emmerson

In 2012, the environmental nongovernmental organization Greenpeace launched a "Save the Arctic" campaign.[1] With support from film stars, environmental campaigners, concerned scientists, and some Inuit groups — but very far from the majority — the world was presented with the dire prospect of an Arctic at risk of rapid destruction from the depredations of Big Oil. Fresh from the *Deepwater Horizon* tragedy in the Gulf of Mexico, assurances as to the technical competence of oil companies and promises of sound environmental stewardship rang more hollow than in the past. A major oil spill would be only a matter of time if drilling were allowed to proceed in offshore areas, environmental activists argued. A pristine environment would suffer catastrophic environmental harm, many times worse than the long-term damage caused by the *Exxon Valdez* spill in 1989. Worse yet, producing oil and gas in the Arctic would fuel global hydrocarbon consumption, thereby undermining efforts to reduce greenhouse gas emissions and, in a cruel irony, contributing to the very processes of global climate change already so acutely felt in the Arctic, which is warming faster than

anywhere else on the planet. In an appeal to a global environmental con-
science, Greenpeace asked whether any boundaries were left for humanity
in its ruthless exploitation of hydrocarbon resources: was nothing off limits
anymore? In place of an alleged rush for the Arctic's resources, Greenpeace demanded an outright ban on exploration and production of hydrocarbons in the Arctic.

The depiction of the Arctic as a place of unparalleled environmental
peril for the future has been mirrored in recent years by the description of
the Arctic as a prospective energy bonanza that promises prosperity to its
residents, wealth to Arctic nations, and increased energy security both for
them and for their customers.[2] Since 2008, when the US Geological Survey
(USGS) published a "Circum-Arctic Resource Appraisal" suggesting that
the Arctic contained 13 percent of the world's "undiscovered" oil and 30
percent of the world's "undiscovered" natural gas, the Arctic has regularly
been featured as one of a suite of new and often controversial frontiers
for hydrocarbon development, alongside ultradeepwater fields, shale gas,
"heavy" oil, and a range of other geographic regions, from West Africa to
the Celtic Sea off the coast of Ireland.[3] Industry experts and energy analysts deem exploitation of any or all of these frontiers necessary to meet
rising global demand for energy, particularly from Asia, and to arrest the
increasing geographic concentration of oil production, with its attendant
implications for producer–consumer relations and for energy geopolitics.
The Arctic is one part of a larger puzzle and a larger shift from traditional
producers and consumers.

The pace of exploration and production in the Arctic has indeed shifted
gears and increasingly moved offshore, into areas where coastal states enjoy economic sovereignty under the United Nations Convention on the Law
of the Sea and where the greater share of Arctic hydrocarbon resources
is thought to lie. In 2011 and 2012 alone, Statoil announced significant
oil discoveries in the Norwegian Barents Sea; Shell pushed ahead with a
controversial and much delayed drilling program for oil in the Beaufort
and Chukchi Seas off the north coast of Alaska; and a string of deals in
the Russian Arctic was announced between Western major oil companies
(ExxonMobil, Eni, and Statoil) and Russia's Gazprom and Rosneft, touting the Arctic's long-term future—both onshore and offshore—as a major hydrocarbon-producing region of the world. In October 2012, a deal
was announced between Rosneft and BP that saw BP part with its share
of TNK-BP and acquire nearly a fifth of Rosneft, opening the way to an
Arctic cooperation agreement. In March 2013, the involvement of China

National Petroleum Corporation (CNPC) in the Russian offshore Arctic was announced as part of Xi Jinping's first foreign trip, as China's president, to Moscow. China's interest in Arctic energy resources is no doubt one reason for China's application—along with Japan, South Korea, and other non-Arctic states—for observer status at the Arctic Council, granted in May 2013.

Beyond Russia, a licensing round for 72 new blocks in the Norwegian Barents Sea was announced in June 2012. A significant number of blocks have already been licensed for oil exploration in offshore Greenland, albeit with limited drilling activity, led by British company Cairn Energy. Further licensing is anticipated in the coming years in Iceland, Canada, Greenland, and across the north.[4] Acquisition of seismic data, both privately and in many cases publicly, has provided additional clues to Arctic prospectivity for oil and gas and has encouraged companies to bid up the price of licenses and to seriously consider greater investment in Arctic exploration.

It is tempting to argue that the Arctic as a whole is coming of age as a hydrocarbon province as a result of increasing accessibility from reductions in sea ice cover and that its future trajectory is set. But the renewed consideration being given to the Arctic as a major potential factor in global supply is happening at a time of unprecedented flux in global energy markets and in a period of relatively low trust for oil and gas companies, amid widespread concerns about global environmental sustainability. Recent years have seen as many reverses as advances in Arctic oil and gas exploration and production. They run from the effective shelving of the massive Shtokman offshore gas development in 2012 as a consequence of the effects of shale gas on North American natural gas prices, to serial delays and cost overruns across the Arctic—Eni's Goliat oil field, Gazprom's Prirazlomnoye oil field—and the effect of tighter environmental regulation and scrutiny on companies' assessments of the costs and benefits of Arctic exploration and production.

Although far from homogeneous, the Arctic frequently presents a unique combination of technical challenges and environmental risks, about which understandable and legitimate public concern exists. For a significant, vocal, and politically active section of the global population, the Arctic is invested with particular emotional resonance, raising the reputational stakes for companies engaging in Arctic development, even where local communities are broadly favorable. In 2012, Christophe de Margerie, the chief executive officer of Total, the French oil company, told the *Financial Times* that he believed the reputational risks inherent in Arctic oil meant that companies should not proceed, although he saw no such risks for Arctic gas exploration, where Total has staked out a strong position in Russia.[5] Costs of production in the Arctic vary widely, as do environmental and geological conditions. The International Energy Agency's cost curve for Arctic oil projects a cost of production range of $35 per barrel to $100 per barrel.[6]

Thus, although some areas of the Arctic are highly likely to undergo large-scale and accelerating development before 2020—particularly offshore in the Norwegian and Russian Barents Sea, onshore in the Russian Arctic, and potentially offshore in the Kara Sea—and areas of existing production, such as the Alaskan North Slope, will continue as producing regions for the foreseeable future even without major further investment, other areas, such as offshore Alaska, Greenland, Canada, and East Siberia, are more distant prospects. They will not be developed at all unless resources are discovered in economically viable quantities, in politically and environmentally permissive contexts, with adequate and safe means of getting the resource to market, and with some degree of confidence about market conditions once production actually begins, potentially 10, 15, or 20 years in the future.

The Arctic may play a major role in regional energy supply—for example, piped natural gas to Europe—and is highly likely to provide some contribution to global oil and gas supply (perhaps up to 10 percent of global oil supply).[7] The implications of Arctic oil and gas for individual countries—Norway and Russia, in particular—are substantial, and in Greenland and North American communities, they could be politically and economically transformative. Should large-scale hydrocarbon development become established in parts of the Arctic, it will lower the barriers to entry for other players, encourage other activity such as shipping, boost infrastructure expenditures, and potentially boost the area's importance as an energy transit corridor, whether for liquefied natural gas (LNG) shipments or for oil. For individual companies, Arctic resources may prove an increasingly substantial part of their portfolio of production and may determine their corporate success.

However, the pace and extent of Arctic hydrocarbon developments overall are far from certain, depending on an interplay of environmental factors, technology, market conditions for hydrocarbons, corporate strategies, national strategies, public acceptance, and politics—both local and global. Individual events—the discovery of a large oil field, for example, or an environmental disaster—may radically and rapidly change assessments of the balance of the Arctic's hydrocarbon peril and promise.

Arctic Energy Resources: A Moving Target

Because of the historically sporadic nature of exploration in the Arctic, the overall number of exploration wells drilled there is in the low hundreds, compared with thousands in the Gulf of Mexico. The relative sparseness of geological data means that most figures for oil and gas, such as the statistical models developed in the USGS 2008 appraisal, are essentially educated guesses based on a range of geological assumptions. So although the existence of Arctic hydrocarbon resources is well known—historically proven as long ago as the 19th century and practically demonstrated—the extent of those resources is not. This situation leaves open not only the possibility of major finds that by themselves would justify the capital expenditures necessary to bring them to production (at least several hundred million barrels of recoverable oil in offshore Greenland, for example), but also the possibility of large expenditures without major finds.

Many Arctics

The Arctic is not a single region, geologically, environmentally, or politically. Conditions vary widely, from the relatively benign climate and temperate conditions of the Barents Sea, which has no sea ice in most offshore areas, except around Svalbard, to much harsher ice conditions in East Siberia and the Chukchi and Beaufort Seas. Although the Arctic is generally considered to contain more gas than oil, some areas are considered to contain relatively more oil—particularly offshore Alaska, Greenland, and the Barents Sea—and even gas-prone provinces may yet reveal large oil deposits.

Regulatory, tax, and royalty regimes differ. Political systems across the Arctic vary, making for a very different set of political risk factors, from Russia, where political pressure, effective expropriation, and contract renegotiation cannot be excluded, to the United States, where public interest litigation and the general decisions of the federal government on offshore leasing in federal waters are crucial to the future direction of oil and gas development.

Nor does agreement exist on how the Arctic should be defined from an energy perspective. Arctic countries often label as *Arctic* any territory or waters above 60° north latitude, although the Arctic Circle itself is somewhat farther north than that. Companies regularly refer to projects as *Arc-*

tic where conditions exhibit certain characteristics—the presence of sea ice or icebergs in particular—although such projects may be much farther south. The Sakhalin projects in the Russian Far East, for example, and even projects off Newfoundland are often listed alongside far more northerly projects.

Given these variations, it should come as no surprise that a multitrack Arctic has begun to emerge with strongly differentiated stories of how future hydrocarbon development may play out across the north.

United States and Canada

The first area to come into large-scale development in the Arctic in the 1970s, and still a major oil-producing region, is the North Slope of Alaska. The drivers then were largely economic and political. Coming into production at the close of a long period when the United States had been the world's dominant oil producer, the opening of the North Slope was explicitly viewed in terms of enhancing national security and improving US energy security. The final permits for the Trans-Alaska Pipeline were approved shortly after the beginning of the Yom Kippur War of 1973, which in turn sparked the Arab Oil Embargo and the first oil shock.

Since then, arguments about whether to expand areas of federal land and water open to drilling—particularly in the National Petroleum Reserve–Alaska, the Arctic National Wildlife Refuge, or offshore—have tended to focus in Washington, DC, around questions of reducing dependence on imports of foreign oil and cutting the price of gasoline for US consumers, on the one hand, and environmental protection, on the other. But crude oil production on the North Slope peaked in 1988 at just under 2 million barrels of oil per day. Production in 2011 was 562,000 barrels per day, having fallen in every one of the previous 20 years, and the North Slope now represents less than 10 percent of US oil production—and a correspondingly smaller share of US oil consumption, let alone overall primary energy consumption—compared with 25 percent of US oil production in the late 1980s.[8] Without increased North Slope oil production, a point may come at which the Trans-Alaska Pipeline can no longer be operated. Although oil could be shipped directly from the north, such a plan would carry its own political opposition.

In this context, the most aggressive exploration program has been that led by Shell in the shallow offshore Chukchi and Beaufort Seas, on which the company has already spent $4.5 billion, including more than $2 billion on the original licenses. Beset by technical challenges, by litigation, by opposition from some Inuit groups who fear the interference of offshore drilling with the whale population, and by broader political controversy—particularly following the *Deepwater Horizon* disaster—Shell's activities have been regularly delayed.

In January 2013, the *Kulluk* rig, while being towed to Seattle for maintenance, ran aground in heavy weather off the coast of Alaska. Having ordered two fast-track inquiries into what had gone wrong for Shell in the Alaskan offshore, the US secretary of the interior concluded that Shell had "screwed up" and would not allow it to continue its work until it had a far more robust integrated management plan.[9] Even before the findings of the inquiries were made public in March 2013, Shell had announced its own pause until at least 2014.

But the pause may turn out to be longer, even if the current US administration remains theoretically committed to safe Arctic development. Other companies looking at offshore Alaskan developments have put their own schedules back. Beyond the geological potential of the American offshore Arctic, Shell's difficulties have made clear the technical challenges and have demonstrated that, in such a closely scrutinized area as the US Arctic, any mishap will invite further questions, criticism, and reputational risk for companies involved.

National and regional economic arguments are made in favor of development, particularly by Alaskan companies and by Alaskan political representatives (who are overwhelmingly supportive). The USGS estimated "undiscovered" Arctic Alaskan oil at just under 30 billion barrels, in addition to known reserves. If production is not maintained, it is argued, a large share of that resource could be stranded. The national effect of increased Alaskan production on American gasoline prices, however, would be at best marginal and would take time. The potential effect on US energy security is more positive in terms of reducing foreign imports but needs to be placed in the context of the current scale of oil imports, forecast increases in US oil production elsewhere, and a broader question of whether long-term energy security is best served by production of resources or by their conservation. Offshore Alaska could become a major contributor to US oil supply over time but is highly unlikely to transform the nation's overall energy posture.

Interest has been increasing in large-scale natural gas production in both the US and Canadian Arctic, but this possibility is highly dependent on price, marketing strategy, and infrastructure: either a gas line to Canada (potentially to contribute to oil sands production in Alberta or to add to US gas supply) or LNG plants exporting to Asia. In Canada, a gas line along the Mackenzie Valley, scuppered in the 1970s by local opposition and un-resolved land claims, was resurrected more recently. The project acquired both local and central government support but ultimately failed tests of economic viability because North American natural gas prices have fallen. South Korean gas company KOGAS (Korea Gas Corporation) has gained a toehold in the Canadian Arctic, expressing the possibility of future LNG shipments.

But in general, the Canadian Arctic, without Alaska's infrastructure and with still harsher environmental conditions, has remained little more than a prospect. Although Arctic oil was first produced on a small scale in Canada at Norman Wells in the 1920s, and test shipments were made in the 1980s, large-scale development has never taken off. Canada's energy superpower status, anticipated and encouraged by Ottawa, is more likely to rest on Alberta than on the Arctic. In eastern Canada, the government of Nunavut could be expected to eye Arctic development positively from the perspec-tive of local economic development, but investors have thus far expressed little interest. In sub-Arctic Newfoundland, oil is already produced off-shore in "Arctic" conditions, with some hope that the local industry can become a launchpad for development in other parts of the Arctic, particu-larly Greenland.

Norway

The Norwegian Arctic is the most environmentally benign area of the Arc-tic, with no sea ice until the waters around Svalbard, and generally more similar to the North Sea than offshore Alaska. Successive governments have been supportive of a northward drive of exploration and production, led by Statoil (in which the state has a majority holding), as a means of contributing to regional development and offsetting declining production elsewhere. (Norway's overall oil production fell to 2 million barrels per day in 2011 from 3.4 million in 2001.[10]) The Norwegian Petroleum Direc-torate has operated extensive license sales and has promised that the sales will continue.[11] Natural gas is already produced in the Norwegian Arctic—in the Barents Sea from the offshore Snøhvit field—and is liquefied at the Melkøya LNG plant, the only LNG plant in the Arctic. Future Norwegian

Arctic natural gas supply could be connected to existing gas lines feeding continental Europe and the United Kingdom, thereby contributing to the energy security of both. In 2010, Norwegian natural gas made up 27 percent of European Union (EU) gas imports and 14 percent of oil imports.[12]

The first oil from Norwegian Barents Sea fields is expected around 2014 from the Goliat field, which is operated by Eni. Additional discoveries made by Statoil at Havis and Skrugard have led that company to boost its exploration for 2013 farther to the south in the Hammerfest Basin, and farther north in the so-called Hoop area. In 2010, a deal reached for delimiting the maritime border between Norway and Russia in the Barents opened the way for exploration in a further portion of the sea, with Norwegian and Russian cooperation at its center. Overall, the Arctic has emerged as a central part of Norway's strategy to retain its role as a major, secure exporter of hydrocarbons for several decades to come and as a major asset in its geopolitical relationship with its much larger neighbor, Russia.

Russia

The Russian Arctic, ranging from the relatively benign Barents Sea region to the much harsher Far East, exhibits the greatest variability in geological and environmental conditions. It is also the most likely area, alongside the Norwegian Arctic, to be an oil- and gas-producing region over several decades. The determination to produce Arctic hydrocarbon resources is strong, closely connected to the strategies of Russia's national hydrocarbon champions, Gazprom and Rosneft, as well as to those of smaller independent players, such as Novatek; to national strategy; and to the domestic political economy.

Although foreign investments in Russia are traditionally viewed as carrying substantial political risk, even if they are made on apparently commercial terms, the attractiveness of the Russian Arctic to Western oil majors is driven in part by the recognition that production of Russia's substantial Arctic resources is considered an overwhelming national strategic and regime imperative. Maintaining oil and gas production and exports is key to the Russian state's fiscal position and to the country's domestic stability and geopolitical influence. (Russia currently produces 10.3 million barrels per day of oil, providing 35 percent of EU gas imports and 34 percent of EU oil imports.[13]) In a broader perspective, Arctic oil and gas development is seen as ultimately encouraging Arctic shipping, shifting the economics of the entire northern coastal region of Russia and potentially of inland areas of Siberia that are connected to the open seas only by north-flowing rivers to the Arctic. Much is, therefore, at stake.

Although oil and gas are already produced onshore in the Russian Arctic and onshore gas production starting up in the Yamal Peninsula is critical to the ability of Russia to maintain its gas output and its position as the largest gas exporter to the EU, interest has increasingly shifted offshore. There, technological weaknesses of the domestic industry have necessitated a string of partnerships with Western companies.

The first of these related to the Shtokman gas deposit, 600 kilometers offshore, originally discovered in the 1980s. However, technical challenges and changes in global market conditions led to multiple delays in proceeding with major investment. Finally, in 2012, the partnership agreement among Gazprom, Total, and Statoil expired, with doubtful prospects for its revival in the immediate future. Yet, at the same time, ExxonMobil, Eni, Statoil, BP, and most recently CNPC have all struck deals that involve—or are highly likely to involve—a strong Arctic component for future hydrocarbon development, thus unlocking an investment stream that government officials estimate could run to hundreds of billions of dollars. Total is linked to Novatek, Russia's largest independent gas producer, with LNG exports slated for 2018.

Russia's key challenges are to develop a technically difficult frontier—more gas than oil prone—and to redirect its export relationships from existing mature markets in Europe to East Asia. These markets (particularly China), however, are likely to seek a diverse set of suppliers of both oil and gas, rather than wishing themselves tied too closely to Russia, with or without its Arctic resources, and Russian LNG may face strong competition from other sources. In short, Russia cannot afford to wait.

Greenland and Iceland

Greenland and Iceland would both be potentially transformed by any major oil and gas production, given the size of their populations: 57,000 and 320,000, respectively. In the case of Greenland, which otherwise depends on an annual subsidy from Denmark (of which Greenland is a part, albeit with self-rule status), economic transformation would be accompanied by a changed political status. The self-rule government in Nuuk, which is responsible for minerals and petroleum licensing and administration, has generally been supportive. Both Greenland and Iceland already have substantial primary energy supplies from hydroelectric and, in Iceland, geothermal sources.

The existence of hydrocarbons in and off Greenland is known, although information on the exact nature of deposits is patchy. A burst of exploration activity in offshore Greenland occurred in the 1970s and 1980s, with a few holes drilled off its western coast. The 1990s saw some ongoing interest in basic geology and seismic acquisition, both public and private.[14] More serious interest returned in the late 2000s, with new licenses awarded and more substantial exploration investment, which is as yet unsuccessful in terms of finding oil in commercially viable quantities. In addition to smaller companies, such as Cairn Energy, other larger companies (including ExxonMobil and Statoil) are present. A new licensing round for offshore northeastern Greenland, considered highly prospective, is anticipated. Although days of ice cover have tended to diminish all around Greenland, except on its north coast, icebergs are still a major hazard, particularly off the west coast, both from broken sea ice from the rest of the Arctic and from Greenland's own glaciers.

Iceland's oil and gas development is far less advanced, is less economically pressing, and would have less dramatic political consequences. Licensing is under way in the Dreki area, off Iceland's northeast coast.[15]

Drivers for Development

Although the particular contexts for Arctic exploration and development are different, the essential drivers for development are the same: geology, access, technology, corporate strategy, geopolitics, and price. These are often strongly interrelated.

From a geological perspective, the Arctic is thought to offer the potential for substantial finds, possibly in concentrations that might make stand-alone developments viable or open a new region. Climate change has improved maritime access, reducing the number of days (if any) of ice cover and opening up possible new energy transit corridors for oil or for LNG, which is expensive to transport, even as onshore infrastructure may become more vulnerable to storms, to rising sea levels, or to melting permafrost. New technologies have helped improve the economics of Arctic development. Statoil's Melkøya plant has demonstrated the feasibility of Arctic LNG. Shell and ExxonMobil would no doubt point to Sakhalin as evidence of their operational Arctic readiness.

Much depends on different corporate strategies. Those of state-related entities, such as Statoil, Rosneft, or Gazprom, are bound to relate directly or indirectly to national strategic objectives, both domestic and external. The Arctic may create some internationalization opportunities, such as between Russian and Norwegian companies in the Barents Sea. For international oil companies, frontier developments (including the Arctic) have become more attractive because other more prospective areas are less accessible. Some consider the Arctic essential to their future portfolio of production, for which the acquisition of Arctic technology, experience, and reputation is key right now. For those companies, the Arctic is a long-term play, with positioning currently under way to exploit that play. If they are left out now, in the future they may find breaking in difficult.

Although Arctic states may have specific concerns related to local employment, community consultation, and potential environmental harm to other activities (such as fishing) or life ways (such as whaling), political support for Arctic development is generally high in the immediately affected local areas. Although much has been made of geopolitical tensions in the Arctic, nearly all prospective hydrocarbon developments are sufficiently close to shore that they are within areas under the sovereignty of one or another of the Arctic states. Only one outstanding maritime border issue exists of relevance to development (between the United States and Canada in the Beaufort Sea), and all Arctic countries have committed themselves to low-tension geopolitics, expressed through the Arctic Council. Although this situation could change and Arctic geopolitics is subject to the potential for spillover from tensions elsewhere, the current characteristic of Arctic politics is cooperation, not confrontation.

Risks and Uncertainties

Development of Arctic oil and gas is nonetheless beset by risks and uncertainties — some local, some global. The geological risks associated with the Arctic, though nothing new in themselves, are often formidable. Many technical challenges have been addressed in other parts of the world, such as icebergs off Newfoundland or sea ice around Sakhalin. Given the relative shallowness of the waters in which most Arctic offshore drilling would likely take place, the technical challenges for water depth are correspondingly reduced. Nonetheless, extreme cold, variations of temperature, and uncertainty around future environmental conditions all place additional burdens on engineering and design. Long Arctic nights make operations during winter more difficult. Weather can change quickly, and even if sea ice is reduced, icing of ships or machinery may present problems for their stability or function. The *Kulluk* incident in Alaska is indicative of the inherent difficulty of operations. Many parts of the Arctic—but not all—are geographically remote, with few transport options, narrow windows of operation, limited accessibility for air transport, and communications challenges. The combination of these factors means that the Arctic will remain a complex and unique risk environment.[16] Climate change creates its own uncertainties.

These technical and operational risks inevitably play through into environmental, political, and reputational risks. The key issue is not so much the risk of something going wrong, serious as that is in itself, as what happens if it does. Operational and technical challenges may be most obvious and most acute in an emergency phase, whether it involves a collision, an explosion, or an oil spill. Preventing an oil spill is clearly the first line of defense, requiring tight regulation, layers of redundancy, fail-safes, and a suite of technical options for dealing with an accident. These measures all incur additional expenses, themselves a factor for the commercial viability of oil and gas development. But if they do not work, for whatever reason, the issue becomes one of preventing the spread of an oil spill and cleaning it up.[17] Given the harshness of operational conditions in some parts of the Arctic—in the American and parts of the Russian Arctic, in particular— preventing oil spills is a major challenge.

The consequences of a major oil spill in the Arctic would be extremely serious environmentally, with major commercial, political, and reputational ramifications far beyond one company. Although activity is under way among companies and with governments to improve knowledge and capabilities, the public has a legitimate interest in ensuring that best practice is adhered to, that technologies are tested and adequate, and that genuine capacity exists to deal with an accident. The Arctic Council countries signed a legally binding search and rescue agreement in 2011, and an oil spill response agreement was signed at the Arctic Council ministerial held in Kiruna in May 2013, but in both cases questions remain about capabilities.

If something were to go wrong, the industry as a whole would be affected, not just the company or companies involved in any accident. Reputational risk attaches itself to Arctic projects even without any control over events or direct responsibility and even if those projects are managed as well, or better, than those in areas of the world that are less closely scrutinized. Financial risk involved in cleanup is hard to measure but could potentially be far greater than in other areas, with political pressure likely to be high and the possibility of a public backlash against operators in other areas. Ultimately, only larger oil and gas companies will be able to bear the capital expenditures involved with the Arctic, will possess the sufficient range of technical expertise and project management to be successful in Arctic offshore projects, and will have the ability to manage the possibility of something going wrong.

Finally, Arctic development is accompanied by global market risks. Given significant flux in the global energy system, investments that may play out over a multidecade timeframe, as is the case in the Arctic, imply a view of possible energy futures, which may be open to change. Arctic gas projects that made commercial sense a few years ago on the basis of LNG exports to North America no longer add up, with the possibility of the United States becoming a significant LNG exporter itself. Arctic natural gas, should it be developed, will have to compete not only with possible US exports but also with supply from Qatar, Indonesia, and Australia. While oil prices continue above $100 per barrel, a wide range of Arctic oil projects may be commercially viable, but a fall in prices would undercut if not eliminate their potential profitability, reduce the incentives for investment in exploration and infrastructure, and stop some commercial interest in the Arctic in its tracks, as in the 1980s. As always, these impacts will be lessened where an overwhelming strategic imperative to production exists and where the state may be compelled to offer generous tax and other conditions for companies to operate—or where a combination of political permissiveness, environmental conditions, and existing infrastructure means that costs and risks are lower.

Whose Arctic, Whose Security?

Ultimately the Arctic's role in energy geopolitics and energy security will depend on what is developed and when. The emergence of the Arctic as an energy province will be uneven. Its trajectory is uncertain. The Arctic's promise is often exaggerated and may not be realized in some areas. Its perils are real, though they vary significantly from project to project and from region to region.

Some assessment of possibilities for the future can be drawn, however, with broad potential geopolitical consequences. The effect of large-scale hydrocarbon development on Greenland would be to promote the possibility of independence, thereby creating a new Arctic coastal state, the first Inuit-led state in the north. In Russia, Arctic oil and gas development should allow that country to remain a major exporter of hydrocarbons, thus retaining a degree of its geopolitical influence. Development of Arctic oil and gas could ultimately encourage broader northern development and a major shipping corridor. In many respects, Russia has the most significant geopolitical stake in the north.

In Norway, Arctic oil and gas will likely prolong that country's role as a major energy exporter and a significant contributor to European energy security in particular. Although parts of the Canadian Arctic may ultimately be opened for oil and gas development, and although these parts could ultimately contribute to centrifugal forces in the Canadian state, the more likely economic developments in the Canadian north involve other minerals. The most likely oil and gas prospects on the North American continent are in and off Alaska. There, the Arctic could provide limited additional supply but would not fundamentally transform US national energy security.

Overall, the Arctic will remain one energy province among many, in a fragmented and changing global energy picture. Should it be developed to any great extent, its political and security salience will be bound to increase, drawing in additional defense expenditures, political attention, and outside players (such as China, Japan, and South Korea) and acting as a potential point of diplomatic and commercial–political leverage for the Arctic states.

The national strategic calculations around Arctic oil and gas are different, as are their domestic and external consequences. But these national interests are only part of the picture and only one influence on what ultimately happens. In addition to the interests of oil companies themselves, many of which are Western and which can be seen as strategic assets in their own right, are the interests of local communities and of local and regional development. In most parts of the Arctic, considerations of economic development weigh more heavily than strategic issues. Indeed, in most Arctic communities, security is best understood as a function of local energy, economic, and environmental security. Through these communities, Arctic geopolitics ultimately relates back to the domestic politics, and even the local politics, of the Arctic and its people.

Notes

1. See Greenpeace's Save the Arctic website at http://www.savethearctic.org.

2. For a more in-depth treatment of the geopolitical and geoeconomic context, see Charles Emmerson, *The Future History of the Arctic* (New York: PublicAffairs, 2010).

3. USGS, "Circum-Arctic Resource Appraisal: Estimates of Undiscovered Oil and Gas North of the Arctic Circle," USGS Fact Sheet 2008-3049, 2008, http://www.anwr .org/images/pdf/USGS_Oil_gas_Arctic_2008_estimate.pdf.

4. Licensing information is available on the websites of the governments involved. See, for example, Government of Greenland, Bureau of Minerals and Petroleum, http:// www.bmp.gl; National Energy Authority, Iceland, http://www.nea.is; and Norwegian Petroleum Directorate, http://www.npd.no.

5. Guy Chazan, "Total Warns against Oil Drilling in the Arctic," *Financial Times*, September 25, 2012.

6. International Energy Agency, *World Energy Outlook 2008* (Paris: Organization for Economic Cooperation and Development/International Energy Agency, 2008).

7. See, for example, Lars Lindholt and Solveig Glomsrød, "The Arctic: No Big Bonanza for the Global Petroleum Industry," *Energy Economics* 34, no. 5 (2012): 1465–74.

8. These statistics are from the US Energy Information Administration website at http://www.eia.gov/dnav/pet/pet_crd_crpdn_adc_mbblpd_a.htm.

9. John M. Broder, "Interior Dept. Warns Shell on Arctic Drilling," *New York Times*, March 14, 2013.

10. BP, *BP Statistical Review of World Energy 2012* (London: BP, 2012).

11. For more information about licensing, see the Norwegian Petroleum Directorate's website at http://www.npd.no.

12. European Commission, *EU Energy in Figures: Statistical Pocketbook 2012* (Luxembourg City: European Union, 2012).

13. BP, *BP Statistical Review of World Energy 2012*; European Commission, *EU Energy in Figures: Statistical Pocketbook 2012*.

14. More information is available on the website of Greenland's Bureau of Minerals and Petroleum at http://www.bmp.gl.

15. For more information about licensing, see the website of Iceland's National Energy Authority at http://www.nea.is.

16. Lloyd's and Chatham House, *Arctic Opening: Opportunity and Risk in the High North* (London: Lloyd's, 2012). See also Fridtjof Nansen Institute and Det Norske Veritas, "Arctic Resource Development: Risks and Responsible Management," Det Norske Veritas, Høvik, Norway, 2012.

17. Nuka Research and Planning Group and Pearson Consulting, *Oil Spill Prevention and Response in the US Arctic Ocean: Unexamined Risks, Unacceptable Consequences* (Philadelphia: Pew Environment Group, 2010). See, for example, Shell, "Preventing and Responding to Oil Spills in the Alaskan Arctic," Shell Exploration and Production Company, Anchorage, 2011, http://s07.static-shell.com/content/dam/shell/ static/usa/downloads/alaska/osp-response-alaska-2011.pdf. Information is also available on SINTEF's website at http://www.sintef.no/home.

Commentary on Part II

Alexander V. Gorban

It is welcome, indeed, to add a Russian perspective to those expressed by authors from Western Europe and the United States on the critical issues in the previous three chapters. More and more, one must recognize the close relationships among energy, foreign, and security policies—and the need to develop integrated national and global approaches to dealing with them. An underlying theme not only for part II but also for this entire book is that governments must catch up with the need to develop more effective strategies both internally and when they are working together.

Europe, Eurasia, and the Arctic are, of course, regions of high interest to the Russian Federation. In addition to the Far East, we are adjacent geographically, and we are closely interconnected in terms of commerce, energy, security, and a long-shared history. Interestingly, each chapter has its own focus: Pierre Noël's chapter on Europe highlights the energy-related disputes, Julia Nanay and Jan Kalicki's chapter on Russia and Eurasia describes the prospects for moving from a zero-sum past to a positive-sum future, and Charles Emmerson's chapter on the Arctic emphasizes the large opportunities for cooperation in achieving the right balance between energy and the environment.

It is probably more accurate to suggest that both differences and areas of agreement exist in each of these cases. From my Foreign Ministry vantage point, I see that our countries wish to find ways to resolve fairly any disputes and to build and widen the areas of agreement. As the authors suggest, large changes in the energy environment present opportunities for either negative or positive interaction, and they give us a chance to make the most of the prospects to collaborate.

In the case of Russia, one must keep in mind that its interests are determined by its dual role as a leading producer–exporter and a growing consumer; hence, the state must strike an optimum balance. Russia's people and industry, located as they are on an enormous continent reaching up to the Far North, depend on secure and affordable energy supplies for their very livelihood. With record production in oil and gas in this new century, Russia is not only self-sufficient but also contributes to the energy security of its neighbors to the west and the east. Thus, we can only welcome the establishment of energy dialogues with the European Union and the United States, and we expect these dialogues to become even more profound in the coming years.

We should recognize, further, that big energy changes are driven by technology as much as by politics. Because of ultradeepwater drilling, for example, large new resources are now available offshore in Russia's Far East and Far North. Because of "fracking," large amounts of unconventional oil and natural gas will reach the market—as is already clear in the United States and will likely become clear in large parts of Europe, Russia, and even China. Eventually, still more petroleum resources will become available in the Arctic, a region where Russia and seven other littoral states have substantial if longer-term opportunities to cooperate through the Arctic Council and other forums.

In his chapter, Pierre Noël draws attention to varying levels of energy security or insecurity in the European Union (EU), related in large part to diversity of supply. A similar analysis can be applied to the countries to the east of the EU. In some countries, such as Ukraine, a strong and understandable desire exists for security of supplies that have long come from Russia. But in other countries, such as Russia or Kazakhstan, an equally strong desire exists for security of demand, which would make possible the large investments in oil and gas production needed in challenging and often remote areas. In the case of Gazprom, for example, multibillion-dollar investments are required to meet the natural gas requirements of its Russian as well as its foreign customers. It is only logical that long-term contracts should make it possible to repay these investments and achieve a reasonable rate of return. Unfortunately, there have been too many instances of third-country diversion, to put it politely, of Russian supplies destined for EU customers, leading, in the short term, to supply interruptions and, in the long term, to alternative underwater pipeline routes in the north and the south. I cannot agree with Mr. Noël that these actions are politically driven; rather, they are necessary responses to illegal activity and to the need to ensure uninterrupted supplies to Gazprom's paying customers.

In their chapter, Julia Nanay and Jan Kalicki point correctly to a fundamental shift of Russian oil and gas supplies to Asian markets. We maintain energy export bridges to both the West and the East, with a continuing interest and commitment to our European and other customers, but we are also engaging increasingly with the Asian markets, which offer growing demand and often more advantageous prices. In this field, Russia's export reorientation is not dissimilar from that of Saudi Arabia in oil and that of Qatar in gas, just to mention two examples. We are also realistic about growing competitive pressures in all regional markets and, therefore, the importance of engaging in early energy trade agreements that will accrue to the benefit of both foreign customers and Russian suppliers. While complementary, long-term supply–demand arrangements will promote global stability and security, it is also logical to balance these arrangements with those appropriate to future domestic shale gas development in Europe as well as potentially in Russia, China, and elsewhere. Russian pipelines continue to operate as state assets regulated by the Federal Tariff Service, the only mechanism of effective state regulation available today, but we certainly see unabated competition in energy exploration, production, and distribution—as is the case with private companies, such as Novatek and LUKoil, which compete vigorously with state-controlled companies, such as Gazprom and Rosneft. As for multiple pipelines in the Eurasian region, Russia favors their development as long as it occurs on strictly commercial terms, rather than on politically driven grounds.

As President Vladimir Putin stated at the first Caspian Summit in Ashgabat in April 2002, "Russia does not have an allergy to the idea of multiple pipelines. It is important only that decisions about pipeline routes are not driven by politics and are justified from the economic and environmental points of view." In this context, I welcome the suggestion of Kalicki and Nanay that Russia and our Eurasian neighbors can pursue mutually complementary pipelines in the future—a prospect in complete harmony with the Eurasian Economic Union now under formation.

Finally, I welcome Charles Emmerson's suggestion that the littoral states cooperate in the environmentally safe development of oil and gas resources in the Arctic. To our mind, protecting the ecosystem of this northern frontier is imperative while at the same time making its resource bounty available for global development and growth. As reflected in the 2011 maritime delimitation agreement between Russia and Norway and in the subsequent cooperation of Rosneft and Statoil in planning resource development in the Barents Sea, important opportunities for both political and commercial cooperation exist in this area. In the future, the Arctic Council can certainly promote cooperation on a multilateral basis. This effort has already begun in rescue and safety and can surely continue with wider measures to protect the environment and achieve safe energy development to benefit all parties.

I might conclude by welcoming the wide range of views on energy, security, and foreign policy represented in the second edition of this book edited by Jan Kalicki and David Goldwyn. I believe this excellent book does an invaluable service of integrating these different dimensions and developing a far-sighted global strategy for this new century.

Part III

The Middle East and Africa

Part III focuses on the Middle East, the world's most volatile and largest oil-producing region; North Africa and the Mediterranean, where resource nationalism and political upheaval have led to diminishing production; and Sub-Saharan Africa, a region both resource rich and resource cursed, which shows fresh signs of orienting itself to increased production and possibly improving governance. The repercussions of the Arab Upheaval could bring wholesale changes on a scale unseen in the Middle East since the aftermath of World War I.

Despite the rise in North American oil and gas production, and despite declining imports from these regions, US interests in the friendly and peaceful evolution of Middle East and North African regimes to more pluralistic governments will remain critical to international peace and security. The prosperity of Sub-Saharan Africa will remain important for human rights, democracy, and moral reasons. Oil will remain a globally priced commodity, leaving the global economy and, therefore, the US economy vulnerable to supply disruptions and price spikes. Additionally, larger

225

shares of investment and production in these regions, especially in Sub-Saharan Africa, could support their emergence as stronger US trade and diplomatic partners.

Addressing these and related issues are J. Robinson West and Raad Al-kadiri, who analyze how recent events in Iran, Iraq, and the Gulf region are affecting regional stability and, by extension, the potential for a significant global supply disruption; Fareed Mohamedi, who focuses on the declining standing of the North African and Mediterranean producing states as important energy sources; and Phillip van Niekerk and Aaron Sayne, who discuss the challenges and opportunities for increased hydrocarbon production in Sub-Saharan Africa.

In chapter 10, West and Alkadiri acknowledge that the Middle East—and the Gulf region in particular—may become a lesser strategic priority for Washington in light of the large-scale development of North American unconventional resources and the US strategic pivot toward East Asia. However, they argue that events in the Middle East will still be crucial to the United States because of the continuing US role in shaping global politics and because of continuing threats from that region to global security. Turning to Iran, West and Alkadiri recognize the impasse over its nuclear program as the most immediate threat to regional stability. They consider prospects for compromise to remain remote and the threat of military action and its associated resource impacts to increase the longer the status quo prevails. West and Alkadiri then turn to Iraq, finding that its fractious and divisive politics are preventing the country from fulfilling optimistic postwar oil production forecasts. They further contend that the Syrian civil war is emboldening Iraq's Kurds and Sunnis, which could bring about even more political paralysis and instability. In this unstable regional environment, they expect Saudi Arabia to support oil prices at the current, relatively high levels, although the Kingdom will oppose any price surge that would weaken global demand and will continue to use its oil revenues to insulate itself from regional unrest, as it has throughout the Arab Upheaval.

In chapter 11, Mohamedi traces the decline of the North African and Mediterranean hydrocarbon sectors. He analyzes several supply-side trends—namely, high oil prices, macroeconomic improvements (including lower debt levels), and entrenched interests that inhibit North African states from offering favorable investment terms to international energy companies. Mohamedi also looks at developments on the demand side, finding that Europe's efforts to diversify its natural gas resources, the rapid growth of US shale gas supplies since 2010, and severe economic recession in Southern Europe all contribute to declining demand for North African hydrocarbon exports. In turn, the turmoil of the Arab Upheaval has scared away both domestic and foreign private investment. Mohamedi adds that, in the longer term, observers are skeptical that regime change will lead to much-needed improvements in economic governance. Even in newly emerging plays in Libya, Israel, and Cyprus, Mohamedi points to geopolitical and geological risks that bring into question whether these resources can be brought to market. He concludes that although the North African states will be challenged with rebuilding their governance structures from scratch while those in the Mediterranean will seek to revive their debt-ridden economies, the energy sector will not be a means through which these much-needed improvements are achieved.

In chapter 12, van Niekerk and Sayne assess how increased oil and gas production in Sub-Saharan Africa would affect American interests. They argue that although American imports of African light sweet crude are declining, expanded African production will be a net positive for the United States. Specifically, they posit that African nations developing their resources responsibly could contribute to American priorities in the region, including democratization, reduced transnational crime, disease eradication, and poverty alleviation. They then analyze prospects for growth, finding that significant opportunities exist regionwide, especially in East Africa, which, fueled by large discoveries in Mozambique and Tanzania, could challenge Australia as the top exporter of liquefied natural gas within a decade. Although viewing most African producers as offering relatively open oil and gas regimes and fiscal systems, thus making foreign investment there attractive, van Niekerk and Sayne recognize that the resource-wealthy producers are prone to poor sector management, weak formal institutions, misguided economic policies, high poverty rates, and corruption. They acknowledge that such problems often aggravate perceptions of inequitable resource distribution, which can lead to intrastate conflict. But they find it unlikely that these tensions are currently serious enough to metastasize into a new large-scale war anywhere on the continent. Van Niekerk and Sayne add that the governments of some consuming and producing countries are finally embracing disclosure laws, which if vigorously enforced may alleviate the corrupt practices that often cause intrastate resource disputes. They conclude that although security and anticorruption challenges remain apparent, both major energy companies and independents enjoy a wide range of attractive investment opportunities in Sub-Saharan Africa.

In his commentary on part III, Abdullah bin Hamad Al-Attiyah, Qatar's deputy prime minister and former minister of energy and industry, argues that his country's collaborative model of hydrocarbon development will be essential as global markets respond to expected demand increases for oil and gas worldwide. He notes that producers and consumers will have to work together to ensure that natural gas and oil prices are sufficient to sustain long-term investment. He expresses more optimism than Mohamedi with regard to the ability of Egypt, Libya, and Algeria to create conditions necessary to facilitate high levels of foreign investment. Al-Attiyah also strikes a comparatively optimistic note on Iraq, saying that the country may have the capacity to overcome the immense challenges it faces and maximize its potential. Yet he shares West's and Alkadiri's view that the Middle East faces high levels of uncertainty and risk, concurring with them that instability in Iran and Syria has the potential to spill over into the broader region with serious consequences. Al-Attiyah concludes by positively assessing US engagement throughout all these regions, predicting that such engagement will endure and, in doing so, contribute to a safer, more secure world for producers and consumers alike.

Chapter 10

Iraq, Iran, and the Gulf Region

J. Robinson West and Raad Alkadiri

Why the Middle East Still Matters for the United States

As the largest oil-producing region on Earth, the Middle East has for decades been a central focus of US foreign and energy policy. Ensuring secure and uninterrupted flows of crude oil to the United States and its allies has been a key strategic tenet of US policy since the Second World War. It has underpinned a longstanding security doctrine involving a large-scale US military presence in the Arabian (Persian) Gulf and drawing US troops directly into two wars in the past 20 years, including the lengthy presence in Iraq. This is not to suggest that Washington's policies toward the Middle East are or have ever been driven by oil concerns alone, as some conspiracists have argued. Nevertheless, protecting the region's rich energy resources has been a major reason successive US administrations have dedicated so much strategic attention to the Middle East.

As the second decade of the 21st century begins, however, there are signs of a shift in US energy and foreign policy. The development of massive unconventional oil and gas resources in North America has given rise to a sense of greater energy independence in the minds of US policy-makers and the public at large. On a geostrategic level, a combination of fiscal pressures at home and the inexorable rise of China abroad is moving the focus of US attention eastward, beyond the Middle East. The pivot of US foreign and defense strategy toward Asia has been a long time in the making, but the signs—both economic and strategic—are unmistakable. Indeed, this pivot was explicit in the early days of George W. Bush's administration in 2001, only for US attention and resources to be diverted back to the Middle East by the tragedy of September 11.

However, although the Middle East may move down the list of Washington's strategic priorities over the course of the coming decades, developments in the region will remain important to US energy and foreign policy-makers for some time to come for three basic reasons. First, energy independence is a chimera that makes for good political rhetoric but that will be difficult to achieve in the United States absent a major change in the country's demand profile. Rising production from unconventional resources in North America and the eventual construction of the necessary pipeline infrastructure to transport those resources to key domestic markets will certainly lessen US reliance on foreign energy sources and will alter the map of global energy flows significantly. But even the most optimistic forecasts do not anticipate the United States being import free over the next decade. US dependence on foreign sources is anticipated to decline from 70 percent in 2007 to about 20 percent of demand by 2020, if imports from Canada are included as domestic production.[1] Indeed, the irony of the situation at present is that the development of North American resources has led to a rise in crude oil imports from the Middle East because of refinery configurations and crude quality differences in certain parts of the United States.[2]

Second, even though the United States will rely more on locally produced oil, crude oil is a globally priced, fungible commodity. Geography will have some effect on price, but not to the extent witnessed in the gas sector, where regional markets are more detached, resulting in a significant decline in local prices because of the upsurge of US production, even as prices elsewhere in the world remain higher. Consequently, although the United States may eventually rely less on oil from the Middle East, the US economy will remain vulnerable to any events there that disrupt supplies from the region and thereby drive global prices up. Ensuring the flow of crude oil from the Middle East may therefore be less of a direct economic imperative for Washington in the future, but the United States cannot buffer itself entirely from the impact of events there. Ensuring stability in the region is of economic importance to Washington and will necessitate continued engagement.

Third, the United States remains the world's only global superpower, and none of its long-term rivals, not even China, is showing any desire to fill that role. Washington's influence in the Middle East may have waned over the past decade, partly because of policy missteps associated with the Iraq War and partly because of economic weakness in the wake of the Great Recession, placing greater onus on regional powers to manage stability in their midst. Nevertheless, US disengagement is not an option, nor is it one that Washington would seriously consider. For all the talk of a pivot to Asia and the realignment of forces that are accompanying it, the US determination to play a global role in shaping international politics—and the realities of its unique military might—will keep the Middle East on the agenda for a long time to come.

Indeed, the policy challenges associated with the Middle East and the risk of resource disruption may become more acute over the next decade. Longstanding problems—such as the Arab–Israeli conflict, Iran's nuclear program, and the threat of nuclear weapons proliferation—continue to fester and will not get easier over time. More important, however, the region is in the midst of a major upheaval that began with the overthrow of a number of authoritarian regimes with the Arab Spring but could end up transforming the political and geographic boundaries of the region in a manner not seen for a century. Events in Syria will be a particularly critical factor determining the evolution of the Middle East over the next decade. Violence there is already spilling over into neighboring states,[3] and regional powers, including Turkey, Iran, and Saudi Arabia, are looking warily at what the fall of the Bashar Al-Assad regime in Damascus could mean for the regional balance of power. Thus, the Syrian civil war is bound to be disruptive. It will shape not just stability in the Middle East but also the region's oil and gas production potential in the medium term by bringing regional rivals into conflict and possibly even forcing a redrawing of regional borders. These factors raise the possibility of significant disruptions to energy flows, with all the concomitant price and economic implications.

The Iranian Wild Card

The most immediate potential threat to stability in the Middle East is the impasse between Tehran and the international community over Iran's nuclear program. The refusal of the Islamic Republic to accept United Nations Security Council–mandated restrictions on the program and its failure to disclose the extent of its activities to the satisfaction of international inspectors have led to growing fears of military action against Iran, spearheaded by either Israel or the United States, to destroy Iran's nuclear weapons capacity. In reality, the immediate prospect of an attack against Iran is exaggerated, despite persistent rhetoric: Israel cannot do it on its own, and the United States has no appetite for preemptive action that risks catastrophic escalation in the region unless there is no other option. Entering its second term, the Obama administration in Washington has signaled that, although its patience with Iran is not limitless, it prefers to continue with its carrot-and-stick approach—ratcheting up sanctions while seeking to reach a grand negotiated bargain that would severely limit Iran's nuclear program for the future.

This strategy has adopted a significant economic tool that can be used not just on Iran but also, indirectly, on the global economy. In Iran, sanctions and restrictions on financial flows have driven up inflation and undermined growth in the nonoil sector. The rapid collapse in the value of the rial in the autumn of 2012, although prompted by a planned devaluation of the currency, illustrates the difficulty of managing an ever more isolated economy and eroding consumer confidence. But it also suggests that Iranian leaders are preparing contingencies for the long haul: they are seeking to reduce imports and extend the cover provided by what are still relatively healthy foreign reserves. This approach will undoubtedly contribute to popular dissatisfaction with the regime, but it is a policy that has worked in the past.

Sanctions on Iran have also had an impact on the global economy, although it has been nowhere near as deleterious as the domestic consequences. The fear of possible military action has introduced a war premium on oil prices that will persist in the market as long as the crisis remains unresolved and will certainly rise much higher—at least temporarily—if an attack on Iran does take place. More important in the longer term, steadily tougher international sanctions, especially the European Union's embargo on crude imports from Iran and ever-tightening financial restrictions, have blocked investment in the country's oil and gas industry and significantly reduced Iranian oil exports to around 1.0 million barrels per day (mmbpd) from a preembargo level of 2.2 mmbpd.[4] These losses have not been disastrous so far: global demand growth remains relatively muted, and rising production from Saudi Arabia and key Gulf states, as well from sources outside the Organization of the Petroleum Exporting Countries (OPEC), have made up for the shortfall in Iranian exports. But these losses have put clear upward pressure on oil prices, as well as tightening the supply–demand picture globally as OPEC spare capacity (especially in Saudi Arabia) has declined.

This picture is unlikely to change any time soon. Absent regime change in Iran, Tehran is likely to remain defiant. This defiance is not simply a matter of national pride, although Iranian leaders insist that the nuclear program is civilian and, therefore, legitimate; it also reflects Iran's own security fears and the conviction of Iranian leaders that the real goal of the United States and US allies is to remove the current regime. Under these circumstances, reaching a compromise on the substance and sequencing of any deal will be very difficult, even assuming that achieving nuclear breakout capability is not Tehran's real objective. Bridging the gap between the international community's and Tehran's perceptions and introducing mutually acceptable confidence-building measures that provide a pathway to a long-term agreement have proved impossible so far, and there is little to suggest that such efforts will get any easier.

That does not mean, at least at this writing, that war is imminent. For all the rhetoric, Western intelligence agencies do not seem convinced that Iran is about to build its first nuclear bomb. But as time passes and the status quo prevails, the threat of military action will inevitably rise, with all the risks associated for energy supplies. Not merely will strikes threaten Iran's own production, but also Iranian retaliation will reduce exports from other regional producers: 17.0 mmbpd of crude and product pass through the Strait of Hormuz,[5] which Tehran has threatened to block in the event of an attack. Its ability to do so will be limited by the international community's determination to open the strait within days, but even a temporary blockade would cause a massive spike in oil prices. Over the longer term, Tehran may respond through asymmetric warfare, targeting production on the Arab side of the Gulf. The failed terrorist attack against Saudi facilities at Abqaiq in February 2006 and the cyber attack against Saudi Aramco in 2012 are sobering reminders of the potential vulnerability of oil and gas infrastructure in the region.

But at the same time, factors that could reduce the risk of confrontation may alter the status quo—notably political change in Iran. The regime's response to postelection demonstrations in 2009 illustrated Tehran's still significant capacity to quash domestic dissent, and the Arab Spring offers reminders of the cost of failure. Nevertheless, time may do what the protestors could not and alter the character of the regime in a material way. The biggest wild card in Iran is not the nuclear program, but rather the longevity of its leader, Ayatollah Ali Khamenei, and the implications his eventual death will have on the sustainability of the current regime. Undoubtedly, a host of players have a vested interest in perpetuating the current system, but Khamenei and his allies have through their repression undermined the legitimacy of the regime and narrowed its base. And in taking sides so clearly in the domestic unrest, Khamenei debased the authority of the Office of the Supreme Leader and with it the credibility of the *vilayat-e faqih* (or rule of the jurisprudent) system of government that was established by his predecessor, Ayatollah Ruhollah Khomeini, who led the 1979 revolution. The Iranian regime managed to avoid a crisis of legitimacy on Khomeini's death in 1989, but Khamenei's passing is likely to bring no such reprieve. What follows will look significantly different from the regime that exists today. It will usher in a period of uncertain—and probably violent—transition, given the hold of the Revolutionary Guard and other security forces, but the prospects for a Persian Spring will rise significantly in the medium term.

Although this transition might reduce tensions in the Gulf and ease pressure on oil prices, whether it will automatically bolster energy supplies from Iran is not clear. Any successor regime will have to deal with the consequences of years of sanctions on the oil and gas sector. Foreign investment may flow again, but the damage has already been inflicted on the resource base through a mixture of mismanagement and the forced shut-in of production that will not easily be recovered. PFC Energy estimates that Iran's production capacity has declined by around 0.5 mmbpd as a result of sanctions,[6] and that decline will only grow as the embargo on the Iranian oil and gas sector tightens. Iran may well recover some of this capacity through investment and new technology, but such improvements will take time. Consequently, hopes that a political resolution will lead to the rapid restoration of Iran's output potential appear fanciful at best.

Iraq: Between Potential and Reality

Indeed, a pertinent example of the potential gap between hopes and reality in the midst of political transition lies immediately to Iran's west. The overthrow of Saddam Hussein's regime in Iraq in 2003 prompted optimistic forecasts of the speed and scale at which the country's oil production would increase. Immediate postwar estimates imagined rapid output expansion, delivered in part by foreign investment in the sector; 6 mmbpd within six years was regarded as an achievable target.

The reality has been much more disappointing. Iraqi production did not consistently reach prewar highs until January 2011. The sector was not opened up to foreign investment until 2009, and even then on only a very limited basis. Moreover, it has quickly become apparent that the production forecasts associated with this investment (almost 12 mmbpd by the end of 2017) are entirely unachievable. If Iraq is able to reach half that figure, it will be a major achievement, especially in light of waning investor appetite.

Ultimately, four factors will determine just how much oil Iraq produces in the next decade. The first is whether sufficient onshore infrastructure (including water injection facilities) can be built to ensure the production and transport of rising volumes of crude. Significant pipeline, storage, and pumping capacity bottlenecks still exist in the south of the country that will limit output potential unless addressed quickly, not just because of immediate transport constraints but also because international companies will be even more reticent to invest the necessary sums to ensure that their projects reach maximum potential.

Whether this situation is reversed is linked to the second factor—namely, whether the Iraqi government improves its decision-making processes, bringing them in line with the terms of the technical service agreements it has signed. Thus far, Baghdad has struggled to meet its responsibilities, not just on the infrastructure side but also through the facilitation of procurement and remuneration. Moreover, its planning assumptions, in terms of both cost and time, have been out of touch with reality, leading to additional delays. These factors, combined with payment delinquency and endless bureaucratic red tape, have undermined the economics of the contracts signed and have been instrumental in convincing companies such as Statoil to divest their stakes in southern projects, while others have slowed down their intended pace of investment.

This situation is unlikely to improve unless the third factor can be addressed—namely, the human resource constraints faced by Baghdad. Years of war and sanctions have led to a toxic mix of isolation and brain drain, robbing Iraq of actual and potential expertise. Reversing this situation will take as much as a generation, thus making the schedule that Baghdad set in 2009 appear even more unrealistic. Irrespective of recent gains in production, which have taken output to historic highs, if Iraq is to keep increasing its output over the next decade, it will have to find a way to compensate for its weak human resources. That effort will almost certainly require the government to alter its investment model to reduce the state's role in the program.

This change does not look feasible because of the fourth and arguably the most overriding factor: the fractious and divisive political situation in the country. Political polarization has risen steadily as critical disputes, particularly over federalism and power sharing, remain unresolved. The resulting turmoil has paralyzed effective decision-making, thus keeping the government from introducing major new initiatives or reforming existing institutions and procedures. Political power and survival is the name of the game, with all factions viewing issues through a damaging and very short-term zero-sum lens.

In this context, the government will find altering the investment framework for the oil and gas sector very difficult. Not only does resource nationalist sentiment remain strong, but also senior government officials fear that their rivals will use any revamp of the investment framework against them, even if it contributes to increased production in the longer term. Moreover, the gradual politicization of ministries over the past decade—turning them into what amounts to political fiefdoms—makes the process of intergovernmental coordination, which is necessary to improve the investment environment, more difficult. The most determined opponents of Prime Minister Nouri al Maliki are also his partners in coalition government, and none of them has any interest in making his policies succeed. Absent the overwhelming victory of one faction in future elections or acknowledgment that broad coalition government is not effective, this situation will persist irrespective of who leads Iraq.

Under these circumstances, the dangers to Iraq's oil production prospects are not merely operational or investment related. Instead, the viability of the state in its present form is increasingly coming into question as interfactional tensions rise and the government fails to deliver basic services. The most dangerous immediate schism is between the federal government in Baghdad and the Kurdistan Regional Government (KRG) in Irbil. Relations between the two sides have witnessed a dangerous deterioration as personal antipathy has added fuel to the fire of disputes over their rival interpretations of federalism. For the Kurds, anything more than a weak confederal system composed of multiple regional administrations (rather than just an Arab and a Kurdish one) is anathema; any alternative—other than outright independence—is seen as an eventual existential threat.[7] For most Arab parties, this division is regarded as a threat to the territorial integrity of Iraq, which they suspect is Irbil's long-term goal. Maliki may be more vociferous than others in insisting that Baghdad's sovereignty must be preserved, but his Arab rivals—both Shia and Sunni—share his opinion. For some Sunnis, greater decentralization of power from Baghdad is seen as an attractive but temporary option until they can find a way of restoring their authority over the central government.

As this seemingly intractable dispute becomes more intertwined with factional and personal rivalries, the risk that it will prompt renewed internecine conflict is increasing. Recent spikes in violence have prompted fears that Iraq is returning to the type of civil war that raged between 2005 and 2008. This is still a possibility, but a more likely scenario in the medium term is that localized conflagrations, provoked by disputes over territory, spark intercommunal tensions. Repeated standoffs between the Iraqi Army and Kurdish Peshmerga forces in disputed territories have so far been resolved peacefully, but the risk of a violent clash keeps rising, especially in the absence of the calming presence of US forces as a buffer between the two. Similarly, tension has risen along fault lines between Sunni and Shia communities in Iraq. Meanwhile, regional events—especially the civil war in Syria—are altering the calculations of different Iraqi factions, prompting greater rigidity as a result of either perceived risk or perceived opportunity.

Syria and the Threat of Regional Conflict

Indeed, spillover from the collapse of the regime in Syria—and the way it shapes the perceptions of both Iraqi factions and the governments of neighboring states—may be the single most important influence on stability in Iraq over the next decade. It is shaping the energy picture along with everything else—particularly in the case of the Kurdistan region of Iraq. The civil war to Iraq's west has convinced some factions—notably the Kurdistan Democratic Party (KDP), which dominates the KRG—that their aspirations for greater autonomy (and eventual independence) are increasingly achievable. The emergence of a Kurdish enclave in Syria not only is an opportunity to extend the Irbil government's regional influence but also heralds the possibility that the KRG will not be the only autonomous Kurdish entity in the Middle East. For KDP leaders, including Masoud Barzani, president of the KRG, the establishment of another statelet modeled on the Irbil administration would provide a useful ally. More important, it would further enshrine the concept of ethnic identity as the basis for quasi-state formation in the Middle East, which Barzani and the KRG are likely to interpret as a major steppingstone to eventual Kurdish independence.

Whether Barzani and the KRG can achieve this age-old dream will be closely linked to oil and gas developments in Kurdistan—critically whether the regional government is able to develop export routes independent of the federal administration in Baghdad. Optimism about Kurdistan's production potential is high (local authorities estimate output in 2015 to be as much as 1 mmbpd[8]), and the contractual terms are attracting the world's largest oil and gas companies despite punitive threats from Baghdad. But absent independent export routes, Irbil will remain reliant on Iraqi government–controlled pipelines through Turkey to get its oil and gas to market, leaving the KRG— and its investors—at Baghdad's mercy fiscally. The federal government has already demonstrated that it is willing to use its control over revenue to limit Kurdish autonomy, and as long as underlying political disputes between Irbil and Baghdad remain unresolved, the Iraqi government has little reason to change course. Only when new pipelines to international markets are built will the Kurds have fiscal autonomy and the ability to guarantee full remuneration and cost recovery to its investors. And at that point, the allure of independence is likely to be too tempting to pass up.

Ultimately, the most critical factor determining Irbil's future options will be Turkish policy and whether the government in Turkey will allow independent export routes. Ankara's tilt toward Irbil—and away from Baghdad—was an important factor encouraging the KRG to challenge the Iraqi government's authority, particularly on the oil and gas front. Indeed, Irbil and the companies that have invested in Kurdistan appear convinced that Turkey would acquiesce to an independent export route across its territory. Until recently, Ankara has done little to belie this belief, regarding Kurdistan not only as a lucrative market for investment, but also as a source of cheap hydrocarbons in the future.

But Turkish leaders, though more sympathetic to Irbil than were their predecessors, are nonetheless wary of creating the basis for an independent Kurdistan. Ankara's preference is for a hydrocarbon- and revenue-sharing deal between the KRG and Baghdad that would reinforce the territorial integrity of Iraq while also promoting Turkish investment across the country. Ankara will see a landlocked Kurdistan that is reliant on Baghdad-controlled infrastructure as far more controllable, no matter how much Irbil protests that independence is not the KRG's goal. If Iraq does begin to split up, Turkey may review its position on independent pipelines, but only to ensure that Ankara maintain maximum leverage on any future Kurdish entity.

Not just the KRG sees the Syrian civil war as a source of long-term political opportunity. A variety of Iraqi Sunni and nationalist groups also believe that regime change to the west—particularly if it brings with it a Sunni-led government—will be to their advantage by altering the regional balance of power in their favor and isolating the Shia-led government in Iraq. At a minimum, these Iraqi opposition groups (something of a misnomer given that many are actually represented in the Maliki coalition government) hope that change in Syria will force Shia parties in Baghdad to be more accommodating of Sunni and nationalist demands. But the gradual collapse of the Assad regime in Damascus has led some Iraqi opposition groups to dream of restoring a version of the old, pre-2003 order in Iraq.

The nationalist perceptions of Iraqi Sunnis are shaped to a large part by the sense of victimization and marginalization they have felt at the hands of successive, Shia-led postwar governments in Baghdad. The absence of real political reconciliation in the country has convinced these groups—and the constituencies they represent—that the new order offers little hope for genuine political inclusion or power sharing. The danger is, however, that these groups will misjudge the effect of the changes that are taking place in Syria and overreach, either by pressing their case too hard with Baghdad or by seeking greater autonomy with the hope of getting political, logistical, and possibly military support from a new regime in Syria. At best, their overreach is bound to increase tension and political polarization in Iraq, further paralyzing the Iraqi government; at worst, it could pull apart the fabric of the existing Iraqi state.

Indeed, both the Iraqi Kurdish and Sunni nationalist responses to the Syrian civil war illustrate how destabilizing the crisis is. Moreover, hopes that the regime in Damascus will fall quickly and that violence will abate look fanciful. Syria is in the process of state collapse, with power diffusing in an unmanaged fashion to local groups. This situation, in turn, has exacerbated the weakness of neighbor states, not just in Iraq but also in Lebanon and Jordan. Hopes of restoring powerful state structures in any of these countries are dim; instead, what is in store is likely to be an extended—and often violent—period of political instability that could, at worst, threaten to redraw the boundaries of the Middle East from western Iran to the Mediterranean Sea.

How Secure Are Saudi Arabia and the Gulf States?

If a period of regional instability persists, its ripple effects will extend to the Gulf states to the south, adding to the pressures—political and fiscal—already created by the Arab Spring. Indeed, unrest in Syria—perhaps more than any other single factor besides the situation in Iran—will shape the regional policy of the Gulf states and, by extension, their domestic stability and energy policy for the next few years. Saudi Arabia and Qatar have adopted particularly active regional foreign policies over the past two years, with Qatar parlaying the huge financial strength that its gas investments have delivered into real political influence as it has sought to mediate domestic crises in a number of Arab states. But for all its success, Qatar faces the same challenges that Saudi Arabia and the other regional hegemons (Iran, Turkey, and Israel) do in pursuing intervention in Syria—namely, balancing its efforts to shape the outcome there with the need to limit the spillover effect of the Syrian civil war into the wider region.

Backing proxies in Syria, as both Qatar and Saudi Arabia are doing, will be key to this balancing effort. But this policy risks heightening the violence and accelerating the collapse of the Syrian state, not only pulling the two Gulf states further into the morass, but also making the violence more difficult to quell. Moreover, in the absence of any regional security framework, such a policy will likely heighten regional competition between rival hegemons (Saudi Arabia and Iran are already at loggerheads, and early signs of tension exist between the Gulf states and Turkey). Syria, therefore, could very quickly resemble Lebanon during its civil war in the 1970s and 1980s, when regional states fought their battles indirectly through allies on the ground. But given Syria's strategic location and proximity to a host of weak states, including Lebanon itself, the destabilizing impact is likely to be much greater.

By virtue of size, distance, political homogeneity, and financial strength, Qatar will be able to protect itself somewhat from the immediate consequences of the escalation of the Syrian conflict and the spillover of violence there. But it cannot hope to remain completely immune from instability elsewhere in the Gulf or any conflict that encourages a more aggressive policy by Iran. Saudi Arabia faces a much more difficult task managing its future, with the risks posed by regional instability compounded by the challenge of its own domestic transition. The deaths of Crown Princes Sultan bin Abdulaziz and his brother Nayef in rapid succession were a reminder—as if any were needed—that the apex of power in the Kingdom is geriatric. The ascension of Salman bin Abdulaziz—who at 76 is comparatively young by the standard of senior princes—to the post of Crown Prince may offer some temporary respite after the passing of King Abdullah bin Abdulaziz, but a shift to the next generation of princes (the grandsons of the Kingdom's modern founder, Abdulaziz al Saud) is only a matter of time. And the likely jostling for power among contenders from the different kingly lines will force a much clearer division of power between rival factions.

Ultimately, the government of Saudi Arabia is likely to prevail in its current form; the ruling family has shown itself to be more robust and cohesive in times of crisis than many analysts have anticipated. Nevertheless, succession issues are bound to divert the attention of senior Saudi princes inward at a time when delicate management of regional crises will be vital. With the region facing what is potentially a once-in-a-century political upheaval, not to mention the ever-present threat of military action against Iran, the risk of Saudi miscalculation will be heightened as long as Saudi Arabia's own house is not fully in order. Domestic competition will exacerbate the risk that rival agendas will cloud policy-making and lead to missteps.

In the midst of this domestic and regional instability, however, one thing is clear: Riyadh will want oil prices to remain at their recent high levels, although not so high as to disrupt foreign markets or weaken demand. Higher spending will continue to be used to buffer the Kingdom from the impact of regional unrest, just as it has during the Arab Spring. Meanwhile, financial power can be translated into wider regional influence, especially with governments whose coffers are relatively bare. But that situation creates an imperative for Saudi Arabia to keep oil prices—and therefore oil revenues—at current high levels, allowing it to balance its domestic and external accounts despite higher spending while continuing to build financial reserves to provide funds in case of an emergency.[9]

This scenario does not mean, however, that Riyadh is likely to drive prices up further in the medium term. Oil policy-makers in the Kingdom recognize the fine balance between prices and demand, especially at a time when the global economy remains fragile. As the only holder of significant spare capacity in OPEC, Riyadh has used its production prowess and the need to protect both price and demand to bolster its financial strength and its strategic relevance—a factor that adds a further element of insurance for the Kingdom. For the foreseeable future, Saudi Arabia will not be replaced in this pivotal role.

This fact has two important implications. First, it puts an onus on Saudi Arabia to keep developing its hydrocarbon resources, both oil and gas. Although both Kuwait and Abu Dhabi have ambitious plans to expand capacity, the Kingdom remains the linchpin of OPEC efforts to maintain spare capacity. Indeed, this role is core to Saudi Arabia's strategic raison d'être.

The government in Riyadh is spending hundreds of billions of dollars to maintain capacity at 12.5 mmbpd, and officials have talked in the past of increasing production capacity to 15.5 mmbpd, although this goal has been mostly shelved since 2008. Meanwhile, Saudi Aramco and the new King Abdullah City for Atomic and Renewable Energy (known as KA-CARE) are focusing considerable efforts to develop natural gas, solar energy, and nuclear energy, which will be critical to substituting oil in local power generation, thereby allowing additional crude to be exported. The importance of these challenges has been recognized at the very highest levels of the Saudi oil and gas industry, with calls for a clear and effective strategy to be introduced over the next decade, including greater energy conservation.[10]

The second implication is that this balancing role will perpetuate the close relationship between the Kingdom and Washington. US officials and the public at large may sometimes question the value of the relationship, but its contribution to the global energy supply and economic stability remains crystal clear. Disruption of these supplies, whether from domestic upheaval in Saudi Arabia or regional events spiraling out of control, would be disastrous for the world economy and, by extension, for the United States as long as the world's only superpower, as well as its allies, remains dependent on hydrocarbons to power its economy.

A Region in Need of Continued US Attention

Turmoil is nothing new in the Middle East. But the current changes sweeping the region are particularly disruptive and could conceivably bring about political transformations not seen since the 1920s. The instability associated with this upheaval will be significant and will shake many of the assumptions about oil and gas supply from the region over the next decade. Some countries—particularly Iraq—will face even more obstacles to increasing output significantly. Certainly, the most optimistic output estimates for the end of the current decade now look out of the question, and a risk remains that regional events will lead to a fragmentation of the country, which would further depress production growth and could reverse recent gains.

This risk reinforces the importance of Saudi Arabia as the central bank of oil for the foreseeable future. It also illustrates the continued centrality of the Middle East to US economic, energy, and foreign policy. For all the determination and strategic imperative for Washington to pivot its focus eastward, its attention will continue to be dragged back to the Middle East and the need to ensure stability there.

Notes

1. PFC Energy, "US: Moving toward Energy Security," PFC Energy Market Intelligence Service, May 2, 2012. See also Margaret Ryan, "EIA Chief: US Could Reduce Oil Imports to Zero," AOL Energy, October 23, 2012, http://energy.aol.com/2012/10/23/eia-chief-us-could-reduce-oil-imports-to-zero-but-might-not-wa/?a_dgi.

2. According to the US Energy Information Administration (EIA), US crude imports from the Gulf have increased from 1,500 barrels per day in January 2010 to 2,500 barrels per day in May 2012. See the table "US Imports from Persian Gulf Countries of Crude Oil" at EIA's website, http://www.eia.gov/dnav/pet/hist/LeafHandler.ashx?n=PET&s=MCRIMUSPG2&f=M.

3. PFC Energy, "Syria: How Much of a Threat to Regional Stability?," PFC Energy Market Intelligence Service, July 31, 2012.

4. These figures are PFC Energy Market Intelligence Service internal estimates.

5. See EIA, "World Oil Transit Chokepoints," EIA, Washington, DC, August 22, 2012, http://www.eia.gov/countries/regions-topics.cfm?fips=WOTC&trk=p3.

6. These figures are PFC Energy Market Intelligence Service internal estimates.

7. This point has been made repeatedly to the authors in meetings with senior Kurdish leaders over the past six years.

8. See, for example, "Hawrami Announces KRG Oil and Gas Strategy," *Kurdish Globe*, September 24, 2012, http://www.kurdishglobe.net/display-article.html?id=1542DF665716C1D274B73E32DEFE562D.

9. According to PFC Energy internal estimates, in 2012 Saudi Arabia needed a crude oil price of around $70 per barrel to balance its current account.

10. For example, Khalid A. Al-Falih, president and chief executive officer of Saudi Aramco, has expressed such sentiments. See Khalid A. Al-Falih, "Addressing the *Real* Sustainability Challenge," keynote address to the Second International Energy Forum, Paris, April 7, 2011, http://www.ief.org/_resources/files/content/events/2nd-noc-ioc-forum/khalid-al-falih-keynote-speech.pdf. See also Syed Rashid Husain, "Aramco's Prudent Investment Recipe Aimed at Posterity," *Saudi Gazette*, October 28, 2012, http://www.saudigazette.com.sa/index.cfm?method=home.regcon&contentid=20121028140999.

Chapter 11

North Africa and the Mediterranean

Fareed Mohamedi

Once deemed an important and abundant source and market for hydro-carbons, North Africa and the Mediterranean have undergone a massive structural change in the past decade. North Africa was seen as a stable source of natural gas and high-quality oil for Europe and even the far-flung markets of the United States and Japan. In fact, it was part of Europe's triad of natural gas suppliers that ensured its energy security. As a market, Europe promised steady long-term growth for natural gas as the European Union (EU) and the European states created a regulatory environment to encourage the use of natural gas for environmental and efficiency reasons.

Today, none of these statements rings true. For political, economic, and market reasons that are related to changes in global oil and gas, most North African countries have seen their hydrocarbon sectors stagnate and are viewed increasingly as unreliable suppliers of energy. Similarly, European demand has stagnated and, in some countries, has even shrunk because of the economic crisis that has enveloped the continent. As the major thrust of the world hydrocarbon markets shifts east in terms of demand and west in terms of supply, the Mediterranean and North Africa will be seen as less important for energy security in the coming decade.

Major Structural Changes on the Supply Side

Even before Mohamed Bouazizi, the Tunisian fruit seller, sparked the revolution in Tunisia, which then spread to the entire Middle East and North Africa, the oil and gas sectors of the region had begun to stagnate. With the rise in oil prices in the early 2000s, the financial strains in most producers of North Africa disappeared. Notably, by the mid-2000s, Algeria had an abundance of funds, low debt levels, and growing foreign exchange reserves—in contrast to a violent civil war and debilitating debt crisis in the 1990s, during which 98 percent of its oil revenues for a period went to service its external debt.[1] Similarly, Libya emerged from strict sanctions as the Muammar Gaddafi regime negotiated its way "out of the cold" with the West and saw a sharp increase in foreign oil company interest in its potentially prolific oil and gas sector. Egypt, which itself had struggled with insolvency in the 1980s, entered a period of high growth in the 2000s, fueled partly by higher gas revenues but also by funds from investors in Europe and the Arabian (Persian) Gulf.

Libya

High oil prices and the general improvement of the economic environment—and international relations in the case of Libya—hardened the stance of the North African producers toward foreign oil and gas companies. Libya's reopening was anticipated with great excitement by international oil companies (IOCs), but when the terms of the various Exploration and Production-Sharing Agreement rounds revealed relatively low rates of return, IOC interest plummeted. The previous regime also did little to build up the acumen, skills, and capacity of its national oil company (NOC), starving it of funds for major projects while Gaddafi family members indulged in outright theft.[2]

Libya had been the scene for pivotal battles between the internationalizing midsize independents (such as Occidental and Amerada Hess) and the large oil companies (such as ExxonMobil, Shell, BP, and Chevron), which enabled the Organization of the Petroleum Exporting Countries to take control of oil pricing. Despite strong sanctions against it, the Libyan government had protected the interests of these companies and anticipated increased investment after the sanctions were lifted. Such investment did not materialize.

Algeria

In Algeria, the reformist oil and gas minister of Algeria, Chakib Khelil, promised sweeping changes in the oil and gas sector and increased autonomy and international expansion of the NOC, Sonatrach. However, entrenched interests and political forces prevented change and forced Khelil's dismissal. Arrests of key members of Sonatrach management, which resulted in decision-making delays, and the prospect of a maturing hydrocarbon region, all topped by hardened contractual terms, prompted an IOC exodus from the country.[3]

For example, BP had expected high output and returns from its In Salah investment but decided to cut its losses and partially exit. After Algeria made petroleum legislation changes in 1986, many foreign companies returned, even those (such as Total) that had seen their assets nationalized in the 1960s. But even after further reforms in the 2006 hydrocarbon law, three bid rounds were largely failures: only 8 blocks were awarded of the 36 offered. Both the major oil companies and the independents have lost interest in Algeria. ExxonMobil and Chevron have no assets there, and Shell is in the process of withdrawing from the country.

Egypt

In North Africa, high population growth and politically motivated fuel subsidies, enabled by higher economic growth, resulted in an upsurge of demand for oil and gas. This increase in demand, in turn, led to greater strain on the oil and gas sectors of the region. Nowhere was this truer than in Egypt. By the 1990s, Egypt's oil production had begun to stagnate and even decline, at the same time as growing domestic demand was eating into the country's ability to export. Oil exports were an important part of Egypt's foreign currency earnings, in addition to foreign aid, tourism receipts, Suez Canal dues, and exports of agricultural goods.

Fortuitously for Egypt, foreign companies—notably Shell—had discovered substantial quantities of natural gas, which initially allowed the government to substitute natural gas for oil consumption. Eventually, gas supplies were so abundant that a liquefied natural gas (LNG) project was developed, and exports to Europe began. Like oil, however, domestic natural gas demand exploded, thereby increasing the pressure on exports—a problem that persists to this day.[4] The 2012 revolution and resulting economic crisis have dampened domestic demand, but the structural problem has not gone away.

The situation is similar in Algeria, to a lesser extent. Political malaise has not yet translated into revolution and economic disruption. As a result, high domestic demand growth continues in the face of stagnating output.

New Asian and Middle Eastern Investors

Along with high oil prices, the competitive landscape had seemed to favor North African producers in the 2000s. National oil companies from Asia and the Arabian Gulf showed keen interest in investing in North African countries. Chinese NOCs invested in Libya and Algeria, as did their Indian, Thai, and Korean counterparts.[5]

Mubadala, Abu Dhabi's offset program fund, which had begun acquiring a global investment portfolio, also invested in Libya in partnership with Occidental. These funds provided a new source of capital for the North African producers, in addition to the other benefits coming from Asia Inc.

In general, the Asian and Middle Eastern companies were more welcome, because they accepted the harsher terms rejected by other IOCs and their governments were less overbearing than the European and US governments. Despite providing new investment resources, however, these companies have not been able to overcome the general stagnation and, in some cases, decline of the oil and gas sectors of the region.

Major Structural Changes on the Demand Side

Three major factors have transformed the landscape on the demand side. First, the international marketplace for gas has fundamentally changed. Europe moved to diversify its natural gas resources by expanding its LNG imports, continuing to import from Algeria, adding a pipeline from the Caspian Sea, and seeking to create more competition with Russian supplies. Although Egypt could also benefit from these moves to diversify, it faced strong competition from Trinidad and Tobago, Qatar, Equatorial Guinea, and Angola—only for all suppliers to see lessening of European demand with the eurozone crisis.[6]

Second, the US market, to which the Algerians had sold LNG in the late 1980s, had promised to become once again an important market for North African producers. This prospect simply disappeared when US shale gas supplies exploded after 2010. Moreover, LNG supplies from other regions that had been destined for the United States were now encroaching on Algerian market share in Europe. More recently, another phenomenon has started to attack overall gas demand in Europe. Cheap natural gas supplies have taken market share from coal in the United States, especially coal usage for power generation. This development, in turn, has led to sharp increases in coal exports to Europe, where natural gas and coal are more expensive than in the United States. As a consequence, European power companies have shifted from gas toward coal despite political pronouncements against greenhouse gas emissions.

Third, the economic collapse of peripheral countries of the eurozone bodes badly for energy demand and expanding markets for the North African producers. In core Europe, France and Germany were important potential markets for the North African producers, but both were not viewed as reliable long-term partners. The French produced nearly 70 percent of their power from nuclear plants, and the Germans had wed themselves to Russian gas supplies for economic and political strategic reasons, which are only beginning to unwind because more competitive alternatives are beginning to emerge. The Germans also unveiled an energy policy that called for greater reliance on renewables, potentially curtailing their dependence on coal. But critical dependence on coal employment and income still makes it unlikely that Germany will forsake coal for gas.

In sharp contrast to core Europe, the countries of peripheral Europe (Italy, Spain, Greece) were natural partners for the North African producers, given their geographic proximity and what appeared to be strong growth prospects in the 1990s. As a result, several natural gas pipelines were built between the southern and northern shores of the Mediterranean. Given peripheral Europe's dependence on North African natural gas supplies, the EU also embarked on a large aid and economic integration project, a significant but smaller version of the assistance given to new EU members.

Sadly for the North African producers, they are now physically tied to precisely the economies that are undergoing a severe recession—a recession that does not look as though it will abate any time soon. In fact, the peripheral countries of Europe have a fundamental structural economic problem. Their inability to generate sufficient jobs led to an income problem, which was partly offset by government spending funded by debt accumulation. Now, however, they must reduce this spending to pay off their accumulated debt. Peripheral Europe must overcome this structural economic crisis before energy supplies can return in abundance from North Africa and again become a long-term energy solution for future economic growth.

The Revolution and Its Energy Consequences

The Arab Spring started in North Africa, but it is symptomatic of similar problems that plague the wider Middle East and North Africa region. The fundamental problem of rentierism based on oil and gas revenues is behind the uprisings in the region.[7] Overdependence on these revenues led to economic policies that discouraged productive investments. Given the capital-intensive and highly technical nature of the oil and gas sector, it generated little employment and had few extended links to the overall economy, in contrast to the energy industry in more developed countries, with its extended downstream and supply chains. Governments also had few incentives, especially in times of high oil prices, to invest in other sectors. Inefficient and poor infrastructure investments led inevitably to periods of high inflation, which critically hurt the poor. Governments overspent to forestall political revolts rather than investing in long-term diversification.

Except for the past few years, there was never enough money to meet the regime's appetite for guns and the popular aspirations for butter. As a result, most of the governments of North Africa got into financial trouble and were forced to go to the International Monetary Fund (IMF) or external aid agencies for assistance. That aid came with economic conditionality that invariably translated into cuts in social welfare programs, which brought with them a rising sense of economic vulnerability for the middle classes and poor.[8]

But structural adjustment policies also opened up commercial opportunities for many of the elite in North Africa. It became a common phenomenon in the North African states for sons of presidents (Gamal Mubarak, son of Hosni Mubarak, or Saif al Islam Gaddafi, son of Muammar Gaddafi) or close relatives (the brother-in-law of Zine El Abidine Ben Ali) to own monopolistic businesses or control critical sectors of the economy. Not only were these elites seen to be making a lot of money—while the rest of the population's income stagnated or fell—but they also were the gatekeepers of the economy and handed out access to important sectors only in return for political subservience. The combination of outright theft by the regimes and cutbacks, especially in a time of plenty, led to the revolt of the populations, sometimes with the support of the regime's key coercive agencies, the military and the secret services.[9]

Rentierism also fed back to hurt the oil and gas sectors. Excessive current spending on subsidies and welfare left less to be retained by the NOCs for investment in the oil and gas sectors. Moreover, subsidies spurred wasteful domestic consumption, which ate into the surpluses for export. This vicious cycle of politically motivated spending, underinvestment in the sector, and stagnating or falling supplies eventually undermined the ability of the dictators to sustain themselves.[10]

Postrevolutionary Prospects

The critical uncertainty today after the revolutions is whether things will change—or even whether one or another revolution will go into a more extreme phase. On that front, there is quite a bit of skepticism that the political revolutions will yield fundamental and needed economic change. Will they put economies on a virtuous cycle of productive development, with growing employment and incomes and, as a consequence, lessening overdependence on the oil and gas sectors?

Although growing domestic economies will need more local oil and gas production, they will also need to be more efficient in the use of such production. Skepticism of this sort of future stems from the pent-up demand for material relief in the population. We have already seen that the first instinct of the new regimes is to spend more on welfare, subsidies, and other forms of income support and distribution. While boosting domestic demand, the revolutions have undermined what little production capacity existed in these countries. Capital flight or expropriations of property from formerly politically connected businessmen undermined these countries' private sectors. Plus, continuing political turmoil has scared away private investment, both domestic and foreign. And in the case of Egypt and Tunisia, both huge recipients of tourist dollars, political instability has caused tourists to flee.

If these countries cannot spawn productive economies, then the prospects for economically secure groups negotiating a better collective future look extremely pessimistic. And without productive economies, the states will not be able to diversify away from oil and gas to other revenue sources. The political consequence will be to sustain the authoritarian or at least illiberal nature of the new regimes, which will revert to using oil and gas revenues to fund their rule.

The other more extreme consequence of the revolutions is state failure, as has been seen in Libya. To one degree or another, most North African states suffered from general weakness that was more a consequence of systemic faults: rentierism and unproductive economies. In the case of Libya, the Gaddafi regime actively undermined any attempts at useful state building as a means to subvert any challenges to its rule. So when the revolt came, it started in the east — an area that Gaddafi had kept suppressed because the previous regime of King Idris had sprung from there — and it led to wholesale collapse of key government institutions, including the military and secret service, as well as other public services. What sprang up in the place of these institutions were primordial clans and militia, either for self-protection or to attack the regime's forces. At this writing, the current Libyan government is a mixture of Islamist groups, previously severely suppressed by Gaddafi, and regional militias. To some extent power has shifted back to the east, with periodic threats from militias and groups from Benghazi calling for outright secession from Libya. As a result, not only does the government remain weak and fractured, but also the prospect of a country falling apart clouds the horizon.[11]

Consequences of the Revolutions for Oil and Gas

Oil and gas sectors require stable sources of capital for investment and a regulatory and investment environment that is secure and stable and that allows private sector players to make profitable returns. Unfortunately, the North African oil and gas sectors seem currently to have none of these attributes.

Algeria

Algeria's oil and gas supplies have stagnated. Government investment in infrastructure and pipelines is chronically delayed by Sonatrach's operational and pricing problems. For example, phases 1 and 2 of the

South West Gas Project are expected to add sufficient supplies to off-set the declines in Algeria's large Hassi R'Mel and Hassi Messaoud gas fields. However, delays in building a major trunk line could delay the gas supplies until 2016. The Algerians are also very keen to develop tight gas, which could generate large new supplies for the country. However, the Algerian government is bogged down in price negotiations with the French company Total. Total wishes to receive a higher price that is based on LNG sales, but the government seeks a lower price, because it may have to use the gas for domestic consumption, including its ambitious petrochemical and power generation projects. Throughout, slow government decision-making, conflicting objectives, and domestic pricing concerns complicate Algeria's future. At great cost, in January 2013, Algerian forces killed 89 jihadists and their hostages after they seized BP's southwestern In Amenas gas complex and reportedly were planning to blow it up—one more brutal reminder of the need to protect more effectively energy infrastructure and workers.

Egypt

Three factors cloud the future of the oil and gas sector in Egypt. Political turmoil has created fears among foreign investors of administrative chaos and regulatory and tax volatility. The Morsi government has tried to stabilize its external finances with a loan from the IMF. One of the conditions of the loan is cuts in subsidies, expected to be £E 70 billion in 2013. There are already indications that these cuts will be implemented very slowly, given their unpopularity and the threat of more political violence. Also, a government bogged down by populist demands is not likely to focus on infrastructure development.

The oil and gas sector will likely continue to experience the payment and approval delays that have plagued it in the past several years. Against the backdrop of deep working-class discontent, strikes are emerging in the oil and gas patch. These strikes not only disrupt production but also make many companies extremely nervous about further investments. In a 2012 exploration bid round, the Egyptian General Petroleum Corporation, the NOC, awarded 11 blocks out of 15, which it saw as a success. In fact, however, foreign investor interest was tepid, with no new players and no tactical moves by existing players to shore up their current positions in the sector.[12]

Libya

Much the same is happening in Libya. Oil and gas production stopped during the civil war, but then foreign companies restored production within a year of the cessation of hostilities. However, new exploration commitments by foreign companies have lagged because of the security situation and uncertain political outlook. The Arabian Gulf Oil Company, the Benghazi-based NOC affiliate, has been at the forefront of postrevolutionary exploratory drilling, especially in the Ghadames Basin.[13]

Foreign oil companies have said that their delays are due to the lack of availability of rigs, but in some cases, the delays are due to severe political disputes. For example, China National Petroleum Corporation has not returned for fear of reprisals for Chinese assistance to the Gaddafi regime and because it is demanding compensation for damages suffered during the civil war. Japanese and other companies are relinquishing blocks and moving away.

These moves may be temporary, and stability may bring Libya back into the investor's spotlight. The new oil minister, Abdelbari Al-Arusi, is an oil man, educated in the United Kingdom. Al-Arusi worked for Sirte Oil before being fired for his Islamist politics. He bridges several political, professional, and regional divides in the ruling coalition and may bring necessary stability to the oil and gas sector.

New Plays, Old Politics

Major offshore gas finds by Noble Energy raise the prospect of Israel's becoming a major exporter of LNG. However, they have also ignited a major political row within the country. Conservationist politicians have called for an export ban on natural gas, which they would like to keep exclusively for home use. Such a measure would provide Israel with energy security virtually forever, they argue. A less publicized reason that many prominent leaders have joined the conservationist call is that exports would enrich and empower influential tycoons such as Ofer Nimrodi, who owns the Israel Land Development Company (ILDC). In their view, tycoons like Nimrodi already control too much of the Israeli economy, and gas exports would just worsen the distribution of income. Israel's recent Arab Spring–like riots over economic and income distribution seem to confirm these developments.

The Zemach Committee of the Knesset ruled for a compromise between the exporters and the conservationists. Companies will be able to export

500 billion cubic meters (bcm) of gas out of total reserves of 950 bcm.[14] However, this ruling was thrown into doubt by ILDC's failure to find gas in the Sara and Mira license blocks, which were viewed as safe-bet fields containing around 182 bcm of gas and 150 million barrels of oil. This failure could energize the conservationists in future elections and further delay the development of LNG projects in Israel.

Gas found off the coast of Cyprus has led to hopes that LNG revenues would lift the island state out of its economic straits. In line with this aim, Nicosia awarded four offshore blocks to international companies.[15] Two of the companies, Total and Eni, are European companies; given the island's dependence on the Europeans for economic help, this award clearly signaled that Cyprus could become another source of European gas. The two other companies, Gazprombank and Novatek, are Russian, and their political connections and deep pockets help Cyprus financially and politically. Notably, no Israeli companies were given any awards, apparently to limit the country's dependence on Israel. This outcome was unexpected, because Cyprus and Israel had signed an understanding to bring Israeli gas for liquefaction to Cyprus. They had even signed a defense treaty, partly as a result of Turkish saber rattling. Turkey claims the gas as part of the internationally unrecognized Turkish Republic of Northern Cyprus. The defense treaty and the Cyprus–Israeli energy cooperation have been factors in the decline in good relations between Turkey and Israel.

What is also notable about the development of Eastern Mediterranean gas is how little interest it has generated among the private IOCs and even the Asian NOCs. Most observers believe that investing in these two zones exposes companies to the vagaries of two of the most complicated geopolitical problems. Turkey has already threatened to exclude any IOCs from its territory if they invest in Cyprus, which seemed not to turn away Total, despite its participation in the Baku–Tbilisi–Ceyhan pipeline, and Eni, which has a stake in the Blue Stream pipeline. But other companies—investors in either Caucasus–Central Asia or the Gulf region—have chosen to stay away from these geopolitically charged regions.

The Mediterranean in Global Context

In conclusion, the Mediterranean has changed quite dramatically and rapidly. No more is it seen as the pivotal region it once was only one to two decades ago. With the rise of Asia, West Asian NOCs are seeking stronger strategic ties with their East Asian brothers and are creating a pan-Asian trading system. East Africa's new discoveries will also add to these supplies. With the rise of North American supplies and Brazilian and Angolan deepwater discoveries, the Atlantic Basin will become another focal point, while some of its supplies could also cross the Pacific. Russia is also starting to turn away from Europe and is seeking new markets in the East.

The Mediterranean region will spend the next decade or two rebuilding its debt-ridden economies on the northern shore and its virtually broken states on the southern shore. Energy will still be an important link between the two shores, and it certainly could make a larger contribution to economic development and growth, but this sector will not be sufficient to revive the economic and political prospects of the region.

Notes

1. These figures are based on historical data of the International Monetary Fund.

2. PFC Energy, "LNOC Strategy and Performance Profile," NOC Strategies Service, May 21, 2012.

3. James Cockayne, "Foreign Investors Look for Streamlined Algerian Oil Bureaucracy as Shell Exits," *Middle East Economic Survey*, September 28, 2012.

4. James Cockayne, "Payment Delays Turn Independents away from Egypt," *Middle East Economic Survey*, October 12, 2012. See also "Growing Gas Shortage Forces Egypt to Import LNG," *Middle East Economic Survey*, October 26, 2012.

5. Xin Ma, "China's Energy Strategy in the Middle East," *Middle East Economic Survey*, June 9, 2008. See also Florence C. Fee, "Asian Oils in Africa: A Challenge to the International Community," *Middle East Economic Survey*, April 24, 2006.

6. See Pierre Noël, "European Gas Supply Security: Unfinished Business," chapter 7 of this volume.

7. Ralph Chami, Ahmed Al-Darwish, Serhan Cevik, Joshua Charap, Susan George, Borja Gracia, Simon Gray, and Sailendra Pattanayak, "Libya Beyond the Revolution: Challenges and Opportunities," International Monetary Fund, Washington, DC, 2012.

8. Chris Toensing, "Tunisian Labor Leaders Reflect upon Revolt," *Middle East Report* 258 (2011): 30–32. See also Mona El-Ghobashy, "The Praxis of the Egyptian Revolution," *Middle East Report* 258 (2011): 2–13.

9. Omar S. Dahl, "Understanding the Political Economy of the Arab Revolts," *Middle East Report* 259 (2011): 2–6.

10. PFC Energy, "Arab Spring: Longer Term Effects," PFC Energy Market Intelligence Service, November 28, 2011.

11. Rafiq Latta, "Security, Politics Dominate Libyan Oil Sector Concerns," *Middle East Economic Survey*, October 26, 2012.

12. James Cockayne, "Egypt Finalizes Bidding Award," *Middle East Economic Survey*, November 16, 2012.

13. James Cockayne, "Eni Returns to Libyan Exploration Drilling," *Middle East Economic Survey*, December 7, 2012. See also, James Cockayne, "Libya's AGOCO

Looks to New Ghadames Production Heartland," *Middle East Economic Survey*, November 2, 2012.

14. Theodore Tsakiris, "Israel Gas Export Options Blurred," *Middle East Economic Survey*, November 9, 2012.

15. Gary Lakes, "Cyprus Awards Four Offshore Licenses," *Middle East Economic Survey*, November 2, 2012.

Chapter 12

Sub-Saharan Africa

Phillip van Niekerk and Aaron Sayne

Sub-Saharan Africa will continue to play a relatively modest but active role in US energy interests in the future. Growing US supplies of light sweet crude are tempering US demand for African hydrocarbons.[1] However, despite security and anticorruption challenges, opportunities for investment remain attractive and varied for both major energy companies and independents.

On a policy level, US interest in increased oil and gas production from Sub-Saharan Africa will continue to hinge on (a) the effects of such production on world markets and regional stability and (b) the potential for the increased investment and production to support high levels of growth in Sub-Saharan Africa, which in turn will bolster Africa's emergence as a trade and diplomatic partner.

Moderate US Role in Exploration and Production
in Sub-Saharan Africa

From Somalia to Namibia, from Mauritania to Mozambique, Africa's energy resources are generating great interest. Currently all but 4 of the continent's 54 nations are either drilling or producing oil or gas. The region accounts for roughly 7 percent of current global crude production. Current signs suggest US interests will have an active but moderate role.

Offshore prospects among established producers on Africa's west coast remain solid. In January 2012, Angola (the second-largest African oil producer, with 9 billion barrels in reserves) followed Brazil by announcing major presalt drilling successes, the precise extent of which remains unquantified. Long one of the continent's most stable suppliers, Angola's government now is chasing 2 million barrels per day (mmbpd) production by 2014, up from less than 1.8 mmbpd in 2011. Gabon likewise has considerable subsalt potential, which could reverse its otherwise declining outputs.

A number of smaller West African states are also expected either to ramp up production or to pump first oil this decade. Ghana leads thus far, with the government targeting 5 billion barrels of proven reserves by 2015. The geology offshore neighboring Liberia and Sierra Leone looks promising, and minor producers such as Mauritania and Côte d'Ivoire are stepping up.

At the same time, investor interest is pivoting toward East and Central Africa. The meteoric rise of natural gas reserves in neighbors Mozambique and Tanzania—where an estimated 100 trillion to 150 trillion cubic feet of gas have been discovered since 2010—leaves the region well placed to become one of the world's top gas producers by 2020. Some analysts predict East Africa could challenge Australia as the top liquefied natural gas (LNG) exporter within a decade. Discoveries of oil in Kenya's Turkana region also greatly boosted East Africa's profile as a crude oil source. Prior to 2012, West Africa's proven reserves trumped the East by 10 to 1. Finally, in the heart of the continent, Uganda is making some progress toward first production from a reservoir in the Lake Albert Basin, which borders neighboring Democratic Republic of the Congo (DRC). With production from South Sudan and new discoveries near Lake Turkana in the north of Kenya, East Africa is set to emerge as a substantial crude oil producer. Accompanying this production will be a new pipeline traversing the region and exiting at the envisaged new deepwater port of Lamu in Kenya.

US concessionaires—particularly mid-level independent operators—recently announced some of the most significant finds in Sub-Saharan

Table 12.1. Supermajor Asset Transactions in Sub-Saharan Africa, by Company and Country, 2008–Second Quarter 2012

Company	Buys	Sales
Chevron	1 (Liberia)	2 (Joint Development Zone, Nigeria)
ExxonMobil	3 (Liberia, Nigeria, Tanzania)	0
Shell	5	9
BP	5 (2 countries)	0
Total	14	11

Sources: Data from Energy Intelligence, Argus, and author interviews with industry experts.

Africa.[2] Recent strikes suggest that lower exploration costs, use of new technology, and willingness to take first-mover risks can pay well in the region. Sub-Saharan Africa also continues to offer top US-based oil field service contractors such as KBR and Baker Hughes opportunities that are lacking in other, less open environments. The United States has little presence in physical trading of energy in Africa, where Europeans and—to a lesser degree—Asians dominate.

US majors ExxonMobil and Chevron have been slower to expand their operations in Sub-Saharan Africa, though executives say their interest in the region remains solid. Both do have major stakes, mostly tied to megaprojects in established producers such as Nigeria, Angola, and Equatorial Guinea. Together these projects yield more than 1 mmbpd. ExxonMobil and Chevron have recently shied away from frontier locations, except for Chevron's move into Liberia. In terms of mergers and acquisitions activity, the two firms have also fallen behind their European counterparts in Sub-Saharan Africa, as shown in table 12.1.

A mix of factors explains ExxonMobil's and Chevron's relatively conservative stances on new Sub-Saharan African investments. Both companies have major technological edges in the deepwater, where most development potential lies. Yet their global project queues and overhead cost structures point them to "hunting the elephants"—fields with a minimum of 1 billion barrels of reserves. This situation effectively priced the majors out of much of the more modest frontier acreage offered in recent Sub-Saharan African

Table 12.2. US Crude Oil Imports from Sub-Saharan Africa, by Country and Production Volume: Average Daily Barrels, 2006–12

Location	Average Daily Barrels		
	2006 (annual)	2011 (annual)	2012 (June)
Nigeria	1,037	767	471
Angola	513	335	346
Chad	95	49	0
Gabon	60	34	45
Equatorial Guinea	57	19	56
Congo-Brazzaville	27	53	22
DRC	0	11	0
Côte d'Ivoire	4	4	0
Mauritania	3	2	0
Cameroon	2	36	64
All countries	10,118	8,935	9,101
Total from Sub-Saharan Africa	1,798	1,310	1,004
Sub-Saharan Africa as a share of total imports (%)	17.7	14.7	11.0

Source: Data from US Energy Information Administration.

licensing bonanzas. ExxonMobil's and Chevron's high public profiles also increasingly make them sensitive to investing in violent, corrupt, or politically unstable places.

Low US Imports from Sub-Saharan Africa

US crude oil imports from Sub-Saharan Africa have declined in recent years, because US production of light sweet crudes displaces those imports. Between 2006 and 2011, US purchases of African crude fell by 27 percent, with further cuts in 2012. Nigerian imports were the most affected, as seen in table 12.2.

The current combination of lower domestic demand; growing domestic light oil production; political calls for energy independence; higher reliance on heavier Canadian and Arabian Gulf grades (mainly from Saudi

Arabia, Kuwait, and Iraq); and shrinking margins for East Coast refiners may continue to stunt US demand for Nigeria's premium light sweet crude, though it is early to forecast a permanent shift away from Nigerian or other African oil.[3] Yet the potential for developments in Sub-Saharan Africa to influence US energy prices is small but not always de minimis. History suggests that sudden, extreme supply disruptions on the continent can contribute to global price hikes, and a disruption in any of Sub-Saharan Africa's major exporters could rock world markets.

The United States imports no natural gas from the region, and increases in domestic gas production from hydraulic fracturing mean that East African gas will find other markets. Chief among these will be Asia, where recently the Fukushima disaster, Indian power blackouts, and market gaps created by delayed LNG projects in Nigeria all suggest favorable conditions for future East African sales.

Asian Competition?

China's three state-owned oil companies are active in Sub-Saharan Africa, though the extent to which this activity represents a threat to Western interests has been overstated. The China National Petroleum Corporation (CNPC) is active in Chad, Mauritania, and Sudan; Sinopec is engaged in Nigeria, Ghana, and Angola; and the China National Offshore Oil Corporation (CNOOC) is playing in Nigeria, Uganda, Equatorial Guinea, and Kenya.

Market and investment trends do not support the common claim that the Chinese are creating a new scramble for Africa by competing with the United States for scarce energy resources. To date, no clear evidence indicates that China's presence in Sub-Saharan African oil is substantially affecting Western supplies or prices. Earlier in the 2000s, Chinese companies did beat out US contenders for a few choice blocks, often by dangling attractive oil-for-infrastructure deals, foremost in Angola.[4] Some in the sector saw such package deals as a fundamental threat to US ways of doing business in Sub-Saharan Africa. But with time, it became clear that the region's energy sector was a relatively minor front in the broader competition between the United States and China.

One common prediction, for instance, had Nigeria taking a major diplomatic and commercial turn toward China, led by shifts in global markets and diplomacy. Instead, high cost sensitivity among Chinese refiners, the slowing of China's commodities boom, and mediocre management of the

Nigeria–China bilateral relationship kept China buying only about 20,000 barrels per day of crude from Nigeria in recent years — or roughly 1 percent of average daily production. At the same time, the United States effectively turned away from Nigeria by buying less crude, and once that happened, China did not rush to pick up what Americans left on the table.[5] Similarly, the few blocks that the Asian tigers won during Nigeria's 2005–07 licensing rounds still sit idle, and a plan for Chinese interests to construct three new greenfield refineries in the country has faltered.[6] Chinese firms have had greater success in less chaotic Angola.

Three main trends define China's position in Sub-Saharan African energy today. First, Chinese firms have made only limited commercial advances with established producers. Shares in Sub-Saharan African energy blocks remain modest, with Malaysia's Petronas holding the most equity on the continent. Most acquisitions have not involved operatorship.[7] Second, although Chinese strategies for entering Sub-Saharan Africa have differed in some respects from those of US firms, the big three Chinese companies participate in Sub-Saharan African blocks through negotiated commercial and technical partnerships, the same as Western players.[8] Third, both emerging and established Sub-Saharan African producers may be looking at Chinese investment more skeptically. Performance records of oil-for-infrastructure deals and oil-backed loans are poor, and the model may be losing favor.[9]

China, it should be noted, is not the only Asian player in Sub-Saharan Africa. Companies from India, South Korea, Taiwan, and Thailand have also invested in African oil and gas. Their overall market shares remain small, despite some high-profile acquisitions.[10] Japan is not a significant producer or buyer of Sub-Saharan African crude oil or gas.

Limited Resource Nationalism

Few Sub-Saharan African governments (or national oil companies) have the technical capacity to conduct deepwater exploration on their own or the bureaucratic capacity and political clout to strike stiff deals with large oil companies. The US supermajors, in particular, are highly skilled and resourced, and the outdated laws and budget shortfalls many emerging producers face tend only to strengthen the companies' hand in negotiations.

Most African producers have relatively open oil and gas regimes, allowing free participation by private firms. This situation can make investments in Sub-Saharan Africa attractive compared to those in much of the Middle

East—for instance, in Saudi Arabia, where the sector is dominated by seasoned state-owned oil companies. Sub-Saharan African fiscal systems are also relatively favorable to operators, and countries have fewer burdensome partnership requirements, local labor quotas, and restrictions on trade and procurement, among other things.

Relations between Sub-Saharan African governments and oil companies can be tense, however, and officials are increasingly assertive at the bargaining table. Some African oil bureaucracies have become quite skilled at running auctions, negotiating supply contracts, and setting oil prices. Laws containing basic fiscal terms are being reworked, most notably in the long-running debate around Nigeria's Petroleum Industry Bill, which is discussed later. A few jurisdictions are also closing loopholes that allow for oil company tax avoidance through, for instance, transfer pricing and nonpayment of capital gains.

Thus far, most energy sector reforms by Sub-Saharan African producers have done a fair job of balancing competing desires to boost public revenue and to optimize investment conditions. Grassroots advocacy has spurred some reform and renegotiation efforts, as ordinary Africans demand to see more benefits of oil production trickling down. Several nations have also mounted ambitious, populist drives to boost local content in their energy sectors. At best, local content initiatives can open spaces for serious indigenous players, as a few stories from Nigeria may suggest. At worst, they devolve into an added tax on investment and corruption risk, as seen elsewhere in Nigeria and particularly Angola.

Corruption and Weak Governance

Most history in older Sub-Saharan African producers, such as Nigeria, Gabon, Equatorial Guinea, and Angola, shows that fast influxes of natural resource wealth encourage corruption, poor sector management, and low-value economic policies—often referred to as "the resource curse."[11] Nearly all of the region's current and future oil- and gas-producing nations regularly score at the bottom of Transparency International's Corruption Perceptions Index and other relevant benchmarks. Most have young and weak formal institutions, patronage- and sharing-based political economies, high poverty, and underpaid civil servants.

The participation of multinationals in African energy sector corruption—most particularly oil field service providers—became clearer throughout the 2000s. Rising enforcement of the US Foreign Corrupt Practices Act (FCPA), which bars US companies from paying bribes to foreign officials to win business, took Sub-Saharan African oil and gas as a focus point.[12] Some US-linked oil company executives cite the FCPA, in particular, as a constraint on how they do business in the region, while acknowledging high levels of underlying corruption, down to the point of final investment decisions.[13] Meantime, nongovernmental organizations such as Global Witness, Revenue Watch, and Human Rights Watch published damaging, well-researched reports and kept up a drumbeat about the dangers of opaque deal-making and weak oil sector management.[14]

The clear global trend is toward more enforcement and disclosure. New legislation, notably the 2010 UK Bribery Act and section 1504 of the US Dodd–Frank Act, could compound the risks of paying bribes if vigorously enforced. Anecdotal evidence also suggests that high-profile money-laundering convictions, asset seizures, and diplomatic measures against African oil kleptocrats—notably by the United States, the United Kingdom, France, and Switzerland—can raise the perceived opportunity costs of graft for opportunistic officials.[15]

For their part, African producers have the option of signing on to a range of multistakeholder transparency initiatives.[16] Major prosecutions for oil-related corruption have been rarer at home, but new producers are writing strong transparency language into their laws and contracts and publishing more information online.[17] Some officials seem to take these issues seriously; others become fluent in Western "good governance" speak as a means to greater investment and legitimacy. Donors continue supporting civil society groups that advocate better management of natural resources.

As an example of the common governance hurdles facing new producers, consider Mozambique. Notwithstanding the country's favorable geology, Mozambique's government needs to address a number of key challenges for Mozambican gas to reach world markets by 2020. Adequate infrastructure and local workers are scarce. New fiscal and commercial terms must be agreed on before major LNG development can start. Complex unitization discussions could delay first production on some projects. A political economy thick with conflicts of interest raises risks of anti-corruption liability. Meanwhile, competition in the global gas market is robust, with Australia and Qatar well out in front; Equatorial Guinea and Angola making gains; and China, India, and the United States looking forward to shale gas booms. Poor official decisions in such an environment could carry stiff penalties.

Security and Stability Concerns

At the policy level, arguably the strongest US strategic interests in Sub-Saharan African energy relate to larger questions of how stability in energy-rich African nations can promote healthy world market performance and other key US priorities, such as democratization, reduced opportunity for transnational crime, eradication of disease, and poverty alleviation. A stable, energy-rich Sub-Saharan Africa aligns with broader US interests in the region and beyond.

Historically, Africa has had few outright oil wars, the one notable exception being Sudan, where a conflict over religion, ethnicity, and regionalism deepened into a battle over the distribution of oil—particularly access to and fees of a pipeline controlled by the north. The dispute continues to simmer, despite a political settlement in 2012; building an alternative line to the east would take two to three years and large amounts of coordinated investment.

The Sudanese oil fields are relatively clearly divided between South and North. The major problem and source of conflict is that the government of South Sudan has been entirely dependent on the pipeline to Port Sudan to export its oil. After the south part of the country became independent in 2011, the government of Sudan upped the transfer fee to extortionate levels—more than 30 times the average transit fee. The government of South Sudan responded by blocking oil production, and the countries veered close to war.

Under prodding from the international community, a deal was struck in Addis Ababa, Ethiopia, on September 27, 2012, the most serious oil deal to date. But it was at best a stopgap measure that is already in danger of breaking down, and the only long-term solution to eliminate tensions over oil is for the government of South Sudan to build a pipeline to the Kenyan coast, where the leading contender is a new deepwater port that is being planned at Lamu.

The most likely course for the pipe is to run from Lake Albert in Uganda across Kenya, pick up the Lake Turkana oil, connect with a line down from South Sudan, and then travel on to the coast. The costs of this enterprise are immense, and the challenge of getting Uganda, South Sudan, and Kenya on the same page is also immense.

Africa's boundaries, often drawn by colonial powers, have a long history of provoking regional conflict, some of it violent. Legal disputes over maritime boundaries lying across potential oil reserves are already stacking up between Angola and DRC; Uganda and DRC; Côte d'Ivoire and Ghana;

Tanzania and Malawi; and Mozambique, the Comoros, and Madagascar. None of these disputes appears likely to degenerate into interstate warfare, however.

There is also a chance that complaints over inequitable oil wealth distribution and official corruption will fuel intrastate conflicts.[18] For many Africans, poverty, income inequality, and youth unemployment will initially be high as state oil proceeds roll in. Strong quality-of-living divides between rural and urban areas, rising citizen expectations, and divisive identity policies around oil can also deepen grievances and provoke violence.

Political transitions and rifts in some countries could also challenge the stated US goal of promoting democratic consolidation in Africa. Following a decline in military-backed dictatorship across the continent, a number of Sub-Saharan African producers—Angola and Equatorial Guinea, for instance—may see major leadership shifts this decade as long-ruling strongmen step down or age out. Some analysts see major generational gaps opening in the politics of Nigeria, Angola, and Mozambique, among others. That these changes will result in significant violence or instability is far from certain.

Insecurity can also curb investment in Sub-Saharan African oil and gas, particularly by the US majors. Perceived conflict and corruption risks convinced Chevron to pull out of Sudan decades ago, and ExxonMobil has largely suspended its expansion plans in weakly governed Chad. Somalia may be hydrocarbon rich, but civil war, terrorism, and organized crime keep it closed.

In a few cases, broader concerns about preventing terrorism on the continent could inhibit US energy policy and investment plans. Some security analysts fear that well-armed local pastoralists and terrorist attacks linked to Somalia's Al-Shabaab militia could frustrate future investments in Kenyan oil and Ethiopian gas. In West Africa, Islamist-linked insurrection has helped delay drilling in Mali's section of the promising Taoudeni Basin.

Perhaps the ultimate concern is that pumping oil in some dusty, disenfranchised parts of the continent could fund regional terrorist cells, deepen secessionist tendencies, or contribute to state failure. Niger, which security sources say hosts various bands of Islamist militants and criminal mercenaries, is claiming reserves in excess of 300 million barrels, with perhaps 20,000 barrels per day currently being pumped and refined locally.

Spokespersons for Nigerian terrorist phenomenon Boko Haram list mismanagement of oil wealth and sectional inequalities as key grievances. However, the vast majority of African oil and gas reserves are well south of the Islamist fault line that crosses through Mauritania, Mali, Niger, Chad, Sudan, and Somalia, and thus far predictions that terrorism in northern Nigeria could spread through West Africa appear overstated.

A Broader Energy Agenda

Sub-Saharan Africa's rising profile in world energy markets is central to its emergence as a trade and diplomatic partner to developed nations such as the United States. Six of the world's fastest-growing economies in 2012 are in Africa, and all but two African countries had growth rates above that of the United States. Though baselines can be low, African markets offer investors returns not readily available in the sluggish US and European economies.

Outlays on oil and gas infrastructure—from offshore platforms to processing plants and pipelines—will dominate foreign direct investment in Africa for the future, just as high commodity prices support some of the high gross domestic product figures recorded. However, burgeoning local markets for mobile phones, innovative financial products, and the exponential growth of internal consumer markets are the real drivers of growth for many countries. Ethiopia and Kenya, two of the fastest growers, are not major oil or mining hubs.

Africa remains paradoxically an energy-poor continent as it gears up to export more of its oil and gas. Electricity supply is spotty in most cities and can be nonexistent in rural areas. The entire installed generation capacity of Sub-Saharan Africa's 48 nations is 68 gigawatts—an amount roughly equal to that of Spain. Without South Africa, the total falls to 28 gigawatts.

Better electrification could be a powerful economic multiplier across the region. With the right policies and infrastructural investments, resource-rich countries in Sub-Saharan Africa could likely sustain their high growth rates and draw tens of billions of dollars in new short- and medium-term investment.[19] The raw materials, whether coal, thermal, gas, or water, are there. Renewable energy breakthroughs in the United States and elsewhere could also provide significant support for many sun-rich, windswept rural areas difficult to connect to national grids.

Improving electricity access in Sub-Saharan Africa should be a winning proposition for US interests.[20] In October 2012, at Georgetown University, US Secretary of State Hillary Clinton asserted that the United States "has an interest in helping the 1.3 billion people worldwide who don't have access to energy. We believe the more they can access power, the better their chances of starting businesses, educating their children, increasing their incomes, joining the global economy—all of which is good for them and for us."[21]

Nigeria: The Cautionary Tale

Paradoxically, Sub-Saharan Africa's energy giant offers the clearest case of promise deferred. Despite favorable geology and deep sector experience, Nigeria is a chronic underachiever, for several reasons.

A sometimes violent rebellion in the oil-producing Niger Delta has undermined security and development. Violence is driven by a tangle of environmental, political, and socioeconomic grievances, often with complex links to organized criminality. A 2009 amnesty for militants featuring large cash handouts and training programs has helped restore calm, along with the fact that Nigeria's president since 2010, Goodluck Jonathan, is an ethnic Ijaw from the Niger Delta. Many unanswered issues remain, however, and long-term peace is far from assured.

As conflict in the Niger Delta was being brought under control, an Islamist rebellion erupted in the country's predominantly Muslim north. The shadowy, diffuse movement Boko Haram launched a campaign of random attacks and suicide bombings on government buildings and churches, costing the lives of thousands of innocents. Though most attacks have been in the north, far from the country's oil patch, they do challenge the state security of a long-time pro-Western and reliable US ally in Sub-Saharan Africa. The Jonathan administration is scrambling to get on top of the situation, and it has made peace moves with factions of Boko Haram.

Ultimately, Boko Haram is a manifestation of deeper political tensions in the country, some of which overlie existing ethnic, socioeconomic, generational, and regional fault lines. Thus far, no signs strongly indicate that Boko Haram attacks will affect oil production or investment. The Nigerian federation also has a long, creative history of sharing oil wealth and power to avoid security crises. Future moments of high political competition—above all, the 2015 presidential polls—will test how far the old settlement mechanisms can keep order both in the north and in the Niger Delta.

After a stint as the world's second major site of expatriate kidnappings, Nigeria now ranks behind only Somalia as a locus of maritime piracy. Pirate operations, in turn, reportedly draw manpower, intelligence, and logistical support from one or more Niger Delta oil theft rings, which together could export tens of thousands of barrels of stolen crude per day into world markets.

High security costs and maturing onshore reservoirs have several of the supermajors pondering limited exit strategies, which in turn will open spaces for smaller foreign and indigenous players. Shell has led in onshore divestments thus far, selling off its stake in four high-producing blocks in the Niger Delta. ConocoPhillips floated plans to divest its modest Nigerian portfolio in July 2012, and four months later Total surprised many by selling a producing deepwater block (oil mining lease 138) to Sinopec for $2.5 billion.

Decades of mixed sector management have also diverted funds away from Nigerian oil and gas development. The country's oil bureaucracy has solid pockets of technical, commercial, and political competence. Top officials often show willingness to adapt to broader industry trends. But a culture of self-dealing, patronage, and chronic politicization blocks much development potential and increasingly stifles optimism in the sector. Questionable bureaucratic meddling can delay contracting and project rollout for years at a time.[22] Meanwhile billions in oil revenues set aside for national development do not reach beneficiaries, mostly because of endemic corruption and waste.

The resulting gridlock appears to be eroding the Nigerian petroleum sector's technical and commercial fundamentals. Oil reserves grew by less than 30 percent during the 2000s—the lowest rate of all major Sub-Saharan African producers apart from Congo-Brazzaville. The last major discovery in Nigeria's much vaunted deepwater is more than a decade old, with more than 20 awarded blocks sitting idle. Even without supply disruptions from theft and sabotage, and even when factoring in gains from the amnesty program, production today is barely at 2005 levels. Government data show output from aging onshore wells falling 10 to 12 percent a year with scarce replacements. According to the consulting group Wood Mackenzie, without serious investment, production could fall 20 percent by 2020.[23] Meanwhile, exploitation of Nigeria's gas reserves—among the largest in the world—was slowed by low political attention, underinvestment, infrastructure deficits, and power sector dysfunction.

Over time, such problems have reduced the government's earnings from oil. Nigeria's aging reservoirs now require billions of dollars in extra operating costs each year to maintain even current production levels. The international oil companies carry the government's share of costs on roughly a quarter of all crude production, attracting average finance charges of 9 percent. Greater reliance on development offshore, which is governed by outdated production-sharing contracts that favor operators, reduces per barrel profits to the nation. One recent government audit suggested the national oil company was technically insolvent at the end of 2009.[24] Lost or trapped investment could top $50 billion, with the costs of lost or deferred production higher still.

The Petroleum Industry Bill, an omnibus oil sector reform bill that is now over a decade in the making, aims to correct many of these problems while boosting government's share of profits. Quick passage would surely ease the sense of drift in the sector and encourage new deals. But the bill has likely been oversold as a catalyst for unlocking investment. The latest draft, which is currently before parliament, is weak on solutions to many possible investment barriers, including bureaucratic interference in contracting and project rollout, joint venture funding issues, national oil company dysfunction, and confusion over government's future role in the upstream. The supermajors complain that the new deepwater fiscals are uncompetitive, though such claims are hard to assess because the bill leaves royalties, rents, and other key terms to later regulation or block-by-block haggling. High corruption risks, the potential for renewed violence in the Niger Delta, and rising prospects elsewhere in the region could affect some plans. And in the country's current highly politicized environment, passing the Petroleum Industry Bill could fall victim to other, more self-interested agendas.

Conclusion

The exploitation of Africa's energy supplies will create more supply diversification and greater flows of oil and gas on to world markets. Revenues from energy are a boost to Africa's growth and emergence in the global economy. Both outcomes coincide with US policy objectives, even as US demand for African oil and gas wanes. The security concerns centering on disputes over borders appear, at this stage, unlikely to escalate into wars, though they will have to be carefully managed. The United States, along with the international community, could play a role in assisting negotiations to mediate and resolve conflict when and if it occurs.

The United States and Europe will remain the leading investors in Sub-Saharan African hydrocarbons, whereas Asian nations—especially

China—will likely be the bigger consumers of African oil and gas. Whether African leaders will lean more to their stakeholders or their customers is not clear, but in setting anticorruption conditions for engagement, the investing nations have a strong hand. Though African oil and gas does not rise to the level of a strategic interest for the United States, the country has a definite interest in promoting democracy, governance, and economic growth among African oil producers.

Finally, the electrification of the continent is a massive project accompanying its burgeoning growth. The continent has the natural resources, and the United States can play a critical role in assisting and marshaling technology and investment in the infrastructure of the continent. Not only is it an economic multiplier that would further unlock Africa's potential, but also it will provide a huge boost to the quality of life and prospects of ordinary Africans.

Notes

1. See Richard G. Newell and Stuart Iler, "The Global Energy Outlook," chapter 1 of this volume.

2. Anadarko, the US operator of Mozambique's hugely promising gas play area 1, predicts that it could be producing more than 60 million metric tons of gas per year (or 8 billion cubic feet per day) by next decade. Houston-based Cobalt International led Angola's presalt finds in the Kwanza Basin, with significant 2012 discoveries from its Cameia-1 well situated in offshore block 21.

3. Meanwhile, according to author interviews with government officials and oil traders, the Nigerian government has firmed up demand by relying more on tenders from Asian refineries and by doubling its oil export sales to Europe. But impending production spikes elsewhere—particularly in Libya or the newer West African producers—could challenge this strategy in the longer term.

4. Most notably, Sonangol Sinopec International, a joint venture between Sinopec and the Angolan national oil company, drew widespread notice in 2006 when it offered $1.1 billion each in signature bonuses for Angola's highly prospective deepwater blocks 17 and 18 (with estimated reserves of 1 billion and 700 million barrels, respectively). In addition to the record-breaking bonuses, Sinopec pledged to invest $200 million in Angolan "social projects."

5. Government data from the China General Administration of Customs show that the country's average Nigerian crude imports actually fell during 2011, just as tapering US sales turned Nigeria into a buyer's market for crude.

6. Furthermore, when Chinese firms tried to persuade Umaru Musa Yar'adua (president of Nigeria from 2007 to 2010) to award them various onshore leases sought by Chevron, ExxonMobil, and Shell, the Nigerian government merely used the offer as leverage in negotiations with the supermajors. For more on the Chinese presence in Nigeria and Angola, see Alex Vines, Lillian Wong, Markus Weimer, and Indira Campos,

Thirst for African Oil: Asian National Oil Companies in Nigeria and Angola (London: Chatham House, 2010).

7. Sinopec's 2009 purchase of Swiss-based Addax Petroleum's upstream business for $7.3 billion increased Chinese holdings, but according to author interviews with analysts, some experts view the sale price as inflated.

8. In Uganda, for instance, CNOOC in 2011 partnered with Tullow Oil and Total on exploration areas 1, 2, and 3A. CNOOC assumed operatorship of two existing exploration licenses in 3A (Kanywataba and Kingfisher), with Tullow and Total operating areas 1 and 2, respectively. This acreage attracted little serious interest from US firms.

9. Most recently, Ghana faulted Sinopec for delaying a gas infrastructure project backed by a $3 billion loan from China Development Bank beyond Ghana's December 2012 presidential elections.

10. Most recently, Thailand's PTT Exploration and Production purchased Cove Energy's stake in several Mozambique gas fields, an early indication of where the interest and market for that gas will be found.

11. For a thorough discussion of these issues, see Charles McPherson, "Governance, Transparency, and Sustainable Development," chapter 19 of this volume.

12. Five of the 10 highest FCPA settlements to date involved contractors paying bribes to win or retain business in the Sub-Saharan African oil and gas sector. The defendants were Panalpina, JGC Corporation, Technip, Snamprogetti Netherlands and Eni, and KBR and Halliburton; total fines paid topped $1.58 billion. Other corporate defendants in the sector to date have included Shell Nigeria Exploration and Production Company, Transocean, Tidewater Marine International, Noble Corporation, Aibel Group, Willbros Group, Paradigm, Vetco Gray, ABB Vetco Gray, GlobalSantaFe Corporation, Pride International, Bristow Group, and Baker Hughes.

13. High-level self-dealing (and some disappointing geology) convinced Exxon-Mobil and Anadarko to exit São Tomé's much hyped Joint Development Zone. In Angola, national oil company Sonangol has routinely forced foreign operators to partner with local firms linked to allies of President José Eduardo dos Santos and the ruling party. Author interviews with Angolan government officials, civil society workers, and oil industry personnel.

14. Notable examples include Arvind Ganesan, "Angola: Some Transparency, No Accountability—The Use of Oil Revenue in Angola and Its Impact on Human Rights," *Human Rights Watch* 16, no. 1(A) (2004): 1–93; "The Secret Life of a Shopaholic: How an African Dictator's Playboy Son Went on a Multi-million Dollar Shopping Spree in the US," Global Witness, London, 2009; Ian Gary, *Ghana's Big Test: Oil's Challenge to Democratic Development* (Boston: Oxfam America, 2009).

15. Perhaps most notably, the British government's convictions in 2011 and 2012 of James Ibori, a former Nigerian governor, and his associates on money-laundering and fraud charges may have substantially curbed illicit transfers of oil wealth to the United Kingdom. Author interviews with UK and Nigerian anticorruption police, oil industry personnel, and other Nigerian government officials.

16. Recent examples include the Natural Resource Charter and Open Government Partnership; most already host some form of the pioneering Extractive Industries Transparency Initiative.

17. For instance, the governments of Congo-Brazzaville, DRC, Liberia, and Ghana now publish contracts; contract disclosure is legally required in Niger, Guinea, and Sierra Leone. Several African governments, including representatives of Liberia, Ni-

geria, and Congo-Brazzaville, are pushing to make contract disclosure a mandatory requirement for membership in the Extractive Industries Transparency Initiative. Author interviews with Extractive Industries Transparency Initiative experts and oil industry consultants.

18. These countries include Mozambique in 2010 and Nigeria, Angola, and Sudan in 2012.

19. Currently, Kenya, South Africa, Ethiopia, Ghana, Mozambique, and Nigeria all have vast electrification projects under way or planned.

20. For a discussion of the policy reforms needed to improve electrification, see the discussion by Charles K. Ebinger and John P. Banks in "Electricity Access in Emerging Markets," chapter 18 of this volume.

21. Hillary Rodham Clinton, "Energy Diplomacy in the 21st Century," address to Georgetown University, Washington, DC, October 18, 2012.

22. In the late 2000s, an audit of the National Petroleum Investment Management Service found 524 bureaucratic steps needed for approval of a multimillion-dollar upstream contract. Average contract approval time is 18 to 24 months, with some projects delayed three to four years. In one notable case, last-minute interference by officials sidelined a $10 billion investment by Shell in its prospective Bonga South field. Author interviews with oil industry personnel and Nigerian government officials.

23. Wood Mackenzie, "Wood Mackenzie's Assessment of the Nigerian Petroleum Industry Bill," press release, September 27, 2012, http://www.woodmacresearch.com/cgi-bin/wmprod/portal/corp/corpPressDetail.jsp?oid=10810748.

24. KPMG Professional Services Nigeria, "Project Anchor: Full Report of the Process and Forensic Review of the Nigerian National Petroleum Corporation, 2011," report commissioned by the Nigerian Ministry of Finance, Abuja, 2011.

Commentary on Part III

Abdullah bin Hamad Al-Attiyah

From my vantage point in Qatar and the Arabian Gulf, I see the success that cooperation among producers, consumers, and national and international energy companies can bring. Qatar began exporting liquefied natural gas (LNG) in 1997 and is today the world's largest LNG exporter. Our oil production has nearly tripled over this time, and our exports of condensate rival those of our crude oil.

Our growth model has been to build a world-class national oil and gas company in Qatar Petroleum (QP) and world-class gas companies in Qatargas Operating Company Limited and Ras Laffan Company Limited, which demonstrate daily the benefits of partnership between QP and the technology and project expertise of the world's leading energy companies. We continue to grow—even as we retain our moratorium on new gas developments for now in an effort to husband our national resources for future generations. In 2009, Qatar produced 3,154 billion cubic feet (bcf) of natural gas. The Barzan Gas Project, a 90:10 joint venture between QP and ExxonMobil, will produce an additional 600 bcf per year when it comes on line between 2014 and 2015.

We, too, are affected by the growth in indigenous natural gas in the United States and the shift in global energy demand toward Asia and here in the Middle East. In 2009, Qatar exported nearly 1,800 bcf of LNG, with Japan, South Korea, and India as our primary destination markets, followed by European markets. We send 2 bcf per day to our neighbors in the United Arab Emirates and Oman through the Dolphin pipeline.

Our model of cooperation, where producers and consumers share risk and reward, investment and expertise, and information about markets and geopolitics, will be indispensable in the period of change that we now face. Globally, we will see a rise in demand for oil and gas worldwide. We will see expansion of access to LNG, and increased demand for natural gas, as underserved nations in South Asia increase their electricity access, use competitively priced natural gas, and mitigate the impacts of climate change by replacing coal or, in some cases, nuclear energy with cleaner-burning natural gas. Producers and consumers will need to ensure that investment is sustained and that prices for natural gas and oil are sufficient to sustain that investment for the long term. My own service, as president of the Organization of the Petroleum Exporting Countries over the years and as host to the Gas Exporting Countries Forum, has been directed to that essential goal.

Qatar's success over the years has been a product of (a) creating a positive, mutually respectful, and highly attractive investment framework to meet global energy demand; (b) investing resource revenues in our own nation; and (c) working in close partnership with the United States, Europe, and our Asian neighbors in trade, investment, and security. These modes of cooperation will be indispensable in the period of uncertainty and potential volatility that we will face in the Middle East and North and Sub-Saharan Africa.

As Fareed Mohamedi so well describes in chapter 11, North Africa and the Mediterranean are undergoing dramatic changes in government and governance. Libya's energy sector has returned swiftly to prewar levels, even as the process of building a new government evolves more slowly. Egypt's energy sector is now focused more internally than externally, and a new government is still developing its long-term strategy. Mohamedi is pessimistic about the ability of Libya, Egypt, and Algeria to create sufficiently attractive investment frameworks in the near term—and in the case of Libya and Egypt, sufficiently secure ones. In his perspective, growth of oil and gas from these nations will be slow, and because of the complexities of developing new fields and export facilities in the Mediterranean, their evolution is also expected to be modest. As a result, he sees Europe's reliance on these nations for natural gas shrinking in favor of other suppliers of piped gas or LNG.

I am somewhat more optimistic. Libya's traditional investors have been steadfast for many decades and may weather the current uncertainty with fortitude. Creative approaches to partnership in Egypt and Algeria may yet provide the investment flows that these nations need to expand national prosperity. And Europe's desire for diversity of supply will grow rather than shrink in the years ahead.

In chapter 10, Robin West and Raad Alkadiri astutely assess that the global nature of the oil market, the strategic nature of oil itself, and the commitment of the United States to exercise its responsibilities as a global superpower will sustain US and Western investment and commitment to the Middle East and the Gulf states. They note Iraq's enormous potential and the challenges it faces in the important work of building the infrastructure, human capital, and political accommodation needed to maximize its potential. Here, too, I am optimistic.

With respect to the Gulf states, it is true that Qatar and our neighbors have elevated our foreign policy engagement to help shape the evolution of our region in positive and prosperous ways for all our people. This development has been historic and highly successful. Our nations all face succession issues, and we have seen—and will continue to see—national resilience in managing those crucial transitions.

But West and Alkadiri also rightly note that our region faces enormous uncertainty and risk in the months ahead. Iran retains its adversarial posture on the nuclear brief, and its occasional statements with respect to the Strait of Hormuz unsettle global markets. We pray that diplomacy will prevail, as we would experience acutely the risks of the failure of that path. We remain concerned about the intransigency of the Middle East conflict and its human and security impacts. The growing violence in Syria, West and Alkadiri note, could also adversely affect neighboring Saudi Arabia, Iraq, Turkey, and Iran, as well as Lebanon, on a continuing basis. They correctly assess the dangers that a spillover could hold for markets and politics.

Finally, like Phillip van Niekerk and Aaron Sayne, we see the hope that newly emerging energy producers in East and Upper West Africa can bring to the development of these nations. We have witnessed Angola's rise as an oil and gas power and its successful partnership model. It is true that many nations have not maximized the benefits of their energy development in the past, but we see the commitment of Nigeria's leadership to modernizing the structure of its energy sector, the security that Asia's demand for oil and gas can bring to the continent, and — like van Niekirk and Sayne — the sustained interest of international oil companies in investing in those nations, even as the primary markets for their resources shift from the West to the East.

As a US partner and ally, Qatar shares the perspective of the authors of each of the chapters that the United States will and should remain committed to the security, stability, and development of its friends and allies in the Middle East and the Gulf, as well as in North and Sub-Saharan Africa. Effective diplomacy, support for democracy, close partnership with allies, and coordinated approaches to development will create a safer and more secure world for producers and consumers. In this respect, this second edition of *Energy and Security*, edited by my friends Jan Kalicki and David Goldwyn, is superbly timed and provides an excellent foundation for a new and effective energy security strategy.

Energy and security are inextricably linked in our region and in the world. Energy is the key to development for us, but the role of governments in providing stable investment climates, secure areas to work in, and partnerships to help share the risks and rewards of this enterprise will be as essential over the next two decades as they were for the past two. We take heed of the importance of this collaboration, and we hope readers in government, business, and academic institutions will as well.

Part IV

The Pacific Rim

Part IV assesses the trends and challenges for energy security in the countries of the Pacific Rim, where the rate of growth in energy demand is the highest in the world. The conduct of the nations of this region will have a heavy influence on the geopolitics of energy worldwide. China is once again reviewing its energy use and antipollution policies, leading to increased efforts to manage energy demand and control carbon emissions—for example, through increased use of natural gas—while overtaking the United States as the world's largest energy consumer in 2013 and continuing (with India) to maintain record construction rates for mostly coal-fired power plants.[1] Externally, China's national oil companies (China National Petroleum Corporation, Sinopec, and China National Offshore Oil Corporation) are stepping up their efforts to capture long-term oil and gas supplies through asset acquisitions enhanced by subsidized government credits and by pipeline and other infrastructure commitments. Furthermore, China is vigorously asserting jurisdiction over islands and their surrounding resources in the South and East China Seas, thereby increasing tensions with Japan, Vietnam, Taiwan, Brunei, and the Philippines, which have their own claims.

At the same time, Australia's catapulting to preeminent gas supplier status in the region will help allay Chinese and, even more so, Japanese worries about energy shortfalls dragging down economic growth. Australia's traditional ally, the United States, needs to decide whether to export oil and gas from increasingly accessible shale resources and thus help lower the highest natural gas prices in the world. This decision is particularly consequential in the wake of Japan's retreat from nuclear power after the Fukushima disaster and debate in Japan about whether to seek future energy security through bilateral or collective arrangements. Like other Asian countries, India must consider how best to fuel its rapidly growing economy and whether enough credible alternatives exist to allow India to comply fully with international sanctions against Iran's nuclear weapons program.

Overall, countries throughout Asia and the Pacific will face a growing choice between destructive competition and collective efforts to seek energy security through limiting demand, augmenting and sharing strategic stocks, and moving cooperatively to increase the availability of energy resources. In each case, US policy and commitment to regional and global energy security can play a significant or even major role.

Part IV contains chapters by Amy Myers Jaffe and Kenneth B Medlock on China, India, and Asia and by Mikkal Herberg on Japan, Southeast Asia, and Australia. In each case, the great challenges for policy-makers are how to expand the circle of cooperation, how to avoid descending into destabilizing competition in a region that still enjoys reserves in only a few countries, and how to promote cooperative behavior in building storage capacity.

In chapter 13, Jaffe and Medlock show how oil and gas producers are reorienting toward growing Asian energy consumers—propelled by increasing populations, income, industries, and vehicles. Growing proportions of exports from Arabian (Persian) Gulf countries go to China and India, which in turn have sought to offset their dependence, initially through bilateral oil deals and subsequently through foreign energy investments and acquisitions supported by subsidized credits. Chinese and Indian ownership of foreign energy assets can have systemic benefits, including an increased stake in a well-functioning, cooperative, and integrated market. But it can also have negative impacts, ranging from investing in pariah states (such as Iran and Sudan) to building blue-water navies that can increase regional military tensions, particularly in disputed areas with high resource endowments (for example, the South and East China Seas).

In China, Jaffe and Medlock detail greatly increased energy-efficiency requirements, which are offset, however, by even greater numbers of vehicles. They also assess its substantial shale gas potential but recognize considerable infrastructure, water supply, and regulatory obstacles to its commercial development. In India, they detail even greater obstacles in infrastructure, bureaucracy, power availability, and subsidized energy prices that make the country increasingly dependent on oil and liquefied natural gas imports.

Jaffe and Medlock recognize, finally, considerable opportunities for cooperation among China, India, and the United States in moderating oil market volatility, including such steps as limiting oil use and coordinating release of emergency stocks during times of supply disruption. US leadership will be needed to capitalize on these opportunities at the same time that differences persist over such important issues as international sanctions against Iran.

In chapter 14, Herberg points out that both Northeast and Southeast Asia have become large net oil importers and share a strong economic and strategic concern for energy security. What is an energy deficit for them is an energy surplus for Australia, a natural gas powerhouse that can become a foundation for increased regional energy security. In Japan, the Fukushima disaster has led to the closing of its nuclear power plants and an intensified search for the alternative energy sources necessary to achieve economic growth. As evidenced by the Senkaku (Diaoyu) Island dispute with China, resource development in disputed areas must receive much more attention, and investments and supply must be secured. Despite huge subsidies and investments, however, Japan has failed to raise its 15 percent equity share of oil imports or to diversify its heavy dependence on Middle East oil. By contrast, its gas diversification has been more robust. Japan relies on several suppliers, including Australia, Qatar, and Southeast Asian countries, but is paying the world's highest prices for long-term contracts. As for Southeast Asia, it has moved overall from a net export to a net import position with rapidly growing demand from its own industry and other consumers. The exception is Myanmar (Burma), which continues to export gas to southern China.

Finally, Australia is enjoying a natural gas production boom off its northwestern coast, and its investment-friendly fiscal and legal regimes help attract the billions of dollars required to fully realize that production, turn it into liquefied natural gas, and transport it to distant Asian markets. Over the entire region looms the threat of nuclear weapon and missile development in North Korea—as well as Iran—and the need to substitute peaceful energy and other forms of cooperation for the increasing risks from those or other quarters. Australia is a natural ally for promoting energy and overall security in Asia as the United States pivots strategically to the region. Other areas in which Australia and the United States could cooperate include Pacific Islands energy security (a potential bridge with China), energy sea-lane security, and possibly regional emergency oil stocks (a potential bridge with other Asian countries, China included).

In his commentary on part IV, J. Bennett Johnston, a former US senator and Senate Energy Committee chairman, shares the view of Jaffe, Medlock, and Herberg that key to the energy security and stability of the Asia-Pacific region is China's relationship with the United States and its own neighbors. Johnston calls for strong leadership to draw China closer to the United States, through cooperation on strategic reserves, energy efficiency, research and development, and the peaceful use of nuclear energy. He lauds Japan's example in maximizing energy conservation and Australia's leadership in creating a regional energy security platform, and he foresees that closer cooperation on energy can pay great dividends for US national security by creating a foundation on which the United States, Japan, China, and Russia can seek to prevent by peaceful means nuclear weapons proliferation worldwide, most urgently in North Korea.

Note

1. Ailun Yang and Yiyun Cui, "Global Coal Risk Assessment: Data Analysis and Market Research," Working Paper, World Resources Institute, Washington, DC, November 2012.

Chapter 13

China, India, and Asian Energy

Amy Myers Jaffe and Kenneth B Medlock III

Asia's economic miracle has been a driving force behind rising global energy use and increasing prices since the 1990s. It is likely to continue to play a pivotal role in the coming years. In fact, Asian players are increasingly important participants in oil and gas investment around the world, and global energy trade and trends in prices will be highly dependent on the future of Asian economic growth and the pace of investment in energy infrastructure.

The growth of Asian demand comes at a time when the oil and natural gas imports of other regions and countries, notably the United States, are beginning to decline.[1] This trend has pushed large oil and gas producers to focus increasingly on Asian markets as a key destination for future sales. This emerging trade pattern already influences the geopolitics of energy, with China's involvement in oil-producing countries now rivaling that of the United States and Europe. In turn, the potential strategic power and reach of oil-producing states may begin to affect rising Asian nations more than it does the historically dominant energy-importing Western nations.

Trends in Asian Energy Demand

Many analysts believe that the rapid increase in oil price from 2005 to 2007 was driven by quickly expanding demand in the developing economies of Asia.[2] Indeed, global incremental demand growth has been dominated by trends in the Asia-Pacific region. This development is evidenced in figure 13.1, which indicates global total primary energy requirement by source, differentiated between the Asia-Pacific region and the rest of the world.[3]

The Asia-Pacific region accounted for 56 percent of the increase in global primary oil demand from 2000 to 2010, and the Baker Institute projects the same region to account for 70 percent of global oil demand growth from 2010 to 2020.[4] Asian giants China and India are leading this surge in energy use, with China alone forecast to represent about 48 percent of the growth in global oil demand through 2020. Much of this dominance is attributable to projected weakness in demand growth in Europe, in particular, but the trend portends a substantial shift in global energy flows.[5]

Population growth is also a major factor. Asia is projected to account for about 50 percent of the growth in world population between 2010 and 2020. By contrast, population growth in the industrial West is expected to be less than 0.3 percent a year to 2020. By 2020, China and India are projected to have 1.4 billion and 1.3 billion people, respectively, and as the living standards of these populations improve, demand for energy resources will expand.

The shifting center of global population to the Asia-Pacific region, coupled with strong economic growth in the region, signals that energy trade will continue to move away from the West. In fact, the Asia-Pacific region has become an important destination for the sale of all major commodities, and rapidly rising imports of oil and natural gas in large Asian economies have been a key driver to rising commodity prices.

China's and India's External Drives for Energy Security

As the need for oil and gas imports in Asian economies increased in the 2000s, concerns about energy security intensified, prompting many governments to find ways to strengthen their footholds in oil-producing regions. By the late 2000s, Asian national oil companies, especially those from China and India, became particularly active in pursuing equity interests in energy assets in the Middle East, Africa, and Latin America.[6] Some analysts have argued that China's oil drive abroad has been commercially

Figure 13.1. Global Total Primary Energy by Source and Incremental Growth, 2000–20

a. Total Primary Energy Requirement

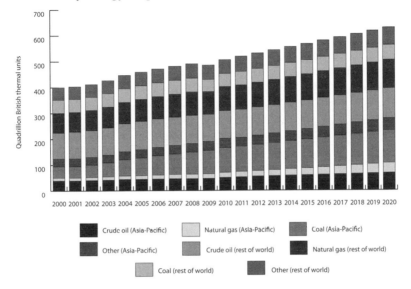

b. Growth in Total Primary Energy Requirement since 2000

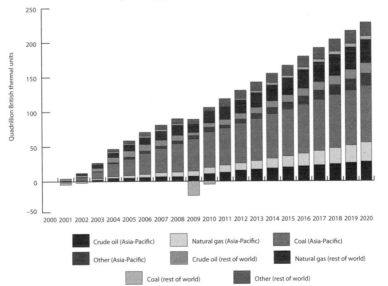

Source: Kenneth B Medlock III, Total Primary Energy Projection, 2012, James A. Baker III Institute for Public Policy, Rice University, Houston, TX.

oriented and is thereby of little consequence to geopolitics.[7] But China's rising involvement in areas rife with conflict—such as Sudan, Iran, and more recently Syria—suggests otherwise.[8]

The shift in Asian energy investment patterns has created several new geopolitical realities on the ground, some positive, some not. On the positive side, China has become more vested in a well-functioning global market, which could, as Yergin, Eklof, and Edwards argue, bring market integration and cooperation, which, in turn, reduce the risk of conflict."[9] However, strategic concerns for both China and India, in particular, have extended well beyond their immediate geographic neighborhoods. The increased need for energy has led Asian powers to focus increasingly on building blue-water navies, thereby raising the level of military competition in the region.[10] Just as friction arises today involving naval units from China, South Korea, and Vietnam in the South and East China Seas, a longer-term consequence could be increased friction between China and India in the sea-lanes of the Indian Ocean.[11]

Indeed, the South and East China Seas, with potentially large resource endowments, will likely be the subject of increasing tensions between China and other Asian economies—notably Malaysia, Indonesia, Brunei, Taiwan, and the Philippines—with their own competing territorial claims. Since 2007, incidents and provocations in the region have increased, spurred in part by a rising interest in surveying and exploiting possible oil and gas resources. China National Offshore Oil Corporation (CNOOC), a state company, has significant oil and gas reserves in areas of the southern and eastern South China Sea that are not in dispute, and it has expressed concerns about resources in disputed waters. The scale of the potential resource at stake is a subject of debate, however, with China's Ministry of Land and Resources putting total South China Sea oil reserves at more than 23 billion barrels, which is significantly higher than most other estimates.[12]

The spring of 2012 saw military tensions escalate between China and the Philippines in the Scarborough Shoal, while Japan and China traded military flyovers in the Senkaku Islands (which China calls the Diaoyu Islands) in the East China Sea. Analysts argue that the latest leadership transition now taking place in Beijing will heighten nationalistic trends, because President Xi Jinping is expected to stand up for Chinese interests more assertively in the international arena, "especially those deemed to be China's 'core interests,' which include issues related to sovereignty over the South China Sea."[13]

Attempts by China and India to secure foreign oil and gas supplies from key oil-producing regions in the Middle East and Africa and tensions over

South and East China Sea shipping lanes have drawn increasing attention from the United States.[14] Similarly, energy security concerns in Beijing and New Delhi are intensifying these rising powers' reactions to US policies.[15] Such changing attitudes could make it difficult to re-create, for example, the kind of US-led international coalition that pushed Saddam Hussein's army out of Kuwait. More generally, it could complicate future US military and energy security policy.

The Role of Rising Oil Demand

China is now the second-largest oil consumer, following the United States, and the International Energy Agency (IEA) forecasts China's oil imports to rise to between 11.4 million barrels per day (mmbpd)[16] and 13.0 mmbpd by 2030, up from around 5.0 mmbpd in 2011.[17] The trend of increasing oil imports is also accelerating in India. India consumed nearly 3.5 mmbpd in 2011, of which about three-quarters were imported. By 2035, the IEA projects that 92 percent of India's oil will have to be imported because its annual demand grows at over 5 percent per year.

Both China and India initially sought commercial bilateral oil supply deals as their energy demand increased in the 1990s. But this strategy eventually gave way to the pursuit of a foreign investment and acquisition strategy, which was supported by loans and other financing from home governments, sometimes at below-market rates or through the provision of infrastructure and aid to governments in oil producing countries.[18] These various financing programs gave Asian national oil companies (NOCs) an advantage in bidding for assets against Western counterparts.

The Role of State Support for NOCs

Each government's support of its NOCs' activities abroad has been aimed at improving energy security and ensuring that its NOCs remain financially strong and able to serve the country's geopolitical interests. In the case of the Chinese government, the financial health of Chinese NOCs was particularly important to the Chinese Communist Party's political position because NOCs play an important role in the overall strength of the Chinese economy, national employment levels, and provision of social services. The financial crisis of 2008 aided the overseas investment strategy because it lowered acquisition costs for energy assets, thereby creating lucrative investment incentives for cash-rich Asian governments. The prevailing view held that overseas oil, gas, and mining assets would appreciate over time. As a result, Asian governments encouraged their NOCs to expand investment in foreign oil and gas assets because such deals were considered excellent vehicles in which to invest national financial surpluses.

China and India were among the most active in promoting global expansion of their NOCs. In some cases, commercial factors also played an important role. For example, the Chinese firms CNOOC, China National Petroleum Corporation (CNPC), and Sinochem were facing the possibility of dwindling domestic resources as older oil and gas fields faced production declines. Moreover, the firms needed a means to supplement domestic revenues, which were increasingly coming under pressure as more private competition entered the domestic energy sector. For competitive reasons, therefore, China's NOCs looked abroad for merger and acquisition opportunities to diversify their asset holdings and book profitable operations outside of China.

"Soft Power" Support of Energy Security

In 2007, China's White Paper on Energy proposed "cooperation for mutual benefit" and "intensifying mutually beneficial cooperation in energy exploration and utilization."[19] This strategy reflects the recognition that energy security strategies could be defeated through traditional conflict (use of military force and embargoes).[20] It also recognizes that "soft power" might achieve what threats could not, including steering many of the 12 Latin American countries that still recognize Taiwan's sovereignty to China's position.[21]

Chinese energy diplomacy has used the country's increasing comparative financial advantages to secure resources. When its foreign exchange reserves boomed, Beijing began offering generous oil credit swaps for up to 10 years to major oil exporters (e.g., $25 billion to Russia and $20 billion to Venezuela). Nevertheless, China still seems to prefer equity participation by its companies, sometimes in regions with substantial commercial risk. Indeed, with government backing, the Chinese NOCs have offered bids that might not have been justified in the private sector given the political and economic risk.

The major Asian NOCs spent roughly $49 billion between 2005 and 2009 acquiring interests in oil and gas assets overseas, according to calculations made by the authors. China's CNPC was among the most active investors during that period, receiving strong government financial support for foreign acquisitions.[22]

Aggressive Chinese Bidding, Cautious Indian Moves

Chinese firms—and to a lesser extent South Korean firms—have been highly active in the oil and gas mergers and acquisitions market and have offered premiums to win assets away from more commercially oriented Western firms. Indian firms, in contrast, have generally been more conservative in their overseas acquisition strategies, tending to focus more squarely on commercial factors than on geoeconomic drivers. As a result, Indian firms such as the Oil and Natural Gas Corporation (ONGC) have lost out on several major acquisitions to Chinese and other firms with more aggressive practices. In fact, ONGC's foreign subsidiary ONGC Videsh Limited is perhaps as well known for its large, failed bids to invest in foreign oil and gas assets as it is for its successful ones. Still, ONGC announced in 2010 that it intends to invest an additional $20 billion—more than twice the sum it had already invested abroad—on foreign assets over the coming decade to help meet India's growing oil import requirements.

China's NOCs, by contrast, have already spent nearly $45 billion on overseas acquisitions since the 1990s. They have equity stakes in roughly 1.2 mmbpd of crude oil production as a result. The trend has been accelerating in recent years, as evidenced by the fact that Chinese NOCs spent about $15 billion in oil and gas acquisitions in 2009 and more than $26 billion in 2010, according to statistics gathered by the authors. More recently, deals have been floated, including CNOOC's $15 billion acquisition of Canadian firm Nexen Inc. in February 2013.

The Geopolitics of Asian Oil and Gas Investment

The overseas investment activity of the Asian NOCs has prompted their respective governments to expand energy diplomacy activities and has pushed Asian countries increasingly into energy geopolitics more generally.

In its early years, the Chinese oil industry's campaign to attain oil and gas assets abroad focused on countries with emerging geopolitical risks or human rights problems, such as Iran, Iraq, Libya, Sudan, Burma, and Venezuela. The strategy was not necessarily ideological; rather, it reflected initial difficulty in competing in areas where US and European firms were already well established. The solution, Chinese strategists felt, was to focus China's international exploration efforts on countries where Western firms would not easily compete.[23] Hence, in the 1990s, many countries under US sanctions were ideal for targeted Chinese investment.

This policy, which was initially greeted in Chinese leadership circles as pragmatic and profitable, is now increasingly presenting problems. China's vast oil, natural gas, and mineral holdings in conflict-prone regions have increasingly enmeshed Beijing in localized conflicts far from its borders and have put a strain on its relations with the United States. For example, through its NOC investments, China became involved in conflicts in Libya and the newly divided Sudan. Moreover, Chinese oil and gas investments in Iran have become an economic and geopolitical liability, given tightening Western economic and banking sanctions against Tehran. China also faces great uncertainties in Venezuela, where the death of President Hugo Chávez is raising questions about the country's future politics and the fate of China's multibillion-dollar loans in the oil sector.

China has also found investments in Africa and Latin America can become problematic because of emerging risks from a lack of political and social stability, sensitive issues related to human rights, problems arising from resource nationalism, the difficulty of managing local community relations, and local environmental problems. China's extensive oil and gas holdings on these two continents are stretching its diplomatic resources and raising questions about its long-term force projection strategies. As China internationalizes its presence beyond its traditional Asian neighborhood, it adds a complicating element to US–China relations.

Relations with the United States will remain important to China's economy, but frictions will likely increase. China's continued support for Iran, in particular, has been a source of tension with the United States. India, in contrast, has taken a more conciliatory approach to US global concerns in its overseas investment strategies. Seeking US backing for both its expanding nuclear programs and its bid for a seat on the United Nations Security Council, India has been relatively more responsive to US regional diplomacy, including efforts to isolate Iran. This geopolitical orientation has been somewhat costly for ONGC, which has been discouraged by its home government from moving forward on pipeline and other projects involving Iran.

Figure 13.2. Chinese Total Primary Energy Requirement by Source, 1992–2030

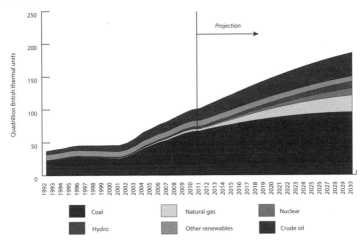

Source: Kenneth B Medlock III, Total Primary Energy Projection, 2012, James A. Baker III Institute for Public Policy, Rice University, Houston, TX.

Chinese Economic Growth: A Driver of Future Oil Prices?

Economic growth throughout Asia has given support to oil and gas markets, and China has played a particularly important role. China's economic and geopolitical rise has been the single largest influence on oil in the 21st century. China is now the world's second-largest economy and largest exporter. It also has the world's largest population, and thus gross domestic product per capita (purchasing power parity) rates remain at the lower-middle-income level, $7,400. Nevertheless, China's real rate of economic growth has been consistently high since the country adopted market reforms in the 1980s and was estimated to be over 7 percent in 2010, despite the global recession.

Strong urbanization has accompanied China's rapid economic expansion, thus prompting a major demographic shift. This shift has included the migration of more than 2 million citizens to cities across the country, requiring billions of dollars in government investment in the basic infrastructure needed to elevate the country to an advanced industrial economy. As indicated in figure 13.2, such a development will propel continued growth in Chinese energy demand.

Although China has made great strides in improving energy efficiency and reducing the environmental impact of its economic expansion, continued growth is certain to increase demand pressure on fuels and other resources and to test the limits of environmental sustainability. By 2040, China's oil use could easily reach levels comparable to current demand in the United States, according to Baker Institute forecasts.[24] This increased demand is projected to occur despite high vehicle-efficiency standards and an ambitious program to promote the use of alternative fuel vehicles. The principal cause is movement of a large proportion of the Chinese population into income brackets where vehicle ownership and use can become an accessible reality.

Soaring Numbers of Vehicles

Despite sporadic government policies to discourage private car ownership, the growth in the number of vehicles on the road in China has soared in recent years. The total vehicle stock in China, which includes cars, vans, buses, and trucks, has more than quadrupled in a decade, from 14.5 million in 1999 to 62.9 million in 2009.[25] The Baker Institute projects this growth will continue, reaching more than 220 million vehicles by 2020 and 750 million vehicles by 2040, contingent, of course, on strong economic growth. This forecast for total vehicle stocks in China is the equivalent of 149 vehicles per 1,000 people in 2020 and 493 vehicles per 1,000 people in 2040.[26]

The effect of strong growth in vehicle stocks, combined with rapid industrialization, has already shown up in China's energy demand, with oil consumption rising from 5.6 mmbpd in 2003 to 9.2 mmbpd in 2010. Given China's limited domestic oil production, net oil imports have also risen significantly to 4.9 mmbpd in 2010, up from 2.0 mmbpd in 2003.

To abate this trend, the Chinese government set forth in 2004 a goal of raising the average fuel economy of new vehicles by 15 percent in 2010, relative to a 2003 baseline.[27] In December 2009, China issued a proposed third-phase standard, which was designed to raise the fuel efficiency of new passenger vehicles to 7.0 liters per 100 kilometers (33.6 miles per gallon) by 2015. This standard is supposed to cover both imported and domestically manufactured vehicles. China is currently considering tightening fuel economy standards for 2020 to 5.0 liters per 100 kilometers, or about 53 miles per gallon.[28]

China has also committed about $15 billion by 2020 to develop electric vehicle infrastructure. In one important policy, Beijing is exempting electric vehicles from the lottery system for license plates begun after 2011 to limit the number of vehicles in that city. Other locales also have electric fleet vehicle and other programs under way. China's Ministry of Industry and Information Technology, Ministry of Science and Technology, Ministry of Finance, and National Development and Reform Commission jointly issued a draft plan in April 2011 calling for production of 1 million "new energy" vehicles each year by 2015, 50 percent of which should be all electric or plug-in electric. This call extends to target sales of 5 million units each year by 2020. However, even if China's plan is successful, the penetration rate of these new vehicles will remain low relative to the total stock of motor vehicles, which is forecast to be in the hundreds of millions.

The expected high growth rate of vehicle stocks means that even with tight fuel efficiency standards China will have difficulty limiting growth in oil use in transportation. The IEA forecasts that nontransportation oil use in China will average about 5.7 mmbpd by 2020 and then remain relatively flat at that level in the 2020s and 2030s.[29] However, rising vehicle stocks will continue to contribute to rising oil demand in China from the transportation sector throughout the 2020s and 2030s, despite rising efficiency standards. Altogether, projections for vehicle stocks mean that China's total oil demand could reach more than 19 mmbpd by 2040, putting China at oil-use levels comparable to those in the United States.[30]

What If China's Economy Falters?

The most important caveat is perhaps that the Chinese economy could falter. The Chinese economy has grown at a very fast rate over the past three decades. This growth has been heavily biased in favor of investment-driven, capital- and resource-intensive, export-oriented industrialization. Some have questioned whether China can sustain its rapid growth given the accompanying internal and external imbalances (investment and trade surpluses) of the Chinese growth model and sociopolitical risks emanating from corruption and growing inequality among various economic sectors, geographic regions, and individuals. Chinese growth has been driven, in part, by extremely high rates of domestic saving, which fueled high rates of investment spending at the expense of private consumption. The country's dramatic shift away from agricultural activities to industrialization and urbanization has fueled real estate and construction markets, but some financial analysts question whether this kind of growth will be sustained in the coming decades. Since 2004, the Chinese government has taken steps to remedy imbalances; however, these problems have continued. Manufacturing activity in China fell at the end of 2011, with both production and new investment slowing in response to Beijing's tightening monetary policy designed to dampen inflation.

Opinion is divided about whether China's leaders can orchestrate a soft landing in light of global economic conditions. For the most part, economic indicators suggest that China can muddle through.[31] However, increasing income inequality, corruption, wage repression, and geographic income imbalances have led some commentators to predict that growing social instability and collapsing trust in the Communist Party leadership could bring about a larger crisis that would curb economic performance more drastically. Slower growth in China would have a dramatic, negative impact on projections for continued growth in oil and gas demand.

China's Shale Gas Potential

China's unconventional natural gas resource base is considered extensive. Estimates of Chinese shale gas potential are uncertain, but preliminary studies show that the country may have more than 700 trillion cubic feet of commercially recoverable resource.[32] Advanced Resources International estimates potential Chinese shale gas resources to be as high as 1,275 trillion cubic feet of technically recoverable resources in place.[33]

Still, substantial barriers to rapid Chinese shale development must be overcome before Beijing can substitute domestic supplies for foreign imports. They concern such issues as (a) a lack of existing pipeline infrastructure, (b) water scarcity in some potentially prolific areas, and (c) appropriate regulatory frameworks for upstream activities. In essence, accessibility, as well as cost and technology, is critical. Market structure, public sentiment related to perceived environmental costs, and government policy are all important factors that determine accessibility.[34] Moreover, a lack of well-defined intellectual property rights protections in the use of proprietary upstream technologies will cause many international firms with the where-

Figure 13.3. Indian Total Primary Energy Requirement by Source, 1992–2030

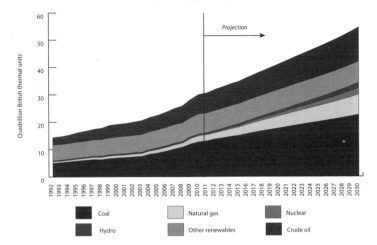

Source: Kenneth B Medlock III, Total Primary Energy Projection, 2012, James A. Baker III Institute for Public Policy, Rice University, Houston, TX.

withal to develop Chinese resources to move very slowly. So although the potential for large-scale development of shale resources in China exists, it is anything but certain, meaning China's imports of natural gas may continue to grow in the coming years.

Growth in India: Portents of Continued Strong Asian Demand

As in China, economic growth and rapid urbanization have spurred India's demand for energy. In 2005, 27 percent of India's population lived in urban areas, but by 2030, this figure is expected to rise to 45 percent.[35] At the same time, Indian gross domestic product growth has averaged 8.0 percent per year since 2000 and is projected to reach average annual growth rates that are only slightly lower over the next decade. Taken together, these factors have yielded energy demand growth in excess of 4.5 percent per year and portend strong growth (over 3.2 percent per year on average) over the next decade. Figure 13.3 indicates the Baker Institute's projection for Indian primary energy demand by fuel source through 2030.

Indian demand for oil and oil products topped 3.4 mmbpd in 2011, driven by robust diesel and gasoline consumption. Fuel subsidies are a major contributing factor to the observed demand growth, which is exacerbated by an expanding middle class that is turning increasingly to private automobiles for better mobility. More than 30 million vehicles were on the road in India in 2010, up from just over 14 million in 2000. According to Baker Institute projections, this number is expected to climb to more than 120 million by 2030. Importantly, oil demand will likely grow with vehicle stocks, but as long as Indian policy-makers fail to remove fuel subsidies, demand will grow even more strongly as the vehicle stock grows. In fact, Indian oil demand is expected to double over the next two decades, making India the world's third-largest oil consumer behind China and the United States.

India's rapidly expanding energy demand is putting pressure on domestic resources. India already imported over 90 percent of its primary oil requirements and about 25 percent of its primary gas requirements in 2011. By comparison, in 2000, India was dependent on imports for about 60 percent of its oil use and completely self-sufficient in gas.[36] Moreover, domestic oil and gas resources are not sufficient to meet projected demand, meaning that India's dependence on imports will continue to rise. This trend of increasing import dependence has raised concerns that lack of access to energy supply could be a significant impediment to sustained economic growth.

Impediments to upstream opportunities by international oil and gas firms and subsidized prices to end users are two issues that present challenges to the development of India's domestic oil and gas resources, which, in turn, exacerbates the trend of increasing import dependence. In oil and gas specifically, the issues become immensely complicated throughout the value chain. For example, the fact that gas must be bought at international prices but is sold at subsidized domestic prices challenges liquefied natural gas (LNG) import infrastructure development. This "buy high, sell low" model creates a disincentive to capital investment. Nevertheless, India does import LNG for domestic use, and a lack of domestic gas production has India exploring pipeline import options from Iran, Bangladesh, and Turkmenistan through Afghanistan and Pakistan. The odds of these projects achieving financing, however, remain very low at present. Domestic subsidies and preferential treatment of domestic energy interests in lease bidding act as impediments to development of India's domestic oil and gas resources, which leaves the country with limited options for meeting projected demand growth.

Similar aboveground issues plague India's coal sector. Inadequate rail infrastructure and impediments to foreign investment in domestic coal production threaten to force India to rely increasingly on coal imported from Australia, Indonesia, and even the United States.

In India, investment opportunities more generally are challenged throughout the value chain. For example, the country's electricity infrastructure is inadequate, and a lack of a proper market structure discourages the type of investment that is needed to ensure stable load flow and sufficient generating-capacity reserve margins. This problem was evidenced clearly when a major blackout in July 2012 reportedly affected more than 620 million people. The cause of the blackout followed sudden weather-related surges in summer demand, combined with increased demand for irrigation pumps in agricultural applications and below-normal hydrogeneration. But the lack of proper pricing signals, the presence of distortionary subsidies, and the lack of investment in generation capacity left the market incapable of rationalizing the impending shortage, thereby triggering a massive failure.[37]

Given the lack of a competitive investment environment, India will likely become increasingly dependent on imports of LNG. This need will force it to establish long-term relationships with LNG providers such as Qatar, Australia, and perhaps eventually the United States. The growing pressure to rely on oil and gas imports is already driving India's foreign and military policies, including its expanded naval presence in the Indian Ocean.

Concluding Observations

In the 2000s, partly driven by increasing needs for energy imports, China, India, and other major Asian economies pursued goals in the Middle East that created difficulties for US diplomacy, including sizable proposed investments and trade with Iran. In recent years, China's policies, in particular, have been in direct conflict with US interests. But China's policies toward the Middle East are multifaceted and are only partially commodity driven. As a result, even though China and the United States have a common strategic interest in maintaining the free flow of oil internationally and, in particular, from the Arabian (Persian) Gulf region, China perceives that its overall strategic interests in the Middle East diverge widely from those of the United States. If the United States is tied up seeking to contain conflicts across the Middle East, it will be harder pressed to focus its attention in East Asia. Notes John Garver:

> A strong Iran resistant to US dictates and at odds with the United States would also force Washington to keep large military forces in the region, limiting the ability of the United States to concentrate forces in East Asia, where China's core interests lie. The 9-11 attacks on the United States were a strategic windfall for China, diverting US attention away from China and East Asia toward the Middle East and Islamic world. That the United States bogged itself down in protracted wars in Afghanistan and Iraq was a further blessing for Beijing. If Washington now were to wade deeper into conflict in the Middle East—this time with Iran—the chances for China's successful rise without having to confront the United States would increase. In this regard, it would not benefit China to help the United States coerce Iran into de-nuclearization and corresponding docility.[38]

Foreign policy differences need to be managed diplomatically and strategically. This axiom applies not only to China's Mideast diplomatic and military trade activities but also to China's aspirations for territories in the South and East China Seas. The United States and its regional allies anticipate a more assertive, nationalistic leadership in the aftermath of the generation transition of the 18th Party Congress in 2012.

The shortcomings of China's and India's "going abroad" investment strategies and the expected increases in oil and gas imports through Asian sea-lanes are driving renewed interest in military expansion in both China and India. But although both countries are expanding their naval presence close to home, neither is well positioned to project power into major producing regions such as the Middle East. That situation forces both countries to rely more heavily on the US naval assets already present in the Middle East at a time when US dependence on foreign oil and gas resources is beginning to wane.

Regardless of nationalistic elements of their publics, Chinese and Indian leaders must recognize that their strategic interests in the energy space are not contradictory and, in fact, align with those of the United States in most respects. Moreover, it is not clear whether China would want to take on a role of power projection even if it had adequate resources. Traditionally, China has devoted its military resources to protecting its interests in its own backyard, including the South and East China Seas and the Taiwan Strait, largely relying on US military presence to protect its interests abroad—particularly in the Middle East.[39]

As US interests evolve in the Middle East, Asian nations will be placed under new pressures. The "oil weapon" previously brandished against the United States and Europe will lose its effectiveness as Western import dependence declines over time through energy-efficiency and environmental policy measures as well as increased domestic production. As the demand locus shifts toward the Far East, Asian powers, not the West, will find themselves most vulnerable to changes in oil policies in the Middle East and Russia. This development will almost certainly change the geopolitics of energy moving forward and recalibrate great-power relations in favor of the United States. But it will also tether Asia more closely to oil-producing states and reduce Western economic leverage over global oil trade. This situation is already apparent in the difficulty the United States and its allies have had in curbing oil exports from Iran in 2012 in an effort to influence Iranian nuclear policy.

The expected change in the pattern of energy trade flows toward Asia will alter foreign relations between the United States and China bilaterally and in the global arena. However, despite strategic differences, the United States, China, Japan, and India will remain among the world's largest economies and represent the largest oil-consuming nations in the world. As a result, each country has common interests in moderating global oil market volatility. Thus, the emerging Asian powers and the United States will continue to have a common interest in reducing global oil use—and hence global dependence on imported oil—through bilateral or global agreements on corporate average efficiency standards for automobiles or other coordinated conservation methods and in coordinating the release of strategic emergency stocks during times of energy supply disruption. Doing so will reduce the chances that other strategic pathologies will lead to conflict over energy supply.

Notes

1. See Richard G. Newell and Stuart Iler, "The Global Energy Outlook," chapter 1 of this volume, and Shirley Neff and Angelina LaRose, "North America," chapter 15 of this volume.

2. Michael Wesley, ed., *Energy Security in Asia* (Oxford, UK: Routledge, 2007).

3. *Total primary energy requirement* is defined as the energy required for all energy consumption. It therefore includes all energy consumed in final uses as well as energy used in conversion (e.g., refining, electricity generation) from primary energy sources

(e.g., oil, coal, natural gas) to final energy sources (e.g., gasoline, diesel, electricity). As such, for example, primary oil demand is oil demand as measured in primary use. This approach is, in fact, a more complete measure of global oil demand because it captures all oil use, including that lost in conversion.

4. In fact, 69 percent of the increase in global total primary energy requirement between 2000 and 2010 came from countries in the Asia-Pacific region, and the same region is projected to account for 65 percent of the growth in total primary energy use from 2010 to 2020.

5. The increase in coal use is particularly striking, and in fact, most of the growth has already occurred and is attributable to China.

6. Dorian, Franssen, and Simbeck note, "China, for example, attempting to diversify oil supply for security reasons, now imports oil from more than 20 countries around the globe." See James P. Dorian, Herman T. Franssen, and Dale R. Simbeck, "Global Challenges in Energy," *Energy Policy* 34, no. 15 (2006): 1984–91, 1985.

7. Xu Yi-chong, "China's Energy Security," *Australian Journal of International Affairs* 60, no. 2 (2006): 265–86.

8. Jareer Elass, Keily Miller, and Amy Myers Jaffe, "China's Relations with OPEC: Challenges for US–Sino Relations," James A. Baker III Institute for Public Policy, Rice University, Houston, TX, September 26, 2012, http://www.bakerinstitute .org/publications/EF-pub-ChinaOPECRelations-092612.pdf.

9. Daniel Yergin, Dennis Eklof, and Jefferson Edwards, "Fueling Asia's Recovery," *Foreign Affairs* 77, no. 2 (1998): 34–50.

10. Walter Russell Mead warns, "A world with half a dozen great powers dueling for influence in the Middle East, with each power possessing the will and the ability to intervene with military force in this explosive region, would be a less safe and less happy world than the one we now live in, and not only for Americans." See Walter Russell Mead, *Power, Terror, Peace, and War: America's Grand Strategy in a World at Risk* (New York: Vintage, 2004), 43.

11. Joshy M. Paul, "The Role of Energy Security in China's Foreign Policy: A Maritime Perspective," *Maritime Affairs* 6, no. 2 (2010): 49–71.

12. For example, the 2010 assessment of the US Geological Survey places the resource an order of magnitude lower than China's Ministry of Land and Resources. See Christopher J. Schenk, Michael E. Brownfield, Ronald R. Charpentier, Troy A. Cook, Timothy R. Klett, Mark A. Kirschbaum, Janet K. Pitman, Richard M. Pollastro, and Marilyn E. Tennyson, "Assessment of Undiscovered Oil and Gas Resources of Southeast Asia, 2010," USGS Fact Sheet 2010-3015, 2010, http://pubs.usgs.gov /fs/2010/3015/.

13. See Bonnie Glaser, "Trouble in the South China Sea," *Foreign Policy*, September 17, 2012, 3. See also Jane Perlez, "China Steps Up Pressure on Japan in Island Dispute," *New York Times,* December 15, 2012.

14. Amy Myers Jaffe and Steven W. Lewis, "Beijing's Oil Diplomacy," *Survival* 44, no. 1 (2002): 115–34.

15. Wesley states, "Asian powers have begun to worry whether by acquiescing to the US energy security umbrella, they are leaving themselves vulnerable to collateral damage arising from Arab anger at US policies." See Wesley, *Energy Security in Asia*, 6–7.

16. Author's calculation using IEA forecasts under the New Policies scenario for total oil demand and domestic production. See IEA, *World Energy Outlook 2012* (Paris: OECD/IEA, 2012), 85, 107.

17. IEA, *World Energy Outlook 2011* (Paris: OECD/IEA, 2011).

18. Paul, "Role of Energy Security in China's Foreign Policy." The Export–Import Bank of China, for example, extended a $2 billion credit to the Angolan government at the generous rate of 1.5 percent interest over 17 years to finance infrastructure construction by Chinese firms.

19. State Council of the People's Republic of China, "China's Energy Conditions and Policies," White Paper on Energy, December 26, 2007, http://www.china.org.cn /english/environment/236955.htm, as quoted in Maite J. Iturre and Carmen Amado Mendes, "Regional Implications of China's Quest for Energy in Latin America," *East Asia* 27, no. 2 (2010): 127–43, 137.

20. Wang Limao, "Some Considerations for the Oil Security of China," presented at the conference on Security of Energy Supply in China, India, Japan, South Korea, and the European Union: Possibilities and Impediments, Clingendael International Energy Programme and International Institute for Asian Studies, The Hague and Leiden, Netherlands, May 20–21, 2005.

21. Melissa Graham, "China Looks South: Problematic Investments in Latin America," Council on Hemispheric Affairs, Washington, DC, November 8, 2010, http://www .coha.org/china-looks-south-problematic-investments-in-latin-america/. Most states recognizing Taipei are Latin American. See Iturre and Amado Mendes, "Regional Implications of China's Quest for Energy in Latin America."

22. CNPC received, for example, a $30 billion loan from China Development Bank to support its global overseas acquisition strategy. China is not alone in this strategy. For example, the Korea National Oil Corporation (KNOC) was supported by government loans. Additionally, KNOC was given access to investment funds made available through South Korea's National Pension Service, which pledged $21.6 billion toward energy project investments, anticipating in 2007 that such investments would provide higher returns than profits available through government bonds and other financial instruments.

23. Yishan Xia, "Woguo nengyuan xingshi ji zhanlue zhi wo jian" [My view on China's energy situation and energy strategy], *Renmin Ribao* [People's Daily], August 10, 2001.

24. Kenneth B Medlock III, Ronald Soligo, and James D. Coan, "Vehicle Stocks in China: Consequences for Oil Demand," December 2, 2011, James A. Baker III Institute for Public Policy, Rice University, Houston, TX, December 2, 2011, http://www.baker institute.org/publications/EF-pub-RiseOfChinaMedlockSoligoCoan-120211-WEB.pdf.

25. Growth in the stocks of personal cars has been even faster, rising to 45.9 million by 2009, with Chinese vehicle sales exceeding sales in the United States in both 2009 and 2010.

26. As a point of reference, the United States currently has about 825 vehicles per 1,000 people against a much smaller total population than China's.

27. The first Chinese fuel consumption standards took effect in 2006, with a second phase in 2008. The new program divided vehicles into 16 weight classes, each with its own standard. As the standards took effect, sales-weighted average consumption dropped to 8.06 liters per 100 kilometers in 2006 from 9.11 liters per 100 kilometers in 2002, which represents an increase from 25.8 miles per gallon to 29.2. However, imported passenger vehicles were exempt, thus allowing consumers to buy larger imported vehicles.

28. By comparison, US efficiency goals are 34.5 miles per gallon for new car sales by 2016 and 54.5 miles per gallon by 2025.

29. IEA, *World Energy Outlook 2011*.

30. Projecting oil demand for transportation use faces many uncertainties, including different rates of economic growth, changes in fuel tax policy, development of urban public transportation networks and rail, density of areas undergoing urbanization, and adoption of new technologies and penetration of alternative fuel vehicles.

31. See, for example, Mahmoud A. El-Gamal, "Chinese Growth Prospects in the Short to Medium Term," James A. Baker III Institute for Public Policy, Rice University, Houston, TX, December 2, 2011, http://www.bakerinstitute.org/publications/EF-pub -RiseOfChinaElGamal-120211-WEB.pdf.

32. See Kenneth B Medlock III, "Estimating Global Shale Gas Development Costs," prepared for documentation of the Rice World Gas Trade Model for the US Department of Energy, 2012. The document is available on request from the author.

33. Vello Kuuskraa, Scott Stevens, Tyler Van Leeuwen, and Keith Moodhe, *World Shale Gas Resources: An Initial Assessment of 14 Regions Outside the United States* (Washington, DC: US Energy Information Administration, 2011).

34. See David G. Victor, "The Gas Promise," chapter 3 of this volume. Market structure in which capacity rights are unbundled from facility ownership has been critical in the United States, just as the producers' ability to negotiate directly with landowners has aligned incentives to expedite development. Furthermore, although public opinion is more muted in China, fear of possible watershed contamination or water use, particularly in regions where water scarcity is already a problem, has led to the implementation of government policy banning or suspending such activities in many regions around the world, including the US state of New York and the countries of France and Bulgaria.

35. Tanvi Madan, *Brookings Foreign Policy Studies Energy Security Series: India* (Washington, DC: Brookings Institution, 2006), http://www.brookings.edu/~/media /research/files/reports/2006/11/india/2006india.pdf.

36. These data are derived from US Energy Information Administration statistics on total oil and gas consumption and imports.

37. See Charles K. Ebinger and John P. Banks, "Electricity Access in Emerging Markets," chapter 18 of this volume.

38. John W. Garver, "Is China Playing a Dual Game in Iran?" *Washington Quarterly* 34, no. 1 (2011): 75–88, 79.

39. Jon B. Alterman, "The Vital Triangle," presented at the Woodrow Wilson Center for International Scholars conference on China and the Persian Gulf, Washington, DC, July 12, 2010, http://csis.org/files/publication/100715_JonPresentationWWC.pdf.

Chapter 14

Japan, Southeast Asia, and Australia

Mikkal E. Herberg

Asia has become the center of gravity for global energy demand growth. Energy consumption has been booming over the past two decades to meet rising transportation needs as well as rising demand for electricity. For its part, rising demand also has meant rapidly rising dependence on imported energy.

As a whole, the region is now a large net oil importer. Hence, energy security is a vital economic and strategic concern across both Northeast and Southeast Asia. Australia's energy security interests, alternatively, reflect a robust energy endowment and, therefore, a rather different mix of concerns. Australia's energy security worries have more to do with ensuring that its rising energy exports have reliable access to energy markets across Asia as well as secure and open sea-lanes to serve those markets.

Hence, the three cases examined in this chapter reflect Asia's wide range of energy endowments, histories, and energy security prospects. Each case also has its particular set of current energy security challenges and specific concerns. Japan is facing a new national energy crisis as a result of the Fu-

kushima earthquake and nuclear disaster that is forcing a profound rethink-
ing of its future energy plans. Southeast Asia's hopes for new oil and gas
supplies in deeper offshore waters of the South China Sea are increasingly
entangled in disputes with China over conflicting maritime territorial claims
and over control of the critical energy sea-lanes of Southeast Asia. And
Australia is facing major new challenges as it seeks to become the world's
largest liquefied natural gas (LNG) exporter in the space of just one decade.

Japan: Energy Security Is National Security

Japan's approach to energy security is shaped by the island state's poor
resource endowment and virtually total dependence on imported energy,
which must be delivered over the sea-lanes. In 2010, 95 percent of Japan's
energy needs were met by imported energy, 83 percent of which was oil,
natural gas, and coal, and another 12 percent of which was made up of
imported uranium to fuel nuclear power generation.[1] The Middle East accounts for 90 percent of Japan's oil needs and more than one-quarter of its
LNG supplies. Hence, energy security for Japan is almost an existential
issue: energy security is national security.

Although Japan remains highly dependent on imported energy, it has
made enormous progress in strengthening its energy security over the past
four decades.[2] The first path was through diversification of energy sources.
Oil powered Japan's economic miracle, and the country grew dramatically
for the two decades leading up to the early 1970s. By 1973, oil accounted
for 75 percent of Japan's total energy, and consequently, the Japanese economy was hit hard by the two 1970s oil shocks, which led to sharp recessions in 1973–75 and 1980–82. Since then, Japan has worked ceaselessly
to diversify its energy mix away from oil toward natural gas, coal, and
nuclear power generation. The early mantra for energy policy became the
two e's of energy security and economic efficiency, which later became
the three e's when environmental protection was added. Between 1973 and
2010, oil's share of energy use was reduced from 75 percent to 42 percent
as oil was replaced by coal, natural gas, and nuclear generation. Use of coal
doubled in volume, and its energy share rose from 17 percent to 22 percent
of total energy as it backed oil out of the power sector and fueled Japan's
growing steel industry.

The share of natural gas increased more than fourfold, from 4 percent
to 19 percent, as Japan practically invented the LNG industry. Tokyo spon-

sored its large trading companies in a string of LNG projects in Indonesia, Malaysia, Brunei, and the United Arab Emirates to feed gas to its large coastal electricity markets. Japan has become the world's largest LNG importer, importing 70 million metric tons (mmt) of LNG in 2010, nearly 30 percent of the global—and one-half of the Asian—LNG market.[3] Japan also built a large nuclear power generation fleet and a nuclear industry that became an export powerhouse. Nuclear generation rose from nothing to 12 to 13 percent of total energy and 30 percent of total electricity by 2010. The government considers nuclear energy to be semidomestic production.

Radical Improvements in Domestic Energy Efficiency

The second way Japan strengthened its energy security was through radical improvements in domestic energy efficiency. Japan's energy efficiency has reached the highest level in the world, improving by 40 percent from 1973 to 2009 in terms of energy used per unit of gross domestic product (GDP).[4] By comparison, in 2009, Germany used 60 percent more energy per unit of GDP, the United States 100 percent more, and South Korea 200 percent more per unit of GDP.[5] Japan has led in industrial energy efficiency as well as pioneering the development of more fuel-efficient vehicles and, more recently, hybrid vehicles.

While Tokyo worked diligently to strengthen its domestic energy foundation, it also pursued multilateral efforts to strengthen its energy security. A founding member of the International Energy Agency (IEA) in the mid-1970s, Japan has joined other IEA members in developing joint emergency oil stocks. It has been a strong proponent of energy security cooperation at the Group of Eight and the Group of 20 and has also been a leader in largely unsuccessful efforts to promote regional energy cooperation in Asia through the Asia-Pacific Economic Cooperation, the Association of Southeast Asian Nations (ASEAN), the East Asia Summit, and the ASEAN+3 (which added China, Japan, and South Korea).

Japan Energy Inc.: From JNOC to JOGMEC

Tokyo also has pursued a second track of its own brand of mercantilist energy and resource diplomacy. After the oil shocks of the 1970s, Tokyo sought to create competitive Japanese national oil companies (NOCs) under the umbrella of the Japan National Oil Company (JNOC). Tokyo initially boosted its direct state support for JNOC in an attempt to secure control of overseas oil supplies that funded a number of smaller oil exploration companies, including Inpex and Japex, to expand Japan's oil acquisition capabilities. This effort was an early forerunner of China's push for its NOCs to gain control of overseas oil and gas resources beginning in the late 1990s. Japan's strategy was led by the Ministry of Economy, Trade, and Industry (formerly the Ministry of International Trade and Industry), which subsidized these companies while it also worked in tandem with the large Japanese trading houses (such as Mitsui and Mitsubishi) that led much of the development of Japan's LNG industry and overseas projects.

Unfortunately, the historical results for oil security have been disappointing. Despite huge subsidies and investments, Japan's overseas equity share of oil imports has remained stable at a modest 15 percent of oil supplies. Under Junichiro Koizumi, who was prime minister from 2001 to 2006, Japan shifted away from an interventionist approach to energy, and Japan's upstream oil industry was reorganized. Tokyo dissolved the troubled JNOC and created the Japan Oil, Gas, and Metals National Corporation (JOGMEC) to better assist Japanese oil and gas companies in their projects abroad.

But with the end in 2006 of the Koizumi years, which coincided with rapidly rising oil and LNG prices and with Beijing's emergence as an aggressive competitor for overseas oil supplies, Tokyo returned to its emphasis on nationally controlled oil supplies, the so-called Hinomaru oil.[6] In the New Basic Energy Policy Act of 2006, the government raised its target for oil imports by Japanese companies from 15 percent to 40 percent of imports by 2030. The Japan Bank for International Cooperation also has been mandated to expand its financial support for Japanese companies in their international oil and gas projects. In the 2010 Strategic Energy Plan, Tokyo set a goal of raising overall energy self-sufficiency from 18 percent to 36 percent by 2030, which implied an enormous increase in Japanese overseas oil and LNG investments.[7] In 2012, the government authorized another $1 billion fund for JOGMEC to support the overseas expansion of Japan's oil and gas industry.

Despite these efforts, Japan has been largely unable to gain national control over significant amounts of oil abroad or to diversify its heavy dependence on the Middle East. Japan lost its single most important oil production concession in the Partitioned Neutral Zone between Saudi Arabia and Kuwait in the early 2000s. Inpex's subsequent efforts to develop the huge Azadegan oil field in Iran had to be abandoned because of US diplomatic pressure and unattractive Iranian contract and operating conditions.

Tokyo has also worked over the past decade to gain access to Russian Far East oil and gas to help diversify its dependence on the Middle East. At one point Tokyo offered to finance the large East Siberia–Pacific Ocean (ESPO) pipeline to bring oil from East and West Siberia to the Pacific Coast. Ultimately, a smaller pipeline was built with Chinese financing supplying 300,000 barrels per day (bpd) to China beginning in 2010. Japan, however, has been able to access some 150,000 bpd of the additional 300,000 that has been transported by rail to the Pacific Coast at Kozmino Bay. That oil is now flowing to the Pacific Coast through the completed ESPO pipeline. Japan has also been importing Russian oil from ExxonMobil's Sakhalin 1 project since 2009. Overall, Japan has been able to source roughly 300,000 to 400,000 bpd from Russia, but this source has been disappointing compared to Tokyo's earlier hopes and has not substantially altered the country's heavy dependence on the Middle East.

Japan's energy security profile in LNG is far more robust, insofar as Japan and its trading companies have successfully developed a diverse range of supplies from nearby and reasonably secure countries. Roughly 27 percent of LNG comes from the Middle East, mainly Qatar and the United Arab Emirates. This LNG must transit the Strait of Hormuz, so these supplies would be at serious risk if conflict were to break out in the Arabian (Persian) Gulf. But traditionally secure and nearby sources in Indonesia, Malaysia, and Brunei historically have accounted for well over half of Japan's LNG supplies since the late 1970s. Malaysian and Brunei supplies have remained steady, but Indonesian shipments have declined by 50 percent since 2003, as Jakarta has increasingly diverted the gas to domestic use. Rising LNG demand has been met increasingly by Australia's North West Shelf project, where Chevron has the leading position, and by new supplies from Russia's Sakhalin 2 project, which commenced in 2009. Japan's companies also have stakes in many of the large LNG projects that are scheduled to come on line after 2015, most importantly from Australia.

Fukushima and Its Fallout

The March 2011 earthquake and Fukushima nuclear disaster have triggered a profound resurgence in Japan's energy security anxieties, most importantly over future LNG supplies. The disaster led to the shutdown of the entire 54-unit nuclear power generation fleet by mid-2012 and the loss of 30 percent of normal electricity supplies. On an emergency basis, the shortfall has been addressed by rationing electricity, restricting supplies, imposing conservation and efficiency measures, and significantly raising electricity prices. At the same time, Japan has sharply raised imports of LNG and crude oil to boost thermal capacity. Despite these measures, electricity production was cut nearly 5 percent for 2011 and declined a profound 12 percent during the hot summer months.[8]

The crisis has triggered major new energy security concerns in Tokyo over reliable and affordable access to its burgeoning but uncertain future LNG needs. In 2011, the power sector accounted for 65 percent of Japan's total LNG consumption.[9] Much higher imports of LNG will be needed in the future. To fill the immediate gap, Japan's annual 2011 LNG imports rose by 12 percent to 79 mmt, and recent forecasts suggest that 2012 imports will rise to 88 mmt.[10] This increase would amount to an annual 18 mmt demand shock compared to a base of 140 mmt per year in Asia's 2010 LNG market and a global 2010 LNG market of around 220 mmt per year. Japan's needs were met by diverting supplies from Qatar, West Africa, and Sakhalin that had been destined mainly for the Atlantic Basin.

Adding to Japan's concerns, its buying spree led to a severe spike in Asian LNG prices. Since the crisis, LNG prices linked to the Japan Crude Cocktail price (i.e., the average price of customs-cleared crude oil imports in Japan) rose from $13 to $16 or $18 per million British thermal units.[11] The Asian LNG premium was already a serious concern for Asian LNG buyers—especially Japan. Beyond energy security concerns, the surge in imports of LNG also drove up Japan's import bill dramatically. The LNG import bill alone rose an eye-popping 52 percent, from ¥3.5 trillion to ¥5.4 trillion ($60 billion) from fiscal 2010 to fiscal 2011 (more than 1 percent of GDP). That increase led to the first trade deficits for Japan in many years.[12] The 2012 bill is likely to be even higher.

Adding to Tokyo's anxieties about LNG is the uncertainty about the outcome of the domestic debate over future nuclear power in Japan. The Japanese public remains deeply opposed to restoring nuclear power, while the government and industry believe that the costs of doing without nuclear energy are too high. Precrisis plans called for nuclear power to rise to 50 percent of generation by 2030, and filling this gap will be extremely difficult and costly. In late 2012, the Democratic Party of Japan government announced a new plan that would restart existing power plants but gradually phase out nuclear power by 2040, as the existing plants reached their 40-year life spans. But the plan was filled with caveats and plans to reassess the decision in the future. Moreover, Japan's national election in December 2012 led to the return to power of the Liberal Democratic Party, which is much more favorable to a return to nuclear generation. The new Abe government announced plans to restart Japan's nuclear power sector gradually as the new, independent Nuclear Regulatory Agency certifies each plant one by one to meet new, tougher safety standards. Nevertheless, in the face of widespread public suspicion of the nuclear industry, there remains significant uncertainty over the scale of returning nuclear supplies, and hence, LNG imports are likely to continue at high levels for the foreseeable future.

The government has responded to this energy security predicament by expanding its energy diplomacy and seeking stronger national access to future LNG projects. Japan is working diligently to access future US shale gas LNG exports, although this effort is complicated by the lack of a US–Japan free trade agreement. The government hopes to import less expensive LNG based on Henry Hub pricing and more flexible volumes.[13] Tokyo is also stepping up support for its oil companies to take ownership stakes in many of the major new LNG projects around Asia and in the United States. Although the Asian LNG market looks very tight until 2016, beyond that point major new Australian and other supplies should reduce some pressure on the market.

In conclusion, Japan has made enormous strides over the past 40 years to strengthen its domestic resilience and claim on future LNG supplies, despite what remains a very uncertain nuclear energy outlook for the future.

Southeast Asia: Changing Energy Export Roles and South China Sea Challenges

Southeast Asia is a diverse region that defies easy categorization into a single set of energy security concerns. It includes net oil exporters and oil importers, LNG exporters, and—most recently—some new LNG importers. It is an increasingly significant coal exporter, and it features extensive intraregional energy trade. But, in broad terms, the Southeast Asian region is significant in a number of ways with respect to global and regional energy trends, and changes in some of its key states are notable.

Traditionally, Southeast Asia has been a major oil and LNG supplier to Northeast Asia. During the 1990s, Indonesia, Malaysia, and Brunei exported 700,000 to 900,000 bpd of oil, mainly to Japan and South Korea, which provided those countries some diversification away from the Middle East. In the early 2000s, Vietnam also became a modest oil exporter to Northeast Asia as its offshore oil production ramped up.

However, this situation has since changed: Southeast Asian domestic oil demand has grown rapidly over the past two decades, and production has plateaued or declined. The change has been most dramatic in Indonesia, where oil output peaked at 1.5 million to 1.6 million bpd during the 1990s but began gradually declining after 2000. With rapidly rising domestic oil demand, Indonesia became a net oil importer in 2003 and now imports nearly 0.5 million bpd. Malaysia remains a modest and steady net exporter, although since the mid-2000s, exports have declined because of rising domestic demand as well as sharply declining production after 2008. And with rapidly growing oil demand in Thailand, the Philippines, and elsewhere in Southeast Asia, the region is now overall a large net oil importer. It depends on imports from outside the region for nearly three-quarters of its oil needs.

Roughly three-quarters of the region's oil imports come from the Middle East; thus, Southeast Asia is exposed to potential supply disruptions in that volatile region. One exception to Southeast Asia's overall decline as an energy supplier to Northeast Asia is the development of new oil and gas pipelines to Southeast China from Myanmar (Burma). Myanmar's rising gas production will begin flowing to China by 2014, along with Middle East oil shipments in transit to China.

A second major shift is from Southeast Asia's historic role as a major LNG supplier to Northeast Asia to its new role as an LNG market as its own gas demand booms. Indonesia, Malaysia, and Brunei have long been major LNG suppliers to Japan, South Korea, and Taiwan, and much of Asia's LNG industry has been based on Japanese investment. Although all three countries remain LNG suppliers to Northeast Asia, these supplies are now beginning to lag. Rising demand in China, Japan, and South Korea is being made up increasingly with volumes from Australia, Qatar, and Russia.

A third key point is Southeast Asia's position abreast key energy sea-lanes between the Middle East and Northeast Asia. Two-thirds of Asia's oil supplies transit the critical sea-lanes of the South China Sea and the Strait of Malacca and the other key regional straits, Lombok and Sunda. The littoral states of Indonesia, Malaysia, and Singapore have national jurisdiction over the actual Strait of Malacca, but the regional powers and large oil importers of Northeast Asia clearly all have major stakes in ensuring reliable and safe passage of oil and LNG tanker traffic through the strait. Use of the Strait of Malacca has become hostage to the broader geopolitical shadowboxing in the region among the United States, China, Japan, and the Southeast Asian states. In 2002, the United States proposed a new Regional Maritime Security Initiative to add to littoral state efforts to safeguard the Strait of Malacca, and in 2005, Japan also proposed a new regional arrangement.

These proposals met with deep Chinese suspicion and were rejected soundly by the littoral states. More broadly, securing the congested and contested sea-lanes of the South China Sea is leading to what increasingly looks like a regional naval arms race. As China's regional maritime power grows with its blue-water naval modernization and its ability to project power into Southeast Asian waters, control of the energy sea-lanes is increasingly a key aspect of the growing US–China struggle for mastery in Asia.

This struggle for Asian mastery fuses energy security with regional geopolitics and is reflected in intensifying disputes over territorial sovereignty in the South and East China Seas between China and neighboring states. Although these disputes have existed for decades, they have heated up recently as the naval capacity of China to enforce its maritime claims has grown and as several Southeast Asian states move to strengthen their claims and capabilities. The rapid rise in regional energy demand and the potential for large oil and gas reserves in these contested areas add to the already toxic mix of motivations over sovereignty, fishing rights, and other resource potential.

The most acute naval incidents in the South and East China Seas have occurred between China, on the one hand, and Japan, the Philippines, and Vietnam on the other. In 2011, 2012, and 2013, Filipino and Chinese naval vessels faced off repeatedly over control of the Mischief Reef, and Vietnam awarded a number of oil and gas exploration blocks located inside Chinese territorial claims, among them a block awarded to India's Oil and Natural Gas Corporation. Responding that Vietnam's claimed blocks are illegally in Chinese waters, Beijing prompted China National Offshore Oil Corporation to put out for bid a line of exploration blocks that precisely track China's maritime claim line and are well within Vietnam's claims. This action–reaction cycle continues to escalate, and the potential for direct military conflicts is increasing. The situation also risks drawing in the United States, which has alliance commitments to Japan and the Philippines. ASEAN has made repeated efforts, supported by the United States, to forge a regional approach, but ASEAN has been divided, and China has been able to use its historically close allies in ASEAN, Myanmar and Cambodia, to prevent such an approach. The outlook for finding solutions is increasingly uncertain, and the potential for open conflict is growing, which suggests that oil and gas exploration and development in the South and East China Seas are likely to be delayed indefinitely.

Australia: The Opportunities and Challenges of Energy Plenty

Australia defies the broader Asian narrative of an energy-short region dependent on imported energy. Australia's story, rather, is as a major energy supplier to Asia, because of its abundant resource base. Hence, its major energy security concerns revolve around ensuring that its enormous energy export industry can secure new markets in Asia to monetize its large endowment and drive Australian economic prosperity, as well as the security of the sea-lanes to transport that energy reliably.

Compared to much more interventionist Asian governments, Australia relies on flexible and transparent energy markets and private investment to ensure its energy security. As the 2012 energy white paper stated, "The cornerstone of the government's energy policy framework is ... through competitive and well-regulated markets that are operating in the long-term interests of consumers and the nation."[14] Australia's location in the Pacific makes it well positioned to take advantage of Asia's booming energy demand. Australia exports two-thirds of its total energy output and is the world's second-largest coal exporter, the fifth-largest exporter of LNG in 2011, and a major uranium exporter. Coal production has doubled since 1990, and Japan is typically the largest export market, taking around 40 to 45 percent of Australia's exports, but China, South Korea, and India are also important export markets. Australia has benefited enormously from the commodity supercycle and from rising prices for steam and metallurgical coal in Asia. Nevertheless, Australia will have to compete with rapidly rising coal exports from Indonesia, which surpassed Australian coal exports in 2011. In the longer term, evidence that the commodity supercycle may be coming to an end with China's slowing economic growth is likely to present new challenges for Australia's heavily resource-based economy.

Oil security for Australia presents a rather different picture. Australian crude oil production peaked in 2000 at 800,000 bpd and has declined gradually to around 550,000 bpd, while demand has gradually risen toward 1 million bpd. Hence, Australia imports nearly half of its crude oil needs. Although government policy maintains that oil security can rely on flexible global markets, the 2012 energy white paper has faced some criticism, which is focused on Australia's rapidly declining domestic refining capacity and near total dependence on imported oil products over the next decade. These critics argue that Australia needs to retain enough refining capacity to ensure product supplies in a strategic emergency. However, the government contends that a diversified products supply market and a healthy regional refining system centered in Singapore can meet Australia's oil product security needs.

Australia's LNG Boom

The most important aspect of Australia's energy boom for Asia is its emergence as a major LNG producer with enormous plans for the next decade. In 2011, Australia exported 26 mmt per year of LNG from the existing Northwest Shelf and Darwin projects. The exports were destined for Japan primarily but also for South Korea and China.

Australia is poised to surpass Qatar as the largest LNG exporter in the world. Seven major LNG projects under construction, with combined investments of $168 billion, put the industry on track to export more than 80 mmt per year by 2021. Seventy percent of the LNG projects currently under construction in the world are in Australia and are concentrated in four major offshore north and northwest projects producing conventional gas and three large LNG projects fed by coal seam gas in the east in Queensland. The largest offshore projects are two Chevron-led projects, Gorgon and Wheatstone, along with major projects led by Woodside (Browse); Prelude, which is a floating LNG project led by Shell; and Ichthys (Japan Inpex). The Queensland coal seam gas projects are led by Shell, ConocoPhillips, and Santos.

The massive expansion of Australian LNG is good news for LNG-short Japan; the other growing LNG markets in South Korea, China, India, and Taiwan; and the new Southeast Asian LNG importers. Nevertheless, Australia's LNG growth faces significant risks and headwinds. Most important, the massive scale of LNG project construction in Australia is rapidly driving up the costs of engineering services, labor, equipment, and port services. Chronic delays attributable to overloaded infrastructure and port congestion are also taking a toll. The cost of labor in the context of Australia's heavily unionized labor market has skyrocketed.

Moreover, the resource boom has driven up the value of the Australian dollar to the point where equipment and capital costs for projects have escalated dramatically. For example, Chevron announced in late 2012 that its Gorgon project costs had risen by 40 percent, from $37 billion to $52 billion. Rising costs across the industry are threatening the viability of future LNG developments planned beyond the seven currently under construction and could even lead to delays in projects currently under construction.

Also, Australian LNG will face strong competition for Asian markets from (a) potentially lower-cost LNG projects in the United States and Canada from the shale gas boom, (b) renewed export competition from Qatar, (c) new Russian supplies from Sakhalin 3 and possibly Vladivostok, (d) West African supplies drawn in by Asia's LNG price premium, (e) Papua New Guinea LNG, (f) potential East African offshore gas, and (g) even possibly Alaskan LNG. In China, Australian LNG also will have to compete with potentially much higher domestic conventional and shale gas production, as well as pipeline gas competition from Turkmenistan, Kazakhstan, Myanmar, and possibly Russia's East Siberia. Japan's LNG needs also are highly leveraged to the very uncertain outlook for nuclear power.

Finally, growing competition to supply high-priced Asian LNG markets suggests that LNG price trends over the longer run are quite uncertain. While the Asian LNG balance seems likely to remain very tight for the next few years, LNG markets look likely to be much more balanced and potentially oversupplied after 2016, with major new supplies coming online and continuing weak LNG demand in Europe. The gradual introduction of US hub-based pricing to Asian LNG markets also creates new uncertainties. Already, several of Japan's large utility LNG buyers have negotiated new short- and medium-term contracts that include a US Henry Hub component to their price formulas. All these factors suggest that the traditional oil-linked Japan Crude Cocktail contract price system that has fed the Asian "premium" is likely to be under growing pressure. This development would not bode well for Australia's higher-cost projects.

In sum, Australia is extremely well positioned to take advantage of Asia's booming LNG and coal demand growth. Despite the economic slowdown from 2010 to 2012, which led to a period of commodity price weakness, gradually strengthening economic growth in China and the West should underpin strong markets for Australia's energy exports, and prospects look excellent. Australia is not called "the lucky country" for nothing.

Energy Security Implications for the United States and the Region

The United States has important long-term strategic interests in Asia's continuing search to strengthen the region's energy security, and the pivot to Asia makes energy security an even more salient dimension of US interests. Japan, Southeast Asia, and Australia are key parts of the regional energy mosaic and, therefore, can play a central role in more secure energy trade. However, the drift in Asian energy security strategies since 2000 has been toward an increasingly zero-sum atmosphere in which national competition over energy supplies and transit routes has prevailed over energy cooperation. China's, Japan's, and Southeast Asia's high and growing dependence on imported oil, combined with the region's heavy reliance on Middle East supplies, have all fed this mercantilist competition. This scramble, in turn, has fed rising oil and LNG prices and strengthened the hands of the producers. Distrust has also reinforced major power strategic rivalry in the region such that, rather than becoming a source of common interest and collaboration, energy security has aggravated the underlying sense of strategic competition and major power rivalry.

In this highly charged atmosphere, achieving much in the way of regional energy cooperation has been difficult, despite obvious common interests. This scenario threatens not only the region's economic stability, in which the United States has a vital stake, but also, quite literally, regional peace, as the recent rising tensions in the South China Sea clearly demonstrate. Therefore, as the United States shifts its strategic attention toward Asia, it needs to make strengthening Asia's energy security and cooperation a much more salient dimension of its regional strategy.

The United States can pursue a range of strategies. The strong US–Australian strategic and economic partnership provides an ideal basis for new efforts to craft regional approaches to securing the energy sea-lanes vital to the region. Australia's unique geographic position facing northward toward the South China Sea but also west to the Indian Ocean makes maritime security and naval power core national goals for Australia. The country's enormous LNG and coal exports depend on secure sea-lanes through the contested and congested seas of Southeast Asia. The new agreement for positioning 2,500 US Marines in the port of Darwin testifies to growing strategic collaboration, as Australia searches for the right balance between its close alliance with the United States and its booming commodity export dependence on China. With less strategic baggage than the United States in its relationship with China, Australia can potentially provide a bridge between the two countries in finding new ways to collaborate on energy sea-lane security. The United States must pursue this opportunity vigorously with Australia, China, Japan, and Indonesia, if it is to be feasible.

US engagement with Southeast Asia through ASEAN, the East Asian Summit, and the ASEAN Regional Forum also presents opportunities to draw the regional powers into new energy security arrangements. These groups now include all the key players and could provide an architecture for regional energy cooperation. For example, ASEAN has discussed for 15 years the need for regional emergency oil stocks but has achieved little. Only Japan and South Korea, as members of the IEA, possess strategic oil stocks, whereas China is building its own national strategic stocks. The region is ripe for drawing all the major players into a regional oil stock system that would strengthen Asia's energy security while beginning to institutionalize energy cooperation. A regional oil stock system could also potentially ease some of the tensions over maritime and energy territorial claims that are currently escalating in the South China Sea. But again, this effort will need a US push if it is to move up on the crowded regional agenda.

Another opportunity for promoting regional energy cooperation would be to strengthen energy security cooperation in the Pacific islands. US Secretary of State Hillary Clinton's participation in the Pacific Islands Forum in August 2012 demonstrated a stronger US interest in the islands, albeit perhaps driven by China's aggressive diplomacy there. But given the positive relationship between the Pacific Islands and China, energy cooperation could also provide another bridge toward US–China energy cooperation. The islands would certainly be important beneficiaries from and contributors to a regional emergency oil stock system.

Energy security provides an ideal platform for a stronger and constructive US role in Asia. If managed properly, it could also be a platform for easing some of the energy and strategic tensions between the United States and China. And energy security will be a critical determinant of Asia's economic prosperity and political stability that is vital to the United States. A major future disruption in oil and LNG supplies will hit Asia's heavily import-dependent economy harder than anywhere else, because Asia is the major importer of Middle East oil and LNG. As the United States shifts its attention and resources to Asia, energy security needs to be high on the list of strategic priorities.

Notes

1. Toshikazu Okuya, Ministry of Economy, Trade, and Industry, "Japan's Energy Crisis," presented to the roundtable on Japan's Energy Security: Outlook and Implications, National Bureau of Asian Research, Washington, DC, January 25, 2012.

2. See Keiichi Yokobori, "Japan," in *Energy and Security: Toward a New Foreign Policy Strategy*, ed. Jan H. Kalicki and David L. Goldwyn (Washington, DC, and Baltimore: Woodrow Wilson Center Press and Johns Hopkins University Press, 2005), 305–28.

3. BP, *BP Statistical Review of Energy 2012* (London: BP, 2012).

4. Ministry of Economy, Trade, and Industry, "Japan's Energy Crisis."

5. International Energy Agency, *Energy Balances of OECD Countries, 2010* (Paris: OECD Publishing, 2010). See also International Energy Agency, *Energy Balances of Non-OECD Countries, 2010* (Paris: OECD Publishing, 2010).

6. For an excellent discussion of Japan's more recent energy security policies, see Reiji Takeishi, "Japan's Energy Security Strategy," in *Energy Security in the North Pacific*, ed. Fereidun Fesharaki, Nam-Yil Kim, and Yoon Hyung Kim (Seoul: Korea Energy Economics Institute, 2009), 208–56.

7. Ministry of Economy, Trade, and Industry, *The Strategic Energy Plan of Japan: Meeting Global Challenges and Securing Energy Futures* (Tokyo: Ministry of Economy, Trade, and Industry, June 2010).

8. Tomoko Hosoe, "Asia's Post-Fukushima Market for LNG: A Special Focus on Japan," in *Oil and Gas for Asia: The Geopolitical Implications of Asia's Rising Demand*, ed. Philip Andrews-Speed, Mikkal E. Herberg, Tomoko Hosoe, John V. Mitchell, and Zha Daojiong (Seattle, WA: National Bureau of Asian Research, September 2012), 43–56.

9. Hosoe, "Asia's Post-Fukushima Market for LNG."

10. Tsutomu Toichi, "Fossil Fuel Option and Japan–US Cooperation," presentation at the Sasakawa Peace Foundation–Woodrow Wilson Center Joint Seminar, Institute of Energy Economics, Tokyo, October 30, 2012.

11. Toichi, "Fossil Fuel Option and Japan–US Cooperation."

12. Tetsuo Morikawa and Hiroshi Hashimoto, "Japan's New Challenge and Possible Solutions in LNG Procurement Activities in the Wake of Less Availability of Nuclear Power Capacity," Institute of Energy Economics, Tokyo, August 2012.

13. Henry Hub prices are open market–based benchmark US natural gas prices that reflect direct gas-on-gas competition. In mid-2013, US gas prices stood at roughly $4 per million British thermal units, only one-quarter of Japan's LNG costs.

14. Department of Resources, Energy, and Tourism, *Energy White Paper 2012: Australia's Energy Transformation*, Canberra, 2012, p. x.

Commentary on Part IV

J. Bennett Johnston

This volume highlights the ways in which US energy policy can advance America's foreign policy and national security interests. The authors of the chapters in this part, "The Pacific Rim," paint these intersections in sharp relief. In my view, the United States can increase its share of global trade, maintain its security umbrella for Asia, forge partnerships to address complex issues such as North Korea's nuclear proliferation, and advance American values in the region through creative partnerships with the great powers of Asia, such as China and Japan, and through cooperation with multilateral organizations such as the Asia-Pacific Economic Cooperation (APEC) forum. Energy can be one of America's most powerful tools in crafting these new relationships.

As the authors of the chapters in part IV point out, energy insecurity in China, India, Japan, and other countries and national policies that favor energy autarky over regional cooperation can cause serious tensions. There is a tendency for Americans and various Asian nations to see China as an oil adversary and to fear its growth and appetite for energy as a threat. As

Amy Myers Jaffe and Kenneth Medlock rightly note, China today seeks to act on its own to achieve energy security. Yet China's actions are quite progressive in some respects. Beijing is curbing demand by raising fuel-efficiency standards, redressing adverse environmental effects by shifting from coal to cleaner natural gas and nuclear power, developing its own resources both by modernizing its national oil companies and by inviting partial foreign ownership in them, and moving to build strategic stocks.

But China also pursues security by bilateral means that put it at odds with US and Western policies. Jaffe and Medlock point out that China seeks access to reserves in such places as Iran and Sudan, where the United States and other countries have deep security and humanitarian concerns. China exchanges arms for oil with suppliers in the Middle East, where China can undermine regional stability and compromise Western security interests. Together with Russia, it has wielded its United Nations (UN) Security Council veto to help shield Syria's Assad regime from UN-authorized intervention to stop the indiscriminate killing of civilians as well as insurgents in the tens of thousands. It also engages in brinkmanship with its neighbors for oil and gas reserves in contested waters.

Nevertheless, effective diplomacy and leverage can still build on shared US, Chinese, and Indian interests in energy security to forge a relationship of cooperation that will allow Beijing and New Delhi to have a greater stake in shared concerns than in divergent interests. The United States can cooperate on new energy-efficient technologies with China, to help curb Chinese demand. It can help China to develop strategic stocks and manage them in a way that does not disrupt the global market. It can exchange information on clean coal and gas utilization strategies and can promote new shale oil and gas investments, which would advance shared environmental and energy security objectives. The United States can share its global energy market data with China in exchange for transparency with respect to China's energy demand and supplies. This kind of cooperation can put US–China discussions on North Korea, Southeast Asia, and global security issues on a more secure footing.

Another component of a wise US Asian energy policy should be to encourage China, India, and Japan to help moderate oil market volatility by supporting multilateral steps to limit oil use and to coordinate emergency stocks during times of supply disruption. US leadership will be needed to capitalize on these opportunities at the same time as differences persist over such important issues as international sanctions against Iran or long-standing territorial disputes in Asia.

Outside the Middle Kingdom, Mikkal Herberg traces a key shift: Southeast Asian fuel exports to Northeast Asia are giving way to both regions becoming large net oil importers with deep concerns for their own energy vulnerability, punctuated by Japan's energy predicament as the country closes its nuclear power plants following the Fukushima disaster. Fortunately, with its favorable resource base and business environment, Australia is now and will increasingly be a gas export power that can help strengthen the foundation for regional energy security.

This point is particularly important, because Australia is not only an energy power, but also a political-military ally sharing US values and goals in Asia and the Pacific. Australia will be even more essential as the United States pivots strategically to this region and as Japan, South Korea, and the member states of the Association of Southeast Asian Nations seek an adequate counterweight to growing Chinese economic and military strength. In turn, China and its Pacific neighbors all share a strong interest in containing North Korean nuclear weapons and missile capabilities and in encouraging Pyongyang to move in the direction of economic reforms, which can be supported more readily if it changes its nuclear course.

Transportation arrangements also present opportunities for cooperation and competition. On the one hand, Russia, China, and South Korea are negotiating a possible pipeline to carry East Siberian gas to these two Asian markets. On the other hand, one of the sharpest competitions bruited today involves the new East Siberia–Pacific Ocean (known as ESPO) oil pipeline from Russia—how much oil will go to Japan or China, in the near and longer term? The opportunity is there to make sure that cooperation prevails in the energy relationship among these major Asian powers. In turn, APEC and the United States should find a more comprehensive solution for the region that promotes the development of sufficient infrastructure to prevent harmful competition.

In the longer term, progress toward regional infrastructure and eventually regional energy reserves can go far in helping highly diverse countries to navigate between the adversarial and the cooperative in Asia and the Pacific. For example, if China were to join in a regional reserve whose members shared the cost of the oil and the storage, it could see a real and dramatic security dividend for cooperation. If that strategic reserve were shared with other nations of Northeast and Southeast Asia, regional tensions would decrease. Likewise, a regional plan for gas and liquefied natural gas infrastructure, with nations helping to ensure long-term demand at market prices, could accelerate gas transportation development and boost the regional economy. The stronger the economic and energy foundation, the greater the growth and, ultimately, the peace of this extraordinarily dynamic region will become.

The key to the advancement of any of these bold ideas remains the leadership of the United States. The US role as investor, bridge builder, and facilitator of multilateral organizations is a historic one. US leadership has been indispensable for lasting peace and security in the Pacific. Sustaining this role in the coming decades will require that America return to those roots and invest its diplomacy in building a true Pacific community.

This forward-looking book makes clear the dividends of a new regional and global energy strategy for US national and economic security. The authors have provided a concrete vision of how energy can support regional and global cooperation instead of conflict in the new century.

Part V

The Western Hemisphere

Part V of our volume turns to the Western Hemisphere, where game-changing technological developments unforeseen just a few years ago are reversing decades of resource scarcity with an abundance that is tilting the balance of energy power away from the Middle East and toward our own hemisphere. Nowhere is this trend more apparent than in the United States, where the application of horizontal drilling and hydraulic fracturing is bringing about dramatic increases in US tight oil and shale gas production. Canadian oil sands production is also surging, and tight oil and gas plays may also be developed if transport options from Alberta and British Columbia are cost-effective. The potential for North American net self-sufficiency in oil, gas, and products is real, if—and only if—all US, Canadian, and Mexican hydrocarbon potential is realized.

Although North America's resource endowment is clearly promising, Canada and the United States will have to overcome significant political and regulatory hurdles to leverage its full potential. This challenge is even more acute in Mexico, where policies resistant to foreign investment, and

323

as a result foreign technology and project management, have led to rapid declines in oil production and imports rather than exports of natural gas.

New energy prospects are also emerging in Latin America. Brazil's deepwater acreage (both above and below the salt layer), Colombia's on-shore fields, and Peru's gas fields have all benefited from competitive fiscal regimes that have attracted private investment and technology with impressive results. More nationalistically inclined producers such as Argentina, Bolivia, and Venezuela continue to decline as they seek either to extract excessive rents or to seize control of private investments once they find success. Although nearly any economic metric would suggest that the more open regional players have achieved more success than those that have kept their hydrocarbon sectors closed, Latin America's difficult history with outsiders remains a key issue in all its producing countries.

Shirley Neff and Angelina LaRose analyze these and related issues in their chapter on North America, where they describe the surprising reversal in the region's energy supply and demand network and its implications. Thomas F. "Mack" McLarty describes the evolving Latin American energy setting and recommends a way forward for US engagement in the region.

In chapter 15, Neff and LaRose find that unexpected growth in US oil and natural gas production and declining domestic demand have dramatically changed the region's landscape, with positive implications for all of North America. They argue that the region may eventually achieve energy self-sufficiency in physical supply, although the global oil market will continue to determine oil prices. Neff and LaRose forecast that US crude production will continue to increase, with Gulf of Mexico offshore and tight oil production gains driving growth. With regard to Canada, they note that oil sands resources there could enable Canadian production to reach 6 million barrels per day by 2035, which is about twice the 2010 production rate. The outlook is not as positive for Mexico, where oil production has been on the decline since 2004. Although Mexico's oil reserves are considerable, Neff and LaRose point out that Petróleos Mexicanos (PEMEX) remains the sole oil operator in the country and does not have the technical capability or financial means to harness fully Mexico's resource endowment. Neff and LaRose then turn to natural gas, noting that large supplies of shale gas in the United States will enable the country to consume a predominantly domestic supply of gas for years to come.

Neff and LaRose assert that this fact will have regionwide effects, because Canadian gas exports to the United States will continue to decline, whereas US gas exports to both Canada and Mexico will proceed on their upward trajectory. They conclude that although North America's resource endowment has the potential to render significant positive effects, some political and regulatory obstacles remain in the way. Among these are (a) the standoff over building more pipeline infrastructure to ease transportation constraints between the United States and Canada and (b) continued resource nationalism in Mexico, which is hampering more robust development of its oil and gas sector.

In chapter 16, McLarty assesses how Latin American energy development may affect the United States. He finds that Latin America's capacity to grow its energy exports, combined with Canada's expanded oil sands development and huge US shale gas finds, could very well bring about a future in which the United States can rely mostly on its own and Western Hemisphere energy supplies. McLarty describes the bifurcated nature of the current Latin American hydrocarbons landscape. He notes that some producers, such as Colombia, Brazil, and Peru, are demonstrating a continuing willingness to open their energy sectors to foreign investment and have reaped production and revenue benefits. Others, including Venezuela and Argentina, remain committed to protectionist policies that are resulting in significant, ongoing declines in output.

McLarty notes that although countries that have embraced liberalization and reform are clearly performing better than those that have not, political and nationalistic concerns in Latin America continue to have just as much influence as economic considerations. He also assesses Latin America's renewable resource potential, arguing that a lack of available capital and robust supply chains, in addition to prohibitive import barriers, continues to hamper foreign investment regionwide. McLarty concludes by recommending that the United States offer strong support to Latin America's reformers and reciprocate their liberalization efforts. Specifically, he calls for the United States to pursue an Energy Compact of the Americas, which would formalize cooperation, investment, research, and technology sharing in the energy sector.

In her commentary, Michelle Michot Foss offers a heavy dose of caution about the prevailing high hopes for North American energy self-sufficiency. Recalling the gas bubbles of the 1980s and the gas overhang of the 1990s, she warns, "The United States and North America are littered with the detritus of bad decisions, many intertwined with questionable policies." Foss takes no issue with the impressive forecasts of resource availability from Neff and LaRose, and also from McLarty. But, as in 2005, she cautions that "It ain't the resource, it's the framework." And here she sees high risks that the United States will take regulatory steps that will "kill the golden goose" and lead to far lower resource deliverability than Neff and LaRose (and Newell and Iler)[1] forecast. Her optimism for the hemisphere is weaker still. Here Foss sees serious backsliding even from the champions of smart frameworks, Brazil and Colombia. Colombia emerged only after a "near death" experience with production decline, and Brazil is sowing the seeds of state dominance and control that dominated the years when it was an energy importer. Politics and state demands for revenue and control are hard to deter in any country. Foss adds a new axiom, warning that "'it ain't just the framework, it's the implementation' and, even more, the ability to forestall erosion of political will and commitment—issues of internal politics—that matter in the long run." All of the strategic implications of the Western Hemisphere tight oil and gas boom hoped for in this part (and others) depend on governments making good decisions about the future. Foss expresses hope, but little confidence, that governments will make better decisions in the future than they have in the past.

Note

1. Richard G. Newell and Stuart Iler, "The Global Energy Outlook," chapter 1 of this volume.

Chapter 15

North America

Shirley Neff and Angelina LaRose

The past decade has seen a total reversal in the energy supply and demand outlook in the United States, a turnabout that has significant positive implications for all of North America. A decade ago, the outlook was for increasing hemispheric imports of oil and natural gas. Supplies of both were declining in the United States and Mexico, while Canadian demand for natural gas was growing to support development of the oil sands. Competing industry proposals for natural gas pipelines from the North Slope of Alaska and the Mackenzie Delta in Canada were under consideration, as were new import terminals for liquefied natural gas (LNG) in the United States and Mexico.

Unexpected growth in US oil and natural gas production, coupled with declining oil demand growth in the United States, has changed the entire landscape. The focus has now shifted to repurposing some of the infrastructure investments, made less than a decade ago, for export, not import, and shifting continental infrastructure to accommodate regional changes in supply.

The application of horizontal drilling and hydraulic fracturing in shale and other "tight" (very low permeability) formations in natural gas plays

Figure 15.1. North American Shale Plays, May 2011

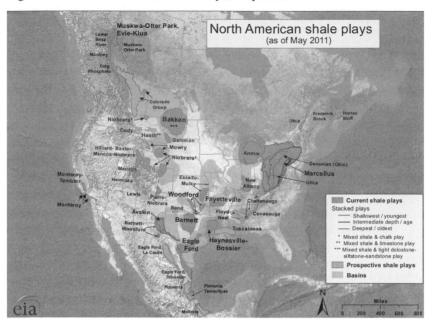

Source: US Energy Information Administration.

in Pennsylvania (Marcellus) and Texas (Barnett), as well as oil in North Dakota (Bakken) and Texas (Barnett and Eagle Ford), is setting off a dramatic change in the profile of US oil and natural gas production (figure 15.1). Opportunities also exist for the parts of the Bakken that extend into Canada and those of the Eagle Ford that extend into Mexico. The Canadian oil sands have also flourished in the higher-price environment of recent years. The dramatic growth in oil production in the United States and Canada has resulted in political rhetoric touting the possibility of "energy independence in North America." Net self-sufficiency is a more accurate way to think of the implications of the growth in production, because the forces of a global, integrated market for crude oil will continue to drive prices. As markets for natural gas and refined products expand beyond the North American hemisphere, those prices will increasingly be influenced by external factors as well.

Oil Production: The United States

US crude oil production, led initially by the deepwater Gulf of Mexico, has increased steadily since 2005, thereby reversing a decline that began in 1986, from 5.2 million barrels per day (mmbpd) in 2005 to an average of 7.0 mmbpd at the end of 2012, the highest monthly production volume in 20 years. In 2012, Texas oil production reached its highest level since 1988, and North Dakota passed California and Alaska to become the second-biggest oil-producing state. Imports of crude oil fell below 8.5 mmbpd for the first time since 1997. The temporary moratorium on deepwater drilling in the aftermath of the BP oil spill in 2010 slowed activity into 2012.

Wood Mackenzie, one of the major industry analysts for the Gulf of Mexico region, issued a report in October 2012, predicting regional production would exceed 2009's peak by 2018 or 2019 at 2 mmbpd of oil equivalent.[1] The report describes the diversity of opportunities and the range of players in the US Gulf of Mexico as unique in the world, with such a wide range of prospects available from small, low-risk fields to giant targets in extreme conditions. Another province that could add to US production, the Arctic north of Alaska, was expected to see drilling start in 2013. By mutual agreement, the US government and private sector players are taking a timeout to ensure sound planning and execution in the harshest of remote frontiers.

US proved reserves of oil and natural gas for 2010 reflected the extent of new development.[2] US proved oil reserves (which include crude oil and lease condensate) rose to 25.2 billion barrels in 2010,[3] the highest volume since 1991. Natural gas proved reserves (estimated as "wet" natural gas, including natural gas plant liquids) increased to 317.6 trillion cubic feet (tcf), the first year US proved reserves for natural gas surpassed 300.0 tcf.

Over the next 10 years, continued development of tight oil, in combination with the ongoing development of offshore resources in the Gulf of Mexico, will push domestic crude oil production higher. Experience and technological advances are expected to continue to improve recovery rates, with production increasing through 2019. The step change in the US outlook is clearly reflected by the US Energy Information Administration (EIA) in its *Annual Energy Outlook 2013*, which raised the forecast for crude oil and lease condensate production in 2020 by more than 35 percent over that forecast in 2005.[4]

Canadian Oil Production

The emergence of unconventional production as the dominant source of supply growth began in the Canadian Athabasca oil sands in Alberta. Canadian oil production in 2012 was just over 3.8 mmbpd, an increase of nearly 25 percent over 2005. Production from the oil sands, initially developed using conventional surface-mining techniques, is increasingly from deeper fields, which are developed using steam drive in situ approaches. Canada has remaining oil reserves of 173 billion barrels, 98 percent of which are oil sands bitumen. According to the *Oil and Gas Journal*, Canada is in third place globally in terms of proved oil reserves, behind Saudi Arabia and Venezuela. Canada's National Energy Board (NEB) expects the recognition of Saskatchewan reserves, coupled with new extraction technologies applied to the oil sands, will further increase Canadian reserves.

The NEB's most recent assessment has forecast oil sands production to triple by 2035, increasing its share to 86 percent of Canada's total oil supply, up from 54 percent currently.[5] By 2035, Canadian crude oil production is expected to reach 6.0 mmbpd, or about double 2010 production rates. Both the NEB and the Canadian Energy Research Institute predict that the oil sands will be profitable for operators, as well as for the provincial and federal governments, at a price of about $90 per barrel (US currency) of West Texas Intermediate (WTI) in 2011.

Oil sands bitumen extraction is energy intensive and requires large volumes of natural gas as fuel and feedstock. In situ processing uses steam-assisted gravity drainage, which involves pumping steam underground to liquefy the bitumen and pump it to the surface. The majority of the growth is expected to occur in the in situ category; 80 percent of the oil sands reserves are considered well suited to in situ extraction, compared with 20 percent for mining methods. Even though the industry continues working on new technologies and efficiency enhancements to decrease the intensity of gas use over time, the NEB, in its update to the 2011 energy market assessment, projected natural gas requirements for the oil sands development to increase "from 0.7 billion cubic feet per day in 2005 to 2.1 billion cubic feet per day in 2015."[6]

Mexican Oil Production

Mexico is one of the 10 largest crude oil producers and net exporters in the world. Three-quarters of Mexico's oil production occurs offshore in the Bay of Campeche of the Gulf of Mexico, over half from two heavy oil fields: Cantarell and Ku-Maloob-Zaap. These heavy "Maya" crudes are largely exported. The remaining quarter of current production is onshore, mainly in the states of Tabasco and Veracruz. The lighter crudes from the onshore fields are kept for domestic refining.

Mexican oil production has been steadily declining since peaking at 3.85 mmbpd in 2004 to 2.94 mmbpd in 2012. The EIA, in its *International Energy Outlook 2011*, noted that despite Mexico's potential resources to support a long-term recovery in total production, the outlook was for continued production decline until 2025 in the absence of a dramatic change in the investment environment. Mexico's state oil company, Petróleos Mexicanos (PEMEX), has two deepwater discoveries in the Gulf of Mexico near the US maritime border. The first was discovered in 2006 but is years from commercial development, given PEMEX's lack of technical capability or financial means to develop projects so remote from infrastructure.[7]

In contrast to the United States and Canada, where the sector is privatized with active investment by domestic and international companies, Mexico has just one oil operator in the country, PEMEX. Reforms have been enacted in recent years to bring in outside industry experts as advisers, to permit incentive-based service contracts with foreign companies, and to give PEMEX greater flexibility in procurement. In 2011, the first production licensing round in more than 70 years resulted in the award of three contracts to incentivize foreign service companies to increase production from some existing mature fields. The future of PEMEX and the oil sector in general was a major topic in the 2012 presidential election, which brought the Institutional Revolutionary Party (Partido Revolucionario Institucional, or PRI) back to power. Although the PRI's support of labor was the rationale for creating PEMEX in 1938, the new president of Mexico, Enrique Peña Nieto, and his economic advisers talk of further reforms that could allow private investment to revitalize the sector.

Oil Market Adjustments, Transitions, and Politics

Until recently, most North American crude grades broadly tracked fluctuations in WTI Cushing prices.[8] Pricing differentials were largely explained by the different quality characteristics of the crude oil in each location and transportation costs to Cushing, Oklahoma, the delivery point of the New York Mercantile Exchange contract, with lighter crudes capturing a premium. The rapid growth of lighter crudes from the Bakken and other tight formations in the mid-continent depressed their relative value. US refineries, especially those in the Gulf Coast, are among the most sophisticated in the world and optimize returns by running the heavier barrels that are less valuable to others; therefore, they are less willing to pay a premium for these lighter crudes.

Transportation constraints in the wake of rising production from fields in western Canada, North Dakota, and Texas are another factor affecting marketing of certain crudes. Limited pipeline capacity has both complicated the logistics and increased the cost of moving crude oil out of the mid-continent to refining centers in the Midwest and Gulf Coast. Rail shipments to East and West Coast refineries are viable alternatives.

Unlike the Bakken, the growth in oil sands was foreseen, and pipeline expansions were planned to move that production to US refineries. In 2010, Enbridge, the Canadian oil pipeline company responsible for 65 percent of the exports to the United States, expanded its system into the Midwest by 450,000 barrels per day (bpd) with the option to expand to 800,000 bpd. At the same time, Enbridge built a parallel pipeline to transport lighter hydrocarbons back to Alberta for use as diluents to process the bitumen. TransCanada, the major Canadian natural gas transmission company, entered the crude oil transportation market with construction of the Keystone pipeline system. The main line from Alberta to Illinois with capacity of 435,000 bpd entered service in 2010; an additional leg to Cushing commenced operation in 2011, thereby increasing TransCanada's total export capacity to 591,000 bpd.

Additional pipeline capacity to export the oil sands crude has run into major environmental opposition in the United States and within Canada. TransCanada's proposed addition, Keystone XL, became a heated political issue in the 2012 US presidential campaign, with environmentalists on one side and energy security interests on the other. The future of the project, which requires a presidential permit for the border crossing, remains a key issue for the US environmental community, which is frustrated over the lack of action to address climate change. Two proposed pipeline projects from Alberta to Pacific ports in British Columbia—expansion of the Kinder Morgan Trans Mountain pipeline and Enbridge's proposed Northern Gateway pipeline—also attract organized environmental and aboriginal opposition. Here the opposition is focused more on oil spills, both from pipelines and potentially from tankers, than on the greenhouse gas emissions associated with the oil sands development.

Within the United States, the unexpected increase in production has led to reversing the flows of existing liquid lines and repurposing sections of gas pipelines to move liquids. Railroads have been playing an increasingly important role in transporting US crude oil to refineries, especially oil production from North Dakota's Bakken formation, where pipeline infrastructure is limited. As additional pipeline capacity that is currently under construction between Cushing and the Gulf of Mexico eases transportation bottlenecks, the downward pressure on mid-continent crude prices should lessen.

US crude oil imports during 2012 fell to the lowest level in 15 years, driven by the increase in domestic crude production, coupled with the growth in alternative transportation fuels required under the federal Renewable Fuels Standard. The decline in demand growth in the transportation sector has also been a significant factor. The economic downturn in 2008–09 had a temporary impact on demand growth, but imposition of three major vehicle fuel economy rules over the past decade and higher prices are having a sustained effect. The EIA has projected that net imports will decline to 32 percent of total consumption in the short term, before increasing to 37 percent as tight oil production begins to decline after 2020 (figure 15.2).

Refining and Products

During the 2000s, as US production declined to a low in 2005 and the average barrel of imported oil was growing heavier, US refiners—especially in the Gulf Coast region—invested in upgrading capacity. The result is that the US refining industry is the most technologically advanced in the world, albeit with variations across the different regions.[9] In the United States, refineries have typically optimized production for finished motor gasoline to meet high US demand. This approach resulted in beneficial trading opportunities with Europe, where diesel was preferred to gasoline. In recent years, by fine-tuning the production mix, US refiners on the Gulf Coast have produced historically high volumes of distillate fuels (a category that includes both diesel fuel and heating oil) and motor gasoline.

The United States, in 2011, exported more petroleum products on an annual basis than it imported for the first time since 1949. This trend has continued as increasing foreign purchases of distillate fuel from South and Central American markets have added to European imports of US distillates.

Figure 15.2. US Dependence on Imported Liquids Declines

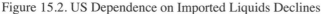
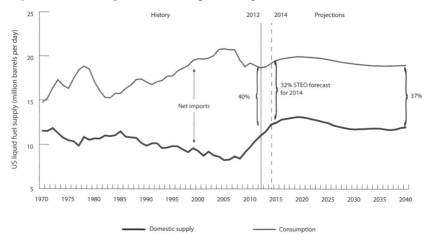

Sources: EIA, "AEO 2013 Early Release Overview," EIA, Washington, DC, March 2013, http://www.eia.gov/forecasts/aeo/er/pdf/0383er%282013%29.pdf; EIA, "Short-Term Energy Outlook," EIA, Washington, DC, March 2013.

Note: STEO = short-term energy outlook.

Transportation Energy Consumption

After nearly two decades of stagnation, then decline, in US average vehicle efficiency, a series of three new standards for cars and light trucks under the CAFE (Corporate Average Fuel Economy) rules are having a notable effect on demand for refined products. The EIA's *Annual Energy Outlook 2012* includes a scenario in which, by 2035, 80 percent of all light-duty vehicle sales that do not rely solely on a gasoline internal combustion engine for both motive and accessory power (including those that use diesel, alternative fuels, or hybrid electric systems) will meet higher fuel economy standards.[10] Evidence exists of greater consumer acceptance and growing demand for more fuel-efficient vehicles, especially as auto manufacturers are including the interior upgrades that drivers have come to expect in new cars.

Natural Gas

Natural gas expansion has been largely a US story. In the past 40 years, the natural gas sector in the United States has oscillated between supply concerns and supply optimism. Enactment of the Power Plant and Industrial Fuel Use Act of 1978, which barred new construction of gas-fired generation, was a response to perceived scarcity. Once gas markets were restructured and commoditized, an "overbuild" of natural gas–fired electric power plants occurred in the 1990s, followed by the construction of LNG import facilities in the mid-2000s.

Now, the advances in drilling technology with the combination of horizontal drilling and hydraulic fracturing have propelled the United States into an age where domestic natural gas supply seems abundant. US production of natural gas increased 25 percent from 2000 to 2012 because of natural gas production from onshore resources and is now at record levels. Other contributing factors include improved site planning and field optimization, multiwell drilling from a single pad, rising associated natural gas production from oil plays, and improved drill-bit technology.

Of the natural gas consumed in the United States in 2012, about 94 percent was produced domestically. The availability of large quantities of shale gas is expected to enable the United States to produce more natural gas than it consumes. Onshore production growth is largely concentrated in shale plays, with production from the Haynesville shale in Louisiana and the Marcellus shale in Pennsylvania leading growth since 2007. Development of other shale resources, such as the Eagle Ford and Barnett plays in Texas and the Utica play in Ohio, is adding to natural gas production levels. The EIA's *Annual Energy Outlook 2013* projects a 44 percent increase in US dry natural gas production, from 23.0 tcf in 2011 to 33.1 tcf in 2040.[11] Almost all of this increase in domestic natural gas production is due to projected growth in shale gas production, which grows from 7.9 tcf in 2011 to 16.7 tcf in 2040.

Shale Gas Production

Although the prospects for shale gas production are promising, considerable uncertainty remains regarding the size and economics of this resource. Many shale formations, particularly the Marcellus, are so large that only a limited portion of the entire formation has been extensively tested for production. Most of the shale gas wells have been drilled in the past few years, so uncertainty exists regarding their long-term productivity. Another uncertainty is the future development of well drilling and completion technology, which could substantially increase well productivity and reduce production costs.

From 1978 to 2003, over 20 percent of the US natural gas gross withdrawals came from offshore resources, largely in the Gulf of Mexico. As more domestic US natural gas production shifts from offshore fields in the Gulf of Mexico to onshore basins, potential natural gas supply disruption risks have shifted as well. The development of shale natural gas plays has created an indigenous supply of natural gas in areas of the United States that have historically relied on regional imports (either from other US producing areas or from foreign imports) to satisfy their natural gas demand. This is particularly true for production of natural gas in the Marcellus shale play, which is located near the major natural gas–consuming region in the Northeast. The development of the Marcellus shale has significantly affected the natural gas supply portfolio in the Northeast.

Northeast Gas Supply

Supply of natural gas to the Northeast traditionally came from Canada, the Gulf region, and the mid-continent producing areas. The completion of the Rockies Express pipeline (terminating in Ohio) in 2009 brought gas from the Rocky Mountains to the Northeast. Then, in 2010, significant regional production from the Marcellus shale play became available. These new supplies from the Rockies and from the Marcellus displaced both Canadian and LNG imports into the Northeast. Expansion of the Northeast pipeline infrastructure, targeted to ease congestion out of the Marcellus and surrounding areas, has placed additional pressure on traditional suppliers and has contributed to both the reversal of a Canadian import point and the expansion of capacity into the West and Midwest for Rockies pipelines.

Pipelines and LNG Terminals

The levels of natural gas imports and exports in the United States have shifted considerably with the growth in domestic production. US net imports of natural gas peaked in August 2007 at 10 billion cubic feet per day (bcfpd). By 2012, average US daily net imports—imports minus exports—were just over 4 bcfpd, the lowest level since 1990.

The decline was the result of a combination of a lower level of imports and a higher level of exports to eastern Canada and Mexico. In 2012, US natural gas imports via pipeline from Canada fell over 10 percent compared with the preceding five-year average. Although gross pipeline imports fell significantly, they still served as a marginal source of supply during times of high natural gas demand or when US pipelines were down for maintenance. For example, when Ruby pipeline, which moves gas from the Rocky Mountains to the West Coast, went offline in December 2011, imports from Canada to the United States rose to about 3.0 bcfpd, up from around 2.5 bcfpd earlier in the month.

LNG imports through US terminals peaked in 2007 at more than 2.1 bcfpd. Average daily deliveries to US LNG terminals were down over 60 percent in 2012 compared with the previous five-year average. Although there are eight LNG import terminals in the United States, two (Everett Marine Terminal in Massachusetts and Elba Island in Georgia) have been receiving the vast majority of LNG cargoes, largely to fulfill long-term contract obligations. Similar to the role of pipeline imports from Canada, Everett also serves as a marginal source of supply during cold snaps, when high prices in the Northeast could attract international cargoes. Higher natural gas prices in competing markets abroad are attracting "spot" LNG cargoes that can be delivered under flexible pricing terms. LNG cargoes have been diverted to take advantage of higher prices at other international markets, including the United Kingdom, Japan, and Belgium, where prices generally traded several dollars higher than at Henry Hub during the year.

US Natural Gas Exports

Although the decline of natural gas imports continues, US exports of natural gas to both Canada and Mexico have increased. Increasing use of natural gas in the oil sands in western Canada has created a market opportunity for US gas to move into eastern Canada. Much of the recent growth in natural gas exports to Canada has been for deliveries on US pipelines to natural gas storage facilities in Ontario.

Exports to Mexico averaged almost 1.7 bcfpd in 2012, nearly 70 percent greater than the preceding five-year average. Mexico has focused on expanding natural gas–fired power generation in the past several years, and the country's Federal Electricity Commission (Comisión Federal de Electricidad, or CFE) has called for additional natural gas–fired genera-tion. In its outlook for 2006 to 2016, the CFE forecast increasing use of natural gas in the electric generation sector, as well as some growth in gas consumption in the industrial sector. These projected increases in demand come at a time of declining natural gas production from PEMEX. In 2011, PEMEX's natural gas production declined 6 percent. Although Mexico has LNG import capacity, low prices have made importing US natural gas via pipeline an economically favorable option.

Both the CFE and PEMEX have proposed projects to expand Mexico's natural gas pipeline system by approximately 40 percent, with an invest-ment of more than $7 billion. To support the growth of Mexican natural gas consumption, the pipeline projects slated to come online between 2013 and 2018 will have a capacity of nearly 6 bcfpd. These projects include three natural gas import pipeline projects that would increase the capacity for US natural gas imports by over 4.5 bcfpd.

According to PEMEX, the southern region of the country contains the largest share of proved reserves. However, the northern region, with its shale gas deposits, likely will be the center of future reserves growth, be-cause it contains almost 10 times as much probable and possible natural gas reserves as the southern region. PEMEX started its assessment of Mexico's unconventional resources in 2010. The oil and natural gas assessment of shale basins resulted in a range of 150 to 459 tcf of technically recoverable resources, with a mean of 297 tcf. As of 2012, minimal test drilling had occurred in these areas. As Mexico considers the development of its own shale resources, the pace and extent of reforms will be critical to attracting expertise and capital. Even with reform, however, the availability of inex-pensive US natural gas imports may hinder the development of Mexico's shale gas.

Mexico may not be the only outlet for the abundance of US natural gas. The combination of high global prices and low US prices has led several companies to apply for permission to construct US LNG liquefac-tion facilities to export domestically produced natural gas. As of March 2013, the US Department of Energy's Office of Fossil Energy has re-ceived 25 applications to export LNG with nearly 30 bcfpd of proposed export capacity; only Sabine Pass in Louisiana and Freeport LNG in Texas have received authorization to export to both countries with which the United States has a free trade agreement and countries with which it does not. Sabine Pass already has signed several long-term export contracts and plans to begin exporting LNG by 2016. Freeport LNG, which was granted a conditional authorization, also has several long-term contracts in place and plans to begin exporting LNG by 2017. Most of the proposed terminals are located at current LNG import facilities and are primarily in the Gulf Coast area.[12]

A combination of increasing natural gas production, a declining US export market, and relatively low natural gas prices has also strengthened Canada's interest in exporting LNG to the world market. Four LNG export projects are planned in western Canada, and one facility is proposed in eastern Canada. Three facilities have received export licenses from Canadian regulators. The first, a 20-year export license, was granted to Kitimat LNG in 2011 and has a planned initial capacity of 700 million cubic feet per day. The location of the western Canada LNG export projects, close to higher-valued Asian markets, has an advantage over the proposed US LNG export projects, which are based along the Gulf Coast.

Although both Canada and the United States have regulatory and political hurdles to LNG exports, Canada also faces infrastructure challenges because, unlike most of the facilities proposed in the United States (which are at the site of existing LNG import terminals, connected to pipelines), Canada would have to build both liquefaction facilities and a pipeline connection to supply areas. Canada-based facilities, which may have to offer oil-indexed LNG prices because of higher investment costs, may be at a competitive disadvantage to facilities based in the United States, which have the prospect of LNG prices linked to Henry Hub.

Export as LNG is only one outlet for natural gas from booming domestic production. The resulting low natural gas price environment has opened the door to expanding domestic markets, which include natural gas–fired electric power generation, increased industrial activity, and natural gas as a vehicle fuel. In the immediate term, increased natural gas use for electric power generation has presented itself as the primary outlet for soaking up available natural gas.[13]

The increased use in natural gas–fired electricity has come at the expense of coal-fired electricity. In March 2012, amid historically low natural gas prices and the warmest March ever recorded in much of the United States, coal's share of total net generation dropped to 34 percent—the lowest level since at least January 1973 (the earliest date for which monthly statistics exist). Despite seasonally low loads, natural gas–fired generation grew markedly and accounted for 30 percent of overall net generation by March 2012.

The decrease in coal use at electric power plants, combined with strong demand from Europe and Asia and relatively high international coal prices, boosted US coal exports to record-high levels in 2012. Total coal exports reached 126 million short tons, breaking the previous record level of 113 million short tons in 1981. Steam coal exports, which grew about 50 percent in both 2011 and 2012, accounted for 98 percent of the total export growth from 2011 to 2012.

Low carbon dioxide (CO_2) prices, relative natural gas and coal prices favoring coal, and the start of the nuclear phase-out in Germany prompted European electricity generators to use more coal. A series of weather- and labor-related international coal supply disruptions in 2011 and 2012 in major supply areas such as Australia, Indonesia, Colombia, and South Africa also drove European and Asian countries to import more coal from the United States.

More than half of US coal exports were to Europe in 2011 and 2012. Year on year from 2011 to 2012, exports to Europe increased by 12 million short tons, or 23 percent; exports to Asia increased by 5 million tons, or 18 percent. Most of the growth of exports to Asia has been driven by demand from China and India.

Impact on Regional CO_2 Emissions

As a result of increased natural gas use in the United States and increased coal use (particularly in Europe), regional emission levels have shifted. Natural gas has approximately one-half the carbon of coal. In 2012, US annual energy-related CO_2 emissions were at the lowest levels since 1994, at 5.3 billion metric tons. Several factors combined to produce this drop, including slower economic growth, weather, and changes in the prices of fuels, which played out differently in major economic sectors. US CO_2 emissions from coal were down 18 percent to 387 million metric tons in the period from January to March 2012, the lowest first quarter CO_2 emissions from coal since 1983 and the lowest for any quarter since April–June 1986. Energy-related CO_2 emissions have declined in the United States in four of the past five years.

The situation in the United States is markedly different from that in Asia and Europe, which saw an increase in CO_2 emissions in 2011 and 2012. This outcome is particularly remarkable for Europe, which has a regionwide climate policy. High natural gas prices combined with low CO_2 emissions prices contributed to this increase.

Policy Issues

Future prospects for North American energy self-sufficiency may depend more on political will than on resources. The political standoff in the United States and Canada over pipeline infrastructure to move large quantities of crude oil could slow production growth. Limits on US infrastructure to import Canadian crudes could lead to higher imports of heavy crudes from the Middle East or Venezuela to satisfy the US Gulf Coast refiner preferences. These substitutions might also negatively affect broader economic benefits, because a smaller share of import payments would be recycled in bilateral trade. Likewise, the ability of the new government in Mexico to implement constitutionally valid reforms in the petroleum sector will be the key to timely development of Mexican deepwater discoveries as well as replication of the US experience with shale resources.

The business model for much of the US Gulf Coast refinery complex is now focused on optimizing value from deep conversion of the world's heaviest crudes into light commercial products. Products are then sold to the highest-value market, increasingly throughout the Western Hemisphere. Although this model may make sense from a business perspective, it might also lead to pressure for the United States to allow exports of lighter crudes. Exports of crude oil would require congressional action. Such action would occur only after extensive analysis, fierce debate, and lobbying on all sides.

Similarly, US policy determinations on LNG gas exports to countries with which the United States does not have free trade agreements may affect US natural gas production. A study commissioned by the US Department of Energy recently concluded that the net benefits of LNG exports to the US economy were positive under all scenarios, that US prices did not migrate to world prices, and that market conditions were likely to limit US export volumes to a level far below the volumes that permit applicants are requesting (in aggregate).[14] But the same report noted sectoral shifts in welfare effects, because wage earners paid modestly higher natural gas prices and resource owners earned modestly higher income. These tradeoffs pose political complications for policy-makers. The question of whether to let the market decide the level of LNG exports or to impose limits through some formula or bureaucratic procedure is to be addressed in 2013.

This new abundance of oil and gas supply poses tradeoffs for policy-makers that did not exist in the long period of relative resource scarcity. Exports of oil, gas, and petroleum products were then unimaginable, but today they are either already happening or awaiting government approval. The income benefits from these high-value exports could support a weak economy, create new jobs, and improve the US trade balance. The geopolitical benefits of a more competitive natural gas market or increased hemispheric supplies of products or surplus light oil are potentially considerable. However, those concerned with environmental impacts challenge the net benefits of the production of oil and gas anywhere. Those who hope to increase petrochemical and manufacturing benefits dispute studies showing that domestic oil and gas prices will not increase appreciably and argue that more economic and job growth would occur in the absence of increased energy exports. The fault lines cross parties, regions, and industries—and bridging them will be a political and policy challenge of the first order.

Notes

1. Wood Mackenzie. "E&P Activity Driving Deepwater Gulf of Mexico Revival," press release, October 3, 2012, http://www.woodmacresearch.com/cgi-bin/wmprod /portal/corp/corpPressDetail.jsp?oid=10826889.

2. *Proved reserves* reflect volumes of oil and natural gas that geologic and engineering data demonstrate with reasonable certainty to be recoverable in future years from known reservoirs under existing economic and operating conditions.

3. US Energy Information Administration (EIA), *US Crude Oil, Natural Gas, and Natural Gas Liquids Proved Reserves, 2010* (Washington, DC: EIA, 2012), http://www .eia.gov/naturalgas/crudeoilreserves/pdf/uscrudeoil.pdf.

4. The comparison is between the *Annual Energy Outlook 2005* forecast under the high oil price scenario and the 2012 Reference Case scenario, recognizing the change in the overall level of oil prices. See EIA, *Annual Energy Outlook 2013 with Projections to 2040* (Washington, DC: EIA, 2013).

5. NEB, *Canada's Energy Future: Energy Supply and Demand Projections to 2035* (Ottawa: NEB, 2011), http://www.neb-one.gc.ca/clf-nsi/rnrgynfmtn/nrgyrprt /nrgyftr/2011/nrgsppldmndprjctn2035-eng.pdf. See also Canadian Energy Research Institute, *Canadian Oil Sands Supply Costs and Development Projects (2011–2045)* Calgary, AB: Canadian Energy Research Institute, 2012), http://www.ceri.ca/images /stories/2012-03-22_CERI_Study_128.pdf.

6. NEB, "Canada's Oil Sands: Opportunities and Challenges to 2015: An Update— Questions and Answers," October 28, 2011, http://www.neb.gc.ca/clf-nsi/rnrgynfmtn /nrgyrprt/lsnd/pprtntsndchllngs20152006/qapprtntsndchllngs20152006-eng.html.

7. EIA, *International Energy Outlook 2011* (Washington, DC: EIA, 2011).

8. West Texas Intermediate, or WTI, is a grade of crude oil with relatively low density and sulfur content that is used as a benchmark in oil pricing and is the underlying commodity of the Chicago Mercantile Exchange's oil futures contracts. Cushing, Oklahoma, is a major crude oil trading hub and has been the delivery and price settlement point for WTI on the New York Mercantile Exchange for more than three decades.

9. Wood Mackenzie, *Outsourcing US Refining? The Case for a Strong Domestic Refining Industry* (Washington, DC: American Petroleum Institute, 2011), http://www.api.org/aboutoilgas/sectors/refining/upload/api_case_for_us_refining_wood mackenziereport.pdf.

10. EIA, *Annual Energy Outlook 2012 with Projections to 2035* (Washington, DC: EIA, 2012).

11. EIA, *Annual Energy Outlook 2013*.

12. Exceptions include the Jordan Cove Energy Project, situated off the coast of Oregon, and the Dominion Cove Point facility, an existing import terminal located on the Chesapeake Bay, south of Baltimore, Maryland.

13. Average capacity factors for the US fleet of natural gas combined-cycle power plants have increased steadily since 2005. Increased use of these plants means that facilities that previously served peaking or, more often, intermediate load needs now contribute more significantly to base load electricity needs. Between 2005 and 2010, average capacity factors for natural gas plant operations between 10 p.m. and 6 a.m. rose from 26 percent to 32 percent. For peak hours—from 6 a.m. to 10 p.m.—capacity factors averaged about 50 percent on a national basis in 2010 compared to about 40 percent in 2005. Both the increasing domestic supply of natural gas and lower natural gas prices, together with the high efficiency of combined-cycle power plants, have contributed to the plants' increased use.

14. W. David Montgomery, Robert Baron, Paul Bernstein, Sugandha D. Tuladhar, Shirley Xiong, and Mei Yuan, *Macroeconomic Impacts of LNG Exports from the United States* (Washington, DC: NERA Economic Consulting, 2012), http://www.ourenergypolicy.org/wp-content/uploads/2012/12/nera_lng_report.pdf.

Chapter 16

Latin America

Thomas F. "Mack" McLarty

Latin America's status as a commodity powerhouse is nothing new. What is new is what the Latin American countries are producing and who is producing it. In recent years, Latin American countries—Brazil in particular— have discovered vast new reserves of oil and gas, transforming the region and world energy markets. New energy leaders such as Brazil, Colombia, and Peru have emerged, while traditional pacesetters such as Venezuela, Mexico, and Argentina have struggled with declining production amid rising domestic demand.

Latin America has the second-largest oil reserves in the entire world, and those reserves are among the world's most promising sources of new production in the decade ahead.[1] This development has profound implications for the region and for the United States. World energy demand is projected to grow by almost half by 2030,[2] and Latin America will have to play an ever-greater role in meeting the energy needs of its own growing middle class and of people around the world.

The United States already imports over one-quarter of its oil from Latin America, and this robust energy trade will likely continue for many decades to come.[3]

If you combine Latin America's capacity to grow its energy exports with massive new shale gas finds in the United States and the expanded development of Canada's substantial oil sands deposits, you will see a potential that was unthinkable just a few years ago: *a United States that is mostly energy self-sufficient, with the overwhelming majority of our energy imports coming from partners in the Western Hemisphere.*

That is an eventuality that every American should welcome, although perhaps not for the reason that many think. "Energy independence" is an idea with great political salience but much less real-world relevance. After all, whether the United States purchases a barrel of oil from Saudi Arabia, Canada, or Colombia does not really matter, because oil is a fungible global commodity. But there is great value in the United States building stronger trade and investment ties with its neighbors, and no more promising area exists for cooperation than energy. A thriving Latin America is manifestly in the US interest. More opportunities for Latin Americans equal more jobs and trade within and between our nations and more stability for the entire region. And despite all of Latin America's progress, plenty still needs to be done.

Income inequality in Latin America is among the highest in the world, and 100 million Latin Americans still rely on traditional biomass such as firewood to meet their basic energy needs.[4] Latin America needs substantial investments in its infrastructure, including $3 trillion in investment in the energy sector, over the next five years.[5] That amount is more than Latin American investors and governments alone can provide. But the investment must come from somewhere because Latin America needs more secure and affordable energy to export and to fuel the vehicles, homes, and businesses of its emerging middle class.

The good news for Latin America is that the energy resources are there. Aside from its vast oil and gas reserves underground, Latin America also has immense energy capacity aboveground. Of Latin America's energy, 28 percent comes from hydropower—more than four times the global average—and the region possesses significant solar and wind energy potential.[6] But having resources is no guarantee that a country will benefit from them. Capitalizing on natural resources requires policies that welcome competition, regional integration, and foreign investment and technical expertise and that resist the temptations of protectionism and overbearing state control. Fortunately, many countries in Latin America have followed the former path for the past few decades.

But implementing policies favorable to foreign investment has always been a delicate balancing act in Latin America for entirely understandable reasons. I have traveled extensively to the region for more than 20 years and have become well acquainted with the deep sensitivities that Latin Americans have about historical imperialism and foreign participation in their energy industries. And in recent years, states such as Argentina, Ecuador, and Bolivia are again asserting more state control over their energy resources. Venezuela, of course, has nationalized key parts of its oil industry and has implemented oil royalty regimes and rules that are often unappealing to international companies. But Latin America stands a much better chance of capitalizing on its energy abundance in the 21st century if it can move beyond the historical baggage of the 19th and 20th centuries.

Although Latin America does have a fraught history with outsiders, international companies are essential partners in modern energy exploration. Recent studies by Ramón Espinasa at the Inter-American Development Bank reveal that Latin American countries with comparatively open energy sectors, such as Colombia, Peru, and Brazil, have enjoyed substantial increases in energy investment and production in the wake of rising oil prices, whereas those with more state involvement have gone mostly in the opposite direction.[7] It is not hard to see why, because energy exploration is a capital-intensive (operating just one deepwater rig can cost more than $350 million a year)[8] and complicated process that requires the best talent and resources from around the world. Very few countries are capable of conducting energy exploration entirely on their own.

As Latin American countries seek continued opening, the United States can be a constructive partner. It already has deep cultural and commercial ties. The United States has 50 million Hispanics and that population is growing,[9] and its trade with Latin America grew faster than its trade with both Asia and Europe over the past decade.[10] There is immense untapped potential for energy cooperation. US companies have capital and scientific and engineering expertise, which can be an essential complement to Latin America's energy development, especially as ambitious deepwater exploration pushes technological boundaries.

The US government and US companies must approach these potential partnerships with the utmost respect and humility. Where reformers seek more openness and integration, the United States should support and encourage them. But it is not the role of the United States to give directives to anyone. As President Barack Obama said at his first Summit of the Americas meeting in Trinidad:

We have at times been disengaged, and at times we sought to dictate our terms [to Latin America]. But I pledge to you that we seek an equal partnership. There is no senior partner and no junior partner in our relations.[11]

Building this new partnership will require American policy-makers to take a more holistic and strategic view of US relations with its southern neighbors. Too much of the discussion in Washington revolves around narrow issues such as narcotrafficking, the machinations of the Castro brothers in Cuba, or battles over bilateral trade deals. These issues are undoubtedly important, but Latin American energy issues should be consuming an ever-greater share of US attention, especially as many critical issues come to the fore in 2013 that will determine whether Latin America continues down the path of energy sector liberalization:

• Brazilian geologists have made the biggest oil discovery in the Western Hemisphere in three decades, but can the oil be reached, how much will foreign companies be allowed to help, and which regions of the country will share the spoils?
• In Mexico, a new president will try to reform the country's constitution to open its oil sector for the first time since 1938, but can he overcome the vested interests that have stymied reform in the past?
• In Colombia, historic market reforms have led to more energy development and production and enabled the country to punch well above its weight in energy reserves in world markets. Will other countries follow Colombia's lead, or are recent moves by Argentina and Bolivia to assert more state control over their energy resources evidence that the Venezuelan model is gaining new appeal?
• Latin America has been a global pacesetter in developing renewable resources such as hydropower and ethanol. The region also has immense wind and solar power potential, but can this potential be translated into production?

These questions and others will ultimately be answered by Latin Americans, and I will attempt to provide some clarity on what they might decide and how the United States can play a constructive role.

Brazil

Any discussion of Latin America's rise as an energy titan must begin with Brazil, the region's most populous country and the recipient of a recent oil and gas windfall that has transformed regional and world energy markets virtually overnight. The speed and scale of the change that has occurred is hard to overstate. Brazil has long been a major commodities producer, and it is the world's biggest exporter of beef, coffee, sugar, and orange juice.[12] But it never produced much oil or gas, with its effect on world energy markets mostly limited to the export of sugarcane ethanol. As recently as 1997, a full two-thirds of Latin American oil imports went to Brazil.[13]

But in 1997, Brazil commenced a historic opening of its energy sector, setting up a concessions system in which the state oil company, Petrobras, would provide competitive bidding opportunities to international companies for exploration and production rights. The energy sector was further liberalized when Brazil deregulated oil and derivative prices in 2002. This opening had two salutary effects. First, it attracted significant amounts of foreign capital and technology to help Brazil discover and develop new energy reserves. And second, it brought a market discipline that enabled Petrobras to become a vastly more efficient and productive company. The results speak for themselves. When Brazil's oil market was liberalized in 1997, the country was producing about 840,000 barrels of oil per day. In 2011, Brazil produced 2.1 million barrels per day.[14]

But the development that turned Brazil from a significant energy player into a true energy powerhouse occurred in 2007, when Brazilian geologists made the biggest oil find in the Americas since the discovery of Mexico's Cantarell field in 1976.[15] The *presalt oil fields*—thus named because they sit under a thick layer of salt deposits in Brazil's offshore Santos basin— cover an area the size of the state of New York and contain anywhere from 50 billion to 200 billion barrels of oil.[16]

Although the presalt areas are responsible for only about 6 percent of Brazil's current oil production,[17] their immense potential has led some experts to predict that Brazil could be producing more oil than Venezuela by the end of the decade,[18] even though Venezuela has the biggest oil reserves in the world.[19] But getting to these reserves will be a significant challenge. The presalt deposits sit under 18,000 feet of water, salt, sand, and rock,[20] with many deposits so far out to sea that platforms need to be built midway between the coastline and the drill rig to house workers. This situation is akin to building a base camp before scaling a mountain peak, and it is just one reason that one commentator called the presalt development "by far the biggest industrial undertaking in Brazil's history."[21]

Presalt development will ultimately be a test case for Brazil's commitment to openness in its energy sector. Brazil's recent discoveries were spurred in part by liberalization that brought in more foreign companies to explore.[22] But Brazil has exerted tighter state control ever since the presalt discovery, creating a state-owned enterprise, Petrosal, to contract out the exploration and production of the fields. Brazil is also requiring the state oil company, Petrobras, to maintain a 30 percent ownership stake in every contract[23] and is mandating the purchase of at least 65 percent of its inputs—such as tankers and drilling rigs—within Brazil.[24]

Petrobras is undoubtedly a world-class company with considerable expertise in deepwater drilling. It is active in 23 countries and fresh off a $70 billion initial public offering, the largest in history. Moreover, the company is putting ample capital behind this and other exploration projects, having recently unveiled a five-year, $225 billion investment plan.[25] But concern is growing that Petrobras may be stretched too thin, with early reports emerging of difficulties finding sufficient suppliers of infrastructure such as drilling rigs and pipelines within Brazil.[26]

Finding sufficient technology, capital, and scale to develop the presalt fields is not the only challenge. Brazil still has not resolved a contentious debate over dividing royalties from presalt oil production—with states like São Paulo, Rio de Janeiro, and Espírito Santo angling to keep most royalties in the area where they are produced, and other regions fighting for the royalties to be paid into a national fund. As a result, oil concession auctions that were initially scheduled for 2011 have been pushed back to 2013.[27]

Energy exploration has become a high-stakes enterprise for Brazil, and that situation has unfortunately resulted in resurgent nationalism and hostility to foreign energy companies in some quarters. Private companies and some members of the Brazilian government alike were taken aback by the politicization of the November 2011 Frade incident, in which some 3,700 barrels of crude oil seeped into Brazil's offshore waters.[28]

The Frade oil spill was, by almost any measure, a minor one that resulted in virtually no damage to fish, wildlife, people, or property (for comparison, the spring 2011 Macondo oil spill in the Gulf of Mexico released 4.9 million barrels of crude oil).[29] Yet Brazilian authorities took drastic action against the international energy companies involved in the spill by impounding passports, suspending operating rights, and pursuing multibillion-dollar civil fines and criminal charges.[30] This overreaction has led some to wonder whether international companies will take the risk of exploring Brazil's presalt oil fields if the reward is limited by a more activist Brazilian government and the threat of severe punishment for mishaps.

Despite the unfortunate Frade incident, I believe Brazilian leadership understands the essential role that international companies have in developing the country's reserves for the benefit of the Brazilian people. And the presalt oil fields remain a promising opportunity for companies with the capital, technology, and long-term time horizon to stay the course. To date, Brazil has effectively struck a middle path with its energy sector, maintaining state control over key resources while still keeping a regulatory framework that allows reasonable competition and providing major state enterprises such as Petrobras the independence to make largely market-based investment decisions. The coming months will provide fuller clarity on whether Brazil intends to stick with this middle course—a course that has served it well over the past decade—or whether it will move to assert fuller state control over its energy assets.

Mexico

While Brazil continues to debate how much to open its oil and gas sector, Mexico is in the middle of a historic debate over whether to open its oil sector at all. Since 1938, foreign oil firms have been constitutionally prohibited from ownership of any oil that they produce, which has severely curtailed foreign participation in Mexico's energy sector.

But that could soon change as Mexico and its state oil company, Petróleos Mexicanos (PEMEX), face significant declines in production and in revenue. Since 2004, PEMEX's oil production has dropped from 3.2 million to 2.5 million barrels per day,[31] and the company lost $7.4 billion in 2011, its fifth consecutive annual loss.[32] Because PEMEX is responsible for 32 percent of Mexican government revenues, this situation is untenable for the Mexican leadership.[33] It has obvious implications for the United States, as well, because Mexico is the second-largest source of US oil imports.

PEMEX's production is not falling because of declining reserves— quite the contrary. Mexico's former energy minister has estimated that the country has 50 billion barrels of potential oil reserves in the Gulf of Mexico—more than twice its current reserves.[34] Mexico also has the world's fourth-largest shale gas reserves.[35] Unfortunately, PEMEX is suffering from years of insufficient capital investment and limited offshore drilling expertise. PEMEX, like many state-run oil companies, has to serve two masters—the state and the market—which often have diametrically opposed priorities.

PEMEX's budget is set by Mexico's congress, and its revenues are used to fund everything from education and infrastructure to the combating of narcotrafficking. They are also used to employ 140,000 politically powerful union members.[36] The upshot is less money for energy investment and exploration.

But change is afoot. In 2011, Mexico opened licensing for performance-based oil contracts to foreign oil companies. And in early 2012, Mexico and the United States signed the Transboundary Agreement, approved by the US Congress in 2013, which, when implemented, will enable them to share communications, training, personnel, equipment, and technology expertise in exploring the 1 million-acre-plus international maritime boundary between the two countries in the Gulf of Mexico.[37]

Mexico's new president, Enrique Peña Nieto, has pledged to go even further. Before he was elected in 2012, he said that PEMEX "can achieve more, grow more, and do more through alliances with the private sector." He called for abandoning an ideology that has "stopped us from taking a much more audacious step in the greater opening up of the energy sector."[38] Because Peña Nieto is the leader of the Institutional Revolutionary Party (Partido Revolucionario Institucional, or PRI)—the party that initially nationalized Mexico's oil industry—he may have the credibility for a "Nixon to China" moment, especially with the opposition National Action Party (Partido Acción Nacional, or PAN) also expressing some openness to energy sector reform. Indeed, the PRI took a promising step forward in March 2013 when it agreed to drop its longstanding opposition to the constitutional energy sector reforms being sought by Peña Nieto.[39]

But this energy sector opening will still not be easy, because Mexico's oil industry is the locus of significant nationalist fervor. The March day in 1938 when President Lázaro Cárdenas kicked out foreign oil companies is still celebrated as a national civic holiday. Moreover, any change to the Mexican constitution requires a two-thirds majority in the Mexican congress, and Peña Nieto cannot get that vote without significant cooperation from the PAN or the Party of the Democratic Revolution (Partido de la Revolución Democrática, or PRD). Mexico's trade unions are a powerful force that has often been resistant to changes in the energy sector and will have a lot to say about any future reform. Still, if Peña Nieto can push reform through, a good possibility exists for constructive partnership between PEMEX and international companies. PEMEX has joint oil ventures with international companies—just not in Mexico. In fact, PEMEX is a co-owner with Royal Dutch Shell of a refinery in Deer Park, Texas, that processes 340,000 barrels of Mexican oil a day.[40]

Time is of the essence. Absent reform, Mexico could become a net oil importer by 2020—an almost unthinkable prospect just a few years ago. And new production in the Gulf of Mexico could take 10 to 15 years to come online.[41] Mexico's political leaders have made a bold pledge for reform. I believe they will ultimately prevail in their efforts because a growing majority of Mexico's leadership realizes that the current oil sector arrangement is simply unable to meet the current and future needs of the Mexican people. Now, the world will have to see if Peña Nieto can follow through.

Colombia Showing the Way Forward, and Venezuela, Argentina, Bolivia, and Ecuador Sliding Back

Fortunately, Latin American countries that want to open their energy sectors can find excellent case studies among their neighbors. Peru has gradually opened up its mining, oil, and gas sectors since the 1990s and achieved spectacular results.[42] Peru now has more than 50 foreign oil companies engaged in exploration, which has helped add approximately 50 million barrels of proven reserves in each of the past two years. Its natural gas production has also been rising rapidly since 2004.[43] Although Chile is one of the most energy-poor countries in South America, it has one of the region's richest economies, thanks in part to its openness to trade and investment, particularly in its thriving mining sector, which has helped Chile become the largest exporter of copper in the world.[44] But Colombia is the country that stands out as a true exemplar of forward-thinking energy reform. It has the largest coal reserves in South America and is the largest source of US coal imports. But unlike its neighbors Brazil, Ecuador, Venezuela, and Peru, Colombia is relatively oil and gas poor, with only 1.9 billion barrels of proven crude reserves.[45]

Nonetheless, Colombia has added as much new crude oil production as Brazil over the past five years, increasing its output by 450,000 barrels a day to almost a million barrels daily.[46] This production gusher has coincided with the most significant energy sector opening in Colombian history. Although the state oil company, Ecopetrol, is the largest oil producer in Colombia, it competes and partners on a relatively level playing field with 70 other international energy companies.[47]

Under former president Álvaro Uribe, Colombia took a series of steps to become more attractive to international investment in its energy sector, offering tax breaks and attractive royalty terms and allowing foreign companies to own 100 percent stakes in oil ventures. The result has been a drastic increase in foreign direct investment in Colombia's oil sector, rising from $278 million in 2002 to $4.3 billion in 2011.[48] Colombia also authorized Ecopetrol to sell shares in public markets, which has helped increase the company's capital spending by a factor of four.[49] These investments have bought new technology, opened new frontiers for exploration, and created optimism that Colombia can add significantly to its current reserves in the future.

If Colombia is pointing a constructive path forward for the region on energy, Venezuela has unfortunately moved in the other direction since the late Hugo Chávez assumed power in 1999. Venezuela certainly has the resources to be a preeminent energy producer, with oil reserves even larger than Saudi Arabia and the second-largest natural gas reserves in the Western Hemisphere behind the United States.[50] But Venezuela's petroleum exports have dropped 50 percent since 1997, in large part because of its hostility to foreign companies and chronic mismanagement and misallocation of resources at the state energy company, Petróleos de Venezuela (PdVSA).[51]

After taking office, President Chávez nationalized key parts of the Venezuelan energy sector and chased out much private capital and expertise with unattractive tax, royalty, and regulatory policies. In 2007, Chávez made a public show of having the Venezuelan army seize the massive oil fields at Faja, saying at the time that the move represented the "true nationalization of our natural resources."[52]

PdVSA has assumed a more central role in the Venezuelan energy sector but has been unable to effectively explore for new reserves or increase existing production. In 2002, President Chávez fired 18,000 PdVSA employees for political disloyalty—many of them talented engineers and managers—and the company and the country have never quite recovered.[53]

PdVSA is a direct extension of the Venezuelan government. Its revenues have been used to fund everything from agricultural and food programs to generous energy subsidies that account for 8.3 percent of Venezuelan gross domestic product.[54] Despite these assistance programs, the Venezuelan people have seen dubious benefits and often face fuel shortages. Many Venezuelans are justifiably angry that the country is forced to import vast quantities of refined petroleum and natural gas despite sitting on some of the most ample energy reserves in the world. President Chávez also used PdVSA to buy political influence throughout the region, sending hundreds of thousands of barrels of discounted oil a day to Central American and Caribbean countries, including, notably, Cuba.

All this spending leaves precious little for badly needed investment. Whereas Brazil's Petrobras is investing $45 billion a year in new technology and infrastructure, PdVSA is investing less than one-quarter of that amount.[55] This underinvestment has led to a precipitous decline in safety protections for Venezuelan oil workers, as evidenced by the explosion at Venezuela's largest oil refinery in August 2012 that killed 42 people. Despite the denials of Venezuelan government officials, independent analysts maintain that mismanagement and deferred maintenance at the refinery are the primary culprits for the accident.[56] Venezuela's underinvestment in its energy sector has also led to a predictable drop in Venezuela's oil production, decreasing from 3.15 million barrels of crude per day in 2000 to just 2.15 million barrels per day a decade later.[57]

If Venezuela were to open its energy sector, it would likely significantly expand its production in relatively short order. International oil companies do continue to operate in Venezuela, and they have the local knowledge and the scale to restore robust exploration and production. Venezuela did have a brief opening in the 1990s before President Chávez took over. But reforms in Venezuela's energy sector are unlikely in the near term. Although Chávez passed away in March 2013, his handpicked heir, Nicolás Maduro, is a committed *chavista* and has given no indication of planning to rethink seriously the country's approach to energy development. The people of Venezuela and the world will have to wait for either a recount or a future election—and likely a new leader—for the country potentially to change course.

Despite Venezuela's precipitous decline in energy production in the wake of nationalization, other countries in the region have recently shown troubling signs of following in its footsteps. In Argentina—South America's largest natural gas producer and a significant producer of oil[58]—President Cristina Fernández de Kirchner seized in 2012 a majority stake in the state energy company, Yacimientos Petrolíferos Fiscales (YPF), from the Spanish company Repsol.[59]

Argentina is seeking to reverse a precipitous reversal that has seen oil output drop by 27 percent from 1998 to 2010 and gas production drop 10 percent since 2004.[60] But the YPF seizure is unlikely to work, especially if Argentina maintains its counterproductive policies. Heavy energy subsidies have made natural gas and electricity over 70 percent cheaper in Argentina than in its neighbors, causing a predictable spike in demand that often leads to energy rationing in winter months.[61]

Argentina's energy sector needs significant investment, but the country has largely been shut out of international debt markets since its economic crisis in 2001. And it is important to note that even before the YPF seizure, international investment had begun to chill in Argentina in response to a series of protectionist policies. For example, Argentina instituted a heavy-handed effort to balance its trade by forcing companies to match their imports with exports, leading in one case to automotive importers having to export soya and wine.[62] Absent a reevaluation of policy, Argentina will likely find attracting the necessary foreign technology and investment to take full advantage of its ample energy reserves very difficult.

In Bolivia—which has the second-largest natural gas reserves in Latin America—President Evo Morales expropriated in 2012 the country's electricity distribution company from a Spanish company.[63] This incident followed the nationalization of Bolivia's oil and gas sector in 2006.[64]

And in Ecuador—which holds Latin America's third-largest oil reserves behind Brazil and Venezuela—the government recently passed a new hydrocarbons law allowing only fixed-rate service agreements for foreign oil companies. Such agreements are much less appealing to prospective investors.[65]

Unfortunately, Latin American countries that choose the path of stronger state control tend to achieve disappointing results. Too much money gets diverted from investment into politically motivated spending, which ultimately leads to less production, less energy for citizens, and a less dynamic economy. The United States can only hope that more of these countries will reconsider their course of action and look toward the positive examples of countries such as Colombia, Peru, Chile, and even Brazil, which, despite some missteps, is generally headed in the right direction.

Renewables: Can Potential Translate into Production?

Although significant hydrocarbon finds justifiably dominate the energy headlines in Latin America, the region is not without substantial renewable resources. The challenge is for countries to develop a policy and investment climate to help emerging sectors such as wind and solar achieve scale.

Latin America's most dominant renewable resource is hydropower, which provides 65 percent of the region's electricity.[66] Although hydroenergy produces no carbon emissions, it can have serious drawbacks, including deforestation, negative effects on fish and wildlife, and displacement of indigenous people. These problems help explain why numerous proposed dam projects—including the $13 billion Belo Monte Dam in Brazil[67] and a $4 billion dam on the Inambari River in Peru[68]—have recently been delayed by courts, regulators, and activists.

Ethanol continues to be a significant transportation fuel in Latin America, although the main producer, Brazil, has slowed its output in recent years as resources and attention have been diverted to oil and gas exploration.[69]

As for solar and wind, the potential is undoubtedly there. The Atacama Desert in Chile has strong and sustained sunlight, making it an ideal location for solar power,[70] and the Patagonia region of Argentina is a promising wind corridor.[71] But these sources are still more expensive than traditional sources of energy and are often situated far from population centers.

Renewable energy in Latin America also has its own unique hurdles, including a lack of available capital and robust supply chains and prohibitive import barriers. As a consequence, Latin America attracted only 5 percent of the world's new investment in clean energy projects in 2011.[72]

Renewables could assume a greater share of Latin America's energy output in the near future if the region's governments made more public investments and took more steps toward regulatory reforms to attract private capital. But for the foreseeable future, oil and gas development will likely be the focus of governments across the region.

Continuing on the Path to Openness

A survey of Latin America's energy landscape reveals that the debate in the years ahead will center on how to harness most effectively the region's significant new finds of oil and gas. Recent years have given us compelling evidence that embracing openness, competition, and integration in the energy sector offers the best chance for Latin American countries to meet the energy needs of their people and to grow their economies. But this finding hardly guarantees that Latin American nations will embrace this path, because the region's energy sector continues to be influenced by historical, political, and nationalistic considerations just as much as economic ones.

The United States needs to strongly support countries and reformers in Latin America that embrace openness, and it needs to reciprocate with continued liberalization of its own. The recent free trade agreements with Panama and Colombia and the elimination of tariffs on Brazilian ethanol are great examples, and the United States should keep moving in that direction. The United States is already playing a constructive role in Latin America, most notably through foreign direct investment. The United States invests more in the region than does any other country. And although the region has seen increased investment flows from other countries, such as Russia and China, the United States remains far ahead. To cite just one example, the United States has invested $105 billion in Brazil as of 2010, 13 times as much as China has invested.[73]

US policy-makers should make every effort to deepen our energy relationship with the region, up to and including the pursuit of a comprehensive Energy Compact of the Americas, which would feature more formalized cooperation, investment, and research and technology sharing in the energy arena. A similar idea was proposed in 2010 by then-Senator Richard Lugar,[74] and it remains a laudable goal even if the backsliding by major players in the region such as Venezuela and Argentina make it a more distant one.

The United States should continue to do the hard diplomatic work of creating a framework for hemispheric energy cooperation, with the hope of attracting new energy partners whenever they are ready to open themselves to the world. Latin America's energy abundance has the potential to deliver more security, stability, and prosperity to the entire Western Hemisphere, and the United States must do everything it can to help Latin America turn that potential into reality.

Notes

1 Andrés Cala, "Brazil Tested by Latin America Energy Populism," *Energy Tribune*, May 15, 2012.

2. Dinakar Sethuraman, "World Energy Demand to Rise 40% by 2030, Chevron's Kirkland Says," *Bloomberg*, June 5, 2012.

3. Nancy E. Brune, "Latin America and US Energy Security," *World Politics Review*, November 9, 2010.

4. Genaro Arriagada, "Leading Energy Policy Issues in Latin America," *Hemisphere* 20 (Spring 2011): 6–10.

5. "Efficiency Drive," *Economist*, September 9, 2010.

6. Paul Isbell, "What Climate Change Means for Latin America," *Hemisphere* 20 (Spring 2011): 19–20.

7. Energy Action Group, "Energy and the Americas: Issues and Recommendations," Americas Society and Council of the Americas, Washington, DC, 2011, 1–14.

8. Clifford Krauss and Elisabeth Malkin, "Mexico Oil Politics Keeps Riches Just out of Reach," *New York Times,* March 8, 2010.

9. Robert B. Zoellick, "Globalization: Made in the Americas," remarks at the Inter-American Dialogue 30th Anniversary Dinner, Washington, DC, June 7, 2012.

10. John F. Hornbeck, "US–Latin America Trade: Recent Trends and Policy Issues," Congressional Research Service Report for Congress, Washington, DC, February 8, 2011, 13.

11. Tim Padgett, "Signs of Spring: US–Latin America Relations Thaw," *Time,* April 20, 2009.

12. Paul M. Barrett and Peter Millard, "Over a Barrel," *Bloomberg Businessweek,* May 14, 2012, 63–69.

13. Arthur Allen, ed., "Report from 29th Annual Journalists and Editors Workshop on Latin America and the Caribbean" (Washington, DC: Inter-American Dialogue, May 6, 2011).

14. US Energy Information Agency (EIA), "Brazil Crude Oil Production by Year," IndexMundi, http://www.indexmundi.com/energy.aspx?country=br&product=oil&graph=production.

15. Peter Millard and Rodrigo Orihuela, "Petrobras Looks Past Lula for Next Big Find: Corporate Brazil," *Bloomberg,* June 25, 2012.

16. Barrett and Millard, "Over a Barrel."

17. Millard and Orihuela, "Petrobras Looks Past Lula for Next Big Find."

18. Allen, "Report from 29th Annual Journalists and Editors Workshop on Latin America and the Caribbean."

19. EIA, "Venezuela," Country Analysis Brief, EIA, Washington, DC, October 2012.

20. EIA, "Brazil," Country Analysis Brief, EIA, Washington, DC, February 2012.

21. Simon Romero, "In Brazil, Energy Finds Put Country at Whole New Power Level," *New York Times,* October 10, 2011.

22. "It's Only Natural," *Economist,* September 9, 2010.

23. "Oil, Water, and Trouble," *Economist,* December 31, 2011.

24. "It's Only Natural."

25. Barrett and Millard, "Over a Barrel."

26. "It's Only Natural."

27. "Brazil Energy Secretary: Time Running Out for Auction of Oil Exploration," *Dow Jones Newswires,* August 13, 2012.

28. Brian Asher, "Brazil Berates Chevron for Frade Oil Spill, but Production to Restart," *Dow Jones Newswires,* July 19, 2012.

29. "Transocean, US Discussing $1.5 Billion Spill Settlement," *Reuters,* September 10, 2012.

30. Barrett and Millard, "Over a Barrel."

31. Allen, "Report from 29th Annual Journalists and Editors Workshop on Latin America and the Caribbean."

32. Eric Martin and Carlos Manuel Rodriguez, "Mexico May Finally Get a Modern Oil Industry," *Bloomberg Businessweek,* July 22, 2012, 9–10.

33. EIA, "Mexico," Country Analysis Brief, EIA, Washington, DC, October 2012.

34. Krauss and Malkin, "Mexico Oil Politics Keeps Riches Just out of Reach."

35. Romero, "In Brazil, Energy Finds Put Country at Whole New Power Level."

36. Krauss and Malkin, "Mexico Oil Politics Keeps Riches Just out of Reach."

37. John M. Broder and Clifford Krauss, "US in Accord with Mexico on Drilling," *New York Times*, February 20, 2012.

38. Ed Crooks and Adam Thomson, "Mexico Reform Crucial to Exxon Investment," *Financial Times*, June 27, 2012.

39. Phillippe Diederich, "Enrique Peña Nieto, Ready to Break Up the State Oil Monopoly," *Voxxi*, March 17, 2013.

40. Krauss and Malkin, "Mexico Oil Politics Keeps Riches Just out of Reach."

41. Krauss and Malkin, "Mexico Oil Politics Keeps Riches Just out of Reach."

42. Polya Lesova and Michael Molinski, "Latin America's New Tigers Forge Ahead: Investor Interest Growing as Colombia and Peru Economies Boom," *Market-Watch*, July 25, 2012.

43. EIA, "Peru," Country Analysis Brief, EIA, Washington, DC, May 1, 2012.

44. Kelly Cregg and Randy Woods, "Top Copper Producer Chile Sees Prices Staying High as China Economy Cools," *Bloomberg*, May 25, 2011.

45. EIA, "Colombia," Country Analysis Brief, EIA, Washington, DC, June 2011.

46. "Gushers and Guns: A Boom and Threats to It," *Economist*, March 17, 2012.

47. Luciana Palmeira Braga and Thiago Neves Campos, "A Comparative Study of Bidding Models Adopted by Brazil, Peru, Colombia, and Uruguay for Granting Petroleum Exploration and Production Rights," *Journal of World Energy Law and Business* 5, no. 2 (2012): 94–112.

48. "Gushers and Guns."

49. "Gushers and Guns."

50. EIA, "Venezuela."

51. EIA, "Venezuela."

52. "Venezuela Takes Control of Final Privately Run Oil Fields," *PBS NewsHour*, May 1, 2007.

53. Allen, "Report from 29th Annual Journalists and Editors Workshop on Latin America and the Caribbean."

54. Arriagada, "Leading Energy Policy Issues in Latin America."

55. Allen, "Report from 29th Annual Journalists and Editors Workshop on Latin America and the Caribbean."

56. Michael Martinez, "Report: Venezuela's State-Run Refineries Afflicted by Mismanagement," *CNN*, August 30, 2012, http://www.cnn.com/2012/08/29/world/americas/venezuela-refinery-problems/.

57. EIA, "Venezuela Crude Oil Production by Year," IndexMundi, http://www.indexmundi.com/energy.aspx?country=ve&product=oil&graph=production.

58. EIA, "Argentina," Country Analysis Brief, EIA, Washington, DC, June 2011.

59. Chris Dolmetsch, "Repsol Sues Bank of New York Mellon over YPF Election," *Bloomberg*, August 1, 2012.

60. Pablo Fernández-Lamela, "Argentina's Energy Pricing Challenge," *Hemisphere* 20 (Spring 2011): 32.

61. "Fill 'Er Up," *Economist*, April 21, 2012.

62. Jude Webber, "Argentina Tightens Import Controls," *Financial Times*, January 11, 2012.

63. Cala, "Brazil Tested by Latin America Energy Populism."

64. EIA, "Bolivia," Country Analysis Brief, EIA, Washington, DC, August 2012.

65. EIA, "Ecuador," Country Analysis Brief, EIA, Washington, DC, October 2012.

66. James Burgess, "Hydropower Provides 65% of Latin America's Electricity Generation." *Oilprice.com*, June 26, 2012.

67. Anna Flavia Rochas and Caroline Stauffer, "Brazil's Belo Monte Dam Risks Delay after Court Order," *Reuters*, August 17, 2012.

68. Clay Risen, "A Mega-Dam Dilemma in the Amazon," *Smithsonian*, March 2011.

69. Vincent Bevins, "Renewables Hit a Wall in South America," *New York Times*, October 25, 2011.

70. Gavin O'Toole, "Red Light for Green Energy in Latin America and the Caribbean," *Guardian*, June 8, 2012.

71. Bevins, "Renewables Hit a Wall in South America."

72. O'Toole, "Red Light for Green Energy in Latin America and the Caribbean."

73. "The New Brazil," *Miami Herald,* April 9, 2012.

74. Office of Senator Richard Lugar, "Lugar Re-introduces Western Hemisphere Energy Compact in Advance of Meeting between US and Brazil Presidents," press release, March 12, 2009.

Commentary on Part V

Michelle Michot Foss

Since the 2005 edition of this book, and given the intervening years of obvious instability in governments, markets, and business conditions, one can point to a number of things that have not changed. These variables will dominate outcomes in the years ahead and considerably affect the energy security conversation.

- Continental drift did not accelerate. The geological and geographic distribution of continental margins and sedimentary basins around the world remains the same even though major, traumatic natural events have caused enormous disruptions in energy markets.
- The richness of major sedimentary basins also remains the same. Nothing has happened to reduce or alter the presence of hydrocarbons and other energy resources in the Earth's crust or our understanding about the occurrence and distribution of energy resources worldwide. We keep demonstrating through resource assessments and research that fossil fuels in various forms are abundant, and we keep finding cleaner and more

361

flexible ways of developing and using them. This trend continues to irritate those who would like to shift the energy paradigm away from these very convenient, efficient forms of energy.

- But, for all of those who believe energy security rests in a different paradigm, we continue to demonstrate that "commerciality" matters regardless of the energy sources or technologies at hand. Frameworks—the crux of the matter and focal point of my 2005 commentary—are still the axis around which everything revolves. I stated then and state now, *"It ain't the resource, it's the framework."*[1] Policies, regulations, market structures, and the institutions charged with creating, managing, and overseeing energy development and use remain weak, fragmented, ill conceived, misunderstood, or otherwise compromised. That is the caveat emptor in what is otherwise a collection of good news presented in chapters 15 and 16 and in other chapters of the book.

Energy deliverability, which for our purposes is the capacity of the global industrial system to provide almost 90 million barrels of oil equivalent per day, requires a great deal of effort. The business of achieving and sustaining commercial energy deliverability rests on the same fundamental components that it has since the early 1900s, although the trappings—energy finance and the enabling force of information technology in the energy business, for instance—have affected considerably how we do things.

In a nutshell, someone has to have an idea. Testing the idea entails access to resources, capital, and people. All of these components require enabling frameworks, including in the first place the motivating idea about where oil and gas might occur, how they might be recovered, and whether this work can be done at a profit. The generation of an oil or gas prospect ("oil is found first in the mind") will happen much more creatively in an atmosphere that fosters entrepreneurship and risk-taking behavior. We know this—both intuitively and firmly—and we can prove it best by looking at the performance of companies across a range of ownership, size, and corporate models and in a variety of settings.

The companies that excel day after day, year after year in achieving their energy deliverability targets and mandates and in returning real, tangible value to their investors, shareholders, and customers (capital destruction being a more likely outcome) are those that are organized and operate in the most competitive and transparent frameworks. Humbling as it may be, even those companies considered best in class can make mistakes. Delivering 90 million barrels of oil equivalent every day, 365 days a year, year after year, with minimal disruptions and remarkably few incidents, is a tough, demanding, and in these times, often thankless business.

Energy enterprise success does not preclude corporate organizations in which governments play a direct role, including that of owner or major shareholder. But as one might infer from Mack McLarty's chapter on Latin America, it is a much less likely incidence. Political interference in economic life—especially in sectors such as energy that have a strong, strategic inference—is a reality and one that seems to be growing in prevalence rather than dissipating.

As this book goes to press, we are in a very long and mature oil price cycle. Politicized rent-seeking behavior has been rampant, driven by internal and geopolitical suasions (the Arab Spring and its corollaries or, more fearfully, emerging resource nationalism and competition in the Pacific Rim and other sensitive regions); the lure of potential new riches (Brazil's presalt and other discoveries); and government revenue needs in general and everywhere, especially in countries marked by years of financial and economic distress and mismanagement (Argentina and, well, Argentina).

In any case, whether by direct extraction of revenue from national oil company cash flows or through indirect, taxed extraction of revenue from public and private companies the world over, a distinct trend is to capture economic rents from oil and gas production to offset what are often considered to be extraordinary profits or to compensate for real or, more typically, perceived socioeconomic and environmental impacts. For many, this approach is a matter of fairness. A common formula is to link profits from oil production in a high oil price context with environmental concerns (read, climate) in an effort to redistribute income in part, or in whole, toward "green" energy technologies that remain difficult to implement, costly, and technically flawed and that provide questionable environmental benefits.

Rarely debated is the expense to energy consumers and customers of higher costs associated with alternative energy technologies, reduced (and thus higher-priced) oil and gas deliveries, and regulatory embrace of utility tariffs that bolster alternative energy schemes by passing through higher costs associated with intermittent energy sources without commercially acceptable options for energy storage. It is simply "part of the deal."

A consequence is killing off the goose before the golden egg is even laid. The conclusions and assumptions in these chapters, in other parts of the book, and indeed, in prevailing views are that US and Canadian unconventional resource largesse and potential exports of oil, oil products, natural gas liquids (NGLs), and liquefied natural gas (LNG) are changing and will change not only the Western Hemisphere but also the world. Just that. But absent some forethought about the quality of frameworks, including fiscal systems for oil and gas and sustainability of the oil and gas investment cycle, this abundance will all come to naught. We will have witnessed a blip that married an extraordinary price cycle and associated production growth with an extraordinary recession to get the surplus supply conditions witnessed today and nothing more.

Colombia, covered in McLarty's chapter, offers the best and perhaps most accessible story of near death and revival in a country's oil business as a result of tackling the hard, unpopular choices to improve a framework. Then again, Colombia almost had no choice. It is a poster child for the theory that near death has to happen before political will kicks in to "do the right thing." Importantly, the job is not finished, and past accomplishments can backslide. Ecopetrol, the main petroleum company in Colombia, is much improved but remains hampered by both opportunities and internal culture. A change of government means new personalities in charge and perhaps an erosion of political will. Brazil offers an object lesson. Its National Agency of Petroleum, Natural Gas, and Biofuels (Agência Nacional do Petróleo, Gás Natural e Biocombustíveis, or ANP) was the model for many countries aspiring to tap global capital markets and international expertise. By all accounts, these exogenous forces were largely responsible for pushing Petrobras into more efficient and competitive commercial behavior. ANP today is a shell of its former capacity and is unable to constrain government intrusion into the massive presalt in ways that could exert permanent damage to the potential of that play. A corollary lesson to the 2005 edition is that "it ain't just the framework, it's the implementation" and, even more, the ability to forestall erosion of political will and commitment—issues of internal politics—that matter in the long run.

The United States and Canada are not spared from these lessons, as the 2005 chapters and commentary demonstrated. Shirley Neff and Angelina LaRose now lay out an impressive array of data and information on US oil and gas production growth. Yet drilling has pulled back sharply as high costs and development uncertainties embedded in resource plays run head on into shrinking margins. Both domestic oil and gas prices are softer and detached from international markets. Little known outside of the United States and Canada is that domestic producers rarely get, these days, even the full price of traded domestic crude, West Texas Intermediate, a direct result of production success and mid-continent infrastructure bottlenecks. Confusion about where the United States is heading with respect to policy and regulatory treatment of oil and gas exploration and production makes investors only more inclined to pull back on drilling capital expenditures.

So far, none of the industry adjustment under way since early 2012 is so very different from the previous wave—and, yes, there was a previous wave. The unconventional phenomenon is not new by any means. As such, a key question—perhaps the critical question—is whether the past is prologue. It is not a pretty story.

The policy initiatives covered by Neff and LaRose in chapter 15 were deployed to neutralize previous policy actions and right a very lopsided natural gas ship. A distinct goal was to provide more price clarity for drilling and production. Congress also included direct incentives in the form of tax credits to foster unconventional drilling and production in coal-bed methane (also termed *coal seam gas*) and tight gas.

Most of the plays pursued during the 1980s and 1990s were largely in the same basins and locations as those that have commanded attention in the 2000s. Indeed, Texas Barnett production was launched in the initial unconventional push. A turnaround in US dry gas production was realized by the mid- to late 1980s, encouraged first by the energy disruptions and high price signals of the late 1970s and early 1980s and then sustained through the oil price collapse of the mid-1980s by drilling and production tax credits. Recessions and demand softness in the 1990s resulted in a glut of gas and prices below the cost of replacement. We fondly termed that era the *gas bubble*. Indeed, many viewed the tax credit–driven gas production as rubbing salt in the wound of excess gas deliverability and low price conditions. Famously, the gas bubble became a prolonged sausage. By 2001, the strong buildout of natural gas–fired power generation with 1995 Energy Policy Act and Federal Energy Regulatory Commission encouragement, along with the booming US economy of the late 1990s and lack of drilling in the prolonged low-price era, all combined to foster the price spikes for which the early 2000s became famous. LNG imports, anyone?

Fast forward to today. Like the 1990s, a gas supply overhang persists as real gains in production collided with painful recession and the warm 2011–12 winter. This time, the oversupply culprit is incremental gas production associated with crude oil drilling in response to continued robust oil prices rather than direct tax incentives. If any policy action merits a closer look, it is the tendency to use monetary easing to bolster the US economy, a habit acquired in the wake of the 1987 stock market crash. An indirect effect is a cheaper dollar, which partly contributes to upward price pressure on dollar-denominated traded commodities such as oil (especially oil, given dependence of producing and exporting governments on dollar receipts from oil sales). Also, as in the 1990s, cheap gas attracts buyers. This time, there is no immediate trigger like the Energy Policy Act's bulk power rule, but the thinking is that fear of regulatory action and the low cost of building gas generation have undermined the coal industry to such an extent that any competitive advantage for coal going forward is hard to imagine.

And yet, today, electric power companies of various stripes are adding solid fuel to their generation portfolios. What gives? For one, the coal industry has become quite motivated to promote its product, given limited upside opportunities (such as environmental activism against exports of relatively clean US coal that could improve the lot of customers forced to use dirtier fuels).

Research and development is yielding adaptations to even the stickiest pollution rules, such as mercury, such that retrofits are turning out to be much cheaper than previously thought. In addition, power engineers argue that coal-fired generation, typically as base load, can more easily and cheaply be ramped up and down to load follow intermittent renewables. This need to meet gaps in demand, or to balance or "follow" the load, can be met by coal rather than gas wherever high-efficiency coal units are running base load, and even when lower-efficiency units are online. Finally, coal takes whatever premium natural gas prices yield. During summer 2011, in the midst of a most uncomfortable drought in Texas, coal generation displaced natural gas when Henry Hub rose to a mere $3. With Henry Hub at $4 during the first half of 2013, electric power producers swung toward coal. Although this might seem to bolster the "cheap gas forever" story, these market conditions do little to provide long-term encouragement for gas production given the predominance of the electric power burnertip as a driver for resource exploitation and sales.

All of this is not to undermine reality. The rapid buildout of gas-fired power generation capacity certainly gained market share for gas within the power segment. But overall, electric power use has been affected by recession and other factors to such an extent that, as with refining, serious questions are being raised about growth prospects. Indeed, contrary to all established norms, some are suggesting that the United States may never see net growth in electric power demand again. Such assertions are symptomatic of the difficulty in parsing confusing economic times. However, a distinct possibility is that recession-induced, pent-up demand could, with better economic conditions, join with slack gas drilling to yield yet another round of natural gas price spikes, albeit less dramatic than in the early 2000s.

Apparently, many in the utility industry fear just such a scenario, and it is not hard to imagine. For one thing, very rosy views of future natural gas resource recovery have been easy to build. To a large extent, there is limited ability outside the oil and gas industry—and even among industry insiders—to fully comprehend the industry's own cost structure. Much of this problem is related to misunderstandings about the geological and engineering considerations in unconventional resource plays. As a result, a widespread tendency exists to understate full-cycle, break-even costs associated with exploration and production in key basins and plays as well as across companies.

Additionally, more complex production streams; fierce decline curves; uncertainty associated with planning infrastructure investment in the face of highly variable outputs of oil, other NGLs, and natural gas; and variability and volatility in "spreads" across different products (oil to gas, oil to NGLs, and NGLs to gas) all interweave, thereby hindering decision-making and affecting investment timing.

Expectations built on natural gas remaining in the $3 to $4 per million cubic foot range with little volatility are likely to be dashed as economic recovery collides with lack of deliverability from dry gas locations. An old axiom remains true: in tough times, with low prices, operators fall back to the best, cheapest producing locations. The best operators can thrive; tough times tend to whittle down competition and eventually put downward pressure on costs. However, capture of the most cost-effective oil and gas resources today means more expensive tranches later because companies must necessarily bring more marginal acreage into production.[2] As it stands, the cheapest natural gas production is associated gas from oil wells or nonassociated gas from condensate locations. Softer prices for oil and NGLs—a distinct possibility going forward and, at present, a reality across the US mid-continent and into Canada—coupled with the many infrastructure and midstream commercialization challenges that are only briefly touched on in chapter 15 could render current views about US self-sufficiency obsolete.

In many respects, the United States as a whole and the largest oil- and gas-producing states have been lucky—less so in Canada and Canadian provinces. A surging natural gas market in the mid-2000s enabled US producers to prove up dry gas leaseholds in unconventional plays. Natural gas prices fell as production gains coupled with softening demand to create a drag on the key Henry Hub index. These events coincided with continued robustness in international oil prices, thereby allowing operators to shift capital expenditures to oil drilling, especially where they can sell into stronger markets.

This transition has been much more difficult to achieve in Canada, mainly because of the remoteness of Canada's unconventional resource plays. The outcome is the shift in oil and gas flows addressed in chapter 15, as Canada's established production in the Western Sedimentary Basin declines and as operators struggle to connect the more remote unconventional locations to markets. Moreover, lower prices for oil and NGLs reduce upstream investment and thus remove tranches of the most inexpensive methane. Eventually, methane deliverability is affected by twin forces: a cheap Henry Hub, which discourages dry gas exploitation, and cheaper domestic oil and NGL prices, which discourage liquids exploitation.

The outcome is ever-higher natural gas prices to attract investment back to gas and yield incremental dry gas production. Eventually, a rising and higher Henry Hub price may enable producers to sustain production of associated oil and NGLs in the face of less attractive oil and NGL prices, should such an eventuality materialize, but a more expensive gas price context certainly would also affect gas demand. And so it goes—and will go—in the complicated world of oil and gas well economics.

Canada's travails also will come in the form of higher costs and difficulties winning support for export fairways that will allow producers of more remote, trapped, and stranded resources to reach viable markets. Meanwhile, Mexico must decide what kind of nation it wants to be. As set up in these chapters, it is both North American and Latin American, a not-so-subtle indication of identity crisis. On the one hand, Mexico wants to promote development of its shale gas resources. Shale gas is a lever that many in government and industry want to use to alter the rules of the game around an intransigent Petróleos Mexicanos, which, like any producer in the United States and Canada, sees no rationale for investing scarce capital in a cheap gas market.

But Mexico's market is cheap only because the country's framework does not allow price discovery. Mexico, which would likely have a much stronger gas price signal, given industrial and electric power demand, is a US Henry Hub price taker. And so, on the other hand, the Mexican government is moving forward to expand cross-border gas pipeline capacity. Mexico's gas imports from the US lower 48 could more than double in short order as these pipeline expansions are realized. How massive gas imports will jive with promotion of shale drilling in a weak upstream framework is a mystery.

A realistic view of Canada and the United States is that the two nations will muddle through a variety of price-cycle events and discordance in opinions and political debate about how and whether oil and gas—and fossil fuels in general—should remain a part of the energy landscape. This prospect seems outlandish when considered in light of how the conversation has evolved to date and the widespread bullishness about the US and Canadian roles as potentially leading producers and exporters.

Yet, in the global supply stack, our domestic resources are high cost with, as previously noted, the prospect of rising costs. Unconventional and frontier resources, if one includes deeper water, Arctic, and other arenas, are more complex, trickier to produce, and more demanding of technology to manage both the cost and the production footprint. None of this is to suggest that industry prowess cannot overcome and stabilize output from these settings. In truth, we would be displacing lower-cost (if not lower-priced; see previous discussion on rent capture) but "material" resource and production opportunities in more politically risky and unpredictable countries and regions that are off limits to industry anyway because adequate frameworks are unavailable and may never be offered. Whether our own, internal political risks can be managed to make this delicate equation work remains to be seen.

Finally, perhaps the biggest framework question of all concerns international trade in energy. I can only repeat my admonition from the first edition:

> The emergence of liquefied natural gas (LNG) and the depth of LNG trade and commercial activity that can be achieved for the Atlantic basin, as well as the potential for gas-to-liquids technology to integrate natural gas more deeply into crude oil applications especially for transportation, mean that "barrels" are no longer relevant. We are moving into an era in which it is "barrel equivalents" that are important and in which we can put aside the tired debate about whether and when we will run out of oil. *Flexible, transparent frameworks also help to facilitate trade flows.* Energy trade is an essential component in both Europe and the Americas as well as globally. Imagine a world in which international comparative advantages could not be exercised and markets not cleared! Well, perhaps some can, but I cannot.[3]

I still cannot imagine it. Gains from trade are compelling, but due diligence is required by all market participants to understand risks and rewards. It is not unusual, and never has been, for some to oppose trade out of fear that current price, cost, quality, or other attributes that they currently enjoy might be threatened. Likewise, it is disingenuous to suggest that there will not be some impacts from trade and the arbitrage associated with different supply, demand, and price conditions and signals. What we believe—what we can show—is that open trade can provide sufficient benefits to outweigh costs. That remains a tough sell no matter how much the world has progressed. Beyond the question of whether open, free trade should be a component of frameworks is the issue of whether investors will pursue sound strategies and what effect those strategies will have on the discourse.

Neff and LaRose provide a comprehensive rendition of the state of development of LNG and other export infrastructure in the United States and Canada, but it is fair to wonder whether this swing of the pendulum is tenable. Almost as many LNG export projects are on the table (end of 2012) as there were import projects in 2006. Convincing the US public to accept accelerated drilling for unconventional natural gas so as to feed worldwide export businesses may be a tall order. The uncertainty around our own domestic natural gas use, as previously noted with regard to electric power, leaves producers with few other options if economies of scale in unconventional plays are to be achieved and sustained. We in the United States simply are not accustomed to thinking of ourselves as energy exporters. A great deal of embedded status quo opinion, activism, and psychology would have to be unwound.

The United States and North America are littered with the detritus of bad decisions, many intertwined with questionable policies. The industrial relics strewn across the western states from the Carter-era Synfuels Corporation activities are one testament to how easy it is to get things wrong. Whether we are any better now at discerning the future remains to be seen.[4]

Notes

1. Michelle Michot Foss, "Commentary on Part V," *Energy and Security: Toward a New Foreign Policy Strategy*, ed. Jan H. Kalicki and David L. Goldwyn (Washington, DC, and Baltimore: Woodrow Wilson Center Press and Johns Hopkins University Press, 2005), 399–406, 399.

2. Over the life of any oil and gas field, unit costs fall as the field reaches peak production but then begin to rise as more work must be done to squeeze additional production from the upstream asset. The same is true across plays and basins as they mature.

3. Michelle Michot Foss, "Commentary on Part V," 400.

4. For more background on US and North American natural gas see the following: Michelle M. Foss, "Natural Gas Pricing in North America," in *The Pricing of Internationally Traded Gas*, ed. Jonathan Stern (London and Oxford, UK: Oxford University Press, 2012), 85–144; Michelle M. Foss, "The Outlook for US Gas Prices in 2020: Henry Hub at $3 or $10?," NG 58, Natural Gas Programme, Oxford Institute for Energy Studies, Oxford, UK, December 2011, http://www.oxfordenergy.org/2011/12/the-outlook-for-u-s-gas-prices-in-2020-henry-hub-at-3-or-10/; Michelle Michot Foss, "United States Natural Gas Prices to 2015," NG 18, Natural Gas Programme, Oxford Institute for Energy Studies, Oxford, UK, February 2007, http://www.beg.utexas.edu/energyecon/documents/MFoss_ngox.pdf.

Part VI

Toward a New Energy Security Strategy

In the concluding part VI, new paths are advanced toward a new energy security strategy for the United States and its partners in this new century. Underlying all the chapters is the recognition that technology is changing fundamentally the energy landscape. Through ultradeepwater drilling, hydraulic fracturing ("fracking"), and horizontal drilling, large new resources of oil and natural gas are shifting the energy balance of power to North America and the Western Hemisphere.

In the 2005 edition of this book, high import dependence was the prevailing condition for the United States, for its partners in the Organization for Economic Cooperation and Development, for China, and for most developing countries as well. In this 2013 edition, the United States and its producing partners in the hemisphere—starting with its two neighbors, Canada and Mexico—are far less dependent: by 2025, the North American countries can become energy self-sufficient and net exporters for the first time in history.

This development is nothing short of a quantum leap in America's energy position and its related economic, national security, and environmental opportunities. What it is *not* is an opportunity to be energy "independent"—despite contrary political rhetoric from the highest levels since the 1973 Arab Oil Embargo. The oil market is global, not national, and price spikes coming from any conflict or natural disaster will affect US markets the same as European and Asian markets. The natural gas market is still truncated—making much lower prices possible in the United States—but it is steadily globalizing as well. If interdependence, not independence, is the order of the day in energy terms, it is even more so in economic and security terms, as all countries combat economic downturns, failed and failing states, and nuclear weapons proliferation—from Iran to North Korea.

Today, the relatively simple if perilous threats of the Cold War and oil embargos have given way to much more dispersed and even more perilous threats: terrorism and religious extremism at the subnational level; corruption and instability at the national level; transnational conflict internationally; and disease, poverty, and environmental degradation at the global level. As is seen in the concluding chapter of this book, the challenge is to develop a multifaceted strategy to deal with these multiple threats—one that integrates energy, economic, environmental, foreign policy, and national security components, rather than treating them separately from each other.

To address these questions, Melanie Kenderdine and Ernest Moniz take a close look at the leading role and prospects of technology in the present energy revolution. Charles Ebinger and John Banks consider the crucial role of electric power in ensuring energy security. Charles McPherson analyzes governance, transparency, and sustainable development. Michelle Patron and David Goldwyn discuss the management of strategic reserves. Michael Levi sets forth the framework and critical tradeoffs among energy, environment, and climate change, and Leon Fuerth then proposes a new paradigm and strategy for advancing US and global interests within this framework. Finally, Frank Verrastro and Kevin Book analyze the challenges of US energy politics, whose resolution will be essential to an effective national strategy.

Presenting a comprehensive assessment of technology and energy security in chapter 17, Kenderdine and Moniz discuss the requirement for goal-driven technology programs to increase US energy security. After reviewing key energy-related security challenges and objectives, they analyze available technology pathways that can address these objectives through further research, development, and demonstration or through technology-enabled policy initiatives. They hone in on the effects of technology on

US energy supply, highlighting (a) the potential for dramatic increases in recoverability of oil and gas fields and (b) the availability of technologies to reduce emissions and water use from unconventional oil and gas development. They consider modeling tools to reduce the use of scarce rare earth materials and to improve our ability to recycle or manufacture alternative materials. Kenderdine and Moniz paint a sobering picture of the proliferation risks of current nuclear fuel cycles and offer alternative pathways for smaller, cheaper, and more proliferation-resistant models. Finally, they suggest technology pathways for dealing with climate change and terrorist threats to critical energy infrastructure, and they consider organizational proposals for ensuring that technology and policy can be properly, or at least much better, integrated.

In chapter 18, Ebinger and Banks focus on the critical issue of electricity access in a world where 1.3 billion people still have none—with profound impacts on education, economic modernization, and living standards. Identifying energy poverty as a major barrier to global development and growth, they show how ending that poverty is critical to political stability and social cohesion and how increased access to electricity is necessary for an effective climate change strategy. In the broader security perspective, electrification can make the difference between failed states and national and regional recovery. Finally, they propose an action plan that would make this issue a top-tier priority, increase financial support, create the necessary governance, pursue decentralized solutions, and support environmentally benign power solutions.

In chapter 19, McPherson argues that transparency and good governance are essential for energy security and sustainable development. He analyzes the principal challenges to good governance presented by oil, including "Dutch disease," market volatility, weak institutional capacity, corruption, and uneven distribution of wealth. He considers models for management of petroleum revenues and ensuing expenditures and advances proposals based on active roles for international, governmental, and nongovernmental stakeholders.

In chapter 20, Patron and Goldwyn analyze how strategic reserves can become a more robust component of a new energy security policy. They describe the history of US strategic reserve policy and ways new threats and economic realities have outpaced the policy. They draw lessons from past failures to use the Strategic Petroleum Reserve (SPR), analyze how the SPR can be used to prompt the Organization of the Petroleum Exporting Countries to release spare capacity, and advocate the SPR's new role of managing market expectations to help prevent price spikes. They propose five steps to revamp SPR policy to reflect the new realities of the contemporary oil market: maximizing export flexibility during a drawdown, modernizing infrastructure, expediting the decision process and incorporating technical market expertise, enhancing cooperation with International Energy Agency (IEA) and non-IEA members, and developing an active communication strategy.

Levi turns to a new framework for energy, environment, and climate in chapter 21 and then considers the tradeoffs among these priorities. He weighs the environmental implications of energy development in both fossil and nonfossil fuels, including controversies over fracking, as well as in nuclear and renewable sources. He examines the legislative, regulatory, and international dimensions of US climate change policy and the ways both market shifts and policy choices will influence progress in reducing the impact of carbon in our environment.

In chapter 22, Fuerth calls for a new paradigm, strategy, and governance for climate change policy, which he believes should be placed on par with national security and energy policies. Arguing that climate change is a real and present security threat, he sees the fracking revolution as a strategic opportunity to "use economic savings from the ongoing shift from coal to gas as a way to propel a second shift from carbon-based fuels to renewables." To achieve this goal, he advances a strategy involving actions that the United States can take on its own, from planning for drought as the new normal to industrial-scale carbon sequestration, and including actions that need to be taken with others, from global instrumentation to coordinated in-time responses to major threats. He calls for "anticipatory governance," which will ensure an integrated response to complex system threats, requiring foresight, networked organization, and feedback systems.

In chapter 23, Verrastro and Book analyze the necessary political foundation that is required for a new energy security strategy. Describing dysfunctions in both the executive and legislative branches, they assess the adverse impacts of a polarized, ideologically driven environment that undermines cohesive and sustained policy initiatives. They point to the new opportunities created by the prospect of North American energy self-sufficiency and identify three alternative future paths: developing a "comprehensive narrative that incorporates the nation's economic, environmental, foreign policy, and energy security goals" as part of a "broader strategy rather than one-off events"; pushing the "green button" and emphasizing regulation to achieve environmental and climate goals; or taking a more incremental approach that balances the pro-production and pro-environment constituencies and also "keeps the administration at the center of the discourse." From a 2013 vantage point, they see pronounced tendencies in the Obama administration toward combining incremental and green-oriented approaches.

In his commentary on part VI, John Deutch offers a gentle critique based on long and deep experience with energy and security policy in Washington, pointing out that the United States lacks a comprehensive energy security policy despite the efforts of presidents of both major political parties. He provides a cheerfully pessimistic view on the likelihood of success at this moment. Deutch agrees with the analysis that Washington repeatedly fails to address long-term problems or organize to address complex nonlinear problems but is skeptical that the political environment will change to correct this situation. He agrees forcefully with the need for electrification to address energy poverty; the reality of climate change; the importance of transparency; and the need for investment in research and development to address energy security, climate, and nuclear proliferation issues. However, he holds modest hope that the current budget environment will permit the United States to pursue these objectives with the generosity that he believes they deserve or that all of the relatively micro strategies offered will have, cumulatively, a big enough influence on the problems these strategies seek to address.

Chapter 17

Technology Development
and Energy Security

Melanie A. Kenderdine and Ernest J. Moniz

This chapter, an update of one written in 2005, discusses the nation's energy security challenges over the next decades, some policy objectives to address those challenges, and a set of aligned technology pathways. Not intended as a comprehensive discussion of all emerging technologies, the chapter instead highlights several new and potentially game-changing technology pathways that could help positively alter the energy security landscape.

We conclude with some thoughts on how to overcome the energy inertia of the past few decades—suggestions for some new fundamentals of *process* and *organization* that can help transform how we produce, distribute, and consume energy; mitigate the associated environmental impacts; promote economic growth; and reduce overall energy security risks.

Global Energy Challenges and US Energy Security

Persistent energy-related challenges to national and economic security, historically and prospectively, include the following:

- The concentration of natural resource supply in regions prone to disruption and the consequent risks of supply interruption
- Climate change and associated natural disasters and humanitarian crises
- The spread of nuclear weapons capabilities through global nuclear fuel cycle development
- Increasingly vulnerable energy infrastructure and supply chains

These core US energy challenges have not changed substantially since 2005, but the playing field and some of the players have changed. These changes add to and complicate the many energy challenges for the United States and the world and have implications for technology development priorities, which are the central focus of this chapter.[1]

Oil security issues, as always, take center stage in energy security debates, but world events are changing their relative importance, both positively and negatively. The *Deepwater Horizon* oil spill and oil rig problems in the Arctic illustrate the problems of producing oil in ever-harsher environments. The Arab Spring has produced significant anxiety in oil markets, manifest in volatile and high oil prices even in the face of lower demand. These high prices have, in turn, put a major drag on the economies of all major consuming countries. In contrast, the dramatic increase in unconventional oil production in the United States and Canada and a larger resource base in the Western Hemisphere are enhancing US energy security and could herald some fairly radical geopolitical shifts in the oil balance of power.

Other issues unrelated to oil have also changed the US energy security calculus. The US shale gas boom is nothing short of extraordinary—both enhancing US energy security and creating similar opportunities for some allies if this experience can be successfully replicated. The news is less positive for the nuclear power industry, which was rocked by renewed safety concerns after Fukushima Daiichi. Also, technologies and fissionable material associated with the nuclear power fuel cycle raise the specter of nuclear weapons proliferation, with Iran serving as the world's latest reminder of this frightening possibility. A new and related energy security concern is the production of rare earth and other critical elements, essential building blocks for many clean energy technologies. China has already flexed its market power in this arena.

In addition, progress under the Kyoto Protocol is stalled, and climate legislation passed only one house of Congress in 2009. While political discourse displays an inability to achieve consensus, the empirical evidence of anthropogenic climate change continues to grow. This evidence argues for adaptation strategies in addition to strategies of carbon dioxide (CO_2) mitigation, such as support for renewable technologies, which meets multiple policy objectives. The policy agenda should also include support for near-term scalable technology options that may be good but not perfect—for example, gas-fired generation in lieu of coal.

Finally, the economic downturn in the United States and elsewhere shines a spotlight on domestic job creation and the need to boost economic productivity. Low-cost, clean, and reliable energy supply is important to stimulate economic recovery and long-term prosperity while mitigating climate change risks. Adequate investment in energy research and development and infrastructure are necessary contributors to success in this endeavor.

As noted, in this chapter we discuss the four high-level energy security challenges for the United States, which we describe briefly in the context of a set of policy options and a research agenda for technology pathways to address them. These policy options could help form the basis of a US energy policy to meet these challenges in a comprehensive and informed manner, as well as serve as a guide for a range of technology investments.

Challenge 1: The Concentration of Conventional Oil and Gas Resources and Critical Materials

Conventional oil and gas resources are heavily concentrated in the Middle East, Russia, Eurasia, and parts of Africa, where almost 70 percent of the world's technically recoverable conventional oil resources are found. In addition, 97 percent of rare earth minerals, important to clean energy technologies, are produced in China, which actively seeks to protect this near monopoly.

These concentrations present significant energy security and technology challenges for the United States that will be exacerbated by energy demand growth. Demand growth will be uneven by fuel and by region. Emerging economies in Asia that are not members of the Organization for Economic

Cooperation and Development (OECD) will represent 60 percent of the increase in the world's incremental oil demand and 32 percent of incremental gas demand by 2035.[2] Importantly, increased natural gas demand in the Middle East will approach gas demand growth in *all* of OECD North America, Europe, and Asia. This increased demand could diminish the availability of gas exports from the Middle East, a key source of global gas supply.

In addition, demand growth will increase the environmental impacts of energy production, distribution, and consumption, thereby placing additional stress on climate-related energy security and elevating the need for new technology and policy solutions. Also, indigenous conventional gas production in Western Europe is in precipitous decline, which could leave key US allies highly dependent on Russian gas, an outcome that could adversely affect US strategic security priorities.

Finally, rare earth elements and other critical materials used in many renewable and energy technologies will grow in strategic and geopolitical importance. Within the OECD, Europe will represent 42 percent of the incremental demand for renewables, with the United States a distant second in business as usual.[3] Absent alternatives to these essential elements, the United States and its allies will become increasingly dependent on those countries that control critical element production.

Technology options are essential for diversifying sources and increasing overall supplies of both conventional and unconventional oil and gas, mitigating the environmental impacts of production, reducing demand through development of oil alternatives and energy efficiency, and developing scalable renewable energy resources that draw only on Earth-abundant materials (see table 17.1).

Unconventional Oil: Changing the Map of the Oil World

A combination of technology advances and a higher floor price for oil is enabling relatively affordable production of *unconventional oil*—oil that cannot be "produced, transported or refined using traditional techniques" because of low porosity, permeability, or density.[4] These sources include oil sands, oil shale, heavy oil, and shale oil (different from oil shale), all with different characteristics and technology needs.

These unconventional oils are also found in unconventional geographic locations: North America, South America, and Eastern Europe rather than the Middle East, Russia, and Africa. As seen in figure 17.1, when unconven-

Table 17.1. Resource Concentration Challenges

Energy Security Challenge	Policy Options for Enhancing Energy and Economic Security	Representative Technology Pathways
The concentration of natural resource supply (conventional oil and natural gas, rare earth elements) and the associated geopolitics create energy and economic security concerns.	• Increase domestic oil production. • Reduce oil demand. • Provide alternatives to oil. • Develop vehicles for alternative fuels and drivetrains.	• Heavy oil and oil sands • Other unconventional oil • Technologies for production in harsh environments • Enhanced oil recovery • Biofuels • Gas to liquids • Hydrogen production • Higher-efficiency vehicles • Hydrogen vehicles • Flex-fuel vehicles • Bifuel vehicles • Electric vehicles • Liquefied natural gas heavy vehicles
	• Promote development of global and domestic natural gas supplies. • Promote development of global gas markets, with efficient and transparent monetization of global gas supplies.	• Technologies to produce unconventional gas in a range of basins, including environmental mitigation technologies • Liquefied natural gas production, transport efficiency, and safety • Compressed natural gas transport • Global gas market design and systems analysis

Table 17.1. Resource Concentration Challenges (continued)

Energy Security Challenge	Policy Options for Enhancing Energy and Economic Security	Representative Technology Pathways
	• Anticipate, reduce, recover, recycle, and replace rare earth elements and other critical materials used for transformative energy technologies. • Diversify sources of supply of critical elements. • Develop new extraction technologies for rare elements.	• Recycling technologies for rare elements • Analytical toolsets to mitigate materials criticality risk • Earth-abundant alternatives for rare earth elements and other critical materials

Source: Authors' compilation.

tional oil resources are included in oil resource estimates, the OECD Americas has as much technically recoverable oil as the Middle East plus Eastern Europe and Eurasia. The large-scale development of unconventional oil establishes the potential for geopolitical pivots, both from and to key regions of the world. This resource distribution also suggests a technology development and investment strategy to increase US energy security by enabling and enhancing North American and hemispheric unconventional oil development.

In general, production of unconventional oils is more difficult and energy intensive than production of conventional oil. Unconventional oils are higher in sulfur and metals, require more processing (more energy and emissions), and have greater impacts on water and land use. In addition, the larger carbon footprint of unconventional oil is an issue of growing concern as unconventional oil becomes a larger percentage of the global oil mix. Life-cycle CO_2 and greenhouse gas (GHG) emissions data for oil sands do not typically include methane losses or emissions associated with land use and infrastructure construction.[5]

These issues can be addressed by investing in a range of technology improvements and options. Better water recycling or better dry or paste tailings technologies could, for example, help mitigate surface-water issues associated with mill tailings from oil sands production. In situ pro-

Figure 17.1. Remaining Technically Recoverable Oil and NGL Resources,
by Region and Type

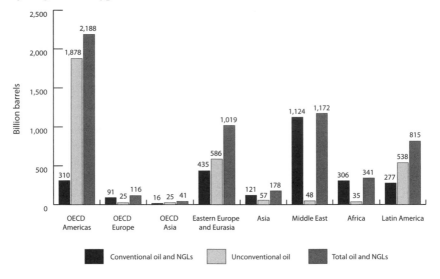

Source: Data from International Energy Agency (IEA), *World Energy Outlook 2012* (Paris: OECD/
IEA, 2012).

Note: NGL = natural gas liquid.

duction and processing of bitumen would diminish surface effects as well
as enhance production of those resources that are too deep for surface
mining. Technologies to reduce the steam-to-oil ratio of thermal recovery
methods would reduce the energy intensity of production.[6] Importantly,
additional research and analysis is needed to more accurately reflect the
GHG emissions associated with unconventional oil in general and oil
sands specifically, as well as to develop technologies to reduce these
emissions.

From Gas Importer to Exporter: The US Shale Gas Experience

By 2005, the prevailing political and industry wisdom—note Alan Greenspan's testimony before Congress in 2003[7] or Lee Raymond's similar view
in 2005[8]—was that the United States and North America were running out

Figure 17.2. Remaining Technically Recoverable Natural Gas Resources, by Region

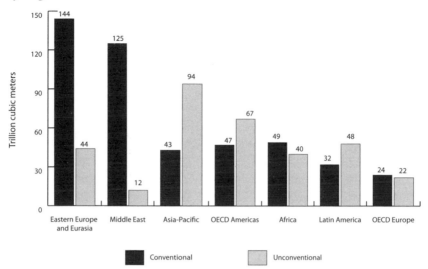

Source: IEA, *World Energy Outlook 2012* (Paris: OECD/IEA, 2012).

of natural gas. Policies were adopted and investments were made to substantially increase US gas imports. Fast-forward just a few years and the United States is the number one gas producer in the world and is preparing for gas exports. This turnaround would be remarkable in any context, but in the United States, it represents a paradigm shift that could greatly enhance its energy security.

As implied in figure 17.2, the replication of the US shale gas experience could have geopolitical implications, bringing major new regional players into gas markets and providing enormous opportunities for non-traditional market players, such as Asia, Latin America, and US allies in Europe. Active support for export of US shale gas expertise and technologies could enhance the energy and economic security benefits of shale gas to the United States and key allies by shortening supply chains, promoting jobs and economic development, and helping to mitigate climate change in the near to mid term.

Enhancing Shale Gas and Oil Production

Both shale gas and shale oil recovery factors could be enhanced through research and technology development. Recovery factors for shale gas are projected to be in the 10 to 20 percent range but are currently widely variable.[9] The production history is short, and more precise understanding will come with experience. Shale oil recovery factors are lower still, typically projected to be less than 10 percent, although experience is limited there as well. Both recovery factors in known basins and opportunities in new basins could be enhanced with new imaging tools and advanced simulation for reservoir modeling, which would allow us to better understand the geology, geomechanics, and geophysics of rock properties;[10] advanced production analysis to inform better well design, completion, and stimulation technologies, including optimal fracture treatments; and general improvements in hydraulic fracturing techniques, such as slot drilling that would expand the surface of a fracture, thereby enabling increased returns and higher recovery factors.[11]

In addition to maximizing production of existing resources, we need additional characterization work for new basins in the United States. Also, relatively little characterization and production in shale gas basins has been done globally. Each shale basin is different, and economic productivity varies greatly. The US experience has enabled global opportunities and will accelerate development, but basin- and region-specific technologies are still necessary in other parts of the world and will take time to develop and deploy.

Mitigating the Environmental Impacts of Shale Gas and Oil Production

The development of technologies to produce shale gas—which took about 20 years—was the result of a highly effective public–private partnership and a time-limited tax credit. The primary beneficiaries of this effort were thousands of smaller independent producers. This profile of players and the speed of the technology development, deployment, and diffusion, however, came with a downside. When the initial deployment rush occurred, best practices and environmental concerns were not well understood by some producers or regulators, and little baseline data were available to analyze potential impacts. Water treatment systems, other infrastructures, and communities were sometimes overwhelmed.

Awareness of environmental issues and impacts is now greater. Widely reported environmental incidents associated with shale gas production have mostly resulted from faulty well completions and surface-water management.[12] Air quality and methane emissions are other issues that need to be managed. Although some distinctions exist, the environmental issues associated with shale gas and tight oil production are similar. Some mitigation options follow:

- *Water pollution impacts.* Although water concerns and impacts vary by geology, geography, and climate, a range of solutions exists for surface- and subsurface-water management issues. They include more environmentally friendly fracturing fluids and complete disclosure of their composition, adherence to best practices, direct reuse of water without treatment, on-site and off-site water treatment and reuse, off-site water disposal, and better well casings and cement seals. These measures should each be reinforced by appropriate regulation. As important, good baseline data are needed to more fully understand the possible subsurface impacts of fracturing over time.
- *Air quality.* The operation of drilling rigs, trucks hauling water, and other industrial activity associated with production can negatively affect air quality. These impacts can be substantially reduced by lower-cost flowback water recycling and the buildout of pipelines for the transport of water to drill sites. In addition, producers are switching from diesel-powered trucks and equipment to natural gas, which will substantially improve air quality. Another issue is GHG emissions. The US Environmental Protection Agency (EPA) recently revised its inventories of methane releases from gas production substantially upward, thereby raising concerns about the value of gas as a lower-carbon transition fuel. A recent analysis by the Massachusetts Institute of Technology of the fugitive emissions from 4,000 shale gas wells suggests that the EPA estimates are high and that "the production of shale gas and, specifically, the associated hydraulic fracturing operations have not materially altered the total GHG emissions from the natural gas sector."[13] Regardless, both an economic incentive for "green completions" and an EPA requirement for them by 2015 should help mitigate this concern.
- *Land-use and community impacts.* Although land-use and community impacts exist for shale gas and oil, shale gas production has tended to occur more often in relatively populated areas, particularly in the Marcellus and parts of the Barnett. Illustrative requirements for infrastruc-

ture, land, and water needs for producing 1 trillion cubic feet of natural gas per year over a 15-year period include the development, construction, and use of between 70 and 100 well pads per year and the net water consumption of 70 million to 200 million barrels per year.[14] This level of water consumption is relatively low compared to that of other uses and types of energy production. For shale gas development, however, large amounts of water are needed all at once for fracturing; this water tends to be procured over short periods and trucked in, sometimes stressing local water sources and area roads. Such levels of land and water use and community impacts prompted the US Secretary of Energy Advisory Board to recommend a range of science-based actions: identification of sensitive or unique areas that should be off limits to development; informing planning, mitigation, and reclamation actions; and field monitoring to inform assessments of land-use and community impacts.[15]

- *Induced seismicity.* Few induced seismicity events—the building of dams; geothermal, oil, and gas production; and other fluid injection— are of sufficient magnitude to be felt at the surface. One case of induced seismicity (seismic events related to human activities)[16] has been associated with hydraulic fracturing and eight with produced water disposal wells.[17] Induced seismicity can be managed by avoiding injections in or near known faults, by minimizing pore pressure through appropriate formation selection, by installing seismic monitoring arrays, and by establishing best practices and protocols.[18] The National Research Council recently recommended additional research associated with energy-related induced seismicity, including data collection, instrumentation, hazard and risk assessment, and modeling.[19]

Conventional Oil and Enhanced Oil Recovery

US and hemispheric energy security would also be enhanced by increasing recovery rates for conventional oil. Conventional oil production is declining at a rate of about 5 percent per year, with average worldwide ultimate recovery factors of around 35 percent.[20] *Enhanced oil recovery* (EOR)—any method of economically recovering oil incremental to that produced by primary (natural drive) or conventional improved recovery methods[21]—represents a significant opportunity for meeting demand growth and offsetting conventional production declines. Worldwide, EOR technologies produce about 3 million barrels per day,[22] or about 3.5 percent of global consumption.[23]

EOR can be applied in both secondary recovery, which primarily uses water flooding and reservoir pressure restoration, and tertiary recovery, which includes thermal processes, gas injection, and chemical treatments. Secondary EOR technologies could take recovery factors to 50 percent, and tertiary technologies could move them as high as 80 percent.[24] Tertiary technologies are, however, more expensive and at various stages of research, development, and deployment. Areas for additional research and development include "smart" water flooding, which is tailored for maximum production; improved in situ combustion processes to reduce surface environmental impacts and lower upgrading costs; various foam agents to enhance the efficiency of water sweeps; acoustic imaging to more efficiently and effectively target resource development; microbial recovery enhancement; and high-pressure air injection.[25]

Increased understanding of the various production zones associated with conventional oil production is also an important target for EOR research and technology development. To date, the focus of EOR has been on *main pay zones* (MPZs), "perforated intervals above a traditional oil water contact." The *transition zone* (TZ) contains both mobile oil and water, with water increasing by depth; and the *residual oil zone* (ROZ) is where oil is no longer mobile and cannot be produced with secondary recovery.[26]

EOR and Opportunities for Carbon Capture and Storage

CO_2 EOR enables roughly 5 percent of US annual crude oil production and uses 65 million metric tons of CO_2 annually. This fraction, however, represents only a small portion of the total theoretical EOR-enabled production, estimates for which range as high as 100 billion barrels of recoverable oil.[27]

Increasing recovery rates from conventional fields will require additional CO_2. Natural CO_2 is delivered to EOR sites via pipeline, but sources are declining. Anthropogenic sources could help meet this need, and MPZs in the United States could theoretically accommodate an additional 235 million metric tons of CO_2 above the current 65 million. State-of-the-art EOR in MPZs or ROZs could produce an incremental 3 million barrels of oil per day by 2030, providing a major opportunity to increase US energy security through technology development.[28]

At the same time, the high cost of integrated carbon capture and sequestration (CCS) projects and federal program structures have slowed large-scale demonstrations of this important technology for reducing CO_2

emissions from combustion of fossil fuels. The need for additional CO_2 for EOR and the attractiveness of additional production at current high oil prices could provide impetus and stimulus for large CCS projects, as well as for the technology and infrastructure development that will be required to capture and transport the CO_2 from point sources. Research is needed to understand reservoir capacities; maximum and optimum injectivity rates; permanence of CO_2 EOR storage; systems analyses for capture, transport, and storage, including the mismatch of CO_2 streams from power generation and oil production needs; and the potential of EOR in TZs and ROZs.[29]

Advanced Vehicles to Reduce Oil Consumption and Enhance Energy Security

Reducing oil consumption for transportation remains a high priority for energy security reasons and potentially for climate change policy. As noted, increased domestic oil production will not divorce the United States from global oil markets and prices and the oil needs of our allies, although it will positively affect the US balance of payments. Furthermore, the transportation sector, fueled overwhelmingly by oil, is responsible for more than one-quarter of total US GHG emissions (on a CO_2-equivalent basis).

Generally, the technology pathways for achieving these goals involve using less oil (i.e., more efficient vehicles) or substituting other fuels for oil. The substitution route has multiple pathways, but each must compete with the desirability of petroleum-derived liquid fuels, which have high-volume energy densities, are easily distributed, and remain relatively inexpensive. Specific pathways include alternative liquid fuels (especially those "drop-in" fuels that are compatible with existing fuel distribution infrastructures), compressed natural gas (CNG), and fuels that require alternative vehicle technologies (electric and hydrogen fuel cell vehicles). Hybrid solutions also exist, such as internal combustion engine–battery vehicles; efficiency gains from integrated internal combustion engine–alternative fuel design; and flex-fuel vehicles that can use different mixtures of liquid fuels (such as gasoline, ethanol, and methanol), thereby allowing consumers to choose from fuels derived from oil, biomass, and natural gas feedstock. We discuss several options of current interest.

The shale gas revolution has revived interest in natural gas as a transportation fuel. CNG is a well-established vehicle fuel globally, with more than 10 million vehicles on the road (generally as bifuel CNG–gasoline vehicles). With current US natural gas and gasoline prices, CNG is attractive from fuel cost and environmental perspectives. However, the range of pure CNG vehicles is typically only one-quarter that of gasoline-fueled vehicles, and the initial vehicle cost is significantly higher. As a consequence, payback periods of a few years require very high mileage use. This limitation and the need for fueling infrastructure point to fleet vehicles with limited range requirements as the most obvious application.

Liquefied natural gas (LNG), another natural gas option, has been advocated as a fuel for long-haul trucks. This alternative faces many challenges: much higher vehicle cost, operational issues such as boil-off, and the need for a relatively expensive specialized fueling infrastructure. In addition, the limited market for such vehicles affects resale value. LNG heavy trucks will likely continue to make inroads in cases where the vehicles travel station to station, representing about 20 percent of the market.

Yet another option is natural gas–derived liquid fuels. Multiple conversion options exist.[30] The most direct is to methanol, a widely available commodity with a history of use in high-performance vehicles. Methanol is a key fuel in the Open Fuel Standard initiative, which would statutorily require new light-duty vehicles to have tri-flex-fuel capability (i.e., to be capable of running on varying mixtures of gasoline, ethanol, and methanol). This requirement would likely create retail competition among fuels, thereby diminishing the strategic value of oil. The incremental costs for producing engines with this capability appear to be modest, but some controversy persists about the capability for meeting stringent emissions constraints. Because of its implications for public policy, this issue merits a dedicated research program in the public domain.

Enhanced efficiency of internal combustion engines offers obvious opportunities for lower oil consumption. One generic approach is downsizing of internal combustion engines operated with turbocharging and higher compression ratios. This method can be reinforced by injecting ethanol, because of its high octane, at high torque,[31] thus demonstrating the importance of integrating engine and fuel design. Substantial efficiency gains (20 to 30 percent) could be realized with modest engine cost increases. "Lightweighting" vehicles—substituting aluminum, magnesium, plastics, and carbon-fiber composites for steel—and improving vehicles' aerodynamic design are key efficiency pathways. In the United States, much higher CAFE (corporate average fuel economy) standards introduced in 2012 (54.5 miles per gallon by 2025 for light-duty vehicles) provide impetus for making such efficiency gains, as well as for developing hybrid and other advanced drivetrains.

Electric vehicles (plug-in hybrids, battery vehicles, fuel-cell vehicles) were given the highest priority for vehicle and fuel precompetitive research and development funding in the 2011 US Department of Energy (DOE) *Quadrennial Technology Review*.[32] This program was part of a larger recommendation that DOE place greater emphasis on transportation relative to stationary sources to reduce both oil dependence and emissions. Electrification would diversify primary fuels for transportation because electricity is generated from coal, natural gas, nuclear, hydropower, and other renewables.

Electric vehicles face many challenges in gaining a large market share. Preeminent among these challenges is the cost reduction of batteries for light-duty vehicles. Although quoted battery costs show considerable variation,[33] an estimate of about $600 per kilowatt-hour is representative for lithium batteries. This cost, which is still quite high, typically produces a range limit of about 40 miles for vehicles operating on battery power only. A reduction to $100 or $200 is needed to spur mass-market penetration, and whether the current technology will reach this performance goal over the next decade or so remains unclear. This cost reduction is clearly a very high research priority, as is exploration of alternative battery chemistries.

Recycling Critical Elements, Anticipating Criticality

The International Union of Pure and Applied Chemistry defines 17 elements—the lanthanides plus scandium and yttrium—as rare earth elements (REEs).[34] They and a number of other elements are essential to many clean energy technologies, such as batteries, catalytic converters, permanent magnets, and lighting. Some of these technologies, if deployed at the scale required to displace conventional energy sources or to alter the trajectory of GHG emissions, would consume more REEs than are being produced with today's mining and processing methods. This *potential* shortage of REEs and other elements that are important for advanced energy technologies (such as tellurium for thin-film photovoltaics) leads to their designation as critical materials or energy critical elements (ECEs).[35]

Some of these elements are rare in the Earth's crust. Others are relatively Earth abundant but are found in low, noncommercial concentrations. Still others are minor coproducts of mining for different metals, such as

Table 17.2. Select Energy Products Using Energy Critical Elements

Energy Product	Energy Critical Elements
Energy-efficient solid-state lighting	Yttrium, europium, terbium
Photovoltaics	Gallium, germanium, indium, silver, tellurium
Auto catalysts, fluid catalytic cracking	Cerium, neodymium, praseodymium, lanthanum
Hybrid automobiles, wind turbines	Neodymium, praseodymium, samarium, cobalt, terbium
Advanced turbine alloys	Rhenium
Cryogenics, advanced nuclear reactors, energy manufacturing	Helium
Fuel cells	Platinum, palladium, cerium, yttrium
High-performance batteries	Lithium, lanthanum

Sources: Modified from American Physical Society Panel on Public Affairs and Materials Research Society, "Energy Critical Elements: Securing Materials for Emerging Technologies," American Physical Society, Washington, DC, 2010, and Laura Talens Peiro, Gara Villalba Mendez, and Robert U. Ayres, "Rare and Critical Metals as By-products and the Implications for Future Supply," Faculty Research and Working Paper 2011/129/EPS/TOM/ISIC, INSEAD, Fontainebleau, France, 2011.

Note: Each element is not used in each of the products.

copper; as such, their production schedules are highly dependent on unrelated mineral production, and strong price signals are often absent. In this instance, the only options for increased production of REEs and ECEs are increased production of the underlying mineral or increased recovery rates for critical materials, an ongoing research focus area.

ECE Energy Applications

About 20 percent of global consumption of critical materials is for clean energy technologies.[36] Some key functions and products that use these and other REEs and ECEs are highlighted in table 17.2. ECEs are important not only for renewable and efficiency technologies; for example, catalytic cracking for refining oil uses cerium and lanthanum, both REEs.

ECEs, US Policy, and Research

Global demand for REEs is expected to increase by 54 percent from 2010 to 2015. The United States is contributing to this increase; demand for rare earths is expected to grow for catalysts by 4 to 7 percent per year, for magnets by 10 to 16 percent per year, and for metal alloys by 15 to 20 percent per year over the next several years.[37] DOE has identified five rare earth metals (dysprosium, neodymium, terbium, europium, and yttrium) as most critical in the short term.[38]

US policy toward minerals has long been the promotion of "adequate, stable, and reliable supply of materials for US national security, economic well-being, and industrial production."[39] The United States is currently almost 100 percent dependent (except for some minor recycling) on imports of rare earths. This situation could be highly problematic from energy, national security, environmental, workforce, and economic perspectives. Options for US production of REEs from existing mines (e.g., the One Mountain Mine in California) are limited, and starting up new mines is a long-term proposition, taking an average of 10 years. Environmental concerns are an important issue. As such, a US research strategy to support US mineral policy and help enable a renewable energy future should include both recycling options for REEs and some ECEs to address near-term concerns and development of replacement options in the longer term, anticipating the range of materials that will become critical in the future.

Recycling of Rare Earth Minerals

Many difficult technical, environmental, and economic issues are associated with recycling REEs. Current methods focus on various separation and dissolution technologies and tend to be expensive and inefficient. Collection systems are inadequate and generate waste and environmentally harmful byproducts. Lanthanum, for example, which is used in refining, could theoretically be recycled and used for high-performance batteries. Spent catalysts are, however, sufficiently hazardous that they require expensive disposal methods. Another example is provided by cerium oxide, which is used in ceramics. It can be recycled, but today the cost of recycling is higher than the element's value.[40] Commercial recycling opportunities are also greatly affected by the extreme price volatility of REEs, generally related to "above-ground" factors. These and other issues have limited recycling of REEs to very small volumes.

Designing, developing, demonstrating, and deploying energy-efficient and sustainable recovery and recycling processes require new approaches. These approaches include the application of intelligent sorting to help minimize energy consumption, waste generation, and harmful byproducts; new separation and purification technologies; and new recovery pathways. The US Geological Survey also suggests two promising functional areas of focus. The first, permanent magnet recycling, appears to be the most technically feasible and could provide benefits for this high-growth-rate sector. The second, replacement of nickel metal hydride (NiMH) with lithium ion, would help decrease the demand pressure on cerium, lanthanum, and neodymium, which could then be devoted to other uses.[41]

Criticality Analysis and Replacement Research

For purposes of this discussion, *criticality* is a shortage or anticipated shortage of a material that is critical for development of efficiency and renewable technologies. *Criticality analysis*, fundamentally a tool to anticipate and analyze replacement options for REEs and ECEs as needed, would enable industry and policy-makers to internalize criticality as a property of materials and would include (a) systems analysis with inputs and feedbacks and (b) market and cost modeling. Informed by criticality analysis, a concurrent research program would include the following:[42]

- Using sophisticated computer modeling of the range of material properties that could continually identify possible replacements for ECEs
- Improving recycling opportunities at each stage of the recycling process
- Developing replacement options with a focus on new devices and materials
- Promoting commercialization opportunities
- Creating educational and workforce development opportunities to ensure commercialization
- Collaborating formally on REE and ECE technology pathways with US allies

Challenge 2: Climate Change and Security

Concern about the long-term security implications of climate change has grown substantially since 2005. The congressional testimony of General Gordon Sullivan, chairman of the Military Advisory Board to the Center for Naval Analysis, summarized the board's findings in a 2007 report as follows:

- First, projected climate change poses a serious threat to America's national security;
- Second, climate change acts as a threat multiplier for instability in some of the most volatile regions of the world;
- Third, projected climate change will add to tensions even in stable regions of the world, and
- Fourth, climate change, national security and energy dependence are a related set of global challenges.

...

Hoping that these relationships will remain static is simply not acceptable given our training and experience as military leaders.[43]

These findings led to a recommendation (among others) that the United States "commit to a stronger national and international role to help stabilize climate changes at levels that will avoid significant disruption to global security and stability" and "commit to global partnerships that help less developed nations build the capacity and resiliency to better manage climate impacts."[44] This recommendation encompasses both mitigation of climate change risks and adaptation to the now-inevitable impacts of climate change.

The board's significant focus on adaptation in less developed nations reflects this reality: many of these societies do not have the financial resources for large-scale climate change preparedness or response and could be prime candidates for instability that could threaten American security and foreign policy interests. This sentiment is echoed in the 2012 Intelligence Community Assessment on global water security.[45] These judgments from the American national security community frame the discussion of climate-related policy objectives and key technology pathways highlighted in table 17.3.

Table 17.3. The Climate Change Challenge

Energy Security Challenge	Policy Options	Representative Technology Pathways
Climate change and associated natural disasters and humanitarian crises, especially in combination with poverty and social change, will increasingly present national security risks.	• Mitigate global warming by "decarbonizing" energy production: — Increase the efficiency of fossil fuel use. — Promote the substitution for coal by natural gas. — Develop and deploy cost-effective technologies with very low carbon emissions. — Effectively integrate large amounts of intermittent renewable electricity and low-carbon alternative fuels into the energy infrastructure.	• Efficient buildings and appliances • Renewable technologies such as solar energy, onshore and offshore wind, engineered geothermal energy, and third-generation biofuels • Advanced nuclear reactors • Carbon dioxide capture and sequestration • Utility-scale storage to facilitate renewables integration • "Smart grid" for renewables and distributed generation integration
	• Provide effective adaptation strategies and technologies to address the consequences of climate change: — Minimize consequences of natural disasters associated with climate change. — Develop resilient strategies and technologies to recover from consequences.	• Smart infrastructure • Refinement of predictions of local and regional impacts of climate change • Development of crops requiring little water as a drought response • Low-cost energy-efficient desalination • Storm surge protection • Social science research to understand societal shifts in response to climate change and extreme weather risk • Ecosystem service preservation

(*continued*)

Table 17.3. The Climate Change Challenge (continued)

Energy Security Challenge	Policy Options	Representative Technology Pathways
	• Explore geoengineering (deliberate large-scale intervention in the climate system) for global warming mitigation.	• CO_2 removal from the atmosphere through ocean fertilization, CO_2 capture and sequestration, and biochar
		• Solar radiation management through space-based reflectors, reflective aerosols, reflective ground and building surfaces, and cloud whitening
	• Minimize energy-related emissions of GHGs other than CO_2.	• Minimization of GHG emissions (especially methane) in hydrocarbon production
		• Detection and elimination of leaks in natural gas delivery systems

Source: Authors' compilation.

Climate Change Mitigation

Clearly, the most direct way to minimize climate change impacts and reduce the associated risks is to dramatically reduce GHG emissions into the atmosphere. More than 30 billion tons of anthropogenic CO_2 is emitted globally each year, making CO_2 the GHG of principal concern. CO_2 also has a long residence time in the atmosphere, measured in centuries, relative to other GHGs. Therefore, it poses a cumulative challenge, and the impacts can be mitigated only by the collective actions of countries at different stages of development—particularly the industrial countries and the BRIC (Brazil, Russia, India, and China) and MIST (Mexico, Indonesia, South Korea, and Turkey) countries.

A significant majority of economists posits that the most straightforward approach to limiting CO_2 emissions would be a cap or a suitable charge. The marketplace would then presumably find the most efficient way to allocate resources to demand reduction, lower-carbon fuel substitution, and "zero-carbon" technology deployment. In whatever form, this cap would confront the ground truth that today's global energy systems are 80 percent fossil fuel based. This conflict was front and center at the 2009 United Nations Climate Change Conference in Copenhagen, where hopes of a global agreement on climate change met the reality that few nations were prepared for an internationally binding agreement, including the world's two largest CO_2 emitters, China and the United States. Near-term prospects for achieving such an international agreement do not appear to be good. More promising is the acceleration of low-carbon technology innovations (both supply and demand) that lower the cost differential to business as usual alternatives.

It is generally acknowledged that the electricity sector will take the lead in the "decarbonization" of energy supply. The three general approaches for this pathway are using less electricity; switching from coal to lower-carbon (natural gas) or zero-carbon fuels (renewables, nuclear, hydro) for power generation; and following fossil fuel combustion with CO_2 capture and storage.

Using Less Electricity

Efficiency and demand management is, of course, a very effective avenue for emissions avoidance and often comes with significant life-cycle economic benefits. For example, the light-emitting diode (LED) requires only 20 to 25 percent of the electricity of an incandescent bulb. A single 60-watt-equivalent LED will use 1,100 to 1,200 kilowatt-hours less electricity and, with a retail electricity price of $0.12 per kilowatt-hour, save $140 per bulb over a 25,000-hour life span.[46] Given that about 13 percent of total US electricity use is for lighting in residential and commercial buildings and that the LED may have additional benefits associated with the 25-fold longer lifetime (particularly in commercial building applications), the cost, energy, and emissions savings could be substantial.[47] Inadequate consumer information and the initial higher capital cost for LEDs are barriers to these savings, suggesting the need for policies to accelerate the adoption of LEDs.

Switching to Zero-Carbon Fuel Options

Solar photovoltaics provide an example of dramatic cost reduction in recent years. The solar resource is enormous compared with societal energy demands, but technology deployment remains modest because of various challenges, such as cost and intermittency absent economic storage options. The price of photovoltaic modules has, however, dropped dramatically in recent years. Uncertainty exists as to whether the drop in price represents true cost reduction or is simply a market response to global oversupply, although real module costs appear to have dropped to around $1 per watt. Balance of system and installation cost declines have been slower, but claims of costs leveling at $0.15 per kilowatt-hour are no longer dismissed. Variability and intermittency still present problems for large-scale deployment and may incur systems integration charges in future regulatory regimes. Nevertheless, the pace of solar energy as a viable zero-carbon option in many contexts is more rapid than widely anticipated just a few years ago.

The story for nuclear power as a continuing major zero-carbon option is more complex.[48] The Fukushima Daiichi accident has clearly cast uncertainty on a "nuclear renaissance" in some countries with large nuclear programs. By 2022, Germany will likely phase out nuclear power. Japan is struggling to balance antinuclear sentiment and its dependence on nuclear power. In contrast, projects in China, Russia, India, and South Korea, where 80 percent of the world's nuclear plant construction is taking place, are moving forward.

In the United States, the first plants to be built in decades are in the early stages of construction. The price tag of $6 billion to $10 billion per plant (typically in the 1,000 to 1,600 megawatt range for new plants), the recent experience in Europe (multibillion-dollar cost overruns for new plants in Finland and France), and the added costs of new environmental regulations in the post-Fukushima environment place enormous pressure on these projects to demonstrate that they can be built on budget and on schedule. These activities are being closely watched by other utilities that are contemplating similar nuclear projects to see whether the financial returns on operations will be sufficient to justify the large upfront capital investment. The uncertainties surrounding US nuclear waste management are another barrier to new plant construction.

New small modular reactors (SMRs) may be able to improve the economics of nuclear power. SMRs, with power ratings from 10 to 300 megawatts, would incorporate natural cooling features designed to work even if external power is lost, as well as underground reactor placement to make them more secure. The entire nuclear reactor core and other components of SMRs would be manufactured on a production line and then shipped and hooked up to conventional power plant facilities. Cost savings would be achieved, in part, through manufacturing economies, not through the economies of scale sought by today's light-water reactors (LWRs). Another key feature of SMRs is the possibility of stretching out the capital commitments of utilities, thereby enhancing opportunities for more favorable financing terms. DOE is supporting private sector construction of "first mover" plants, but SMRs are a long-term proposition, and whether their promise can be realized in practice will be clear only when some are built.

The negative environmental impacts associated with shale gas *production* must be balanced with the environmental benefits of natural gas *consumption*, enabled by shale gas and the associated low prices. When combusted in modern power plants, natural gas emits about 50 percent less CO_2 than coal. US CO_2 emissions in the first quarter of 2012 were the lowest they have been since 1992. This drop is attributed in part to the "decline in coal-fired electricity generation, due largely to historically low natural gas prices."[49]

Modeling suggests that gas-fired generation is a critical bridge to a no-carbon future. Under a scenario of major reductions in CO_2 emissions by 2050, the progression from high-carbon to low-carbon content is fairly obvious: coal is displaced by natural gas, and then the natural gas is displaced by zero-carbon options. The message: we need to pick up the pace on zero-carbon technology innovation to ensure that the gas bridge can lead to carbon-free generation in this half-century.[50]

Applying Carbon Capture and Sequestration

The CCS option could enable the continued use of coal (and ultimately gas) on a large scale while dramatically cutting CO_2 emissions. Carbon capture challenges differ from those of sequestration.[51]

Today's CO_2 postcombustion capture process is derived from the petrochemical industry and is too expensive at scale. Alternative approaches include design of more advanced solvents and novel technologies such as membranes, phase-change absorbers, and stimuli-responsive capture. Coal combustion in a pure oxygen atmosphere rather than air would also lower capture costs. Interesting precombustion options exist as well—including coal gasification—that could offer multiple benefits: cleaner power generation, the conversion of coal to liquid fuels, and hydrogen production for various uses.

On the sequestration side, over its life span, a single utility scale coal-fired power plant will produce billions of barrels of CO_2 to be stored underground. Multiply this amount by many hundreds of plants and the CCS "industry" would be the size of the oil industry! This huge enterprise, however, would manage waste (unless CO_2 beneficial use is viable at enormous scale), not a high-value product like oil. Subsurface capacity is likely adequate over time, but multiple, decades-long, highly instrumented demonstration projects are needed in different geologies, each at a scale of megatons of CO_2 per year. Such projects are important for examining the effects of large cumulative injections, injectivity, microseismic limits,[52] and other operational issues to inform appropriate regulation and help monetize long-term liabilities. No project to date fully meets these needs, and the decades-long developmental time scale conflicts with the urgent need for scalable emissions reductions.

Geoengineering

The persistent inability of the global community to mount a credible climate change mitigation plan and the urgency this inaction induces call for a prudent exploration of all alternatives, including *geoengineering*—the intentional intervention in the global climate system to slow climate change or minimize its consequences. Some geoengineering approaches include the distribution of aerosols in the atmosphere or mirrors in the stratosphere to reflect incoming sunlight, actions to increase reflectivity of sunlight at the Earth's surface (including rather simple actions such as requiring white roofs for buildings), and ocean fertilization to absorb more CO_2.

This research pathway is currently even more taboo than adaptation, discussed later in this chapter. The reasons are clear: the unintended consequences of drastic geoengineering solutions to climate change could rival the impacts of its anthropogenic causes. A simple example: aerosol or mirror interventions would not ameliorate continued acidification of the oceans because of the continuing increase of CO_2 atmospheric concentrations. Another unintended consequence could be geopolitical tensions arising from single states acting without international concurrence or consideration of the global consequences. Research into political issues of international cooperation should be a parallel to research in the various technology pathways. All geoengineering pathways can and should be thoroughly questioned and researched on the basis of unintended consequences. It should be emphasized that launching a geoengineering research program is not an endorsement for geoengineering actions; the program may well reinforce their unattractiveness and give greater impetus and urgency to mitigation.

Other Greenhouse Gases

Although CO_2 is clearly and understandably the major focus, other GHG emissions are important, including methane, which is receiving increasing attention as the United States produces, transports, and consumes more natural gas. Methane is generally acknowledged to be a much more potent GHG than CO_2 (an equivalence factor of about 20) but with much shorter residence time in the atmosphere (roughly a decade versus over a century). Data on methane emissions from the entire gas system are out of date. The government should support an expanded data collection and publication effort on emissions from the entire supply chain to inform both technology and regulatory improvements if necessary; this effort could be extended to other large-scale sources of methane emissions.

Challenge 3: Nuclear Proliferation and Nuclear Power

A unique security concern raised in the energy sector is that of possible nuclear weapons proliferation facilitated by the spread and expansion of nuclear power.

Background

The Treaty on the Nonproliferation of Nuclear Weapons (known as the *Nonproliferation Treaty*, or NPT) requires that signatories, except for the P-5 weapons states (China, France, Russia, the United Kingdom, and the United States), forgo nuclear weapons development in exchange for assistance in developing peaceful uses of nuclear technology. Even though nonsignatory nations (India, Pakistan, Israel, North Korea, and Iran) have taken steps—some initially undetected—toward, or have achieved, nuclear capability, the NPT is generally viewed as successful in restraining the spread of nuclear weapons in recent decades. We focus only on the proliferation risks associated with the nuclear power fuel cycle, not with dedicated weapons programs.

Here, the central issue is control and elimination of weapons-usable fissionable material, either highly enriched uranium (HEU) or plutonium. HEU can be obtained with essentially the same low-enrichment uranium technology (mostly centrifuges) used for today's LWR fuel. Plutonium, in contrast, is separated from irradiated nuclear fuel in fuel cycles currently operating in some countries, notably France. The separated plutonium is then fabricated into new nuclear fuel for use in LWRs. Unfortunately, a huge amount (more than 250 tons) of separated plutonium is now in storage; the International Atomic Energy Agency defines *significant quantity* ("the approximate amount of nuclear material for which the possibility of manufacturing a nuclear explosive device cannot be excluded") as 8 kilograms.[53]

The plutonium separated from commercial irradiated nuclear fuel (with residence time in the LWR of a few years) is not pure, and its radiation background and high-heat-level characteristics make it relatively harder to use in high-performance nuclear explosives.[54] High-yield reliable nuclear weapons, however, are not required in many contexts: a crude device with a significantly lower nuclear yield could still be effective for national aims in certain regional contexts and for terrorist groups.

The plutonium quality for use in nuclear explosives can be degraded further if it is left together with other transuranic elements in the irradiated fuel. There are proposals for "advanced" fuel cycles that would do this and then recycle the whole lot into fuel for reactors with a fast neutron spectrum. This approach would render these materials effectively unusable in nuclear weapons for many decades. Of course, if the fission products are also left with the fissionable material, the spent fuel is useless for a nuclear explosive (although not for a "dirty bomb" that has no nuclear explosive yield). This option is employed in the once-through fuel cycle used in the United States, where spent fuel is not reprocessed but is instead stored for eventual direct disposal.

This excursion is meant to underscore the point that fuel-cycle technology choices matter to proliferation risks. In general, the objective of any of these various technology pathways and the associated institutional arrangements should be to minimize the spread of enrichment and reprocessing facilities under national control and to enhance international monitoring and security of fissionable materials (table 17.4).

Table 17.4. The Nuclear Power Challenge

Energy Security Challenge	Policy Options	Representative Technology Pathways
The global expansion of nuclear power and associated nuclear fuel technologies could spread nuclear weapons capabilities.	• Enhance safeguards, monitoring, and detection capabilities for fissionable materials and for fuel-cycle operations.	• System design of fuel-cycle facilities that integrates proliferation resistance (safeguards by design) • Development of advanced remote detectors for fissionable materials and associated fuel-cycle activities, including environmental monitoring
	• Deploy nuclear fuel cycles that minimize proliferation risks.	• Research, development, and demonstration of proliferation-resistant reactors, fuels, and fuel cycles • Spent fuel waste management • Deep borehole nuclear waste disposal

Source: Authors' compilation.

Technical Approaches to Fuel-Cycle Proliferation Challenges

A variety of reactor designs, fuels, and fuel cycles have been proposed to diminish the proliferation risks associated with nuclear power. As noted, the "bookend" reference points are the once-through fuel cycle using LWRs and the plutonium-recycle approach. Within this context, nonproliferation goals can be advanced through technical means that enhance transparency for the international community, confirm the security of nuclear materials for operators, and raise the bar against diversion.

Reducing Diversion Opportunities

The once-through cycle used in the United States has no weapons-usable material from normal operations; spent fuel is targeted for disposal in a deep geological repository. As such, diversion from enrichment operations or clandestine replication of the technology presents the greatest proliferation risk of this fuel cycle. One option for risk management is to eliminate or greatly reduce the need for the enrichment technology that could be misused or replicated to make HEU.

Another option also exists. The plutonium-breeding fuel cycle has dominated the discussion of self-sustaining nuclear power for half a century, driven by concerns about uranium supply. Past research focused on a high *breeding ratio*—the amount of fissionable material produced relative to the amount in the reactor fuel—with a goal of maximizing uranium supplies. It also led to the development of a fast-spectrum plutonium breeder reactor whose initial fuel loading would have a large amount of plutonium produced by LWRs. High-growth scenarios for breeder reactors also assumed substantial LWR deployment and associated enrichment to produce enough startup plutonium.[55]

Uranium is in fact plentiful under any credible nuclear power growth scenario for at least a century.[56] Relaxation of the high breeding ratio requirement opens up many more reactor and fuel-cycle options. Possibilities include using low enrichment uranium rather than plutonium as the initial fuel and diminishing the need for so many LWRs, which would, in turn, reduce the need for uranium and enrichment capacity. This option needs to be revisited in view of a greatly changed uranium supply profile.

Fuel-cycle operations can also place barriers to diversion. Some fuel forms, such as tristructural-isotropic fuel designed for high-temperature gas reactors, would require a more complex reprocessing approach than the standard approach for LWR irradiated fuel. High burnup fuels—fuels that can tolerate much longer residence times in the reactor core before refueling—would have higher neutron and heat levels, making them less attractive for nuclear explosives. As already noted, absent additional separations, recycling of all the minor actinides along with plutonium effectively would remove the nuclear explosive risk but would increase the costs and fuel fabrication challenges; hence, this option may not be commercially viable. These are only a few of the ideas for reactor, fuel, and fuel-cycle technology that limit proliferation risk, sometimes incrementally, sometimes dramatically. The latter generally face more research, development, and demonstration (RD&D) needs and longer development cycles for potential commercial viability.

Encouraging Waste Management and Nonproliferation

Spent fuel contains a very significant amount of plutonium, with obvious connections between waste disposal and nonproliferation, which places a high value on physical security and surveillance. Importantly, a nation's failure to successfully manage spent fuel disposal limits global options for minimizing proliferation risks.[57]

Consider the "fuel leasing" option (the Assured Nuclear Fuel Services Initiative is a specific example).[58] Under this arrangement, the nuclear fuel supplier would retain ownership of the fuel, lease it to the producers in another country for use in power production, remove the spent fuel after a short cooling period, and then manage the nuclear waste as it does for its own domestic program. Leasing is especially appropriate for small national programs, which are the norm for early-stage nuclear power programs (e.g., Iran).

The willingness of the fuel supplier (or cooperating third-party country) to accept and dispose of the spent fuel is one of the biggest challenges of this approach. However, precedent is found in the return of irradiated fuel from US-supplied research reactors explicitly for nonproliferation purposes. Absent a broadly accepted domestic spent fuel storage and disposal strategy, however, even if spent fuel amounts were only a small fraction of total US spent fuel, this nonproliferation option is effectively blocked. The Blue Ribbon Commission on America's Nuclear Future has laid out a roadmap for a revitalized US nuclear waste management program,[59] but although many actions need to be taken in the near term, its execution will take decades.

The US waste management research and development program has been largely constrained from pursuing different technology pathways. This situation needs to change: a renewed emphasis on RD&D could provide some new directions. Research that clarifies the technical limits for very-long-term and reliable storage of spent fuel on the scale of a century or more would provide an important option.[60] A very different direction would be deep borehole disposal, in which waste would be disposed of in a "well," several kilometers below the earth's surface.[61] The feasibility and economics of such an approach have dramatically improved because of the immense progress in drilling technology in the past two decades. This option, when combined with spent fuel partitioning, could limit borehole disposal to transuranic elements only. This approach would isolate a very small volume for disposal and yet ameliorate the greatest concerns

Table 17.5. Technology-Based Safeguard Objectives

Enrichment Plants	Reactors and Fuel Fabrication	Reprocessing Plants	Waste Sites
• Detect concealed enrichment plants.	• Detect concealed production reactors.	• Detect concealed reprocessing plants.	• Detect diversion of nuclear material or spent fuel.
• Detect production of highly enriched uranium or excess amounts of low enriched uranium in declared plants.	• Detect covert production of nuclear material. • Uncover diversion of nuclear material from declared inventories.	• Uncover undeclared use of facilities for separation or purification activities. • Detect diversion of nuclear material.	

Source: Authors' compilation.

about long-term radioactivity, heat, and toxicity of spent fuel or high-level nuclear waste.

Developing Safeguards

The principal focus of technology-based safeguards has been timely detection of fissile material theft or diversion from nuclear fuel-cycle facilities, complementing physical security and facility inspections.[62] Table 17.5 summarizes technical objectives at various stages of the fuel cycle, taken from a 2005 American Physical Society report.[63]

Terrorist and other threats are increasing just as nuclear reactors and fuel-cycle facilities are being deployed more widely. This challenge has placed additional burdens on the need for inspection; the situation in Iran illustrates the importance of detecting undeclared facilities. This effort could be advanced, in part, through new safeguards and enabling technologies, such as modeling and simulation of complete plant operations and material flows and integrated sensor, information, and communications systems.

Undeclared enrichment capability that could be used to make weapons-grade HEU is a growing concern.[64] Detection of centrifuge plants is already challenging (again, Iran is an example) because such plants have a relatively small operational footprint, and the footprint for some next-generation technologies could be smaller still. A current example is laser isotope separation, which may be reaching a commercial stage. Furthermore, other enrichment approaches could be used for proliferation purposes in small operations without regard to their commercial viability for high throughput. It is important that the United States actively keep abreast of the entire range of isotope separation technology pathways with a focus on batch operations, not just commercial viability. Understanding those special components and materials needed for all such technologies is key to detection.

A few of the areas for safeguards technology research and development are safeguards by design, real-time process monitoring, data integration, and environmental monitoring.[65] A variety of commercial and national laboratory facilities can be used in the United States for demonstrating and refining the new safeguards technologies that emerge from an expanded research and development program.

Challenge 4: Energy Infrastructure and Security

Two weather events in 2012 have helped refocus attention on climate change, energy infrastructure, and energy security. During Hurricane Sandy, 8 million homes lost power, and damages from this single hurricane could total over $60 billion. The "superderecho" that struck primarily in the Mid-Atlantic states in the summer of 2012 left 5 million homes without power for several days. Importantly, the derecho left large portions of the federal defense and homeland security workforce without power, access to computers, and telephone services (even 911 services went down), raising serious security issues.[66]

Disruption of these power networks has far-reaching economic, health, safety, and security impacts and serves as a stark reminder of how the nation's critical energy infrastructures literally serve as lifelines for, and key enablers of, our modern world. The United States has a direct interest in ensuring the security of these and other infrastructures, threats to which come in the following general areas:

- Climate-related and other natural events
- Malevolent attacks on supply chains or other key infrastructures

Table 17.6. Infrastructure and Supply Chain Challenges

Energy Security Challenge	Policy Options	Representative Technology Pathways
Energy infrastructure and supply chains are lengthening, diversifying, and becoming increasingly information technology–dependent, making them more vulnerable to both natural disasters and malevolent acts.	• Protect high-density targets against modern threats.	• "Low-tech" with regulatory requirements
	• Improve the robustness and resilience of energy delivery networks.	• Cyber security • Resilient grid architectures, including hardware and software • Distributed generation • Superconducting cables
	• Enable infrastructure to match power generation fuel sources.	• High-deliverability storage

Source: Authors' compilation.

- Threats to the infrastructures of key US allies and US military installations around the globe

Some policy options and technology pathways to address the infrastructure and supply chain challenges are highlighted in table 17.6.

Climate-Related and Other Natural Events

Public awareness of the risks of climate change has been raised by a growing set of *domestic* events—the intensity and cost of storms, extended drought, and near-record wildfires. It has been reinforced by an equally disturbing set of *global* indicators, including sea-level rise, disappearing Arctic sea ice, and melting of the Greenland ice sheet, at and beyond the previously anticipated upper limits.

Adaptation and the Electricity Infrastructure

The current US electricity grid—on which many other critical infrastructures now rely, including energy production and distribution, water systems, and telecommunications—is designed to withstand single and isolated events but is not adequate to withstand the widespread storm surges and sustained high winds of an event like Hurricane Sandy.

This inadequacy has prompted discussions on adaptation research to harden and make the nation's electricity infrastructure more resilient. "Smart grids" and a comprehensive plan for "elegant failures and recovery" of the nation's power system have been discussed for some time but have been slow to materialize beyond the current focus on smart metering. A specific focus on adaptation and energy infrastructure preparedness could add to the economic impetus for smart grid deployment. In addition, the US government should redouble its research support for microgrids and other distributed generation. Moreover, new building materials and land-use options, along with supportive building and creative insurance incentives, are needed.

Adaptation has often been resisted as a strategy because it might lessen the drive to mitigate. Climate inaction and urgency, however, now make the pairing of mitigation with adaptation the only responsible pathway for altering the trajectory of GHG emissions while simultaneously addressing the near-term risks and impacts of a changing climate. Mitigation is, in fact, key to managing the costs of adaptation, which could be enormous. Of course, unintended consequences must be carefully explored before major projects are implemented. Protections against storm flooding in certain low-lying areas could, for example, exacerbate ecological damage in neighboring seashore environments. A highly elevated level of analysis is needed for prudent actions. The adaptation focus should elevate recognition of the importance of mitigation and emphasize for the public how climate change can damage the economy now, not just in the future.

Adaptation is a global issue that demands local solutions. A concerted international program is needed for climate change adaption technology transfer to the least developed nations, paid for by industrial nations and the large emerging economies—a pathway generally supported by, as noted, the US national security community. The local or regional nature of these problems and the need for tailored responses, however, make global resources much more difficult to mobilize.

Electromagnetic Radiation

Another area of concern is the possible, if controversial, issue of power grid disruption from electromagnetic radiation associated with solar storms.

Such disruption is identified as a "black swan event" in a recently released report of the National Intelligence Council, which noted, "Solar geomagnetic storms could knock out satellites, the electric grid, and many sensitive electronic devices. The recurrence intervals of crippling solar geomagnetic storms, which are less than a century, now pose a substantial threat because of the world's dependence on electricity."[67] Mitigation options and requirements are being reviewed by the Federal Energy Regulatory Commission (FERC), which issued a notice of proposed rulemaking in December 2012 for reliability standards to address the impacts of electromagnetic radiation on bulk power systems. Technology and best practice options can be synergistic with many of those needed for adaptation, so research investments could have dual application.

Growing Interdependencies between Gas and Electric Infrastructures

Yet another remarkable change in the US energy profile since 2005 has been the increased use of natural gas in power generation and the degree to which it is displacing coal. In fact, at one point in 2012, natural gas generation reached parity with coal. This turnaround has been largely enabled by shale gas development.

Not surprisingly, this development is increasing the interdependencies between the electric and natural gas infrastructures, making power generation more dependent on natural gas (including those infrastructures that produce it and move it to consumers) and conversely making gas systems more dependent on electricity. This growing relationship poses new challenges for reliability and resource planning for both sectors. A recent report summarizing a series of Gas–Electric Coordination Technical Conferences held by the FERC highlights some of these key issues, including scheduling issues associated with mismatched operating schedules, coordination and information sharing, and future capacity planning and resource adequacy.[68]

These operational, contract, regulatory, investment, and capacity-planning issues need careful consideration and review, and research is needed to address issues of interdependency. Additional modeling capabilities would provide greater analytical insight into the reliability, investment, and security needs associated with these relationships. Another specific area of interdependency concern is gas storage. Most gas storage is filled up in the summer and drawn down in the winter. Power generation requirements, as gas-fired generation increases, may require high-deliverability storage with multiple cycles.

Malevolent Attacks on Supply Chains or Other Key Infrastructures

Moving energy long distances from supply to demand centers creates a range of opportunities for attacks on supply chain infrastructures, thereby raising energy and economic security issues for the United States.

Oil and Gas Supply Chains

In 2012, the Turkish government reported that terrorists attacked the Baku–Tbilisi–Erzurum gas pipeline twice within three weeks, and Somali pirates successfully hijacked a Greek oil tanker. Disruption of oil supply chains, regardless of their location, affects the price and availability of US oil supplies. A strategy for producing more unconventional oil closer to demand centers—in Eastern Europe, China, or in the Western Hemisphere, for example—could reduce risks.

Also, although there is no global gas market and the United States has abundant supplies, attacks on LNG tankers, other LNG-related facilities, and long-distance gas pipelines create security risks for key US allies in OECD Europe and Asia. In an incident related to a contract dispute, Russia shut off gas through its pipelines in 2009. Although the incident was not caused by a malevolent attack, four countries in Eastern Europe lost 100 percent of their gas supplies in the middle of winter, and many others lost substantial percentages. Supporting environmentally responsible conventional and shale gas development in parts of Europe, Northern Africa, and the Eastern Mediterranean would reduce supply chain risks for key US allies.

Cyber Security of the Electric Grid

The electric grid is critical to US security at many levels, but the control of this infrastructure resides largely in the hands of private operators, thereby complicating efforts to combat cyber attacks on the nation's power systems. Also, operations, smart metering, two-way communications, and power dispatch are increasingly reliant on information technology and computer networks between utilities, thus increasing opportunities for such attacks as well as the damage they can inflict.

Failures of these systems could be the result of either accidents or malevolent attacks from disgruntled employees, criminals, terrorists, or countries. The risk of such attacks is complicated by the constant evolution of the nature of such attacks. The transition to "cloud computing," for example, raises an entirely new set of issues not contemplated just a few years ago. Bureaucratic confusion adds to the concern: the FERC recently set up an Office of Energy Infrastructure Security to "identify, communicate, and seek comprehensive solutions to potential risks to FERC-jurisdictional facilities from cyber attacks and such physical threats as electromagnetic pulses,"[69] but no single agency in the federal government has authority or jurisdiction over the full range of issues associated with grid cyber security. State levels also have overlapping and competing authorities. These issues need to be sorted out to improve the nature and timeliness of information sharing between the private sector and the government (including intelligence agencies).

The Role of Technology in Energy Security

In recent decades, we have seen significant innovation in areas such as information technology, communications, and biotechnology. We have also seen innovation in the energy space—for example, advanced three-dimensional seismic exploration, ultradeepwater drilling, and unconventional fuels, which are game changers. Moreover, the unprecedented level of investment in clean energy technology over the past decade is cause for optimism.

The difficulties in rapidly capturing innovation advances in the energy space generally stem from several reasons that also affect clean energy. The explanation lies partly with the absence of policy that would coherently and convincingly limit CO_2 emissions, because such a climate change–driven policy would incentivize the energy system toward zero- or low-carbon technologies, the very antithesis of the current system dominated by fossil fuel combustion. Such a policy, however, confronts the reality of the scale and nature of today's global, multitrillion-dollar, capital-intensive energy enterprises with well-established efficient supply chains, delivery infrastructures, and customer bases. These enterprises are commodity businesses: they have cost sensitivities that tend to limit the initial introduction of disruptive technologies (absent policy-driven mechanisms), and their large capital needs make innovation very expensive, especially in the demonstration phase. The consequences of decisions on which technologies and infrastructures to invest in and deploy will likely last for decades, and reward structures favor reliability over innovation. These characteristics all place high barriers to displacement of incumbents.

Other features of the energy space affect the pace and range of innovation. Importantly, energy technology innovation seldom provides consumers with new functionality. Rather, it provides alternative pathways to light, heat, mobility, and other essential services, thereby placing significant boundary conditions on the scope and nature of change. Also, the introduction of new energy technologies depends strongly on policies, not market forces, to gain major footholds in the marketplace. These features, coupled with the fact that energy businesses provide essential services throughout society, invite extensive regulation and complex politics and geopolitics. As such, the deployment of energy technologies is often deeply influenced by public policies that can help condition and open up new energy markets.

Getting these policies right is highly challenging for a range of reasons. First, policy coherence requires the ability to weave together and align multiple policy threads: environment, diplomacy and security, natural resources, land and food, and others. A current example that engages the equities of several departments and demonstrates the complexity is the licensing of US LNG exports. Factors in the balance include the price of natural gas for domestic consumers; jobs in the gas industry; the role of natural gas and natural gas liquids as a base for expanded domestic manufacturing; and support for a key ally, Japan, that is desperate for new gas supplies post–Fukushima Daiichi and has supported US security policy elsewhere—in particular, Iran sanctions that limit its oil export options.

Also, in several key aspects, the structure of the DOE, which is the principal source of federal energy RD&D support, reflects a 1970s energy marketplace. The suitability of some of these structures for the 21st-century global energy marketplace deserves reexamination to help guide more coherent and relevant energy policies and energy science and technology investments. Program innovations such as ARPA-E (Advanced Research Projects Agency–Energy) and the Energy Innovation Hubs are a good start. ARPA-E promotes an innovation culture that accelerates the transformation of scientific discoveries and inventions into clean energy technologies for the marketplace. Energy Innovation Hubs establish multidisciplinary integrated teams of basic and applied scientists and engineers for a sustained focus on various specific critical DOE energy missions, such as state-of-the-art nuclear reactor simulation, new types of batteries, and reduced risk regarding the availability of energy technology critical materials.

Integrated Energy Policy

Coherence requires more effective integration of the myriad policy threads and equities. These equities include multiple federal departments and committees in Congress, as well as state and local governments that play a strong role—indeed often a leading role—in innovative policies. The tools available to stimulate technology innovation are also diverse (direct support of RD&D plus a variety of economic incentives, regulations, standards, and government procurement programs) and need to be fit to purpose.

Addressing this fragmentation of responsibilities and perspectives, the President's Council of Advisors on Science and Technology (PCAST) advanced a recommendation for the establishment of a quadrennial energy review (QER) that would do the following:[70]

- Lay out an integrated view of short-, intermediate-, and long-term objectives for federal energy policy in the context of economic, environmental, and security priorities.
- Outline legislative proposals to Congress.
- Put forward anticipated executive actions (programmatic, regulatory, fiscal, and so on) to be coordinated across multiple agencies.
- Identify resource requirements for the RD&D and innovation incentive programs.
- Provide a strong analytical base for research investments and the associated policy and incentive structures.

Accomplishing these objectives will be a challenge. The cross-government convening power to implement such a QER process resides in the Executive Office of the President (EOP), but the EOP does not have the operational and analytical capacity for such an undertaking. The DOE, with appropriate EOP leadership and guidance, is the obvious agency to organize and staff an executive secretariat for this purpose, supporting a robust interagency process for the EOP to produce decision recommendations for the president that reflect a balance of equities and are based on serious analysis.

The analytical capability needed for this outcome, however, needs strengthening, including the development of highly sophisticated modeling and other engineering and economic analysis tools, informed by a broad, deep, current, and extensive understanding of both domestic and global energy markets. The Energy Information Administration within the DOE is certainly a major asset in this regard, but its independence from policy development needs to be preserved. Building this capacity in a way that earns the trust and respect of all parties—the administration, Congress, states, nongovernmental organizations, and industry—will take time. Essential ingredients for success include a range of inputs from these and other quarters and a high degree of transparency. The goal would be both a process and a plan that has bipartisan and multiregional support, essential to core stability in energy policy across administrations.

In addition to creating the process and structures to more effectively integrate equities with policies, PCAST was concerned that federal research support have a planning horizon consistent with long-term innovation cycles. It was the sentiment of PCAST that the QER might form the basis for multiyear congressional budget authorizations that could buttress private sector confidence in committing resources to clean energy technology investments as well as provide a more appropriate funding profile for successful energy research and development.

In recognizing the organizational and intellectual challenges posed by the QER, PCAST recommended both a multiyear approach to the first full QER and an initial installment focusing exclusively on technology. The DOE did, indeed, produce the *Quadrennial Technology Review*, which recommended some rebalancing of the DOE RD&D portfolio toward the oil dependence challenge through advanced vehicle development—particularly electrification of transportation.[71] This initial effort was largely confined to one department (the DOE) and, as such, did not exercise the cross-government coordination that is central to the QER. Its success, however, paved the way for the next step: weaving together the multiple energy policy threads, including those of economic and national security. Such a measured approach is needed to move away from fragmented policies, technologies du jour, and frequent policy shifts that complicate private sector clean-tech decisions.

The essential role of technology in energy production, distribution, and consumption has changed little since 2005. However, with 35 years of public energy research, development, demonstration, and deployment experience—both good and bad—and expanded security imperatives, the time is right to reexamine how both the administration and Congress can innovate an energy policy development process appropriate for the 21st-century marketplace and for the overarching challenges of energy supply, security, and climate change risk mitigation.

Notes

1. Melanie A. Kenderdine and Ernest J. Moniz, "Technology Development and Energy Security," in *Energy and Security: Toward a New Foreign Policy Strategy*, edited by Jan Kalicki and David Goldwyn, 425–60 (Washington, DC, and Baltimore: Woodrow Wilson Center Press and Johns Hopkins University Press, 2005).

2. US Energy Information Administration (EIA), *International Energy Outlook 2011* (Washington, DC: EIA, 2011).

3. EIA, *International Energy Outlook 2011*.

4. Annu Mital, "Unconventional Oil and Gas Production Opportunities and Challenges of Oil Shale Development," testimony before the Subcommittee on Energy and Environment, Committee on Science, Space, and Technology, US House of Representatives, Washington, DC, May 10, 2012.

5. Deborah Gordon, "Understanding Unconventional Oil," Carnegie Papers, Energy and Climate, Carnegie Endowment for International Peace, Washington, DC, May 2012.

6. Unconventional Oil Subgroup of the Resource and Supply Task Group, "Unconventional Oil," Paper 1-6, North American Resource Development Study, National Petroleum Council, Washington, DC, September 15, 2011.

7. Alan Greenspan, "Natural Gas Supply and Demand Issues," written testimony before the Committee on Energy and Commerce, US House of Representatives, Washington, DC, June 10, 2003.

8. Lee Raymond, speech at the Reuters Energy Summit, New York, June 21, 2005.

9. Personal communication with Francis O'Sullivan, Massachusetts Institute of Technology Energy Initiative, 2013.

10. Ernest J. Moniz, Henry D. Jacoby, and Anthony J. Meggs, eds., *The Future of Natural Gas: An Interdisciplinary MIT Study* (Cambridge, MA: Massachusetts Institute of Technology, 2011).

11. Ernest E. Carter, "Novel Concepts for Unconventional Gas Development of Gas Resources in Gas Shales, Tight Sands, and Coal Beds," Final Report, Carter Technologies, Sugar Land, TX, February 19, 2009.

12. Moniz, Jacoby, and Meggs, *Future of Natural Gas*.

13. Francis O'Sullivan and Sergey Paltsev, "Shale Gas Production: Potential versus Actual Greenhouse Gas Emissions," *Environmental Research Letters* 7 (2012) 044030, 5.

14. Florence Gény, "The Changing Debate around Shale Gas: From Enthusiasm to Responsible Development," presentation at Chatham House Fossil Fuels Expert Roundtable, London, July 5, 2011.

15. Secretary of Energy Advisory Board, *Shale Gas Production Subcommittee 90-Day Report* (Washington, DC: US Department of Energy, 2011).

16. Murray W. Hitzman, written testimony before the Energy and Natural Resources Committee, US Senate, Washington, DC, June 19, 2012.

17. National Research Council, *Induced Seismicity Potential in Energy Technologies* (Washington, DC: National Academies Press, 2012).

18. Mark D. Zoback, written testimony, Committee on Energy and Natural Resources, US Senate, Washington, DC, June 19, 2012.

19. National Research Council, *Induced Seismicity Potential in Energy Technologies*.

20. Alain Labastie, "Increasing Recovery Factors: A Necessity," *Journal of Petroleum Technology* (August 2011): 12–13.

21. Perry M. Jarrell, Charles Fox, Michael Stein, and Steven Webb, *Practical Aspects of CO_2 Flooding* (Richardson, TX: Society of Petroleum Engineers, 2002).

22. Labastie, "Increasing Recovery Factors."

23. Sunil Kokal and Abdulaziz Al-Kaabi, "Enhanced Oil Recovery: Challenges and Opportunities," in *World Petroleum Council: Global Energy Solutions* (London: World Petroleum Council, 2010), 64–69.

24. Kokal and Al-Kaabi, "Enhanced Oil Recovery."

25. Total, "EOR Maximizing Recovery Factors," Total, Paris, 2009. See also Vladimir Alvarado and Eduardo Manrique, "Enhanced Oil Recovery: An Update Review," *Energies* 3, no. 9 (2010): 1529–75.

26. Peigui Yin, Shaochang Wo, and David Mohrbacher, "Preliminary Mapping for Potential EOR Development of Transition and Residual Oil Zones in the Bighorn Basin, Wyoming," Enhanced Oil Recovery Institute, University of Wyoming, Laramie, 2011.

27. MIT Energy Initiative and Bureau of Economic Geology at the University of Texas, *Role of Enhanced Oil Recovery in Accelerating the Deployment of Carbon Capture and Sequestration* (Cambridge, MA: Massachusetts Institute of Technology, 2010).

28. MIT Energy Initiative and Bureau of Economic Geology at the University of Texas, *Role of Enhanced Oil Recovery*.

29. MIT Energy Initiative and Bureau of Economic Geology at the University of Texas, *Role of Enhanced Oil Recovery*.

30. Moniz, Jacoby, and Meggs, *Future of Natural Gas*.

31. Leslie Bromberg and Daniel R. Cohn, "Effective Octane and Efficiency Advantages of Direct Injection Alcohol Engines," Massachusetts Institute of Technology Laboratory for Energy and the Environment, Cambridge, MA, 2008.

32. DOE, *Quadrennial Technology Review* (Washington, DC: DOE, 2011).

33. MIT Energy Initiative, *Electrification of the Transportation System* (Cambridge, MA: Massachusetts Institute of Technology, 2010).

34. See the US Geological Survey website, "Rare Earths Statistics and Information," at http://minerals.usgs.gov/minerals/pubs/commodity/rare_earths/.

35. American Physical Society Panel on Public Affairs and Materials Research Society, "Energy Critical Elements: Securing Materials for Emerging Technologies," American Physical Society, Washington, DC, 2010.

36. DOE, *US Department of Energy Critical Materials Strategy: December 2010* (Washington, DC: DOE, 2010).

37. Keith R. Long, *The Future of Rare Earth Elements—Will These High-Tech Industry Elements Continue in Short Supply?*, USGS Open-File Report 2011–1189, 2011.

38. DOE, *US Department of Energy Critical Materials Strategy: December 2011* (Washington, DC: DOE, 2011).

39. Marc Humphries, "Rare Earth Elements: The Global Supply Chain," CRS Report for Congress 7-5700, Congressional Research Service, Washington, DC, June 8, 2012, 1.

40. Thomas G. Goonan, "Rare Earth Elements: End Use and Recyclability," USGS Scientific Investigations Report 2011-5094, US Geological Survey, Reston, VA, 2011, http://pubs.usgs.gov/sir/2011/5094/pdf/sir2011-5094.pdf.

41. Goonan, "Rare Earth Elements."

42. Personal communications with Joel Clark, Materials Science and Engineering and Engineering Systems Divisions, Massachusetts Institute of Technology, 2012 and 2013.

43. Gordon R. Sullivan, testimony before the US House of Representatives Select Committee on Energy Independence and Global Warming, Washington, DC, April 18, 2007, http://www.cna.org/reports/climate/testimony/2007-04-18. See also CNA Corporation, *National Security and the Threat of Climate Change* (Alexandria, VA: CNA Corporation, 2007).

44. Sullivan, testimony before the US House of Representatives Select Committee on Energy Independence and Global Warming.

45. Defense Intelligence Agency, "Global Water Security," Intelligence Community Assessment 2012-08, Defense Intelligence Agency, Washington, DC, 2012.

46. This savings is reduced by the difference in cost between the LED and the 25 replaced incandescent bulbs. A 4 percent discount rate over 25 years (assuming 1,000 hours of operation per year) would reduce the net present value of the benefit by nearly 40 percent; a significant benefit remains.

47. EIA, *Annual Energy Outlook 2012 with Projections to 2035* (Washington, DC: EIA, 2012), tables 4 and 5.

48. Ernest J. Moniz, "Why We Still Need Nuclear Power: Making Clean Energy Safe and Affordable," *Foreign Affairs* 90, no. 6 (2011): 83–94.

49. EIA, "US Energy-Related CO_2 Emissions in Early 2012 Lowest since 1992," *Today in Energy* (blog), August 1 2012, http://www.eia.gov/todayinenergy/detail.cfm?id=7350.

50. Moniz, Jacoby, and Meggs, *Future of Natural Gas*.

51. Stephen Ansolabehere, Janos Beer, John Deutch, A. Denny Ellerman, S. Julio Friedmann, Howard Herzog, Henry D. Jacoby, Paul L. Joskow, Gregory McRae, Richard Lester, Ernest J. Moniz, and Edward Steinfeld, *The Future of Coal: Options for a Carbon-Constrained World: An MIT Interdisciplinary Study* (Cambridge, MA: Massachusetts Institute of Technology, 2007).

52. Ansolabehere et al., *Future of Coal*.

53. International Atomic Energy Agency (IAEA), *IAEA Safeguards Glossary: 2001 Edition* (Vienna: IAEA, 2002), 23.

54. Robert Serber, *The Los Alamos Primer* (Berkeley and Los Angeles: University of California Press, 1992).

55. Mujid Kazimi, Ernest J. Moniz, and Charles W. Forsberg, eds., *The Future of the Nuclear Fuel Cycle: An Interdisciplinary MIT Study* (Cambridge, MA: Massachusetts Institute of Technology, 2011).

56. Kazimi, Moniz, and Forsberg, *Future of the Nuclear Fuel Cycle*.

57. Kazimi, Moniz, and Forsberg, *Future of the Nuclear Fuel Cycle*; Blue Ribbon Commission on America's Nuclear Future, *Report to the Secretary of Energy* (Washington, DC: 2012).

58. John Deutch, Arnold Kanter, Ernest J. Moniz, and Daniel Poneman, "Making the World Safe for Nuclear Energy," *Survival* 46, no. 4 (Winter 2004–05): 65–80.

59. Blue Ribbon Commission on America's Nuclear Future, *Report to the Secretary of Energy*.

60. Blue Ribbon Commission on America's Nuclear Future, *Report to the Secretary of Energy*.

61. Kazimi, Moniz, and Forsberg, *Future of the Nuclear Fuel Cycle*.

62. Kazimi, Moniz, and Forsberg, *Future of the Nuclear Fuel Cycle*.

63. Nuclear Energy Study Group, "Nuclear Power and Proliferation Resistance: Securing Benefits, Limiting Risk," American Physical Society, Washington, DC, 2005.

64. Kazimi, Moniz, and Forsberg, *Future of the Nuclear Fuel Cycle*.

65. Kazimi, Moniz, and Forsberg, *Future of the Nuclear Fuel Cycle*.

66. Michael G. Frodl and John M. Manoyan, "Energy Security Starts with Hardening Power Grids," *National Defense*, November 2012.

67. National Intelligence Council, *Global Trends, 2030: Alternative Worlds* (Washington, DC: National Intelligence Council, 2012), xi, http://globaltrends2030.files .wordpress.com/2012/12/global-trends-2030-november2012.pdf.

68. FERC, "Staff Report on Gas–Electric Coordination Technical Conferences," Docket AD12-12-000, FERC, Washington, DC, November 15, 2012.

69. See the description of the Office of Energy Infrastructure Security on the FERC website at http://www.ferc.gov/about/offices/oeis.asp.

70. PCAST, "Report to the President on Accelerating the Pace of Change in Energy Technologies through an Integrated Federal Energy Policy," Executive Office of the President, Washington, DC, November 2010.

71. DOE, *Quadrennial Technology Review*.

Chapter 18

Electricity Access in Emerging Markets

Charles K. Ebinger and John P. Banks

Ensuring access to affordable energy for the world's population has been on the agenda of governments and other institutions worldwide since the oil price shocks of the 1970s staggered the world economy. Although the price spikes had a devastating impact on the macroeconomies of all nations, the skyrocketing costs of imported oil in developing countries had an especially destabilizing effect.[1] In India and Pakistan, farmers either could not obtain oil or had to pay staggeringly high prices to run their tube well irrigation pumps. In much of Asia and Africa, the oil price rise led to a surge in demand for fuelwood, forcing women and girls to spend many more hours a day searching for fuel far from their villages. At the same time, the demand for fuelwood led to accelerated deforestation and rising

The authors would like to thank Kartikeya Singh for his inputs, drawn from his recent work, "Equitable Energy Access and Climate Change: Opportunities for Innovation," Implementing Climate Pragmatism Framing Document 1, Consortium for Science, Policy, and Outcomes, Washington, DC, 2011.

emissions of greenhouse gases (GHGs), both from the greater use of fuel-wood and from the removal of large forests that had previously served as global carbon sinks. In the desert regions of the world, the destruction of already fragile vegetation for use as energy led to growing desertification and the first climate change refugees.[2]

Although these events increased the focus on energy in the world's poorest nations — reflected in the demand by the Group of 77 at the Conference on International Economic Cooperation held in Paris in 1977 for enhanced energy access — the world development community was slow to recognize the critical role that energy, in requisite volumes and at affordable prices, plays in all key development issues. Too often energy was viewed as a subsidiary issue to addressing a host of socioeconomic human development challenges, such as poverty eradication, improved health, higher crop yields, greater access to markets for goods and services, and female empowerment.

Access to electricity is particularly important for most measures of human development, economic modernization, and living standards.[3] Although there has been progress — the electrification rate in developing countries increased from 25 percent to 76 percent from 1970 to 2010 — an unacceptably high percentage of the developing world's population remains without access to power.[4]

Commencing in the late 1980s, global discussions on how to combat climate change complicated targeted action on energy poverty, as emerging market nations were in a very different position with regard to their past contributions to GHG emissions and their financial, institutional, and technological capacity to reduce emissions to adapt to climate change. This diverse reality from the position of the major industrial nations was recognized at the United Nations (UN) Conference on Environment and Development — the Earth Summit — in Rio de Janeiro in 1992. With the creation of Agenda 21 at the summit, the Conference of Parties noted not only the importance of technology transfer, financing, and human capacity building as critical for sustainable development in emerging market countries, but also the responsibility of the major industrial nations to assist them in addressing climate change.

The result, however, was that climate change — specifically the debate over the respective responsibilities and burdens between developed and developing countries in an international climate framework — became the policy focus. In addition, the issue of clean energy has moved to the top of the international agenda, although there has been no consensus on what constitutes clean energy. For example, is it limited to renewables such as wind, biomass, solar, run-of-the-river hydro, geothermal, energy efficiency, and conservation? Or does clean energy also include cleaner-burning natural gas, advanced and more thermally efficient coal, carbon capture and sequestration (CCS) for coal and gas, nuclear power, and large-scale hydro?

In short, energy poverty historically tended to be a second-tier policy priority—a component of achieving broader economic and development goals—or, throughout the 1990s and into the 2000s, was largely considered in a separate silo, playing second fiddle to climate change and the development of clean renewable energy resources. This second-tier position was starkly illustrated in the UN's failure to specify energy as one of the Millennium Development Goals (MDGs).[5]

In the past five years, another complicating factor has emerged: the global economic downturn. Although the investment needs of the world's poorest countries continue to rise, many of the world's wealthiest economies are in financial crisis, focusing on domestic challenges with little appetite—or capacity—to allocate resources to international efforts.

We have now reached a critical juncture for implementing solutions to address energy poverty and, specifically, to expand electricity access. The failure to meet this challenge will have drastic impacts on emerging market economies, efforts to eradicate poverty, and the stability of the global climate, all of which will affect US security interests. The United States will need to accelerate and coordinate its efforts across the government to focus on supporting nationally tailored and appropriate balances between conventional and clean energy; on sustaining technical assistance for policy, institutional, and governance reforms; and on expanding financial support and technology transfer.

Energy Poverty and Its Geopolitical Impact

Developing countries are assuming an increasingly important role in global energy: the International Energy Agency (IEA) projects that more than 90 percent of increased energy demand and carbon dioxide (CO_2) emissions growth between now and 2035 will be in nonmember countries of the Organization for Economic Cooperation and Development (OECD).[6] In addition, $23 trillion of investment is required in the energy supply infrastructure of these countries.[7]

Several core factors drive demand and investment needs in developing countries, including population growth, urbanization, an expanding middle class, and energy subsidies. Most important, however, is the fact that 1.3 billion people—or 20 percent of the world's population—have no access to electricity (see table 18.1). Despite expectations that more people will gain access in the coming decades, the total number without access remains close to 1 billion people in 2030. In Sub-Saharan Africa, the number actually increases 11 percent. Moreover, largely obscured in these data is the fact that, by some estimates, as many as 2 billion other people in the developing world have very limited access to electricity, perhaps one appliance and several light bulbs.[8]

This energy poverty has highly detrimental effects on quality of life. Per capita consumption of electricity is strongly correlated with a variety of human development indicators such as life expectancy, school enrollment, and availability of water (see figure 18.1). Access to electricity allows children to study at night, provides refrigeration and powers life-saving medicines, and creates opportunities for cottage industries that improve family income and generate employment.

Some countries struggle not only with a lack of basic access to electricity, but also with unreliable existing power supplies. Pakistan suffers from widespread power outages with devastating economic results: in a November 2012 assessment of the Pakistani economy, the International Monetary Fund noted that "A key structural impediment to growth is the problems in the energy sector, which have resulted in widespread and unpredictable power outages."[9]

Thus, emerging market countries are confronted with a daunting challenge: how to meet growing energy demand and expand electricity access to maintain economic growth, to raise income levels, and to create jobs while simultaneously addressing energy security concerns and mitigating environmental impacts. Failure to meet these multiple, complex energy development needs has a direct impact not only on economic growth and human development but also on political stability. The UN estimates that 47 percent of the population in developing countries is under the age of 24.[10] Failure to meet the rising expectations of these young people by providing jobs and a pathway to the middle class will sow growing dissatisfaction, potentially leading to increased political instability. Moreover, failure to mitigate the environmental consequences of energy use—especially use of fossil fuels—also can lead to civil discontent. A growing environmental activism in many developing countries that protests, for example, industrial

Table 18.1. Number of People without Access to Electricity by Region

Region	2010				2030			
	Rural	Urban	Total	Share of Population (%)	Rural	Urban	Total	Share of Population (%)
Developing countries	*1,081*	*184*	*1,265*	*24*	*879*	*112*	*991*	*15*
Africa	475	114	590	57	572	83	655	42
Sub-Saharan Africa	474	114	589	68	572	83	655	48
Developing Asia	566	62	628	18	305	29	334	8
China	4	0	4	0	0	0	0	0
India	271	21	293	25	144	8	153	10
Rest of developing Asia	291	40	331	31	161	20	181	14
Latin America	23	6	29	6	0	0	0	0
Middle East	16	2	18	9	0	0	0	0
World	*1,083*	*184*	*1,267*	*19*	*879*	*112*	*991*	*12*

Source: IEA, "Projections for the New Policies Scenario," in *World Energy Outlook 2012* (Paris: OECD/IEA, 2012), 535.

Figure 18.1. Energy Development Link to Human Development, 2011

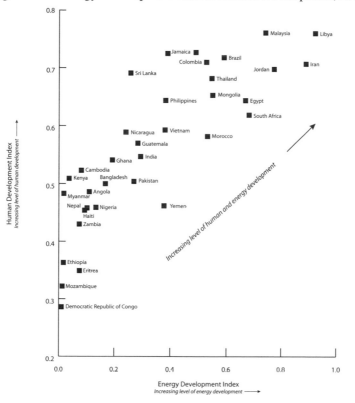

Sources: For Human Development Index data, United Nations Development Program, http://hdr
.undp.org/en/statistics/. For Energy Development Index data, http://www.worldenergyoutlook
.org/resources/energydevelopment/theenergydevelopmentindex.

Note: The Energy Development Index measures per capita commercial energy consumption, per
capita electricity consumption in the residential sector, share of modern fuels in total residential
sector energy use, and share of population with access to electricity.

growth, industrial accidents, and industrial pollution, has led to increased
public opposition in countries such as China.[11] Hu Jintao, the former president of China, declared in a speech, "We must be clearly aware that development is of overriding importance and stability is our overriding task. If
there is no stability, then nothing can be achieved, and what achievements
we have made will be lost."[12]

The energy challenges of emerging markets will play an increasingly important role in US foreign policy. Energy poverty and attendant anemic economic modernization are destabilizing and fuel the creation of failed states that pose a threat to US interests. Indeed, there is a direct correlation between political stability and electrification, as evidenced by the Failed States Index produced annually by *Foreign Policy* and the Fund for Peace. Figure 18.2 presents the 2012 index's ranking of the most vulnerable nations with their corresponding electrification rates, illustrating that the majority of the most vulnerable states in the world have electrification rates well below 50 percent.

Second, the inability to expand electricity access in a manner consistent with curtailing the adverse effects of energy use, especially GHG emissions, can accentuate political and social instability. The US national security establishment recognizes this threat. The 2008 US National Intelligence Estimate stated that global climate change "will worsen existing problems—such as poverty, social tensions, environmental degradation, ineffectual leadership, and weak political institutions."[13]

In 2010, the US Department of State conducted its first Quadrennial Development and Diplomacy Review, in which it recognized that addressing energy poverty was a critical component of overall energy policy.[14] The Department of State went on to assert that a new geopolitical reality is influencing US foreign policy: "Emerging powers and 21st-century centers of global and regional influence, including Brazil, China, India, Indonesia, Mexico, Nigeria, Russia, South Africa, and Turkey, define today's geopolitical landscape."[15]

Burgeoning demand for energy in less developed countries, especially in Asia, could pose a challenge to the United States. As large emerging markets in this region turn to imports to meet their rising thirst for fuel, competition will increase for resources and for more transport of fuels through strategic chokepoints. For example, 20 percent of the world's liquefied natural gas (LNG) trade is shipped through the Strait of Hormuz, and all of Qatar's LNG exports—the world's largest—pass through the strait destined for Asian markets.[16] US military strategy may need to be altered to reflect this changing dynamic, especially if other countries, such as China and India, move to deploy their own military assets to protect import sources and routes.

Energy- and climate-related issues in the developing world also are having a direct impact on US trade policy. For example, the rise of China as a competitor in solar technologies has led the US Department of Commerce

Figure 18.2. Failed States and Electrification Rates, 2009

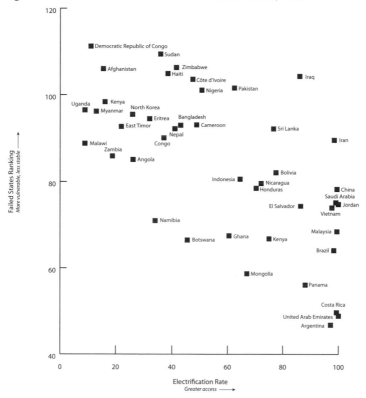

Sources: Electrification rates as of 2009 from the IEA database in *World Energy Outlook 2011* (Paris: OECD/IEA, 2011), http://www.worldenergyoutlook.org/resources/energydevelopment /accesstoelectricity/. Failed States Index as of 2012 from *Foreign Policy* and the Fund for Peace.

Note: The Failed States Index is produced annually by *Foreign Policy* and the Fund for Peace. The higher the numerical ranking, the more at risk a country is. Countries with rankings above 90 are considered at very high risk. The data reflect the following categories: demographic pressures, movement of refugees or internally displaced persons, vengeance-seeking group grievance, chronic and sustained human flight, uneven economic development, poverty, sharp or severe economic decline, legitimacy of the state, progressive deterioration of public services, violation of human rights and law, security apparatus, rise of factionalized elites, and intervention of external actors. For more information on the Failed States Index, see http://www.fundforpeace.org/ global/?q=fsi-grid2011.

to investigate China's alleged illegal trade practices, including the dumping of cheap solar products in the US market. This investigation led to an October 2102 decision to levy tariffs on solar products imported from China.[17] As more emerging market countries develop clean technologies to meet their energy and development needs, similar trade disputes will likely occur.

Finally, US climate diplomacy is critically linked to the situation in emerging markets. Crafting a post-Kyoto global climate framework is vital to ensure not only that developing countries are bound by emission reduction targets, but also that those countries have viable, scalable pathways to meet their electricity needs and are supported by bilateral and international efforts to provide technology transfer and financing mechanisms. Domestic policy, both in the United States and in host government nations, is also a critical component in this process. As Todd Stern, chief climate negotiator for the United States, has stated, "the real key to bringing down emissions is national action. And the action that is at the heart of the matter is the transformation of the energy base of our economies."[18]

Key Energy Trends and Issues in Emerging Markets

Several important trends and issues will have a major effect on addressing the energy and development needs of emerging market countries in the coming decades. However, because the prospects for specific regions and fuels are addressed in detail elsewhere in this volume, the following discussion highlights the interrelationships of selected policy choices related to expanding electricity access.

Nuclear Energy

The challenges of meeting electricity demand, reducing energy imports, promoting economic growth, and lowering CO_2 emissions have prompted many emerging market countries to consider nuclear energy. As a result, most new nuclear capacity in the coming decades will be added in developing countries. Of nuclear reactors currently under construction worldwide, 69 percent are in China, India, and Russia (China alone accounts for 40 percent of the global total).[19] The United Arab Emirates (UAE) has broken ground on the construction of its first units, and Turkey, Jordan, and Vietnam are also well along in their plans to introduce nuclear power. A handful of other countries are exploring the nuclear option.

Nevertheless, the substantial financial requirements, small grid size, long-term commitment required, lack of human resource capacity, underdeveloped safety and nonproliferation culture, inadequate or absent stakeholder engagement, and other factors effectively limit the number of countries that can realistically pursue atomic energy. However, if small modular reactors (SMRs) can be developed that are both technically and commercially viable, some of these challenges can be addressed.[20]

Oil and Natural Gas

A number of developing countries are poised to become oil and natural gas producers or to expand production significantly.[21] These resources can provide income that can be used for pressing social and development needs in health, education, and infrastructure, as well as to help expand energy access. In particular, natural gas will play a much larger role in the power sector of emerging market countries in the coming decades.

Nonetheless, the development and use of oil and gas—either for domestic consumption or export—face considerable obstacles. The appropriate legal and regulatory frameworks governing resource extraction, foreign investment, and operations need to be established; adequate and sustainable indigenous human resource capacity needs to be developed; and the supporting infrastructure, including drilling rigs, pipelines, storage facilities, ports, and, in some cases, LNG facilities, needs to be built. In the case of those developing countries with potential shale gas resources,[22] the lack of the requisite expertise in hydraulic fracturing and horizontal drilling,[23] absent or embryonic regulatory frameworks to support large-scale shale gas exploration, and inadequate infrastructure and access to water resources will slow development.

Shale gas production in the United States has the potential to have a dramatic influence on the electricity sector in the developing world. With booming shale gas production in the United States severely limiting the domestic market for coal-fired generation, coal exports are at record levels in 2012, including emerging market countries such as Brazil, China, and India.[24] In addition, large volumes of US shale gas production have spurred interest in developing US exports of LNG to some of those same markets.

For the oil and gas producing states in the Arabian Gulf, population and economic expansion, along with highly subsidized electricity prices, is driving double-digit electricity demand growth rates. As more and more domestic oil and gas production is used to generate electricity, the hydrocarbons available for export are plummeting, along with revenues from export sales.[25] Rather than end subsidies, some Gulf states, such as Saudi Arabia and the UAE, are looking to other electricity supply options—including renewable energy or nuclear power plants—to free up oil and gas for export.

Finally, oil importing developing economies often use more oil in electricity generation than do OECD nations. For example, in the Middle East, oil accounts for 40 percent of power generation, and in Africa, 12 percent of power generation is fueled by oil.[26] The IEA estimates that for all end uses, the oil import bill for less developed countries has increased from about $20 billion in 2000 to $100 billion in 2010, accounting for 5.5 percent of their gross domestic product.[27]

Coal

The IEA projects that the increase in coal demand for power generation in non-OECD countries will be "three times greater than the corresponding decline in demand in the OECD."[28] With abundant coal resources, China, India, Indonesia, Kazakhstan, Mongolia, Pakistan, South Africa, Turkey, and Vietnam all rely on coal for a substantial portion of their growing power generation requirements. Another recent analysis suggests that, although China and India account for 76 percent of proposed new coal-fired power plants globally, 10 other developing countries are planning to build new plants (Cambodia, Dominican Republic, Guatemala, Laos, Morocco, Namibia, Oman, Senegal, Sri Lanka, and Uzbekistan).[29]

With coal resources viewed as a way to combat poverty and expand access—as well as protect the tens of thousands of workers in the coal industry of some poorer nations—it is incumbent on governments not only to look at alternatives to fossil fuels, but also to find cleaner ways to burn coal that are both technically and commercially viable. Finding mechanisms to support innovation, financing, and technology transfer of supercritical and ultrasupercritical combustion technology, CCS techniques, and coal gasification approaches is vital. As one analyst recently stated, "no matter what one thinks about coal, this much is clear: cleaning it up has to be a central part of any climate strategy."[30]

Institutional Reforms

A variety of institutional reforms (legal, regulatory, and governance) is crit-ical for developing countries if they are to expand energy access. The case of India provides a telling example. Although the blackout in northern India in August 2012, which left 600 million people without power, was blamed initially on technical and operational issues, longstanding institutional ob-stacles (bureaucratic red tape, arcane land acquisition processes, an overly complex regulatory system, coal transportation bottlenecks, corruption in coal leasing, inadequate upstream coal pricing, and heavily regulated re-tail electricity rates) played a much larger role.[31] Expanding grid access in emerging market countries requires a policy framework that is conducive to private sector participation and that includes the implementation of an effective, independent regulatory regime; cost recovery in the tariff sys-tem; transparent subsidy regimes; and mechanisms for funding noncom-mercial grid expansion into lower-income rural areas. The development of smaller-scale minigrids or microgrids in rural areas using distributed generation represents a major opportunity for areas where expansion of the national grid is prohibitively expensive and commercially unviable.

Financing

For universal energy access, an estimated $35 billion to $50 billion per year will be needed between now and 2030, a daunting challenge considering that in 2009 total expenditures were $9.1 billion.[32] However, low-income energy consumers in emerging market countries spend nearly $37 billion annually on inefficient sources of energy such as candles, matches, and batteries, owing to the lack of more efficient, modern energy sources. [33] The scale of the challenge is demonstrated by the IEA's 2011 Energy for All scenario, which estimated that by 2030 an additional 220 gigawatts of power generation capacity will be required to meet the world's expanding energy needs, with 45 percent "generated and delivered" through national grid extensions, 36 percent in minigrid development, and 20 percent in off-grid solutions. Most of the on-grid capacity is projected to be fired by fossil fuels (often coal), whereas the minigrid and off-grid capacity will be predominantly renewable sources of power. Each pathway has different financial, institutional, technical, and market challenges that need to be addressed.

Clean Energy Technology Investment

Many developing and middle-income countries are setting priorities for alternatives to fossil fuels by implementing policies to support using renewable resources in power generation. These policies—including clean energy tax incentives, feed-in tariffs, renewable energy standards, government procurement policies, development of carbon markets, and issuance of green energy bonds—are spurring greater deployment of clean energy technologies. From 2006 to 2011, China, India, Brazil, Argentina, and South Korea experienced growth rates in renewable energy capacity above 40 percent. Over the next decade, the Pew Charitable Trusts projects annual investment growth rates in clean energy of 10 to 18 percent in Asia, Africa, the Middle East, and Latin America.[34]

Water and Energy Nexus

The link between water and energy is an area of growing concern. The US Office of the Director of National Intelligence has stressed the importance of water in the coming decades, stating:

> We assess that from now through 2040 water shortages and pollution probably will harm the economic performance of important trading partners. Economic output will suffer if countries do not have sufficient clean water supplies to generate electrical power or to maintain and expand manufacturing and resource extraction.[35]

The water–energy nexus is especially critical for policy-makers in developing countries. Water scarcity is prevalent in many regions, with Sub-Saharan Africa and the Middle East accounting for the largest share.[36] Thermal sources of power generation use large quantities of water for cooling. Consequently, capacity additions of gas- or coal-fired power generation, as well as nuclear reactors, will require water for cooling. Water is also required for energy production, including the production of coal and shale gas. These energy-related water needs will need to be assessed in light of other requirements for drinking water and agriculture.

Furthermore, many countries, especially in the Middle East, will require greater desalination capacity to produce fresh water for drinking supplies. This increased desalination will require a large, reliable power supply. As a result, Saudi Arabia and the UAE have identified nuclear energy as an option in their power portfolios in part to address rising desalination needs.

Energy Access and the Global Community: A New Sense of Urgency

The past five years have seen an increased focus on energy poverty and electricity access as a top-tier policy issue. In 2009, the World Health Organization (WHO) and the United Nations Development Program (UNDP) issued a report in response to the growing realization that without massive increases in the quantity and quality of global energy services, the MDGs were unlikely to be achieved. The WHO and UNDP report represented a clarion call to the world community that progress in expanding energy access had been painfully slow and that "[p]olicies and national programmes must be drastically enhanced to tackle in a significant way energy poverty."[37] The report stated that this progress could not be done without a clear understanding of energy access, regional and national trends, rural and urban disparities, and the range of energy sources typically used in the households of the poor.[38] The IEA, which has been addressing energy poverty in its annual *World Energy Outlook* since 2002, joined the UNDP and the United Nations Industrial Development Organization in 2010 in declaring that "the UN Millennium Development Goal of eradicating extreme poverty by 2015 will not be achieved unless substantial progress is made on improving energy access."[39]

Energy for a Sustainable Future

The coalescing of these organizations and others around the urgency and importance of elevating energy poverty as a policy priority served as a catalyst for UN Secretary-General Ban Ki-moon to form the Advisory Group on Energy and Climate Change in 2009. The group is designed "to address the dual challenges of meeting the world's energy needs for development while contributing to a reduction in GHGs."[40] In 2012, Ban launched an initiative called Sustainable Energy for All (SEFA) with three main objectives: ensuring universal access to modern energy services, doubling the global rate of improvement in energy efficiency, and doubling the share of renewable energy in the global energy mix—all by 2030.[41]

By mid-2012, $320 billion in commitments had been pledged to the three SEFA objectives from more than 50 countries, but only 10 percent was to meet the universal access goal.[42] However, the IEA's Energy for All case estimates that nearly $1 trillion is required by 2030 for the access goal alone, $602 billion for universal electricity access, and $76 billion for universal access to clean cooking facilities.[43]

At the Rio+20 summit in June 2012, SEFA was prominently discussed. Perhaps the most important surprise was the willingness of world business leaders to urge political leaders to move forward with the initiative and not wait for a consensus on a global climate treaty.[44] With financial returns on investments in the developed world near historically low levels, business leaders see energy growth in the emerging markets as an opportunity for double-digit returns and are eager to help create the institutional environment that will allow business to flourish. Despite the high-level attention paid to energy poverty issues at Rio+20, no binding commitments were reached, although leaders agreed to develop sustainable development goals to build on the MDGs after 2015.

Energy Access and US Foreign Policy: A New Direction Under Way

For the United States, energy policy, national security, development assistance, the domestic economy and trade, and the global climate framework are becoming inextricably linked. It is imperative that the United States has a comprehensive, integrated energy–climate approach that not just incorporates but also prioritizes the eradication of energy poverty—specifically the expansion of electricity and broader energy access in the world's poorest countries.

Although skeptics argue that in an era of fiscal austerity we would do better spending the money at home or, at a global level, dedicating our resources to reducing world hunger, eradicating deadly diseases, or addressing other serious challenges, such views are short-sighted, albeit understandable. Access to electricity is the foundation for improving health, living standards, and economic opportunity in developing countries. Without this underpinning, we have a heightened risk of more failed states with impoverished, alienated populations that can accentuate the spread of global instability and environmental degradation. Building this foundation, therefore, is squarely in the US national interest.

Several critical actions are required. First, addressing energy poverty and expanding electricity access needs to be elevated to a top-tier policy priority, thereby occupying a critical place in overall US foreign policy in general and in energy, climate, and development policy specifically. The Obama administration has taken important steps in this direction at the highest levels. "Energy cuts across the entirety of US foreign policy," said Secretary of State Hillary Clinton in October 2012. "It's a matter of national security and global stability. It's at the heart of the global economy. It's also an issue of democracy and human rights."[45] To make this policy focus operational, the US Department of State created the Bureau of Energy Resources to address the three pillars of energy strategy: energy diplomacy, energy transformation, and energy poverty.[46]

Second, most analyses indicate that the level of financial support required to provide electricity to everyone in the developing world must increase dramatically. As noted, all sources must increase their contribution, but it is particularly incumbent on the world's wealthiest economies to do more. Given its wide-ranging interests at stake, the United States should lead in providing financial assistance in this endeavor, and in recent years, the Obama administration has launched several programs and has allocated funding, including support for the SEFA initiative.[47] In addition, the United States was instrumental in forming the Clean Energy Ministerial, a global forum that marshals the resources of the world's major economies at the highest levels to focus on three goals: improve energy efficiency worldwide, enhance clean energy supply, and expand clean energy access.[48]

Third, emerging market countries need more than money. A broad array of institutional, regulatory, and governance preconditions must be in place to support the expansion of electricity access. The United States should increase its support for reforms in this area, and, indeed, Secretary Clinton highlighted good governance as a cornerstone of addressing energy poverty.[49] But new leadership in emerging market countries must be committed to ending corruption and to making serious institutional and regulatory changes. The commitment must include phasing out subsidies to encourage energy efficiency and, above all, strengthening the rule of law, which is so vital to attracting private sector investments.

Fourth, decentralized power solutions need to play a vital role in providing electricity in developing countries, especially throughout much of Sub-Saharan Africa and South Asia, where rural electrification rates are well below the global average. Although scaling up the deployment of minigrid and off-grid systems—mostly based on renewable technologies such as solar, biomass, minihydro, and others—faces many regulatory, institutional, and financial barriers, policies and business models are emerging to address them.[50] In the area of financing, for example, promising innovative approaches are being implemented in microfinancing, microleasing, "pay-go" payment systems, and mobile banking.[51]

Fifth, US policy should recognize that, in addition to assisting developing countries with the deployment of clean energy technologies, we must support the efforts of those countries with large fossil fuel or hydro resources to develop and use them in the most environmentally benign manner possible. In particular, financing and collaborative efforts will be required to develop and to transfer more efficient coal combustion technologies such as ultrasupercritical systems as well as CCS for both coal- and gas-fired power plants. As noted by the IEA, a large amount of on-grid fossil fuel capacity will be required in the coming decades.[52] The United States should work to ensure that this capacity is deployed in the cleanest manner possible. Examples of such efforts include the US Department of State's Unconventional Gas Technical Engagement Program, with China, India, Jordan, and Poland participating, and the US Department of Energy's Fossil Energy Protocol between the United States and China.

Many in the development and energy communities oppose taking advantage of domestic fossil fuel resources in developing countries, arguing that it runs counter to environmental objectives, even though some countries may have no viable short-term alternatives. This view illustrates the different objectives and agendas of the climate and development communities: "There has been a tendency to exclude some energy mixes and technology options on the basis of carbon emissions and their impact on climate change, promoted mainly by those who are unaware that providing access to energy for the poor would entail a low level of emissions."[53] For example, the IEA states that achieving its Energy for All scenario would increase CO_2 emissions by 0.6 percent in 2030.[54]

Another critique is that the use of fossil fuels runs the risk of the "resource curse," in which the wealth generated by oil, gas, and coal investment can hinder economic development and thus does not benefit the poor. Whereas extreme poverty certainly persists in some countries blessed with natural resources, emerging evidence suggests that there is no "significant deterministic evidence of a direct negative relationship between the abundance of natural resources and income per capita levels," but rather "intangible wealth in the form of governance quality is a key determinant to the outcome of natural resource abundance as a blessing or a curse."[55] This finding confirms the view that supporting policy, institutional, and governance reforms is a critical component of any effort to use these domestic resources in the pursuit of alleviating energy poverty.[56]

US policy is on the right track, but more needs to be done in the areas highlighted in this chapter through a more "whole of government" approach. In particular, a focus on fiscal austerity and the boom in US domestic hydrocarbons cannot be allowed to shift the progress of US policy away from the objectives of eliminating energy poverty and expanding electricity access. Failure to maintain this momentum will mean the emergence of more failed states posing grave challenges to the global community and the United States.

Notes

1. Many terms are used to refer to the countries we examine here. Some are specific, formal definitions used by international organizations. The World Bank uses designations that are based on income level: low-income, lower-middle-income, and upper-middle-income countries (http://data.worldbank.org/about/country-classifications/country-and-lending-groups#Upper_middle_income). The United Nations has a category called Least Developed Countries (http://www.unohrlls.org/en/ldc/25/). The International Energy Agency (IEA) refers to the Organization of Economic Cooperation and Development (OECD) and non-OECD countries to describe those countries that are or are not members of OECD, a group of more advanced industrial economies created in 1961 to foster economic growth. In this chapter, we use the terms *emerging market countries* and *developing countries*, consistent with the IEA's use of the term *non-OECD countries*. Note that the IEA treats Eastern Europe and Eurasia as a separate grouping. For regional groupings see IEA, *World Energy Outlook 2012* (Paris: OECD/IEA, 2012), 649.

2. See Independent Commission on International Development Issues, *North–South: A Program for Survival* (Cambridge, MA: MIT Press, 1980), 160–71. See also World Commission on Environment and Development, *Our Common Future* (Oxford, UK: Oxford University Press, 1987).

3. The term *energy poverty* refers to the lack of access to affordable, modern forms of commercial energy for a variety of activities. *Energy access* refers to access to a broad range of commercial energy sources, such as electricity for lighting and other uses and liquefied petroleum gas, kerosene, and other fuels for cooking and heating. *Electricity access* refers specifically to access to power, whether from a centralized grid or off-grid and minigrid sources. In this chapter, we focus on electricity access, given its importance for a wide range of economic activities, including basic services for improving standards of living, and its central role in climate change. This emphasis is not meant to diminish the importance of other energy sources and uses. Indeed, seminal work has been done recently by several institutions (most notably the United Nations, the IEA, and the World Health Organization) that highlights not only the vital goal of improving access to fuels and technologies for cooking and heating but also the severe health impacts of continued use of traditional fuels in these activities.

4. IEA, *World Energy Outlook 2012*, 535.

5. World leaders agreed to the MDGs at the United Nations in 2000 to focus the international community's efforts on eradicating extreme poverty by 2015. The eight specific goals are (a) ending of poverty and hunger, (b) universal education, (c) gender equality, (d) child health, (e) maternal health, (f) combating of HIV/AIDs, (g) environmental sustainability, and (h) global partnership. The only mention of energy is under environmental sustainability, which calls for targets on carbon dioxide emissions (total, per capita, and per $1 gross domestic product purchasing power parity). The rest of the issues under this goal are related to making sustainable development policies, providing access to safe drinking water, preventing biodiversity loss, and improving the lives of slum dwellers. For more information about the MDGs, see the UN's website at http://www.un.org/millenniumgoals/.

6. See IEA, *World Energy Outlook 2012*. These estimates are based on the IEA's New Policies scenario. This growth predominantly will be in the power and transport sectors and will rely heavily on coal, gas, and oil. Consequently, the IEA expects global energy-related CO_2 emissions to increase 23 percent by 2035, with non-OECD countries accounting for nearly all of this growth.

7. See IEA, *World Energy Outlook 2012*, 74. Non-OECD countries account for 64 percent of all global investment requirements in energy supply infrastructure and 59 percent of all power supply requirements.

8. Coal Industry Advisory Board, "The Global Value of Coal," IEA, Paris, 2012, http://www.iea.org/publications/insights/name,15212,en.html.

9. International Monetary Fund, "IMF Executive Board Concludes First Post-Program Monitoring Discussions and the Ex-Post Evaluation of Exceptional Access under the 2008 Stand-By Arrangement with Pakistan," Public Information Notice 12/135, International Monetary Fund, Washington, DC, November 29, 2012.

10. United Nations, *World Population Prospects: The 2010 Revision* (New York: United Nations), http://esa.un.org/unpd/wpp/.

11. Keith Bradsher, "Saying No to Growth in China," *New York Times,* November 7, 2012.

12. Hu Jintao, address to a meeting commemorating the 90th anniversary of the founding of the Communist Party of China, July 1, 2011.

13. Thomas Fingar, "National Intelligence Assessment on the National Security Implications of Global Climate Change to 2030," statement of the deputy director of National Intelligence for Analysis and chair of the National Intelligence Council before the House Permanent Select Committee on Intelligence, House Select Committee on Energy Independence and Global Warming, June 25, 2008.

14. US Department of State, *Leading through Civilian Power: The First Quadrennial Diplomacy and Development Review* (Washington, DC: US Department of State, 2010), http://www.state.gov/s/dmr/qddr/.

15. US Department of State, *Leading through Civilian Power*, 13.

16. Javier Blas, "Corridor of Power," *Financial Times*, October 5, 2012.

17. John McArdle, "US Commerce Department Levies Stiff Tariffs on China's Solar Panel Imports," *ClimateWire*, October 11, 2012.

18. Todd Stern, address to Dartmouth College, Hanover, NH, August 2, 2012.

19. These figures are based on data in the Power Reactor Information System of the International Atomic Energy Agency, http://www.iaea.org/PRIS/WorldStatistics /UnderConstructionReactorsByCountry.aspx. Moreover, some nuclear plans are very

ambitious, with China targeting 40 gigawatts (GW) of nuclear capacity by 2015, up from 10.8 GW today, whereas India, with 4,400 megawatts (MW) of installed capacity, plans to have 63,000 MW by 2032.

20. *Small modular reactors* are generally defined as those with a capacity up to 300 MW. SMRs offer some advantages for emerging market countries: lower construction costs and cost savings from modular assembly, suitability for smaller electricity grids, and application for nonelectricity needs such as desalination. However, there are also challenges related to deployment in developing countries: some estimates suggest the overall costs may be higher per kilowatt-hour than much larger conventional nuclear plants. Given that SMR deployment may involve more sites that are more widely dispersed, how spent fuel will be handled needs to be addressed, including cost, environmental protection, and local acceptance. In addition, the risk of nuclear proliferation is a concern in some countries, given the possibility of smaller, remotely located facilities.

21. For example, French Guiana, Ghana, Kenya, Tanzania, and Uganda have recently discovered commercially recoverable resources of oil, and existing producers Brazil, Iraq, Kazakhstan, and Vietnam are expected to increase production substantially. In the past several years, large discoveries of natural gas have been made offshore in Mozambique and Tanzania. In addition, commercial gas discoveries in the Eastern Mediterranean offshore of Israel and Cyprus provide a potential source for domestic consumption, as well as for consumption in neighboring economies in desperate need of fuel for power generation (e.g., Egypt, Jordan, Lebanon, and the West Bank and Gaza).

22. A recent US government study of world shale gas raised estimates of technically recoverable resources by 40 percent, with several emerging market countries identified as having large shale gas reserves, including Argentina, Brazil, Algeria, Libya, South Africa, and China.

23. A number of emerging market countries, especially China and India, have invested in North American plays to gain the requisite experience. For an example of a recent investment, see "Indian Oil Companies Buy Joint Stake in Niobrara Shale Holdings," *EnergyWire,* October 5, 2012.

24 According to the US Energy Information Administration, coal exports are on pace in 2012 to increase 24 percent over the previous year. In May through June 2012, US coal exports to Brazil, China, and India accounted for 21 percent of total exports. See US Energy Information Administration, "US Coal Exports on Record Pace in 2012, Fueled by Steam Coal Growth," *Today in Energy* (blog), October 23, 2012, http://www .eia.gov/todayinenergy/detail.cfm?id=8490.

25. See J. Robinson West and Raad Alkadiri, "Iraq, Iran, and the Gulf Region," chapter 10 of this volume, for a discussion of the dilemma confronted by the Gulf producers. Reduced export revenues hinder the ability of governments to meet their budget requirements, including expenditures to curtail civil unrest such as witnessed during the Arab Uprising.

26. The global average is about 5 percent, and in OECD countries it is 3 percent. See IEA data for 2009 at http://www.iea.org/stats/.

27. See IEA, "Energy for All: Financing Access for the Poor," OECD/IEA, Paris, 2011, 8. The calculation is in 2010 US dollars. The IEA states that this group of countries "includes India and the oil-importing countries within the United Nations classification of least developed countries (available at www.unohrlls.org). This group has a

combined population of 1.8 billion people and accounts for 65 percent of those lacking access to modern energy."

28. IEA, *World Energy Outlook 2011* (Paris: OECD/IEA, 2011), 85.

29. Ailun Yang and Yiyun Cui, "Global Coal Risk Assessment: Data Analysis and Market Research," Working Paper, World Resources Institute, Washington, DC, November 2012.

30. Richard K. Morse, "Cleaning Up Coal," *Foreign Affairs* 91, no. 4 (2012): 102–13, 112.

31. Charles K. Ebinger and Govinda Avasarala, "Emerging Power Crisis," *Foreign Policy*, August 1, 2012, http://www.foreignpolicy.com/articles/2012/08/01/emerging_power_crisis.

32. See United Nations, "Energy for a Sustainable Future: The Secretary-General's Advisory Group on Energy and Climate Change," United Nations, New York, April 28, 2010, and IEA, "Energy for All." The $9.1 billion figure is from the IEA report.

33. International Finance Corporation, *From Gap to Opportunity: Business Models for Scaling Up Energy Access* (Washington, DC: International Finance Corporation, 2012), 12.

34. Pew Charitable Trusts, "Who's Winning the Clean Energy Race, 2012" Pew Charitable Trusts, Washington, DC, 2013, 7.

35. Defense Intelligence Agency, "Global Water Security," Intelligence Community Assessment 2012-08, Defense Intelligence Agency, Washington, DC, 2012, iv, http://www.transboundarywaters.orst.edu/publications/publications/ICA_Global%20Water%20Security%5B1%5D%20%281%29.pdf.

36. The United Nations Department of Economic and Social Affairs states, "Water scarcity is defined as the point at which the aggregate impact of all users impinges on the supply or quality of water under prevailing institutional arrangements to the extent that the demand by all sectors, including the environment, cannot be satisfied fully." See United Nations Department of Economic and Social Affairs, "Water Scarcity," http://www.un.org/waterforlifedecade/scarcity.shtml.

37. WHO and UNDP, *The Energy Access Situation in Developing Countries: A Review Focusing on the Least Developed Countries and Sub-Saharan Africa* (New York: UNDP and WHO, 2009), i.

38. The report was sobering in its major findings, especially beyond electricity access: modern fuels and improved cook stoves to meet basic cooking needs are out of the reach of the majority of people living in developing countries, especially in rural areas; 56 percent of the people in developing countries rely primarily on fossil fuels (i.e., coal and traditional biomass with little or no access to modern forms of energy); only 27 percent of those who use solid fuels, nearly 800 million people, have modern cook stoves; almost 2 million people die each year from diseases caused by indoor cooking using biomass and coal; and emissions from burning open fires make significant contributions to GHG emissions of CO_2. See WHO and UNDP, *Energy Access Situation in Developing Countries*.

39. UNDP, United Nations Industrial Development Organization, and IEA, "Energy Poverty: How to Make Modern Energy Access Universal?," OECD/IEA, Paris, September 2010, 7.

40. United Nations, "The Secretary-General's Advisory Group on Energy and Climate Change: Summary Report and Recommendations," United Nations, New York, April 28, 2010, 7.

41. For more information about SEFA, see the initiative's website at http://sustainableenergyforall.org/.

42. IEA, *World Energy Outlook 2012*, 531.

43. The IEA defines *access to electricity* to involve "more than a first supply connection to the household; our definition of access also involves consumption of a specified minimum level of electricity, the amount [of which] varies based on whether the household is in a rural or an urban area. The initial threshold level of electricity consumption for rural households is assumed to be 250 kilowatt-hours (kWh) per year and for urban households it is 500 kWh per year.... [T]he average level of electricity consumption per capita across all those households newly connected over the period is 800 kWh in 2030." See IEA, "Energy for All," 12.

44. The United Nations Conference on Sustainable Development took place in Rio de Janeiro, Brazil, on June 20–22, 2012. Referred to as "Rio+20" to mark the 20th anniversary of the 1992 United Nations Conference on Environment and Development, the conference focused on two themes: (a) a green economy in the context of sustainable development poverty eradication and (b) the institutional framework for sustainable development. See the conference's website at http://www.uncsd2012.org/about.html.

45. Hillary Rodham Clinton, "Energy Diplomacy in the 21st Century," address to Georgetown University, Washington, DC, October 18, 2012, http://www.state.gov/secretary/rm/2012/10/199330.htm.

46. Clinton, "Energy Diplomacy in the 21st Century."

47. Specifics of US support are provided on the Department of State's website at http://www.state.gov/r/pa/prs/ps/2012/06/193500.htm.

48. More information can be found on the Clean Energy Ministerial's website at http://www.cleanenergyministerial.org/about/.

49. Clinton, "Energy Diplomacy in the 21st Century."

50. International Finance Corporation, *From Gap to Opportunity*.

51. For a description of these and other mechanisms along with real-world examples, see the website of Arc Finance at http://arcfinance.org/.

52. See IEA, "Energy for All," 26.

53. See Practical Action, "Energy Poverty: The Hidden Energy Crisis," Schumacher Centre for Technology and Development, Rugby, UK, 2009, 5, http://practicalaction.org/docs/advocacy/energy_poverty_hidden_crisis.pdf. Thanks to Kartikeya Singh for clearly outlining this view and the following point.

54. IEA, *World Energy Outlook 2012*, 529.

55. Otaviano Canuto and Matheus Cavallari, "Natural Capital and the Resource Curse," Economic Premise Note 83, World Bank, Washington, DC, May 2012, 5.

56. Combating corruption is also part of this effort, and the US government has moved to join the Extractive Industries Transparency Initiative, a global standard that advances the transparency of payments from natural resources. For more information, see the initiative's website at http://eiti.org/.

Chapter 19

Governance, Transparency, and Sustainable Development

Charles McPherson

Issues of governance, transparency, and sustainable development are central to foreign policy engagement with petroleum-rich developing countries and emerging economies.

Together these countries hold 94 percent of the world's oil reserves and account for 88 percent of the world's exports of oil. They also account for 96 percent of world reserves of natural gas and, excluding Canada–US trade, close to 70 percent of the world's export trade in natural gas.[1] Resource wealth on this scale inevitably attracts foreign policy attention out of concern for supply access, investment opportunities, and global market stability.

Dependable access to oil and gas supplies has been critical to all major petroleum consumers as well as their close partners. This concern over access has increased these countries' diplomatic presence in the developing petroleum producers and has led to substantial investments. Investments are typically made through countries' national oil companies (NOCs), often in competition with US investors but under different standards of

444

conduct, which may crowd out US companies. Or such investments may simply take the place of US investment in countries ruled off limits either by US foreign policy or by the policies of the host countries themselves.

In addition to supply access and investment issues, the dominant position of developing and emerging economies in oil and gas trade underscores their relevance to energy market stability. Supply disruptions on the part of the major producers, whether deliberate or the result of internal conflicts, could have a major impact on market and price volatility and on global economic performance.

Other outcomes in oil-rich developing countries present different but equal challenges to US foreign policy objectives in the areas of growth, human development and human rights, political and social stability, prevention of violent conflict and containment of terrorism, democratization, freedom of speech, public–private sector balance, and market-oriented economics.

Looked-for positive results in each of these areas have proved elusive. Most oil-rich developing countries have records of serious economic and social underperformance and have experienced significant social and political unrest and often violent conflict. Ironically, failures can, in good part, be traced to the resource endowment itself.

Successfully addressing this "paradox of plenty"[2] will depend on reforms across the entire petroleum sector value chain, from policy articulation, through best practice legislation and institutional and fiscal design, to decisions on the saving and expenditure of sector revenues and the mitigation of adverse environmental and social impacts. Progress under those headings will be determined in good part by the political context. Restoring good governance and introducing transparency, both too often undermined by oil wealth, will be critical to the reform process.

Fortunately, the governance and economic dimensions and even the political economy of the paradox are now reasonably well understood, and a consensus is emerging on appropriate responses. When it comes to helping countries that are dependent on oil revenues to follow paths of sustainable development, the fundamental issue is political will. Although exercising that will must primarily be the responsibility of the local government, responsibility must be shared by all stakeholders—the governments of major petroleum-importing countries, the home countries of global oil and gas investors, industry, civil society, and international financial institutions and organizations. Given the close fit of issues in most oil-rich developing countries with US foreign policy concerns, it would seem entirely correct that they be prominently featured in any new foreign policy strategy.

Are Oil Wealth and Sustainable Development Compatible?

Whether petroleum resources are translated into sustainable development depends on the management or mismanagement of sums of money that can be enormous, in both absolute and relative terms. Figures for a selection of non–Middle Eastern countries suggest the potential for good and the room for abuse: at $100 per barrel of crude oil, annual oil rents accruing to Mexico are estimated at $100 billion; to Venezuela, $90 billion; and to Nigeria, $60 billion.[3]

Given sums like those, it is not surprising to find that dependence on oil and gas in many petroleum-producing states, particularly in the developing world, is high. For example, oil accounts for 40 percent of Nigeria's gross domestic product (GDP), 90 percent of its government revenues, and 95 percent of its foreign exchange earnings. The respective numbers for Venezuela are similar: 30, 55, and 70 percent. Even a country such as Mexico, which in recent years has succeeded in diluting its dependence on oil in GDP and export terms, still depends on oil for more than 30 percent of its government revenues.[4]

Given their scale and relative significance, it seems reasonable to expect oil and gas revenues to be major drivers of development in the countries concerned. Unfortunately, positive results are hard to find.

During the past decade, a growing body of research has documented the underperformance of resource-abundant developing countries relative to resource-deficient developing countries. One of these studies shows that between 1960 and 1990, countries that were resource poor, whether large or small, significantly outperformed resource-rich countries in terms of per capita GDP growth.[5]

GDP growth per capita is just one dimension of a country's well-being, albeit a very important one. However, the evidence to date with respect to other indicators of sustainable development is equally disturbing. As an example, oil-producing Cameroon was poorer in 2007 than it was in 1985. It has also scored badly against a broad range of widely accepted governance metrics.[6]

Numerous studies have shown that democracy and oil are not readily compatible, and these studies have exposed a strong positive correlation between oil and corruption.[7] Oil has had a troubled history of negative social and environmental impacts. Another discouraging finding is that states that are dependent on oil revenue disproportionately experience social and political unrest and often violence.[8]

Governance and Oil: An Uneasy Mixture

In the disconnect between oil wealth and sustainable development, governance scores are perhaps the most worrisome in that they are causal. The failures in governance that put sustainable development at risk may have predated oil development in many countries. However, much evidence exists that the arrival of significant oil wealth can itself undermine governance, at a minimum exacerbating preexisting problems.[9]

What is it about oil wealth and oil revenue dependency that creates this challenge to good governance? A list of the most common answers would include the following:

- *Dutch disease*. This "disease" was named for the problems experienced by the Netherlands following the discovery and initial exploration of vast reserves of natural gas. The rapid growth in petroleum exports led to an appreciation of the exchange rate, resulting in an increased price of nonpetroleum exports, and put upward pressure on the costs and prices of nontraded domestic goods and services, thereby diminishing their competitiveness and eroding the diversity and balance of the domestic economy. The disease has been identified in almost all countries where petroleum exports play a major economic role.
- *Volatility*. The oil industry is notorious for its violent cyclical behavior. Volatility makes life difficult in itself, especially if cyclical swings are not predictable. Difficulties are compounded by the frequent inappropriateness of policies and decisions associated with these swings. Bad decisions or investments made in boom years are very difficult to undo in bust years.
- *Expansion of the public sector*. The popular perception of oil as "strategic" has led governments to take a prominent role in the sector. Significant sector revenues mask the inefficiencies that commonly result and encourage governments to move into other sectors that they see as strategic, thereby spreading inefficiency and crowding out private sector participation, which many argue offers the best chance for economic growth and diversification.[10]
- *Inefficient investment*. Oil wealth often comes suddenly, with new discoveries or an upward spike in prices. In developing countries, the new wealth typically exceeds the institutional capacity to ensure its efficient investment.
- *Excessive credit expansion*. When oil revenues get into the domestic banking system, they will very likely result in excessive credit expansion, thereby fueling inflation and threatening financial stability.

- *Weak institutional capacity.* Oil is likely to undermine a more efficient civil service because, on the collection side, revenues are typically concentrated and require relatively small staffs to administer and, on the disbursement side, institutional accountability is limited.
- *Diminished accountability.* Oil revenues provide a government with a source of income independent of its citizens. Where oil revenues are significant, this independence diminishes the need for accountability, and at the same time increases government's ability to buy off or intimidate opposition. Significant petroleum revenues make it easier for governments to postpone much-needed economic reforms and may encourage initiatives in the opposite direction.[11]
- *Political sensitivity.* Oil wealth provokes strong emotional responses related to its "national patrimony" qualities. There is a strong temptation to use this sensitivity to score political points and achieve political outcomes that may be—but are more likely not—consistent with sound development policy.
- *Revenue-sharing demands.* Sharing public revenues among different social and geographic groups is a challenge under any circumstances. Difficulties intensify in the case of oil revenues, not only because of their scale but also because their sources are virtually never evenly distributed within a country.
- *Corruption.* Last, but far from least, is the corrosive influence of corruption. Petroleum wealth is a lightning rod for corruption at every stage in the revenue chain, from taxation and collection through expenditures. Where corruption is deeply rooted, little attention will be paid to meeting any of the challenges listed previously. Longer-term structural improvements and the enhancement of accountability are of little interest when the focus is on near-term theft for the benefit of a few. Corruption is greatly facilitated by the all too common lack of transparency when it comes to oil revenues.[12]

Many of these challenges overlap. Nevertheless, the list is daunting, and it is not surprising that the governance record of so many oil-dependent exporting states has been poor.

Addressing the Issues

Successfully addressing the foregoing challenges will require determined action by the oil-rich government and other stakeholders across the entire petroleum sector value chain. Viewing the sector as a chain is useful because it suggests interdependence of the actions required under each heading or link.[13]

Policy, Legal, and Contractual Framework

An agreed vision for the petroleum sector is all too often lacking, yet it is critical to guiding sector legislation and oversight. Topics covered in any sector policy statement should include, nonexhaustively, the following: sovereignty over resource endowments, intentions with respect to key provisions of sector laws and contracts, institutional roles and responsibilities, fiscal objectives, intentions with respect to sector revenue management, and the mitigation of adverse social and environmental impacts. New, emerging oil producers, such as Ghana and Uganda, have produced comprehensive policy documents, which encourage public discussion and debate.

Sector laws, contracts, and regulations should closely reflect announced policies. Together with decisions on sector organization and a fiscal regime, they provide the detailed framework essential to sector investment and the conduct of operations.

Institutional Framework

Clarity on the roles and responsibilities of the various government ministries and agencies charged with sector oversight is vital to successful sector management.[14] Although core responsibility typically resides in the sector ministry, a variety of other ministries and agencies—finance, environment, economic planning, the central bank, and so forth—may be involved, thereby placing a premium on coordination, which has proved more difficult to achieve in practice than on paper.

National oil companies deserve special mention. Most oil-rich developing countries have chosen to establish or maintain NOCs. These companies often play critical roles in sector oversight, operations, and fiscal administration, in competition with the sector and finance ministries and with agencies such as the revenue authority. A number of observers have pointed out serious systemic governance risks associated with NOCs. These risks are now widely recognized, and remedies have been identified—enhanced transparency among them. NOCs remain popular, however, risks notwithstanding.[15]

Among the most critical decisions related to sector organization is whether to accept private sector participation and, if so, in what form. The benefits of private participation can be considerable both in terms of access to finance and technology and in terms of sharing of risks. Most oil-rich developing countries, with the exception of some Middle Eastern states, actively seek private participation.

Fiscal Design and Administration

The design of the fiscal regime applicable to petroleum is central to ensuring that resources are efficiently exploited; investor interest is maintained; and revenue flows to the host government are timely, dependable, and adequate. Although there is growing understanding of what constitutes good petroleum fiscal design, a number of difficulties are still encountered in practice. These difficulties include finding the appropriate competitive level of fiscal take; ensuring governments a progressive share of project rents (i.e., a share that increases as profitability increases); and creating incentives for cost containment.

The robustness of a fiscal regime (i.e., its ability to adjust government take automatically to different or changing circumstances) is especially valuable given the volatility of sector prices and the variability of cost conditions.[16] Good fiscal design can help fiscal administration by limiting opportunities for investor tax evasion or tax "management" and by reducing the number of disputes and the need for special exceptions. That said, it is no substitute for good administration. Good administration requires adequate skills, salaries, and resources in terms of both labor power and technology. These qualities are not often found in developing countries, leading many to argue that fiscal design should be simplified accordingly. Sacrificing good design to accommodate administrative weakness, however, is very likely to result in greater—not fewer—demands on administrators. Poor design will almost certainly result in pressures from either the government or the investor to renegotiate or to issue exemptions or side-letter adjustments, thus increasing, rather than decreasing, administrative complexity. It is much better, then, to focus on building capacity.[17]

Monitoring and controlling the considerable fiscal flows in the petroleum sector will require clear definitions of the roles of the different agencies involved—usually a regulatory agency and, in all likelihood, the NOC, the central bank, and the ministry of finance—and clear procedures for interagency reconciliation of reported revenues. Regular and public reporting and audits are an essential part of the process. They are frequently lacking in developing countries, however, opening the door to corruption and revenue loss.

Revenue Management

Once revenues are anticipated or collected, a well-articulated plan for their management is essential. Management objectives may comprise any or all of the following: spending on consumption or investment, saving until there is a better match between revenues received and the local economy's absorptive and institutional capacity, stabilization of budget revenues, expenditures in the face of revenue volatility, and saving for future generations.

Pursuing these objectives inevitably involves tradeoffs. The most fundamental tradeoff is that between current spending and saving. Those supporting early increases in spending in response to positive shocks point to essential poverty reduction needs and, importantly, the opportunity for substantial returns on social and physical infrastructure expenditures in economies typically starved of investment.[18] Those who argue for caution on current spending point to (a) the limited ability of most oil-rich developing economies to absorb sudden increases in revenues without running the risk of steep inflation and Dutch Disease and (b) institutional weaknesses in the same countries, which raise the likelihood of wasteful investment through ineptitude or corruption.

A seminal study by the International Monetary Fund (IMF) looked at the responses of 26 oil-rich developing countries to the positive oil price shock of 1999 to 2005.[19] The IMF study found that while most countries moved from an overall budget deficit to a budget surplus, their nonoil deficits increased sharply as a result of nonoil tax reductions and dramatic increases in nonoil spending. Furthermore, spending increases in most cases were above long-term sustainable levels based on any reasonable projection of future oil revenues. As a result, countries in the sample greatly increased their vulnerability to any future negative oil revenue shocks.

Oil funds have become a popular choice for parking any saved revenues. These funds are typically designed to smooth the flow of oil revenues into the budget, provide a cushion in the event of unprecedented negative revenue shocks, transfer wealth to future generations, or some combination of the three. Given the very large sums involved, governance of oil funds has become a major focus. Key features are professional management, independent oversight, regular published audits, and maximum transparency.[20]

Expenditure

Expenditure of petroleum sector revenues is often the main vehicle to apply wealth to pressing near-term humanitarian concerns and poverty reduction and to longer-term goals of sustainable economic growth and diversification. Setting expenditure priorities can be greatly helped by a Poverty Reduction Strategy (PRS).[21] Now a World Bank and IMF requirement, the PRS is prepared by the government on the basis of extensive stakeholder consultation, and it articulates a poverty reduction implementation program. Typical priorities include health, education, infrastructure, and the environment.

Recent years have seen a growing emphasis on "investment in investing."[22] This strategy is based on (a) the potential for revenues from economic growth to ultimately vastly outstrip oil revenues in contributing to economic well-being, (b) the recognition that private sector participation is essential to growth, and (c) the fact that most oil-rich developing countries score very badly on creating the conditions for private sector investment.[23] Investment in investing would entail removing the legal and institutional barriers to private sector participation and increasing the emphasis on development of the social and physical infrastructure to complement and encourage private investment.

The back end of the expenditure process—making sure that revenues go where they are intended to go—is the province of budget screening and Public Expenditure Reviews (PERs). Budget screening tests propose current expenditures and investment projects for economic robustness and fit within overall budget strategies. PERs are a standard World Bank product, although by no means exclusive to it.[24] PERs identify lapses in implementation, areas in need of improvement, and recommendations for future practice. In addition to increasing the effectiveness of expenditures, PERs can assist in the detection and deterrence of corruption.

The largest losses in the whole petroleum value chain probably occur at the expenditure stage, through wasteful or premature investment or expenditure, nontransparency, political favors, and especially corruption.

Social and Environmental Policies

Neglected in the past, social and environmental concerns are now prominently featured in resource policies and legislation. Coverage goes beyond the prevention or mitigation of any adverse impacts to include the generation of net economic benefits beyond revenues and special attention to social equity. Laws and contracts commonly call for the generation of local content in hiring practices, in the provision of goods and services, and in direct investment and ownership. Social equity concerns are reflected in local community development plans and agreements linked to oil operations. Women have suffered disproportionately from the resource curse. As a result, gender equity has received particular attention.[25]

Political Context

Delivering on this reform roadmap is far from easy. There has been progress, in that the issues described in the preceding section and the recommended policy responses outlined here are now well recognized. Reform implementation is, however, another matter—a matter of political will that, in turn, depends to a large extent on the political context.

A growing body of academic research has concerned itself with political regime typologies and their relationship to the management of oil wealth. Where time horizons are short (e.g., in predatory autocracies or unstable, factional democracies), the prospects for delivery on a governance or sustainable development agenda are remote. If the political context is one of a rooted democracy, time horizons are extended, and the likelihood of responsible resource wealth management is greatly increased.

Political context has its greatest impact on reform agendas that have to do with division of the political and monetary spoils already generated by oil wealth: institutional clarity, tax administration, and revenue management and expenditure. Governments of oil-rich states are less likely to interfere with reforms that are focused on attracting investment and generating revenues in the first place.

Good Governance and Transparency

Good governance is essential to success at each link in the oil and gas value chain. Transparency, in turn, is fundamental to all aspects of governance. It is not only a critical component of good governance but also one of the most important instruments available to leverage adoption of good governance across the value chain. As such, it has received growing attention from stakeholders at all levels—international, regional, and national.

Powerful arguments have been advanced in favor of greater transparency in the management of petroleum sector wealth:[26]

- *Building of trust.* Available and accurate information on oil and gas operations and finances is essential to building trust among stakeholders. It defuses suspicion with respect to revenues generated and their management and is the starting point for democratic debate on critical issues such as spending priorities.
- *Accountability.* Transparency along the petroleum value chain will act to increase accountability in both the executive and the legislative branches of government at all levels, thereby reducing opportunities for corruption and potential waste of funds. Transparency will put similar pressure on industry behavior, including, importantly, the behavior of NOCs.
- *Macroeconomic management.* Readily available credible data are essential to effective economic management, budget decisions, and forward planning.
- *Access to finance and investment.* International financial institutions (IFIs), both public and private, and investors are increasingly demanding enhancements in transparency. Because of transparency's importance to good governance, lack of transparency is seen as a major obstacle to the creation of a favorable investment climate.
- *Security.* The favorable influence of transparency on governance and avoidance of the resource curse is expected to have a positive impact on global stability and security. In 2008, US Senator Richard Lugar noted that the resource curse "exacerbates global poverty, which can be a seedbed for terrorism, it dulls the effect of our foreign assistance, it empowers autocrats and dictators, and it can crimp world petroleum supplies, breeding instability."[27]

The focus on transparency in oil and gas—and in other extractive industries, notably mining—has led to two influential international campaigns with resource revenue transparency as a key objective: Publish What You Pay (PWYP) and the Extractive Industries Transparency Initiative (EITI).

PWYP and Dodd–Frank Legislation

The PWYP campaign is a coalition of about 150 international and local nongovernmental organizations (NGOs). Skeptical of getting credible resource revenue numbers from governments—especially from governments of countries where transparency has been an issue—PWYP has lobbied to have oil, gas, and mining companies individually publish their payments made to governments.

The PWYP's untiring campaigning has brought results. In 2010, the US Congress passed the Dodd–Frank Wall Street Reform and Consumer Protection Act, which requires all companies registering on the New York Stock Exchange to publish details of all payments made to governments related to the exploitation of petroleum and mineral resources.[28] In August 2012, the US Securities and Exchange Commission (SEC) issued comprehensive instructions for the filing of payments information. Compliance begins with fiscal years ending after September 30, 2013.

Although the oil industry generally supports transparency, it objects to the Dodd–Frank legislation on the grounds that Dodd–Frank would put it at a competitive disadvantage vis-à-vis companies not coming under the requirements of the law, particularly in host countries opposed to publication of payments data. The SEC has rebuffed this objection and will allow no exemptions to its ruling. Supporters of the legislation have stressed that the law covers 90 percent of internationally operating oil companies, including some companies from emerging market economies such as China, India, Brazil, and Russia.[29]

The European Union has declared similar intent, and the European Commission is expected to issue detailed rulings on the filing of payments information with the European exchanges by year-end 2012.

Extractive Industries Transparency Initiative

Inspired by PWYP, EITI was launched by British Prime Minister Tony Blair at the 2002 Johannesburg Summit on Sustainable Development. The EITI Principles call for ensuring that resource payments made and received are properly accounted for and contribute to sustainable development and poverty alleviation.[30] A decade after its founding, EITI has been endorsed by 37 resource-rich countries, 16 of which are now deemed fully compliant with its criteria. It has also garnered widespread donor country and industry endorsement.

While perhaps the most prominent resource transparency initiatives, PWYP and EITI are not alone in pursuing their agendas. A considerable range of bilateral programs, IFI initiatives, and other NGO campaigns are active, with remits that often go beyond strict revenue transparency and extend to other governance and transparency objectives along the petroleum value chain, such as contract and licensing transparency, budget transparency, and expenditure transparency. Recognizing that the volume and complexity of information works against real actionable transparency, proponents of a number of initiatives have focused on building the capacity required to understand and respond to sector information.

There is a great deal for which these programs and initiatives should be congratulated. Some observers, however, see cause for concern.[31] The governance and transparency agenda gained international prominence with astonishing speed over the past decade, but continuation of this momentum is not certain. Key country players, such as Russia, China, and most of the Middle East, have shown no interest, nor have their NOCs. The list of countries endorsing EITI and issuing reports includes only 12 of the 38 countries counted by the IMF as oil rich.[32] Among those missing are Algeria, Libya, Mexico, Venezuela, Colombia, Angola, Equatorial Guinea, Russia, and most Middle Eastern countries.[33] Furthermore, concern has been expressed that a number of countries registered as endorsing or fully compliant with EITI criteria are only nominally committed, following the formal requirements of EITI with little effect on business as usual.[34] In a recent statement, the chair of EITI noted that the initiative was still not measuring up to the EITI Principles and underscored the need to do much more on follow-through to have a significant effect on sustainable development and poverty alleviation.

Stakeholder Roles

Getting positive results from petroleum wealth will depend on the active commitment of all stakeholders. This section examines each of their roles and that of the United States in particular. By working together in alliances, responsible stakeholders can multiply their effectiveness in addressing resource wealth issues. The modalities of such alliances are now being actively explored in a number of different global and country contexts.

Host Governments

The governments of petroleum-producing developing countries are the recipients of the lion's share of petroleum revenues and must play the central roles in developing, legislating, and administering the policies and programs required to deliver beneficial developmental effects. Though the issues to be addressed are admittedly difficult, they have much more to do with political will than with economic or technical complexity.

Governments of Oil-Importing Countries

Oil-importing countries can play critical supporting roles by providing development funding, advice, and technical assistance to producing countries and by applying diplomatic and economic leverage. These countries are the home countries to most international oil industry investors and can further influence host country outcomes by requiring high standards of governance and transparency of those investors, as exemplified by the US Dodd–Frank legislation and planned action by the European Union. These efforts by members of the Organization for Economic Cooperation and Development are notable. China, India, South Korea, and their NOCs should be similarly pressed to adhere to international good governance norms in their dealings with oil-producing developing countries.

Industry

Increasingly, industry investors are paying serious attention to ethical, social, and environmental issues. Their performance in this regard is beginning to affect not only their license to operate in many countries, but also their ability to raise capital as social awareness increases in importance among the investment criteria of professional fund managers.

Major industry players are adopting internal codes of conduct and putting in place corporate social responsibility programs that are designed to address the ills perceived to be associated with petroleum wealth. Some of these programs are directed at the symptoms of government failure—for example, in the provision of public health, education, or other social infrastructure. Others focus on improving government performance through technical assistance in capacity building. The private sector's commitment to transparency principles, whether at the individual company or at the aggregate sector level, will be critical to advancing the governance agenda.

In the end, it is extremely important to recognize that (a) what the private sector can afford to fund in these areas is orders of magnitude less than what the government can finance out of the revenues it receives from the private sector, (b) private sector oil and gas companies generally do not have a comparative advantage in delivering social goods, and (c) private sector expenditures in this area are often deductible against tax at favorable rates and as such may constitute a very expensive source of development finance. In other words, where the delivery of benefits from oil and gas is concerned, the primary focal point should be government rather than industry, notwithstanding industry's important contributions and goodwill.

NGOs, Civil Society, and the Media

NGOs, civil society, and the media play valuable roles in informing the public and in keeping other players' feet to the fire.[35] International NGOs and civil society can play an important role in advising governments and local counterparts on emerging global best practices. Local NGOs, civil society, and the media, by leveraging their grassroots connections, have the potential to be particularly effective in promoting best practices, especially on expenditure and on social and environmental issues. NGO outreach has been important in building local capacity to interpret information on industry contracts, operations, and finances as it becomes available.

International Financial Institutions, Bilateral and Multilateral Development Agencies, and International and Regional Forums

IFIs and bilateral and multilateral development agencies are the leading providers of technical assistance to oil-rich developing countries across the petroleum value chain and can use their funding leverage to press for reform. Certainly the World Bank and the IMF have been preoccupied for some time with using their policy and lending instruments and related conditionality to address issues of resource wealth management. Both institutions identify governance as a key requirement for translating resource wealth into sustainable benefits and transparency as a fundamental building block.

Bilateral programs have also been effective in support of capacity building and good governance. Agencies of the US government, the UK Department for International Development, Norway's Oil for Development, and Germany's GiZ (Deutsche Gesellschaft für Internationale Zusammenarbeit, or German Society for International Cooperation) have been especially active.

International forums such as the Group of 8 (G-8) and the Group of 20 (G-20) have succeeded in raising awareness of resource curse issues and of the need for action. The New Partnership for Africa's Development (NEPAD) has added resource revenue management and transparency to its regional agenda.

United States

The concerns reviewed in this chapter have direct bearing on US foreign policy objectives, and the United States remains an indispensable player in their mitigation. The case for US engagement is strong, even if threats to US oil supply security have diminished. Other expressed foreign policy objectives listed earlier in this chapter and in this book's introduction remain valid and need urgently to be addressed.

The United States already has a prominent role in advancing the global governance and transparency agenda, paying particular attention to oil-rich developing countries. Relevant programs include the Treasury Department's assistance on oil revenue management through its Office of Technical Assistance; the State Department's Energy Governance and Capacity Initiative and its Bureau of Energy Resources, which focus on the promotion of good governance; and the technical assistance programs of the Department of the Interior, the Department of Energy, and the US Agency for International Development. Transparent reporting of resource revenues and expenditures is one of the conditions of access to the US government's Millennium Challenge Account.

Multiple initiatives have unfortunately fragmented and diluted the US message (and profile), underscoring the need for better future coordination. International coordination on oil governance and transparency is also critical. It is under way, and the United States is well placed to lead in this area.

Summary and Recommendations

Sustained development measured against a broad range of indicators— economic growth and poverty alleviation, human development, political and social stability, containment of violence and corruption, safeguarding of democratic and human rights, and gender equity—has eluded many or most oil-rich and gas-rich developing countries. Beyond the tragic direct consequences for the countries concerned, this failure undermines not only policies supporting global oil and gas market stability and supply security, but also the wider foreign policy agenda of the United States and other major developed countries.

It will take a concerted effort by all stakeholders in industrial and developing countries alike to turn these failures around. The producing countries must take the lead in that effort by showing the political will to deliver the good governance and transparency essential to responsible management of their petroleum wealth.

A critical role still remains for other stakeholders in supporting the governments and civil society of oil-rich developing countries with required funding, technical assistance, and corporate social responsibility activities. These stakeholders can also exert healthy leverage on producing governments through the conditioning of development funding on oil wealth management performance; through political forums such as the G-8, the G-20, and NEPAD; through global and local public information campaigns; and through binding actions exemplified by the Dodd–Frank legislation in the United States. Given its relevance to a range of political, economic, social, and security objectives, the promotion of good governance and transparency in the petroleum sectors of oil-rich countries deserves an important place in the foreign policy agendas of donor countries, the United States foremost among them.

Notes

1. These calculations are based on BP, *BP Statistical Review of World Energy 2012* (London: BP, 2012).

2. The phrase was coined by Terry Lynn Karl in her pathbreaking book of the same title, which examined the social and economic troubles experienced in major petroleum-producing developing countries. See Terry Lynn Karl, *The Paradox of Plenty: Oil Booms and Petro-States* (Berkeley: University of California Press, 1997). The phenomenon is equally often referred to as the *resource curse*.

3. These figures are author estimates.

4. These figures are author estimates.

5. Richard M. Auty, ed., *Resource Abundance and Economic Development* (Oxford, UK: Oxford University Press, 2001). The comparison is especially startling when performance is measured against the experience of small oil-exporting countries, whose oil dependence is likely to be high. Between 1970 and 1990, GDP per capita in these countries grew at 0.8 percent, versus 2.1 to 3.7 percent in resource-poor countries. More recent research—using longer period and larger samples—challenges these findings but still suggests that oil-rich states have performed well below their growth potential. See Michael L. Ross, *The Oil Curse: How Petroleum Wealth Shapes the Development of Nations* (Princeton, NJ: Princeton University Press, 2012).

6. These results are reported in Bernard Gauthier and Albert Zeufack, "Governance and Oil Revenues in Cameroon," in *Plundered Nations? Successes and Failures in Natural Resource Extraction*, ed. Paul Collier and Anthony J. Venables (Basingstoke, UK: Palgrave Macmillan, 2011), 27–78.

7. Ross, *Oil Curse*. See also Charles McPherson and Stephen MacSearraigh, "Corruption in the Petroleum Sector," in *The Many Faces of Corruption: Tracking Vulnerabilities at the Sector Level*, ed. J. Edgardo Campos and Sanjay Rajan (World Bank, Washington, DC, 2007), 191–220.

8. See Ian Bannon and Paul Collier, *Natural Resources and Violent Conflict: Options and Actions* (Washington, DC: World Bank). See also Paul Collier, "Economic Causes of Civil Conflict and Their Implications for Policy," in *Turbulent Peace: The Challenge of Managing International Conflict*, ed. Chester A. Crocker, Fen Osler Hampson, and Pamela Aall (Washington, DC: United States Institute of Peace, 2001), 143–62. For the cases of Nigeria, Russia, and Iran, see Paul Collier and Anthony J. Venables, "Key Decisions for Resource Management: Principles and Practice," in *Plundered Nations? Successes and Failures in Natural Resource Extraction*, ed. Paul Collier and Anthony J. Venables (Basingstoke, UK: Palgrave Macmillan, 2011), 1–26. Paul Williams acknowledges the link between resource wealth and violence but qualifies it, pointing to a range of additional factors. See Paul D. Williams, *War and Conflict in Africa* (Cambridge, UK: Polity Press, 2011).

9. A World Bank study of the Middle East and North Africa traced the region's poor growth performance directly to weak governance and especially highlighted the strong correlation between underperformance in governance and the presence of oil. "Riches from hydrocarbons ... have handicapped the emergence of institutions of good governance," according to the authors of the report. See World Bank, *Better Governance for Development in the Middle East and North Africa: Enhancing Inclusiveness and Accountability* (Washington, DC: World Bank, 2003), 152.

10. Collier and Venables, "Key Decisions for Resource Management."

11. A headline makes the point: "Russian Oil Boom Washed away Economic Reform Impetus," *Washington Post*, January 8, 2001. Thane Gustafson made a similar point 10 years later, arguing that oil price increases have underwritten bad policies and have allowed political elites to buy off the opposition. See Thane Gustafson, "Putin's

Petroleum Problem: How Oil Is Holding Russia Back—and How It Could Save It," *Foreign Affairs* 91, no. 6 (2012): 83–96.

12. McPherson and MacSearraigh, "Corruption in the Petroleum Sector."

13. Three influential web-based initiatives take this approach, providing valuable insights into the diagnosis of the resource curse and possible remedies: the Natural Resource Charter (http://naturalresourcecharter.org), the Extractive Industries Source Book (http://www.eisourcebook.org), and the Extractive Industries Value Chain (http://www-wds.worldbank.org/external/default/WDSContentServer/WDSP/IB/2009/05/07/000333038_20090507044239/Rendered/PDF/484240NWP0Box31ei1for1development13.pdf).

14. This point is underscored in IMF, *Guide on Resource Revenue Transparency* (Washington, DC: IMF, 2007). The *Guide* codifies principles for resource-rich countries in handling resource revenue and tailors the IMF's Code of Good Practices on Fiscal Transparency to the specific needs of resource-rich countries.

15. See, inter alia, David G. Victor, David Hults, and Mark Thurber, eds., *Oil and Governance: State-Owned Enterprises and the World Energy Supply* (Cambridge, UK: Cambridge University Press, 2012); Charles McPherson, "State Participation in the Natural Resource Sectors: Evolution, Issues, and Outlook," in *The Taxation of Petroleum and Minerals: Principles, Problems, and Practice*, ed. Philip Daniel, Michael Keen, and Charles McPherson (New York: Routledge, 2010), 263–88; Charles McPherson, "National Oil Companies: Evolution Issues and Outlook," in *Fiscal Policy Formulation and Implementation in Oil-Producing Countries*, ed. Jeffrey M. Davis, Rolando Ossowski, and Annalisa Fedelino (Washington, DC: International Monetary Fund, 2003), 184–203; World Bank, *A Citizen's Guide to National Oil Companies* (Washington, DC, and Austin, TX: World Bank and University of Texas, 2008).

16. Thomas Baunsgaard, "A Primer on Mineral Taxation," Working Paper 01/139, IMF, Washington, DC, 2001) gives a good introduction to petroleum taxation objectives and instruments. See also Philip Daniel, Michael Keen, and Charles McPherson, eds., *The Taxation of Petroleum and Minerals: Principles, Problems, and Practice* (New York: Routledge, 2010); Silvana Tordo, "Fiscal Systems for Hydrocarbons: Design Issues," Working Paper 123, World Bank, Washington, DC, 2007.

17. See Jack Calder, "Resource Tax Administration: The Implications of Alternative Policy Choices," in *The Taxation of Petroleum and Minerals: Principles, Problems, and Practice*, ed. Philip Daniel, Michael Keen, and Charles McPherson (New York: Routledge, 2010), 319–39.

18. Collier and Venables, "Key Decisions for Resource Management."

19. Rolando Ossowski, Mauricio Villafuerte, Paulo A. Medas, and Theo Thomas, *Managing the Oil Revenue Boom: The Role of Fiscal Institutions* (Washington, DC: IMF, 2007).

20. An argument sometimes advanced against transparency in petroleum sector operations is that unwarranted pressure to increase spending will build up once the availability of fiscal resources from that sector is made known. However, informing the public and fostering constructive debate seems like the better strategy. The existence of oil resources cannot be kept secret, and a lack of information on resulting revenues can be a source of debilitating social and political tensions.

21. For more information about Poverty Reduction Strategies, see the World Bank's website at http://www.worldbank.org/en/topic/poverty.

22. Collier and Venables, "Key Decisions for Resource Management." See also precepts 9 and 10 of the Natural Resource Charter.

23. See the country scores at the International Finance Corporation's website, http://www.doingbusiness.org.

24. For more information about Public Expenditure Reviews, see the World Bank's website at http://web.worldbank.org/WBSITE/EXTERNAL/TOPICS/EXTPUBLIC SECTORANDGOVERNANCE/EXTPUBLICFINANCE/0,,contentMDK:20236662~ menuPK:2083237~pagePK:148956~piPK:216618~theSitePK:1339564,00.html.

25. Ross, *Oil Curse*, chapter 7.

26. See, inter alia, Terry Lynn Karl, "Ensuring Fairness: The Case for a Transparent Fiscal Social Contract," in *Escaping the Resource Curse*, ed. Macartan Humphreys, Jeffrey D. Sachs, and Joseph E. Stiglitz (New York: Columbia University Press, 2007); Peter Rosenblum and Susan Maples, *Contracts Confidential: Ending Secret Deals in the Extractive Industries* (New York: Revenue Watch Institute, 2009).

27. As quoted in Thorsten Benner and Ricardo Soares de Oliveira, "The Good/Bad Nexus in Global Energy Governance," in *Global Energy Governance: The New Rules of the Game*, ed. Andreas Goldthau and Jan Martin Witte (Washington, DC, and Berlin: Brookings Institution and Global Public Policy Institute, 2010), 287–314.

28. The applicable provision is section 1504 (the Cardin–Lugar provision). For the full text of the Dodd–Frank Act, see http://housedocs.house.gov/rules/finserv/111 _hr4173_finsrvcr.pdf.

29. Oxfam America, "SEC Brings Oil and Mining Transparency Provision of Dodd–Frank to Life," press release, August 23, 2012, http://www.oxfamamerica.org/press /pressreleases/sec-brings-oil-and-mining-transparency-provision-of-dodd-frank-to-life.

30. The EITI Principles are listed on the EITI's website at http://eiti.org/eiti /principles.

31. Benner and Soares de Oliveira, "Good/Bad Nexus in Global Energy Governance."

32. See IMF, *Guide on Resource Revenue Transparency*, annex 2.

33. Iraq is a notable exception. It is a candidate for EITI compliance and has issued one report.

34. The Cameroon case is described in Gauthier and Zeufack, "Governance and Oil Revenues in Cameroon," and in Benner and Soares de Oliveira, "Good/Bad Nexus in Global Energy Governance."

35. Examples of high-profile, often controversial NGO campaigns include Global Witness, *A Crude Awakening: The Role of the Oil and Banking Industries in Angola's Civil War and the Plunder of State Assets* (London: Global Witness, 1999), http://www .globalwitness.org/sites/default/files/pdfs/A%20Crude%20Awakening.pdf, and Global Witness, *All the President's Men: The Devastating Story of Oil and Banking in Angola's Privatised War* (London: Global Witness, 2002), http://pwypdev.gn.apc.org/sites /pwypdev.gn.apc.org/files/All_the_Presidents_Men.pdf. Both publications address oil revenue management issues in Angola. See also Catholic Relief Services, *The Bottom of the Barrel: Africa's Oil Boom and the Poor* (New York: Catholic Relief Services, 2003), http://pqpublications.squarespace.com/storage/peacebuilding/Bottom%20of%20the% 20barrel.pdf; Human Rights Watch, *Angola Unravels* (London: Human Rights Watch, 1999), http://www.hrw.org/reports/1999/angola/; Human Rights Watch, *Some Transparency, No Accountability: The Use of Oil Revenue in Angola and Its Impact on Human Rights* (London: Human Rights Watch, 2004), http://www.hrw.org/en /reports/2004/01/12/some-transparency-no-accountability.

Chapter 20

Managing Strategic Reserves

Michelle Billig Patron and David L. Goldwyn

The United States created the Strategic Petroleum Reserve (SPR) in 1975, in the wake of the 1973–74 Arab Oil Embargo, to protect the country against a physical disruption in the supply of oil. US planners believed that if the United States and its allies could provide 90 days of import cover, they could protect their economies from harm and leave adequate time for a diplomatic or military response.

Global oil demand has since grown dramatically, the world has become more dependent on supply from unstable countries, threats to global oil supplies have increased, and the role of financial investors in oil markets has expanded. Although US imports are declining because of rising domestic oil production and demand conservation, high oil prices continue to pose significant risks to the global economy from which the US economy cannot insulate itself. For us to meet these challenges, the US strategic

---

The views in this chapter reflect only the authors' personal opinions.

oil response strategy must evolve. We must shift our SPR policy focus from replacing US oil imports to managing global oil disruptions through greater SPR export flexibility, creation of a product reserve, and improved international coordination. The decision-making process for deploying the SPR must be expedited and must use greater oil market expertise. If modernized and wielded effectively, the SPR can be a powerful tool to manage oil disruptions and increase oil market stability.

In this chapter, we describe the history of US strategic reserve policy, the structural changes to US oil flows, and how new threats and economic realities have outpaced US energy policy. In concluding, we propose a new policy for managing US and global strategic stocks.

The Evolution of US Strategic Reserve Policy

The United States responded to the 1973–74 oil crisis by creating its own stockpile of crude oil and by forging a multilateral coalition of consuming countries that would maintain and share their own strategic stocks. The oil markets of the 1970s were very different from today. Oil was sold through term contracts, the US government regulated oil and natural gas prices, and the Organization of the Petroleum Exporting Countries (OPEC) controlled all of the world's excess capacity of oil, because no nation held sovereign stockpiles. The Arab Oil Embargo created a physical shortage of crude oil targeted at the United States and the Netherlands that could not be replaced from other sources. In this world, the United States defined *energy security* as physical availability of supply.

In 1974, US Secretary of State Henry Kissinger led the formation of the International Energy Agency (IEA), and in 1975, Congress passed the Energy Policy and Conservation Act (EPCA),[1] which created the SPR. The SPR was designed to equip the United States with enough oil to replace imports for 90 days in the event of a major disruption. The rules for tapping the SPR were restrictive.[2] In addition, to create a defensive coalition that could share the burden of overcoming an embargo, the IEA agreed to an emergency response policy. Each member committed to hold 90 days of import cover in either government stocks or government-mandated, but privately held, stocks. Members agreed to draw on these stocks only by consensus and committed to an oil-sharing policy. If one member suffered a shortage of more than 7 percent of its previous year's oil imports (as both the United States and the Netherlands had experienced during the

1973–74 embargo), other countries would share their oil with the ally in need.[3]

By 1979, it was becoming clear that physical shortages of less than 7 percent could render severe economic damage. Following the supply interruptions related to the 1979 Iranian Revolution and the Iran–Iraq War, which started in 1980, the IEA introduced a policy whereby each member agreed to cut oil imports by 5 percent from the previous year to create a supply cushion. However, countries proved unwilling to suffer economic pain for the collective good.

From 1979 onward, IEA members agreed to consult each other in the event of an oil disruption and to coordinate the release of their strategic stocks. Such coordinated releases have taken place on three occasions: January 1991 associated with the US invasion of Iraq, September 2005 following the Hurricane Katrina losses, and June 2011 following the war-related losses in Libya.[4]

Congressional politics and the relatively high cost of oil posed challenges to filling the SPR. When the EPCA was enacted, it provided a US policy goal of 1 billion barrels of oil.[5] The SPR hovered below 600 million barrels through the 1990s.[6] In 2001, the Bush administration committed to fill the SPR in the wake of September 11. The reserve reached its capacity of 727 million barrels in 2009. In 2012, the SPR contained roughly 696 million barrels, enough for 80 days of import cover.[7] Commercially held stocks (which can also be counted toward the 90-day import cover requirement) hold another 96 days of import cover, for a total of 172 days of import coverage. If US imports drop by 25 percent from 8.9 million barrels per day (mmbpd) in 2012[8] to 6.7 mmbpd by 2020, the SPR will be more than adequate for meeting the IEA threshold of 90 days import cover.

Even if US net imports go to zero, the SPR will retain its importance as a national security tool to protect against global supply disruptions that could seriously affect prices or otherwise harm the United States and its allies. Moreover, just as domestic production has rebounded over the past few years, this positive trend could abate or even reverse, pushing the United States back on a course of greater import dependence.

The Role of the SPR

The SPR can be a powerful tool for replacing physical supplies of oil, for deterring politically motivated embargos and countering OPEC's restraints of supply, and for calming market fears and dampening speculative price inflation. At times, the United States has used the reserve to great effect. At other times, the country has failed to use the reserve despite compelling conditions, or it has undermined the benefits by slow decision-making.

Replacing Physical Supply

The SPR has been used to replace long- and short-term disruptions of physical supply because of war, weather, and instability in a producer country.

The Gulf War in 1991

The first emergency SPR drawdown took place in response to the August 1990 Iraqi invasion of Kuwait. The invasion led to a global price spike, with West Texas Intermediate (WTI) oil prices jumping from a monthly average of $17 per barrel ($26 in 2010 dollars) in July to more than $35 in September ($52 in 2010 dollars). This price increase followed the losses of Kuwaiti and then Iraqi oil because of United Nations (UN) sanctions. Saudi Arabia scrambled to tap its excess capacity and replace the lost oil. Meanwhile, for almost a year, US policy-makers debated whether to tap the reserve, with no one driving the process to a decision. The United States finally agreed to release 33.75 million barrels on the eve of Operation Desert Storm as part of collective IEA action to release 75 million barrels. The announcement in January 1991 resulted in an immediate price drop from $32 WTI ($48 in 2010 dollars) to $21 WTI ($31 in 2010 dollars). The Gulf War drawdown demonstrates the SPR's potential as a positive influence on the market, but it also highlights the need for prompt action when supplies are disrupted. By the time of the emergency drawdown, the United States was already mired in a deep recession.

Hurricane Katrina in 2005

President George W. Bush declared a severe energy supply disruption in September 2005, when roughly 1.4 mmbpd of oil production[9] and 4.9 mmbpd of refining capacity (during the height of Hurricane Katrina)[10] were disrupted. The US Department of Energy approved emergency SPR loans eventually totaling 9.8 million barrels and then offered 30 million barrels of crude oil for sale (approving 11 million barrels of bids) as part of collective IEA action to make 60 million barrels available. Following these actions, WTI prices fell from $69 to $66 a barrel and then slowly moderated as infrastructure was restored over the next few months. Perhaps more important, the Katrina release put a ceiling on oil prices that prevented a sharp uptick in prices. The emergency highlighted the danger of concentrating US refineries and strategic stocks in the Gulf Coast, an area prone to weather disturbances, and demonstrated the value of developing US strategic stocks of petroleum products, because the United States depended heavily on IEA product stocks in Asia and Europe to cover the shortfall.

The Libyan Uprising of 2011

The third SPR drawdown took place in June 2011 in response to the February 2011 Libyan uprising against the Gaddafi regime, which disrupted production of more than 1.6 mmbpd of oil.[11] Brent crude oil prices steadily climbed from a monthly average of $104 a barrel in February 2011 to $126 in April 2011.[12] Diplomacy with Saudi Arabia lagged, as both sides waited to assess the conflict and its impact on supplies and prices. Riyadh pledged to replace the lost supply and eventually supplied an additional 1 mmbpd to markets.[13] By April 2011, the opportunity for a rapid, robust release of oil supplies with desirable effects had passed.[14]

Nevertheless, the United States continued to push for IEA support for a coordinated release. Countries were reluctant to put stocks on the market, but the United States obtained support from the United Kingdom, France, and Germany for IEA action. The IEA and SPR sale came in June 2011 and involved a nominal 60 million barrels. All 30 million barrels of crude from the United States were sold. Other IEA members pledged to release the equivalent of an additional 30 million barrels, but they added less than 8 million physical barrels of oil and products. The majority of the remaining IEA pledge was conducted through reductions in required stock levels, but the sale of industry stocks was not mandatory.[15] Brent crude prices initially dipped from $115 to $105 a barrel for a few days in June, but they quickly rebounded with market concerns that the additional oil would be delayed for several months and would likely be offset by Saudi production cuts. Oil prices slid again in August 2011, primarily because of European economic concerns.

The Libyan sale took place months after the disruption, undermining its potential market impact. The sale underscored the importance of releasing SPR oil early in a crisis to prevent a sharp run-up in prices. It also high-lighted weaknesses in the IEA system whereby reductions in industry stock levels did not necessarily translate into physical sales.

Bridging Swaps

The SPR has been used to bridge short-term gaps in market supply when weather or delivery lags create shortages. The SPR is used to loan or swap oil so that the market can be supplied promptly and the SPR can be repaid in kind.[16]

After ice on rivers and roads prevented deliveries of heating oil to New York and Connecticut by barge or truck in the winter of 1999, President Bill Clinton authorized a swap in February 2000 to create the Northeast Home Heating Oil Reserve. He authorized another swap in September 2000 of 30 million barrels to address an anticipated shortage in heating oil supplies when low inventories combined with a severe winter forecast and scheduled refinery maintenance to keep oil prices high. Although WTI crude prices dropped from $37 to $31 a barrel within two weeks of the swap award, critics argued that using the SPR to address the US heating oil market would create an arbitrage window pulling crude to Europe, where product prices were higher.[17] Nevertheless, upward of 34.5 million bar-rels were exchanged in 2002 and 2003.[18] President Barack Obama loaned oil to refiners affected by Hurricane Isaac in August 2012[19] and loaned 2 million barrels of low sulfur diesel to the US Department of Defense for distribution to emergency responders in November 2012 in the wake of Superstorm Sandy.[20]

Failures to Act

In many cases, the United States has failed to deploy the reserve despite circumstances that would justify a release. These missed opportunities re-sulted in price run-ups that may have been avoidable and uncertainty as to when the US government would release stocks in future crises.

From the fourth quarter of 2002 through the first quarter of 2003, a se-ries of supply disruptions took place that presented a case for deployment of strategic reserves. First, Petróleos de Venezuela (PdVSA) employees went on strike to protest the Venezuelan government's replacement of the state company's board of directors. The strike disrupted nearly 3 mmbpd of production, including 1.4 mmbpd of exports to the United States.[21] The George W. Bush administration refused to use the SPR, and the US wholesale price of gasoline and heating oil spiked to more than double the 2002 levels.

These disruptions took place during the run-up to the second Gulf War. Oil traders expected a repeat of the 1991 drawdown decision and declined to buy inventories for fear of being caught short if SPR oil was released. Yet in March 2003, with WTI oil prices at $34 a barrel, global excess capacity at 1.5 mmbpd to 2.0 mmbpd, and US crude oil and product inventories at record lows, the Bush administration again declined to tap the reserve. The decision confused the market and delayed commercial transactions to replace disrupted supply. Prices hovered around $30 per barrel for the remainder of the year, a marked change from historic prices.

Deterring Embargoes and Eliciting OPEC Response

The original purpose of the SPR was to deter a repeat of the 1973 Arab Oil Embargo. We have not experienced an embargo since 1973. The existence of the SPR and IEA reserves is one factor contributing to this success. Whereas producers have threatened embargoes, the ability of the US and IEA reserves to easily replace that oil for long periods of time has helped deter producers and reassure markets. With oil producers increasingly dependent on Asian consumers, an embargo constitutes an increasingly self-defeating exercise.

Another use of the SPR has been to prompt OPEC to release spare capacity. Although OPEC's ability to constrain production exceeds the ability of strategic reserve holders to replace it, the seller of the marginal barrels of oil (such as the United States when selling SPR oil) helps set the price. With billions of paper barrels now traded daily on futures markets, financial investors greatly magnify the effect of a stockpile release or purchase. This trading has enabled US administrations to elicit production increases from OPEC with the implicit or explicit threat of an SPR drawdown. For example, concerns over an SPR release—as well as broader economic setbacks—following the Libyan disruption in February 2011, prompted Saudi Arabia and other Arabian Gulf countries to put more than 1.2 mmbpd on the market, albeit after a few months' delay. This and other examples demonstrate that the threat of an SPR release can command OPEC's attention and remains a crucial part of America's foreign policy toolkit.

Managing Market Expectations

Perhaps the most controversial and, in our view, increasingly important task of strategic reserve policy is managing market expectations to help prevent price spikes. Markets anticipate future prices, shortages, and surpluses and act immediately in response to those expectations. This practice, often referred to as speculation, can be a rational economic response to looming crises. But these fears can cause enormous price swings, which can inflict swift pain on vulnerable economies.

In May 2012, the US government successfully telegraphed a potential drawdown as sanctions were tightened on Iran. In 2012, the United States and the European Union implemented measures to curtail Iran's ability to export oil[22] at the same time as market concerns grew over possible military conflict between Iran and Israel. Saudi Arabia, Kuwait, and the United Arab Emirates increased oil production by 1.2 mmbpd between January and June to help meet demand and reassure markets. US diplomacy moved to preserve the option of a coordinated IEA and SPR release in the event sanctions put significant upward pressure on oil prices. The Group of 20 (G-20) issued its first statement on the oil market in its history, signaling the intention of members to use strategic stocks if needed.[23] This signal coincided with a steady decline in Brent crude prices until August, despite the formal implementation of sanctions on July 1, 2012. Other factors weighed on prices, including concerns about economic weakness in China and Europe.

This strategy broke down in August 2012. Faced with climbing oil prices and Brent crude above $115 a barrel, the White House attempted to remind the market of its willingness to use the SPR. While the Group of Seven finance ministers issued a follow-on statement elevating their concern about oil markets and willingness to address future tightness, IEA Executive Director Maria van der Hoeven issued statements claiming that market conditions did not warrant a release.[24]

Declining to use the reserve also influences markets and creates expectations. In 2004, Vice President Dick Cheney famously stated that it would take a loss of 5 mmbpd to 6 mmbpd of supply to justify an SPR release. That volumetric limit—not provided in the law—served as an informal signal to the market that any lesser disruption would not be addressed.

Lessons Drawn

We draw four key lessons from these experiences. The first is that the policy of the US government on responding to events that cause severe oil market disruptions is highly inconsistent. Looking at historical practice, the market cannot anticipate whether the United States will respond swiftly to replace supplies following a disruption or how soon after a disruption the country will make a decision.

Second, it will always be hard to predict the length and size of a disruption, particularly if it is gradual and from multiple sources. Part of what undergirded the refusal of the Bush administration to release SPR oil during the 2002 Venezuela strike or the 2003 Gulf War was the fear that an even greater disruption, such as an attack on Saudi Arabia's oil facilities, might occur. The length and severity of the 2011 Libyan disruption was also unclear. Any calculation of the need to use strategic reserves will always call for an assessment of current market conditions and availability of OPEC and private stocks. But uncertainty of future conditions and the potential for additional disruptions should not prevent prompt decisions to address the situation now. Furthermore, waiting for clear and defined physical disruptions is unrealistic in today's global markets. We will not see physical shortages of oil, but rather we will see price swings that signal that the oil market must be rebalanced. In any event, the cost of economic harm from delayed action is likely to be greater than any negative impact of prematurely oversupplying the market.

Third, when deploying the reserve, a large and swift response is often most effective. The goal of the deployment is to reassure markets that disrupted supply will be replaced so that price-inflating uncertainty can be avoided. If the United States indicates that it will use the SPR in a robust fashion to address an emergency, traders and consumers can see where the replacement supply will come from. No harm is done if the barrels are not fully subscribed, as this partial fulfillment merely shows that demand is not as strong as the market projected or that the current price is too high. Whereas the 2011 Libyan release was fully subscribed, the 1991 Gulf War and 2005 Katrina releases were not. In the latter cases, market participants found the supply they needed, and the security blanket of the SPR created confidence that shortages were unlikely.

Fourth, a consistent, declaratory policy plays a key role. A widely heard market aphorism is "Buy the rumor, sell the fact." Markets react instantly to news that shapes their expectations. So the power of a stated policy to replace disrupted supply can influence market expectations and reduce volatility when it provides assurance that supply losses will not be absorbed without some relief. Note that saying nothing also sends a signal and influences market perceptions.

New Oil Market Realities

In the decades since the SPR was created, the nature of the oil markets and the threats to US and global energy security have changed dramatically. OPEC supplies 40 percent of global oil production today versus 55 percent in 1973,[25] and the markets depend on a larger set of countries that are increasingly prone to economic, political, and social instability. The unpredictable nature of these suppliers creates uncertainty in the oil market and raises the risk of disruption.

More Frequent Disruptions

Over the past five years, oil supply disruptions have become more frequent, with security- and sanctions-related outages accounting for more than 80 percent of the annual volumetric loss. Other key factors include technical problems, labor strikes, and weather-related outages. The level of unplanned oil supply outages experienced from January to July 2012 reached 535 million barrels, or 2.5 mmbpd, with more than 20 countries contributing to the loss.[26] The increase in disruptions is directly related to the uprisings in North Africa, turmoil in Iraq and Sudan, international sanctions against Iran and Syria, and unplanned technical problems in North America and the North Sea. Although disruptions are nothing new, their increased frequency and overlap present a new challenge to policy-makers. It is increasingly likely that a major disruption will be caused not by one large-scale event but rather by a series of smaller outages.

Fewer Cushions

OPEC spare capacity has not kept pace with growth demand in either volume or percent. Spare capacity was about 2.4 mmbpd in the first quarter of 2012—or 3 percent of global demand—a very thin operating cushion to respond to the outages discussed previously.[27] Nearly all the world's excess oil production capacity is held by Saudi Arabia, Kuwait, and the United Arab Emirates.[28] Historically, Saudi Arabia has reliably put supplies on the market at times of crisis—most recently as part of a multilateral effort to curtail Iran's ability to export oil in 2012. But its ability to increase production much further is uncertain in the near term. At 10 mmbpd,[29] the Kingdom produced at record levels in the summer of 2012 and close to its effective capacity. Riyadh floated a 15 mmbpd production capacity goal but appears to have shelved that possibility, given the uncertain outlook for prices and non-OPEC volume as the production of North American shale liquids expands. If spare capacity continues to lag global demand growth and private inventories do not make up the difference, we must decide whether we are willing to use the reserve to adequately protect our economy against a major price shock.

Role of the Futures Market

The growth of futures trading is changing the market landscape. Close to 720 mmbpd are now traded on ICE (Intercontinental Exchange) Brent contracts,[30] eight times the amount consumed globally, with billions more traded on the NYMEX (New York Mercantile Exchange) and associated over-the-counter markets. These instantaneous oil trades, influenced by information as events happen and projections of the effect of new supplies or shortages, greatly magnify the impact of a disruption or, conversely, a stockpile release. Prices rapidly adjust to bring oil demand and supply in balance, but they may do so at a sharp economic cost.

Declining US Oil Imports

US imports are now in decline, falling from 12.4 mmbpd in 2005 to 8.9 mmbpd in 2012.[31] If net US imports continue to decline at the current rate, they will drop to under 5 mmbpd in 2020 and roughly 2.6 mmbpd by 2030, with most imports coming from Canada. This decline represents a major paradigm shift with important implications for the SPR. Although the US physical oil supply is less likely to be directly affected by a disruption outside of the United States and Canada, US crude and product prices will still reflect international benchmarks. The United States will have strong strategic interest in using the SPR to help manage global supply disruptions but will need to shift its policy objective away from replacing US imports. This shift will require greater flexibility to export SPR oil.

Refined product exports are generally permitted without licenses. But current SPR oil exports must receive a license from the US Department of Commerce's Bureau of International Security and Nonproliferation, and exporters must prove that the oil export will result in the import of refined product that would not otherwise have been available.[32] As the United States becomes a growing product exporter, it will be nearly impossible for companies exporting unrefined oil to meet this condition.

Tanker restrictions pose another obstacle. The Jones Act (Merchant Marine Act of 1920) requires that any shipping between US ports use US-flagged vessels owned and crewed by US citizens or permanent residents. Because of the limited availability of US-flagged oil vessels, the Jones Act makes shipping crude from the Gulf Coast to Atlantic Coast refineries difficult. On occasion, the White House has waived the Jones Act to allow for marine shipment of SPR oil between the Gulf Coast and the East Coast. Except for Superstorm Sandy and Northeast fuel disruptions in 2012, these waivers have generally met with a strong backlash from the domestic marine industry and its political supporters.

Equally important are the growing infrastructure constraints to delivering SPR oil to the market as a result of changes in domestic US oil flows. The reversal of the Seaway pipeline, which used to carry crude from the Gulf Coast to Cushing, Oklahoma, eliminated a means to push SPR crude to the middle of the country. Similarly, the other key crude oil pipelines in the area now carry mostly domestic instead of imported foreign oil, with little room for incremental SPR barrels. Furthermore, increased pipeline, dock, and port congestion may make it difficult to release oil at the maximum rate of 4.2 mmbpd. Once the United States no longer imports foreign oil for use in Gulf Coast refineries, the drawdown rate capacity could very well fall to 1 mmbpd to 2 mmbpd, calling into serious question the ability of the SPR to respond to global outages.

A New Policy

A strategic reserve strategy designed in the 1970s is inadequate for a market in which price shocks are the primary threat and the United States continues to reduce its dependence on foreign oil imports. Unless the United States modernizes its reserve policy and updates its infrastructure, the nature of global markets dictates that our country and our allies will continue to hedge through continued purchases from Saudi Arabia, Russia, and other producers. This activity would be reckless and foolish at best. Five steps are required for the United States to revamp its strategic reserve strategy to take into full account the realities of the contemporary oil market.

Step 1: Maximize Export Flexibility during an SPR Drawdown

Declining US crude imports and rising product exports require shifting our SPR policy focus from replacing US oil imports to managing global oil disruptions through greater SPR export flexibility. Although the US physical oil supply is less likely to be directly affected by a disruption outside of the United States and Canada, our nation has a strategic interest in using the SPR to help manage global supply disruptions. Current US regulations severely restricting the export of SPR oil need to be revised. One option is for the president to make a national interest determination (or "finding") that unrestricted SPR flows are beneficial to the US economy. A second option is for Congress to pass legislation that ends or revises SPR restrictions and limitations under the Jones Act.

Step 2: Modernize Infrastructure

The preceding section on new oil market realities analyzed the emerging infrastructure constraints to delivering SPR oil to the market. Given those challenges, we must study the drawdown capacity for waterborne SPR oil from the Gulf Coast under different US production and export scenarios. And then we must analyze alternatives that would maximize drawdown, including expanding port facilities or relocating some SPR oil to the East or West Coasts.

Hurricane Katrina, together with more recent storms, highlighted the vulnerability of US petroleum product supply to severe refining outages. With US Gulf Coast refineries forecast to expand capacity and produce more in volume and global share, our vulnerability to a disruption caused by weather will only increase. This likelihood calls for a feasibility assessment of developing strategic petroleum stocks and possibly locating them outside the US Gulf Coast. Given current fiscal constraints, the United States could finance a future product stock through mandatory industry requirements or, perhaps, through a swap of SPR oil for products. The latter option could become more attractive if US imports decline more rapidly than currently expected and if the level of SPR is deemed more than sufficient.

Step 3: Expedite SPR Decisions and Incorporate Technical Market Expertise

As we have seen, even a well-intentioned wait-and-see strategy ends up delaying action until the window of maximum effect closes. Given the nature of modern oil markets, we are less likely to see major physical disruptions, and we will need to use price as an important signal of market imbalance. SPR releases need to be swift and robust to create confidence that the market will be sufficiently supplied. No harm is done if the barrels are not fully subscribed.

To reach a quick decision, relevant policy-makers need greater access to technical market expertise. The decision to deploy the reserve is made at the political level. At times, policy is led by the White House and, at other times, by the agencies. Whereas SPR decisions are inherently political, the nature of the markets demands that the White House have the analytical capacity to understand these issues with sophistication and to make timely decisions before market considerations undermine the effect of a release. This requirement will become even more important as changes in US oil flows begin to have a significant effect on the availability and price of different qualities of crude. To this end, the US Energy Information Administration should increase its complement of qualified energy economists for advice to the executive and legislative branches. In turn, the White House should consider secondment of such an economist from the Energy Information Administration or from the US Department of Energy's SPR office. Another option is to establish an ad hoc advisory group of outside experts.

Step 4: Enhance Cooperation with IEA and Non-IEA Members

The IEA has developed quick and effective mechanisms to consult and coordinate stock releases among members. Most of the discussion and logistics can be worked out in a matter of days, if not hours. However, tension between the United States and the IEA executive director over the need for a release in the summer of 2012 suggests a weakness in the system.[33] We must work with our partners in the IEA to establish a set of circumstances and market conditions that warrant discussion of an SPR draw. In addition, the 2011 IEA stock release exposed the failure of large incremental physical volumes to be released in the market as a result of lowering the compulsory industry stock requirement, one mechanism that countries can use to meet their IEA obligation. The IEA should review whether it should create enforcement mechanisms that would result in the release of more physical barrels from changes in industry stock requirements.

The United States and the IEA also need to establish a formal mechanism to coordinate with non-IEA countries that are building strategic stocks, most notably China, which now holds more than 105 million barrels and plans to expand to 90 days coverage (800 million barrels according to current demand estimates). Efforts to expand the IEA to include China have met with resistance on all sides. One option is to explore the possibility of using the G-20 or the Major Economies Forum as a place for cooperation. The outlook for lower US imports and continued restrictions on US exports may increase Chinese vulnerability to global disruptions because China will be exposed to a direct loss from non-US producers and be unable to access US replacement supplies. Therefore, China may become more eager to coordinate SPR policy with the United States and the IEA to attempt to ensure that US SPR oil is available to respond to global disruptions.

Step 5: Develop an Active Communication Strategy

In a world where markets react swiftly to media sound bites, policy-makers should know how to talk about SPR use and how to discuss this message with the IEA and holders of spare capacity. Major challenges to an effective communications plan are the ambiguous US agency responsibilities, the institutional weakness of the IEA executive director position, and the US episodic failure to engage key counterparts on these issues until mired in a supply crisis.

Putting a well-staffed, clearly authorized White House official in charge of policy coordination would go a long way toward developing a strong and effective position and would help the White House coordinate which agency engages the IEA, the Saudis, the Russians, or the Chinese. The

IEA executive director has a superb public platform, backed by the IEA's analytical capabilities. But the institutional framework of the IEA makes it more responsive to events than proactive in addressing supply concerns. Although the IEA runs highly effective simulation exercises and scenarios, the need for speed during crises puts the primary burden on the United States—and primarily the White House—for coordinating direct contact and communication strategies with suppliers and reserve holders. The United States should be ahead of the curve and develop a series of SPR contingency talking points for use in different scenarios. Such talking points can obviously be adjusted to reflect the nuances of any circumstance and should, where possible, be developed with IEA partners.

Conclusion

The changing North American energy landscape will not relieve the United States from the need to use the SPR to address price shocks caused by disruptions of oil supply. But these changes require that the United States consider how it will use the reserve in an environment of declining imports. With some forethought and changes in policy and infrastructure, we can make the SPR a powerful tool for a world of growing political instability. But failure to act will trap SPR oil in the United States and reduce an already thin system of buffer stocks, thereby leading to greater price volatility.

Notes

1. Public Law 94-163, S.622 was introduced in the US Senate on February 7, 1975, by Senator Henry M. Jackson (D-WA). The legislation was reported from the Senate Committee on Interior and Insular Affairs with Amendment, S. Rept. 94-26. It passed the Senate and House on December 18, 1975, and was signed into law on December 22, 1975.

2. Only the president can authorize the drawdown of the SPR. The EPCA specifies that the SPR may be tapped to counter "severe energy supply interruption," to honor energy-sharing agreements with other IEA members, and to respond to price hikes that can have "a major adverse impact" on the US economy. This provision was amended in 1990 to allow for less stringent short-term drawdown requirements.

3. Terrence R. Fehner and Jack M. Holl, *Department of Energy 1977–1994: A Summary History* (Washington, DC: Department of Energy, 1994). See also Alice Buck and Roger Anders, "Institutional Origins of the Department of Energy," in *The Department of Energy: 25 Years of Service*, ed. Charles Oldham (Tampa, FL: Faircount, 2002), 24–49.

4. The Office of Fossil Energy discusses the three events on its website at http://energy.gov/fe/services/petroleum-reserves/strategic-petroleum-reserve/releasing-oil-spr.

5. Robert L. Bamberger, "Strategic Petroleum Reserve," Issue Brief for Congress, Congressional Research Service, Washington, DC, April 2003, 16.

6. US Energy Information Administration (EIA), "US Ending Stocks of Crude Oil in SPR," EIA, March 15, 2013, Washington, DC, http://www.eia.gov/dnav/pet/hist/LeafHandler.ashx?n=PET&s=MCSSTUS1&f=A.

7. The Office of Fossil Energy includes this information on its website under "SPR Quick Facts and FAQs" at http://energy.gov/fe/services/petroleum-reserves/strategic-petroleum-reserve/spr-quick-facts-and-faqs.

8. EIA, "AEO2013 Early Release Overview," EIA, Washington, DC, 2012, http://www.eia.gov/forecasts/aeo/er/.

9. EIA, "The Impact of Tropical Cyclones on Gulf of Mexico Crude Oil and Natural Gas Production," EIA, Washington, DC, 5, http://www.eia.gov/forecasts/steo/special/pdf/2006_hurricanes.pdf.

10. EIA "Impact of Tropical Cyclones," 2.

11. EIA, "Libya," Country Analysis Brief, EIA, Washington, DC, June 2012, http://www.eia.gov/countries/cab.cfm?fips=LY.

12. In 2011 and 2012, the Brent crude classification was seen as a more reflective global oil price benchmark. Because of the growing volumes of stranded North American production near the delivery point of WTI at Cushing, Oklahoma, WTI became relatively disconnected from global pricing.

13. These figures are from the US Energy Information Administration (EIA) International Energy Statistics database at http://www.eia.gov/cfapps/ipdbproject/IEDIndex3.cfm.

14. Refiners that could process heavier Saudi replacement crude grades increased their use rates, while simpler refiners (mostly in the Mediterranean) that required the lighter grades displaced by the conflict reduced their runs.

15. The Office of Fossil Energy discusses the 2011 release on its website at http://energy.gov/fe/services/petroleum-reserves/strategic-petroleum-reserve.

16. Congress approved additional drawdown authorities in 1990, which increased the president's flexibility to use the SPR, following West Coast supply interruptions associated with the *Exxon Valdez* Alaskan oil spill in 1989. The provisions authorize a limited drawdown without the declaration of a severe energy shortage or the need to meet IEA obligations. Such drawdowns are limited to 30 million barrels over two months. See Anthony Andrews and Robert Pirog, "The Strategic Petroleum Reserve: Authorization, Operation, and Drawdown Policy," Congressional Research Service Report for Congress, Washington, DC, June 18, 2012.

17. Robert L. Bamberger, "US Home Heating Oil Price and Supply During the Winter of 2000–2001: Policy Options," Congressional Research Service Report for Congress, Washington, DC, August 2001, 8–9.

18. The final awards called for the 30.0 million barrels to be replaced by 31.2 million barrels in 2001 and 2002. Tight market conditions prompted the US Department of Energy to delay deliveries into 2002 and 2003 in exchange for more oil, thereby raising the total exchange amount to 34.5 million barrels. The Office of Fossil Energy discusses the situation on its website at http://energy.gov/fe/services/petroleum-reserves/strategic-petroleum-reserve/releasing-oil-spr.

19. For a discussion of the loan following Hurricane Isaac, see the Office of Fossil Energy's website at http://energy.gov/fe/services/petroleum-reserves /strategic-petroleum-reserve/releasing-oil-spr.

20. US Department of Energy, "Energy Department to Loan Emergency Fuel to Department of Defense as Part of Hurricane Sandy Response," press release, November 2, 2012, http://energy.gov/articles/energy-department-loan-emergency-fuel-department -defense-part-hurricane-sandy-response.

21. These figures are from the EIA International Energy Statistics database at http:// www.eia.gov/dnav/pet/pet_move_impcus_a2_nus_ep00_im0_mbbl_m.htm.

22. On July 30, 2012, President Obama signed an executive order that expanded existing sanctions against Iran that were established under the 2012 National Defense Authorization Act. The expansion was aimed at preventing countries from establishing new mechanisms to pay Iran for oil products, by which they would circumvent the sanctions. The exceptions given under the act also apply to the executive order. See Office of the Press Secretary, "Fact Sheet: Sanctions Related to Iran," press release, http:// www.whitehouse.gov/the-press-office/2012/07/31/fact-sheet-sanctions-related-iran.

23. The declaration, which was issued in Los Cabos, Mexico, on June 19, 2012, in part read, "G20 members will remain vigilant of the evolution of oil prices and will stand ready to carry out additional actions as needed, including the commitment by producing countries to continue to ensure an appropriate level of supply consistent with demand. We welcome Saudi Arabia's readiness to mobilize, as necessary, existing spare capacity to ensure adequate supply. We will also remain vigilant of other commodity prices." The full text of the declaration is available from the University of Toronto's G20 Information Centre at http://www.g20.utoronto.ca/2012/2012-0619-loscabos .html.

24. "IEA Sees Oil Market as 'Sufficiently Supplied,'" *Oil and Gas Journal* 110, no. 8c (2012), http://www.ogj.com/articles/print/vol-110/issue-8c/general-interest/iea -sees-oil-market-as-sufficiently.html.

25. EIA, *Annual Energy Review 1997* (Washington, DC: EIA, July 1998), table 11.4, 273, http://www.eia.gov/totalenergy/data/annual/previous.cfm.

26. PIRA Energy Group, "Unplanned Supply Outages Rise to 2.5 MMB/D," press release, July 31, 2012.

27. EIA, "OPEC Spare Capacity in the First Quarter of 2012 at Lowest Level since 2008," *Today in Energy* (blog), May 24, 2012, http://www.eia.gov/todayinenergy /detail.cfm?id=6410.

28. According to the EIA, "OPEC members serve as the swing producers in the world market because only OPEC producers possess surplus crude oil production capacity, most of which is in Saudi Arabia. EIA projects that OPEC surplus production capacity will average 2.3 million bbl/d in 2012 and rise to an average 2.6 million bbl/d in 2013." See EIA, "Short-Term Energy Outlook: Highlights," EIA, Washington, DC, August 2012, http://www.eia.gov/forecasts/steo/archives/Aug12.pdf.

29. IEA, "OPEC Crude Oil Supply," *Oil Market Report*, August 10, 2012, http:// omrpublic.iea.org/archiveresults.asp?formsection=full+issue&formdate=2012&Submi t=Submit.

30. Lananh Nguyen, "London Overtakes New York as Brent Oil Beats WTI," *Bloomberg*, August 1, 2012, http://www.bloomberg.com/news/2012-08-01/brent-beats -wti-oil-trading-as-ice-eclipses-nymex.html.

31. EIA, "AEO2013 Early Release Overview."

32. Code of Federal Regulations, "Short Supply Controls," Title 15 Commerce and Foreign Trade, section 754.2(f), http://www.gpo.gov/fdsys/pkg/CFR-2011-title15 -vol2/xml/CFR-2011-title15-vol2-sec754-2.xml.

33. Mikael Holter and Kristin Myers, "IEA Head Says Oil Market Doesn't Have Serious Supply Outage," *Bloomberg*, August 28, 2012, http://www.bloomberg.com /news/2012-08-28/iea-head-says-oil-market-doesn-t-have-serious-supply-disruption .html.

Chapter 21

Energy, Environment, and Climate: Framework and Tradeoffs

Michael Levi

Energy has always been inseparable from environmental issues. This chapter surveys the local and global dimensions of the energy–environment relationship, with a focus on US oil and gas and efforts to address related challenges. It then examines ways to address tensions among multiple energy-related goals.

Energy and the Local Environment

Energy production and use inevitably affects the local environment. Understanding the many ways this happens is essential to developing ways to square environmental and other goals.

US Oil and Gas Development

Production of oil and gas in the United States has long raised concerns about local environmental impacts. For several decades, until recently, this concern focused primarily on offshore oil and gas development and Alaska. The history of offshore oil development has generally been one of improving safety performance punctuated by major accidents that have spurred government action.[1] By 2010, confidence in the safety of offshore drilling was on the rise, with President Barack Obama bucking past precedent for Democrats and announcing an expansion of offshore drilling. Only weeks later, a blowout at the deepwater Macondo well in the Gulf of Mexico sent crude gushing into the ocean for nearly three months, setting a record for the largest US oil spill ever. The result has largely been a return to previous fights over offshore oil and gas development, with most environmental groups remaining opposed, while industry and its supporters continue to be enthusiastic.

Alaska has also been a focus of fights between industry and environmentalists for decades. Industry has long been focused on Alaska because of opportunities to profitably extract oil even when crude prices were low. Environmental groups have been focused on Alaska in part because of the industry interest, but also because of the often sensitive nature of the environment there. Historically, this tug-of-war has played out over section 1002 of the Alaska National Wildlife Refuge, a 1.5 million acre parcel of land on Alaska's northern coast, which analysts estimate could produce upward of a million barrels of oil a day at its peak, were it developed.[2] More recently, with rising oil prices and melting Arctic ice, offshore exploration and production in Alaska have become the new focus. Offshore drilling in Alaska poses special environmental challenges, because standard oil spill cleanup techniques may not work in the presence of significant amounts of ice and because seasonal shifts can complicate emergency operations.[3]

With the rapid rise of shale gas and tight oil production in recent years, however, environmental concerns have shifted to onshore development in the continental United States—and particularly to hydraulic fracturing. These concerns focus on three main challenges: water, air, and community impacts.

Hydraulic fracturing has been used for more than a half-century, but new concerns about water contamination have surfaced. These concerns have arisen in part because of the rapid growth in the use of hydraulic fracturing in areas of the country that are new to oil and gas development (or that have not seen intensive development for generations) and in part because modern hydraulic fracturing in shale plays involves water at least an order of magnitude greater for each well than past applications have required. People have raised concerns that fracking fluids injected in the ground could contaminate aquifers. General agreement exists that with proper well construction practices, groundwater contamination will not happen. But there is less agreement as to the frequency of departures from proper practices and the potential consequences. Concerns have also been raised that the large volumes of wastewater produced from wells may be improperly disposed of, thereby contaminating water supplies. Broader agreement exists that improperly managed produced waters can damage— and on occasion have damaged—local water supplies.

Concerns about air quality typically focus on the use of diesel in generators at sites where drilling and hydraulic fracturing are performed and on the venting of volatile organic compounds (produced along with methane as part of natural gas) into the atmosphere. Such air issues can be difficult to address because their effects are cumulative: no single well will cause a large-scale problem alone. These issues are, however, generally amenable to simple technology solutions, which can greatly reduce venting and diesel use. Several states have already pushed developers in this direction, and as of this writing, the US Environmental Protection Agency is in the process of doing the same for venting nationwide.

Shale gas and tight oil development has also raised less traditional concerns surrounding community impacts. Areas that have not typically been host to industrial activity have often found integration of development into their communities difficult. Rapid influxes of people, money, and equipment have created and exacerbated divisions, thereby helping to generate local opposition. Moratoria and bans on development have proliferated in part as a result.

Beyond drilling itself, oil and gas development of all kinds has long faced obstacles related to pipeline development. Community opposition, for example, has long stymied efforts to build gas pipelines in the Northeast. From 2011 on, environmental and landowner groups have focused intense scrutiny on the Keystone XL pipeline, which would move oil and diluted bitumen from the Canadian oil sands and North Dakota to Gulf Coast refineries. A mix of concerns about climate change, local impacts of oil sands production in Alberta, and potential spills along the pipeline route has driven their efforts. As of this writing, a federal decision on whether to allow the pipeline to be built is pending. The combination of local concerns and climate worries is likely to encourage similar opposition to pipelines in the future.

Energy Use and Local Air Pollution

Fossil fuel combustion also creates environmental damages. I focus here on risks from the power sector and from transportation, which together accounted for 72 percent of US oil, 92 percent of US coal, and 34 percent of US natural gas use in 2011.[4]

Recent work focused on power plant emissions has emphasized damages from sulfur dioxide (SO_2), the largest source of local environmental harm from the power plant fleet. (As of 2011, power generation accounted for 66 percent of US SO_2 emissions.[5]) One recent study indicated that the US coal-fired power plant fleet causes damages of $46 billion (constant 2000 dollars) each year that are due to SO_2 emissions and $53 billion if small particulate matter, nitrogen oxides, and other emissions are included.[6] The same study estimated that total environmental damages from the US gas-fired power plant fleet were approximately $900 million, nearly two orders of magnitude lower.

Shifting from coal to natural gas in power generation can greatly reduce air pollution near power plants. (Shifting to renewable or nuclear energy, of course, can reduce those emissions to zero.) The National Energy Technology Laboratory has estimated that an advanced 550-megawatt coal-fired power plant will produce 1,514 tons of SO_2 emissions annually, whereas a similar natural gas combined-cycle plant will produce a negligible amount.[7] Particulate matter emissions from a natural gas plant would be an order of magnitude lower than from a coal plant, whereas nitrogen oxide emissions from gas plants are negligible.

The use of gasoline and diesel in cars and trucks has also led to significant local environmental impacts. These effects have, however, declined radically in recent decades as a result of improving efficiency and increasingly stringent environmental regulations. Between 2006 and 2011, SO_2 emissions from vehicles declined by a factor of 10, whereas between 1980 and 2010, vehicle emissions of volatile organic compounds declined by a factor of 4. But fuel combustion for transportation still causes significant environmental damage. Recent analysis in support of the US government's 2012–16 fuel economy rules indicates that particulate matter and sulfur dioxide emissions are the largest sources of environmental damages.[8] Estimates in the same analysis imply that combined benefits from reductions in those two sources of pollution attributable to greater fuel economy should be nearly as large as benefits from reduced exposure to oil market volatility.[9] That said, SO_2 emissions from transportation account for barely more than 1 percent of total SO_2 emissions in the United States. Transportation emissions of small particulate matter, in contrast, account for 8 percent of the US total.

Alternative Energy Development

Many people have long pressed for alternative energy development in part to address the many environmental (as well as security) challenges associated with oil and gas. Yet development of alternatives is far from immune to environmental opposition.

Nuclear power, an alternative to natural gas in power generation, has long engendered intense opposition from environmental and some local groups, which have focused primarily on reactor safety and on disposal of radioactive waste. Until recently, however, nuclear power enjoyed increasing acceptance in the environmental community. But as with offshore drilling, a major accident—in this case the Fukushima nuclear disaster in Japan—has set that trend back sharply.

Renewable energy has also attracted opposition. To be sure, wind and solar power do not entail risks comparable to those associated with oil spills and contamination from poorly drilled wells. But renewable energy, even when operating properly, can have particularly outsized impacts on land. Vaclav Smil, for example, has argued that generating 1 kilowatt of solar power requires 100 to 250 square meters of land and that generating a similar amount of wind power requires roughly 1,000 square meters of land.[10] This contrasts, by his estimates, with 1 to 10 square meters for the same amount of coal-fired power (including the impacts of coal mining) and 0.5 to 5 square meters for a similar amount of gas-fired power. Improvements in the efficiency of renewable energy generation are driving down land requirements, and a shift to unconventional natural gas production is driving up the amount of land required to produce natural gas, but given the yawning initial gap between fossil and renewable sources, fully bridging it is difficult.

Renewable energy introduces another environmental challenge: many optimal sites for wind and solar generation (i.e., the windiest and sunniest places) are not served by the current electricity grid and thus require buildout of new transmission infrastructure. Construction, though, can face significant environmental resistance. As with pipeline infrastructure, infrastructure for renewable energy can present special challenges, because transmission lines cross large numbers of individual properties.

Biofuel production also has large land-use impacts. One recent study estimated that meeting current US biofuel production goals without new productivity increases would require displacing 80 percent of the current US crop harvest.[11] New technologies could ameliorate this situation, but even then, how biofuels production could be made radically less land intensive is difficult to see. Some assume that algae-based biofuel production could deeply reduce the amount of land necessary for biofuel production, but because algae still need to be exposed to sunlight, there are strong limits to how far that approach can reduce land requirements. Algal biofuel production does not, however, require access to productive farmland.

Climate Change

Burning coal, oil, and natural gas to produce energy releases carbon dioxide (CO_2) into the atmosphere. In 2009, coal combustion accounted for 43 percent of global energy-related CO_2 emissions, oil accounted for 37 percent, and natural gas accounted for 20 percent.[12] All scenarios that ultimately stabilize atmospheric greenhouse gas (GHG) concentrations—and thus limit climate damages—eventually see global CO_2 emissions drop close to zero. Hence, in the long run, they demand that any remaining fossil fuel use be paired with efforts to capture and sequester the resulting emissions. In the interim, shifting from coal to natural gas can cut emissions roughly in half.

Fossil fuel combustion for energy production is the dominant source of global and US GHG emissions. As of 2005, the most recent year for which comprehensive estimates are available, the energy sector accounted for 75 percent of world GHG emissions (70 percent of global emissions were from fossil fuel combustion) and for 96 percent of world CO_2 emissions.[13] As of 2010, fossil fuel combustion accounted for 79 percent of US GHG and 94 percent of US CO_2 emissions. Another 5 percent of US GHG emissions came from methane released by oil and gas systems and coal mining.[14] Curbing GHG emissions from energy—and particularly energy-related CO_2 emissions—must thus be central to any effort to mitigate climate change.

Efforts to identify the lowest-cost opportunities to reduce energy-related CO_2 emissions typically end up focusing on buildings and on the power sector. Buildings can often be improved to reduce their energy use, cutting direct demand for fuel (oil and gas for heating) and for electricity; shifting direct fuel use from oil to natural gas can also cut emissions. Shifting from coal to gas as a power plant fuel and to more efficient power plants also ranks among the lowest-cost ways to reduce emissions, in part because substituting natural gas for coal in power generation results in approximately a halving of GHG emissions.[15] Steps to cut oil use in cars and trucks, whether through greater efficiency or through the substitution of non-fossil-based fuels, typically register as considerably more expensive when judged by their costs per unit of reduced emissions. From a broader national perspective, though, they can often be attractive, because they can help push down oil prices and reduce US exposure to volatile global oil markets, benefits that individual consumers will neglect in their decisions absent government policy.

US Climate Change Policy

The threat of climate change has become a significant part of the US policy debate in recent decades. Debates over US climate policy have typically centered on three questions: How big a problem is climate change? How much should the United States do about it? And how should it pursue whatever goals it sets?

Despite clear scientific evidence that climate change is occurring, is driven in substantial part by human-caused emissions, and is poised to accelerate, many US politicians continue to debate whether climate change is real. Members of Congress regularly challenge the widely accepted view that people can influence the Earth's climate. Although, anecdotally, recent extreme weather appears to have had some influence on public opinion, one-quarter of the American people still believe that the world has not warmed over the past hundred years, and another quarter of those who believe that it has blame natural causes for most of the trend.[16] This situation is a weak foundation upon which to build policy and helps explain partly why the United States has found pursuing aggressive emissions-cutting efforts difficult. Public opinion is not entirely immobile and can be moved by acts of nature and by concerted efforts by leaders to educate and persuade. It is impossible to predict where those efforts will ultimately lead the United States.

People who believe that climate change is real and significant still often differ over how much the United States should do about it. Historically, this argument has focused mostly on whether US emissions-cutting action is worthwhile absent similar steps from other countries. Americans and their elected representatives have argued that unilateral action would put US firms and workers at a competitive disadvantage while barely shifting the world's emissions path. More recently, debate has focused less on these international dimensions and more on the perceived costs of taking action to cut US emissions, with lawmakers opposing US action regardless of what the rest of the world does.

Those who wish to address US emissions despite these arguments typically focus on several types of policies. The first are broad measures that would set overall goals for US emissions (or for emissions from particular sectors) and use a mix of regulation and market forces to achieve them. For most of the past decade, discussion of this type of policy focused on cap-and-trade legislation. Such legislation would set a maximum level of emissions for the US economy, distribute emissions permits totaling that cap, and require that firms hold enough permits to cover their emissions. Firms could buy and sell those permits among themselves, thereby ensuring that emissions were reduced at the lowest possible cost; this is the "trade" part of cap-and-trade.

A related scheme, known as a clean energy standard, has recently become popular among some analysts and policy-makers. It would require that utilities generate an increasing fraction of their electricity from clean sources. Scholars and policy analysts have also long discussed the possibility of taxing carbon emissions, which should, in principle, have the same practical effect as a cap-and-trade system. A popular view, however, has long held that imposing a carbon tax in the United States is not politically possible, even though arguably it is the most efficient way to achieve the desired result.[17]

Mainstream estimates of the cost of reducing emissions through price-based mechanisms such as cap-and-trade or carbon taxes are typically modest. The US Energy Information Administration (EIA), for example, has estimated that a system with permits priced at $15 per ton of CO_2 in 2013 and rising 5 percent each year would cut US emissions by 20 percent (relative to 2010 levels) by 2035, while shaving 0.6 percent off US gross domestic product in that year. (The EIA projects that a more ambitious system would cut US emissions by 67 percent and reduce US output by less than 0.1 percent more.)[18] Estimates such as these should be treated carefully—this one, for example, relies on the availability of abundant nuclear power—but they still provide useful indicators. Using mechanisms like a clean energy standard would have slightly higher costs because the set of acceptable emissions-cutting actions would be smaller, but if designed properly, they would still be net winners.

With price-based mechanisms politically unpopular, policy-makers have increasingly turned to direct regulation of emissions sources. New automobile fuel economy standards promulgated in 2012 were justified in part by the climate benefits they would deliver. New standards for new power plants, which would effectively prevent new coal plant construction, were justified similarly. US regulators have estimated that new fuel economy standards for cars and light trucks with model years between 2017 and 2025 will reduce cumulative US GHG emissions by 2 billion metric tons of CO_2 over the life of the vehicles affected, an amount equivalent to more than one-quarter of US annual emissions.[19] Similarly, scholars have estimated that modest regulation of stationary sources (including power plants) under the Clean Air Act could reduce annual US emissions by the equivalent of more than 6 percent of 2005 emissions levels by 2020.[20]

In general, when the benefits of a new regulation clearly outweigh the associated costs, top-down regulation can be an effective approach. When the balance is less clear, these sorts of regulations can end up turning out to be far less justified in retrospect. For the most part, this prospect is likely to prevent aggressive and inflexible climate regulations from being imposed in the first place.

A final group of people concerned with climate change has pushed for a fundamentally different approach focused instead on technology innovation. A full discussion of technology policy is well beyond the scope of this chapter (see chapter 17 of this volume for a thorough discussion). For the most part, though, while analysts generally agree that accelerating innovation is an essential part of an effective climate strategy, they mostly believe that it must be paired with price- or regulation-based measures to directly drive substitution of lower-carbon energy for higher-carbon fuels.[21]

International Climate Change Actions and Negotiations

The United States, of course, cannot deal with climate change alone. Most GHG emissions are produced outside the United States, and without deep reductions from other major emitters, stabilization of atmospheric GHG concentrations will be impossible. As a result, debate over climate policy regularly focuses on what happens elsewhere in the world.

That discussion has often focused on international climate negotiations. Success in dealing with climate change has typically been identified closely with success in negotiating an international treaty that mandates country-by-country emissions reductions to safe levels. From 2007 to 2009, international climate negotiations focused squarely on concluding a successor treaty to the Kyoto Protocol. These negotiations culminated at the 15th Conference of the Parties to the United Nations Framework Convention on Climate Change in Copenhagen, Denmark, in December 2009. The parties were unable to agree to a treaty but instead negotiated what became known as the Copenhagen Accord, a political agreement that was quickly attacked in most of the world and not formally adopted by the Conference of the Parties. The Copenhagen Accord had four critical elements: (a) agreement to aim to keep global temperature increases below 2°C; (b) emissions-cutting commitments from developed and developing countries (to be submitted early the next year); (c) a commitment by developed countries to contribute $30 billion to assist developing countries by 2012 and to raise up to $100 billion annually for the same purpose by 2020; and (d) an agreement from all to develop a process of "consultation and analysis" that would review countries' mitigation efforts.

The Copenhagen Accord was quickly assailed for being weak and then contested, leading to two years of fighting over its future, the future of the Kyoto Protocol, and the appropriate next steps for the climate regime. In December 2011, in Durban, South Africa, the parties agreed to seek a new agreement by 2015, to come into force by 2020. Nothing indicates that this effort will be any more successful than the one that culminated in Copenhagen, and little progress was made on it at the first post-Durban negotiations in Doha, Qatar, in late 2012, which focused mainly on other issues.

An emphasis on treaty negotiations can, however, be misleading: it is possible to negotiate an ambitious treaty but for emissions reductions to fall short; it is also possible, in principle, to collectively cut emissions to safe levels without a significant treaty. Countries often pursue emissions-cutting steps for reasons other than climate change mitigation and will continue to do so in the future. China, in particular, will continue to seek improvements in energy efficiency regardless of whether a global climate treaty emerges. Indeed, the commitment it made in 2009 to cut its carbon intensity (emissions relative to economic output) by 40 to 45 percent between 2005 and 2020 was mostly a consolidation of existing efforts that were aimed at nonclimate goals. The United States will similarly pursue emissions-cutting measures, whether to improve energy security, to promote clean energy industries, or to deal with climate change (such as through power plant regulations), with the hope that others will reciprocate in a virtuous cycle, even absent an international agreement.

Moreover, countries can coordinate their actions and build on each other's progress through mechanisms other than a global climate treaty. Countries are already moving toward linking cap-and-trade systems through unilateral rules that allow each system to accept credits from others. The Major Economies Forum, long focused on preparing for United Nations negotiations, may eventually expand its focus to include coordination of concrete measures, such as fuel economy standards or trade regulations. Similarly, the Group of 20, having agreed to phase out inefficient energy subsidies in 2009 (with only limited success in implementation), has recently admitted climate finance to its agenda. A process known as the Clean Energy Ministerial, which was spearheaded by the US Department of Energy and launched in 2010, has proved to be a practical forum for developing technology cooperation efforts that can accelerate innovation and deployment. The Clean Energy Ministerial has also been a model for public–private cooperation at the international level. Ultimately, the most important issue is what countries are doing and will do about their emissions, however those plans are coordinated (if they are at all). Whether those steps are mandated in a treaty is a secondary issue.

Alas, countries' actions and announced intentions to date are insufficient to reduce global GHG emissions to levels that experts, diplomats, and policy-makers have focused on as potentially safe. One recent study examined the various pledges that countries have made to reduce their emissions through 2020. These pledges almost certainly present an upper limit to what they will actually deliver.[22] The study concludes that emissions in 2020 will be more than 10 percent above the upper limit of what is consistent with an even chance of keeping temperature increases below 2°C, a typical focus of international talks. Other studies are even more skeptical.

Part of the shortfall in recent ambition and policy effort on climate change has likely been due to economic weakness in the developed world. Economic recovery in the United States would not automatically lead to stronger action on climate change, but it would create an atmosphere in which the costs and benefits of climate policy would be more likely to be debated on their merits, thus allowing policy to move forward. The link between strong climate policy and economic health appears to be more attenuated in Europe, where enthusiasm for action on climate is relatively high in the first place. But European progress on the economic front can only help propel climate action forward. In Japan, decisions on the future of nuclear power are for now the biggest variable in determining future performance on climate change.

Synergies and Tensions

Many energy options can help ameliorate security, local environment, and climate concerns at the same time. Renewable energy and energy efficiency are the clearest opportunities on this front, though whether and under what circumstances they are cost-effective opportunities to address the three types of concerns is a separate matter. Most energy options, however, present more difficult decisions. The classic dilemma surrounds domestic oil and gas development, which provides some contribution to national security but results in local environmental risks associated with extraction. This tension can be ameliorated through responsible industry practices and prudent regulation. Ultimately, though, the only way to resolve remaining tensions is through informed deliberation.

The tradeoffs become more complex when they involve natural gas. Given the fragmented nature of global natural gas markets, increased opportunities for domestic natural gas production can substantially reduce the domestic price of natural gas, leading it to displace coal. Similarly, regulations that encourage the substitution of natural gas for coal should be expected to increase natural gas prices and hence intensify extractive activity. This situation presents a tension between environmental goals, although natural gas–fired power plants are far less polluting than coal-fired plants. (Coal extraction, of course, has its own local environmental consequences, which would be reduced through coal-to-gas substitution.) If regulation (rather than greater opportunities for development) is used to drive greater natural gas use in the power sector, there may also be tensions with security goals, because at some point, increased domestic demand could force the United States to become dependent on gas imports.

Climate change poses a newer and in some ways more vexing set of tradeoffs. Consider oil first. Considerable disagreement exists over whether and how much increased domestic oil production will exacerbate climate change. Much attention has focused on whether domestically produced oil is more carbon intensive—essentially, whether its production entails greater emissions—than the alternative. This issue is something of a distraction, because the main climate impact of oil comes when it is burned, not when it is extracted. The key question, then, is how much global oil consumption will increase as a result of increased US oil production.

The answer depends on three critical variables: the sensitivity of oil demand to lower prices; the sensitivity of oil production in market economies to lower oil prices; and the response of states that control oil production more directly, most notably in the Organization of the Petroleum Exporting Countries. To the extent that these producers offset any increase in US supply by reducing their own (to stabilize prices), the climate impact of increased US production will be small; so too, however, will be the impact on prices, limiting (though not eliminating) any US security benefit from the production increase. At the other end of the spectrum, if other countries do not offset any increase in US production, the climate impact will be larger; so too, though, will be the security and economic benefits.

Natural gas presents another conundrum for climate policy. In recent years, low natural gas prices have led to the substitution of natural gas for coal, thus reducing US CO_2 emissions. Inexpensive natural gas, however, also has two countervailing effects: it leads to greater energy consumption in general (as a result of lower prices), and it deters investment in zero-carbon energy, including renewable and nuclear power.

Broad agreement exists, though, that these impacts have so far been much smaller than the shift from coal to gas. The bigger question surrounding natural gas involves the future—particularly the longer-term US emissions trajectory. Deep cuts in US emissions—Barack Obama and John McCain both spoke of cuts of approximately 60 to 80 percent by 2050 during the 2008 presidential campaign—are incompatible with continued large-scale combustion of natural gas unless the resulting CO_2 emissions are captured and sequestered underground. Policy will need to steer the US energy system toward zero-carbon fuels, whether they be renewable energy, nuclear power, or gas or coal combined with carbon capture and sequestration. This was true before the recent decline in natural gas prices and remains true; the only change is in the competition.

How should US policy navigate these tensions?[23] GHG emissions are primarily the result of fossil fuel combustion, not production, though the two are, of course, related. US climate policy should thus focus on the consumption side of the equation, disincentivizing or restricting GHG emissions as appropriate. Meanwhile, US production policy should focus on ameliorating local environmental concerns (while also addressing security and economic needs) when making decisions regarding access to oil and gas resources, rather than trying to constrain US production in the name of climate safety.

Notes

1. Democratic Policy and Communications Center, "Clean Energy Jobs and Oil Company Accountability Act: Background on Offshore Drilling and Moratoriums," US Senate, Washington, DC, 2010, http://dpc.senate.gov/files_energybill/background_offshore.pdf.

2. Donald L. Paul and Nancy L. Johnson, "Global Access to Oil and Gas," Topic Paper 7, Global Oil and Gas Study, National Petroleum Council, Washington, DC, July 18, 2007.

3. See Charles Emmerson, "The Arctic: Promise or Peril?," chapter 9 of this volume.

4. US Energy Information Administration (EIA), *Annual Energy Review 2011* (Washington, DC: EIA, 2012).

5. Technology Transfer Network Clearinghouse for Inventories and Emissions Factors, "National Emissions Inventory (NEI) Air Pollutant Emissions Trends Data," US Environmental Protection Agency, Washington, DC, 2011, http://www.epa.gov/ttnchie1/trends/.

6. Nicholas Z. Muller, Robert Mendelsohn, and William Nordhaus, "Environmental Accounting for Pollution in the United States Economy," *American Economic Review* 101, no. 5 (August 2011): 1649–75.

7. US National Energy Technology Laboratory, "Supercritical Pulverized Bituminous Coal Plant," in *Cost and Performance Baseline for Fossil Energy Plants, Volume 1: Bituminous Coal and Natural Gas to Electricity—Final Report* (Washington, DC: US Department of Energy, 2007), http://www.netl.doe.gov/KMD/cds/disk50/PC%20Plant%20Case_Supercritical%20with%20CCS_051507.pdf. See also US National Energy Technology Laboratory, "Natural Gas Combined-Cycle Plant," in *Cost and Performance Baseline for Fossil Energy Plants, Volume 1: Bituminous Coal and Natural Gas to Electricity—Final Report* (Washington, DC: US Department of Energy, 2007), http://www.netl.doe.gov/KMD/cds/disk50/NGCC%20Plant%20Case_FClass_051607.pdf.

8. US National Highway Traffic Safety Administration (NHTSA), *Final Regulatory Impact Analysis: Corporate Average Fuel Economy for MY 2012–MY 2016 Passenger Cars and Light Trucks* (Washington, DC: US Department of Transportation, NHTSA, March 2010). Specifically, these are the environmental emissions for which the regulatory impact analysis projects the greatest reductions from the higher fuel economy standards.

9. Author's calculations based on NHTSA, *Final Regulatory Impact Analysis*, 14.

10. Vaclav Smil, "Power Density Primer: Understanding the Spatial Dimension of the Unfolding Transition to Renewable Electricity Generation," University of Manitoba, Winnipeg, Canada, 2010, http://www.vaclavsmil.com/wp-content/uploads/docs/smil-article-power-density-primer.pdf.

11 W. Kolby Smith, Cory C. Cleveland, Sasha C. Reed, Norman L. Miller, and Steven W. Runing, "Bioenergy Potential of the United States Constrained by Satellite

Observations of Existing Productivity," *Environmental Science and Technology* 46, no. 6 (2012): 3536–44.

12. International Energy Agency, *World Energy Outlook 2011* (Paris: OECD/IEA, 2011).

13. Data are from the World Resources Institute's Climate Analysis Indicators Tool (CAIT) database, May 2012, at http://www.wri.org/project/cait/.

14. US Environmental Protection Agency, *Inventory of US Greenhouse Gas Emissions and Sinks: 1990–2010* (Washington, DC: US Environmental Protection Agency, 2012).

15. A small number of scholars have recently argued that methane leakage from natural gas operations renders gas worse for climate change than coal, but their work has been consistently rejected by others who have studied the issue. See Robert Howarth, Renee Santoro, and Anthony Ingraffea, "Methane and the Greenhouse-Gas Footprint of Natural Gas from Shale Formations," *Climatic Change Letters* 106, no. 4 (2011): 679–90. See also Lawrence M. Cathles III, Larry Brown, Milton Taam, and Andrew Hunter, "A Commentary on 'The Greenhouse-Gas Footprint of Natural Gas in Shale Formations' by R. W. Howarth, R. Santoro, and Anthony Ingraffea," *Climatic Change Letters* 113, no. 2 (2012): 525–35; Lawrence M. Cathles, "Assessing the Greenhouse Impact of Natural Gas," *Geochemistry, Geophysics, Geosystems* 13, no. 6 (2012); Ramón A. Alvarez, Stephen W. Pacala, James J. Winebrake, William L. Chameides, and Steven P. Hamburg, "Greater Focus Needed on Methane Leakage from Natural Gas Infrastructure," *Proceedings of the National Academy of Sciences* 109, no. 17 (2012): 6435–40; Michael Levi, "Comment on 'Hydrocarbon Emissions Characterization in the Colorado Front Range: A Pilot Study' by Gabrielle Pétron et al." *Journal of Geophysical Research* 117, no. D21 (2012), doi:10.1029/2012JD017686; Michael Levi, "Climate Consequences of Natural Gas as a Bridge Fuel," *Climatic Change* (January 2013), doi:10.1007/s10534-012-0658-3.

16. Pew Research Center for People and the Press, "More Say There Is Solid Evidence of Global Warming," Pew Research Center for People and the Press, Washington, DC, October 15, 2012, http://www.people-press.org/2012/10/15/more-say-there-is-solid-evidence-of-global-warming/.

17. For an argument for cap-and-trade measures, see Robert N. Stavins, "A US Cap-and-Trade System to Address Climate Change," Discussion Paper 2007-13, Hamilton Project, Brookings Institution, Washington, DC, October 2007. For a carbon tax, see Gilbert E. Metcalf, "A Proposal for a US Carbon Tax Swap," Discussion Paper 2007-12, Hamilton Project, Brookings Institution, Washington, DC, October 2007. For a clean energy standard, see Joseph E. Aldy, "Promoting Clean Energy in the American Power Sector," Discussion Paper 2011-04, Hamilton Project, Brookings Institution, Washington, DC, May 2011.

18. The estimates are from side cases for EIA *Annual Energy Outlook 2012 with Projections to 2035* (Washington, DC: EIA, 2012). They can be retrieved at http://www.eia.gov/oiaf/aeo/tablebrowser/.

19. Office of Transportation and Air Quality, "EPA and NHTSA Set Standards to Reduce Greenhouse Gases and Improve Fuel Economy for Model Years 2017–2025 Cars and Light Trucks," Regulatory Announcement EPA-420-F-12-051, US Environmental Protection Agency, Washington, DC, August 2012.

20. Dallas Burtraw and Matt Woerman, "US Status on Climate Change Mitigation," RFF Discussion Paper 12-48, Resources for the Future, Washington, DC, October 2012.

21. For an argument that innovation support should be combined with carbon pricing, see Robert N. Stavins, "Repairing the R&D Market Failure," *Environmental Forum* 28, no. 1 (2011): 16. For an argument that innovation policy alone is sufficient, see Roger Pielke Jr., *The Climate Fix: What Scientists and Politicians Won't Tell You about Global Warming* (New York: Basic Books, 2010).

22. United Nations Environment Programme, "The Emissions Gap Report: Technical Summary," United Nations Environment Programme, Nairobi, Kenya, 2010.

23. For prescriptions from a national security perspective, see Leon Fuerth, "National Security, Energy, Climate Change: New Paradigm, New Strategy, New Governance," chapter 22 of this volume.

Chapter 22

National Security, Energy, Climate Change: New Paradigm; New Strategy; New Governance

Leon Fuerth

One of the axioms of the American grand strategy is that assured access to oil and gas from overseas producers is an existential matter. Where energy is concerned, the United States has relied on a network of relationships with secular, authoritarian governments in the energy-producing regions—mainly, the Middle East—that are held in place by mutual economic inter-dependencies and backstopped by American military power. This paradigm is now very seriously challenged:

* In the short term, extreme political turbulence in the Middle East raises serious questions about future relationships with successor and survivor governments across the region.

The views herein represent those held by the author in his personal capacity and in no way express an official viewpoint on behalf of the institutions with which he is affiliated.

- In the medium term, geostrategic rivalries over access to energy resources in the Arctic and in the South China Sea have raised the possibility of military confrontation involving US allies, China, and other countries.
- In the longer term, the rapidly emerging reality of climate change—itself a consequence of profligate use of fossil fuels—is introducing an unprecedented new form of risk to international stability.

New Paradigm: Energy–Climate–National Security Interaction

The tendency is to deal with these risks by segregating them, but they are in fact interactive. The national security community is paying serious attention to the short- and medium-term challenges, but it is only just beginning to think about the longer-term challenge from climate change. Within this community, there is a lingering attitude that we have time to deal with climate change *after* we deal with the supply problem and a lingering skepticism that the effects of climate change could ultimately threaten the existing order.

The premise of this chapter, however, is that climate change is *now* a rapidly developing strategic threat to national security, with a sharply rising trajectory, and we do not, in fact, have the luxury to continue to slow-walk an effective response to climate change. Past energy consumption translates into oncoming levels of climate change that cannot be stopped in their tracks but might yet be held to levels that are sustainable by the international system. However, ongoing consumption levels are stoking climate change to levels that will strain and might exceed the adaptive capacity of the international system—and projected levels of energy consumption will drive climate change to levels that can induce systemic collapse.[1]

Abnormal rates of glacier melt in the Himalayan Plateau—caused by climate change—directly affect the vital interests of every nation that depends on water from that source, including three nuclear-armed states whose relations are always problematic: China, India, and Pakistan. The transformation of the Arctic could well lead to a lose–lose competition for prospective competitive advantage for access to its resources. Peak oil appears to be receding as a near-term concern, but further down the road, peak water is advancing to replace it. The already recorded effects of climate change are comprehensively exceeding the upper ranges of what used to be viewed as conservative estimates. Meanwhile, massive diplomatic efforts to deal with the problem through an enforceable, universal set of treaty obligations have stalled out.[2]

World energy requirements will continue to grow, and one way or another much of that growth will depend on the use of fossil fuels—mainly coal—in China and India. The atmosphere will therefore continue to accumulate carbon dioxide (CO_2) from industrial consumption, which, in turn, will stoke the environmental crisis that is already loaded into the planet's climate system. Climate change is now markedly under way, with effects that can be measured throughout the entire planetary biosphere, including the atmosphere, the oceans, and the land.

We do not know how far this process will take us, partly because we do not know how long it will be before humankind gets a grip on the process. But we do understand that climate change has the potential to exceed the adaptive capacity of the international system as we know it. War is only one of many consequences of climate-induced collapse, but it is a special case because the major military powers are diplomatically leveraged in such a way that a conventional war over resources—be they energy or water—has to be regarded as a possible detonator for war on a large scale, even up to and including a nuclear exchange. There is nearly cosmic irony in the likelihood that a nuclear exchange involving large numbers of weapons could itself induce massive, abrupt climate shift—nuclear winter—on a scale sufficient to prevent recovery.

Some may think that this scenario is extreme. And it is. Nevertheless, it is important to point out that the 20th century was a succession of waking nightmares of such scenarios, beginning with a singularity—the assassination of one man in Sarajevo—followed by a string of cataclysms, including two world wars, and then by a cold peace that was based on the very real threat of mutual assured destruction. The physical capability to carry out nuclear destruction still exists, although we tend to put it out of our minds. It exists, in fact, abundantly. The weapons carried by a single nuclear-armed submarine could halt civilization in its tracks. Unrestrained consumption of carbon-based fuel will accelerate climate change and magnify the ultimate level of damage it causes, adding new, increasingly dangerous flashpoints for conflict to those that already exist. Nuclear technology carries great benefits that are indissolubly linked to great dangers. What stands between the best and the worst consequences of these capabilities is human foresight and wisdom. What are the odds that our luck will hold?

We need a game-changer, and maybe one is at hand. American dependence on foreign sources of energy is easing because of the rapid application in the United States of new technologies, especially hydraulic fracturing, or fracking. Of course, natural gas is a fossil fuel, and its use is at best a palliative where climate change is concerned. Seen in strategic context, however, there may be a chance to harness the fracking revolution. The United States is making a potentially revolutionary shift from energy importer to net energy exporter. This development can reduce the leverage of overseas suppliers, making the United States less sensitive to the threat of supply disruption or manipulation of markets; it can help shift the US economy away from coal as the primary source of power for electrical energy generation; it can afford the United States greater flexibility as an agent for international change; it can shift the balance of business advantage toward locating manufacturing in the United States; and it can help build the case for a next-generation smart national electricity grid linking diverse sources of energy into a robust system—efficient, responsive to regional shifts of demand, and resistant to accidental or deliberate harm.[3]

US national security and international stability require assured access to increasing amounts of energy—not just for the US economy alone, but for the maintenance of the globalized economic system as a whole. However, from here on out, both US national and global stability also require that we bring climate change under sufficient control to prevent it from overwhelming the adaptive capacity of individual nations and, ultimately, of the international system as a whole.

Accomplishing this goal will require a new, integrated strategy that aims to reconcile very powerful forces that are at tension with each other. The argument presented here is that we have arrived at an inflection point where it is possible to accomplish this. We have the possibility to use economic savings from the ongoing shift from coal to gas as a way to propel a second shift from carbon-based fuels to renewables. It is also possible that the hitherto missing element—political will—may now be generated by gathering public experience of climate change as a material reality. This is potentially the basis for a new strategy.

New Strategy: Multifaceted Challenge and Multifaceted Response

Under a succession of administrations, US energy strategy has amounted to little more than an aggregate of default positions, characterized by near fatalistic acceptance of US vulnerabilities, masked by magical political thinking. The actual results: until only recently, deeper US dependence on foreign sources of oil and gas—notwithstanding decades of political rhet-

oric about energy independence—and economic growth that was shack-
led to decisions made by producers' cartels, which set prices for oil and
gas. More results: US growth that was distorted by the impact of recycled
energy revenues, invested to suit the purposes of sovereign funds; our
security mortgaged to the defense of foreign suppliers against external ag-
gression and internal disorder; pressures for US support of antidemocratic
governance within the major producing states, as part of the price for doing
business with them; and US failure to create a domestic national energy
system that was robust enough to handle the consequences of damage from
either natural or humanmade causes. And, above all else, the result was US
failure to provide effective leadership for responding to climate change on
a global basis despite at least 20 years of advance warning about its consequences, so that we have now reached the point where the measured rate of
temperature change is on course toward levels deemed to be catastrophic.

Coming to grips with climate change has become a national security
priority on par with ensuring access to energy. The need to manage both of
these priorities as interactive parts of a complex whole is a *new* paradigm.
Doing so will require a multifaceted, phased global strategy that concurrently ensures a balance between energy supply and demand, at economically sustainable prices; responds to the already unfolding consequences of
climate change; and arrests the buildup of greenhouse gases in the atmosphere at levels low enough to head off massive environmental, economic,
and social damage.

The United States cannot solve these problems outside the reality of a
globalized energy market, nor can it exempt itself from the planetwide effects of climate change. This circumstance, however, does not mean that
the United States must await action by others as a precondition for acting to
protect its own interests and those of the global commons. On the contrary,
our ability to act with others will be strongly affected by initiatives that we
should take on our own, for ourselves.[4] The following two sections illustrate
the actions that we can take on our own, concurrently with other actions
that need to be undertaken in concert with others. A successful strategy will
have to deal with both categories as part of an interactive whole, rather than
attempt to deal with them serially.

Actions That Can Be Taken on Our Own

Many actions are possible without the cooperation of other countries.

Plan for Food Price Spikes and Shortages as the New Normal

The impact of climate change on US agriculture has ramifications for global food prices, with cascading political effects in countries that are both politically vulnerable and strategically important. Our operating assumption must be that abnormal weather conditions that are highly damaging to US agriculture will not abate and may intensify. Under those conditions, mandatory requirements for converting corn to ethanol place stress on both US and foreign food markets. In the short term, US policy-making must navigate between the goal of stabilizing the domestic cost of fuel and the international costs of foodstuffs.

Plan for Drought as the New Normal

Climate change is associated with persistent drought in major agricultural regions of the United States. In the short term, efficiencies must be found, both in the use of water for irrigation and in its use for urban and industrial purposes. In the medium term, the impact of protracted, nationwide droughts on rivers will create disputes among jurisdictions *within* the United States and *between* the United States and both Mexico and Canada, which have agreements with us for sharing water. A comprehensive review of the way that these agreements are codified and a search for ways to sustain them under radically stressed conditions are both needed. In addition, over the longer term, persistent drought will speed the exhaustion of major aquifers such as the Ogallala. At some point, this process will threaten the foundations of agriculture as currently practiced in the US western states, with powerful domestic and international effects.

Plan for Higher Sea Levels and Storm Surges

Major coastal cities will be exposed to flooding, which will lead to demands for the construction of defenses. The lead time for designing and constructing these defenses is sufficiently long, however, to risk their being overtaken by rising sea levels and by the growing intensity of storms. The costs for such defenses will be high and justified only prospectively by the social and economic consequences of failure to undertake them in time to have them in place and at a level of robustness able to deal with the upper end of possible challenges. Modeling of climate change effects has some time ago clearly warned of events such as the flooding of portions of New York City, as was seen in Superstorm Sandy in 2012.[5]

Plan for an Ultralow-Carbon, High-Efficiency Energy System

For both security and economic reasons, the United States needs to modernize its energy infrastructure on a nationwide basis to include an ultra-high-voltage DC smart grid that is able to move energy from one end of the country to the other with minimal losses and is designed for resilience against cyber attacks and disruptions owing to natural causes. At the same time, the carbon intensity of the US economy must be sharply reduced by a phased series of adaptations, in the short term by promoting the substitution of gas for coal, in the medium term by promoting even higher levels of efficiency through a carbon tax, and in the longer term by developing solar power reservoirs in regions of the country where solar power can be generated far in excess of local and regional demand and distributed across a national smart grid on a transregional basis.

Plan to Decelerate Carbon Dioxide Deposition in the Atmosphere

The most direct way to do so is to reduce the consumption of carbon-based fuels, but that step requires major adjustments for which many are loath to pay. The alternative is carbon capture, a still developing technology[6] that promises more energy from carbon-based fuel, without climate change. It is time to stop debating this technology on any basis other than the facts, and the only way to get the facts is to construct test-bed facilities on an industrial scale.[7]

But that investment requires due diligence not yet in evidence. There is, for example, a need to confront, rather than to gloss over, the possibility that carbon capture will create an ultra-long-range risk to the environment, as a consequence of the release of tremendous volumes of stored CO_2. Proponents of deep storage for CO_2 claim that it is safe for millennia. The problem is that we also wish for human civilization to persist for many millennia, and decisions made in our time must have the survival of distant generations in mind in addition to our convenience in the present. We take seriously the risks involving storage of radioactive waste that contains isotopes that have half-lives measured in thousands of years. We also take seriously the risk of releasing into the biosphere genetically modified life forms capable of uncontrollable reproduction outside laboratory conditions. If the idea of carbon capture is that it is possible to withhold CO_2 from the atmosphere in quantities sufficient to make a difference on the scale of climate change, then an obvious question arises about the permanence of that sequestration.

Plan for Climate Change as a Real, Imminent Security Threat

In the realm of military thinking, it is standard practice to consider worst-case scenarios as a way to avoid settling on insufficiently robust courses of action, just because they are cheaper upfront. Also, in military thinking, it is standard to pay serious attention to low-probability, high-damage events (e.g., nuclear war). Where climate change is concerned, however, our thinking tends toward best-case outcomes, for no real reason other than the inconvenience of the possible truth.[8] Planning for climate change needs to shift toward worst-case scenarios, especially because trends in the physical evidence are all pointing in that direction.

Plan for Synergistic Responses between Climate Change and Other Security Threats

An effective US domestic energy policy can diminish vulnerability to terrorism. Technology can now enable a shift in the architecture of the national energy system away from reliance on highly concentrated forms of generation and transmission and toward systems that are more dispersed. A consequence of this shift is to reduce the set of ultra-high-value targets for terrorist attack: not just by direct, kinetic forms of assault, but by cyber strikes through the Internet. Smart networks can be designed from the ground up to be more resilient against cyber attacks than the present patchwork of systems.[9]

Actions That Need to Be Taken in Concert with Others

Many necessary actions can be accomplished only with the cooperation of other countries.

Bolster International Law

The United States should, as an act of self-interest, ratify the United Nations Convention on the Law of the Sea. It also needs to work to develop multilateral rules for navigation in Arctic waters that are opening up as the result of climate change—as well as for development of energy sources located on or under the sea-bed in the Arctic.[10] The present regime is based on the sovereign interests of states with territorial claims in the Arctic. With the opening of this region, treating the Arctic as a closed domain will run up against the interests of other countries' economic interests—most notably, those of China. We need to establish international controls to prevent national authorities—or even highly empowered private entities (persons or corporations)—from undertaking geo-engineering projects with the potential to do serious, long-term damage.

Water scarcity will put great stress on existing international agreements for sharing river water. The water rights of nations that are parties to these agreements can be exercised unilaterally to build dams and divert rivers in ways that negate the intent of these agreements. The mere statement of an intent to divert shared water for unilateral purposes carries with it the potential for conflict.

Accelerate Research

Accelerating research is essential to improve, for example, the ability of food crops to withstand drought and to grow in salt-damaged soil.[11] We will need the equivalent of multiple Green Revolutions to ensure that crop production can meet global demands and can do so by means that are sustainable. There will be tremendous incentive to rely on genetic modification of crops and animal life (including marine life) to achieve higher productivity under more demanding environmental conditions. Modification of life forms is becoming steadily easier to accomplish, but complications from their permanent release into the biosphere are problematic and will require greatly strengthened international rules and forms of monitoring.

Promote Collaborative Planning for In-Time Responses to Major Threats

A change in the monsoon cycle could be relatively abrupt and would have massive consequences for billions of human beings. The time to think through palliative responses is now, when first signs may be evident, rather than after circumstances have changed enough to remove all uncertainty. Similarly, the time to think through the consequences of the permanent inundation of regions inhabited by hundreds of millions of persons is already at hand.[12]

Action to Slow Climate Change

The United States has already proposed international action to reduce soot as a way to slow ice melt, so as to gain time for other, harder-to-organize measures that would attack the problem at its source—release of greenhouse gases into the atmosphere. We have to slow the rate at which climate change attacks the global cryosphere and use the added time to institute a more effective basic response to climate change on a global level.[13] Methane is an even more powerful greenhouse gas than CO_2, and it is a by-product of agriculture and animal husbandry. Ways to reduce the contribution that these activities make to climate change need to be added to the global research agenda, alongside measures to reduce the production and release of CO_2.

Global Instrumentation

We need to instrument the planet to permit constant monitoring of climate change, including the impact over time of measures undertaken to limit greenhouse gases. US national technical means can provide an invaluable stream of information about the effects of climate change and also about the efficacy of measures that may be taken to reduce climate change and contend with its effects. However, there is a tendency to overestimate what these systems can do.

A total system must be created that can integrate the outputs of civilian space-based systems for Earth observation. In addition, we need to plan for terrestrial measurement systems that will have to be installed and operated on the territories of many nations, under international supervision and with universal access to their output. There is a very much mistaken belief that both classified and commercial space-based platforms are going to be at hand for the indefinite future. The fact is that existing civilian systems are already past their programmed lifetimes, and replacements have not been funded. It is time to plan for the data streams that will be needed to manage the interaction between energy and the environment, over an indefinite period of time, and to provide reliable funding for these systems.

Anticipatory Governance for Dealing with Complexity

Linear thinking is based on the assumption that it is possible to differentiate between prime movers and driven elements in a given system and that, having done so, it is then possible to permanently determine the relationship between them with mathematical precision. Linear systems are therefore, by definition, predictable, even if they are complicated. In theory, problems related to linear systems can be completely and permanently solved.

Complex systems, however, have no central driver: all elements are simultaneously and continuously interactive. Policies designed for complex issues must therefore contend with uncertainty not just at the outset, when decisions are first made, but also continuously thereafter. All policy options must be considered in the context of alternative possible future consequences, especially those that are unintended. Choices of policy are never more than provisionally valid and must be reviewed on the basis of actual—as opposed to predicted—results. The objective of systems for managing responses to complex issues must be continuous management, based on sampling results and comparing them to explicitly designated indicators of performance (*feedback systems*).

Energy, climate change, and national security can be properly understood only as elements of a complex system, rather than as three separate and independent domains of policy. An effort to apply linear thinking to such a complex system exposes the United States to unintended and disproportionate consequences. For example:

- *The linear approach separates economics from politics, even in the most fragile developing countries.* Typically, the economic approach—which is often dominant in the policies of donor governments—calls for the elimination of energy (and food) subsidies on grounds that they block market signals. These subsidies, however, are all that stand between the ability of the poor to get by and disaster. When governments in countries whose populations live hand to mouth follow this tough love approach to economic policy, the results include massive political unrest, long-term radicalization, and—ironically—serious economic damage as foreign investors pull back. Climate change will reduce the margin for survival and will therefore lower public tolerance for the "right" economic policy.

- *The linear approach says that slashing US dependence on imported energy is the best way to deal with the energy cartels.* However, if energy revenues fall precipitously, then governments in the producing nations can be rapidly destabilized. And because the developing world continues to depend heavily on the energy exports of these countries, thinking about unintended consequences is necessary.
- *The linear approach says that discovery of oil and gas reserves brings prosperity to developing countries.* However, rapid development of energy reserves encourages corruption and social inequality, which, in turn, feed into radical resistance.
- *The linear approach assumes that technologies can be scaled upward without consequence.* Advocates of fracking, for example, stress reduced energy costs but minimize the risk that this technology could cause severe water contamination and that its widespread use could drastically reduce the availability of water for agriculture.
- *The linear approach to the use of ethanol from corn is to push for maximum utilization as a way to hold gasoline prices down.* Climate change, however, tends to restrict the output of grain and thereby turns ethanol policy into a forced choice between the price of food and the price of fuel.
- *The linear approach to climate change is to see the solution as the sum of multiple smaller advances in, for example, efficiency.* Unfortunately, climate change may provoke a nonlinear physical response to CO_2 levels beyond a certain threshold of concentration in the atmosphere, which the evidence of acceleration strongly suggests that we have already exceeded.
- *The linear approach pushes for a solution to CO_2 through capture and deep storage.* Storage of such quantities of CO_2 in geological formations may present long-range unknowns similar to those relating to ultra-long-term storage of radioactive waste. Assurances to the contrary from advocates of this technology are no more trustworthy than any other expression of self-interest. Self-policing is almost invariably a sham. There is a need for due diligence involving not only national but also global institutions.
- *The linear approach to climate change suggests that one way to catch up with the problem could be post facto, through geoengineering on*

a planetary scale. Geoengineering, however, involves fantastically scaled-up applications of laboratory concepts or even of totally untested schemes for blocking absorption of solar energy in the atmosphere and the oceans. At these scales, what is involved is the risk of uncontrollable environmental damage on a planetary scale. Proponents of these ideas should not be relied on for due diligence in the absence of law and effective regulation.

It is possible to recognize the presence of complexity and to develop a manifold strategy for responding to it—and yet to fail, for want of the capacity to actually execute such plans. To manage planning for complex systems, such as the interaction of energy, climate change, and national security, policy-makers need to develop systems with certain attributes:

- *Foresight*, which means the ability to link short-term behavior to long-term goals
- *Networked organization*, which refers to the ability to organize flexible collaborations across bureaucratic or even sovereign jurisdictions
- *Feedback systems*, which have the ability to adapt policy and programs rapidly to consequences

These qualities have become common attributes in the business world. The government of the United States, however, is organized on the basis of linear principles that are out of date. Foresight, networked organization, and feedback are not totally absent, but they are unevenly present, randomly distributed among agencies of the government as residual products of local happenstance rather than as elements of an overall design for the executive branch as a whole system.

Governance as we know it is under severe stress, and the entire US executive structure needs to be upgraded. But the design of this change—and the impulse to undertake it—must come from the presidency. This office alone has the potential for attaining long-sighted, whole-of-government, self-synchronizing behavior.[14]

Conclusion

The ultimate goal of statecraft is to align awareness, resources, and action. A strategy for dealing with the security implications of energy and climate change is a major conceptual challenge. Nevertheless, such a strategy can certainly be designed—provided that climate change is recognized as a major, advancing threat to national security and provided that energy and climate change are treated as equally vital priorities.

Whether the politics involved in such a strategy can be managed is a much more difficult question. So far, managing the politics has not been possible in the United States, and it is likely to be just as challenging elsewhere in the world, especially in countries with rapidly developing economies.

Nevertheless, the physical facts of climate change are what they are, and they are frightening. So let us assume that a change of attitude will take place when climate change reaches a certain level of shock and awe. Perhaps this moment is nearing, but when it comes, the question will be whether a strategy comprising many moving parts, working under conditions of urgency and duress, can be implemented by systems of governance that chronically lag events and that suffer from the effects of organization based on turf rather than on the combined requirements of management in relation to overall mission.

Taken as a complex system, energy and climate change constitute a challenge with major consequences for ourselves as Americans, for our contemporaries everywhere on the planet, and for future generations. We have built a global civilization that is based on the unlimited use of fossil fuels. This system generates immense wealth (at least for some) at the expense of releasing forces that are already destabilizing the global climate. If we have not already gone too far to limit the process and if we are smart enough to change the future by anticipating the consequences of our actions, this destabilization can be kept within levels that can be tolerated by the international system as we know it.

Every civilization, however, exists within an environmental niche, and when—for whatever reason—those niches are destroyed, so too have been the civilizations that depend on them. It is hubris to believe that industrial civilization is immune to the destruction of the planetary climate systems that sustain it. Nature has a way to balance the books if *Homo sapiens* isn't up to the job.

Notes

1. The US National Intelligence Council has available on its website (http://www .dni.gov/index.php/about/organization/national-intelligence-council-nic-publications)

a series of global and regional climate change documents and conference reports, including Defense Intelligence Agency, "Global Water Security," Intelligence Community Assessment 2012-08, Defense Intelligence Agency, Washington, DC, 2012; Office of the Director of National Intelligence, "2012: Global Water Security Map," US National Intelligence Council, Washington, DC, 2012; CENTRA Technology and Scitor, "Southeast Asia: The Impact of Climate Change to 2030—Geopolitical Implications," US National Intelligence Council, Washington, DC, 2010; CENTRA Technology and Scitor, "Mexico, the Caribbean, and Central America: The Impact of Climate Change to 2030—Geopolitical Implications," US National Intelligence Council, Washington, DC, 2010; CENTRA Technology and Scitor, "Russia: The Impact of Climate Change to 2030—Geopolitical Implications," US National Intelligence Council, Washington, DC, 2009; CENTRA Technology and Scitor, "North Africa: The Impact of Climate Change to 2030—Geopolitical Implications," US National Intelligence Council, Washington, DC, 2009; CENTRA Technology and Scitor, "India: The Impact of Climate Change to 2030—Geopolitical Implications," US National Intelligence Council, Washington, DC, 2009; CENTRA Technology and Scitor, "China: The Impact of Climate Change to 2030—Geopolitical Implications," US National Intelligence Council, Washington, DC, 2009.

2. For a framework and analysis of the tradeoffs among energy, environment, and climate issues, see Michael Levi, "Energy, Environment, and Climate: Framework and Tradeoffs," chapter 21 of this volume.

3. For a wider discussion of the homeland and national security aspects, see Leon Fuerth, "Energy, Homeland, and National Security," in *Energy and Security: Toward a New Foreign Policy Strategy*, ed. Jan H. Kalicki and David L. Goldwyn (Washington, DC, and Baltimore: Woodrow Wilson Center Press and Johns Hopkins University Press, 2005), 411–24.

4. See Al Gore, *Earth in the Balance: Ecology and the Human Spirit* (New York: Plume, 1992); Al Gore, *An Inconvenient Truth: The Planetary Emergency of Global Warming and What We Can Do about It* (New York: Rodale, 2006); Al Gore, *The Assault on Reason* (New York: Penguin, 2007); Al Gore, *Our Choice: A Plan to Solve the Climate Crisis* (New York: Penguin, 2009); Al Gore, *The Future: Six Drivers of Global Change* (New York: Random House, 2013); Al Gore, "The Climate for Change," *New York Times*, November 9, 2008.

5. Cynthia Rosenzweig, "Using Regional Models to Assess the Potential for Extreme Climate Change," Columbia University Center for Climate Systems Research, New York, 2004. The period of time during which US national policy has been frozen because of organized campaigns of denial of climate change represents at least a lost decade during which we might have been planning a response.

6. The Massachusetts Institute of Technology's 2007 Future of Coal study calls for testing at least three carbon capture and sequestration technologies, one of which is now being tested by the Mongstad project in Norway. See Stephen Ansolabehere, Janos Beer, John Deutch, A. Denny Ellerman, S. Julio Friedmann, Howard Herzog, Henry D. Jacoby, Paul L. Joskow, Gregory McRae, Richard Lester, Ernest J. Moniz, and Edward Steinfeld, *The Future of Coal: Options for a Carbon-Constrained World: An MIT Interdisciplinary Study* (Cambridge, MA: Massachusetts Institute of Technology, 2007). In 2012, the National Research Council addressed the seismic risk of carbon capture and sequestration. See National Research Council, *Induced Seismicity Potential in Energy Technologies* (Washington, DC: National Academies Press, 2012).

7. The largest commercial carbon sequestration to date is at the Gorgon liquefied natural gas project in western Australia.

8. Gore, *An Inconvenient Truth*. See also Leon Fuerth, "Security Implications of Climate Change," in *The Age of Consequences: The Foreign Policy and National Security Implications of Global Climate Change*, ed. Kurt M. Campbell, Alexander T. J. Lennon, and Julianne Smith (Washington, DC: Center for Strategic and International Studies, 2007), 71–80.

9. See Daniel Yergin, "Energy Security and Markets," chapter 2 of this volume.

10. See Charles Emmerson, "The Arctic: Promise or Peril?," chapter 9 of this volume.

11. A good research baseline is available from the US National Academy of Sciences, including these reports: Polar Research Board, *Scientific Value of Arctic Sea Ice Imagery Derived Products* (Washington, DC: National Academies Press, 2009); Board on Atmospheric Sciences and Climate, *Verifying Greenhouse Gas Emissions: Methods to Support International Climate Agreements* (Washington, DC: National Academies Press, 2010); Board on Atmospheric Sciences and Climate, *Monitoring Climate Change Impacts: Metrics at the Intersection of the Human and Earth Systems* (Washington, DC: National Academies Press, 2010); Board on Atmospheric Sciences and Climate, *A National Strategy for Advancing Climate Modeling* (Washington, DC: National Academies Press, 2012); John D. Steinbruner, Paul C. Stern, and Jo L. Husbands, eds., *Climate and Social Stress: Implications for Security Analysis* (Washington, DC: National Academies Press, 2012); Board on Atmospheric Sciences and Climate and Water Science and Technology Board, *Himalayan Glaciers: Climate Change, Water Resources, and Water Security* (Washington, DC: National Academies Press, 2012); Polar Research Board, *Seasonal to Decadal Predictions of Arctic Sea Ice: Challenges and Strategies* (Washington, DC: National Academies Press, 2012).

12. For a broader discussion of social consequences, see Steinbruner, Stern, and Husbands, *Climate and Social Stress*, a report prepared under the direction of the Committee on Assessing the Impact of Climate Change on Social and Political Stresses, of which the author was a member. See also Henry Pollack, *A World Without Ice* (New York: Penguin, 2009); Sylvia A. Earle, *The World Is Blue: How Our Fate and the Ocean's Are One* (Washington, DC: National Geographic, 2009).

13. Vice President Al Gore initiated this program, which was launched in 1993 by the US Department of Defense and Intelligence Community through the environmental task force and project MEDEA (Measurements of Earth Data for Environmental Analysis) in an effort to aid analysis of ongoing changes in the Earth and provide improved strategic warning of potentially catastrophic threats to US and global populations. Shut down by the George W. Bush administration, it was revived in 2009 but faces renewed budget pressures. For more information, visit the website of the Federation of American Scientists at http://www.fas.org/spp/military/program/sp97/defense.html.

14. See Leon Fuerth, with Evan Faber, *Anticipatory Governance: Practical Upgrades* (Washington, DC: George Washington University and National Defense University, 2012); Leon Fuerth, "Operationalizing Anticipatory Governance," *Prism* 2, no. 4 (2011): 31–46.

Chapter 23

The Challenge of Politics

Frank Verrastro and Kevin Book

For the past 40 years, US energy policy has been largely predicated on the dual notions of resource scarcity and growing demand, especially for oil and, to a lesser extent, natural gas. With the astounding success in the development of unconventional shale gas and tight oil resources, however, a new energy reality is emerging. This new reality couples the enormous availability of fossil fuel resources with flat-to-declining domestic oil demand and a range of options for using natural gas. Against the backdrop of a changing global energy landscape, the advancement of technology, higher prices, and limitations on federal spending, this new reality deepens traditional policy dilemmas for decision-makers and creates some new ones.

Special thanks to Molly Walton and Michelle Melton for their insights, extraordinary research, and editing assistance in the preparation of this chapter.

Energy policy-makers typically strive to incorporate at least three discrete and often competing goals: supply security, environmental protection, and economic growth. Priorities may shift with broader political initiatives and world events, but all three goals factor into every energy policy deliberation. Add to that pressures to fine-tune policies that also simultaneously promote resiliency, enhance competitiveness, protect food and water supplies, *and* produce outcomes that are acceptable to a wide range of political constituencies and the process gets exponentially more complex and challenging.

In the past, the politics of energy in the United States tended to reflect regional resource differences, available infrastructure, and demand preferences as well as party ideologies. Democrats tend to be "greener," favoring incentives for alternative and renewable fuels, conservation, and efficiency. Republicans generally support increased resource access, fewer regulations, greater states' rights, expanded production of traditional fuels, and portfolio choices dictated by free markets.

The tension between energy production and environmental stewardship is nothing new. Thanks to cheap and reliable energy, America became a nation of big dreams, large houses, and long distances. Once established, efforts to transform the nation's energy system or make the national energy mix cleaner require substantial mitigation and remediation investments, a dynamic that makes it easy to think of supply security and economic growth as intrinsically linked—and inversely proportional to environmental protection.

That narrative, of course, is not always true. China is learning today what the United States learned in the late 1960s—namely that the cumulative impacts of pollution and other externalities can also undermine investments and economic growth. The Chinese example demonstrates that both an economic and a sociopolitical case can be made for mitigation when pollution jeopardizes productivity and public health, though it should be clear that the comparative health risk between the United States and China under current standards is markedly different.

The Convergence of Energy and Environmental Goals

Until the early 2000s, for a variety of reasons, the United States has been able to balance successfully (except under the most dire circumstances) economic and energy security considerations along with environmental improvement. At times, all three objectives have been closely aligned. The 1969 National Environmental Policy Act led to slightly more than a decade of progressive environmental legislation. In the 1970s, under both Democratic and Republican administrations, Congress passed or upgraded a variety of statutes, including the Clean Air (1970), Clean Water (1972), Endangered Species (1973), and Safe Drinking Water Acts (1974).

In parallel, Congress moved ahead on the energy security front, largely in response to the Arab Oil Embargo, with adoption of the Energy Policy and Conservation Act (1975); the Energy Tax Act, the Powerplant and Industrial Fuel Use Act, and the Public Utilities Regulatory Policy Act (all in 1978); and the Energy Security Act and amendments to the Outer Continental Shelf Lands Act (both in 1980). Through these and related efforts, the nation built its energy security policy base, including the establishment of CAFE (corporate average fuel economy) standards, the Strategic Petroleum Reserve, and (in tandem with other members of the Organization for Economic Cooperation and Development) the International Energy Agency.

Yet even as America's environmental and energy security policies raced concurrently toward new goals, they did not cancel each other out for a very simple reason: both policy initiatives were in their infancy, and plenty of low-hanging fruit was available. Over the decades that followed, as the nation successfully cleared ever-higher environmental hurdles, each improvement came at somewhat higher cost. Meanwhile, even though the US energy intensity of gross domestic product declined steadily, absolute energy demand continued to grow and domestic oil production continued to fall, thereby increasing America's import dependence.

Both trends increased the tension between energy security and environmental protection, but outright conflict between the disparate policy goals did not become a defining national policy debate until midway through President George W. Bush's first term. The environmental lobby had become more actively engaged, partly as a consequence of President Bush's abandoning support for the Kyoto Protocol in 2001 after backing it during his campaign. The Bush White House also liberalized coal production regulations, reinterpreted power plant air emissions rules, and lobbied Congress to open Alaska's Arctic National Wildlife Refuge to oil and gas drilling.

The 9/11 terror attacks and the subsequent wars in Afghanistan and Iraq made supply security the top driver of US energy policy. After two decades of relative affordability, oil prices escalated sharply, reflecting geopolitical tensions and rapid demand growth overseas. At home, electric power shortages highlighted the vulnerability of a congested, undersupplied grid. Steep natural gas production declines put pressure on supplies for manufacturing, power generation, and home heating.

Panicked by rising fuel prices, lawmakers and executive branch agencies focused intently on ways to diversify transportation fuel supplies for both civilian and military purposes. Congress debated the Renewable Fuel Standard (RFS), a national requirement for refiners to blend biofuels into gasoline. The US Department of Defense initiated its own diversification campaign, the Joint Battlefield-Use Fuel of the Future program, aimed at producing synthetic diesel and jet fuels from coal and renewable sources.

Surprisingly, around November 2004, when Russia ratified the Kyoto Protocol, pathways toward the goals of supply security, environmental protection, and economic growth began to converge. The convergence continued until approximately September 2008, when Lehman Brothers collapsed. Interestingly, this convergence seems to have happened largely because things got worse, not better—especially on the energy side of the equation.

In 2005, transportation fuel security and gasoline prices became such a high priority for Washington policy-makers that a Republican-led Congress abandoned proposals for a federal trust fund to protect MTBE (methyl tertiary butyl ether)[1] producers from liability lawsuits and adopted the Energy Policy Act of 2005, which included the ethanol mandate. Supply concerns persisted, however. In 2007, a Democrat-led Congress augmented CAFE standards for the first time in three decades and augmented the RFS, more than quadrupling the nation's biofuels blending target.

On the environmental front, 2005 marked the beginning of the first phase of the European Union's Emissions Trading Scheme for greenhouse gases. But in Washington, global warming had become so contentious that lawmakers abandoned the president's power plant emissions law after four years of work. Democrats and Republicans could not agree to add a fourth pollutant—carbon dioxide—to the three on which they had agreed (nitrogen oxides, sulfur dioxide, and mercury).

Then, surprisingly, things started changing, subtly at first and then dramatically. By the spring of 2006, two Senate committees held a "climate summit" to debate the form (rather than the necessity) of climate legislation. In February 2007, a coalition of industrial emitters and green groups calling itself the US Climate Action Partnership went before Congress to advocate economywide carbon emissions regulation. And in stark contrast to the 2012 presidential campaign cycle, both 2008 candidates—Senator Barack Obama (D-IL) and Senator John McCain (R-AZ)—presented themselves to voters as supporters of climate change legislation.

From Convergence to Realignment: Scarcity Aligned Energy Policy Priorities, Adequacy Unraveled Them

What produced this unexpected convergence of the historically disparate goals of supply security and environmental protection? The uniting force, at least for a little while, turned out to be energy scarcity. For policy-makers confronting a world where supply appeared to be irretrievably declining and demand appeared to be intractably growing, low-carbon sources such as ethanol and renewable energy were widely viewed as diversification imperatives. If economic growth depended on conserving scarce hydrocarbons, then policies that reduced carbon dioxide emissions were likely to be closely aligned. Policy-makers could easily justify subsidizing hybrid and electric cars and plug-in hybrids (powered by non-fossil sources) as a means to replace gas guzzlers, "peak shaving" solar panels, and wind farms to spare natural gas. They could justify efficiency upgrades and demand-management technologies that saved British thermal units for all purposes. In a world where the same policies could deliver both climate security and energy security, unifying US energy policy within the framework of an economywide, cap-and-trade system for greenhouse gases made sense.

Crisis and Disruption

The 2008–09 financial crisis destabilized the energy side of supply–environment convergence by suppressing—then destroying—demand and by eliminating the unifying notion of resource scarcity. Demand contractions are usually temporary, however, and the convergence might have resumed after the financial collapse. But by 2010, the United States clearly was sitting on somewhere between 50 and 100 years' worth of economically recoverable, low-carbon fossil energy in the form of natural gas. By 2011, the same combination of horizontal drilling and hydraulic fracturing that had freed unconventional gas from the tight pores of the Barnett, Haynesville, Fayetteville, and Marcellus shales would also be heralded as the mechanism for freeing unconventional crude from tight oil formations in the Bakken and Eagle Ford.

The "Threat" of Resource Abundance

For all of its obvious benefits (e.g., job creation, new investment, trade balance reduction, energy security, and the environmental advantages of using lower-carbon natural gas to displace coal in power generation), the notion of having decades (or more) of fossil fuel abundance in the United States and the rest of North America has not met with universal acclaim. The absence of a low-carbon pathway to a more sustainable energy future has caused many in the environmental community to oppose long-lived oil and gas projects as they perpetuate a fossil fuel future for decades to come. For environmental stakeholders, fracking is not a solution but a new problem unto itself. As a consequence, questions about groundwater safety, water use at scale, methane emissions, well integrity, community impacts, and— more recently—induced seismicity linked to large volumes of wastewater disposal in injection wells have come to the fore.

For the energy industry, technology advancements and improved best practices hold the key to prudent development of these resources in a safer, smarter, and cleaner manner and in a way consistent with the public interest. For policy-makers, however, the dilemma is how to reconcile efforts to improve or enhance economic objectives and energy security while simultaneously protecting the environment and addressing the threat of climate concerns. In addition, as large volumes of low-priced gas compete with higher-cost clean fuels and technologies such as nuclear energy, wind, and solar power, finding the right balance to advance research and alternative, cleaner technologies and efficiency while maintaining a robust conventional fuel market now become a policy priority.

Too Many Cooks: The Challenge of Fragmented Policy-Making

In an ideal world, the formulation of a comprehensive and balanced national energy policy would begin with timely and accurate data, incorporate solid analysis, and then balance the tradeoffs required between competing or conflicting economic, security, and environmental objectives. Policy-makers would share unbiased information to arrive at long-term strategic decisions to keep the nation on track. Flexible and adaptive rules and regulations would accommodate technology advances, foreign policy priorities, changing market conditions, and public sensitivities and perceptions.

In short, were one to have the luxury of designing US energy policy from first principles, one could hardly imagine that anything resembling the current system would emerge. Instead, today's energy policy apparatus is highly fragmented and largely reactive and, in many cases, treats energy policy separately from environmental, industrial, and social policy despite intrinsic links.

The Executive Branch

The Founding Fathers may have anticipated a more unitary executive, but even the top tier of this executive comprises multiple players. The Executive Office of the President seeks to coordinate and focus decision-making across a vast array of cabinet and independent agencies. As a result, most big energy decisions run through a maze of reviewers that include the Office of Management and Budget, the National Economic Council, the National Security Council, the Domestic Policy Council, and the White House Council on Environmental Quality.

Outside the White House, different agencies play different principal roles. For example, the US Department of the Interior (DOI) controls mineral access to federal lands and waters, the US Department of Energy (DOE) finances precompetitive research and development (R&D) and innovative commercial-scale projects, and the US Environmental Protection Agency (EPA) regulates air and water pollution from moving and stationary sources. The EPA also oversees biofuels mandates and, in conjunction with the US Department of Transportation, vehicle fuel economy. The Treasury Department administers energy tax policies ranging from consumption and production subsidies to the tax treatment of large, multinational energy companies. The US Department of Agriculture funds biofuels and bioenergy infrastructure, and so on.

The Congress

Jurisdiction in the Congress is equally if not more challenging. In the House of Representatives, the Energy and Commerce Committee oversees most energy and environmental policy matters within the DOE and EPA, whereas the Natural Resources Committee oversees federal lands issues regulated by the DOI. The Senate divides the same portfolio differently, with the Energy and Natural Resources Committee responsible for DOE and DOI and the Environment and Public Works Committee responsible for EPA. Both chambers' tax-writing committees—the House Ways and Means Committee and the Senate Finance Committee—set energy tax policy too, but they often pursue different agendas, set different priorities, and build consensus through different processes.

The legislative process is shaped by a small number of relatively powerful gatekeepers and decision-makers. Leadership generally controls the agenda, the timing, and the form in which legislation eventually gets to the floor for debate and consideration. About 6 percent of legislation proposed in either chamber of Congress passes into law; the rest tends to pass into obscurity. Leaders of decision-making committees within the House and Senate wield substantial influence over legislative outcomes because they control their committees' agendas.

Ideology and Partisanship

In November 2012, just after the election, Senator Richard Lugar (R-IN) delivered a speech on overcoming what he called "political disunity" to effectively address emerging national security threats. In his remarks, Senator Lugar, a moderate Republican and ranking member of the Senate Foreign Relations Committee, noted that current partisan divisions in American politics are "much sharper" than in past decades. He lamented that unlike earlier times, "even in crises, Congress has been unable to muster a consensus for legislative action" and that many members now focus on emphasizing areas of disagreement rather than pointing to legislative achievements—which often require compromise.[2]

Senator Olympia Snowe (R-ME) expressed many of the same concerns in explaining her decision not to seek reelection. Columnists and historians have echoed similar sentiment, citing Congress's penchant for "pointless busy work and ideological signal sending" rather than for genuine efforts to address pressing issues.[3] And although adopting legislation is not the only measure of an effective legislative body, the 112th Congress has been roundly criticized as one of the worst ever for being not only inactive but also ideologically motivated to the point of obsession in choosing which measures to act on. (For example, the House voted, largely along strict party lines, over 35 times to repeal the Affordable Health Care Act, though no similar measure was ever likely to be adopted in the Senate and, consequently, any action in the House was unlikely to become law.[4])

Hyperpartisanship and extreme polarization are frequently cited as the primary reasons for such performance. A *National Journal* review of historical Senate vote ratings charted the ideological "middle ground" represented by the overlap between the most conservative Democrat and the most liberal Republican and found that it had disappeared entirely over the course of the past 30 years.[5] A number of historians and political commentators suggest that this phenomenon may also be growing within the general public. Such commentators argue that as "representatives," these members are merely reflecting the voters who elected them to office or at least the more vocal and organized portions of those constituencies.

The Influence of Local Economics on National Energy Policy

Congressional leaders' considerable authority to gate legislation raises an important question: what determines how such leaders vote on energy policy? Likewise, for all the control leaders enjoy, they still need support from rank-and-file members before they can send legislation to the president's desk. This raises another important question: what determines how rank-and-file members vote on energy policies?

In our representative democracy, national energy policy decisions are much like other policy decisions in that they often reflect home-state economic links, largely because lawmakers in both chambers are elected locally. The effects of these home-state biases (e.g., farm state, coal state, coastal state, tourism focus, and high or low population density) can show up in different ways because of different demographic characteristics and decision protocols within the House and Senate. One of the great strengths of this country is its diversity. In legislative terms, however, diversity can be an impediment to national policy-making, where a premium is placed on achieving consensus. Furthermore, the combination of more parochial and ideological stances often leads to suboptimal policy solutions for the nation at large.

The Influence of Sophisticated Advocacy

Much has been written about the increased role and influence of lobbyists and advocacy groups in the legislative and policy processes. Our intent here is not to reexamine the role of political action committees and campaign donations—that topic would generate a chapter of its own. Suffice it to say that as stakeholders have become more aware of the implications of certain policies for their particular interests, the level of sophistication and analysis they bring to the table to argue their case has dramatically increased. On a positive note, the proliferation of analytical reports and modeling exercises has clearly produced a more diverse mosaic of outcomes for policy-makers to consider when contemplating legislative or regulatory changes, although it may have made the policy process murkier.

Like the late senator Daniel Patrick Moynihan (D-NY), former senator Sam Nunn (D-GA) is fond of noting that "everyone is entitled to his or her own opinion, but the facts are the facts." In today's policy world, however, effective advocates come well equipped to the conversation armed with their own forecasts, models, and inevitably their own sets of assumptions, which they use to construct their own sets of "facts." With no clear-cut answers to complex questions, policy-makers are frequently left to sift and sort through lots of data and analyses and to make assumptions they deem reasonable. They then move on an issue, often with incomplete information and under unreasonable time constraints, especially in response to crises.

Major US Energy Laws Are Rare, and Reactive: It Takes More Than a Village; It Takes a Supply Shock

The political challenges of applying a uniform national policy to the diverse resource demography of the United States are so significant that federal lawmakers are reluctant to take them on unless and until a serious physical interruption of the energy supply chain leaves them with no alternative course of action. Four decades ago, supply crises propelled a series of major laws. The 1973 Arab Oil Embargo spurred the Energy Policy and Conservation Act in 1975. Echoes of that first supply shock led to the 1978 Energy Tax Act, which kicked off 33 uninterrupted years of federal subsidies for fuel alcohols. The 1979 Iranian Revolution and the removal of price controls on domestic oil prompted passage of the 1980 Energy Security Act, the imposition of a windfall profits tax, and the subsidization of alternative fuels from coal, thus spurring the first wave of incentives for renewable energy.

More recent examples also exist. The oil supply interruption resulting from Iraq's invasion of Kuwait in 1990 and the 1991 Gulf War drove the

1992 Energy Policy Act across the finish line, thereby initiating a new wave of renewable energy subsidies and alternative vehicles targets, even though many of the other policies treated by that law had been actively debated for years prior to passage. A similar dynamic accompanied passage of the Energy Policy Act of 2005, a utilities-focused measure motivated by two notable electric power supply interruptions, the 2000–01 California power crisis and the 2003 East Coast blackout. That law also brought into force two unrelated policy mechanisms: the RFS and the DOE loan guarantee program for innovative technologies. President Bush's signature on the Energy Policy Act of 2005 had scarcely dried when Hurricanes Katrina and Rita devastated the Gulf Coast, flooding refineries and shutting down pipelines. The resulting gasoline and diesel shortages across the country put in motion the 2007 Energy Independence and Security Act, which dramatically expanded the RFS and reinvigorated the nation's long-static fuel economy standards by setting ambitious new targets.[6]

Decision Criteria along the Energy–Environment Continuum

We typically distinguish between energy and environmental policies because they tend to be crafted by different decision-makers who are guided by different decision criteria. At various times, however, decision-makers frame energy policies more broadly than this two-dimensional framework might imply, reaching into the realm of industrial and social policy.

Figure 23.1 offers a simplified view of energy, environmental, industrial, and labor or social policies, framing each in terms of (a) whether it operates on the supply or the demand side and (b) how the government subsidizes (i.e., pays into) or monetizes (i.e., takes payment from) activities within each category.

The Evolution of the Obama Administration's Energy Policy

All presidents come into office with at least two immediate priorities: their own agendas and the legacy issues carried over from the outgoing administration. Add to this mix the current state of the economy and geopolitical affairs, which inevitably influence both the daily calendar and issue priorities.

In the case of the Obama administration, inherited legacy issues included a rapidly deteriorating economic situation, a growing budget deficit, and

Figure 23.1. A "Sources and Uses" View of Energy and Environmental Policies

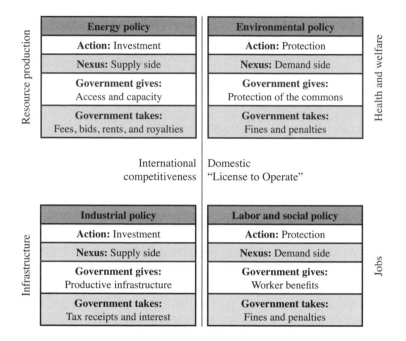

Source: ClearView Energy Partners LLC.

ongoing conflicts in Iraq and Afghanistan. On the energy front, it is worth recalling that when the 2008 election cycle was getting under way, oil prices (summer of 2007) were just shy of $65 per barrel, and net oil imports accounted for just under 60 percent of domestic consumption. The notion of "peak oil" was still very much in vogue for certain analysts and press accounts, and the phenomenon of high and rising prices driven by demand growth in China, India, and elsewhere seemed to reinforce the scarcity notion. By the summer of 2008, oil prices had more than doubled, resulting in larger US trade imbalances, and gasoline prices breached $4 per gallon, underscoring the need for an energy system transformation and a more sustainable energy future. When coupled with calls for climate action at Copenhagen,[7] this convergence of objectives produced a new energy formula, comprising the following objectives:

- Reducing and reversing the trend of rising oil imports and improving the balance of payments outflow
- Using higher prices to promote efficiency and alternative fuels research and use
- Promoting new technologies and, in the process, green jobs
- Advancing a global climate accord and the need for a cap-and-trade regime to stem the growth of greenhouse gases

This agenda was also reflected in the administration's choice of key personnel to manage this transformation, including Nobel laureate Steven Chu to head the Energy Department, Lisa Jackson to serve as EPA administrator, and Carol Browner (a former EPA administrator) to serve as the focal point for the combined energy and climate change agenda within the White House.

The new administration was not ignorant of the fact that fossil fuels (oil, natural gas, and coal) constituted more than 85 percent of primary energy consumption. Rather, it was committed to change that proportion, using higher prices, climate change, and the stimulus to advance that goal.[8] The administration also believed that, with higher prices, oil companies were doing "just fine" and their "subsidies" and tax preferences could be put to better use elsewhere.[9]

But then the world began to change—quickly, it seemed, although these changes had been in the works for years. Prices that had been rising for more than six years laid the foundation for new supply-side investment. Hydraulic fracturing and extended-reach horizontal well technologies that had been under development for decades began to perform on par with, and better than, conventional wells. New investment in the ultradeepwater Gulf of Mexico and the Canadian oil sands continued as—unexpectedly to most—shale gas production offset conventional well declines and as domestic natural gas supplies began to increase markedly.

Behind the scenes, the same formula would soon unlock tight oil formations, but in the foreground, global economic reversals had sent crude oil prices plummeting by more than $100 per barrel between July and December of 2008. By then, victorious President-Elect Barack Obama and his new administration were well on their way to fashioning an agenda built on their campaign pledges. The first tangible manifestation of the green agenda arrived with the February 2009 American Recovery and Reinvestment Act. This economic stimulus effort aimed at twin goals of greening the energy mix while creating a new economic sector—and plenty of jobs—centered around green energy technologies, a goal that would prove to be overly optimistic.[10]

By the summer of 2009, a subtle shift began to emerge, and the fact that oil and gas would be with us for "decades" began showing up in President Obama's speeches, but conventional energy sources remained subordinate to the promotion of, and preference for, cleaner fuels. By early 2010, although he remained committed to the cleaner fuels agenda, the president announced his support for expanded offshore oil and gas development, based in no small part on the industry's exemplary historical record in safely drilling thousands of wells in the offshore and taking stock of significant technology advances in seismic surveys, well design, and ultradeepwater drilling technologies.[11] Less than three weeks later, however, the Transocean rig *Deepwater Horizon* exploded and sank, killing 11 men and creating the largest oil spill ever seen in the Gulf of Mexico.

Some may question the imposition of a full-scale moratorium following the *Deepwater Horizon* accident, but with the collaboration and commitment of both industry and the government, a more rigorous safety and spill containment system was quickly deployed. In less than a year, industry was back to work in the Gulf and admittedly safer, smarter, and better prepared—no small accomplishment.

Against the backdrop of the Arab Spring and the Fukushima disaster, President Obama outlined his "Blueprint for a Secure Energy Future" in May 2011, which publicly called for more oil and gas development (as well as efficiency, renewables, and clean alternatives).[12] The Secretary of Energy's Advisory Board and the National Petroleum Council issued reports calling for prudent development of the nation's oil and gas resources and emphasized the role of best practices with a renewed focus on safety, environmental protection, and interaction with affected communities.[13]

In his 2012 State of the Union address, the president continued to emphasize the transformation and the need for cleaner forms of energy, but he also made clear that the nation needed an "all of the above" approach with respect to making an America that was "built to last."[14] By embracing the "all of the above" approach, the administration pragmatically signaled the emergence of new fossil fuel–based resource opportunities even as it continued to press for cleaner fuels. And although a number of high-visibility issues remain unresolved at this writing (e.g., the Keystone XL pipeline, liquefied natural gas exports, infrastructure development, the future of coal and nuclear energy, and upcoming EPA regulations and climate initiatives), the prospect of a new domestic energy reality appears to be slowly taking hold—one that simultaneously enhances the country's energy security, bolsters the economy, and improves the environment.

So What Can We Expect Going Forward?

The November 2012 election returned President Obama to office for another term. The voters also sent back to Washington a divided Congress similar to the gridlocked group that composed the dreaded 112th. So what can and should we expect?

At this writing, the Doha round of the most recent United Nations climate change negotiations has concluded with an "agreement" to extend the increasingly ineffective and beleaguered Kyoto Protocol for a few more years while work continues toward the development of a new agreement that would presumably enter into force in 2020. This action was taken concurrent with the Doha conference's admonition that the lack of progress on limiting emissions growth makes it increasingly unlikely that global temperatures can be kept from rising more than 2°C, the previous target established to avoid the more catastrophic impacts of climate change. The group also adopted language urging more financial and technical support for the most vulnerable countries, although it failed to create a mechanism for handling such assistance and only a handful of nations actually made concrete financial pledges to cover such assistance.

The global energy landscape continues to shift in new and interesting ways, and the United States would do well to put itself in a position to be resilient and opportunistic in the face of these changes. A transformation is already under way, and the ability to prudently and responsibly access unconventional oil and gas here at home should be welcomed because it gives some breathing space in which to find and deploy scalable replacement technologies and reliable alternatives that will make the US energy future both sustainable and more secure for the long haul.

Given the unavoidable fiscal constraints that the United States faces, the overhang of debt is likely to restrict the administration's ability to finance significant new domestic and international initiatives going forward.

The "inbox" issue highlighted at the beginning of this chapter now includes initiatives and decisions either unresolved or carried over from the president's first term—not least, Iran's nuclear ambitions, the Syrian conflict, the Keystone XL pipeline, liquefied natural gas exports, fracking regulation, rebuilding efforts associated with Superstorm Sandy, and gun control after the incident in Newtown, Connecticut—as well as newly developing crises and events and pressures from constituencies that made the president's reelection possible.

That said, the pathway forward with respect to energy policy is likely to follow one of the three following courses, or possibly a combination of the various routes:

- *Comprehensive narrative and follow-through: pro-development, but to a point.* The administration could decide to be proactive in addressing key components of the energy story by developing a comprehensive narrative that incorporates the nation's economic, environmental, foreign policy, and energy security goals and seeks to establish links and define tradeoffs so that individual policy decisions can be viewed as part of a broader strategy rather than as one-off events. This strategy would give investors some certainty and clarity in approach and could possibly optimize and accelerate the necessary buildout in infrastructure. Following this approach would require a presidential "endorsement" of natural gas (and oil) development but in a way that emphasizes its compatibility with renewables; requires continuous improvement and best practices in accessing, transporting, processing, and consuming the fuels; and does not undermine the realization of the climate objectives that are likely to remain a centerpiece of administration policy.
- *Push the green button.* With a divided Congress, the administration could continue down a path that emphasizes regulation to achieve its objectives. The EPA and other federal agencies already have a number of rulemakings in the pipeline and, absent congressional intervention, would be permitted to finalize pending regulations. This approach would allow the president to satisfy environmental supporters early in the second term before turning to more business- and economy-friendly initiatives. Adopting such a course of action would, however, turn the outcomes over to the courts to resolve, thus absorbing considerable time, effort, and expense—and could cost the president as well in terms of damaging his efforts with Congress. The approach also carries the additional burden of producing a substantively undesirable outcome even

though it removes the administration from direct culpability. Republican efforts in the House to overturn or defund those regulatory activities would likely meet with opposition in the Democratic-led Senate and, in any event, would not survive a presidential veto. The strategy could become a flashpoint for future congressional races, but the president could use intervention down the line if political or economic pressure became too burdensome, or he could use the arsenal of fully deployed regulation as collateral to extract a workable compromise with Congress on a variety of issues.

- *Give a little, take a little.* An alternate approach would be more passive, allowing the market to work and releasing or intervening in rulemakings in a way that gives all sides a little something but strives to ensure balance. Certain regulations would be strict and promote a bright-line perception of protecting the environment at all costs, whereas others might be more lenient and more supportive of production. Executing this strategy, however, runs the risk of displeasing both pro-environmental and pro-production constituencies, which are equally passionate about their positions. However, it keeps the administration at the center of the discourse. If successful, such a strategy could promote compromise and concessions on certain issues but also require clear-cut policies on key pieces of the agenda.

Obvious costs and benefits are associated with each of the approaches in political, constituency, and substantive (optimization) terms, and a divided Congress necessarily puts more focus on the actions of the executive branch, although management of state and local issues is expected to be dispositive in a number of cases, such as permits and siting of facilities. In all cases, presidential leadership will be required.

In large part, the administration's approach in the second term is expected to be dictated (at least in the early going) by the state of the economy and the president's personal (legacy) priorities on big-ticket issues. But other key issues will also loom large, including the role of various constituencies; fact- and science-based analyses addressing areas of impacts; the form and architecture of the White House decision apparatus; and personnel staffing for key (including cabinet- and subcabinet-level) slots dealing with energy, economic, foreign policy, and environmental interests. Relations with Congress will also influence or determine (aside from regulations) which initiatives proceed first and which will be successful.

The 2013 Outlook

Since the original drafting of this chapter in December 2012, a number of actions and events further reinforce our view that the Obama administration's second term will likely occupy the policy space between our "give a little, take a little" and "green button" trajectories. The nominations of Ernest Moniz (DOE), Sally Jewell (DOI), and Gina McCarthy (EPA) to replace departing cabinet members Steven Chu, Ken Salazar, and Lisa Jackson, respectively, suggest the desire to couple a knowledgeable and pragmatic competency with a continued greenish hue.

In the first part of 2013, President Obama gave three speeches that provide insight into his energy policy agenda. January's inaugural address unmistakably articulated that "we will respond to the threat of climate change, knowing that the failure to do so would betray our children and future generations."[15]

In February, the president's State of the Union speech highlighted a pragmatic focus on economic growth, pairing a commitment to "keep cutting red tape and speeding up new oil and gas permits" with a call to divert a portion of oil and gas revenues to an Energy Security Trust to fund clean energy R&D. The president also reinforced his strong call for climate action with his admonition that "if Congress won't act soon to protect future generations, I will."[16]

Finally, speaking on March 15 at the Argonne National Laboratory, the president expanded on the R&D vision of the Energy Security Trust, highlighting that its purpose is to "shift our cars and trucks entirely off oil." Despite thematic similarity to first-term goals, the Argonne speech repositioned the transformation agenda as a long game to be played by "scientists [who] are working on getting us where we need to get 10 years from now, 20 years from now."[17]

Outside of critical funding measures, congressional partisan gridlock seems poised to continue through the 2014 midterm elections. As during the latter two years of President Obama's first term, this situation reinforces the relevance of White House energy policy stances but limits the viability of major initiatives.

In his ensuing commentary on this chapter, John Deutch expresses correctly, in our view, considerable pessimism about both the domestic policy-making process (US energy policy, first and foremost, reflects domestic politics) and the substance of that policy. And although calls for a coherent national energy policy abound, various stakeholders have very different views of what that policy should be. As the US and the global energy landscape continues to evolve, we would suggest that a policy framework that is flexible, adaptive, collaborative, and responsive to the economic, security, and environmental needs of the day, while still anchored in longer-term goals and aspirations, may be the best for which one can hope.

Notes

1. MTBE is an organic gasoline additive used to raise the octane number. Its use has declined in the United States because of ethanol legislation and concerns about its seepage into groundwater.

2. Richard Lugar, "Overcoming Political Disunity to Address Emerging National Security Challenges," address to the CNA Nitze Award and 70th Anniversary Event, Alexandria, VA, November 17, 2012.

3. Tina Dupuy, "Ideology Trumps Accomplishment as 112th Congress Pursues Futile Bills," *Atlantic*, July 27, 2012, http://www.theatlantic.com/politics/archive/2011/07/ideology-trumps-accomplishment-as-112th-congress-pursues-futile-bills/242313/.

4. Ezra Klein, "14 Reasons Why This Is the Worst Congress Ever," *Wonkblog* (blog), July 13, 2012, http://www.washingtonpost.com/blogs/wonkblog/wp/2012/07/13/13-reasons-why-this-is-the-worst-congress-ever/.

5. Dino Grandoni, "Senate Gridlock Explained in One Chart," *Atlantic Wire*, March 8, 2012, http://www.theatlanticwire.com/national/2012/03/us-senate-now-completely-polarized/49641/.

6. Energy policy sometimes takes the form of riders within programmatic funding legislation, such as the periodic bills to reauthorize farm programs or the Highway Trust Fund. In recent years, jobs bills and similar stimulus measures have brought energy-related policy riders across the finish line.

7. "UN Head Calls for Urgent Climate Action," *United Press International*, December 11, 2008, http://www.upi.com/Top_News/Special/2008/12/11/UN-head-calls-for-urgent-climate-action/UP UPI-61001229011806/.

8. Barack Obama, "Remarks by Senator Barack Obama, Presumptive Democratic Presidential Nominee on the Subject of Energy," Michigan State University, Lansing, MI, August 4, 2008. The prepared text of the speech was published by the *New York Times* and is available at http://www.nytimes.com/2008/08/04/us/politics/04text-obama.html?pagewanted=all&_r=0. See also Barack Obama, "Remarks by the President on Energy," in the Grand Foyer of the White House, Washington DC, June 29, 2009, http://www.whitehouse.gov/the_press_office/Remarks-by-the-President-on-Energy.

9. Such comments are typical of the ongoing debate between industry and the administration about whether certain preferences (e.g., intangible drilling and development costs, manufacturing and foreign tax credits) should be considered as legitimate or as dispensable subsidies.

10. Barack Obama, "Remarks by the President on Energy."

11. Jeff Mason and Tom Doggett, "Obama Opens New Oil Drilling Offshore in Climate Drive," *Reuters*, March 31, 2010, http://www.reuters.com/article/2010/03/31/us-usa-oil-drilling-idUSTRE62T06520100331.

12. "Blueprint for a Secure Energy Future," White House, Washington, DC, March 30, 2011, http://www.whitehouse.gov/sites/default/files/blueprint_secure _energy_future.pdf.

13. Secretary of Energy Advisory Board, *Shale Gas Production Subcommittee Second Ninety Day Report* (Washington, DC: US Department of Energy, 2011), http://www.shalegas.energy.gov/resources/111811_final_report.pdf. See also National Petroleum Council, *Prudent Development: Realizing the Potential of North America's Abundant Natural Gas and Oil Resources* (Washington, DC: National Petroleum Council, 2011).

14. Barack Obama, State of the Union Address, US Capitol, Washington, DC, January 24, 2012, http://www.whitehouse.gov/the-press-office/2012/01/24/remarks-president -state-union-address.

15. Barack Obama, Inaugural Address, US Capitol, Washington, DC, January 21, 2013, http://www.whitehouse.gov/the-press-office/2013/01/21/inaugural-address -president-barack-obama.

16. Barack Obama, State of the Union Address.

17. Barack Obama, "Remarks by the President on American Energy," Argonne National Laboratory, Lemont, IL, March 15, 2013, http://www.whitehouse.gov /the-press-office/2013/03/15/remarks-president-american-energy-lemont-illinois.

Commentary on Part VI

John M. Deutch

My assignment is to offer comments on the seven excellent chapters in part VI, "Toward a New Energy Security Strategy." Taken as a whole, these chapters illustrate the enormous diversity of energy security issues that occupy policy-makers and energy market participants; how intertwined these energy security issues are; and the different analyses required to understand problems that have quite various technical, economic, and social aspects. Taken together, these chapters do not constitute a comprehensive energy security strategy, although they do point to some of the important issues that must be considered in thinking about such a comprehensive strategy.

The chapters vary in their assessment of how much progress has been made both nationally and globally in dealing with energy security as a whole. Melanie Kenderdine and Ernest Moniz brilliantly align a menu of energy "technology pathways" with fundamental energy security objectives. Charles Ebinger and John Banks's call for more emphasis on energy poverty, Leon Fuerth's analysis of the failure to deal with climate change, and Charles McPherson's reminder about the governance shortcomings in many oil and gas markets made me wish for more evaluation of "macro" energy issues.

A thorough analysis of "micro" issues such as approving the Keystone XL pipeline, handling natural gas exports, managing the Strategic Petroleum Reserve (SPR), regulating deep offshore drilling, reducing the environmental impact of unconventional oil and gas production, and deciding on biofuels subsidies is vital for the day-to-day energy matters of business and governing. But also important to keep in mind is that the overall objectives of energy policy are to reduce the environmental impacts of energy activities, to prevent conflict over energy supply and distribution, to make a gradual transition to a post fossil fuel–based economy, and to maintain a global market for energy that is transparent—with prices that reflect real costs—and that allows access for both supplier and consumer countries, whether rich or poor.

Part VI of this volume gives the reader an opportunity to assess the totality of US energy policy and where the country has come since the appearance of the first volume in 2005—indeed, in the four-plus decades since the first Arab Oil Embargo riveted the nation's attention on energy. My reading of this volume confirms the view that the country still does not have an adequate energy security policy, despite the call to action of every president and the widespread public recognition of the importance of energy issues to the future welfare of this country and the world. Perhaps unintentionally, the authors further discourage me about the progress the country is likely to make on energy matters, and I am pessimistic about whether careful attention to important loosely linked individual micro issues will, over time, result in a significant cumulative effect. The reader will note my pessimism in some of my comments on the individual chapters, and I apologize for this view. However, I do urge the reader to use the opportunity presented by this volume to reflect on what fundamental change and action is needed to launch an energy policy with a greater possibility of providing for the future.

Kenderdine and Moniz do a world-class job in chapter 17, "Technology Development and Energy Security." They align technology pathways with energy security policy objectives in an informative and useful way. Their menu of representative technology pathways admirably includes some new areas that are not part of the current research and development portfolio of the US Department of Energy (DOE) or other agencies. For example, adaptation is highlighted as an important technology objective, although their list of representative technology options that support this policy objective is somewhat vague and deserves to be elaborated. Quite correctly, the authors include the objective of exploring geoengineering and the need to protect the large and vulnerable energy infrastructure from disasters caused by acts of nature or human action (e.g., cyber attacks). Both energy experts and government officials will find this chapter very helpful.

Of course, not everything can be done in a single chapter, but it would have been most welcome if Kenderdine and Moniz had indicated some sense of *priority* among the different technology pathways. The authors do not mention the constrained budget outlook and the challenge this situation poses to the concrete management issue of allocating scarce budget dollars to the large and expensive technology pathway menu they identify. Some areas are relatively cheap to pursue and have significant prospect of expanding knowledge; others are quite expensive and have uncertain and long-term payoffs. The discussion of the role of technology in energy security is of some interest but curiously does not mention the central question of relative emphasis of government support for technology creation, technology demonstration, and technology deployment. Kenderdine and Moniz do not express a view of DOE's *ability* to execute the technology development program they envision or the role of the different performers: industry, universities, and government laboratories.

Kenderdine and Moniz conclude their chapter with a very important suggestion that the federal government should improve its capacity for integrated energy policy analysis with the goal of achieving "both a process and a plan that has bipartisan and multiregional support, essential to core stability in energy policy across administrations." A comprehensive, multiyear, quantitative energy plan has not been produced since the National Energy Plan of the new DOE in the Carter administration, which served as the basis for the pathbreaking energy legislation of 1978 and 1979. Unlike Kenderdine and Moniz, I consider the initial Quadrennial Technology Review, produced by DOE, a disappointment because its scope is far from the Quadrennial Energy Review proposed by the President's Council of Advisors on Science and Technology, and the DOE report is fatally absent of any numbers describing the cost and effectiveness of any government energy policies and programs.[1]

In chapter 18, Ebinger and Banks address the geopolitical impact of energy poverty in developing countries. They correctly point out that electrification in developing countries is strongly correlated with social and economic development. They explore the challenges to continuing electrification: the capital cost of electricity capacity is high, so developing countries choose lower-cost and less efficient generating options, relying largely on coal or fuel oil. The carbon dioxide emissions from growing electricity generation and other energy use, of course, contribute to world greenhouse gas emissions. Ebinger and Banks rightly note that developing countries will bear the heaviest social disruption and economic damage from the resulting climate change, thus compounding the burden of energy poverty.

Market reform, financing, clean energy technology, and especially efficiency improvements are all needed if electrification is to proceed more expeditiously. Water scarcity in many developing countries makes the challenge greater because energy production requires water in large quantity. Ebinger and Banks describe the international initiatives to place greater priority on meeting the growing energy demand from poorer nations. Especially noteworthy is the ambitious Sustainable Energy for All initiative, launched by the secretary general of the United Nations in 2012.

Ebinger and Banks strongly and unequivocally express the view that "It is imperative that the United States has a comprehensive, integrated energy–climate approach that not just incorporates but also prioritizes the eradication of energy poverty—specifically the expansion of electricity and broader energy access in the world's poorest countries." They list needed "critical actions"—making the eradication of energy poverty a foreign policy priority, providing more money, emphasizing distributed power systems, making available cooperation and concessionary financing for large-scale clean energy technologies—and conclude by saying "a whole of government" approach is needed.

I salute Ebinger and Banks for drawing attention to the challenge of meeting the energy needs of countries in poverty. Typically, US attention focuses on the big energy actors: the Organization for Economic Cooperation and Development; major resource holders in the Middle East; and the large, rapidly growing, emerging economies, especially China, India, Brazil, Indonesia, and Mexico. This focus leaves out a lot of people in the world in Africa, Asia, the Caribbean, and Latin America. Ebinger and Banks take my breath away, however, with their list of needed priority and crucial actions. I doubt that the US government and political system are willing to put policy priority or resources on reducing energy poverty. Furthermore, no evidence indicates that the US government is capable of organizing itself for a "whole of government" approach on such a subject. The likeliest outcome is another Department of State–Department of Energy announcement of a new "program," of which there are many examples, such as the Clean Energy Ministerial, the unconventional oil and gas engagement program, and DOE's clean energy technology agreement with China. The sum of these initiatives seems to me to be good intentions rather than action, but this conclusion reflects my pessimistic frame of mind. Ebinger and Banks press the urgency of action but do not offer any case, much less a convincing case, that our system of government is up to it.

McPherson will make some readers uncomfortable by his unvarnished description in chapter 19 of how oil and gas development corrupts many of the nations that are major producers and resource holders. This story is not new, but McPherson does a very thorough job of describing the dangers to social and economic, as well as political, development that accompany natural resource plenty. Undesirable outcomes such as poor economic growth, asymmetric income and wealth distribution, public investment, tax evasion, and government corruption do not seem to differ greatly if the operating entity is a national oil company or an oil company owned by an international investor: the massive flow of money is what matters. The oil and gas production conveys power to a major resource holder that constrains reform efforts by countries such as the United States that wish to encourage human rights and reasonable economic equity. The net result is that the opportunity presented by depletable resource plenty for lifting the welfare of individuals is lost.

McPherson gives an account of what is being done to improve the governance and transparency of oil and gas activity around the world. This action includes initiatives to require accurate financial reporting, prompted by Publish What You Pay, and government and international public interest efforts, such as the Extractive Industry Transparency Initiative. Although he is somewhat optimistic about what has been accomplished, he gives reasons for concern about future progress.

More generally, McPherson itemizes the roles for other actors to try to influence the transparency between governments and producers: stockholders, governments of oil importing countries, multilateral institutions, industry, nongovernmental organizations, and the media. The US record is mixed between speaking out for good and transparent government and tolerating how industry works out immediate problems. I doubt there is any prospect of changing this pattern, and I do not expect the United States will assume any greater leadership position on this issue than it has up to the present.

Michelle Patron and David Goldwyn, the esteemed coeditor of this volume, present an informative and I believe unique account of the DOE's

SPR policy in chapter 20. They argue that the SPR is a powerful tool that permits US policy-makers "to manage oil disruptions and increase oil market stability."

In the Carter administration, as a DOE official, I appeared before the House Energy and Commerce Committee to explain the administration's SPR program. Representative David Stockman of Michigan (soon to be President Ronald Reagan's first director of the Office of Management and Budget) asked me, "Mr. Deutch, shouldn't the Strategic Petroleum Reserve more properly be called the Tactical Petroleum Reserve?" His point was that the capacity of the SPR was so much smaller than the daily flow of world oil that any release from the SPR (even when coordinated with releases from the national petroleum standby stockpiles of other International Energy Agency members) would have no quantitative effect on the world oil market. Accordingly, SPR releases are entirely tactical in nature, signaling to short-term oil market traders that the US government has the resolve and intent to deal with a disruption brought about by war or calamity, such as Operation Desert Storm in 1991 or Hurricane Katrina in 2005.

In some cases, the immediate market response to a release or threat of release from the SPR has been a sharp reduction in a price spike. In other cases, when no release from the SPR has been made, one cannot disprove the optimistic view that, had there been a release, the retreat from a price spike would have been more rapid. Nor can one prove or disprove that the threat of a release effectively dampened an incipient price spike.

Patron and Goldwyn review the evidence and almost make the case for the SPR. But they go further, swallowing Stockman's tactical purpose hook, line, and sinker, stating: "Perhaps the most controversial and, in our view, increasingly important task of strategic reserve policy is managing market expectations to help prevent price spikes. Markets anticipate future prices, shortages, and surpluses and act immediately in response to those expectations." I do not think it is so easy to "manage market expectations," and I particularly doubt the ability of government bureaucracies to do so effectively or in a timely manner. Patron and Goldwyn point out fairly that the emergence of the large global futures market in oil, not present in the later 1970s, changes the dynamic of oil price volatility, and they are quite correct to emphasize that the value of the SPR is not determined by the level of US oil imports.

Patron and Goldwyn describe the clever innovation that authorizes the SPR to bridge perceived short-term gaps in market supply by swaps that permit the loan of oil from the SPR to suppliers with repayment in the future. This mechanism permits the US government to avoid price risk on the round trip of oil release and replacement. This arrangement to avoid price risk hints that the US government is not always sure about its ability to anticipate future market prices, an ability that underlies the notion of managing market expectations.

In arguing for an SPR policy, curiously Patron and Goldwyn do not mention its cost. In addition to the not insignificant cost of operating the SPR, the SPR incurs a substantial inventory cost for the United States. At a West Texas Intermediate price of $100 per barrel, the 700 million barrel SPR has an inventory value of about $70 billion, which means that annual carrying cost is $70 billion times the government borrowing rate. At today's exceptionally low rates, the SPR is relatively affordable; if real interest rates return to historic levels, the question of the affordability of SPR policy may have greater saliency.

In chapter 21, Michael Levi presents an overview of energy and climate issues in the context of energy and national security. His framework for assessing tradeoffs among energy, the environment, and climate is a useful precursor to the prescriptive chapter that follows. Although I can add little to his analysis and sensible suggestions, I concur with his conclusion that US energy policy should "focus on ameliorating local environmental concerns (while also addressing security and economic needs) when making decisions regarding access to oil and gas resources."

Leon Fuerth is a national security commentator and policy practitioner who has an exceptional ability to identify critical issues and propose imaginative solutions. He does not disappoint in chapter 22, "National Security, Energy, Climate Change: New Paradigm, New Strategy, New Governance." He makes three absolutely correct points that deserve the reader's closest attention.

First, the continued pace of emission of greenhouse gases into the atmosphere ensures that adverse climate change will occur. The change will result in global economic and social disruption, thereby increasing the risk of controversy and conflict between nations and endangering the stability of the international order as we know it. Quite so. We need not pause to decide whether climate should be classified as a traditional "national security" threat. Fuerth makes the case that action is needed now to minimize the extent of the social, economic, and political harm that the world is destined to bear as a result of prodigal human activity.

Fuerth's second point is that the United States must adopt a new multifaceted strategy to deal with climate change. True to his reputation for salience and directness, he suggests two lists of actions: the first to be taken unilaterally, and the second to be taken in concert with others. They are ambitious lists, and I offer a couple of comments, again consistent with my pessimistic frame of mind.

Fuerth proposes measures needed to *adapt* to the inevitable change that is coming, a far different approach from the failed, fancy cap-and-trade emission reduction proposals of the first Obama administration, which sought to avoid climate change through mitigation. Fuerth's calls for US plans to deal with food spikes, drought, higher sea levels, and storm surges are wise, but the cost will be high (something will need to be given up), and the government is not organized to execute such efforts. I would have welcomed Fuerth's thoughts on how these measures might be accomplished; the past several decades of US energy policy do not make me optimistic.

That progress on climate change requires international cooperation is evident, and Fuerth makes some interesting programmatic suggestions: global instrumentation, energy research and development, near-term control of black carbon and emissions of noncarbon greenhouse gases, and joint planning for response to major climate catastrophes. I am less enthusiastic about his suggestion of using international law as a mechanism to prompt change.

Fuerth's third and final point is especially important. He connects the climate change problem with the more general problem of the government's evident inability to deal with the complexity inherent in the problems it confronts. He describes in eloquent detail the shortcomings of "linear thinking," as he calls the current approach, for dealing effectively with the complexities and links of a problem like climate change. Elsewhere Fuerth has written about practical changes that are needed to create "anticipatory government" to deal with complexity.[2] We may need to wait for progress on climate change until some of these more fundamental changes occur.

In chapter 23, Frank Verrastro and Kevin Book address "The Challenge of Politics." I wonder how they were convinced to agree to write this chapter. Verrastro is an experienced Washington observer of energy policy; he knows how the sausage is made, and he must have known that the clearer he was about the story of politics and energy policy the more depressing his account would be.

Verrastro and Book remind us that "Energy policy-makers typically strive to incorporate at least three discrete and often competing goals: supply security, environmental protection, and economic growth. Priorities may shift with broader political initiatives and world events, but all three goals factor into every energy policy deliberation." The chapter takes the reader in a clear and interesting way through many of the fits and starts of US policy efforts over the past decades, from the pathbreaking environmental and energy legislation of the 1970s; through the climate change debates, the efforts to improve energy security after 9/11, and concerns about Middle East stability; to the current ambivalence about the unexpected unconventional oil and gas resource plenty in North America.

Verrastro and Book offer some compelling explanations for the lack of success of US energy policy. They say there are too many "cooks." They mention the White House agencies (the Office of Management and Budget, the National Security Council, the National Economic Council, the Domestic Policy Council, and the Council on Environmental Quality), cruelly omitting the Office of Science and Technology Policy and Council of Economic Advisers; point out the split responsibilities of the departments and agencies (the DOE, the US Environmental Protection Agency, the US Department of Transportation, the US Department of the Treasury, and the US Department of Agriculture); but leave out the US Department of the Interior. An equally large number of congressional committees is involved in energy and environment. Ideology and partisanship are always present, but solid analysis based on accurate data is not. And, of course, regional interests and industry advocacy are an expected part of the US political system.

Verrastro and Book suggest that a supply shock often is needed to launch legislation. This observation is true, but it does not always result in good or effective legislation. Consider the energy subsidies launched as part of the stimulus package or the California and federal responses to the 2001 California and 2003 East Coast power outages. Verrastro and Book do not offer a net assessment of energy policy in the first Obama administration, but it is hardly an inspiring success story.

Verrastro and Book conclude by speculating on three pathways forward for energy policy in the second Obama administration, which they term (a) pro-development, but to a point, (b) push the green button, and (c) give a little, take a little. These are realistic and reasonable policy directions, but they are incremental to a high order. Nothing indicates that the politics of energy will result in a stable long-term energy policy for the nation that will provide secure and affordable energy; avoid the dangers of climate change; and begin the long, but necessary, transition from an economy dependent on fossil fuels to one expanding its use of carbon-free fuels, nuclear power, and renewable sources of energy.

Notes

1. DOE, *Quadrennial Technology Review* (Washington, DC: DOE, 2011). See also PCAST, "Report to the President on Accelerating the Pace of Change in Energy Technologies through an Integrated Federal Energy Policy," Executive Office of the President, Washington, DC, November 2010.

2. Leon Fuerth, "Operationalizing Anticipatory Governance," *Prism* 2, no. 4 (2011): 31–46. See also Leon Fuerth, with Evan Faber, *Anticipatory Governance: Practical Upgrades* (Washington, DC: George Washington University and National Defense University, 2012).

Conclusion: Energy, Security, and Foreign Policy

Jan H. Kalicki and David L. Goldwyn

For nearly four decades, the United States and its closest allies have depended mostly on fossil fuels for their energy, power, and mobility. Some
foreign suppliers were close and reliable partners, but others did not share
many US values, and still others did not share the country's broader interests. The United States was often constrained when suppliers took actions
adverse to political goals, including those regarding democracy or human
rights, when energy sanctions might impair key supply relationships or
investments. Multilateral sanctions against countries from Sani Abacha's
Nigeria to Saddam Hussein's Iraq to Iran under the ayatollahs were hard to
undertake because of fears of major supply disruptions or other countries'
overriding desire for access to oil.

The authors wish to thank Daniel Yergin for his careful review and helpful suggestions
for this final chapter.

Incremental oil supply in the hands of only a few states of the Organization of the Petroleum Exporting Countries (OPEC) left dissatisfied consumers with the poor alternatives of weak diplomacy or economic pain. When their interests coincided with those of the United States, countries such as Saudi Arabia provided spare capacity, particularly as their economic stakes increased in the West. For example, these countries shared US strategic interests during the Cold War and following Iraq's invasion of Kuwait, and they do so today in countering the threat of nuclear weapons proliferation in Iran. When that spare capacity was unavailable or insufficient or their domestic revenue needs trumped global economic stability, the fact that the United States was a growing source of incremental oil and gas demand (and imports) made the American economy particularly vulnerable to restrictions of oil and gas supply.

Superimposed on this geopolitical and geoeconomic maelstrom were growing divisions between energy producers and consumers, both with a largely zero-sum mentality. Producers were disposed to take advantage of oil price hikes, and consumers of price dips, rather than taking the longer-range steps together to build greater balance between supply and demand and greater collaboration in support of market stability.[1]

As we pointed out in the first edition of this book,[2] as a nation Americans were myopic to both the security and the environmental consequences of their consumption, and because of inadequate planning and difficult politics, the United States underinvested in the technologies that could alter this path. US energy security has required diversifying both the sources of supply and the types of fuels used. By 2004, US energy companies had developed the advanced technology required to extend their petroleum reach to the ultradeepwater oceans and their geographic reach to Australia, the Arctic, and new areas of West Africa. The United States had begun to increase a still modest and relatively expensive share of renewable energy (mainly solar and wind power) in its fuel mix and to expand the share of nuclear energy in electric power generation.

Reducing Long-Term Dependence

However, the United States and its partners had not reduced significantly their long-term dependence on fossil fuels nor diminished measurably their vulnerability to foreign suppliers. In this book's first edition, we and our contributors called for new policies to reduce dependence and increase efficiency at home so that the United States could lead on energy and climate policies abroad. We also called for a reorientation of US foreign policy to promote transparency and political opening to the extent possible, while acknowledging that doing so would entail determined effort and a long transition. Even with progress in Western policies, the United States and its partners all faced what seemed an inevitable growth of Asia's dependence on the Middle East for energy supply and a potential erosion of America's broader energy, economic, and political influence if Asia made the same development mistakes as the West, but with even graver environmental consequences.

Times have changed.

A New Pivot Point

Remarkably, the United States and its partners are at a pivot point in history where they can diversify dramatically global supplies of oil and gas, lessen the potential of Middle East instability to shock the global economy, reduce greenhouse gas (GHG) emissions more quickly, and enable the United States—for a change—to use energy as a powerful and positive tool of foreign policy. The following possibilities would have seemed fantastic in 2004, or even in 2008:

- Incremental oil demand can be met by North America as well as the Middle East.
- The world's largest gas exporters could be Australia and the United States, rather than Russia and Qatar.
- The United States (or such partners as Australia and Canada) could directly compensate consuming countries for reducing imports of Iranian oil by selling them equivalent supplies of oil and gas.
- By 2020, the United States, China, and India could cut GHG emissions substantially by substituting natural gas for coal, whether domestic or imported.
- US companies could help Central, Eastern, and Western Europe; Latin America; and Asia diversify supplies by producing domestic natural gas or importing it from the United States.
- The United States could help engineer its own—and a global—economic recovery by reducing energy costs for Europe and Asia through exports of US energy and technology.

These were fantastic ideas when the first edition of this book was published in 2005, but they are opportunities now within reach.

Many aspects of the US energy security posture will remain the same, at least in the next few decades. The oil market is global. Price shocks anywhere affect prices everywhere. The share of fossil fuels in the global energy mix most likely remains well over 70 percent until 2035. But the United States has the power to enhance its own security and shift the energy balance of power strongly to its advantage by leveraging US technology, US markets, and the US role as guardian of the world's sea-lanes—shared in the future, one hopes, with other like-minded powers—to create a more interdependent, stable, and climate-friendly system.

The United States will make this pivot, however, only if it adopts domestic policies that ensure its continued progress in reducing its demand for fossil fuels while expanding its supply, if the US continues on the path of decarbonizing power generation and transportation, and if it adopts foreign policy strategies to promote energy security in its broadest sense.[3] These strategies can and should be pursued through technology, economic, political, and defense policies:

- *Technologies* are now at hand to enhance production, from deepwater to shale; to increase efficiency dramatically in transportation, power, and end uses in buildings, lighting, and appliances; and to step up development of renewable fuels. With more aggressive efforts on deployment, the United States can advance its ability to reduce and sequester carbon emissions from gas and power production as well as transportation.[4]
- *Economic initiatives* already produce significant results. They range from tax incentives for frontier production to step changes in transportation, industrial, and residential efficiency. Greater access to the offshore continental shelf,[5] particularly in the eastern Gulf of Mexico and the mid-Atlantic, and to federal lands for oil and natural gas production from shale[6] will increase fuel supplies, produce new jobs, and generate new revenues for the Treasury. In turn, as President Barack Obama suggested with his 2013 proposal for a new Energy Security Trust Fund,[7] these revenues could be used for alternative transportation technologies or, more broadly, for new infrastructure spending to upgrade power grids and harden critical sites against conventional or cyber attacks— and generate new jobs and growth in the process.
- *Political initiatives* can increase energy cooperation across borders, as Russia and Norway demonstrated in their 2011 agreement on delimita-

tion and development of the Barents Sea and Arctic Ocean. Spurred by this groundbreaking agreement, the Arctic Council has begun to chart the cooperative and safe development of that potentially enormous but environmentally sensitive resource. Such initiatives are needed urgently in the contested areas of the South and East China Seas, which have reached military crisis proportions between China and Japan over the contested Senkaku (Diaoyu) islands and their anticipated, lucrative resource base.[8]

- *Defense capabilities* are needed to help ensure the security of energy development and transportation. The importance of such capabilities was demonstrated dramatically by redundant security measures that defended Saudi Arabia's giant oil-processing facility at Abqaiq against al Qaeda attack in 2006. A similar attack against Algeria's remote In Amenas natural gas plant in 2013 was much more lethal, with hostage taking and at least 69 deaths,[9] even though terrorists did not succeed with their plan to blow up that facility. The urgent need for cyber defense capabilities was underlined by a 2012 cyber attack likely launched by Iran, suffering under international sanctions. Uranium enrichment facilities in Iran were attacked earlier by the so-called Stuxnet virus, so Iran launched its attack against Saudi Aramco and Qatar Petroleum's RasGas. That attack on Saudi and Qatari facilities, labeled "Shamoon," disabled at least 30,000 computers and would have interrupted production of millions of barrels per day had it been fully successful, resulting in a major blow to oil markets and the global economy.[10]

Can the United States Execute This Energy Pivot?

The ability of the United States as a nation to make this pivot is uncertain. First, much higher government coordination and policy direction are required to pursue the necessary technological, economic, political, and defense measures, not only individually but also as an integrated strategy.

Second, the window of opportunity will thrive only if the United States maintains both the investment signals and the safety measures required to sustain domestic and foreign leadership.

Third, US political leaders, on both sides of the aisle and at both ends of Pennsylvania Avenue, will need to abandon some of the comfortable but destructive orthodoxies of the past. The country will need truly to endorse and have confidence in an "all of the above" strategy.[11] It will need to support domestic fossil fuel production and smart, cost-effective regulation of its impacts. The country will need to support exports of US energy and technology and imports of foreign-built solar panels and heavy oil suited to America's complex refineries. The country will need to be unembarrassed about supporting the current fossil fuel boom and unrelenting in its pursuit of technologies of the future, from cyber-secure power grids to carbon sequestration, battery technology, and other modes of electricity storage.

What are the key drivers that have created this new paradigm, how is power being rebalanced in the world of energy, and what steps must the United States take to reap the security rewards of the evolving energy landscape? After decades of frustrating diplomatic efforts of producers and consumers in "getting to yes," we suggest a new approach we call a *global energy security system* (GESS)—or "getting to GESS."[12]

Technology Is the Driver; Industry, the Partner; Government, the Enabler

The remarkable change in US energy fortunes comes, once again, mostly because of technology and private initiative. Reduced US energy demand is also attributable—beyond the immediate impacts of recession—to strides in energy efficiency. Over the past 10 years, cumulative savings from increased US energy intensity are equivalent to roughly 5 years of current Saudi production. Over the next 10 years, they can amount to as much as 6 more years of Saudi production.[13]

Hydraulic fracturing ("fracking") and horizontal drilling are now commercializing natural gas and tight oil from US shale formations, all the way from Texas to North Dakota to the American Northeast. The impact of this change is enormous: technology now makes possible development and production of vast amounts of "unconventional" fuels, which are present in many parts of the world.[14]

The other major cause of today's watershed in energy production comes from ultradeepwater production in the Gulf of Mexico, as well as in other oil and gas provinces offshore eastern Canada and Brazil, West and East Africa, and Australia, and prospectively in or near the Arctic. Here again, new drilling and seismic technology makes possible the tapping of huge reserves of oil and gas[15]—with the West's largest energy and service companies taking the lead in these extremely complex and expensive projects.

Although technology and industry, small and large, are the prime actors, public policy has also played a significant role in these developments. The US Department of Energy invested in advanced seismic technology and experimentation in combining hydraulic fracturing and horizontal drilling. US tax policy promoted both deepwater drilling in the Gulf of Mexico and onshore drilling through accelerated depreciation of drilling costs. Often government, from the US Geological Survey to the Advanced Research Projects Agency–Energy, is the catalyst for new geological discoveries and new technologies in the United States, which are then augmented by private sector research and development (R&D), investment, and management of complex projects. Public policy performs a key role, too, on legal and fiscal terms; public health, safety, and the environment; and commercial advocacy and pressure for the rule of law in foreign trade and investment. Governments, at all levels, must strive for continuous improvement in standards and for smart, timely, and cost-effective regulation so that enterprises can invest in these large, challenging, and expensive projects in a predictable and stable environment.

The Geopolitical and Geoeconomic Stakes Are Far Reaching, but So Are Safety and Climate

Advances in demand reduction, taken in combination with the surge in discovery and production of unconventional and deepwater fuels, can transform North America from a net importer to a net exporter of oil and gas by 2030.[16] Reduced dependence on oil and gas imports from unstable or unreliable suppliers has far-reaching implications, not only for North America but also for many other regions with similar opportunities. The playing field is leveling between traditional producers and consumers, between the old OPEC and an emerging, new system of energy and security.

While seizing the geopolitical and geoeconomic opportunities, the United States must produce new resources with safety and the environment as top priorities. All companies—including the smaller independents—need a strong safety culture, from ensuring well bore integrity in deepwater or deep shale beds, to securing the safe disposal of water produced from "tight" hydrocarbon plays, to careful siting and security of nuclear operations. The independent Center for Sustainable Shale Development (CSSD), established in 2013 with foundation financing and academic, environmental, and industry support, is an encouraging step in the right direction.[17] The

CSSD establishes clear performance standards and welcomes third-party audits of company compliance.

We believe these safety and environmental risks can be minimized so that unconventional fuels and deepwater production can be key to the shift under way in the geopolitical landscape. Already Europe has become less dependent on a single fuel source—Russian natural gas—by diversifying its imports with liquefied natural gas (LNG), alternative pipelines from North Africa and the Caspian, and new deepwater development in the North Sea. Over time, shale gas development in the United Kingdom and, potentially, Eastern Europe may reduce this dependence even further.[18] Having several fuel sources, in turn, will make consumer states less vulnerable to price pressures and supply disruptions—and will encourage supplier states to diversify fuel exports as well as their economies overall.

The same diversification is occurring, if in smaller measure, in other high-consuming regions. In Asia, China is seeking to reduce its dependence on coal and the attendant pollution. It is diversifying its oil and gas imports with pipelines from Russia and Central Asia and with LNG from Australia, thereby limiting its dependence on the Middle East. Additional, potentially vast shale gas deposits can supplement less plentiful development of onshore sour gas and offshore crude to reduce that dependence further.[19] However, not unlike Eastern Europe (at least until recently), India, Japan, South Korea, Taiwan, and other major consumers are not so fortunate—especially since Tokyo's decision (which it may have to revisit) to shut down nuclear power plants following the Fukushima Daiichi disaster in March 2011. The challenge and opportunity will be to ensure that these countries, too, can access abundant new sources of supply, from Australia and Southeast Asia to Canada—as they already have begun to do—supplemented potentially by US exports, which will require important new decisions from Washington.[20]

Similarly, in Latin America, Brazil is developing new ultradeepwater, subsalt resources, and Argentina, Colombia, and Brazil are about to explore potentially significant deposits of shale gas and tight oil. To the north, Mexico, under the "new PRI" (Partido Revolucionario Institucional, or Institutional Revolutionary Party) is on the verge of major energy reforms that, if enacted, could permit large-scale foreign investment through joint ventures, at least offshore, for the first time since the nationalization of the energy industry in the decades following the Mexican Revolution in the early 20th century. All these countries face substantial populist and fiscal challenges, but their progress will go far to reduce dependence on supplies from more radical regimes, most notably Venezuela. Caracas, in turn, is entering a post-Chávez era with serious economic challenges, which could lead it to establish more normal energy ties, begin to restore Petróleos de Venezuela to its former greatness, and help create a more stable and democratic era in Latin America.[21]

Africa is beginning to develop more of its energy resources, with offshore production in the west, exploration in the east, and large shale deposits in South Africa and elsewhere. This activity adds to the oil and gas production in the north of the continent, opening new doors to Africa's economic development and expanding economic links with Mediterranean countries and the American and Asian markets.[22] The challenge in this and other major supplier regions is to contain the "resource curse," which enriches a corrupt few, widens the gap between a global 1 percent and 99 percent, withers development of nonenergy sectors from agriculture to manufacturing, and creates fertile ground for extremist forces—as demonstrated bloodily in the crescent from northern Nigeria to the Maghreb.[23]

Producer–Consumer Relations Are Rebalancing Fundamentally

The consequences of more plentiful and dispersed energy are profound. The era of global and regional energy hegemons is coming to an end. Whereas at its height OPEC held crucial leverage over global oil supplies and prices, now it must contend with growing internal divisions and major non-OPEC producers such as Russia, increasingly North America, Norway, and potentially Brazil.[24] Soviet, then Russian, gas production and transportation dominated the Eurasian landmass; now its traditional customers are importing, developing, and transporting new sources of supply, foreign and domestic.

Growing production in North and South America is also rebalancing the scales of geopolitics. By 2014, the US Energy Information Administration (EIA) expects that US imports of liquid fuels, including crude oil and petroleum products, will drop to about 6 million barrels per day (mmbpd), about half their peak levels of more than 12 mmbpd during 2004 to 2007,[25] with self-sufficiency in North America in prospect by 2030.[26] This situation will put downward price pressure on the oil market and diminish dependence on unstable or unreliable regimes elsewhere in the world.

North America is approaching a critical juncture where all or some of the following key changes can come into place: greatly increased production, greatly reduced imports, growing Canadian exports, a US decision to export more than products, and Mexican reforms leading to an energy renaissance in the south. Even if only some of these changes take place—and they certainly will—North American energy can play a larger strategic role on the world stage.[27]

The United States is now the world's number one gas producer, and within a decade US oil production could well match or exceed that of the world's top producers, Saudi Arabia and Russia. Even if production levels are somewhat less because of political or regulatory constraints, a US or combined North American energy role can lay a new foundation for strategic cooperation with the leading gas and oil producers, both members of OPEC and nonmembers. Moreover, expectations of such a role can provide immediate benefits. As a front-burner example, countries that still import Iranian crude, even if in lower amounts—such as China, India, Japan, and South Korea—will be better able to terminate those imports as part of international sanctions if they have credible substitute assurances. Substitute supplies have been forthcoming from Saudi Arabia, Qatar, and the United Arab Emirates; they should also be forthcoming from North America and Australia, leading to greater Pacific alignment on critical issues of energy and security.[28]

Just as important, the broader relationship between producers and consumers is also changing in fundamental ways. This trend began with the Arabian Gulf region,[29] whose market share has dropped from 23 percent of total US oil imports in 2001 to 16 percent in 2011.[30] Here the critical producer is Saudi Arabia, historically the global "central banker" of oil, which holds most of the world's spare capacity, increased its output to 9.3 mmbpd by the end of 2012[31] and can increase its production by a further 2.0 mmbpd within a matter of months. Although its own domestic demand will grow apace as it proceeds with industrialization and continued energy price subsidies as a way to garner domestic support, Saudi Arabia is still using much of that increase for external political and economic purposes: to compensate for forfeited Iranian barrels and thereby reinforce the global sanctions regime, to prevent OPEC price hawks from raising prices above $100 to $110 per barrel, and, of course, to meet its own budget needs. Despite mutual frustration and disappointment, especially over Syria (where sharp differences appear to be lessening), the Islamist surge, and Palestinian issues, US–Saudi alignment continues to play a pivotal role, both in the Middle East and globally.

Ironically, over the longer term, the Saudis themselves aspire to produce oil from shale and natural gas from offshore resources. They are moving ahead with plans to explore seven new prospects in the Red Sea and Arabian Gulf, which seem more promising than the Empty Quarter. In fact, Ali Al-Naimi, the Saudi oil minister, went so far as to state in March 2013 that future unconventional fuels may well save Saudi Arabia billions of dollars in continued maintenance of more expensive spare capacity for conventional oil.[32]

Less well understood, perhaps, is the changing face of producer–consumer relations. What have been the world's top two consumers—the United States and China—are moving aggressively to diversify production sources and types, with far more domestic resources available, of course, to the United States than to China. What have been the world's top two producers—Saudi Arabia and Russia—are escalating their consumption as their economies develop and industrialize.[33]

Increasingly in the energy arena, consumers are producers, and producers are consumers. Hence, the mostly confrontational or, at best, sterile relations of the past can now become more cooperative and interdependent, a change that is reflected in interesting ways. Faced with growing energy needs as their economies rebound at home, Russia and Saudi Arabia are emphasizing new supplies—offshore and shale in Russia, and offshore and large-scale solar, nuclear, and efficiency initiatives in Saudi Arabia.[34]

Institutionally, the producer–consumer International Energy Forum, headquartered in Riyadh, is pursuing initiatives for oil and gas transparency and data collection, and the International Energy Agency (IEA) continues to seek to engage nonmembers Russia, China, and India in dialogue and at least as observers, which will help both sides better understand each other's views. The fact that all three countries are also members of the Group of 20, the World Bank, and the International Monetary Fund causes them to consider the important energy–economic relationship even more closely.

Even more profoundly than institutional development, global energy policies are beginning to move, albeit unevenly, in more complementary directions. The US lurch to fossil fuel promotion in the Bush–Cheney administration was followed by an opposing lurch to nonfossil promotion under President Obama and his short-lived energy and climate czar, Carol Browner. The strategy under Obama has since evened out to a more balanced "all of the above" fuel and energy strategy,[35] which is advocated by industry and embraced by both Republicans and, now, many more Democrats. The longtime Saudi focus on oil was followed by a frustrating search for onshore natural gas; now, again, a more up-to-date approach is beginning to pay dividends, as Saudi Arabia pursues shale gas, gas offshore, and nuclear and renewables. Russia, another key player, is still making the transition from command and control to a more inclusive, transparent, and competitive strategy. Formerly the "state within the state," Gazprom can no longer simply dictate terms to domestic companies such as Novatek or foreign companies such as Bulgargaz.[36]

Prospects for Price Stability Are Better

Although the world of commodity prices certainly offers no guarantees, the chances of maintaining a more stable and predictable price range have improved for several reasons. The first is that more sources of oil and natural gas, including those in North America, will be available to meet growing demand from an eventual recovery. The second is the growing interdependence between traditional consumers and producers, as well as the blurring of lines between these two groups, such that both sides are increasingly motivated by both producer and consumer incentives.

The third is that North America, and to a greater or lesser extent other consuming regions over time, is moving so substantially toward net energy sufficiency that cooperation is increasingly a matter of choice rather than necessity. A fourth is that the United States, with reduced imports, will be in a far stronger position to use its strategic reserves to replace disrupted supply overseas if it modernizes its system for deploying those reserves.[37] In short, many old energy adversaries are becoming potential energy partners that can share the benefits of a new system of both energy security and economic growth—and guard against the risks of any future downturn.

Strategic Moves toward a Global Energy Security System

The energy watershed that technology is providing in ultradeepwater production and unconventional fuels creates what is perhaps a once-in-a-lifetime opportunity to sharply increase global prospects for energy security—and for energy, growth, climate, and foreign policies to mutually reinforce one another as they have never done before. What is possible to achieve, we believe, is nothing less than a new global energy security system that promotes economic growth, limits and reduces carbon in our environment, and furthers important foreign policy goals. Of course trade-offs will occur among these goals, but a more unified strategy will help rationalize near-term and long-term priorities for the United States and its allies and partners.

Getting to GESS requires priority initiatives in domestic and foreign policy, reorganization of the structure of energy-related decision-making, strong federal and state leadership, and proactive "coalitions of the concerned." On pages 558–59 is a summary table, with each initiative then described in greater detail.

Domestic Policy Initiatives

To be credible in its global policies, the United States must pursue them at home. The most important of these policies are (a) embracing hydrocarbon exports, with consideration for countries that offer reciprocity in market access or security cooperation; (b) allowing inward investment in the US energy sector, with due protection of critical infrastructure and US security objectives; (c) supporting environmental policies and regulations that limit GHG emissions, advance the decarbonization of the energy system, and put the country on a credible path to meet its Group of Eight GHG reduction commitments; and (d) sustaining federal investment in R&D to address the key outstanding technology gaps in the pathway to a cleaner energy economy.

Exports

The United States will enjoy surpluses of natural gas and, for some period, light oil, given the configuration of its more complex refinery system for heavy oil. At present, huge differentials exist between the prices of US natural gas and crude oil, on the one hand, and international benchmarks, on the other hand, because these hydrocarbons are trapped in the United States for policy or infrastructure reasons. From a domestic perspective, limits on exports of products and monopolies on transportation within the United States produce great inefficiencies. Over time, artificial barriers will lead to decreased production, higher prices, and lost value to the US economy. In parts of 2012 and 2013, natural gas prices were below the cost of production in many places because the US market is oversupplied in key regions. Associated gas is flared in the Bakken region because it cannot be monetized in an area that does not need the gas. The East Coast imports gasoline (and crude oil) from Europe or

Summary Table: Getting to GESS

Initiative	Energy Impacts	Foreign and Security Impacts	Economic Impacts	Environmental Impacts
Propagate the unconventional energy revolution abroad.	• Increase global oil and gas supply. • Enhance indigenous energy security. • Expand share of gas in energy mix.	• Reduce dependence on foreign suppliers. • Expand non-OPEC supply. • Counter external pressures. • Offset Gazprom control. • Offset demand for gas from Iran. • Reduce Venezuelan regional influence. • Balance Middle East influence in East Asia	• Increase supply; lower prices. • Improve balance of trade for energy importers. • Lower transport costs. • Create more jobs, greater growth. • Increase resistance to monopolies. • Help end energy poverty.	• Reduce GHG emissions below coal's. • Make gas cost competitive with coal outside the United States. • Find an alternative to gas flaring and longer oil shipments. • Use leverage to relieve restrictions on rare earth minerals. • Ensure high safety and environmental standards.
Create a competitive global gas market.	• Make gas accessible in new markets. • Develop new gas sources. • Promote infrastructure development. • Open up access.	• Reduce vulnerability to cartel-like national and regional behavior. • Open space for alternative regional cooperation (e.g., Ukraine with European Union, Caucasus with Turkey).	• Help allies and partners obtain needed energy at a better price. • Create gas-on-gas competition rather than current regionalization. • Break monopoly and erode oil-linked pricing schemes.	• Natural gas trumps coal as global feedstock if price is lowered and discontinuities are limited.

Forge greater coordination of emergency response measures.	• Limit crisis impact from natural disasters or market disruption. • Increase effectiveness by expanding to product stocks.	• Forge coalition of the concerned to supplement IEA system. • Increase oil and gas supply to Asian consumers actively supporting energy security, sanctions initiatives.	• Limit price disruptions from market shocks. • Improve effectiveness of response by expanding quantity of global reserves.	• Limit fuel switching from gas to coal by ameliorating price impacts of gas supply disruptions.
Lead multilateral effort to end energy poverty.	• Support electrification. • Encourage fuel diversity. • Open up new energy markets. • Expand grids. • Increase transparency.	• Provide World Bank and OECD support. • Emphasize developing country stakes. • "Drain the swamp" through education and training.	• Improve energy access to promote jobs and economic growth.	• Limit biomass burning. • Expand sustainability.
Commit to global engagement and protection of sea-lanes.	• Protect against physical disruption of energy supplies.	• Cooperate with allies and potential adversaries. • Implement cost sharing.	• Prevent major price disruptions from delayed shipments.	

Asia rather than Texas because US-flagged ships are legally required to move crude or product within US boundaries even if the Jones Act fleet is booked.[38] US-produced crude is heavily discounted compared with other crude streams because it is trapped in the United States, thus creating tax revenue losses for US producing states and profits for foreign suppliers.

The United States should embrace hydrocarbon exports carefully but deliberately.[39] Although the market will be limited over time for US LNG exports, gas-on-gas competition is already eroding the link between crude oil and natural gas prices that punishes Europe and Asia with prices that are multiples higher than US prices. US policy allows unlimited LNG exports to countries that have free trade agreements with the United States (only South Korea is a significant importer in that category) but requires a special national interest determination for all others, including allies, such as Japan, and countries subject to restricted gas supplies, such as Ukraine. We believe that the US Department of Energy ought to permit any qualified enterprise to obtain a license to export LNG and should allow the Federal Energy Regulatory Commission and the market to determine which projects come to market. But as a second-best option, the United States ought to allow some consideration for countries that demonstrate extraordinary cooperation with its policies, such as forswearing imports from countries of concern.

Growing US production of light oil will create surpluses of those crude streams. This oil, which is highly sought by countries with less complex refining systems than those of the United States, will be either shut in or inefficiently blended with cheaper crudes if the United States continues to prohibit its export. Why not exploit the US comparative economic advantage for a collective security advantage by allowing the export of crude oil to countries such as Japan, India, or South Korea if they cooperate, for example, with US sanctions on Iran? Or why not allow export to countries within the Western Hemisphere, where Venezuela has sought political influence by subsidized sales of crude oil and products to Central America and the Caribbean? Or why not permit export of oil as well as LNG to countries that sign free trade agreements with the United States or offer reciprocal access to their markets?

Inward Investment

The ability to invest in the US energy sector, both to learn the technology and to profit from the boom, is a powerful draw. The United States will rightly limit foreign investment if the investor poses a risk of compromising the country's critical infrastructure. It will limit investment by state-controlled entities if the home country of that investor is adverse to important national security concerns.[40] The United States should recognize that this opening to foreign investment is a powerful tool. The most sensitive—and perhaps most important—example of its potential use is China. If the US national security goal is for China to rely on the market for supply, open its own market for investment, and restrain investment in countries of concern, why not put a real counteroffer on the table by offering China access (and oil exports as well) on a reciprocal basis and then helping it produce more of its own energy supply? From a GESS perspective, for the United States to press for no more imports from Iran is challenging if the United States continues to stall on substitute energy supplies from its own shores. Far more effective would be to share energy resources with those allies and partners willing to respond to US security concerns.

Environmental Policy

The United States has come to the point where it must accept that failing to address climate change is a safety and security risk. At a national level, extreme weather poses risks to critical infrastructure; at an international level, countries will need to consider methods of adaptation for those regions where mitigation will come too late. This strategy will require that policies be in place to move the nation—and the planet—toward a lower-carbon future to avoid permanent physical and environmental damage and a new set of security risks and consequences.[41]

We believe that the United States should work to export the shale gas revolution and demonstrate that it can reduce GHGs by adopting natural gas now and increasing renewables over time. To do so, however, it needs credible policies on safety and GHG reduction at home. These policies have two components: market incentives and regulation. To reach a pathway of long-term GHG reduction that promotes natural gas as a bridge, we believe, as many others do, that a revenue-neutral carbon tax provides the swiftest, fairest, and most efficient path. Enacting this tax would take bipartisan leadership and courage not yet seen from either party, but the day will come when it must take place. Until then, regulation provides the likeliest path. US Environmental Protection Agency (EPA) rules to constrain air toxins and other preventable emissions (largely from coal) should be adopted. The EPA effort to promulgate a practical rule for green completions of gas wells holds promise for future rules. With these rules in place, a shadow price on carbon will favor natural gas, but coal can invest in technologies to reduce its carbon footprint in a market that rightly puts a price on its externalities.[42]

As we have learned from *Deepwater Horizon* and other disasters, industry's license to operate will depend on embracing strong, well-enforced safety regulation. If the United States is to promote shale gas abroad, it needs to ensure safe practice at home. The country has learned a great deal about how to regulate well. For shale development, industry has embraced, after a bad start, disclosure of fracturing fluids and a wide range of state regulations on seismic assessment, cement integrity testing, water access, and recycling and community impact. A recent study has shown that the United States has many new best practice regulations, although not all of them apply in every state.[43] Through the CSSD and other initiatives, industry will need to raise standards for all operators in all jurisdictions to have a politically sustainable model that countries abroad will also emulate.

Federal R&D

The federal government plays—and for decades has played—an indispensable role in technology development. The country is close—but not close enough—to bringing to commercialization the technologies that can move it further toward a low-carbon economy. As Melanie Kenderdine and Ernest Moniz masterfully detail in chapter 17, additional research is needed to

- Create batteries that can store renewable energy.
- Develop new, small, and proliferation-resistant modular reactors that can bring nuclear energy to developing economies.
- Devise methods to capture as well as safely store carbon dioxide.
- Develop ways to recycle or access the rare earth and energy-critical materials needed for a carbon-free future.

But the United States can dramatically improve its own self-sufficiency through methods to increase oil and gas recovery from existing fields. A true test of commitment to an "all of the above" strategy by those who support fossil fuel development will be their commitment to a robust federal R&D program.

Foreign Policy Initiatives

For all the comfort that growing US self-sufficiency provides, a common thread among our contributors is the challenge posed by the rapidly growing energy demand of the non–OECD (Organization for Economic Cooperation and Development) world to the energy system and the climate. The demand for power and mobility from developing Asia, in particular, but also the Middle East and Africa poses serious national security questions: How will these countries produce electricity? What kind of fuels will they choose? Who will provide them? Will their infrastructure be locked in soon? Will conflict arise over the competition for energy resources or over the absence of access to electricity itself?

In our view, getting to GESS requires a robust set of foreign policy strategies to ensure that the United States uses this moment to secure a rebalance of power in the energy system. The core elements of this strategy are (a) propagating the unconventional energy revolution to as many new countries as possible; (b) creating a competitive global gas market for security and climate, as well as economic, reasons; (c) leveraging reduced US imports to forge an improved coordination of emergency responses to supply disruptions; (d) using diplomacy to foster closer alignment of producers and consumers; (e) leading a serious multilateral effort to end energy poverty; and (f) making a sustained commitment to global engagement and protection of sea-lanes.

The United States has begun major strides along this path. To her great credit, US Secretary of State Hillary Clinton made energy effectively a fourth pillar of US foreign policy, in addition to diplomacy, defense, and development. Supported by special envoys and a newly established Bureau of Energy Resources, she launched new international initiatives for transparency and shale gas, pursued energy policy dialogues with consumers and producers, and made energy security and development top priorities for her department.[44] In addition, the State and Treasury Departments have led the way in organizing effective international sanctions targeted against Iran's energy trade and financial flows, putting significantly more pressure against Iran's development of a nuclear weapons capacity.

We hope that Secretary of State John Kerry will build on this legacy, with foreign policy initiatives that will move the needle in this new energy environment. Multiple security challenges could benefit from energy security solutions. Close at hand, nuclear proliferation risks in Iran and North Korea demand immediate attention. Although military force may become the only viable alternative, the election of Hassan Rohani as Iran's new president in June 2013 may possibly provide a window for an accord to cap nuclear enrichment—in return, for example, for reduced sanctions, an international enriched fuel bank, and renewed energy trade. In Pyongyang, Kim Jong-un and, even more so, the increasingly powerful military leadership must come to face a stark choice between (a) escalated sanctions, where China is induced to cut off fuel and other supplies, and (b) stringently verified termination of militarily useful nuclear and missile programs. However unlikely in the near term, North Korea should understand that it has the alternative of resuming economic liberalization and using civilian food and fuel supplies, including low-enriched uranium for civilian reactors, to replace plutonium programs and encourage a market opening.

Propagating the Unconventional Energy Revolution
to as Many New Countries as Possible

The fastest way to ensure a long, if not lasting, diversification and shift in the weight of oil and gas production away from the Middle East (and Russia) is to help other nations take advantage of the shale revolution so that they can produce their own supplies at lower cost and greater security. In some cases, shale will be insufficiently porous to be developed; in other cases, the geology may be favorable, but the investment regime, infrastructure, and regulatory framework have not yet developed to replicate the American success. But the latter can be learned. Efforts begun under Secretary of State Clinton can be greatly enhanced to expose other governments to the network of laws and rules that enable the United States to have a competitive and robust energy market. Whereas US companies will promote their own technology and compete for investment opportunities, governments are better suited to advise on rules that permit open access to pipelines, on environmental impact assessments, and on safety standards. In other areas, legal, tax, and investment advisers can provide useful insights to the competitive landscape in which countries must operate.[45]

More broadly, the potential foreign policy and climate benefits of propagating the unconventional energy revolution are vast and, in terms of immediate influence, unmatched by any other climate or security strategy. A few examples underline the potential power of such an initiative:

- By helping India and China develop large-scale sources of gas, such efforts can create alternatives to dirty coal and address growing domestic concerns about pollution of the environment at the same time as further limiting Iran's primary export markets.
- By helping European countries break Russia's hold on gas supply, these strategies can reduce the Kremlin's coercive leverage and release urgently needed resources for their own development. In the longer term, this effort can encourage a more cooperative Russian approach to energy security and broader European issues.
- By helping Africa capture flared gas and deliver electricity, these initiatives can open new development windows together with the opportunity to contribute to ending energy poverty in the continent.

Creating a Competitive Global Gas Market for Security and Climate, as Well as Economic, Reasons

As many of our contributors note, the world has multiple regional gas markets but not yet a global gas market. Piped gas dominates the market, thereby allowing monopoly pricing or unjustified high correlation of natural gas prices to oil prices. These discontinuities enable coal to be far more competitive than natural gas for the world's major emitters and obstruct the kind of transition from coal to gas that has led to such rapid and dramatic GHG reductions in the United States. For nations seeking rapid and large-scale centralized access to electric power, natural gas generation is superior to both nuclear power and, until its intermittency can be resolved, renewable energy.[46] Nations should and will pursue both those sources as well, but the real choice today is between gas and coal. The United States can accelerate the advent of a truly global and competitive gas market by clearing the way for its own LNG exports, by encouraging market pricing and gas development abroad, by supporting LNG access and interconnections, and by promoting open access in energy transportation.

Leveraging Reduced US Imports to Forge an Improved Coordination of Emergency Responses to Supply Disruptions

The most recent use of the coordinated emergency response system, following disruption of Libyan supplies in 2011, revealed some important weaknesses. Whereas the United States uses its Strategic Petroleum Reserve (SPR) to put actual barrels on the market, the IEA system often does not. China, with growing strategic stocks, participates on an ad hoc basis.

As US imports shrink, the country will be able to not only replace its own imports if disrupted, but also—if the rules and pipeline infrastructure allow—sell barrels to export to a global market. This ability is an important foreign policy tool, and it will inure increasingly to the benefit of Asian consumers, who will feel price spikes at least as sharply as US consumers. The United States should use this tool to forge a "coalition of the concerned" to supplement the IEA system and should use this opportunity to forge closer alignment on emergency response policy with non-IEA members.

Using Diplomacy to Foster Closer Alignment of Producers and Consumers

The United States now has a rare opportunity to use diplomacy to seek closer energy alignment between the United States and key energy producers and consumers, such as Saudi Arabia, Russia, and Canada in oil; Australia, Russia, and Qatar in gas; Germany, Denmark, and China in renewables; and China, India, and Japan as energy consumers. In most, if not all, of these fields, US leadership is on the upswing, and productive discussions could be organized on promoting energy trade, investment, and efficiency; fighting energy poverty; and creating a new energy roadmap for the future. Such a roadmap could focus on technology cooperation, institutional development, and win–win solutions to disputed energy areas, building on such good examples as the Russian–Norwegian agreement on their sectors of the Barents Sea and the Arctic Ocean. The United States and these key potential allies share needs for large-scale deployment testing in areas such as carbon sequestration.[47] In a time of severe budget constraints, the United States should foster collaborative multilateral efforts, with a focus on including China and India as investors and even test sites for these critical technologies.

Leading a Serious Multilateral Effort to End Energy Poverty

More than 1.4 billion people do not have access to electricity. Energy poverty and energy access are important development, security, and climate challenges. The risks that dysfunctional electricity systems pose to Pakistan, Nigeria, and Iraq are but three examples of where ineffective pricing, misguided policy, and often corruption can increase geopolitical instability that puts vital US interests at risk. The solutions to these complex problems involve mobilizing the political will to reform at the head-of-government level and providing technical advice on restructuring, targeting subsidies, and integrating gas and renewables into broken systems.

These solutions require large-scale, long-term efforts, but they are at the nexus of climate, security, and development. Unfortunately, large-scale US foreign assistance is no longer available in this area, except in crisis or postconflict areas. Rather, the United States now supports multilateral loans for renewable energy instead of hydrocarbon-related projects (unless they have sequestration!)—a serious handicap to World Bank efforts in this area. The United States and its OECD partners should reverse this course and focus diplomacy as well as financial and technical assistance on electrification, which, in turn, could be the greatest single tool for meeting development needs, limiting climate change, and promoting stability and trade.[48]

Making a Sustained Commitment to Global Engagement and Protection of Sea-Lanes

The United States should not mistake its good fortune in increased self-sufficiency as cause to retreat from global engagement. As noted at the outset, North America may become energy self-sufficient—not requiring any fuel imports—within the next two decades. Does that mean that the United States can become "energy independent," as so many politicians like to say, or even pare back its global commitments in the exhausting wake of Iraq and Afghanistan? At least, surely, the United States need not be the guardian of oil flows from the Middle East or the military escort for countless oil and LNG shipments from the Gulf to China and other Far East destinations.

The answer, however, is no. Strictly in energy terms, the oil market is global, and the gas market is moving in that direction. Any disruption of these markets will affect prices not only in a single unstable region but also across the world. Beyond strictly energy, turning one's back on those struggling for security and a better life will invite a repeat of earlier Western retrenchments—from Eastern Europe in the 1950s, which made more likely the Berlin and Cuba crises of the 1960s, or from Afghanistan and Pakistan in the 1980s, which opened the door to the Taliban and its al Qaeda guests. That said, unilateral military efforts can and should give way to coalitions of the concerned, in which like-minded states can join in protecting the sea-lanes as well as critical infrastructure required for energy and other collective security.

The true significance of energy self-sufficiency is that the United States can and should use the resulting strategic leverage to exercise, with its allies and partners, more rather than less influence in global affairs. In this sense, GESS is made possible by combining diplomatic and economic efforts, backed by military capacity as required, to ensure the availability of fuels for all those material things most take for granted in everyday life, including electric power and transportation; food, water, and medical services; and communication on Earth and in the cyber sphere.

Reorganization of Energy-Related Decision-Making

Achieving GESS will require coordinated national and international action, but energy-related decision-making is, unfortunately, largely dysfunctional at the national and global levels. As with other issues, US energy decision-making has been built incrementally over time, with different responsibilities assigned to at least 10 different departments and agencies in the executive branch and with more than 30 congressional committees and subcommittees that more often reinforce shared turf with executive agencies than promote a unified strategic view.

This wide range of energy-related functions can be melded together only by White House leadership. Vice President Al Gore achieved this objective to a significant extent through his joint commissions with Russia, China, and other states in Eurasia and the Middle East. Faced with the same kind of dysfunction, the Obama administration experimented with bilateral commissions cochaired by Secretary of State Clinton and her deputies, to which other US agencies were sometimes loath to devote resources that they could use for their own programs and counterparts. An elaborate process ensued, with limited substantive results, certainly in the energy sphere. The White House also experimented with a short-lived appointment of Carol Browner, a former EPA administrator, as the energy and climate coordinator. Browner focused her activities on domestic environmental issues that continued under her successor and through senior directors at the National Economic Council, the National Security Council, the Council of Environmental Quality, and the Domestic Policy Council—in other words, in an effort just as fragmented and pulled in as many different policy directions as the rest of the executive branch.

The United States can do better. Even without regrouping agencies, the new energy secretary, Ernest Moniz, is in the process of reinvigorating the international policy function, one would hope paying at least equal attention to the 80 percent fossil piece of the pie as to the 20 percent nuclear and renewable piece. The State Department can build its Energy Resources Bureau to field qualified and effective diplomats in more key energy posts, in tandem with energy attachés from the Department of Energy and foreign commercial officers from the Commerce Department, who have been missing in action from commercial energy issues since the Clinton administration. Plans are now underway for quadrennial energy reviews, cochaired by two White House offices (Domestic Policy Council and Office of Science and Technology Policy, with the Energy Department providing the secretariat), corresponding to similar defense and development reviews—a welcome step in the right direction.

It is clear that the White House can and should do better. Instead of an alphabet soup of mid-level energy players, a lead senior official is required to coordinate energy with related national security, economic, environmental, and domestic issues. Recognizing the critical nature of energy resources and access, presidents and prime ministers of other countries frequently engage in person with their counterparts on these issues. For example, President Vladimir Putin has engaged personally for years in negotiating the Nord Stream and South Stream pipelines with foreign leaders—in each case insisting on at least 51 percent Russian control—because he understands their strategic implications for the Kremlin. Likewise, in China, energy access and assets have been at or near the top of the list of priorities for President Hu Jintao and now President Xi Jinping. The Chinese president meets personally with presidents of major resource holders from Saudi Arabia to Iran, Kazakhstan, Turkmenistan, and Venezuela, and the Chinese national oil companies—China National Petroleum Corporation, Sinopec, and China National Offshore Oil Corporation—reinforce China's interests around the world. The results of engagement at these senior levels—as opposed to engagement by a few US assistant or deputy assistant secretaries, however qualified—speak for themselves.

An energy task force of the US Bipartisan Policy Center, cochaired by President Obama's former national security adviser, General James Jones; President George H. W. Bush's former EPA administrator, William Reilly; and two former senators, Byron Dorgan (D-ND) and Trent Lott (R-MS), has made further proposals to raise the energy policy game of the US government.[49] The Bipartisan Policy Center proposes a new National Energy Strategy Council, chaired by the secretary of energy, which would address in a single, high-level forum all energy-related issues, including energy resource, national security, environmental, and domestic issues. It also proposes quadrennial energy reviews as counterparts to the quadrennial defense, diplomacy, and development reviews that already take place. Any or all of those ideas would help bring order to the chaos of US decision-making in this critical arena, although our view would be that high-level coordination is required from the White House, perhaps through an assistant to the president staffed at a level equivalent to the head of the National Economic Council, rather than by a cabinet officer responsible for a single department.

At the international level, the world also suffers from institutions of the past. OPEC in Vienna has long gathered producers to deliberate on oil markets and determine production quotas, but it represents a limited proportion of the oil market and steers clear of natural gas. The IEA in Paris does an excellent job gathering OECD consumers to analyze and deliberate about both the oil and the gas markets, as well as energy efficiency and other energy sources—and importantly, it coordinates the SPR and the emergency response policies of its members. But it does not include increasingly important consumers such as China and India, which while participating together with other countries as observers are neither OECD members nor anxious to accept predetermined IEA requirements. The International Energy Forum in Riyadh does valuable work in compiling data and increasing the transparency of both the oil and the gas markets, but it has yet to fulfill ambitions for it to be a productive focal point for consumer–producer dialogue.

Analyzing this imperfect state of affairs, William Ramsay, a former IEA deputy executive director, urges less attention to institutional development than to action-oriented "minimalist" groups brought together by shared interests and focused on shared initiatives.[50] This approach dovetails with our suggestion earlier in this conclusion that leading oil, gas, and renewables producers and consumers meet and take the lead on such issues as energy trade, investment, efficiency, and energy poverty, as well as creating an energy roadmap for the future.

Federal and State Leadership

Unfortunately, the US Congress has become so polarized that one can more easily visualize its playing a blocking rather than a constructive role in moving US energy policies forward. A very positive force had been Senator Richard Lugar (R-IN), chairman and later ranking member of the Senate Foreign Relations Committee, until a Tea Party candidate ran against his bipartisan approach, defeated him in the primary, and then deservedly lost in the general election. That said, one should never say never, and wider agreement on "all of the above" fuel and energy policies and recognition of the opportunities of energy self-sufficiency may possibly create a new platform for responsible bipartisan action, or even legislation, in the future.[51]

If congressional action does not occur, however, any US policy leadership will need to come both from the federal government, acting within its statutory authority, and from the state governments. Both are consequential to America's new energy pivot point, with its opportunities and challenges. In the case of ultradeepwater drilling, both the federal and littoral state governments have regulatory authority, for example, to approve the license, supervise the drilling operation from a safety and environmental standpoint, and intervene in the case of an accident beyond the operator's capacity to control.

In the case of hydraulic fracturing and shale gas and oil, state governments take the lead in developing and enforcing regulations for their use and development. The challenge is to ensure that the smaller players adopt the same exacting environmental and safety requirements that the majors have embraced. Such regulation is important not only because health and safety should be paramount, but also because even a single serious incident could change the political climate for the entire industry. Anyone who needs convincing should look no further than the *Deepwater Horizon* and Fukushima Daiichi disasters.

Both federal and state governments play an active role on an even wider and more disturbing set of challenges: the growing amount of carbon in the atmosphere. At the federal level, a cap-and-trade bill was passed by the House but not by the Senate in 2009,[52] and it is likely to remain in a coma despite increasing evidence of climate damage, including the sequential devastation of the Gulf and Northeast Coasts by "once in a century" hurricanes and storms. However, the executive branch has the statutory authority to pursue regulations based on finding carbon dioxide to be a pollutant. And the executive and legislative branches both face fiscal problems so overwhelming that a carbon tax may even get a further look as an effective economic as well as environmental vehicle.

As a heads-up to the Obama administration, the EIA is now forecasting that substituting natural gas for coal will play an important role in causing

US energy-related emissions to decline by 1 percent annually until 2035, and the administration could meet its target of a 17 percent reduction of 2005 carbon dioxide levels by 2020, even without legislative action.[53] Another key factor contributing to projected annual emissions declines is the changing US energy demand structure and profile after years of research, development, and policy encouragement.

In addition, states in the United States and overseas can and do take actions of their own. Between California's cap-and-trade climate requirements and the Northeast's adoption of shared carbon emissions standards, states are taking initiatives where Washington fears to tread. Furthermore, unlike the United States, the European Union is pressing ahead with its own emissions trading system, and major consumers such as China are setting new efficiency, emission, and fuel standards that are driven not only by pollution but also by good economics. Even with US negotiators tied down by Congress, a growing likelihood exists that a climate consensus will develop around them and become reflected ultimately in agreements reached by groups of governments in the post-Doha negotiations.

Coalitions of the Concerned

The preceding review of domestic and foreign policy initiatives, energy-related decision-making, and federal and state leadership underlines the increased links among these topics and the difficulty faced by existing national and global institutions in addressing these links effectively. Yet the global realignment of energy resources and their increased potency to significantly affect the most important global challenges call for transcending existing bureaucratic and institutional barriers.

As we have seen, no longer are there only energy "producers" or "consumers"—there are mixes of both. No longer are "domestic" and "foreign" energy policies divorced—the 21st-century energy system requires inputs from both. Sovereign governments continue to affect the system, but to have meaningful influence, they require support from international institutions, state or regional governments, and above all the enterprises that develop and produce the resources. The limitations on productive action become painfully evident when energy ministries simply meet with each other or when global conferences are held on climate change without the necessary building blocks of consensus.

Where most of the productive activity now takes place, and where even more such activity can occur in the future, is in smaller and more focused "coalitions of the concerned," which encompass the stakeholders that are most engaged and are most able to make a difference. After they reach consensus, they can then expand the discussion to include other parties that will have more limited contributions to make but whose support will make the consensus more effective. The challenge, of course, is not to exclude key players, on the one hand, nor to include parties that will likely disrupt the development of the initial consensus, on the other.

In the field of energy, the minimum requirement should be to include affected government authorities and the leading national and international oil companies, whose cooperation will be critical to the success of the initiative. The following priority action list illustrates the way this process might develop, although coalitions of the concerned should be able easily to expand or diminish in number and to sunset as they achieve their goals:

- *Transparency.* Achieving transparency is critical to good governance, corporate responsibility, and protection of public safety. The international Extractive Industries Transparency Initiative, the brainchild of Tony Blair when he was British prime minister, includes a growing number of government and industry participants who are committed to disclosure of sufficient information to promote the responsible allocation of resource revenues and the deterrence of corruption.[54]
- *Investment.* Huge investments are required to produce the energy needed by future generations,[55] which will be forthcoming from external sources only if investors are assured that their investments will be protected under rule of law and that their returns will not be disrupted by radical changes in fiscal and regulatory requirements. Actions by states and investors to demonstrate that contracts will be observed under enforceable bilateral investment treaties can be strengthened further by multilateral and global agreements that protect and promote international investment.
- *Development.* As noted previously, ending energy poverty is key to helping create new opportunities for people at the economic and social margins and to draining the swamp of extremist or terrorist activities. It is critical to creating an educated citizenry capable of active civic participation in their communities. Targeted actions by development agencies and ministries, working with power specialists and companies, should be undertaken with a view to achieving early success stories in the areas most negatively affected.

- *Spare capacity and strategic reserves*. These reserves are critical to maintaining energy market stability and to substituting for supply shortfalls resulting from, for example, the overthrow of Libya's Gaddafi regime or international sanctions against Iran. Here a combination of consultations—on Saudi excess capacity between the United States and the Kingdom; on Gulf Cooperation Council excess capacity among Saudi Arabia, Kuwait, and the United Arab Emirates; on strategic reserves among IEA members; and on non-IEA reserves with China, Japan, and Russia—is appropriate, depending on the circumstances. US efforts to modernize its own strategic reserves, by increasing physical, legal, and bureaucratic ability to swiftly export SPR oil as US imports decline, can be a catalyst to securing multilateral cooperation.[56]

- *Energy diplomacy*. Diplomacy can serve a critical role in managing tensions over development, transportation, and other issues. Foreign investment in the energy sector, particularly in upstream assets, is itself a sensitive issue in a wide range of countries and is often the subject of consultations at the highest levels. Alternative pipeline routes—for example, through Russia, Ukraine, or the Caspian states—are of such consequence that they are addressed by chiefs of state and special energy envoys. Disputed areas also require diplomatic intervention to be resolved, either on a boundary basis, as between Russia and Norway, or on a joint development basis, as between Kuwait and Saudi Arabia or, prospectively, in the South and East China Seas.

- *Climate policy*. Policy on climate will likely develop more quickly if government and private sectors can reach more focused levels of consensus with environmental experts and groups.[57] Instead of lurching between carbon and green policies, a positive and pragmatic government role would be to bring adherents of each set of policies together behind practical steps to limit and then reduce GHGs in the atmosphere. The climate skeptics need to accept that the GHG threat is real and a better path is needed. Environmental advocates need to embrace natural gas and its ability to reduce GHG emissions faster than any other fuel. Although they may not limit world temperature rises to 2°C by 2050, natural gas and expanded use of electricity will limit and reverse GHG levels, which are rapidly increasing at this time, while giving room to develop more advanced, low-carbon technologies, including long-life batteries, carbon capture and sequestration (CCS), second-generation biofuels, and effective and acceptable storage facilities for nuclear waste. Some of these technologies already have a head start—for example, in the largest commercial-scale CCS plant in the world at the Gorgon natural gas project at Barrow Island off the northwest coast of Australia. Energy savings in the range of 30 percent are now being achieved commercially for the US government and industry in the United States, just as the US and European Union governments are raising significantly corporate average fuel economy standards for autos and trucks. All these steps can demonstrate substantial commercial *and* environmental progress and can be replicated in other countries — leading to large savings as well as carbon reductions.

• *Commercial advocacy.* This aspect is increasingly important as companies from certain countries come bearing gifts in the form of grants, soft credits, or even outright bribes. For example, Chinese companies have been particularly proactive in associating their upstream development proposals with pipelines and road and building projects, all on preferential terms as well as state subsidized credits. France and Germany permitted their companies to receive tax credits for bribes, thinly disguised as consulting fees or facilitation charges, until the 1990s, when that practice was ruled out for all OECD members. Export credit and investment insurance agencies have made considerable progress to agreed standards of behavior; in turn they need to engage, directly or through the OECD, other government agencies that have not yet made similar undertakings. Even with a more or less level playing field, commercial proposals increasingly need to be augmented by high-level government contacts to achieve favorable outcomes.

Getting to GESS

Energy plays such a central role in the United States and the world that it inevitably affects security and foreign policy, as well as economic, social, and political issues all at the same time. In 2005, the first edition of this book[58] called for integrating US energy, security, and foreign policy, and clear progress has been made in the State Department and, more broadly, in US declaratory policy, as set forth in a wide-ranging speech given by National Security Adviser Tom Donilon at Columbia University in April 2013.[59]

The first edition of this book also called for concerted multilateral consumer policies, and advances have been made in responding to energy gaps from the Libyan conflict and in marshaling international sanctions against

Iran. It called for strengthened energy defenses, which are evidenced in improved coordination of augmented energy stocks; nevertheless, US energy defenses are still painfully vulnerable to cyber attack, as is so much of the nation's critical infrastructure. In addition to the "hard power" of energy, it called for advances in energy's "soft power," which are reflected in greater attention to energy diplomacy and to bilateral and multilateral coordination.

Still, an all-of-government approach to energy policy has not yet been achieved. Foreign and national security policy has yet to be integrated effectively with energy and economic policy. International performance is uneven in the face of high-level, focused, and integrated foreign, energy, and commercial policies by Chinese, Russian, and other competitors.

A far-sighted strategy that recognizes and capitalizes on the critical role of energy in the full range of foreign, national security, and economic policies—a global energy security strategy—will pay great dividends, from generating jobs at home to promoting greater opportunity and security at all levels of society.

This broader policy frame is not a task just for engineers and geologists, though they play an essential role. It is a task for leaders at all levels—from the world to the national to the state and local stages. Smaller groups must take the steps required first—the "minilateralist" approach—before they are adopted by larger ones, in Congress or at the United Nations climate forum. Local interests may continue to resist, but an overriding common interest in energy, economic, and climate security will cause the policy to advance.

Each region offers opportunities to advance, segment by segment, the Global Energy Security System (GESS) advocated here. In Africa, for example, policy should focus on electricity market reform. In Europe, increased competition and a unified market are priorities. China, India, and the Nordic countries could be natural partners in pressing CCS and other R&D cooperation. In Latin America, an opportunity exists to advance Mexican reforms, plan for a post-Chávez Venezuela, and join with North America in increased energy trade and exports. In Asia, the United States can make common cause with China in its transition from coal to gas and stepped-up energy efficiency, as well as provide energy exports and assurances to Japan and South Korea as they face off North Korean threats and increase their support of international sanctions against the Iranian nuclear weapons program. In the Arctic, the eight members of the Arctic Council have the opportunity to fashion a cooperative approach to development and protection of the environment.[60] Finally, in tandem with Canadian oil and

Australian gas, increased US oil and gas production can be the single most important catalyst for achieving GESS across the board.

Like the other great domestic and foreign policy choices of our times, the energy policy opportunity is so large that it calls for—it demands—the kind of bipartisan leadership that characterized the cooperation between Senator Arthur Vandenberg, Republican chairman of the Senate Foreign Relations Committee, and the Truman administration, leading to the adoption of the Marshall Plan and the establishment of the North Atlantic Treaty Organization after World War II. Senator Vandenberg was a die-hard isolationist until he recognized that the postwar global challenges required a complete change, and he became a pivotal internationalist in the US policy debates that ensued. The world of energy illustrates a parallel path. As noted at the outset, North America may be energy "self-sufficient" within the next two decades, but that does not mean that energy independence can or should be the goal.

No, energy self-sufficiency requires that the United States can and must exercise more, not less, influence in global affairs, which continue to be influenced fundamentally by fuel availability for power and transportation, national defense, communication and electronics, and virtually every other item taken for granted in everyday life. For all this, the prescription is not isolationism or autarky[61] but a robust strategy to promote energy security in tandem with foreign, economic, and environmental policy, with due attention to opportunities developing in each region of the world. This book provides a roadmap toward accomplishing that goal.

Notes

1. As an interesting historical note, in 1999, Ali Rodríguez, who was then Venezuela's energy minister and OPEC's president, suggested a per barrel oil price band of $22 to $28, which many OPEC leaders continued to promote from 2000 to 2005, despite the extreme difficulty of enforcing such a band in the face of collapses or gluts in demand. Seeking to counter this argument, Rodríguez told the visiting US energy secretary, Bill Richardson, in October 2000 that OPEC would release "automatically" an extra 500,000 barrels per day if oil prices reached $28 per barrel or more for 20 consecutive days. See Ello Ohep, "US Richardson and Venezuela Rodríguez Agreed on Stable Oil Prices and an Increase of 500,000 Barrels of Oil," *Petroleumworld.com*, October 22, 2000. See also John Kern, "Is an Oil Price Band Credible?," *Commodities Now* (London), March 31, 2010.

2. Jan H. Kalicki and David L. Goldwyn, eds., *Energy and Security: Toward a New Foreign Policy Strategy* (Washington, DC, and Baltimore: Woodrow Wilson Center Press and Johns Hopkins University Press, 2005).

3. For a more expansive definition of energy security, see Daniel Yergin, "Energy Security and Markets," chapter 2 of this volume.

4. See Melanie A. Kenderdine and Ernest J. Moniz, "Technology Development and Energy Security," chapter 17 of this volume.

5. Bureau of Ocean Energy Management, "Assessment of Undiscovered Technically Recoverable Oil and Gas Resources of the Nation's Outer Continental Shelf, 2011," Fact Sheet RED-20111-01a, Bureau of Ocean Energy Management, Washington, DC, November 2011.

6. According to 2012 data from PFC Energy's North American Onshore Service, the federal government holds title to 30.8 percent of the total US "mineral estate" but thus far has generated only 7.5 percent of oil and natural gas produced from shale.

7. See Colleen Curtis, "What You Need to Know about the Energy Security Trust," *White House Blog*, March 15, 2013, http://www.whitehouse.gov/blog/2013/03/15/what-you-need-know-about-energy-security-trust.

8. In addition to Japan, China has offshore disputes with Brunei, the Philippines, Taiwan (which it considers its own territory), and Vietnam.

9. At least 69 deaths were recorded, including 39 hostages, 1 Algerian security guard, and 29 militants. A total of 685 Algerian workers and 107 foreigners were freed. Three militants were captured. See "Q&A: Hostage Crisis in Algeria," BBC News Africa, January 21, 2013, http://www.bbc.co.uk/news/world-africa-21056884; "Algeria Details the Deaths at In Amenas Siege," *Euronews*, January 21, 2013, http://www.euronews.com/2013/01/21/algeria-details-the-deaths-at-in-amenas-siege/.

10. "Cyber Attacks in the Spin Cycle: Saudi Aramco and Shamoon," *Analysis Intelligence* (blog), November 1, 2012, http://analysisintelligence.com/cyber-defense/narrative-of-a-cyber-attack-saudi-aramco-and-shamoon/.

11. "All of the above" energy policies have attracted bipartisan consensus. Industry advocacy led to Republican congressional support, followed in 2011 by the White House's "Blueprint for a Secure Energy Future," White House, Washington, DC, March 30, 2011, http://www.whitehouse.gov/sites/default/files/blueprint_secure_energy_future.pdf. Time, budgets, and regulations will tell whether that support is more than rhetorical.

12. In 1981, Roger Fisher and William Ury wrote a book titled *Getting to YES: Negotiating an Agreement without Giving In* (New York: Penguin), which suggests a negotiating method called "principled negotiation or negotiation of merits." Although their arguments have considerable weight, they are only remotely related to the GESS approach advocated here.

13. US Energy Information Administration (EIA), *Annual Energy Review 2011* (Washington, DC: EIA, 2012). See also EIA, "AEO2013 Early Release Overview," EIA, Washington, DC, 2012, http://www.eia.gov/forecasts/aeo/er/; International Energy Agency (IEA), *Monthly Oil Market Report*, December 2012.

14. Shale exploration is only at initial stages outside the United States, and whether the same amount of porous formations will be found as in the much more highly developed US remains to be seen.

15. See David G. Victor, "The Gas Promise," chapter 3 of this volume.

16. See the New Policies scenario in IEA, *World Energy Outlook 2012* (Paris: OECD/IEA, 2012).

17. See William K. Reilly, "Valuing Safety Even When the Market Doesn't Notice," chapter 4 of this volume. See also the CSSD's website at http://www.sustainableshale.org.

18. See Pierre Noël, "European Gas Supply Security: Unfinished Business," chapter 7 of this volume.

19. See Amy Myers Jaffe and Kenneth B Medlock III, "China, India, and Asian Energy," chapter 13 of this volume.

20. In the course of meetings in May 2013 with regional leaders in Costa Rica, President Obama said that the United States was likely to make LNG exports by 2020—a decision made formally by the Department of Energy. See Richard McGregor and Ed Crooks, "Obama Backs Rise in US Gas Exports," *Financial Times*, May 5, 2013.

21. See Thomas F. "Mack" McLarty, "Latin America," chapter 16 of this volume.

22. See Fareed Mohamedi, "North Africa and the Mediterranean," chapter 11 of this volume, and Phillip van Niekerk and Aaron Sayne, "Sub-Saharan Africa," chapter 12 of this volume.

23. See Charles McPherson, "Governance, Transparency, and Sustainable Development," chapter 19 of this volume.

24. See Amy Myers Jaffe and Edward L. Morse, "OPEC: Can the Cartel Survive Another 50 Years?," chapter 5 of this volume.

25. Ed Crooks and Anna Fifield, "US Oil Imports to Fall to 25-Year Low," *Financial Times*, January 8, 2013.

26. See Richard G. Newell and Stuart Iler, "The Global Energy Outlook," chapter 1 of this volume.

27. See Daniel Yergin, "Energy Security and Markets," chapter 2 of this volume.

28. Southeast Asia is potentially another source, but as Herberg shows, territorial disputes in the South and East China Seas will be a high hurdle to energy security cooperation with member states of the Association of Southeast Asian Nations, will be a serious impediment to relations with Japan, and could significantly complicate relations with the United States and Australia. See Mikkal Herberg, "Japan, Southeast Asia, and Australia," chapter 14 of this volume.

29. See J. Robinson West and Raad Alkadiri, "Iraq, Iran, and the Gulf Region," chapter 10 of this volume.

30. EIA, "US Imports by Country of Origin," EIA, Washington, DC, December 28, 2012, http://www.eia.gov/dnav/pet/pet_move_impcus_a2_nus_ep00_im0_mbbl_a.htm.

31. IEA, *Monthly Oil Market Report*, December 2012. Saudi oil production had reached a peak of 9.7 mmbpd earlier in 2012, before being reduced in response to increased supplies from other sources when market demand had also grown more slowly.

32. Minister Naimi told an Asian investment conference that Aramco will drill seven shale gas wells, citing "rough estimates" of 600 trillion cubic feet of shale gas and such large amounts of shale oil that expensive maintenance of spare capacity may no longer be necessary. "It is not a question of whether Saudi Arabia has spare [oil] capacity," he said. "It is a question of whether we need to spend billions maintaining it at all." He did not mention the challenges of infrastructure and water availability but added that "new commercial reserves such as shale oil are good news for the global economy" and "will ensure even greater stability of markets and prices" in the future. See Ali Al-Naimi, "Asia and Saudi Arabia: Partners in Prosperity," luncheon keynote address, Credit Suisse 16th Asian Investment Conference, Hong Kong, March 18, 2013.

33. Starting in 2013, China became the world's number one energy consumer. Although Russia has often exceeded Saudi Arabia in production, Saudi Arabia is capable of higher production levels if it chooses to exceed OPEC quotas.

34. The solar, nuclear, and efficiency campaign in Saudi Arabia is promoted by a new cabinet-level agency that is led by a member of the ruling family, the King Abdullah City for Atomic and Renewable Energy (KA-CARE).

35. As emphasized in GESS and increasingly in official policy, an inclusive strategy is required not only for fuels but also for technologies. See Melanie A. Kenderdine and Ernest J. Moniz, "Technology Development and Energy Security," chapter 17 of this volume.

36. See Julia Nanay and Jan H. Kalicki, "Russia and Eurasia," chapter 8 of this volume.

37. See Michelle Billig Patron and David L. Goldwyn, "Managing Strategic Reserves," chapter 20 of this volume.

38. The Merchant Marine Act of 1920, better known as the Jones Act, requires that all goods transported by water between US ports be carried in ships flying the US flag that are built in the United States, owned by US citizens, and crewed by US citizens or permanent residents. Waivers have been granted in cases of national emergencies or strategic interest, such as the Department of Homeland Security's blanket waiver following wide-scale fuel shortages caused by Superstorm Sandy in November 2012.

39. As natural gas increasingly displaces higher-carbon coal to fuel electic power plants in the United States, larger amounts of coal are and will likely continue to be exported to the major Asian and European markets, where coal remains cost competitive, until they too can access lower-carbon natural gas at competitive prices. See Charles K. Ebinger and John P. Banks, "Electricity Access in Emerging Markets," chapter 18 of this volume.

40. The United States also has legitimate concerns over fair play: where a bidding war arises for a US asset, government-subsidized entities should not be allowed to outbid nonsubsidized bidders.

41. See Leon Fuerth, "National Security, Energy, Climate Change: New Paradigm, New Strategy, New Governance," chapter 22 of this volume.

42. See Michael Levi, "Energy, Environment, and Climate: Framework and Trade-offs," chapter 21 of this volume.

43. Alan Krupnick, Hannah Wiseman, Nathan Richardson, and Madeline Gottlieb, "A Review of Shale Gas Regulations by State," Resources for the Future, Washington, DC, 2012, http://www.rff.org/centers/energy_economics_and_policy/Pages/Shale_Maps.aspx.

44. For an excellent presentation of her initiatives, see Hillary Rodham Clinton, "Energy Diplomacy in the 21st Century," address to Georgetown University, Washington, DC, October 18, 2012, http://www.state.gov/secretary/rm/2012/10/199330.htm.

45. The World Bank and US and European Union development agencies have funded an extensive network of such advisers. In addition, the nongovernmental International Trade and Investment Center, based in Washington, DC, holds seminars around the world that bring trade and investment experts together with foreign government officials.

46. Gas and renewable fuels can play complementary roles in that the former can respond instantly and the latter are intermittent and, after substantial capital investment, have essentially no fuel cost.

47. Melanie A. Kenderdine and Ernest J. Moniz, "Technology Development and Energy Security," chapter 17 of this volume.

48. See Charles K. Ebinger and John P. Banks, "Electricity Access in Emerging Markets," chapter 18 of this volume.

49. Energy and Infrastructure Program, "The Executive Branch and National Energy Policy: Time for Renewal" (Washington, DC: Bipartisan Policy Center, 2012).

50. William C. Ramsay, "Energy Sector Governance in the 21st Century," chapter 6 of this volume.

51. See Frank Verrastro and Kevin Book, "The Challenge of Politics," chapter 23 of this volume.

52. The American Clean Energy and Security Act was passed by the US House of Representatives by a vote of 219 to 212. See John M. Broder, "House Passes Bill to Address Threat of Climate Change," *New York Times*, June 26, 2009.

53. EIA, *Annual Energy Outlook 2012 with Projections to 2035* (Washington, DC: EIA, 2012). See also David Hone, "Can the United States Meet Its Energy Emissions Target?," National Geographic Society, *The Great Energy Challenge* (blog), September 9, 2011, http://www.greatenergychallengeblog.com/2011/09/09.

54. See Charles McPherson, "Governance, Transparency, and Sustainable Development," chapter 19 of this volume.

55. The IEA has estimated an annual investment requirement of $1.5 trillion per year for energy infrastructure to meet future demand. Personal communication with Fatih Birol, chief economist of the IEA, October 18, 2011.

56. See Michelle Billig Patron and David L. Goldwyn, "Managing Strategic Reserves," chapter 20 of this volume.

57. See Michael Levi, "Energy, Environment, and Climate: Framework and Trade-offs," chapter 21 of this volume.

58. Kalicki and Goldwyn, *Energy and Security: Toward a New Foreign Policy Strategy*.

59. Tom Donilon's speech was forward looking in many ways on energy and national security policy. He spoke to the need to integrate domestic and foreign energy policy, underlined that "energy and climate are critical elements of US national security," and stated that "we are poised to control our own energy future"—which must happen through continued US engagement in global affairs. Although a significant step forward, the speech was silent on the actions required to prevent "stove-piping" and to achieve both an all-of-government and a coordinated international approach. Donilon highlighted climate issues more than energy's essential contribution to economic growth. He spoke about Canada and other countries but oddly did not mention three of the most critical oil and gas producers outside North America: Australia, Russia, and Saudi Arabia. See "Remarks by Tom Donilon, National Security Advisor to the President, at the Launch of Columbia University's Center on Global Energy Policy," April 24, 2013, http://www.whitehouse.gov/the-press-office/2013/04/24/remarks-tom-donilon-national-security-advisor-president-launch-columbia-.

60. See Charles Emmerson, "The Arctic: Promise or Peril?," chapter 9 of this volume.

61. Thanks to William Ramsay for his input on this point.

About the Contributors

Abdullah bin Hamad Al-Attiyah is deputy prime minister of the state of Qatar, chief of the Emiri Diwan, president of the Administrative Control and Transparency Authority, former minister of energy and industry, and former chairman and chief executive officer of Qatar Petroleum. He has also served several times as president of the Organization of the Petroleum Exporting Countries (OPEC) Ministerial Conference.

Raad Alkadiri is partner and heads both the global risk practice and the Iraq advisory practice at PFC Energy. He has served as Iraq policy adviser to the UK Foreign and Commonwealth Office, has worked as Middle East analyst and deputy managing editor of Oxford Analytica, and has taught at St. Andrews University in Scotland and at the Johns Hopkins School of Advanced International Studies.

John P. Banks is nonresident fellow in energy security at the Brookings Institution and adjunct professor at the Johns Hopkins School of Advanced

International Studies. He has worked as an energy management consultant in developing countries, at Nexant (successor to Bechtel Technology & Consulting), and at BearingPoint (now Deloitte).

Kevin Book is managing director of research and cofounder of ClearView Energy Partners LLC. He has worked as senior vice president of Energy Policy, Oil, and Alternative Energy at FBR Capital Markets Corporation.

John M. Deutch is Institute professor emeritus at the Massachusetts Institute of Technology. He has served as US director of central intelligence, under secretary and then deputy secretary of defense, and under secretary of energy.

Charles K. Ebinger is senior fellow and director of the Energy Security Initiative (ESI) at the Brookings Institution and adjunct professor of electricity economics at the Johns Hopkins School of Advanced International Studies. He has advised more than 50 governments; previously served in several energy consulting firms (IRG, Stone & Webster, and Nexant); and taught at Georgetown and Case Western Universities.

Charles Emmerson is senior research fellow at the Royal Institute of International Affairs (Chatham House) in London. He is the author of *The Future History of the Arctic*, a book about the emerging geopolitics and geoeconomics of the Arctic region under conditions of climate change. Prior to writing his book, he served as an associate director of the World Economic Forum and was responsible for its global risk work.

Michelle Michot Foss is chief energy economist at the Center for Energy Economics, University of Texas at Austin. She was founder and executive director of the Institute for Energy, Law, and Enterprise and assistant research professor at the University of Houston Law Center, and she served as director of research at Simmons & Company.

Leon Fuerth is research professor of international affairs at the George Washington University. He has been a distinguished research fellow at the Center for Technology and National Security Policy at the National Defense University. He has also served as national security adviser to Vice President Al Gore and as a National Security Council principal during the Clinton administration.

David L. Goldwyn is president of Goldwyn Global Strategies LLC. He has served as Secretary of State Hillary Clinton's special envoy and coordinator for international energy affairs, assistant secretary of energy for international affairs, national security deputy to the US ambassador to the United Nations, and chief of staff to the under secretary of state for political affairs. He is a nonresident senior fellow at the Brookings Institution, a member of the National Petroleum Council, and an alternate member of the US Extractive Industries Transparency Initiative Steering Group.

Alexander V. Gorban is director of the Department of Foreign Economic Cooperation, Ministry of Foreign Affairs of the Russian Federation.

Jane Harman is director, president, and chief executive officer of the Woodrow Wilson International Center for Scholars. Representing the aerospace center of California during nine terms in Congress, she has served on the House Energy and Commerce Committee, the Armed Services Committee, the Intelligence Committee, and the Homeland Security Committee.

Mikkal E. Herberg is research director of the energy security program of the National Bureau of Asian Research and senior lecturer on international and Asian energy at the Graduate School of International Relations and Pacific Studies, University of California at San Diego. He has served as director for global energy and economics at ARCO.

Stuart Iler is a research analyst with the Duke University Energy Initiative.

Amy Myers Jaffe is executive director of energy and sustainability at the University of California at Davis. She has served as director of the Rice University Energy Forum and as Wallace Wilson fellow for energy studies at the James A. Baker III Institute for Public Policy.

J. Bennett Johnston is a partner at both Johnston & Associates and Johnston Development Company. He represented Louisiana as a senator from 1972 to 1996, and he also served as chairman of the Senate Committee on Energy and Natural Resources.

Jan H. Kalicki is senior scholar at the Wilson Center and Kennan Institute, chairman of Eurasia Foundation, and counselor for international strategy at Chevron. He has served as White House NIS ombudsman and counselor to the US Department of Commerce in the Clinton administration, on the State Department policy planning staff under Secretaries Kissinger and Vance, and as chief foreign policy adviser to Senator Ted Kennedy. He also taught at Brown (where he was assistant to the president and co-directed its center for foreign policy development), Georgetown, Harvard, Princeton, and the London School of Economics.

Melanie A. Kenderdine was most recently executive director of the Energy Initiative at the Massachusetts Institute of Technology. She was previously vice president of the Gas Technology Institute and director of policy for the US Department of Energy.

Chakib Khelil, an international energy consultant, served 11 years as Algeria's minister of energy and mines (1999–2010), two terms as president of the OPEC Ministerial Conference (2001 and 2008), and as president of the Gas Exporting Countries Forum (2010). At the World Bank, he was energy specialist and adviser for Africa and Latin America (1980–1999).

Angelina LaRose is team leader, natural gas markets, in the Office of Petroleum, Natural Gas, and Biofuels Analysis, US Energy Information Administration.

Michael Levi is David M. Rubinstein senior fellow for energy and the environment at the Council on Foreign Relations and director of the council's program on energy security and climate change. He has been a science and technology fellow at the Brookings Institution and has also served as director of the Strategic Security Project at the Federation of American Scientists.

Richard G. Lugar was US senator from Indiana and served as chairman of the Senate Committee on Foreign Relations from 1985 to 1987 and from 2003 to 2007. In the intervening years, he was ranking member of the committee. He focused much of his Foreign Relations Committee work on dismantling weapons of mass destruction and on promoting US energy security.

Thomas F. "Mack" McLarty is president of McLarty Associates, chairman of McLarty Companies, and past chairman of Arkla. He was chief of staff and special envoy for the Americas under President Bill Clinton and was a member of the National Petroleum Council and the National Council on Environmental Quality under President George H. W. Bush.

Charles McPherson is an international consultant on petroleum and minerals policies and taxation. He served as resource tax policy adviser, Fiscal Affairs Department, International Monetary Fund, and as senior adviser in the Oil, Gas, Mining, and Chemicals Department of the World Bank. He has also held senior international government negotiation positions at two major oil companies.

Kenneth B Medlock III is James A. Baker III and Susan G. Baker fellow in energy and resource economics at the James A. Baker III Institute for Public Policy. He is also senior director of the institute's Center for Energy Studies and adjunct professor of economics at Rice University. He has served as a corporate consultant at El Paso Energy Corporation.

Fareed Mohamedi is vice president of industry analysis, Statoil. He has worked at PFC Energy, Moody's Investors Service, the Institute of International Finance, Wharton Econometrics, and the Ministry of Finance and National Economy in Bahrain. His work has focused on the political economy of oil- and gas-producing countries and the strategies of national oil companies.

Ernest J. Moniz was most recently Cecil and Ida Green professor of physics and engineering systems, director of the Laboratory for Energy and the Environment, and director of the Energy Initiative at the Massachusetts Institute of Technology. He served earlier as US under secretary of energy and associate director of the White House's Office of Science and Technology Policy.

Edward L. Morse is global head of commodities research at Citigroup. He has also headed commodities research at Credit Suisse. He has been chief energy economist at Lehman Brothers, cofounder of PFC Energy, executive adviser at Hess and Phillips Petroleum, president of Petroleum Intelligence Weekly, deputy assistant secretary of state for international energy policy, and lecturer at Princeton University.

Julia Nanay is managing director at PFC Energy, where she leads the Russia and Caspian Service. Her focus over the past 15 years has been analysis and advice on the oil and gas sectors of the Russian–Caspian region and on the countries and companies investing there.

Shirley Neff is senior adviser to the US Energy Information Administration. She also served as senior adviser to the Commission on the BP Oil

Spill. She has been an economist for the US Senate Committee on Energy and Natural Resources, president of the US Association for Energy Economics, and adjunct professor at Columbia University.

Richard G. Newell, former administrator of the US Energy Information Administration, is the Gendell professor of energy and environmental economics at Duke University's Nicholas School of the Environment, director of the Duke University Energy Initiative, and research associate at the National Bureau of Economic Research.

Pierre Noël is senior fellow for economic and energy security at the International Institute for Strategic Studies, based in Singapore. Until January 2013, he had been senior research associate and director of the Energy Policy Forum at Cambridge University. He has worked with the European Council on Foreign Relations and with the French Institute for International Relations.

Michelle Billig Patron was most recently senior director of PIRA Energy Group. Before joining PIRA, she was an international affairs fellow at the Council on Foreign Relations. She worked as international policy adviser at the US Department of Energy from 1999 to 2003 and served as energy attaché at the US Embassy in Beijing.

William C. Ramsay is professor at Sciences Po in Paris and special adviser to the Energy Center of the French Institute for International Relations. He was deputy executive director of the International Energy Agency from 1998 to 2008 and previously US deputy assistant secretary of state for international energy, economic, and foreign policy sanctions.

William K. Reilly, former administrator of the US Environmental Protection Agency under President George H. W. Bush, is senior adviser to TPG Capital and founder of Aqua International, which invests in the water sector. He has been president of World Wildlife Fund and has served with the Council on Environmental Quality. In 2010, President Barack Obama appointed him to cochair the Commission on the BP Oil Spill.

Aaron Sayne is principal at 104 Consulting, where he provides due diligence, risk management, and policy analysis for clients in the African energy sector. He has served as a financial crimes investigator and defense attorney for oil and gas companies.

James R. Schlesinger is counselor and trustee of the Center for Strategic and International Studies and is chairman of the board of the MITRE Corporation. He was the first US secretary of energy and has also served as secretary of defense, director of the Central Intelligence Agency, and chairman of the Atomic Energy Commission.

Phillip van Niekerk is managing director of Calabar Consulting, a company that focuses on business and politics in Africa. He is former editor of South Africa's *Mail & Guardian* newspaper and has 30 years of experience working as an award-winning investigative journalist, foreign correspondent, and adviser to foreign investors.

Frank Verrastro is senior vice president and James R. Schlesinger chair for energy and geopolitics at the Center for Strategic and International Studies. Prior to his current position, he directed the center's Energy and National Security program. He served as senior vice president at Pennzoil Company and as US deputy assistant secretary of energy. He has also been a White House staff member.

David G. Victor is professor at the School of International Relations and Pacific Studies at the University of California at San Diego, where he heads its Laboratory on International Law and Regulation. He has served as director of the Program on Energy and Sustainable Development at Stanford University, where he was also a professor at Stanford Law School.

J. Robinson West is founder and chairman of PFC Energy. He has served as US assistant secretary of the interior and as deputy assistant secretary of defense for international economic affairs. He has also been a White House staff member.

Daniel Yergin is vice chairman of IHS and founder of IHS Cambridge Energy Research Associates. He is the author of *The Quest: Energy, Security, and the Remaking of the Modern World*. He received the Pulitzer Prize for his history of world oil, *The Prize: The Epic Quest for Oil, Money, and Power*. His other books include *The Commanding Heights: The Battle for the World Economy*.

Index

Index